MW01631343

Storytelling in Christian Art from Giotto to Donatello

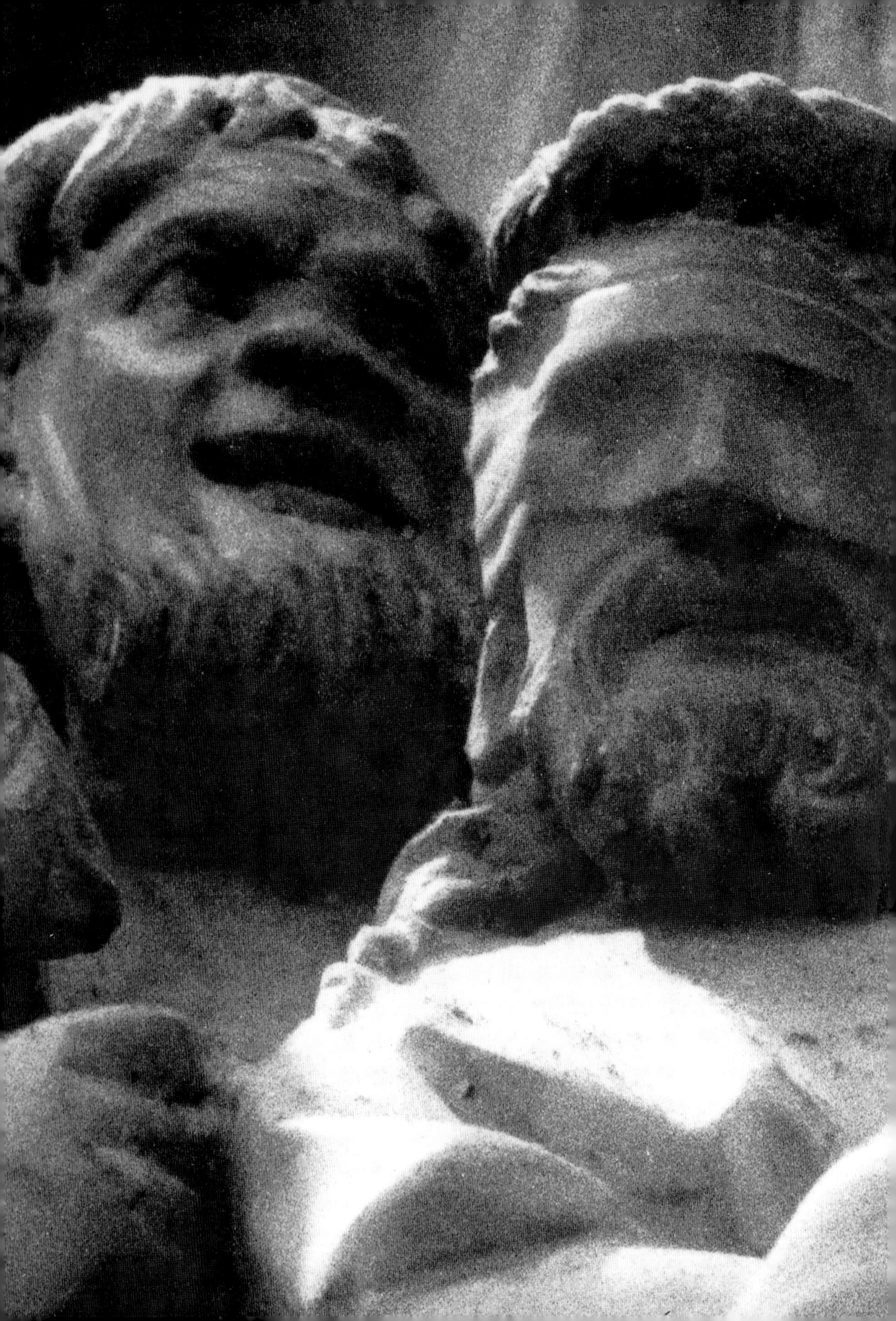

Storytelling in Christian Art from Giotto to Donatello

Jules Lubbock

Yale University Press
New Haven and London

Designed by Laura Bolick

Printed in Singapore

Library of Congress Cataloging-in-Publication Data

Lubbock, Jules.
Storytelling in Christian art from Giotto to Donatello/ Jules Lubbock.
p. cm.
Includes bibliographical references and index.
ISBN 0-300-11727-2 (cl : alk. paper)
1. Narrative art, Renaissance–Italy. 2. Art, Early Renaissance–Italy. 3. Christian art and symbolism–Italy–Medieval, 500-1500. 4. Bible–Illustrations. I. Title: Storytelling in Christian art. II. Title.
N7952.A1L83 2006
704.9´48409024–dc22
2005030956

A catalogue record for this book is available from
The British Library

frontispiece Giovanni Pisano, detail from the Mocking of Jesus, Pisa Cathedral Pulpit, 1302–11

CONTENTS

For Maggie
With Love

ACKNOWLEDGEMENTS

Books are collaborative. Michael Podro and Margaret Iversen have given advice, criticism, encouragement and inspiration throughout, as well as reading much of the book in draft. Michael Baxandall first guided me to think about the relief sculpture of Ghiberti and Donatello. Julian Gardner directed my initial study of pictorial narrative and the late John Shearman did his best to teach me the basic principles of historical method, which I hope I have come to value more than I did in the late 1960s. I have been most fortunate to be a member of the splendidly collegial Department of Art History and Theory at the University of Essex; colleagues have read drafts of chapters and given critical attention to my arguments. I owe a particular debt to Val Fraser for her invaluable support in the early stages, to Thomas Puttfarken, Peter Vergo, Deborah Povey, John Nash, Lisa Wade, Simon Richards, Caspar Pearson as well as to Jonathan White and Kay Stevenson of the Department of Literature. My colleagues in RATS (Renaissance Architecture and Theory Scholars) subjected my views on the invention of perspective to their customarily stringent criticism, and I am also grateful to Richard Williams of the University of Edinburgh and to Michael Ann Holly, Director of the Fellowship Program at the Clark Art Institute, Williamstown, Mass. for inviting me to give papers on that subject. Paul Hills invited me to lecture at the University of Warwick on the subject of 'Visible Speech'. Chris Thompson, Eric Fernie, Joanna Cannon, Laura Jacobus, David Bindman, Francis Ames-Lewis,

James Hall, Diana Norman and Libby Armstrong have generously responded to my queries and requests. Jeffrey Judelson and Sandy Sullivan provided encouragement. Many students over the years have contributed in the process of teaching, listening, looking, finding flaws and coming up with their own ideas, particularly during the department's annual fortnight study visit to Florence. I hope it is not invidious to single out Jessica Rutherford, Neil McKenna, Amy Schwartz, Odette Livingstone-Smith and Michael Wiersing who kept e-mailing me on his travels round the world asking when the book would be published.

One of the most important and pleasurable aspects of the project was the photographic campaign, funded by the University of Essex Research Promotion Fund and the British Academy. Geoff Crossick, Tim Benton and Paul Hills enthusiastically supported me in obtaining that funding. Barry Woodcock made prints from my first negatives of the Giovanni Pisano pulpits and Ghiberti's Baptistery doors and worked on the diagrams. I greatly enjoyed working with Antonio Quattrone, a true maestro, from whom I commissioned photographs of the Donatello Head of St John and of the Scrovegni Chapel. Valentina Bandelloni of Scala was especially helpful. Jennifer Iles typed the first draft with her customary skill and drafted the diagrams The book could not have been written without the staff and resources of the Library of the Warburg Institute; I am also indebted to the British Library, the Albert Sloman Library at the University of Essex, the London Library, the National Art Library and to the staff of the Library of the Clark Art Institute, Williamstown who worked tirelessly to find books and articles during the summer Fellowship Program of 2005. The University of Essex's generous allocation of study leave assisted by the British Academy's study leave programme provided uninterrupted time for research and writing.

This book was incubated at Yale University Press, first by John Nicoll and then when he retired Gillian Malpass adopted it with her customary enthusiasm. Kevin Brown, Sarah Faulks and Emily Angus all made important contributions. The criticisms of two anonymous readers were invaluable. Laura Bolick designed the book and guided it through the press with great skill, no easy task where the relationship between word and image is so intricate.

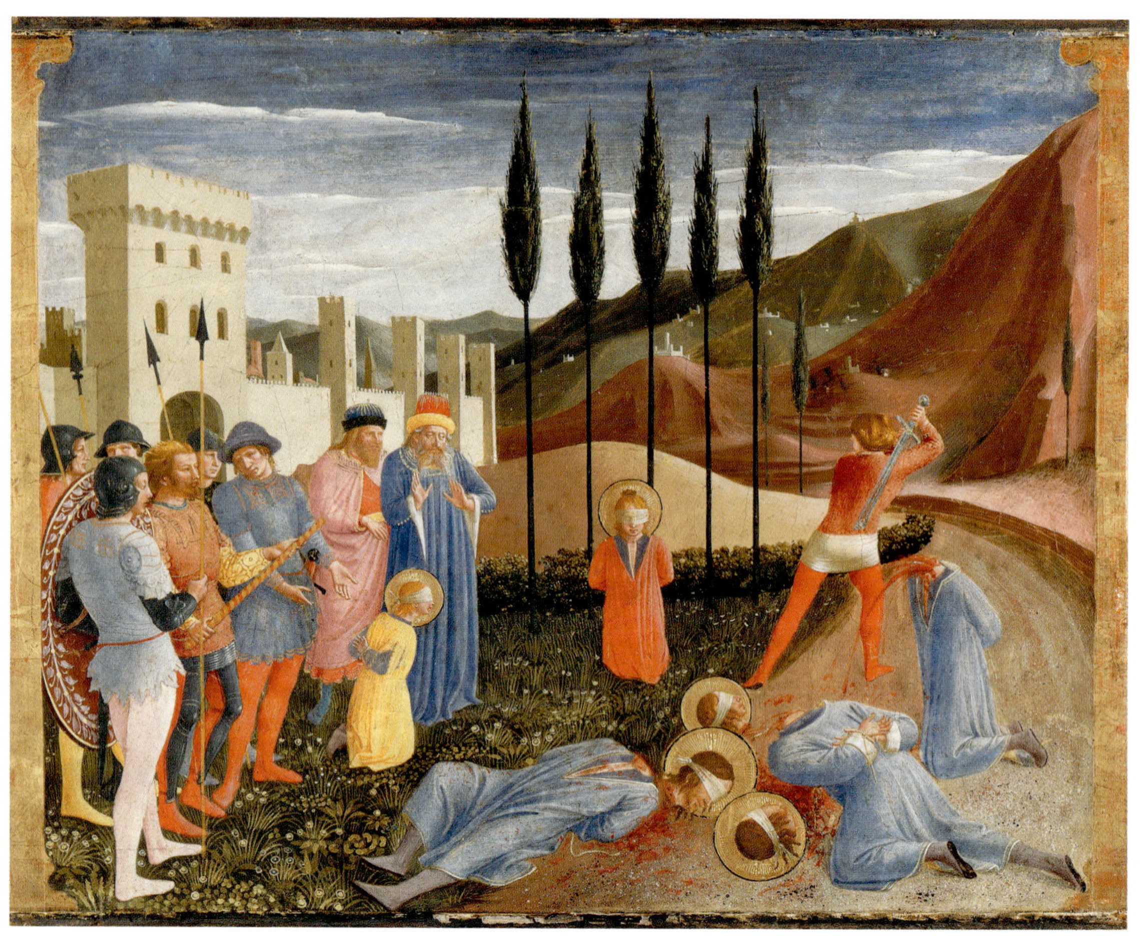

1. Fra Angelico, The Beheading of Saints Cosmas and Damian, predella panel from the altarpiece for the high altar of San Marco, Florence, c. 1440–42, Musée du Louvre, Paris.

PREFACE

My interest in narrative pictures painted and sculpted in Italy during the early Renaissance was aroused when I was an earnest young student forty years ago. I remember being struck by a small painting by Fra Angelico showing the beheading of five saints (Fig. 1). The sense of the rhythm of the executioner swinging his sword as he moved around the circle of kneeling martyrs, three already beheaded, two awaiting their fate; the simplicity of the background with its five cypress trees and the five towers of the walled city; the pure and brilliant colours and clear morning light all helped to stimulate the vivid impression that the event was actually taking place before my eyes. I felt that I could 'read' the picture as easily as a book.

Once upon a time this was probably the dominant mode of engaging with pictures. Narrative was considered to be the most difficult and prestigious branch of painting, but for most of the twentieth century, perhaps because of the very practices of modern art, other concerns have replaced it.[1] The history of style, formal analysis of composition, iconography, the development of representational techniques and skills, social history and the theory of art have succeeded one another as the latest fashion in art-historical writing about the Renaissance. All have their place, but the neglect of narrative is regrettable. Likewise the fact that such images were made to assist instruction in Christian doctrine, serving religious and moral ends to which aesthetic ingenuity was the means, is also somewhat neglected.[2] This book is an attempt to remedy the situation by focusing upon a small group of important narrative images from the period 1300–1465. Almost all of these are biblical cycles by artists considered to be major such as Giovanni Pisano, Duccio, Giotto, Ghiberti, Brunelleschi, Donatello and Masaccio. Inevitably some artists have been omitted, but this is not intended to be a comprehensive history of pictorial narrative in the period even though various historical themes are suggested.

The chapters consist of detailed analytical descriptions[3] of the works and a group of photographs some of which have been specially taken, showing the images both from the ground and from other positions from which I believe they were designed to be viewed, rather than photographed frontally on scaffolding, as is customary.[4] No photograph can be an adequate substitute for seeing the work in its original context particularly because this art was designed for specific locations inside or outside churches, and much of it was relief sculpture. But some photographs are better than others in suggesting the best angles for looking, and they may excite the reader enough to visit, or revisit, the originals.

The introduction provides a brief account of storytelling in general and Christian Art in particular. The conclusion draws some generalisations about the context and circumstances in which artists approached the task of making these images and how they might be read.

There are two parts. Part one includes some seminal works of the first decade of the fourteenth century. I have taken liberties with the strict chronological order by beginning with Duccio's Maestà for the high altar of Siena Cathedral of 1308–11, before turning to Giotto's somewhat earlier Scrovegni Chapel in Padua of 1303–05 and finally addressing Giovanni Pisano's two sculpted pulpits of 1298–1301 for St Andrea in Pistoia and of 1302–11 for Pisa cathedral. The problem of the best order in which to tell a story is one with which all these artists were familiar. The Trial of Jesus, a section from Duccio's Maestà, the subject of the first chapter, acts as an introduction to pictorial narrative. Giotto's frescoed chapel for Enrico Scrovegni is more complicated and has been treated as a whole. Still more demanding upon the viewer, though for different reasons, are Giovanni Pisano's pulpits, partly because they are relief sculptures. Part two examines works produced in the first seven decades of the fifteenth century, in chronological order.

The first part also sketches an implicit debate between these three great artists at the beginning of the fourteenth century, particularly between Giovanni Pisano and Giotto, one favouring a more impassioned and the other a more restrained approach to pictorial narrative. Because they left almost no statements of their intentions, these have to be inferred from their works. In the second part, their successors Brunelleschi, Ghiberti, Donatello and Masaccio, take up the discussion, disagreeing with, competing with and trying to improve upon the work both of their predecessors and of one another to produce the best approach to narrative. All were artist-intellectuals and one of them, Ghiberti, has left a considerable body of writing which helps us to understand his views.[5]

What emerges is a dynamic story in which the work both of contemporaries and of predecessors was not perceived as something relatively primitive to be improved upon, as lower points on an ascending graph of progress towards greater naturalism, but as self-sufficient works of art forming part of a living tradition from which artists continued to learn even two centuries after the originals had been produced.

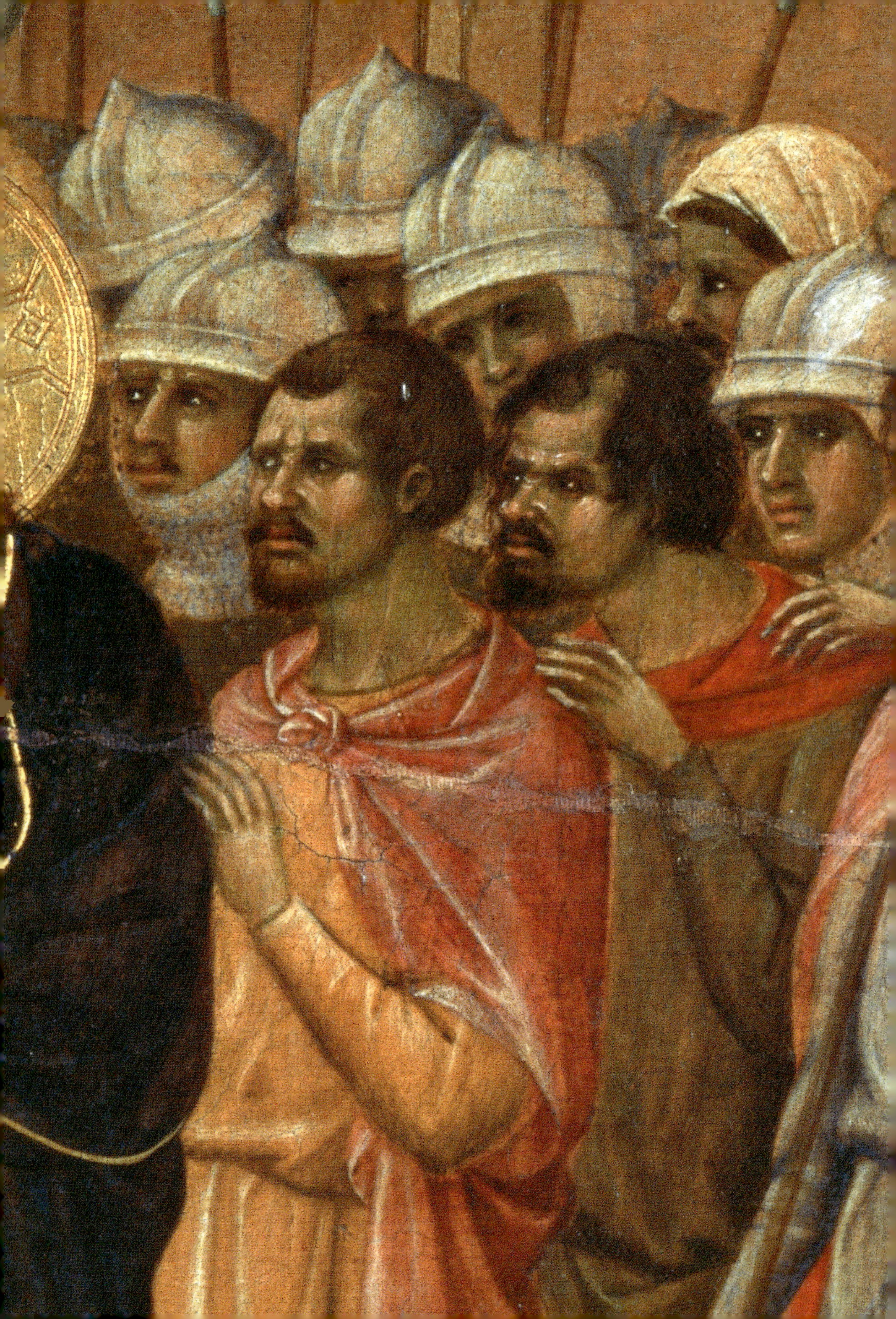

INTRODUCTION

STORYTELLING AND CHRISTIAN ART

Why do we tell stories?

We tell stories constantly. We tell stories about our friends, our family, our colleagues at work as well as about events in the larger world of politics, war, sport and culture. Much of our time we listen to, read or watch stories about real and imaginary people, through gossip, the newspapers, television, radio and now the internet: films, soap operas both fictional and real, plays and novels.[1] Our appetite for stories, hearing them and talking about them, is powerful, perhaps as great as for food, love, sex or the ambition for wealth and power. Yet little attention is given to this. Suppose storytelling were suddenly forbidden. We simply would not know about events that occurred in our absence. As a result we would be powerless because our lives, both as individuals and as members of groups, depend upon knowing what is going on around us – 'Have you heard what old so-and-so is up to?'[2] Were storytelling prohibited we would have to stick together all the time to make sure that our interests were not being adversely affected. Large societies would become impossible. Storytelling, then, is one of the foundations of complex human society without which there could be no division of labour, little social co-operation and only a subsistence standard of living.

Detail of Figure 6

A recent book lends scientific support for this, claiming that:

> about two-thirds of conversation time is devoted to social topics. These include discussions of personal relationships, personal likes and dislikes, personal experiences, the behaviour of other people . . .[3]

Gossipy conversations replace the grooming sessions of apes and monkeys which perform the role of social bonding, but which consume too much time when groups grow larger. If storytelling were prohibited we might well have to return to grooming.

The other side of the coin is that secrecy, deception and censorship, between individuals and within society, are the most effective methods of controlling events whether in national or international politics, work or domestic and social life. By ensuring that someone *does not know* the true story about an event until too late to act, we render them powerless.[4] Our desire for stories is related to obtaining, and retaining, love, sex, food, wealth, power and esteem, by fair means or foul.

Censorship and control

Because storytelling is integral to social life, with so important a bearing upon conduct and morality, great importance has been attached to the control even of imaginary stories let alone stories of real events. Among the earliest and most influential arguments in favour of the State taking legal control of storytelling were those advanced by the Athenian philosopher Plato (429–347 BC) in his *Republic*. In a discussion of how the rulers or Guardians of his ideal city state should be educated, storytelling was first on his list of topics, such was his sense of its importance.[5]

Listening to stories in infancy marks the very start of education, and because the minds of toddlers are so impressionable, anything they are told will leave a permanent mark. Therefore, even children's stories must obey the law. Plato proposed six laws to control subject matter including one dictating that the gods should always be portrayed as good, and never shown quarrelling or taking revenge on one another, to ensure that the Guardians would 'honour the gods and their parents, and know how important it is to love one another'. As a result Homer's *Iliad* and *Odyssey*, almost the equivalent of the Bible in Greek culture, would have had to be largely rewritten or even banned altogether in Plato's *Republic*, because of his insistence that the rulers should only be exposed to models of the best behaviour in their formative years. Nowadays, Plato's prescriptions for subject matter may appear somewhat extreme; but they don't differ in kind from proposals to control children's access to videos, films, television and the internet.

Laws to control the style of storytelling

Plato had a second line of argument, one which seems more peculiar to us, but was widely accepted in the Athens of the fifth century BC and almost everywhere in Europe and the Mediterranean until quite recently. We do not simply take in stories and absorb their lessons about the world. Rather, when we read about Zeus seducing a young woman, we involuntarily imitate his feelings and behaviour, becoming inflamed with lust. Representations of people's behaviour in stories, according to Plato, have the extraordinary effect of overpowering the reader's judgement, of infecting the emotions like a disease and, particularly in a young man or woman, so carrying them away that virtuous intentions are replaced by vicious actions, just as a disease can overpower a healthy body. Although disputed by Plato's student, Aristotle, this idea had a powerful legacy. Within the Renaissance some people took a similar line. In the Fifth Canto of *The Inferno*, Francesca tells Dante that it was reading about the love affair of Lancelot and Guinevere in a contemporary French romance that caused her and her lover Paolo to lose their self-control and make love, leading to their murder by her husband and their eternal punishment.[6]

> One day we reading were for our delight
> Of Launcelot, how Love did him enthral,
> Alone we were and without any fear.
>
> Full many a time our eyes together drew
> That reading, and drove the colour from our faces,
> But one point only was it that o'ercame us.
> When, as we read of the much-longed for smile
> Being by such a noble lover kissed,
> This one, who ne'er from me shall be divided
> Kissed me on the mouth all palpitating.
> Galeotto was the book and he who wrote it.
> That day no further did we read therein.

Paolo and Francesca are overwhelmed by reading the erotic description of Lancelot kissing Guinevere, and imitate them as they read. The French romance is condemned by Dante as the instigator of their adultery. Reading erotic stories lands you in Hell. Stories can be dangerous.

In Plato's view such a total identification with the characters and the imitation of their behaviour was particularly pronounced the closer a story was to drama in its employment of dialogue and direct imitation (mimesis) rather than indirect narration and reported speech (diagesis). Plato stipulated that stories must be told in reported speech without dialogue. He made an exception for speeches by good characters, because the other side of the coin is that everything should be done to encourage people to imitate the best behaviour. Many early Renaissance artists adopted a similar approach, leading the spectator to identify with good people.

Plato went even further. He insisted that the style of storytelling should exclude entertaining descriptions of thunder, wind, the noise of wheels, the barking of dogs, the baaing of sheep and the twittering of birds. The style should be uniform and severe. It is often inaccurately claimed that Plato wanted to banish all poets, painters and artists from his *Republic*. What he actually says is that he would only exclude such descriptive and dramatic poets and storytellers, but would permit those who 'are severe rather than amusing', those who write in the austere style of a good man, a Guardian – in short writers of philosophical and moral stories like Plato himself. This idea was to have great influence upon later artistic practice and theory.[7] To exemplify what he had in mind he did indeed rewrite the opening lines of Homer's *Iliad* in plain speech, turning all the dialogue into reported speech and cutting out Homer's flowery language, so that the passage is terse and grave, almost biblical in character.[8]

Plato's position is often misrepresented as one of outright dislike, even wilful philistinism towards storytelling and the arts in general. On the contrary, however, he appears to have been overawed by their power. He seems to have believed that there was almost no difference between a story and real life. People respond to stories, particularly in the theatre (and films, had he known of them), as if they are living out those actions. Because of this Plato wanted to put a certain distance between the listener and the story, to make it more artificial, to destroy the illusion, so that one would be aware that a story is only a story, and be able to retain one's rational control over the narrated events, instead of being swept away by emotion, spectacle and illusion.[9]

The argument did not rest there. Aristotle (384–322 BC) while agreeing with his former teacher that stories should be serious in subject matter and stripped of sensationalism, argued that the arts do not in fact have this mesmerising effect. One responds to stories and other representations in a different, more detached way than to real-life events. People acquire the knowledge that a story is not real and that whatever emotions they feel will soon be over.* Because of this, stories and other forms of imitation can be

*But small infants are not so sure about the boundaries between the real and the represented, and between a real lion and a soft toy.

useful as well as entertaining. In life, a spider or a corpse might frighten us out of our wits or drive us away in disgust. But an exact and life-like depiction can be pleasurable and enable us to study the object dispassionately. Perhaps it can even increase our capacity to control our feelings through understanding. At a more profound level, the representation of a tragic event would have the same result.[10]

Stories, and the imitative arts in general, did not hold the same dangers for Aristotle as for Plato. They were already distanced from reality by their very nature as imitations; emotional involvement was not dangerous; the best stories, moreover, were a potential source of knowledge and could even constitute a branch of philosophy.[11] The precondition for this was that the subject of the story should be serious, that it should be well told and well constructed.[12] The plot was central to good construction, events should follow one another in a sequence that is 'probable or necessary'.[13]

What bearing do these arguments have upon stories told by means of visual images rather than words, and upon Christian Art in particular?

The origins of Christian art

From its earliest days as a Jewish sect, even before the compilation of the Gospels, Christianity used the historical stories of what became the New Testament, alongside those of the Old, as an essential component in religious instruction. In addition to the stories about the events of Jesus' life, Jesus himself had taught his disciples by telling parables as well as through his moral and theological pronouncements. The Gospels are collections of such stories and sayings embedded in the narrative of Jesus' birth, mission, trial, death and resurrection. As Christianity, with its mission to convert the gentiles, developed into a religion distinct from Judaism, so techniques of instruction and conversion had to be adapted. Early Christians, like the Jews, had largely observed the second commandment, proscribing both the fabrication and the worship of representational images.*[14] Nonetheless by the middle of the third century AD images were being made in both mosaic and fresco for Christian tombs in the catacombs, the underground cemeteries cut deep into the rock on the outskirts of Rome, beyond the walls. Subjects included stories from both the Old and the New Testaments, including the Fall of Man, Abraham's Sacrifice, the Crossing of the Red Sea, Samson and the Philistines, Jonah and the Whale, the Baptism of Jesus, The Raising of Lazarus, the Last Supper and the Resurrection.[15] In many cases the compositions of these pic-

*'Thou shalt not make unto thee any graven image, or any likeness *of any thing* that *is* in the heaven above, or that *is* in the earth beneath, or that *is* in the water under the earth: Thou shalt not bow down thyself to them, nor serve them: for I the Lord thy God *am* a jealous God', Exodus 20, 4–5.

tures already observe the formulaic conventions which were still followed in the early Renaissance and beyond, and which facilitated the recognition of the subject without the need for titles.[16] Until AD 312 Christianity, however, was a faith whose position within the Roman Empire was sometimes precarious; churches were small and inconspicuous, often located in private houses.[17] It was not until the Emperor Constantine's victory at the Battle of the Milvian Bridge in AD 312, which he attributed to the intercession of the Christian God and Constantine's subsequent toleration of Christianity, that he and his family set in train the construction of public churches, basilicas, on a monumental scale. These were decorated with grander versions of the subjects previously confined to the catacombs.[18] For example, the mausoleum in Rome of Constantine's daughter Constantina, Sta Costanza, dating from about AD 351–2, included mosaics of the Sacrifice of Cain and Abel, Noah Building the Ark, Moses Striking the Rock and Susanna and the Elders, and there was a parallel cycle of New Testament scenes.[19] Thus it was not until the mid- to late fourth century that such images began to play a major role in the decoration of churches and in religious instruction and conversion.

Pope Gregory the Great's doctrine of Christian art

Two centuries passed before a definitive doctrine concerning the employment of pictures for the purpose of Christian instruction and worship was formulated. In AD 598 and again in AD 600 Pope Gregory, one of the four great Fathers of the western Church, wrote two letters to Serenus, the bishop of Marseilles, who was at the time bent upon destroying religious images in the churches of his diocese, on the grounds that many Christians were worshipping the images, thereby breaking the second commandment.[20] It seems, however, that the result of Serenus's iconoclasm was to alienate most of his flock, who withdrew from communion. Gregory ordered Serenus to stop his campaign. Although the pope agreed with Serenus that images must not be worshipped, he nonetheless considered that the best way to prevent this was to explain to people why they should not behave in this way, instead of alienating them from Christianity by destroying the pictures themselves, which were popular instruments of instruction and conversion and consequently useful to the Church. In his second letter of AD 600 Gregory argues as follows:

> For it is one thing to adore a picture, another through the story [historiam] of a picture to learn what must be adored. For what writing offers to readers, a picture offers to the ignorant who look at it, since in it the

ignorant see what they ought to follow, in it they *read* [my italics] who do not know letters; whence for gentiles a picture is a substitute for reading.[21]

In his earlier letter Gregory explains that pictures are displayed in churches:

> in order that those who do not know letters may at least *read* [my italics] by seeing on the walls what they are unable to read in books.[22]

Although Gregory makes clear that the book, the Bible, is the best means of instruction, and that a picture is merely a substitute in which 'the illiterate . . . might learn what has been said', nonetheless he seems to be implying that it is possible to *read* a picture in much the same way as one reads a written text. In addition he employs the Latin word 'historia' indicating that he was probably referring to pictures that depict stories, allegories and doctrines, rather than devotional images of Jesus, the Virgin Mary or the saints.[23] The implication is that just as the literate, those who could read Latin and Greek, can read the words on the pages of a book to learn the substance of a story, so too an illiterate (which could simply mean someone without those languages) can 'read' the story from the visual images, and tell the story either to him- or herself, either in silence or reading aloud to others.[24] A picture, therefore, is not a mere reminder of a written text, nor an illustration, it is a text in its own right, a witness to the events or a statement of doctrine just as much as the verbal record.

> And indicate that what displeased you was not the sight of the story revealed through the *witness* [my italics] of a picture, but that adoration which had inappropriately been exhibited to the pictures.[25]

To summarise Gregory's position: he is making two claims for the value of painting for the church.

1. Pictures are a form of text recording the experience of those who witnessed biblical events and those of the saints.
2. Like written texts, pictures can be read and studied. Such didactic images are an important means for teaching Christian doctrine and for conversion.[26]

Let us take each of these points in turn.

Image as eyewitness

St Gregory's doctrine of pictures as witnesses to biblical and miraculous events and as books to be read and studied by the unlearned, took deep root. To understand one way in which his doctrine could be interpreted in Florence seven hundred years later, in the first decade of the fourteenth century, at exactly the time when Giovanni Pisano, Duccio and Giotto were making the works to be discussed in Part 1, let us listen to the learned and influential Dominican monk Fra Giordano da Rivolto (c.1260–1311), who was born a few miles from Pisa and was almost an exact contemporary of these artists.[27] In the church of Sta Maria Novella, the headquarters of the Dominican Order in Florence, on the feast day of the Epiphany, 6 January 1305, Fra Giordano delivered two sermons on the Adoration of the Magi, celebrated on that day.[28]

His first sermon provides such a vivid insight into contemporary ideas about narrative images that I shall quote from it at some length. Fra Giordano began with a question: how do we know many details of the Adoration which are not recorded in St Matthew's Gospel?

> The Fathers had many questions to ask about these Magi. They wanted to know what motivated the Magi to come on their journey, who these Magi were and where they came from, what was their status, and how many of them there were, and how long their journey had taken them? The Fathers asked all these questions because the Evangelist does not say.[29]

Fra Giordano provides some answers from other written texts before turning to what seems a rather surprising source to those of us reading his words seven hundred years later.

> The Fathers also asked questions about the Magi's rank or status. This could be understood purely through the word Magi. In one language Magi means philosophers and very learned men; but in another it signifies great lords or kings . . . But there happens to be another major source of evidence, namely the first paintings of them which came from Greece, where paintings are the book of the laity, and of everybody else as well. *This is because, to begin with, all paintings came from the disciples: in order to provide the maximum amount of information the figures of the first saints were painted from life showing their appearance, their circumstances and the way they were. Thus we find that Nicodemus painted Christ on the cross in a beautiful picture* [my italics], showing Christ's appearance and bearing so that whoever saw the picture fully saw almost all the circumstances, so well have they been portrayed, because Nicodemus was present at Christ's crucifixion, both when Christ was placed on the cross and when he was taken down from it. And through that painting a great miracle occurs, from whence derives the feast of the Holy Saviour.
>
> Likewise we also find that St Luke painted a portrait of Our Lady, showing her precisely as she was. That painting is nowadays in Rome and is preserved with great devotion.

The disciples made those paintings in order to give people the most accurate record of the events, so that these paintings, and especially the old ones which came from Greece in ancient times, are of great authority, because in them the many disciples who painted recount the said things. And they provided copies for the world, which possess great authority, *as great as that of books*.

Through those paintings from Greece we know for certain that the Magi were great lords because they are painted with king's crowns on their heads. Hence, in addition, it can be known how many there were. There were three and thus the three are depicted together. Tell us, what emotions did those Magi feel? They were moved by great faith and devotion. Faith indicated to them that Christ had been born, which was the reason for their journey; devotion moved them to believe that he was not an earthly but a heavenly king.[30]

It is only surprising that Giordano failed to mention the common belief that the Magi took their own painter with them to record the event.[31]

For Fra Giordano then, pictures function as something more than the 'book of the laity', they are also for 'everybody else as well' – including the learned, literate clergy. For although the Gospels do not tell us everything about the events of the life of Jesus, his earliest disciples and followers expressly made eyewitness pictures to provide the 'maximum amount of information' and 'the most accurate record of the events'. Fra Giordano's idea was not original, it seems to date back at least to the eighth or early ninth century, towards the end of the Iconoclastic Controversy, and perhaps even earlier to the time of Pope Gregory I himself.[32] A plea to the iconoclastic Emperor Theophilus in AD 836 provides an example.

> The holy apostles, who 'from the beginning were eyewitnesses and ministers of the Word'[33] even as they had heard and seen and their hands had handled the Word of Life, so they adorned the holy Church with painted pictures and mosaics representing the likeness of Christ, the God-man, and this *before they had written the God-inspired Gospels* [my italics] . . . they delineated the heavenly salutation of the archangel Gabriel to the holy Virgin Mary at Nazareth . . .[34]

Because Jesus' closest followers had made the original paintings as eyewitness records even before writing the Gospels, both these images and copies made from them 'possess great authority, as great as that of books'. According to Fra Giordano and others who shared his views and opinions, we should not regard the pictorial heritage as a didactic substitute for the Gospel, nor as mere translations of the scriptures into images, but as an independent visual testimony to Jesus' life, which complements the Bible, possessing equal authority.

Perhaps Gregory had something similar in mind in his phrase, 'the story revealed through the witness of a picture.' Both Bible and pictures, therefore, need to be read together.

The central figure in this justification for paintings of the Christian story was the evangelist St Luke (Fig. 2). From perhaps as early as the fifth century, some believed that he had painted the portrait of the Virgin Mary from life.[35] But by 1355 when the Sienese Guild of Painters drew up their statutes, St Luke was acknowledged not only as the patron saint of painters but also as the model of the literate artist to whom painters aspired in fulfilling the Gregorian conception of Christian Art.

The preamble to the statutes of the painters' guild opens with the conventional Gregorian doctrine:

> Whereas, by the grace of God, we are visualizers of the miraculous things which occurred through virtue and by virtue of the Holy Faith for the benefit of those coarse people who do not know how to read . . .

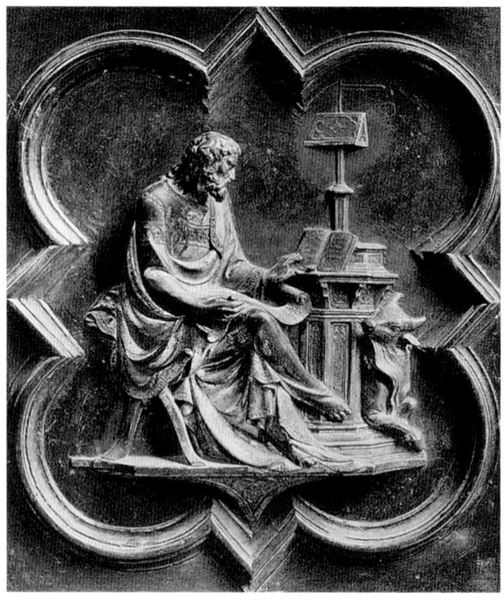

2. Lorenzo Ghiberti, *St Luke*, bronze relief from the second, north doors of the Baptistery, Florence, 1403–24. Ghiberti's portrayal of St Luke shows the saint transcribing from a book or possibly comparing his sources. St Luke was the author of the gospel and was also reputed to be the painter of the Virgin Mary. As such he was adopted by painters' guilds as their patron saint, the model of a literate and learned painter to which many artists aspired.

It concludes with the following account of St Luke, patron of the Guild, whose feast day was to be observed by the painters:

> the venerable and glorious St Luke, who was not only the painter who portrayed the stature and bearing of the glorious Virgin Mary, but was also the author of the account of her most saintly life and of her most holy conduct, whereby our Guild is honoured.[36]

The Sienese painters revered St Luke because he was both a writer and a painter. By implication therefore he was their model for the contemporary artist, who should be highly literate as well as being a skilled visualiser. As I shall show in the conclusion, there is strong evidence that all the artists discussed in this book could read and write Italian, and some may have had a little Latin. In addition, the Sienese painters are making an implicit claim that visual images are as effective as words in representing matters spiritual, and are not restricted merely to depictions of material reality.

According, then, to Fra Giordano in 1305, on the one hand, and to the painters of Siena in 1355, on the other, certain canonical images had the same authority as the scriptures because they derived from the same source – the eyewitness testimony of the early disciples and followers of Jesus. Foremost among these was St Luke, the paradigm of this double witness of Jesus in both word and image, who had been entrusted with the Virgin Mary's testimony, even though he had not known Jesus personally.

The holy scriptures and the canonical images are, as Fra Giordano argues, complementary and mutually illuminating. Pictures can help us to interpret biblical texts, just as the texts help us to understand the pictures. Picture and text should be read together.

Reading pictures

Turning now to the second major point made by St Gregory: what exactly did he mean by 'reading' a picture?

First, it is clear that Gregory did not regard paintings as mere passive reminders of stories that had been heard in sermons or in the liturgy. His careful choice of words suggests that the spectator would be actively engaged in reading the image. It has been ingeniously argued by Celia Chazelle that Gregory derived this concept from the writings of St Augustine (AD 354–430), Bishop of Hippo and author of his *Confessions* and *The City of God*, who like Gregory is also venerated as one of the four Fathers of the Western Church.[37] There is no escaping the fact that Augustine was primarily a man of words who was dismissive of the visual arts as a means of communication in general, let alone of Christian instruction.[38] He was also a student of Plato. In one of his few remarks on the visual arts he claims that when we look at a painting we merely look, recognise what it represents and praise it. Scornfully he likens that process to the activity of an illiterate who can only admire the beauty of the calligraphy of a handwritten manuscript, but is incapable of understanding what the letters and words stand for or what they mean.[39] For Augustine, words are the principal means whereby human beings communicate with one another.[40] Nonetheless, he recognised that words were only one kind of sign among many, and that there were occasions when God had used other types of sign to communicate with mankind. One was the performance of miracles.[41] A miracle such as the feeding of the five thousand, which appears to break the laws of nature, draws our attention to the miraculous nature of God and of his works. Miracles, then, were visual signs designed by God in the form of events. It was not enough, however, for people merely to observe the miracle, to be dumbstruck by it and to praise God. To act in this way, according to Augustine, was to behave like the illiterate who admired the handwriting without understanding the words, or someone who looked at a painting only to praise its formal qualities and craftsmanship. Miracles were not simply signs, those signs were also part of a language which needed to be read, as he put it: 'they have their own language'. There were four stages in the proper response to a miracle: first, the miraculous event itself arouses the senses; then, the senses arouse the mind and the mind in turn interrogates the miracle in an effort to understand the nature of the invisible God, who is made manifest by the miracle. In short, one must go beyond the stage of marvelling at the miracle and admiring God; one must, so to speak, 'read' the signs of the events in the miracle in order to understand its meaning.

> It is not enough to contemplate Christ's miracles. We ourselves must analyse the miracles which speak to us of Christ: indeed, when they are properly understood, they have their own language.[42]

So the educated Christian sees the miracle, praises God, reads the miracle and then goes on to study it so as to understand what it signifies, just as a literate person who sees the letters on the page is roused by the beauty of the book and its calligraphy to read the words and understand their meaning.

Chazelle suggests that St Gregory extended St Augustine's notion of reading miracles to reading paintings of the miraculous events in the scriptures and in the lives of the saints.[43] Augustine's few observations on painting did in fact warrant Gregory to take this step. Augustine's scorn for pictures is that of a Platonist: pictures are deceptive, fictive representations of reality which cannot provide us with knowledge, make no intellectual demands upon the spectator and do not constitute a language. He even compares them unfavourably with mime in theatrical dances which is, in his view, a kind of language. The signs made by such dancers are like the language of words in that their meaning arises from 'human convention and agreement', they are not like natural signs such as smoke which signifies fire. The mimed gestures of the dancers are a language created with the intention of communicating ideas, and constitute a language which has to be learned: 'if a person unfamiliar with these frivolities goes to the theatre, his rapt attention to them is pointless unless someone tells him what the movements mean'. A frivolous luxury the dance may be, but at least it requires knowledge and effort from its audience. Works of visual art, on the other hand, are not only luxuries but are also intellectually undemanding, 'except', Augustine grudgingly concedes, 'when it makes a difference why or where or when or by whose authority one of them is made'.[44] What he meant by this is somewhat obscure. Perhaps he meant that when an image is made for the purpose of Christian instruction, in a church, by the proper ecclesiastical authorities, it might not be a mindless luxury for the passive admiration of form and colour, but part of a system of what he called 'visible speech' – *verba visibilia* – to be observed, admired, read and interpreted, just like a miracle.[45] This, it is suggested, is what St Gregory had in mind when he claimed that illiterates could 'read' a picture in the same way as a literate person reads a verbal text.

We need also to bear in mind that for Augustine reading the scriptures themselves was not a passive process of recognition and reminder but a thoroughly active and often arduous process of deciphering obscurities and metaphors, an activity which he considered to be highly pleasurable:

> no one disputes that it is much more pleasant to learn lessons presented through imagery, and much more rewarding to discover meanings that are won only with difficulty.[46]

Within the early Renaissance, the writer Giovanni Boccaccio in his 1374 *Life of Dante* made a similar point about poetry.

> It is obvious that everything that is acquired with toil has more sweetness in it than that which comes without trouble. The plain truth, because it is so quickly understood with little effort, delights us, and is forgotten. So, in order that truth acquired by toil should be more pleasing and that it should be better preserved, the poets concealed it under matters that appeared to be wholly contrary to it. They chose fables, rather than any other form of concealment, because their beauty attracts those whom neither philosophic demonstrations nor persuasions could have touched. What then shall we say of poets? Shall we suppose that they are madmen, like those carping fools, speaking and not knowing what they say? On the contrary, they are profoundly intelligent in their methods, as regards the hidden fruit, and of an excellent and beautiful eloquence as regards the bark and visible leaves.[47]

The implicit object of criticism is a purely formal response to a work. Beauty is a means of whetting the appetite for a strenuous intellectual engagement with the content of a text or an image. Beauty should not be an end in itself. The difficulty of puzzling out the meaning of an image can be a further source of pleasure designed to encourage us to seek a deeper understanding. With this in mind, let us see how we can read these pictures with pleasure and understanding.

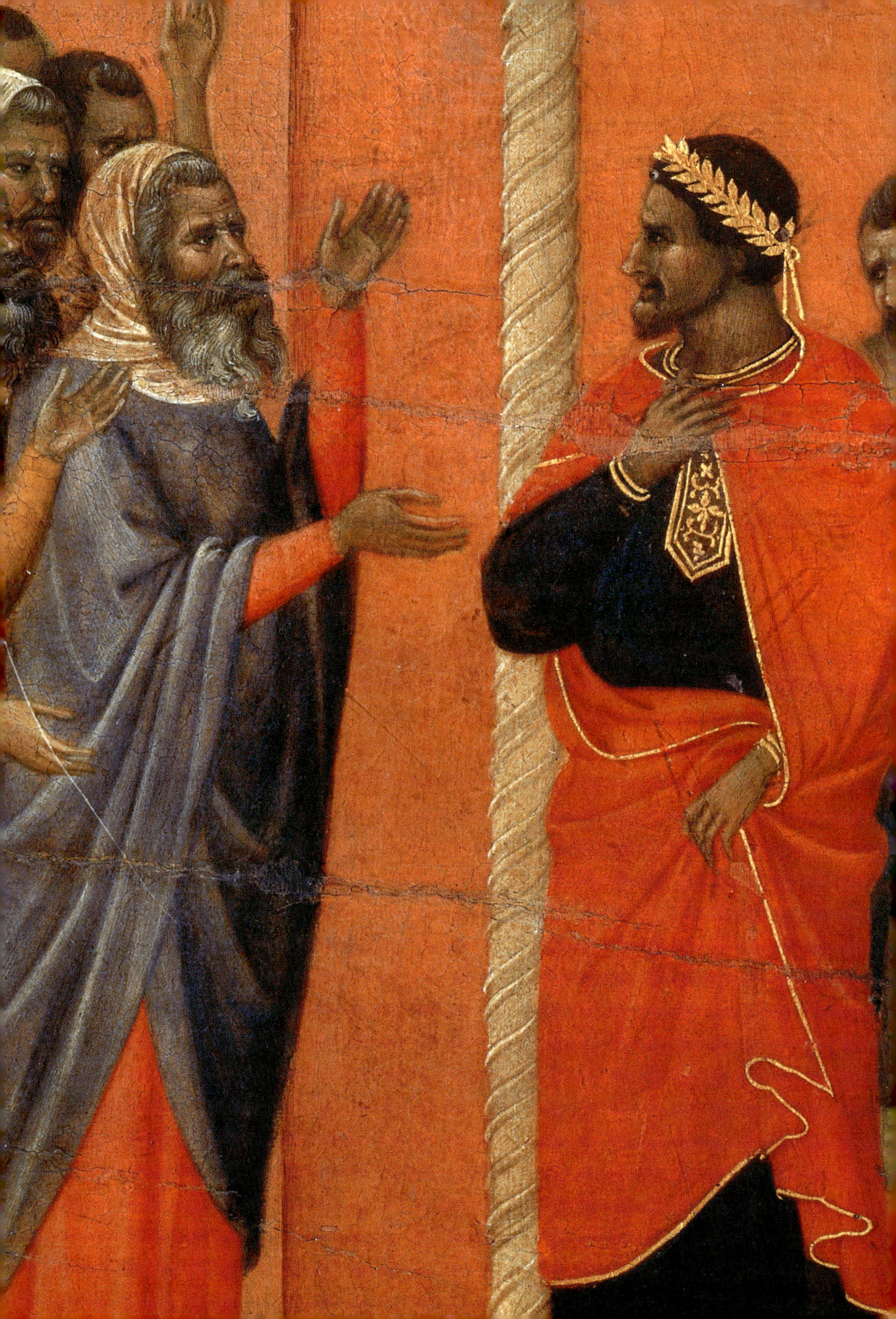

PART 1

1298–1311

Detail of Figure 10

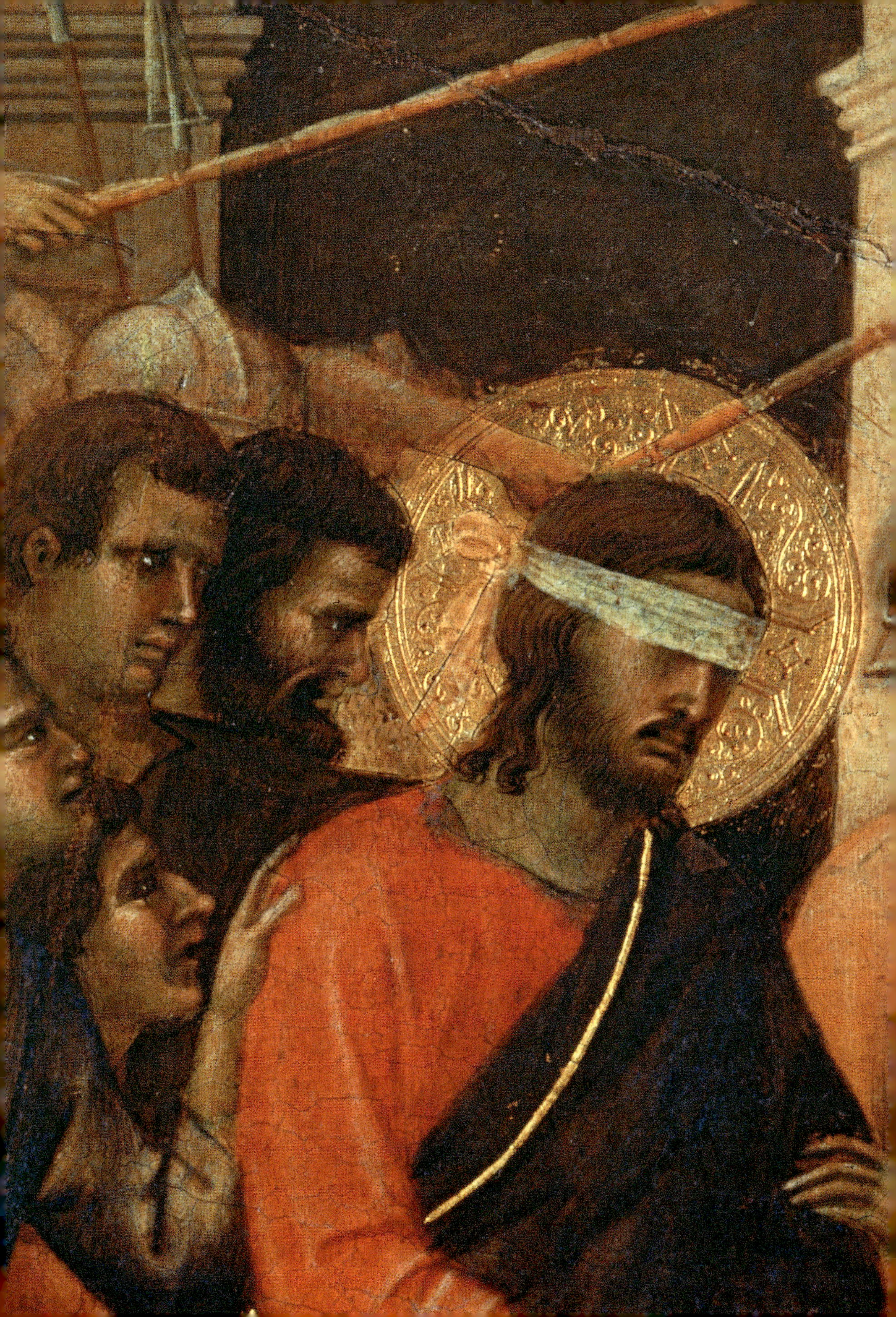

I

DIVINE AND EARTHLY JUSTICE IN DUCCIO'S MAESTÀ

First I shall examine one section of a work which illustrates some of the ways in which narrative pictures can be read – the eleven scenes recounting Jesus' Trial on the back of Duccio's Maestà.[1]

The installation of his altarpiece for the High Altar of Siena cathedral in June 1311, the occasion of a public holiday when the whole population of the city followed the huge altarpiece in a procession from Duccio's workshop to the cathedral by way of the town square, the Campo, to the accompaniment of church bells, trumpets, pipes and castanets, is one of the most magnificent artistic ceremonies to have been recorded in a surviving fourteenth-century description.[2] It was as if Mary, the Mother of God, heavenly advocate and ruler of Siena, was being enthroned in her palace, the new cathedral of the city. The wooden altarpiece, sixteen feet high and fifteen wide and painted on both sides,[3] would have dominated the view of the interior from the entrance (Fig. 3), framed by the perspective of the dark green and white marble columns, raised high on the altar, rich with applied gilding in contrast to the shadowy interior, lit by candles and surmounted at the end of the church by the stained-glass window depicting the Virgin's Death, Assumption and Coronation, which completed the story of the life of the Virgin.[4]

In addition to the great Maestà of the Court of Heaven on the front (Fig. 4), the altarpiece also recounted the Christian story, in about fifty-eight scenes,

Detail of Figure 8

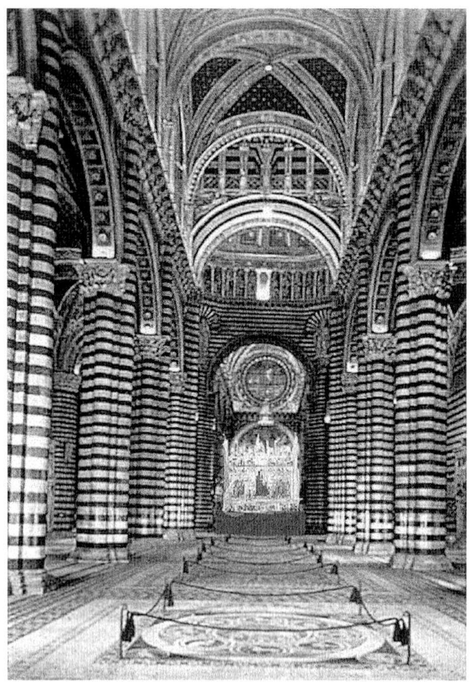

3. View of the interior of Siena Cathedral with a photomontage of Duccio's Maestà suggesting how it might have appeared when installed on the high altar.

of which fifty-two survive.[5] On the front these took the form of a predella beneath the Court of Heaven, showing seven scenes of Jesus' birth and childhood, while there were possibly eight scenes of the life of the Virgin above. The back of the altarpiece (Fig. 5) was devoted to about forty-three scenes of Jesus' ministry, trial, death and resurrection, of which forty survive, making it far and away the most elaborate narrative altarpiece ever created, containing around twenty scenes more than Giotto's earlier fresco cycle in the Scrovegni Chapel, probably finished in 1305, which has thirty-nine.[6] Duccio devoted no fewer than eleven scenes to the Trial of Jesus compared to two in the Scrovegni Chapel. This was unprecedented.[7] One reason may relate to the well-documented concern on the part of the government of Siena for the proper administration of justice during a period of appalling civil conflict. There is ample evidence for this in legislative documents[8] and also in two famous fresco paintings in Siena Town Hall. The first is by Duccio's pupil, Simone Martini, painted about 1315. Like the Maestà it also shows the Virgin in Majesty, only here she also presides over the council meetings or parliament of Siena. The infant Jesus carries a scroll of real parchment embedded in the plaster inscribed with words exhorting his mother's magistrates to observe justice: *Diligitate iustitiam qui iudicatis terram* – Love justice, you who rule the earth.[9] The second is the so-called Allegory of Good and Bad Government in the Room of the Nine, or Cabinet Room, next door to the Council Chamber, painted by Ambrogio Lorenzetti in 1338–40.[10]

The Maestà, however, is earlier than either, and its trial sequence is the first pictorial manifestation of Siena's commitment to justice. As such it will provide the focus for my account of Duccio's narrative. It demonstrates how pictorial narrative could be employed for the difficult task of representing abstract concepts; it also shows how the spectator has to engage actively with the work in order to make sense of it. At the same time it illustrates the nature of an eyewitness depiction of these events and how Jesus' conduct is held up as a standard for us to imitate. Later I will examine Giotto's interpretation of the

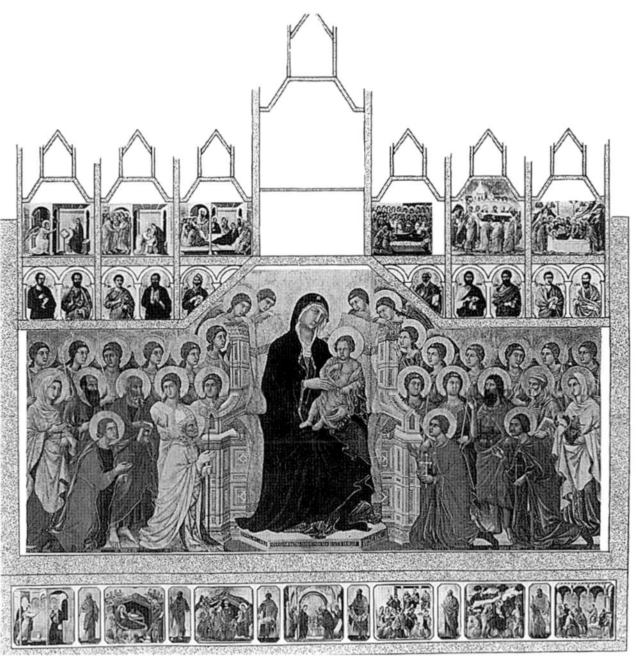

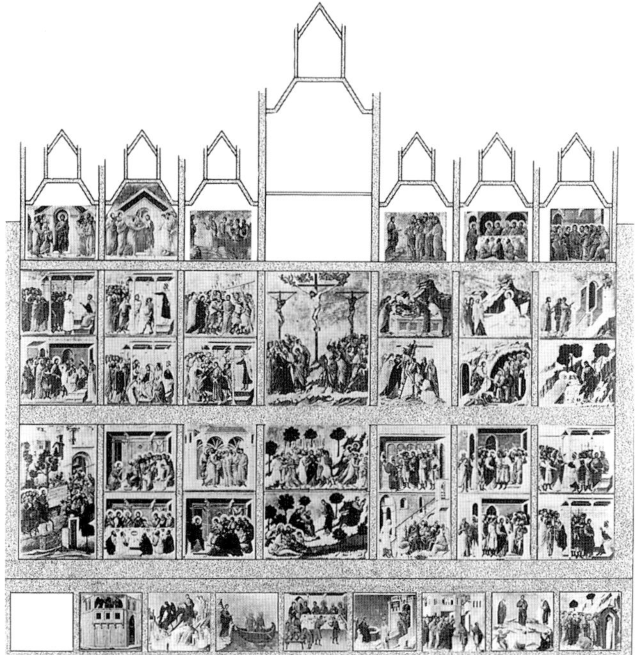

4 (*top*). Duccio di Buoninsegna, reconstruction by John White of the front of the Maestà for the high altar of Siena Cathedral, 1308–11.

5 (*bottom*). Duccio di Buoninsegna, reconstruction by John White of the back of the Maestà for the high altar of Siena Cathedral, 1308–11.

same subject (Figs 33–5), and Giovanni Pisano's highly selective meditation in his Passion panel on the Pisa Cathedral pulpit (Figs 76–86). In contrast to both Duccio's treatment is extended and painstakingly analytical.

Because no earlier artist had to my knowledge represented the scenes of the Trial in such detail, Duccio must have studied the biblical text with great care, selecting his episodes and devising his images. As a preliminary, therefore, someone, either Duccio himself or some ecclesiastical dignitary, had to write the script or programme of the story. There is considerable dispute as to whether artists or clerics were responsible for the choice of texts or programmes.[11] But Italian translations of the Latin Bible, the Vulgate, existed at this time as well as translations of the *Diatesseron*, a second-century compilation which wove the four Gospels together into a single text.[12] There is strong evidence that many artists were able to read and write, and more important, that they could transform a verbal account into visual imagery.[13] That was the task of the literate painter as defined by the 1355 statutes of the Sienese painters' guild. Leon Battista Alberti in his *De Pictura,* On Painting, of 1435 advocates the most careful preparation of the verbal outline of a story, what he called its 'invention' and what film-makers nowadays call the script, as the essential preliminary to pictorial composition.[14]

For the Trial of Jesus this was no easy matter; there are four accounts of the Trial of Jesus in the four gospels (each sung in the Mass on the four days in Holy Week leading up to Good Friday) which differ and even contradict one another. Since almost every episode in Duccio's sequence can be found in the *Diatesseron* it seems quite possible that he used it. Even so the scriptwriting would have involved careful selection and editing. One detail alone is missing from the *Diatesseron* – the first scene (Fig. 6) showing St Peter sitting round the fire in the hall in the midst of Annas's servants.[15]

The theme of the sequence is justice and it centres upon what a Christian in the fourteenth century would have considered the true story of the Trial of Jesus, perhaps one of history's most momentous miscarriages of justice. Both in its form and subject matter Duccio's Trial manifests rules of storytelling similar to those set out by Plato in his *Republic*, followed more closely perhaps than any other sequence in this book. The depiction is detached and unencumbered by inessential descriptive detail. Everything is related to the action that is being performed, as Aristotle and subsequently Alberti insisted.[16] Each scene is set parallel to and across the plane of the panel. There are no oblique viewpoints inviting one to identify with any of the characters. In comparison to the figures in Giovanni Pisano's sculptures Duccio's characters are emotionally restrained, more than Giotto's.

In the Gospel accounts and in Duccio's rehearsal of them, Jesus is examined or tried by no fewer than four judges: Annas, the High Priest's father-

6. Duccio, Jesus interrogated by Annas the priest; below St Peter denies being one of Jesus's disciples. The first of a sequence of panels from the back of the Maestà recounting the Trial of Jesus, tempera on panel, Museo dell' Opera del Duomo, Siena.

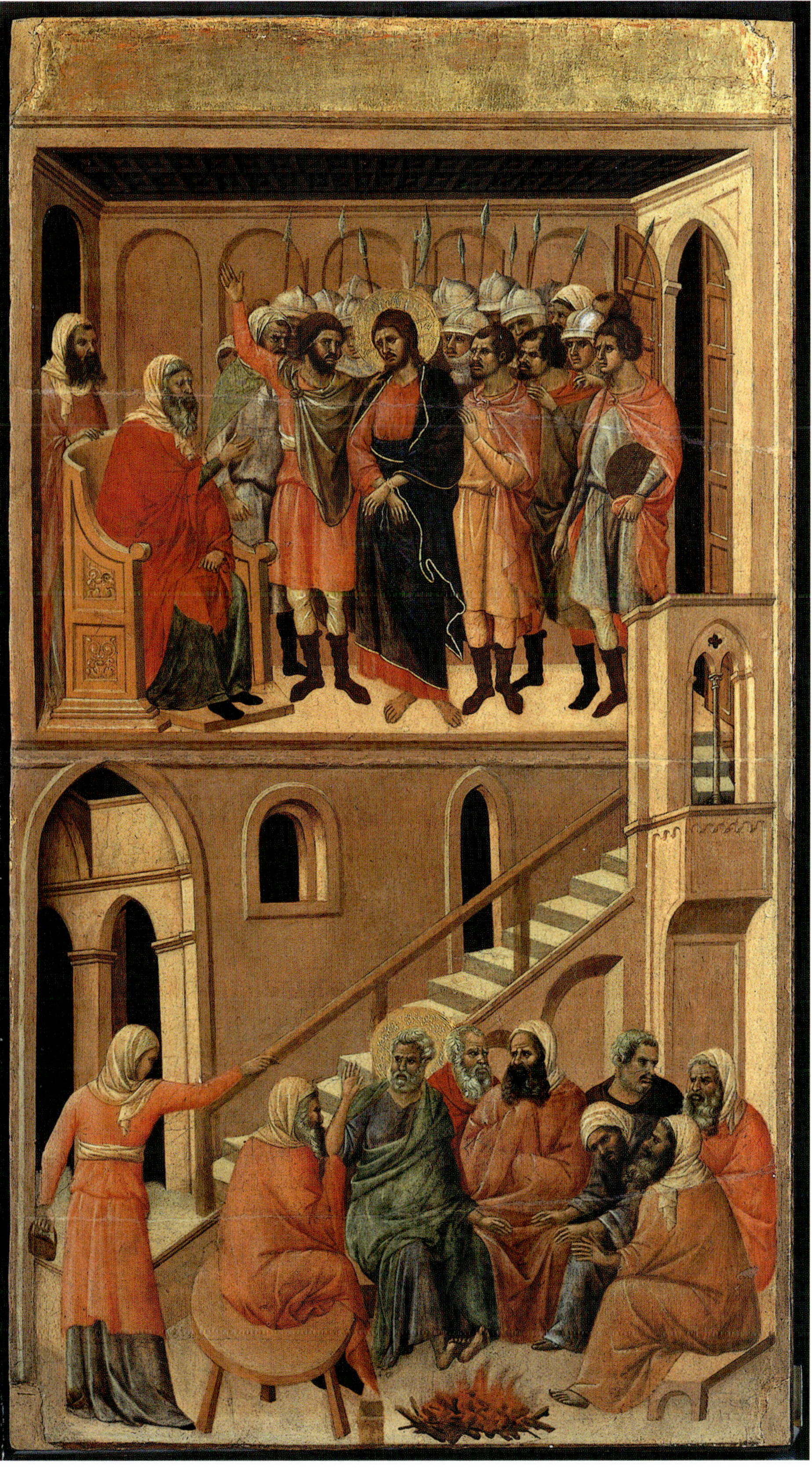

in-law (Fig. 6); Caiaphas, the High Priest (Figs 7–8); Pontius Pilate, the Roman prefect or governor of Judæa (Figs 9, 10 and 12–15); and Herod, the tetrarch of Galilee (Fig. 11).[17] The central issue is whether Jesus had committed blasphemy by claiming to be the Christ or Messiah, King of the Jews and Son of God. Throughout, Jesus either keeps his silence or gives brief answers to questions.

Although a script can be compiled to fit each of Duccio's pictures, in some respects the pictures are even more terse than the biblical story, and the correspondence is not always exact. Duccio does not represent any of the spoken dialogue between Jesus and his judges. In the scene before Annas, in the first scene before Caiaphas and in the first scene before Pilate the Bible records Jesus answering his judges; only in the scene before Herod and in most of Pilate's later interrogations does Jesus remain silent. But Duccio, in all five scenes of interrogation (Figs 6, 7, 9, 11 and 12), depicts Jesus in an almost identical attitude, his arms crossed and bound at the wrists, his eyes and head lowered and his mouth resolutely shut. In contrast his judges and captors question him, tear their clothes in exasperation, beat him, flog him, humiliate him but to no avail – he holds his peace. Through this representation of passive resistance in the face of repeated efforts at coercion an impression of the charade of earthly justice is built up, scene by scene. This interpretation seems to correspond to that of Jacobus de Voragine's observations in his *Golden Legend,* one of a number of texts which provided a gloss on the scriptures upon which some painters drew. 'Why,' asks Jacobus, 'did the Lord, in the course of his Passion remain silent before Herod, Pilate and the Jews?' In the Gospels Jesus did not remain *totally* silent, but it was the overall impression of non-cooperation that Jacobus rightly emphasised. In his view, Jesus' judges were unworthy of an answer because no matter what Jesus said, they would have distorted and perverted it.[18]

Duccio's telling of the story, then, is austere, beginning quietly in the first scene in the palace of Annas where Jesus was taken after his capture (Fig. 6). Annas questions him about his teachings while below, St Peter, having followed Jesus, is sitting in the courtyard toasting his toes in the midst of the officers. When asked by the doorkeeper whether he is one of Jesus' disciples St Peter denies it.

By unifying the two scenes in a cut-away cross-section of a palace, the two storeys/stories connected by an open staircase, Duccio used a simple means to convey the simultaneity of the two episodes – while Jesus is being interrogated and beaten, St Peter denies their relationship.[19] The fact that this takes place in the dead of night is suggested by the blackness seen through every doorway, window and the ceiling of Annas's room. It is an unassuming scene, whose effect turns upon the relationship between Jesus and St Peter which their juxtaposition invites one to interpret. Because St Peter is placed directly underneath Jesus the viewer is encouraged to perceive similarities and contrasts between them: St Peter is free, Jesus is bound; St Peter sits in the warmth of the fire surrounded by companions, Jesus stands alone, beaten by enemies; out of cowardice, St Peter lies in reply to the maid's question, courageously Jesus refuses to answer Annas's question. These are antitheses. Attention is also drawn to a single similarity: St Peter's hand, raised in denial of his master, echoes the hand about to strike Jesus. From the beginning of the Trial Jesus' conduct is presented as an object of imitation, that of St Peter and the priests as behaviour to be avoided.

Jesus is sent by Annas to Caiaphas, the High Priest (Fig. 7). According to St Mark, Jesus, after repeated questioning which he refused to answer, finally admits to being Christ and the Son of God. According to St Matthew, Jesus replies, 'You said it.' Either way both accounts agree that Caiaphas treats Jesus' reply as an admission that he is guilty of blasphemy and should be executed. But Duccio shows Jesus with his hands bound and speechless.

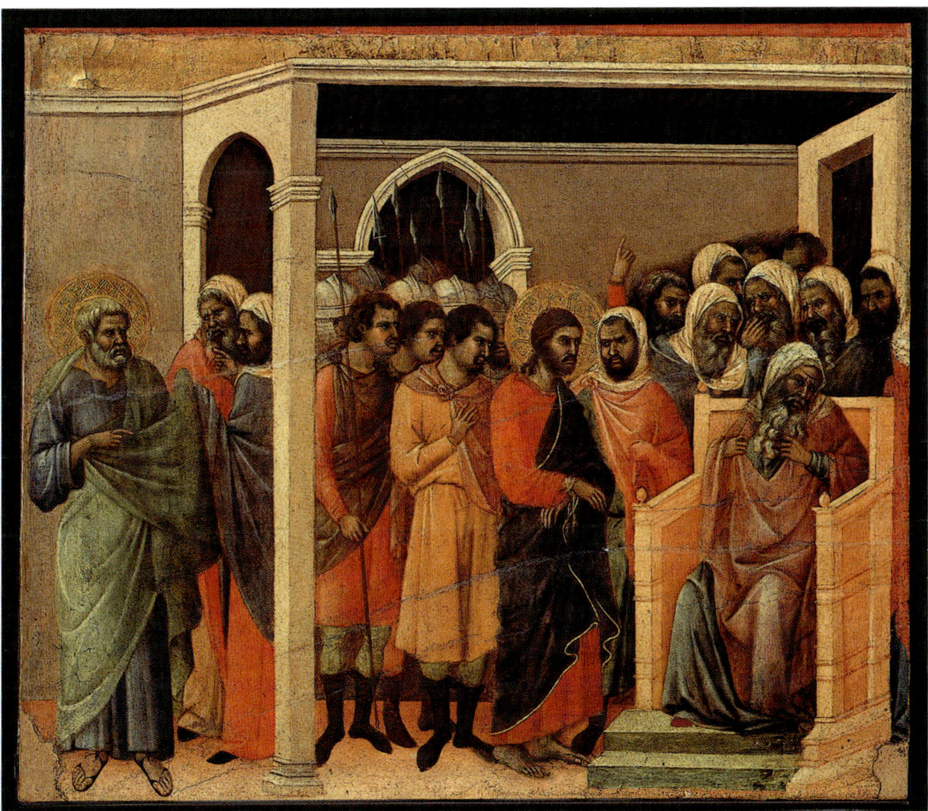

Fig. 7. Duccio, Jesus interrogated by Caiaphas the High Priest and St Peter's second denial, Museo dell' Opera del Duomo, Siena.

In the first and lower of the two scenes Caiaphas tears his clothes, in the fourteenth century a sign of anger. Another sign of his fury is the way he turns his head away from Jesus, refusing even to look at him. Meanwhile Peter, standing in the porch, again denies any connection with Jesus. In the upper scene (Fig. 8) Jesus is blindfolded, beaten and humiliated while the priests surrounding Caiaphas seem to conspire. Meanwhile Peter, still in the porch, once again denies any association with Jesus. It is dawn, the early morning light strikes the inside of the arch behind Jesus, the cock crows at Peter's third denial. I will discuss the architectural setting of these two scenes later; here let me merely note their predominantly grey and miserable colouring and claustrophobic sense of enclosure.

According to St John's Gospel the Jews did not have the right to impose the death penalty themselves,[20] so they needed to convince the Roman governor that Jesus was guilty of claiming to be the Messiah. The trial begins in

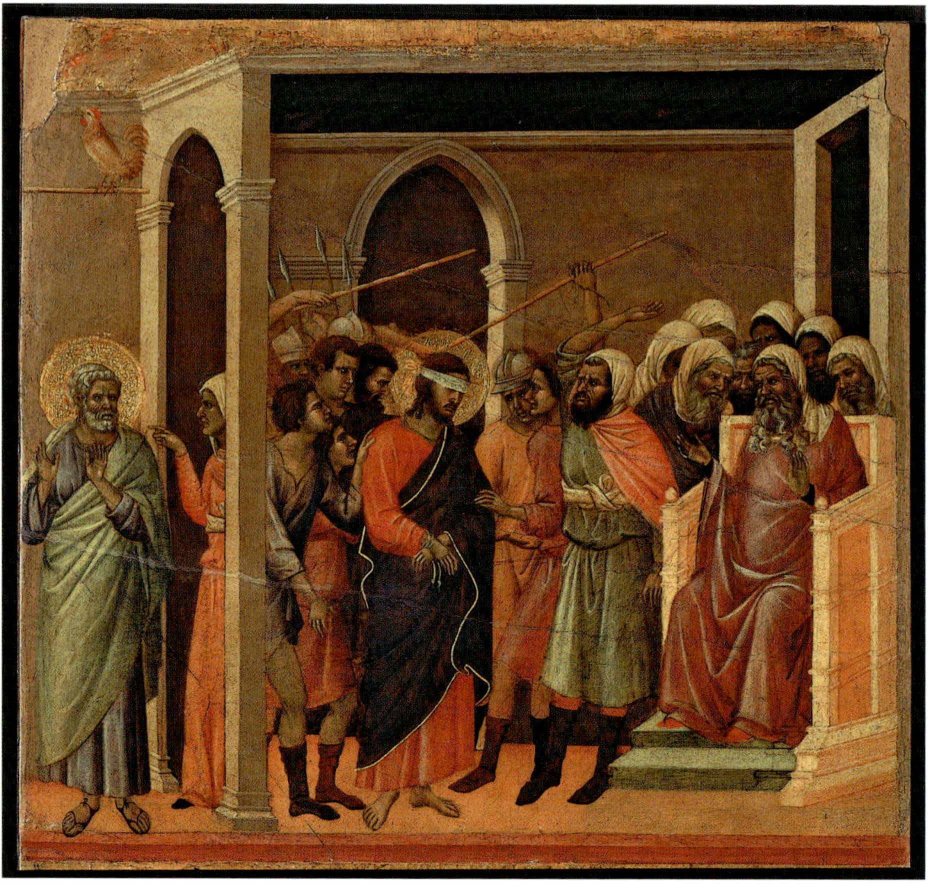

8. Duccio, Jesus mocked by order of Caiaphas and St Peter's third denial. Museo dell' Opera del Duomo, Siena.

earnest. The three scenes of interrogation before the Jews have been a prelude to the process of Roman law. In the *Golden Legend,* Jacobus de Voragine observes that Pilate had begun 'his judging on the basis of truth, but he did not abide by the truth'.[21] That is the gist of Duccio's pictorial interpretation of Jesus' trial conveyed by the successive shifts and changes from one scene in the sequence to the next.

The first, and lower, scene of the Trial before Pilate (Fig. 9) corresponds to the sources except that, as before, Jesus holds his silence. It takes place in what the Latin Vulgate calls the 'praetorium', the palace of the praetor or chief magistrate, the 'hall of judgement' in the English Authorised Version, but the Italian translation of the *Diatesseron* calls it a 'corte' or courtyard, to which Duccio's depiction, central to his representation of the trial, corresponds. We are shown a small open loggia in the corner of a courtyard, the timbers of its roof supported by three slender and finely carved twisting marble columns and by corbels on the rear wall. The three columns lie along the plane of the painting subdividing it into three. On the left, the area outside the loggia is defined by the left-hand marble column and by the rear wall which runs on beyond the frame without any further articulation. This outer area is further subdivided by the pilaster on the rear wall which corresponds to the left-hand marble column, so that the area outside Pilate's court is divided into an outer and an inner forecourt, the significance of which will become apparent. In the middle of the scene there is a central space bounded by two columns and finally, on the right-hand side, is the innermost space, bounded by two columns and the right-hand wall.[22]

This seemingly simple architecture is rich in significance. First, in contrast to the palaces of Annas and Caiaphas (Figs 6–8) this is a highly ordered public environment with clearly marked boundaries. Second there is the innermost area on the right where Pilate sits upon his judicial bench, a simple structure, it should be noted, unlike the thrones of the priests and Herod. Next is the central area, corresponding to the dock, where the accused prisoner stands guarded by Roman soldiers. Finally, on the left, in the forecourt outside, are the accusers, or the mob. The contrast with the first three trial scenes could not be greater. There, little order was to be found: judge, soldiers, priests and the accused are huddled together around the priest's throne. Jesus is beaten and humiliated at will. A travesty of justice is taking place within a private chamber, whose privacy moreover, is emphasised by St Peter's exclusion from it, by the black openings that form the doors and windows, black because it really is night, but also because the proceedings take place secretly under the cover of darkness.

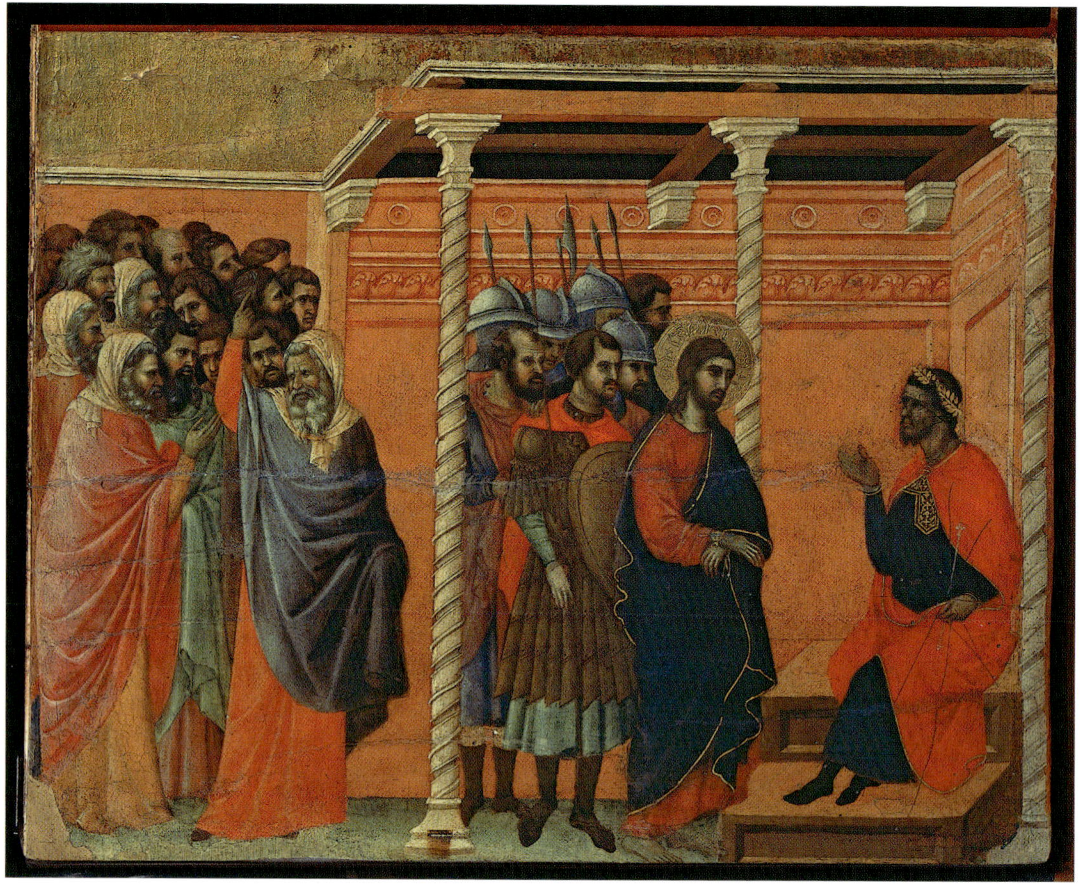

9. Duccio, Jesus's trial by Pontius Pilate, the Roman governor. Museo dell' Opera del Duomo, Siena. In this and subsequent scenes Duccio uses the changes in the positioning of figures in relation to the three columns to convey the progressive breakdown of Pilate's authority and of the administration of justice.

Not only is Pilate's court ordered, it is also rich and dignified, not with fancy thrones but with the rich red of the courtyard walls, the decorated frieze and delicate marble columns. Pilate himself wears a scarlet robe of office worn over a royal-blue ultramarine robe trimmed with gold, identical to that worn by King Solomon, the embodiment of earthly justice, in the later scene of Christ in Limbo, and the obverse of Jesus' robes. The palace of Caiaphas is drab and so are his robes. In arriving at Pilate's court the magnificence of Roman law offers hope of justice. It has recently been suggested that Duccio drew upon Roman coins in order to distinguish Pilate and his court, which is classical, from those of the Jews which are contemporary Italian gothic in style, maybe associated in Duccio's mind with the anarchy and injustice of contemporary politics.[23] Whether or not that association is correct, architecture and symbolic space are crucially important to the unfolding narrative.

A final point. Duccio plays fast and loose with the perspective of his courtyard. Instead of placing the three columns firmly on the ground on the front plane of the painting so as to overlap the human figures behind them, as if the viewer is looking at the drama through the screen of columns as even empirical perspective dictates, figures stand in front of one column or another and the columns disappear behind them and do not meet the ground. These columns, therefore, do not obey the basic rules of perspective but rather follow what Hogarth called 'false perspective', employed here by Duccio to develop his theme.

In the first scene (Fig. 9) the priests wait outside the praetorium, according to St John 18, v. 28, 'lest they should be defiled, but that they might eat the Passover'. The dignity of the precinct of the magistracy is impressive, observed in practice by the republics of Siena and Florence. Not only do the priests remain outside but only one of them intrudes into the secondary subdivision of the outer courtyard, and then barely so. No figures overlap the left-hand marble column, neither in front of it nor behind, giving rise to the almost comic effect that the bodies of the two leftmost soldiers of the seven, who possess only two pairs of legs between them, are cut off behind the column where one would expect their bulk to protrude a little on its left-hand side. Within the court Jesus, as much protected from the priests by the soldiers as guarded by them, is interrogated by Pilate: 'Art thou the King of the Jews?' Jesus does not answer. The soldiers listen intently.

The viewer moves to the next scene (Fig. 10), immediately above. Pilate has walked to the threshold of his courtroom. With his elbow barely protruding outside the boundary column and cloaked in his authority, he has delivered his verdict to the Jews: 'I find no fault in this man.' Duccio depicts their response. 'They were the more fierce', according to St Luke. They gesticulate angrily, the raised hands of their leader edging across the no-man's-land between pilaster and the sacred divide of the first marble column which is almost imperceptibly narrower than in the picture below. The boundary is threatened but maintained. Nonetheless there is tension in the air conveyed by the narrowing gap between the high priest's hand and Pilate's elbow; it is a stand-off and Pilate has to find an instant solution to buy time, if possible to pass the buck and prevent a riot. His manoeuvre is to send Jesus to be

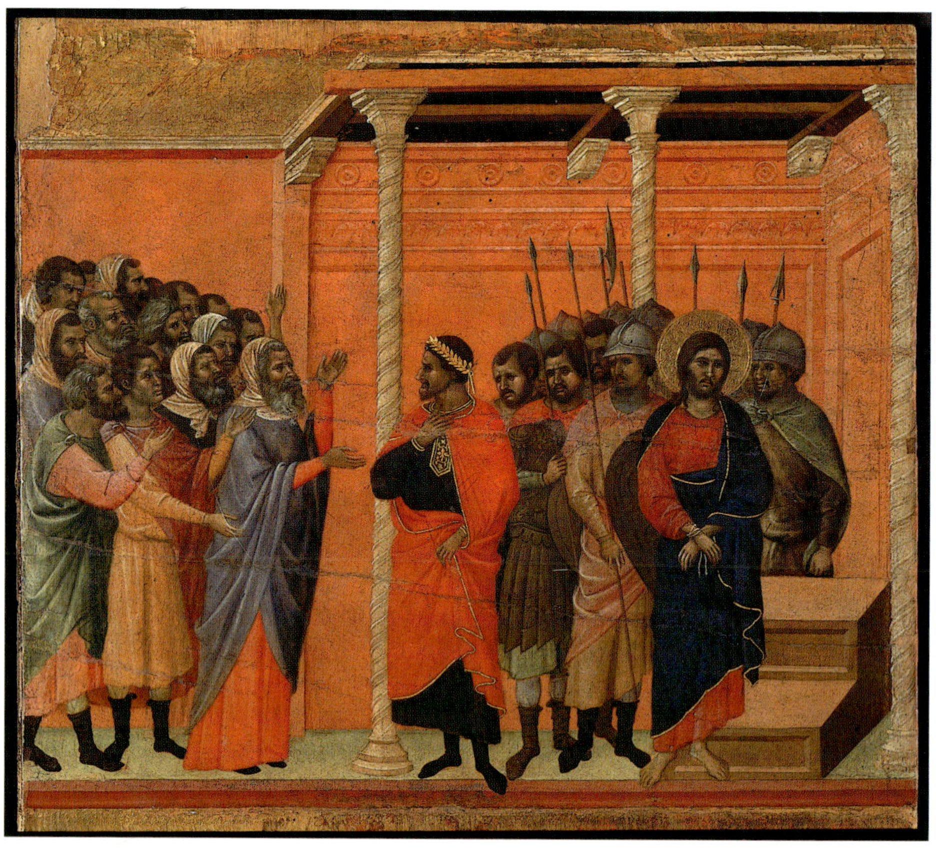

10. Duccio, 'They were the more fierce'. Pilate tells the Jews that he could 'find no fault in this man'. Museo dell' Opera del Duomo, Siena.

examined by King Herod, who has jurisdiction in Galilee, from where Jesus comes, and who happens to be in Jerusalem for the Passover.

This marks the end of the first 'chapter' of five scenes (Fig. 5). The four scenes showing Jesus before Caiaphas and Jesus before Pilate suggest a set of antithetical relationships, some of which have already been noted. The sombreness of Caiaphas's court in the left-hand pair contrasts with the splendour and apparent beneficence of Pilate's; the court of Caiaphas is closed and private, Pilate's open and public, with defined boundaries; Caiaphas rages at the prisoner, Pilate questions him in an open-handed style; under Caiaphas's jurisdiction the prisoner is beaten for not answering, under Pilate he is pro-

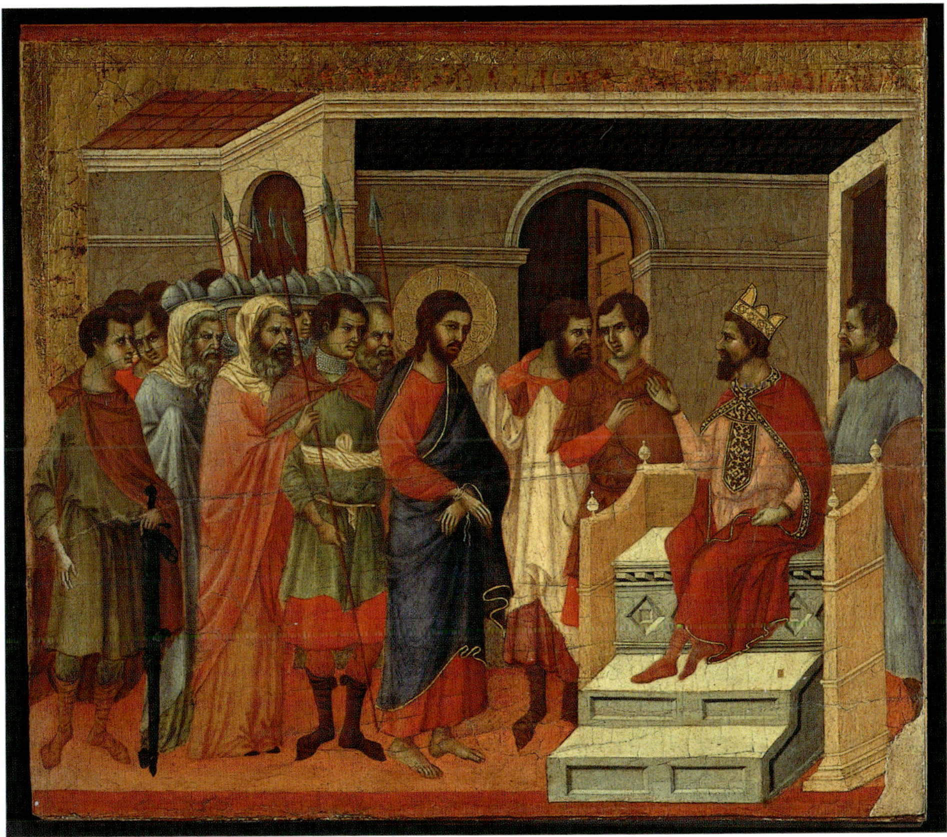

11. Duccio, King Herod interrogates Jesus. Museo dell' Opera del Duomo, Siena. Herod's court like those of the priests is less ordered architecturally than Pilate's. Duccio may also have used a more medieval style of architecture to differentiate their courts from the classical style of Pilate's.

tected by soldiers from his accusers; in Caiaphas's court, judge, jury, accusers and guards are all mixed together, in Pilate's each component of the judicial procedure has its place.

Herod's interrogation opens the next chapter (Fig. 11). The setting is a reminder of Caiaphas's court – grey walls and grand throne, priests, soldiers, prisoner all jumbled together. Herod questions Jesus, out of theological interest we are told by St Luke, but Jesus remains silent.

Why did Duccio introduce this scene, so subdued in comparison to the previous two? Maybe that is the point. The apparent reduction in tension and the law's delay heightens the tension later. Indeed, in the next scene above,

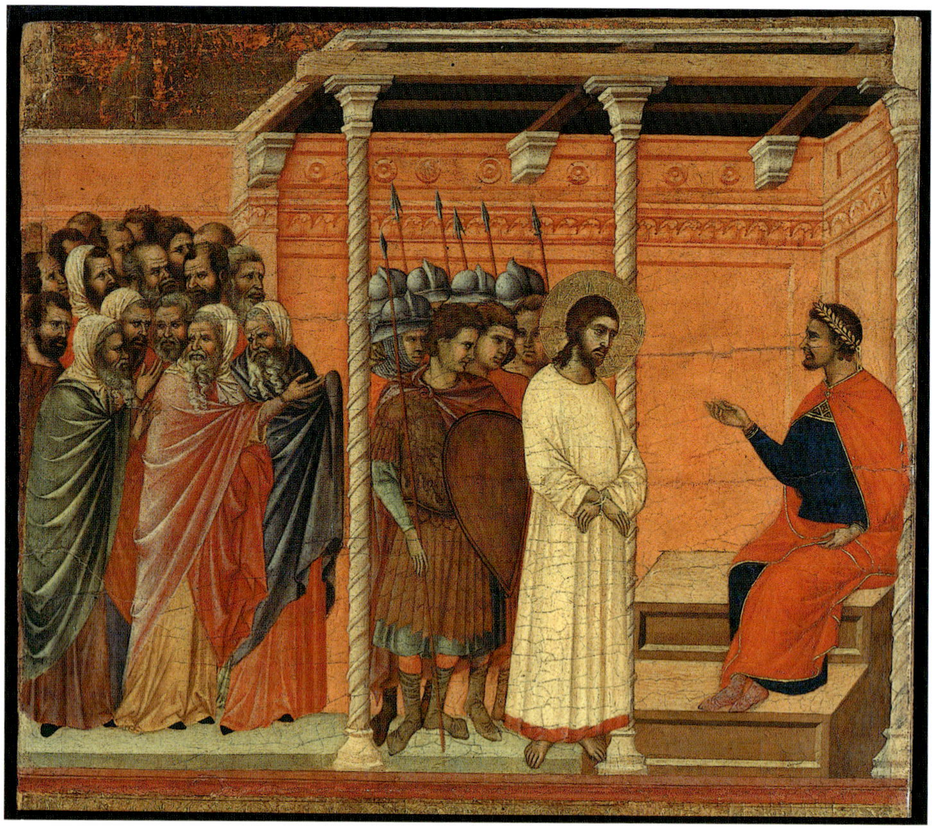

12. Duccio, Pilate examines Jesus after his return from Herod. Museo dell'Opera del Duomo, Siena.

where Jesus is re-examined by Pilate (Fig. 12), the composition appears at first glance to be a replica of Pilate's first examination: an extra helmet, an extra soldier, a couple of extra legs, Jesus' white robe in which Herod had draped him, interpreted by the *Golden Legend* as the sign of a simpleton and fool who stays mute[24] – these seem to be the only differences between the two paintings, which reflect the biblical texts in which Pilate once again questions Jesus but is unable to find fault in him.

But as one dwells on Duccio's image, trying to understand the reason for this apparent repetition, significant differences begin to emerge: the crowd of Jews has grown and the robes of the chief priests, still to the left of the unobstructed boundary column, now hang so close to it that the gap is almost closed. Their reiterated gestures in Jesus' direction give us the sense that while judicial order still prevails inside the court, outside the pressure of the mob is building remorselessly upon the representative of Roman law, and of justice. And there are other almost imperceptible differences: Pilate's bench, previously in front of the central column, is now behind it, though this is concealed by Jesus' robe and foot; Pilate's scarlet cloak now overlaps the right-hand pillar. Pilate is now in profile, he is tense and imperious, where before he seemed more at ease with his authority.

Despite the growing tension, Pilate tells the priests that after repeated cross-examination he can still find no fault in Jesus, 'I will therefore chastise him, and release him.' Duccio does not represent this scene of Pilate returning to the threshold of his court to give his verdict, but his order and his action are represented (Fig. 13). 'Then therefore Pilate took Jesus and scourged him.'

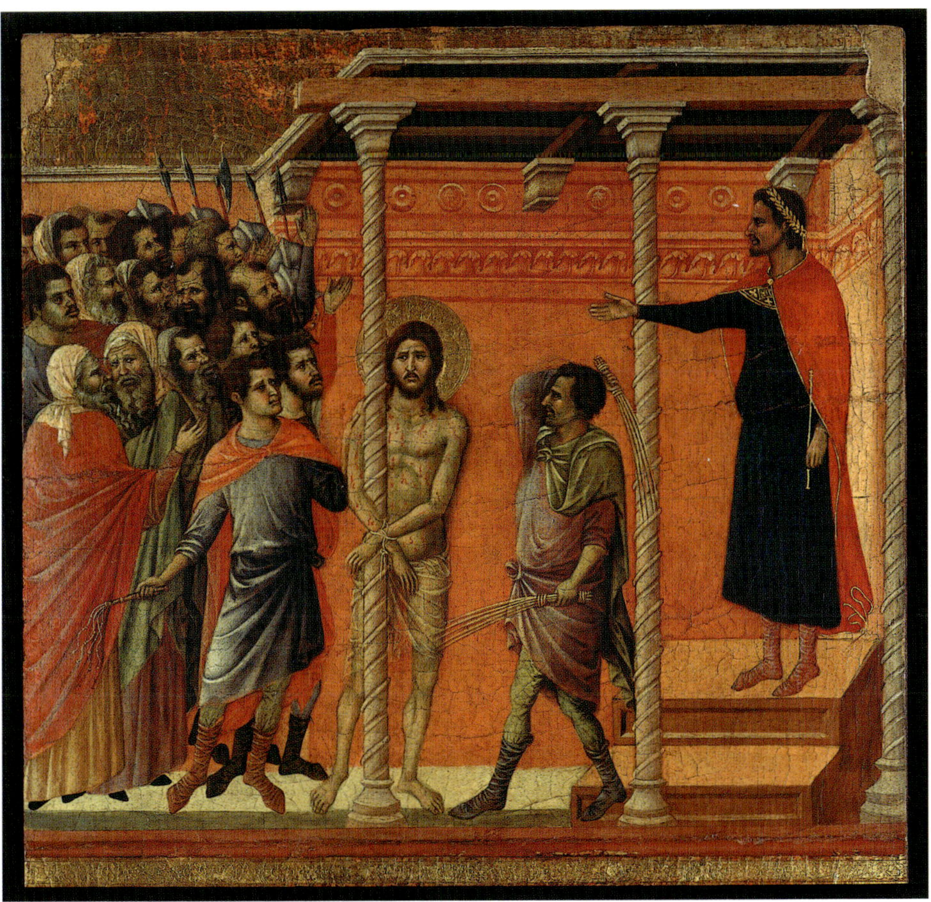

13. Duccio, The Flagellation. Museo dell' Opera del Duomo, Siena.

Pilate has now given in to the mob, for, having found Jesus innocent, having given his verdict that there is no cause for the death sentence and that the prisoner should be released, he nonetheless has him flogged. The scene, representing that, displays all the subtlety of Duccio's serial technique and his use of architecture.

First, the quasi-sacred boundary between courtroom and forecourt has been breached; second, Pilate looks as if he is no longer in control, even though he is now standing upon his judicial bench issuing the command, where before he was seated. But judicial order has not yet broken down completely. The courtroom is still occupied only by Pilate with one of his men and the prisoner. Significantly it is Pilate's soldiers who have moved into the forecourt, temporarily recovering a little territory from the Jews. This can also be read as the soldiers shifting their allegiance towards the Jews, the winning side, as the military are wont to do. One soldier whips Jesus who is roped to the boundary column, which becomes the pillar of justice, only an arm and a leg protruding into the inner section of the forecourt. Jesus' head and torso, so to speak, remain within Pilate's jurisdiction, but there is a suggestion that his body is slipping out of the Roman governor's authority, with the implication that the governor is beginning to lose control of his courtroom. It is another manifestation of Duccio's economy to use part of the architecture as the whipping post, and it reinforces our sense of the function of the building as well as the system of justice. Even as he is tortured, however, Jesus begins to triumph. His beautiful body dominates the picture, he does not flinch or recoil, his full face is shown for the first time and he even seems to be supporting the pillar of justice to which he is lashed. Again, Jesus is presented as an object of imitation in contrast to the Roman governor.

What gives us the feeling that Pilate is no longer in control? Partly it is the bridging of the divide; partly, a small detail, the position of Pilate's bench *behind* the central column is now no longer concealed; partly that Pilate is having to stand to assert his authority; but most telling, the distance between the middle and right-hand column, defining the area of Pilate's tribunal has shrunk and the space in the forecourt has grown. Thus Pilate, commanding though his posture may be, seems increasingly hemmed in. The change is almost imperceptible, but it is all the more effective. Duccio clearly wished to convey the way that justice and authority are undermined by cowardice and compromise with the mob, thus in the next scene of the Mocking (Fig. 14) the mob has virtually taken over Pilate's courtroom, with a continuous mass of figures running from forecourt into the praetorium, both in front of and behind the boundary column and with a Jew kneeling in mock homage before Jesus within Pilate's tribunal area. Now Pilate, however regally he may

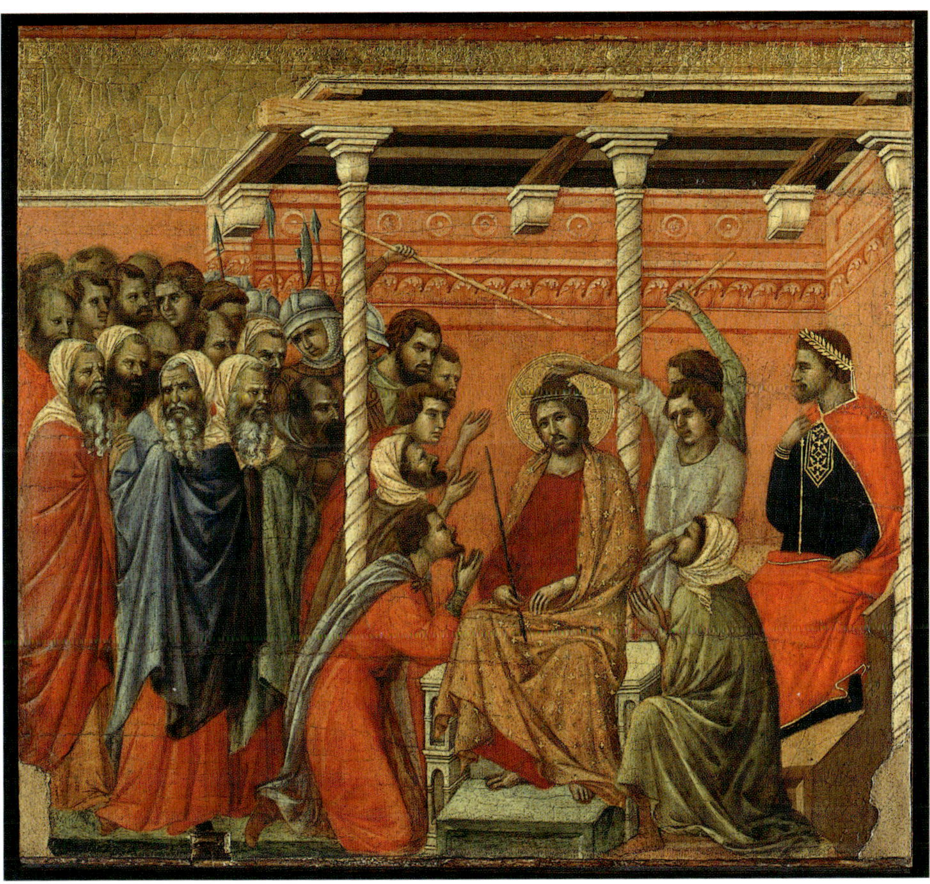

14. Duccio, The Mocking of Jesus. Museo dell' Opera del Duomo, Siena.

posture, is squeezed into a corner, his bench disappearing behind the kneeling figure. At the same time the splendour and impartiality of Roman justice, symbolised by the clear boundaries of judicial order, has broken down into the anarchy and confusion of the priestly and royal courts from which the accused could expect no justice, and the analogy is drawn to the mocking and scourging inflicted upon Jesus by Caiaphas in the previous chapter. We should also take stock at this point of the fact that in his representation of the battle for territory in the courtroom Duccio is doing far more than illustrating his text. Studied carefully, as St Gregory would have us do, the visual nature of the narrative enriches our understanding of the trial and is not translatable into words.

At this point another transformation has taken place. For the first time Jesus, now enthroned and robed in a cloth of gold, in Matthew a scarlet cloak, looks out of the picture directly at the spectator. Although it is a mock coronation Jesus is now the central commanding presence, he emerges as the true king, the embodiment of real justice, which is being humiliated as a result of Pilate's cowardice in yielding to the demands of the mob. Hence Jesus' sorrow. Moreover, one can trace the transformation of Jesus from the abject victim of the earlier scenes to the still sorrowful but increasingly dominant figure of these two scenes.

Looking back, one might say that Pilate's authority was maintained so long as he protected the prisoner's rights, but as soon as Pilate ceased to do so, his authority manifestly shrinks, while that of Jesus grows. This may very well have been Duccio's method of conveying the idea expressed in St John 19, 10–11.

> Then saith Pilate unto him, 'Speakest thou not unto me? Knowest thou not that I have power to crucify thee, and have power to release thee?' Jesus answered, 'Thou couldest have no power at all against me, except it were given thee from above.'

Earthly justice depends upon ideal or divine justice, here abused by the mob.

Finally, in response to the mob's repeated demand Pilate yields to their call for the death penalty, and washes his hands of all responsibility for his decision (Fig. 15). In this last scene the solid mass of the mob and the soldiers fills the entire forecourt and the first bay of the praetorium, the crowd is placed in front of the boundary column so that, visually, half of Pilate's palace and the pillar of justice seem to have been swept away with Jesus on his way to crucifixion. Pilate standing upon his bench, is left not even half a palace; his audience chamber has become a little cloakroom, a privy in which to wash his hands, a room so low that he almost bangs his head against its ceiling. Even his scarlet cloak has grown shorter. All vestiges of the magnificence of judicial order signified by the clear boundaries marked out by the columns have been destroyed in this grotesque travesty of justice. Duccio's treatment of the architecture reveals the progressive ebbing of Pilate's authority as he caves in to the mob.

★ ★ ★

Duccio is sometimes regarded as a rather charming, infinitely touching, typically 'primitive' painter. There is indeed great charm to be found even in so serious a sequence as this – in St Peter toasting his toes by the fire in the

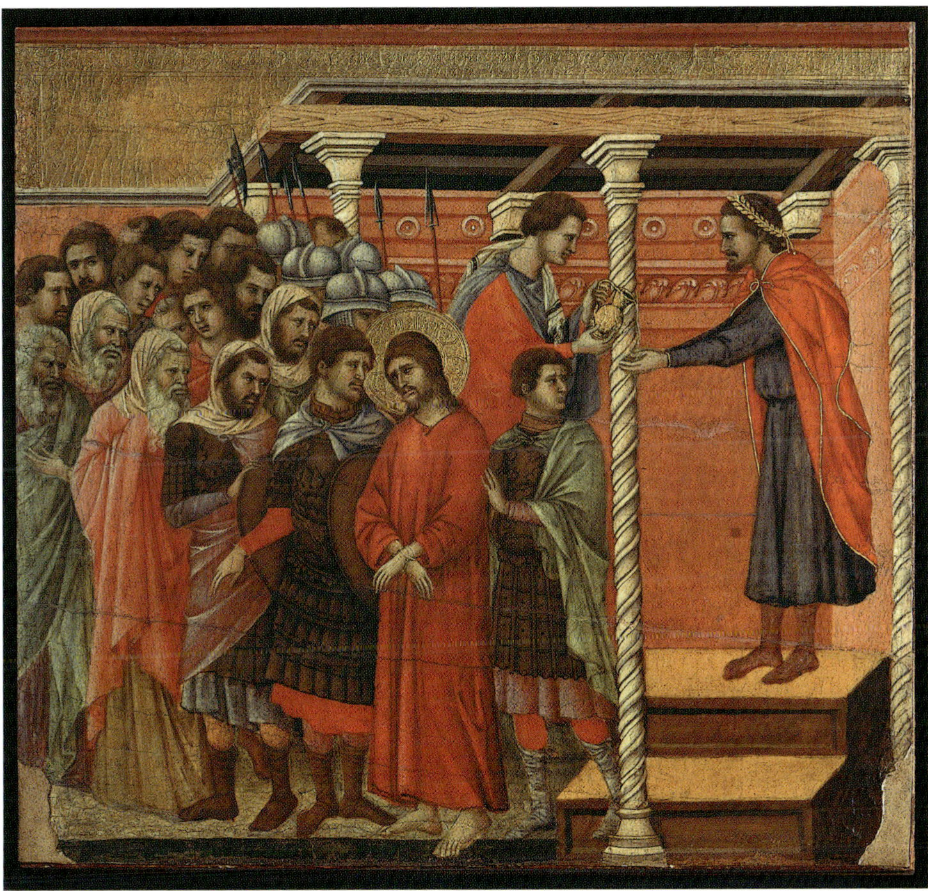

15. Duccio, Pilate washes his hands and Jesus is taken to be crucified. Museo dell' Opera del Duomo, Siena.

courtyard of Annas's palace (Fig. 6). There is also great finesse in Duccio's depiction of the light of dawn on the inside of the arch (Fig. 8) and the sketchy painting of the heads of the men at the back of the crowd (Fig. 12). But the sequence of the 'Trial of Jesus' demonstrates that Duccio's seeming artlessness conceals a highly intellectual painter who used the biblical account to offer his own reflections upon the nature of human rights and true justice, its independence and impartiality symbolised by clear boundaries between judge, accused and plaintiffs but, more important, dependent upon the ideal of divine justice for its standards and the courage to maintain those standards against the blackmail of mob rule and violence. This is perhaps the most serious responsibility of any state, but when Duccio made his Maestà it was of overriding importance to Siena struggling to sustain a just government of the merchant class in the face of the constantly conspiring nobility, with tyranny as the extreme solution to the breakdown of social order.

This intricate and forceful visual representation of the struggle between justice and injustice employs the greatest economy of means to the most complex ends, and illustrates Duccio's approach to many of the features of pictorial narrative.

Duccio's Trial sequence also fulfils many of the requirements of Christian Art derived in part from Plato's conception of a serious, philosophical art and subsequently developed by St Augustine and St Gregory. No detail is unrelated to the subject: even the light of dawn striking the inside of the arch in the court of Caiaphas contributes primarily to the narrative rather than drawing one's attention to the artist's naturalistic skill. The episodes follow one another in Aristotle's 'probable and necessary sequence'; the images can be read as if they were words in a book. They make considerable demands upon the spectator to interpret what is happening, and it does indeed prove rewarding to 'discover meanings that are won only with difficulty' as one dwells on the images. Above all, the sequence helps one imagine how the trial might have taken place, enriching the biblical record without contradicting it. Although the format of many of the scenes follows pictorial precedent, the sequence of the trial as a whole was unusual and cannot fully be understood without knowledge of the Gospels.

Although Duccio does not provide the psychological insight into what was going on inside the minds of the protagonists, he does demonstrate that painting can successfully represent abstract ideas of importance and complexity – in this case, the nature of justice. He achieved this principally through his employment of a sequence of images of the events which took place in the four courts of Annas, Caiaphas, Herod and Pilate. Most significant is the Pilate sequence, where the changes in the way that the participants occupy the architecture from one scene to the next, make manifest the struggle for power between the Jews and Roman justice. At the simplest level the sequence is temporal, but its purpose is not to suggest the passage of time as such, something of a red herring in the discussion of pictorial narrative, but to establish an ordered series of events which enables the spectator to work out the shifts and changes which occur from one scene to the next.[25] The first scene in Pilate's court is one of order and splendour, with Pilate in control (Fig. 9). This architectural formality, with its clear physical boundaries, signifies the proper administration of justice through the strict observance of legal procedure. In the succeeding scenes we observe its progressive disintegration under the remorseless threat of physical violence from the Jewish mob, until the very fabric of Pilate's courthouse is overwhelmed and due process lies in ruins (Fig. 15).[26] The step-by-step encroachment of Pilate's territory provides a distinctively visual enrichment of the Bible story, corresponding to Jacobus de Voragine's gloss quoted earlier.

The Pilate sequence is interwoven with events at the other courts. The visual comparisons set up between them draw one's attention to contrasts or antitheses between the initial authority of Roman and the degeneracy of Jewish justice. They also establish a framework through which we can take stock of how Pilate's court increasingly resembles the Jewish courts, in its confusion, impropriety and injustice. The sequential changes in the architecture and the arrangement of figures within it, act as an extended metaphor for the breakdown of justice.

Finally it must be remembered that the sequence not only enriches our understanding of the trial of Jesus but also serves a moral purpose: the conduct of Jesus, steadfast, courageous, unflinching in the face of injustice and torture, is a constant, offered as a model for imitation, as against the inconstancy of St Peter, the priests, Herod and Pilate, ducking and weaving in the face of changing circumstances.

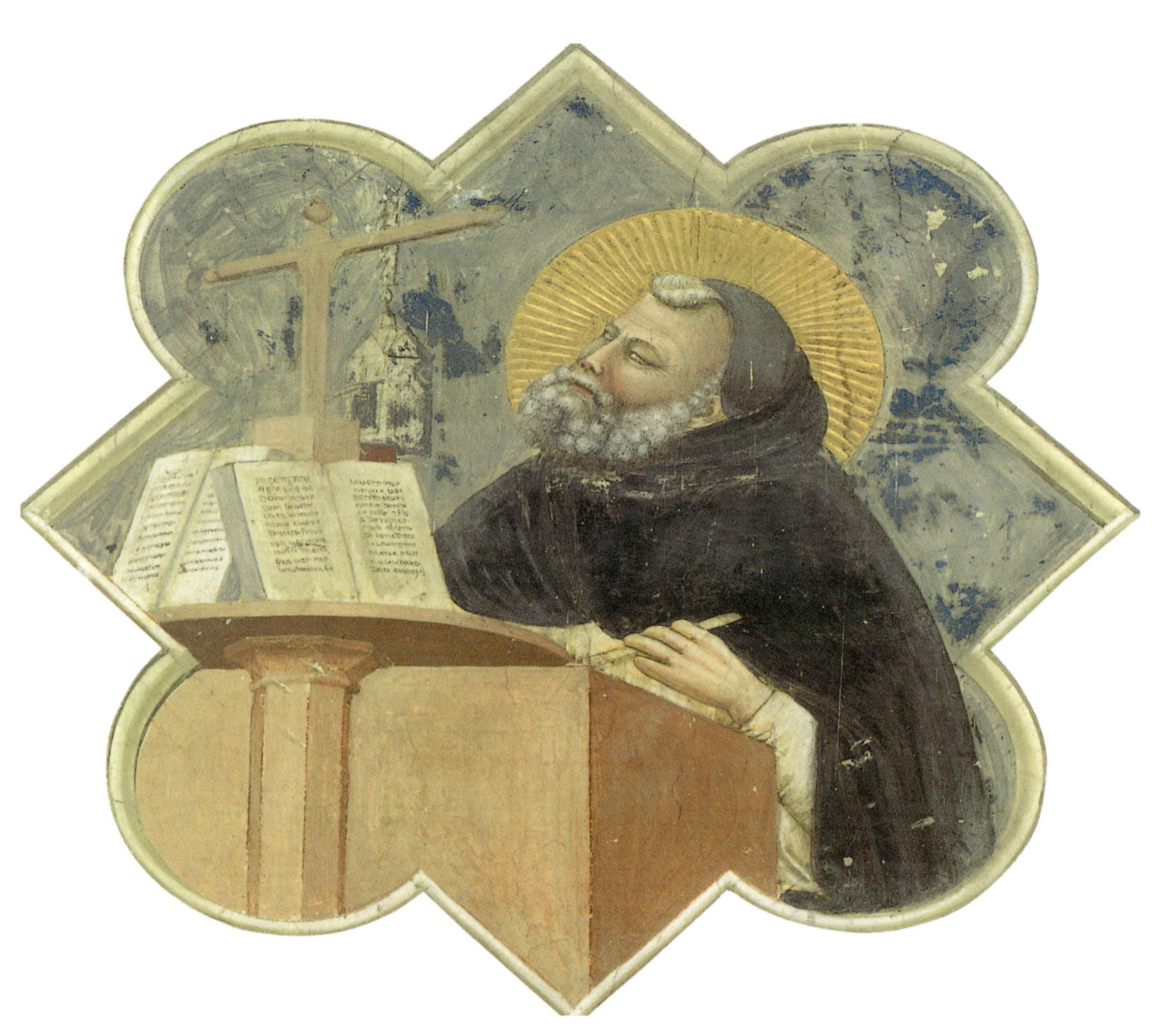

II

GIOTTO: SCROVEGNI'S TEMPLE

Painting and architecture

The narrative cycles which are the subject of this book constituted a public art treating major religious, ethical and even legal issues through the depiction of biblical stories. Such art was integral to the fabric of public places, churches, which the local population and pilgrims visited for worship, instruction and political meetings, just as it was integrated into the church service, Gospel readings, preaching and liturgical drama. Duccio's Maestà was the image upon which one's attention focused when one entered Siena Cathedral (Fig. 3); the Pisano pulpits (Figs 44 and 72) were small-scale architectural structures attached to the choir screen. The Scrovegni Chapel in Padua (Figs 16–17), however, is significantly different in that not only are the paintings physically part of the structure of the building, because fresco painting is physically bonded to the plasterwork, but Giotto related the individual episodes of his cycle to the liturgically significant spaces of the chapel.[1] The full subtlety of this will emerge, but first a brief account is needed to show how the physical space of the chapel is subdivided and how the individual scenes relate to it.

The basic shape of the chapel is that of a rectangular box with a barrel-vaulted ceiling and a small chancel opening out of the far end through a

Detail of Figure 32

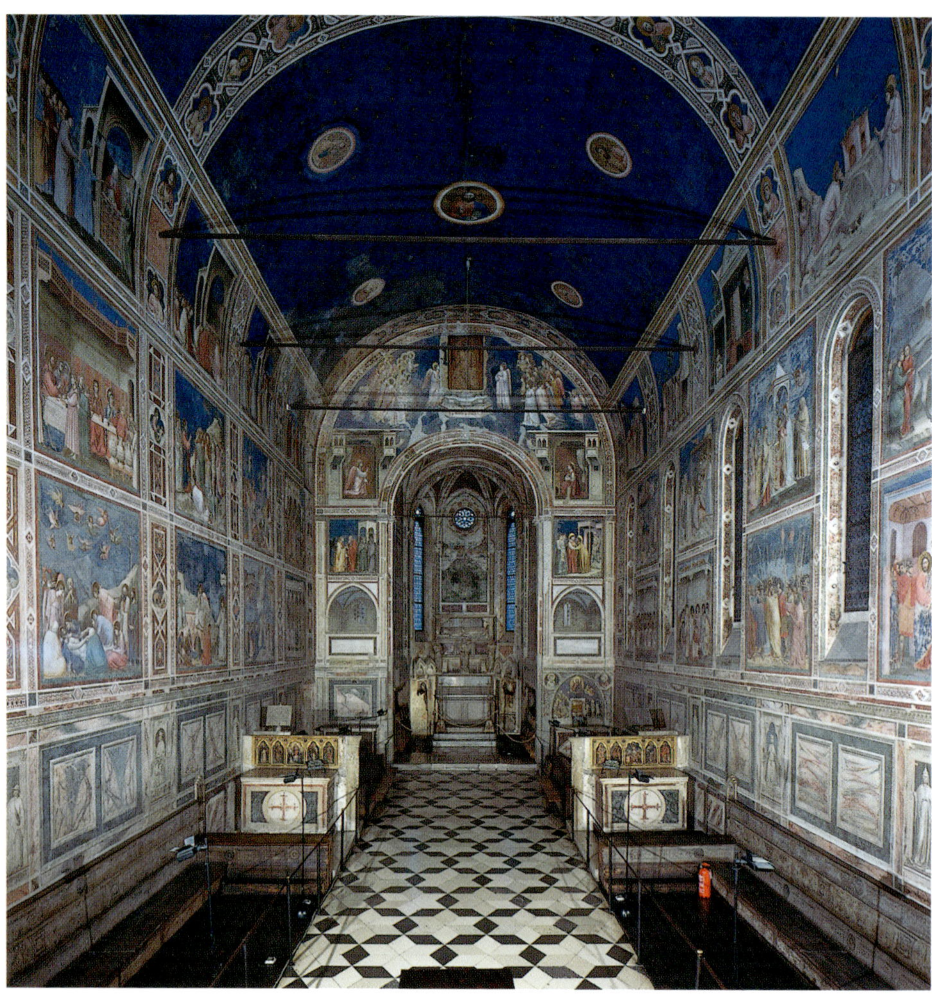

16. View of the interior of the Scrovegni Chapel, Padua, looking east towards the sanctuary and high altar, painted in fresco by Giotto, c. 1303–5.

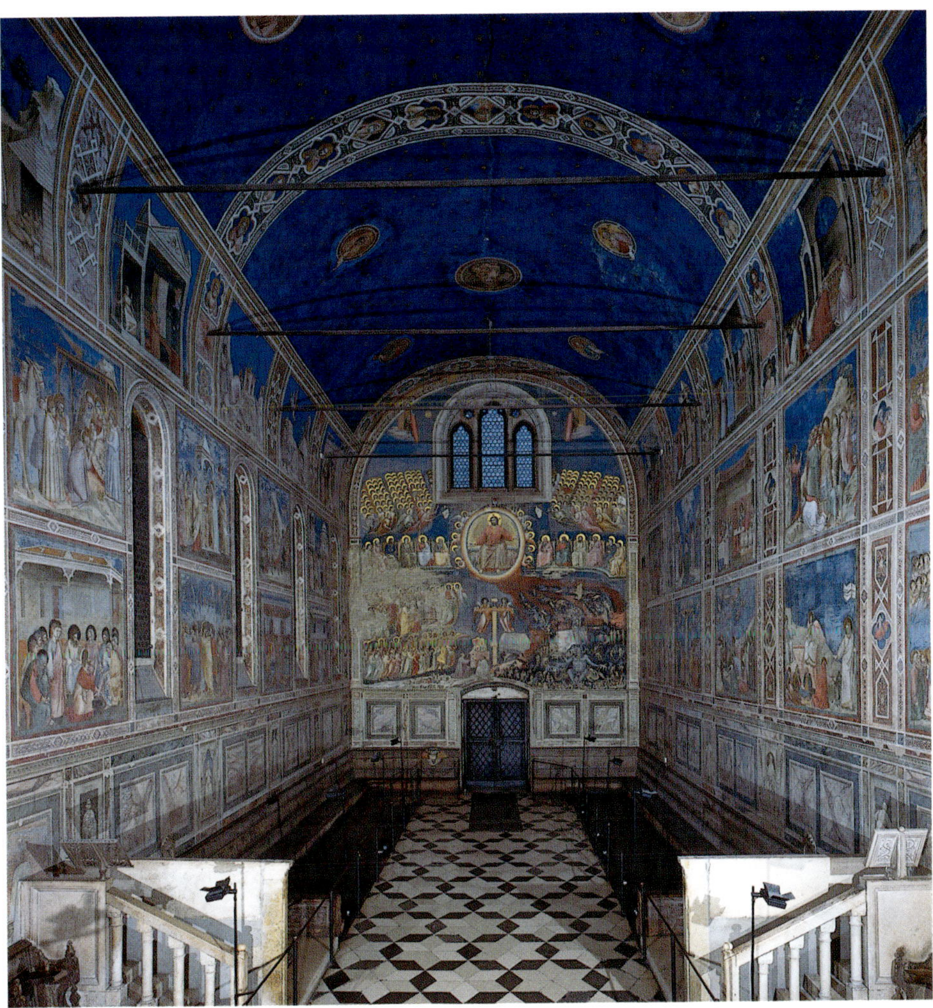

17. View of the interior of the Scrovegni Chapel looking west towards the main door and the fresco of The Last Judgement.

rounded arch that echoes the curve of the ceiling. There are six tall lancet windows in the south wall and a three-light window on the west entrance wall. On the rear wall of the chancel behind the high altar on which stands a statue of the Madonna and Child, is the tomb and effigy of the donor Enrico Scrovegni, whose mausoleum the chapel was intended to be. These sculptures are attributed to Giovanni Pisano. Mass was to be celebrated here for the souls of the Scrovegni family, whose palace was adjacent to the chapel.[2] In addition Giotto arranged the sequence of images to reinforce the chapel's liturgical symbolism, and this in turn informs the significance of the paintings. On the wall surrounding the arch Giotto painted a pair of empty vaulted chambers on the lower storey, a pair of narrative images on the next level, and the Annunciation taking place in a pair of small turret rooms at the top, either side of the arch.[3] Thus the arch is transformed into a magnificent gateway opening onto the chancel, a transformation of a Roman triumphal arch into Christian form. Above, in the blue celestial regions, the scene taking place in the Court of Heaven, usually described as God sending the archangel Gabriel on his mission to the Virgin, probably represents the council meeting to decide man's salvation. God presides, seated upon his throne in the centre,[4] attended by Mercy and Peace on his right, with Truth and Justice to his left surrounded by an angelic host. This scene is described in *Meditations on the Life of Christ,* often used by artists to enlarge upon the scriptures and the pictorial tradition, probably written by a Franciscan at the turn of the fourteenth century.[5]

What does the arch signify? It frames the altar where the daily miracle of transubstantiation takes place during Mass, and it is given the appearance of a city gate.[6] The scene of Gabriel's Annunciation to Mary, that she will give birth to the Son of God, the moment of Jesus' incarnation when Mary conceives, takes place pictorially across and above the altar upon which the bread and wine become Jesus' flesh and blood. The Virgin of the Annunciation was said to open the path leading to Paradise, and the Annunciation was often depicted on either side of the chancel arch. The chapel was dedicated to Sta Maria della Carità, popularly associated with the Feast of the Annunciation. An enactment of the Annunciation had been performed on the site of the Roman Arena in front of the chapel since before 1278, and was probably performed on Lady-day, 25 March 1305, the most likely date for the consecration.[7] Such plays continued to be performed until the seventeenth century. Ritual, liturgical drama, painting, sculpture and architecture work together.[8]

The fresco cycle is divided into chapters, which are also related to the architecture (Fig. 18). The frescoes tell the story of the redemption of mankind, which begins with the heavenly council meeting. There follow six chapters recounting the story of Mary and Jesus arranged in three horizontal tiers. On the south wall at the highest level, where the wall starts to curve into the vault, begins the story of Mary. The first chapter (Figs 20–1) starts to the right of the council meeting and proceeds in six frescoes to the entrance wall, portraying the events leading up to Mary's birth to elderly parents Joachim and Anna. The second chapter, her infancy and marriage, is depicted on the wall opposite at the same level (Fig. 19), also in six stories, running from the entrance wall back to the arch across which the Annunciation takes place. In the middle tier, the next chapter telling of Jesus' birth and infancy, introduced by the Visitation on the wall of the arch, leads back towards the main entrance, while the fourth chapter, located on the north wall opposite, recounts the events of his adult life and ministry, terminating on the arch with the scene of Judas receiving the thirty pieces of silver. On the lowest tier, the fifth chapter depicts the Last Supper, the capture and trial of Jesus (Figs 29–30 and 33–5), while the sixth and final sequence (Fig. 19) opposite treats his death and resurrection. Thus the cycle follows the path of a downward spiral running clockwise round the chapel, descending from the heavenly vaults to our earthly level where Jesus is crucified, rises from the dead, ascends to heaven and where the Holy Spirit descends upon the disciples in the Pentecost. The direction of the sequence is emphasised by the action within most of the frescoes which runs from left to right, though this rhythm is occasionally modified to mark the beginning, middle and end of each chapter.

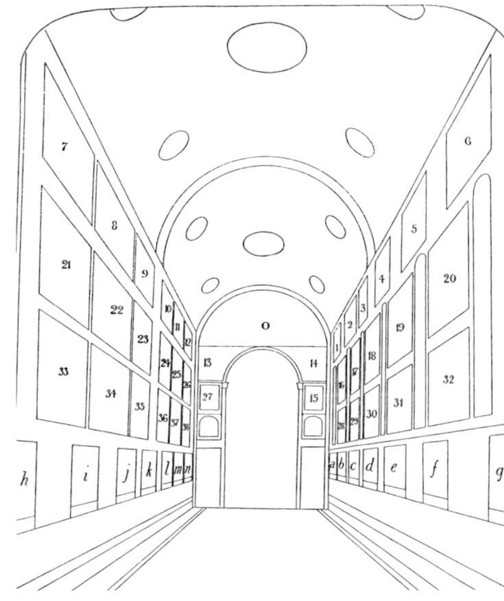

18. Diagram of the Scrovegni Chapel, Padua, looking east, showing the position of the frescoes. From John Ruskin, *Giotto and his works in Padua*.

There is also a delicately marked caesura within each of the six chapters. On every tier the two episodes nearest the chancel appear to be associated with a sacred domain and those closer to the main door to an earthly one.*

*On the right or south wall the alignment is necessarily less precise because the position of the windows gives rise to a different arrangement of frescoes in the lower two tiers. On the north wall there are six frescoes in each tier so that the caesura lies between the fourth and fifth frescoes in each tier. On the south wall, however, there are six frescoes in the upper tier only and five in the two lower tiers, so that the caesura lies between the second and third frescoes in the upper tier but bisects the Adoration of the Magi and Jesus washing the disciples' feet beneath.

Within the sacred domain, for instance, are scenes of Joseph's betrothal to the Virgin Mary, Jesus' Entry into Jerusalem and his Ascension to heaven; outside are the Flight into Egypt, the Massacre of the Innocents, Jesus' Passion and Crucifixion. This division is marked by the images of Anger, on the north wall and by Temperance opposite, while a roundel (Fig. 16) of Jesus blessing the spectator beneath, is located in the centre of the vault just within the boundary. The two altars on each side of the chapel marking the boundary of the choir and sanctuary also reinforce the caesura, but it seems that they were not erected until 1595. The original layout of the main chamber of the chapel and the location of the sanctuary is uncertain.[9] The position of the two existing altars, however, coincides with the images of Anger and Temperance so that there are reasonable grounds for believing that the caesura in the narrative corresponded to an original sanctuary.

Below the lowest tier of narrative are seven allegorical images of the Virtues facing seven Vices, painted in grey to simulate stone carvings, separated from one another by highly deceptive illusionistic marble panels.[10] Below this is a painted marble dado which originally reached to the floor. Finally, the entire entrance wall is occupied by the Last Judgement (Fig. 17), so that the end of each of the three chapters on the right-hand or south wall and the beginning of each chapter on the left-hand or north wall is marked by the scene of divine justice, like a refrain, in which the virtuous are rewarded and the wicked punished in fulfilment of God's decision to save mankind.[11]

An examination of the first sequence of the life of Mary will show in more detail how the positioning of individual frescoes and sequences enriches their significance and that of the chapel as well.

Pictorial sequence

The story of Joachim and Anna (Figs 20–1) occupying the uppermost tier on the south wall, has a clearly defined beginning, middle and end, both to the story and to the design of the sequence, and also demonstrates how the logical relationships between parts of the story are manifested.

The written legends relate how Joachim, a very wealthy sheep farmer, a charitable and virtuous citizen of Jerusalem, visited Solomon's Temple to make his ritual offerings at a religious festival. The priest rejected these, driving Joachim from the Temple on the grounds that his marriage was childless. As a result, and in great distress, he left his wife and home for the wilderness, to fast for forty days and forty nights until God responded to his prayers.[12]

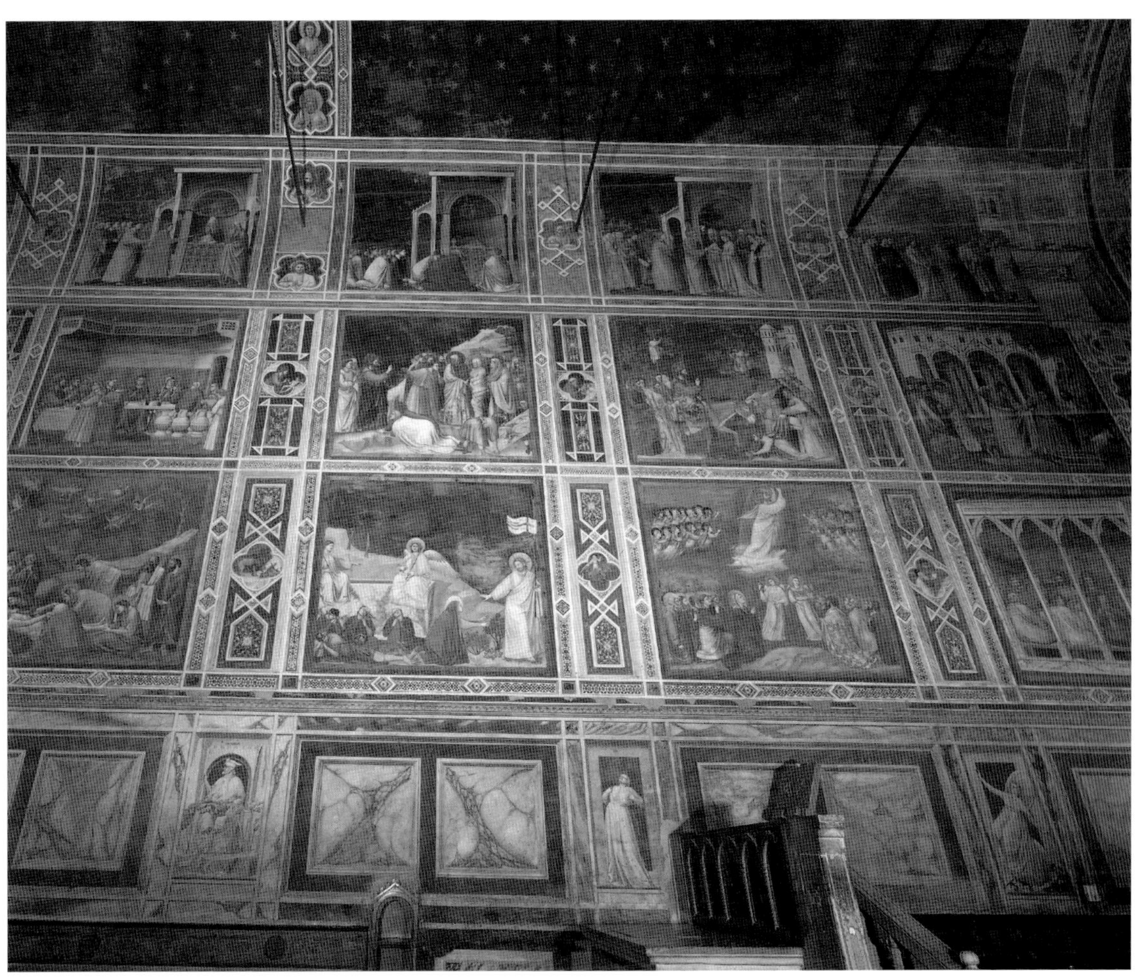

19. View of part of the north wall of the Scrovegni Chapel. In the upper tier there are four scenes of the Betrothal of the Virgin Mary; scenes from the Ministry of Jesus are shown in the middle tier, and of his Passion and Resurrection in the lower tier. In the tier beneath the narrative frescoes there are representations of the vices of Injustice, Anger and Inconstancy. The altar beneath Anger separates the sanctuary from the main body of the chapel and also marks a boundary between frescoes to its left and right.

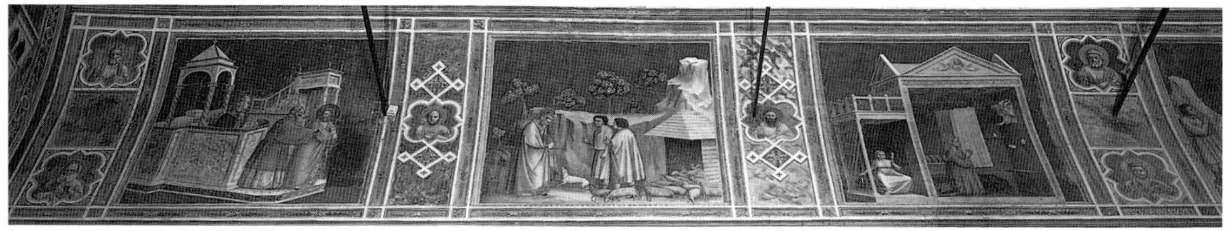

20. Scenes one to three (see Fig. 18) of the story of Joachim and Anna in the uppermost tier of the south wall of the Scrovegni Chapel. This photograph, like Fig. 21, is taken from the position of a spectator looking upwards from the floor of the chapel.

In this abridged account of the first two episodes, each action follows clearly through cause and effect, and these links are designated by appropriate conjunctions: 'on the grounds that', 'as a result', 'until'. Not so in the corresponding frescoes. In the first (Fig. 22), adjacent to the triumphal arch, we observe two actions taking place simultaneously in the surroundings of the Temple sanctuary. To the left of centre, somewhat hidden from view within its walls we see a priest in front of the altar blessing a man whose head is just visible. To the right, standing on the raised dais which marks the threshold, a second priest is pushing Joachim, identified by a golden halo and carrying his sacrificial lamb away from the sanctuary and off the edge of the dais. From our standpoint below he seems to be leaning forward at such an angle that he will fall. Here are two sentence-like images: one priest blesses a man within the sanctuary; another pushes Joachim out.[13] Is there any relationship between these two juxtaposed events, and if so what is it? The spectator has to infer the nature of the relationship. In this instance that is not very difficult. It is an antithesis: acceptance, rejection; benediction, banishment; inclusion within the religious community, exclusion from it; the fertile and the infertile.[14]

The second fresco is set in the wilderness (Fig. 23). On the left stands Joachim, now upright on stable ground but sunk in depression; towards the right his two shepherds look at one another, seemingly puzzled by his condition and by his failure to respond either to their presence or to the dog who jumps up joyfully to greet his master. There are several juxtapositions which call for interpretation. First, the relationship between this and the preceding fresco (Fig. 20), separated by a strip of wall decoration which both masks and condenses the distance between the temple sanctuary and the rocky wilderness. That time has elapsed may be inferred from the journey Joachim appears to have made from the sanctuary to the wilderness, and in the corresponding psychological change from hurt bewilderment to total dejection and

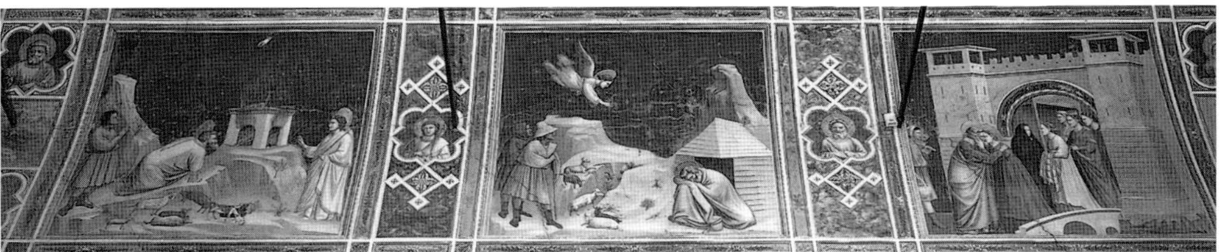

21. Scenes four to six (see Fig. 18) of the story of Joachim and Anna in the uppermost tier of the south wall of the Scrovegni Chapel.

withdrawal from the people and creatures around him. But far more significant is the implied causal relationship between the two frescoes: *as a result of* his exclusion Joachim has fled to the wilderness where he has withdrawn into himself – he feels deserted by man and by God. Within the second fresco two further sentence-like actions reinforce the sense of Joachim's state of mind; these are in the form of negations: Joachim does *not* respond to the friendly dog; he does *not* respond to the shepherds, and in their response to this situation the shepherds themselves hang back, puzzled by the cause of their employer's affliction and concerned by what has befallen him. Finally one may perhaps read a further antithesis, as well as a similarity, into the contrasted pattern of the two frescoes where the tall rock on the right of the second fresco mirrors the high ciborium covering the altar in the first scene. It is this rocky landscape which, in the fourth scene (Fig. 21), will become the site of the natural sanctuary in which Joachim's sacrifice is offered again and accepted by God.

This is not an exhaustive analysis, but it shows how in looking at pictorial narratives we have to interpret and supply the logical relationships implied by the juxtapositions both within and between individual images. In this example I have found no fewer than four major logical relationships – causation, antithesis, similarity and negation – as well as the suggestion of temporal sequence.[15]

It should also be noted that, as in Duccio's Trial, the visual depiction of the story, were it to be translated back into words, would differ significantly from the original verbal narrative, where there is no mention of another man being blessed, of dogs or puzzled shepherds nor of a natural sanctuary. Moreover where the logic employed in the verbal story is brisk and causal, the pictorial logic is more complex and reflective.

What emerges is that while there is a direct and unproblematic equivalent between a depiction of an action and a simple sentence – the priest shoves Joachim out of the Temple; the dog barks to greet its master – all the con-

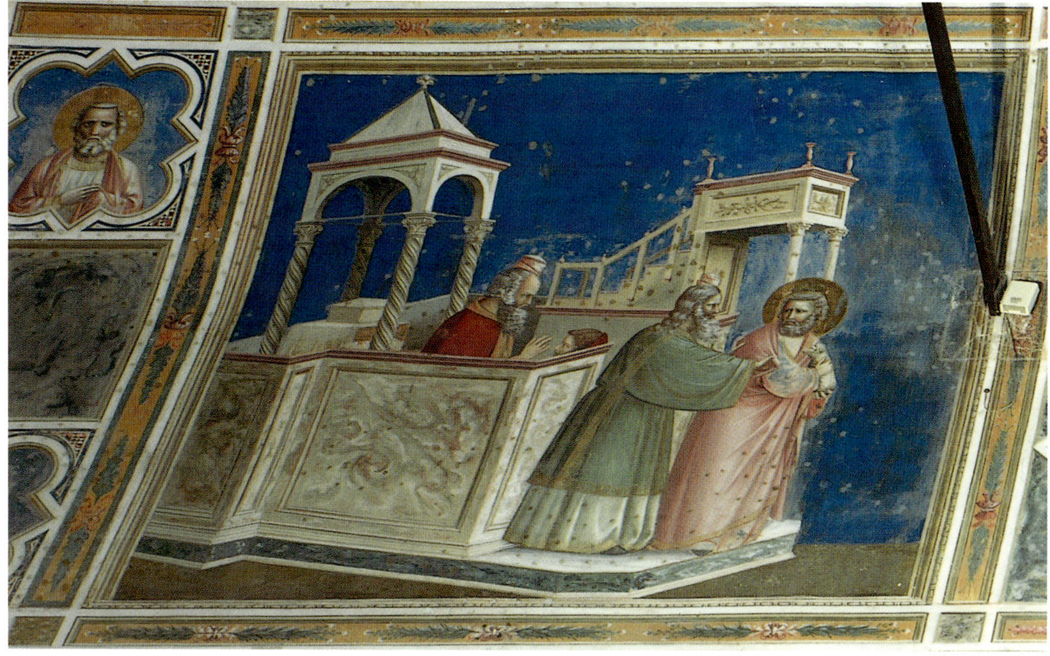

22. Giotto, Joachim's Expulsion from the Temple in Jerusalem, south wall of the Scrovegni Chapel, detail of Fig. 20.

junctions which are essential to storytelling as Aristotle described it, and which any verbal account would make apparent, have to be reconstructed by the spectator from juxtapositions carefully designed by the artist. The spectator has to perform much of the business of the storyteller or narrator by working out the relationships which supply Aristotle's conception of 'probability and necessity'.[16] This is a point of great importance, in reading the pictures, the spectator behaves in many ways like the narrator of a verbal text; he tells the story to himself as he pieces it together. The works of Duccio and Giotto are similar in arousing this response, though in Giotto there is perhaps a greater variety of more complex logical relationships.

The second fresco illustrates another aspect of the spectator's role. The left-hand shepherd seems to be glancing out of the corner of his eye towards his mate – or is it towards the spectator? Through the shepherd's complicity with the spectator, Joachim is isolated still further from the ring of characters, both within and outside the picture, who are arrested and perplexed by his

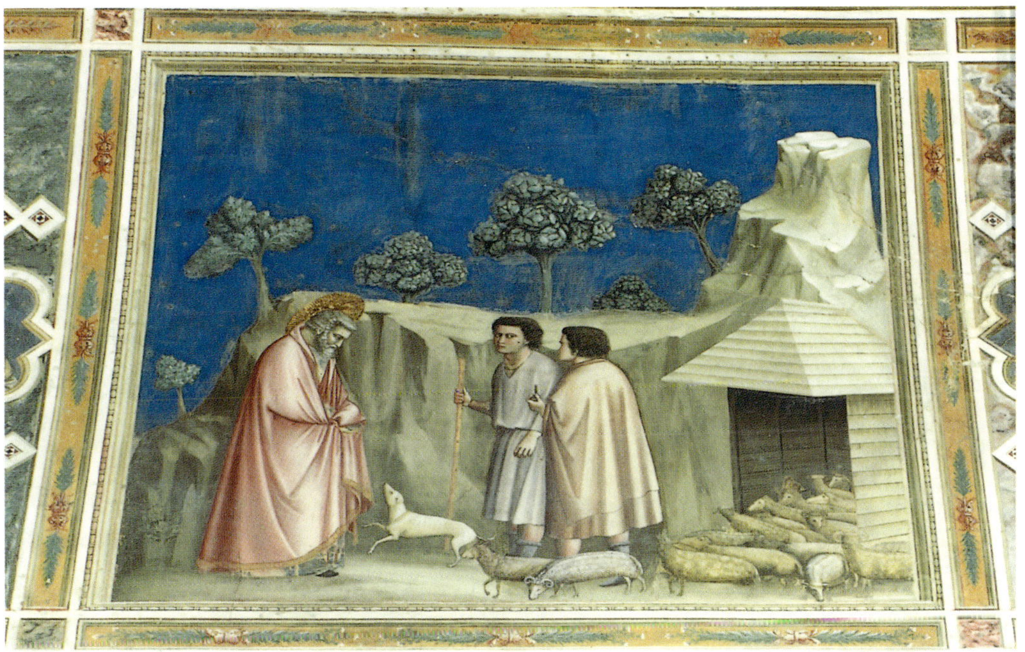

23. Giotto, Joachim in the Wilderness, south wall of the Scrovegni Chapel, detail of Fig. 20.

immobility. The double-take makes one feel like a third shepherd sharing their puzzlement, so that one is enabled to some degree to share their viewpoint.

The scene also introduces the wilderness or desert, a key symbolic location within Giotto's story as it is in the Bible, in contemporary preaching and within late medieval romances.[17] This is the location of almost one-third of the frescoes, twelve of the thirty-nine. In addition to three scenes in the Joachim sequence, the Birth of Jesus and his Adoration by the Magi, the Holy Family's Flight into Egypt, the Baptism, the Raising of Lazarus, the Crucifixion, the Lamentation over Jesus' corpse, his Resurrection and his Ascent into Heaven take place in the wilderness. The wilderness is ambivalent: on the surface it is an inhospitable and barren place, a wasteland; yet it is also a place where animals graze, where outcasts find refuge and a site of meditation and of spiritual regeneration. Thus, while Joachim is cast out of the Temple sanctuary, on entering the wilderness he takes the first steps in his own spiritual enlightenment, with consequences for the salvation of mankind.

Finally, the deepening emotional gloom is reinforced by a shift in lighting and colour from the bright and colourful scene of festivities in the Temple to the grey shadowy tones of the rocky wilderness.*

The story continues: Anna, who grieves both on account of her barrenness and Joachim's desertion, is taunted by the maid. Anna prays for a child. In response, an angel appears to tell her that she is pregnant with a baby daughter. She is to go to the Golden Gate of the Temple in Jerusalem where she will meet her husband. Simultaneously, Joachim makes a sacrifice to God in the wilderness and in answer an angel appears to him in his sleep telling him to return to Anna, who will bear him a daughter. He meets Anna at the Golden Gate, she runs forward and they embrace.

'Meanwhile back at home, Anna . . .'. By showing the angel appearing to Anna inside her bedroom (Fig. 24) – the texts have the scene taking place in a garden – Giotto marks a clear change of location and by that means suggests both the conjunction 'meanwhile' and the adverbial phrase 'back at home' which introduce the parallel story of Anna. The fresco is placed outside the 'sanctuary' of the chapel. Colour and light convey deeper desolation befitting Anna's state of widowhood, in the words of the *Protevangelium*. The reflections from the green walls of Anna's bedroom and the porch cast her and particularly her maid, in a light which anticipates the pallor of the body of the dead Jesus in the Lamentation (Fig. 38).[18] The combination of this green with Anna's orange robes creates a disharmony also used in the Lamentation. Both pictures represent loss and mourning. Nonetheless there is a ray of hope in the angel's pink wings and light blue robe, squeezing into the room through the small window, while Anna's golden robes are her bridal garments into which she had changed from her mourning clothes in order to pray. This shift in light and colour intensifies in the next three pictures. Furthermore the figures of the maid, Anna, the angel and, in the next fresco, Joachim kneeling before the altar, all direct one's attention upwards towards the hand of God which appears in answer to his prayer (Fig. 21). The angel in the fifth fresco of Joachim's Dream seems to dive down from a point between the two scenes, high in the heavens, from where the hand of God seems to have descended. The angel also appears to point downwards to the Golden Gate in the final scene. In Joachim's Sacrifice brightness returns, Joachim seems to be warmed by the flames of the altar. The colours prefigure those of the Resurrection. In the next scene, Joachim's Dream, the light is still brighter, build-

*This is evident within the chapel but colour photographs, particularly when artificially lit, do not represent it well.

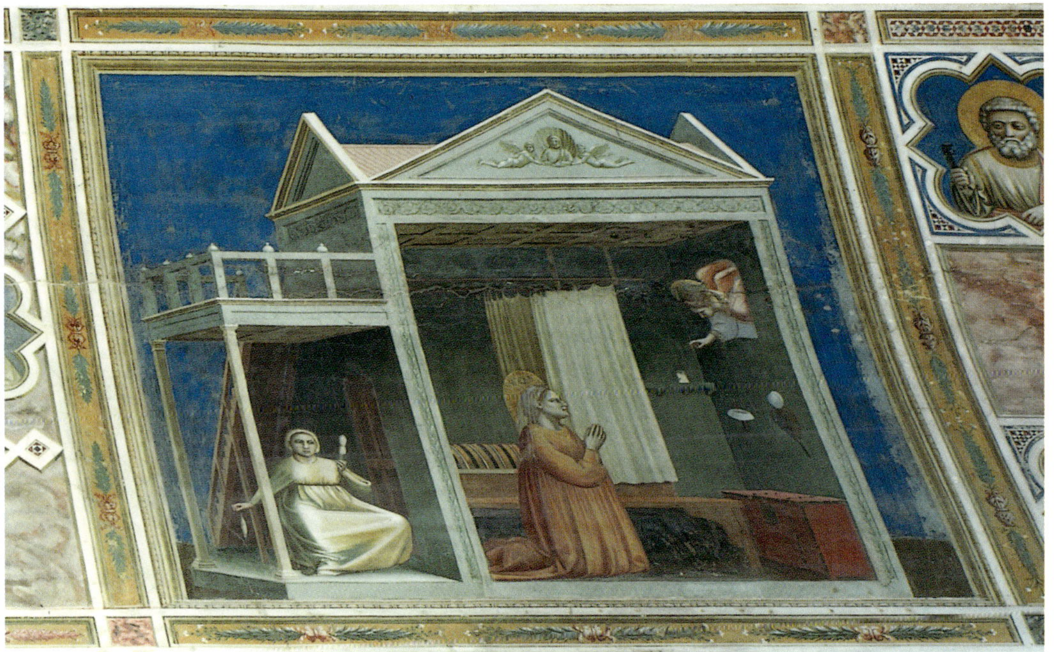

24. Giotto, The Angel's Annunciation to Anna, south wall of the Scrovegni Chapel, detail of Fig. 20.

ing up to the climax of the Golden Gate. The settings of Joachim's Sacrifice and Dream also constitute a natural sanctuary in the wilderness where Joachim finds God, in contrast to the Temple in Jerusalem where his offering was rejected. This is reinforced through visual rhymes and echoes.

The sequence concludes (Fig. 25) with the Meeting at the Golden Gate of the Temple in a tender embrace. Anna, still wearing her bridal robes, holds the back of Joachim's neck, stroking his beard with her other hand as she inclines her head to kiss him on the lips, their bodies forming an arch as they stand on the threshold of the bridge leading to the gate: 'Anna stood at the gate and saw Joachim coming and ran and hung on his neck, saying: "Now know I that the Lord God hath greatly blessed me: for behold the widow is no more a widow, and she that was childless shall conceive."'[19] This is one of Giotto's most moving scenes, it is tender, erotic even, though the kiss itself is the moment of the Virgin's conception.[20] The event is witnessed by three smiling women coming out of the gate dressed in white, red and green robes, the colours of the three Christian virtues, Faith, Charity and Hope, who are also depicted in the same order on the lowest register, directly beneath. Their brilliant robes, Anna's golden wedding dress and Joachim's pink cloak create a fanfare of colour bringing to a harmonious climax the gradually warming colours and the general brightening of the two previous scenes. In the words of Pseudo-Matthew, 'And there was such great joy amongst their friends and family that all Israel rejoiced.' Giotto, however, introduces a single contradictory note in the woman shrouded in black separating the couple from the virtuous onlookers, perhaps intended as an omen of the ensuing tragedy.[21]

When we cast our eyes over the whole chapter (Fig. 20–1) from a vantage point in the centre of the chapel we become aware of subtle formalities. Both the dais of the sanctuary in the first scene and the bridge to the Golden Gate in the last, are angled toward the centre of the sequence, answering one another and giving visual expression to the beginning and end of the chapter. This also suggests an overarching antithesis: in the first scene Joachim is cast out of the Temple by the priest, perhaps representing the Jewish religion; in the last scene Joachim is passionately embraced by the mother of the Virgin, who symbolises the Church.

Giotto uses the story of Joachim and Anna from the apocryphal gospels as a prelude to some major themes in the cycle. Yet the first chapter has its own balance and completeness. Giotto's construction of this sequence, enabling the spectator to supply the logic of the story, is so dextrous as to lead one to

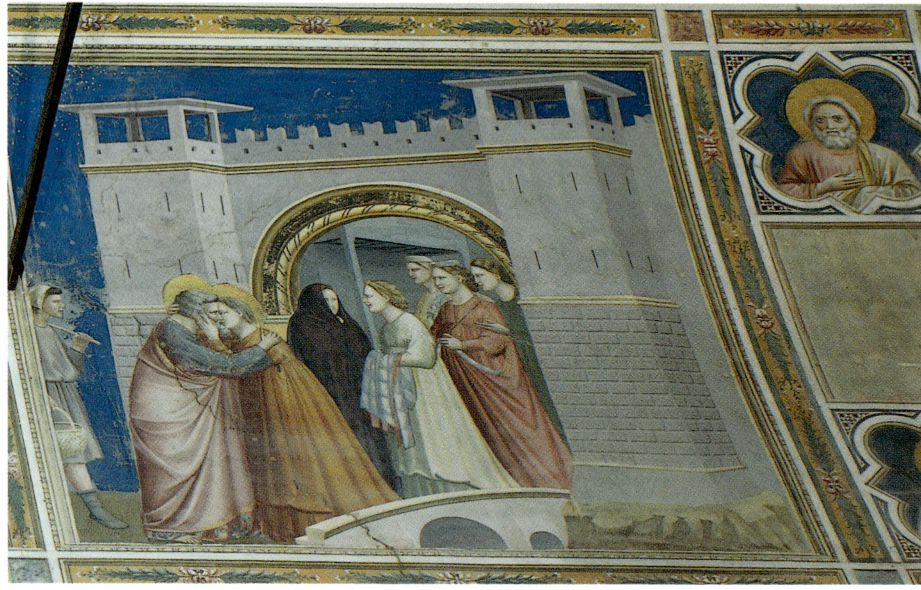

25. Giotto, The Meeting of Joachim and Anna at the Golden Gate of the Temple in Jerusalem, south wall of the Scrovegni Chapel, detail of Fig. 21.

argue that although there may be no precise pictorial equivalent to verbal syntactical markers 'thus', 'therefore', 'in contrast', 'meanwhile', nonetheless we can read pictures in a similar way. It is as if there were a syntax.

When we turn to examine more closely the relationship between the architecture within the frescoes and that of the Chapel itself we notice that the rounded arch of the Golden Gate itself, its flanking towers topped with open loggias (Fig. 25), resembles the actual chancel arch (Fig. 16) at the far end of the chapel, in whose loggias the Annunciation, and hence the Incarnation, takes place, just as the Virgin is conceived through her parents' kiss on the threshold of the Golden Gate. By this means Giotto strengthens the symbolism of the arched entrance into the chancel as the entrance of mankind into the heavenly Jerusalem, made possible by God's decision to save humanity through the incarnation of the Holy Spirit in Jesus. When the Messiah comes, according to Jewish tradition, he will enter the Temple through the Golden Gate, and Christians believed that on Palm Sunday Jesus entered Jerusalem through this gate.[22]

A further possibility arises, that the Scrovegni Chapel as a whole may have been intended as a copy or imitation of the Temple of Solomon. Solomon's Temple was a similar long, tall and thin building, its interior measuring 60 cubits long, 20 wide and 30 high.[23] The interior of the Scrovegni Chapel has almost identical proportions and is approximately the same size – it is long, narrow and tall.[24] The wall dividing the oracle of Solomon's Temple, within which stood the ark of the covenant, was located at a point that divided the main chamber in a ratio of 1 : 2, the same as that between the 'sanctuary' area to which I have referred and the rest of the chamber in the Scrovegni Chapel. Solomon 'made windows of narrow lights' in the Temple.[25] The Temple had a single main chamber with a porch in front of it the same width as the building, so too did the Scrovegni. The Temple seems to have been sited next to Solomon's Palace; the Scrovegni Chapel was next to Scrovegni's palace.[26] Both were palace chapels.[27] Many churches, however, are supposedly modelled upon the Temple;[28] what makes this identification significant for the interpretation of Giotto's narrative cycle is that the Temple itself is represented in at least nine of the frescoes – Joachim's Expulsion, the Meeting at the Golden Gate, the Presentation of the Virgin in the Temple, the three scenes of the Betrothal of the Virgin, Jesus' Presentation in the Temple, Jesus among the Doctors, the Cleansing of the Temple. We have already seen that several of these scenes are related to the architectural arrangements of the interior; next we shall see how subtle that relationship could be.

Complete as the first chapter appears to be, it marks but one step on the path to mankind's redemption; Joachim and Anna are not shown entering the

Golden Gate, they embrace on the threshold of the bridge, at the farthest point from the high altar of the chapel. That promise, or hope of redemption, is partially fulfilled in the next chapter, depicting the birth and marriage of their daughter, the Virgin Mary, which also brings us, as we pursue our journey round the chapel, back within the 'sanctuary' area. Giotto devotes no fewer than four frescoes to the marriage (Fig. 19), more than to Jesus' ministry or to his trial. It is hard to improve upon the explanation provided by John Ruskin, who draws attention to the fact that the individual pictures within these extended pictorial cycles were governed by rules unlike those which apply to an individual framed painting or 'tableau':

> we find the masters of the 14th century dwelling on moments of the most subdued and tender feeling, and leaving the spectator to trace the undercurrents of thought which link them with future events of mightier interest and fill with a prophetic power and mystery scenes in themselves so simple as the meeting of a master with his herdsmen among the hills, or the return of a betrothed virgin to her house.
>
> It is, however, to be remembered that this quietness of character was much more possible to an early painter, owing to the connection in which his works were to be seen. A modern picture, isolated and portable, must rest all its claims to attention on its own actual subject; but the pictures of the early masters were nearly always parts of a consecutive and stable series, in which many were subdued, like the connecting passages of a prolonged poem, in order to enhance the value of meaning of others. The arrangement of the subjects in the Arena Chapel is in this respect peculiarly skilful . . .[29]

The Virgin chapter may be regarded as just such a connecting passage, not dissimilar to a lengthy bridging passage in a Beethoven symphony whose quietness and sense of immanence intensifies the power of the moment when the new subject is stated. At the same time the figures within this chapter seem to move slowly but relentlessly towards the altar of the chapel, culminating in the final fresco of the Virgin's Procession and, most important, the Annunciation. Since the scene of Joachim's Expulsion we too have been moving in the same direction, towards the Incarnation. We will also observe the felicity with which Giotto uses the caesura between the 'sanctuary' and the rest of the chapel.

The third and fourth scenes (Fig. 26) show the process by which Mary's husband is chosen. The high priest ordered that all eligible bachelors of the house of David must bring rods to the altar of the Temple. Only one would blossom and the Holy Spirit in the form of a dove would appear on its top.

The owner of the blossoming staff would become Mary's husband. In the third scene we see the young men bringing their rods to the altar housed in its apse. According to the apochryphal Pseudo Matthew this is the altar of the Holy of Holies in the Temple.[30] The rounded arch of the apse in the fresco echoes the arch of the actual chancel. In the next fresco, located in the area just outside the 'sanctuary' of the chapel, they all kneel before the altar upon which the rods are piled. One man, who wrings his hands as if urging a horse to win, expresses their collective anticipation. Joseph hides at the back. In the next fresco, situated significantly within the 'sanctuary' on the other side of the boundary, all are standing again, Joseph is now centre stage, his rod has burst into life with its leaves and flowers and the dove, symbol of rebirth and of the Holy Spirit, which also alludes to the Incarnation enacted across the chancel arch. Here the ceremony of betrothal takes place within the Holy of Holies in front of the apse of the Temple. The unsuccessful young men, to the left of the building, break their sticks in anger and one makes to strike Joseph on the back just as the priest is joining him and Mary in matrimony. Because the same building is employed in each of the three scenes, our attention is directed to the step-by-step unfolding of the story, a feature that Duccio may have imitated in his Trial sequence. In the sixth and final fresco, Mary, in solemn procession, is welcomed home by an exuberant trumpet fanfare (Fig. 27), the players' cheeks puffed out as they blast out the march. This is the forte passage for which Giotto was holding back.[31] In our own journey we have now turned a full circle, from the spiritual despair and desolation of Joachim's ejection from the sanctuary of the Temple to the flowering of hope in the same location. But in the turrets of the chancel arch (Fig. 16) where the Annunciation takes place, all is once more quiet and solemn, full of mystery, the Holy Spirit represented only by the empty space in the arch between Gabriel and Mary. The sense of immanence and mystery which surrounds it is entirely appropriate to the location of the Annunciation within the 'sanctuary' or Holy of Holies of what one might call Scrovegni's Temple.[32]

The composition of the individual fresco

Next I will look in more detail at the variety of compositional logic at work in individual frescoes. Three examples from the middle sections of the cycle demonstrate Giotto's range.

There are two apparently contradictory aspects of Giotto's art. On the one hand he can be highly rational in analysing the pictorial requirements for

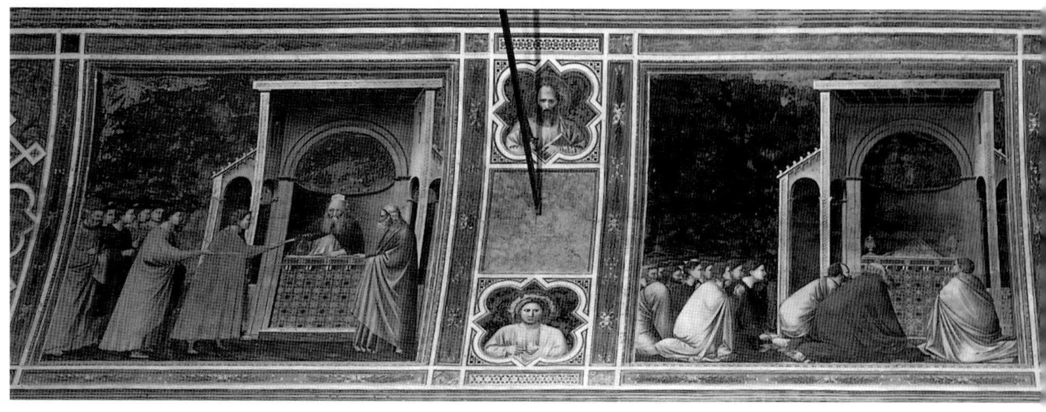

visualising a story and correspondingly clear where the action naturally manifests itself in bodily movements. On the other hand, as in his Last Supper (Fig. 29), he can express inward feelings and mental states in complex actions involving concealment, as well as in miraculous events. In the first example, the Raising of Lazarus (Figs 19 and 28), he finds means to visualise a psychological transition from scepticism to belief; in the Last Supper (Fig. 29) he depicts an enigmatic event in a correspondingly enigmatic way; and in the Betrayal (Fig. 30), a more straightforward drama is told with a vivid sense of the logic of events, treated with grave reserve.

The Raising of Lazarus is an example of Giotto's compositional logic compressing a long rather meandering story into a single image. The Gospel explains how Jesus, knowing that Lazarus is ill, allows him to die. Jesus does this in order to raise him from the dead, as a sign of his powers and as a symbol of the resurrection.[33] The compositional formula for this subject had been formulated as early perhaps as the second or third centuries and is found in the Roman catacombs; even the phase of the action depicted by Giotto was long established.[34] After the tomb has been opened, Martha and Mary, the sisters of Lazarus, remain on their knees, continuing their appeal to Jesus, when he cries in a loud voice, 'Lazarus, come forth.' At this the dead man, still bound like a mummy, comes out of the cave and Jesus orders that the shroud be removed. These three causally connected phases are compressed into a single image.[35] The distinctiveness of Giotto's depiction turns upon the central figure in green robes standing between Jesus and Lazarus. This man has the index finger of one hand on his chin as he gazes at Lazarus, and his other hand is outstretched towards Jesus. One hand seems to express doubt, the other is caught on the wing, rising in astonishment like the hands of the man behind him which are already raised. This transitory gesture, emphasised

(*above and page 57*) 26. Giotto, the Betrothal of the Virgin Mary: The suitors bring their Rods to the High Priest in the Temple; The Suitors Pray for their Rods to Blossom; The Betrothal of the Virgin Mary; The Virgin's Procession Home. Upper tier of the north wall of the Scrovegni Chapel, detail of Fig. 19, corresponding to 9, 10, 11 and 12 in Fig. 18.

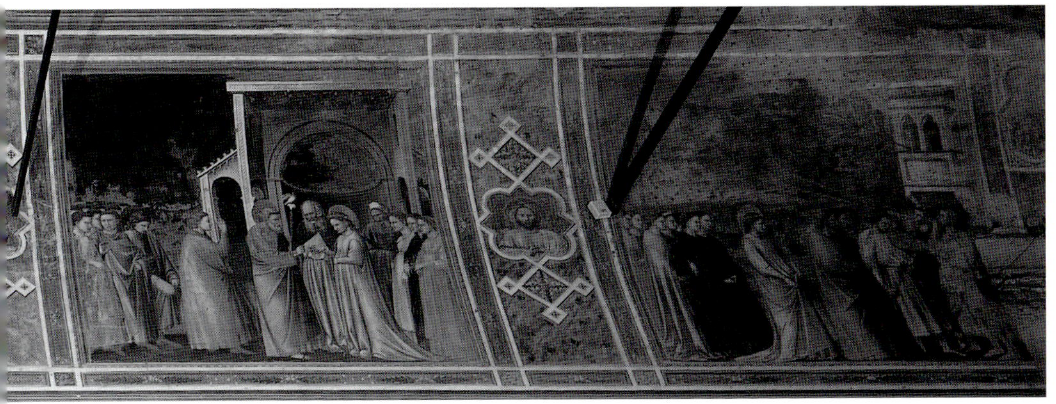

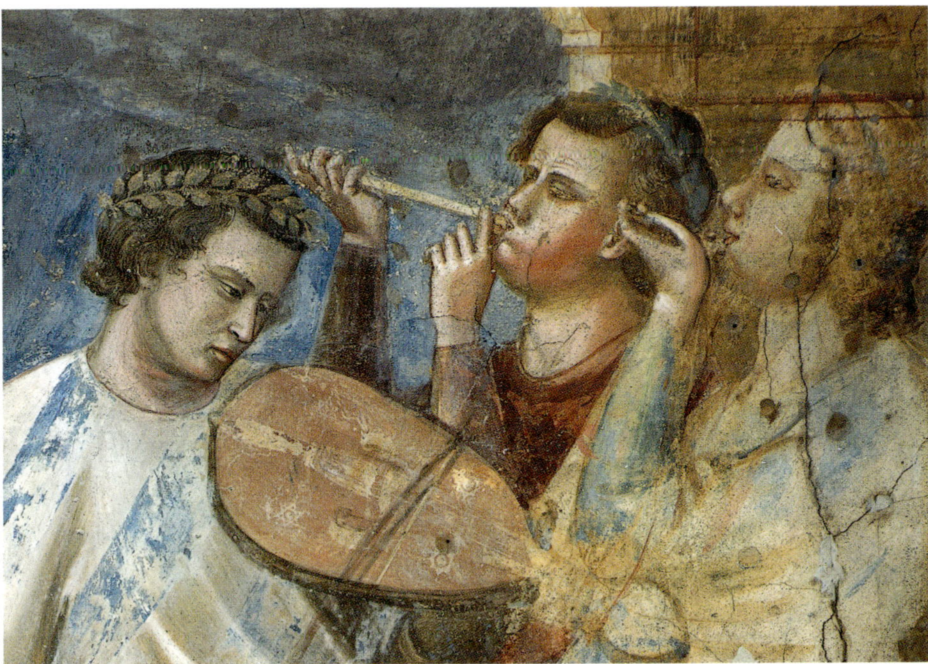

27. Giotto, detail of the musicians in The Virgin's Procession Home, upper tier of the north wall of the Scrovegni Chapel.

by the stereoscopic effect of the outstretched hand, whose foreshortened fingertips are highlighted, seems to capture the very moment of Lazarus's own transition from death to life, before his body begins to stir. But Giotto also conveys the chief point of the miracle: to prove to the Jews that Jesus is the Son of God. The man in the centre, with others behind him, is caught at the turning point when his expression changes from scepticism to belief.

In the biblical account of the Last Supper (Fig. 29), Jesus' announcement of his imminent betrayal is highly enigmatic. The disciples' uncertainty about the identity of the traitor arouses mutual suspicion; in addition they seem

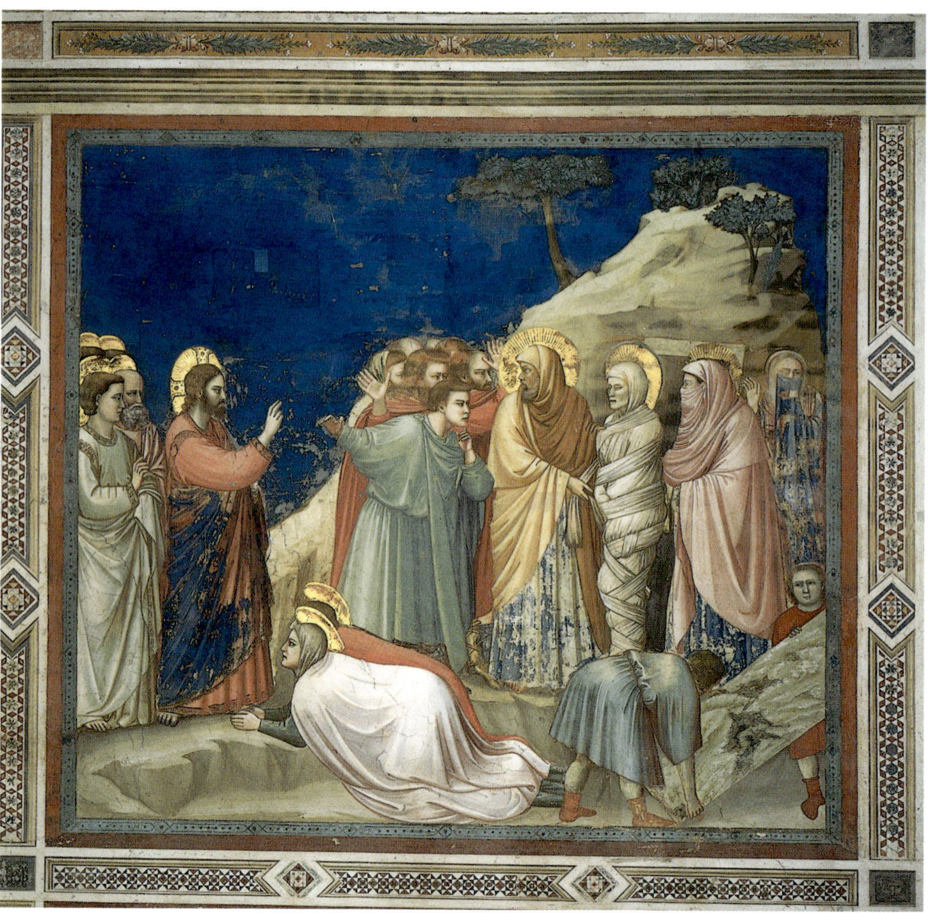

28. Giotto, The Raising of Lazarus, middle tier of the north wall of the Scrovegni Chapel, corresponding to 24 in Fig. 18.

incapable of reading the sign which Jesus provides: the traitor will dip with him in the dish or take a piece of bread from him.[36] This poses a difficult problem of visual representation, since the essence of the story lies in the fact that the full situation is concealed from most of the participants, who cannot see what is happening. But for obvious reasons it is almost impossible in visual images to represent things that cannot be seen. We have already seen how both Duccio and Giotto handled the similar but less difficult problem of depicting negative statements. An artist has to provide enough visual information for the story to make sense to the spectator but not too much. It is a type of problem that we will encounter again in plots of great complexity, involving incomprehension, deceit or conspiracy, inherent in many stories. Verbal narrative, on the other hand, can represent such aspects of a plot without great difficulty.

It is worthwhile quoting in full the account provided by the *Diatesseron*, from which Giotto seems to have worked, italicising those passages bearing directly upon his fresco.

> When Jesus had thus said, he was troubled in spirit, and testified and said, Verily, verily, I say unto you, that one of you shall betray me. (John 13, 21) *And they began to be sorrowful, and to say unto him one by one, Is it I? and another said Is it I, Master?* (Mark 14, 19) *And he answered and said, he that dippeth his hand with me in the dish, the same shall betray me.* The son of man [the son of the virgin, in the Italian] goeth as it is written of him: but woe unto that man by whom the son of man is betrayed! It had been good for that man if he had not been born. (Matt. 26, 23) *Then the disciples looked one on another, doubting of whom he spake.* (John 13, 22) *And they began to inquire among themselves, which of them it was that should do this thing.* (Luke 22, 23) *Now there was leaning on Jesus' bosom one of his disciples, whom Jesus loved.* Simon Peter therefore beckoned to him, that he should ask who it should be of whom he spake. He then lying on Jesus' breast saith unto him, Lord, who is it? *Jesus answered, He it is, to whom I shall give a sop* [a piece of bread in the Italian] *when I have dipped it. And when he had dipped the sop, he gave it to Judas Iscariot, the son of Simon. And after the sop Satan entered into him.* Then said Jesus unto him, That thou doest, do quickly. Now no man at the table knew for what intent he spake this unto him. For some of them thought, because Judas had the bag, that Jesus had said unto him, Buy those things that we have need of against the feast; or, that he should give something to the poor. (John 13, 23–9) Then Judas, which betrayed him, answered and said, Master, Is it I? He said unto him, Thou hast said it. (Matt. 26, 25).[37]

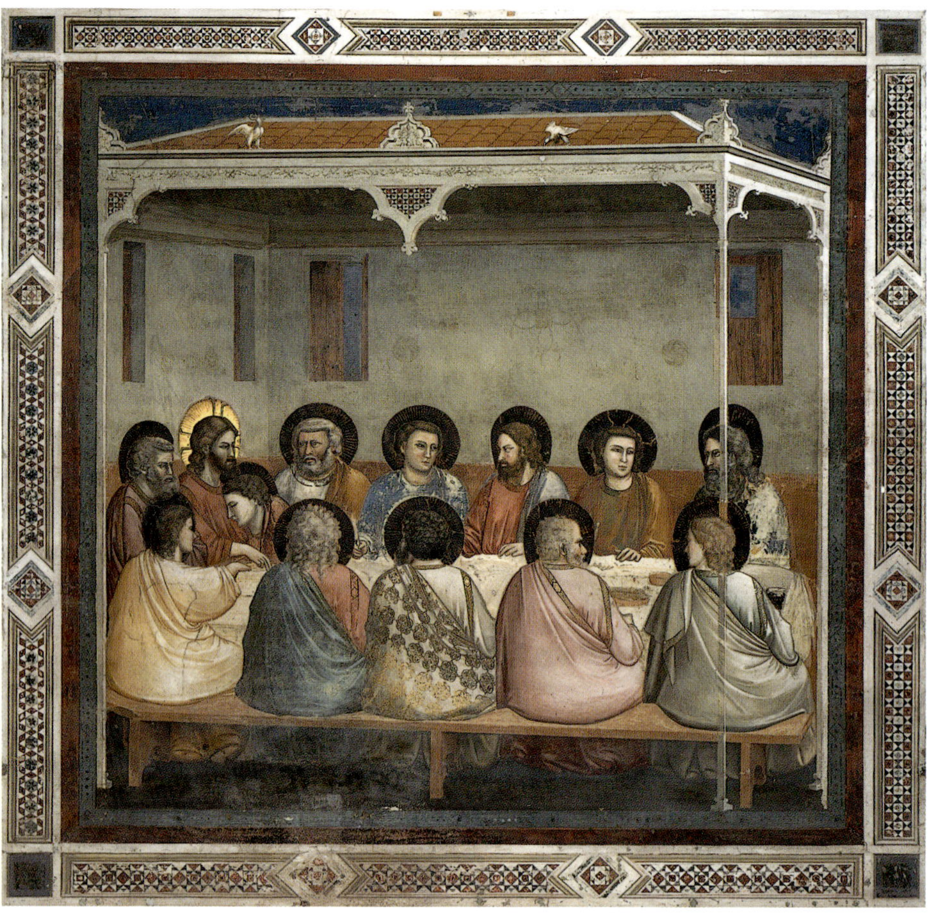

29. Giotto, The Last Supper, lower tier of the south wall of the Scrovegni Chapel, corresponding to 28 in Fig. 18.

At first glance, Giotto's picture seems unremarkable, even boring: thirteen men doing very little, seated in rows either side of a table almost parallel to the picture plane, five of them with their backs turned towards us. Then one notices that most of the figures are paired, each looking towards the other; alternatively one can read them as pairs looking *away* from one another. The ambiguity of this pattern conveys a sense of movement strongly suggestive of their perplexity: 'Then the disciples looked one on another, doubting of whom he spake. And they began to inquire among themselves, which of them it was that should do this thing.' This is one phase of the event that Giotto represents. But he also shows Judas dipping his hand in the dish with Jesus.

So absorbed, however, is each disciple in his own personal guilt, doubt and suspicion that Judas's action passes unnoticed – not one of them has his eyes on it. Indeed Giotto has depicted it so unobtrusively, while the pattern of the disciples scrutinising one another is so insistent, that initially it may even escape our attention – it is as if a gap has opened up between Judas and the disciple to his right through which only the spectator can momentarily catch a glimpse of the two hands in the same bowl.

Giotto's solution to the problem of representing actions which pass unnoticed, is like a magician's sleight of hand. The attention of each disciple is diverted, and so too, initially, is that of the spectator. Perhaps the solution is less than perfect, but it does indicate Giotto's thoughtfulness and ingenuity in extending the resources of painting to depict complex and covert events, and it provided a model for later artists, such as Ghiberti in his relief of Joseph and his Brothers (Fig. 138).[38]

The Betrayal of Jesus (Fig. 30) is again different in character. The story is almost identical in the three accounts given by Matthew, Mark and Luke, upon which Giotto drew. After Jesus' prayer in Gethsemane Judas leads an armed mob to capture the man whom he will identify with a kiss. Jesus says, 'Judas, betrayest thou the Son of Man with a kiss?'[39] St Peter draws his sword to cut off the ear of the High Priest's servant. At this, Jesus orders St Peter to 'put up again thy sword into his place: for all they that take the sword shall perish with the sword.'[40] Giotto does not represent this command, not directly at least, but rather through the juxtaposition of the figure of Temperance (Fig. 43) beneath and to the left, as we shall see subsequently. The disciples desert Jesus and flee. One of them, who is wearing only a linen robe, is grabbed by the mob, but escapes naked, leaving the cloth behind in the hands of his would-be captor.[41]

What is remarkable about Giotto's depiction of a scene whose overall composition had long been standardised? In one image he compresses a rapid succession of events with a sure grasp of the causal relations between them. In the centre, both men in profile, Judas, having enveloped Jesus in his capacious yellow cloak, is about to kiss him. Jesus stares into Judas's eyes with extraordinary restraint as if the accusing question is passing through his mind, unspoken. Anticipating the kiss, the robed figure in the right-hand foreground, unmentioned in the Gospels but invented by Giotto, points Jesus out to armed officers, giving them the order to close in upon him. In the final fresco of this chapter, the Death Sentence (Figs 33–4), this gesture is echoed by that of the High Priest. Meanwhile, on the left-hand side the action has moved on. One man who has just grabbed hold of Jesus is attacked by St Peter, who lunges forward with his knife and cuts off his ear. Behind St Peter,

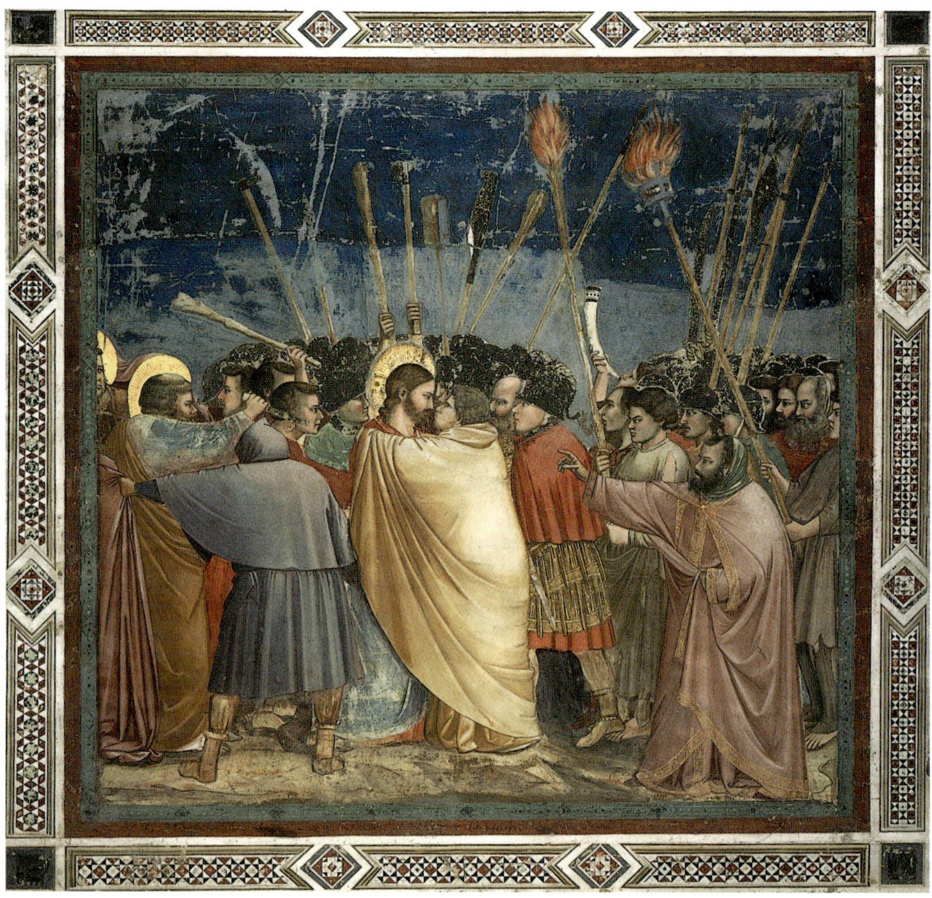

30. Giotto, The Betrayal of Jesus, lower tier of the south wall of the Scrovegni Chapel, corresponding to 30 in Fig. 18.

the other disciples run off, the head of one of them, marked by a halo, is half-concealed behind the left-hand frame, his cloak is just slithering off his body, winding round behind St Peter's head; the cloak of another disciple, whose body is not visible, is held by a grey-hooded figure with his back towards us. Just as the cloak is looped through the crowd, so everything is interconnected: one action leads to another in the confusion surrounding the incident which is, nonetheless, depicted in an image of great clarity. A tiny detail illustrates this delicate triggering of the chain of cause and effect: the soldier in a red cloak to the right of Judas is just on the point of bringing the full weight of his heel down upon the bare toes of the man behind him, but has not yet done so. The picture is like an intricate piece of machinery connected by pulleys and tripwires. There is, moreover, a similar intricacy relating this fresco to the chapter of which it is the centre – the disciples flee, as if to a haven, in the direction of the Last Supper (Fig. 16); Judas and the Jews come at Jesus from the direction of the two courts in which he will be tried (Fig. 17).

The Betrayal closely corresponds to the conventional characterisation of Giotto as a naturalistic painter of human events. Compared to Duccio's depiction of the same event Giotto's intellectual rigour is impressive. Each action is closely interrelated with the others, compressed into a single image, whereas Duccio separates the kiss, Peter's retaliation and the fleeing disciples in an episodic fashion, an example of what is often referred to as continuous narration. Giotto's Betrayal best epitomises his taut causal logic, but the sleight of hand employed in his Last Supper also depends upon the same quality.

Order and obliquity

One implicit assumption so far has been that we read the frescoes sequentially in the biblical order of events;[42] a second is that we look at each fresco frontally. It is undeniable that this is the dominant order, unfolding majestically as we journey downwards following the spiral from its starting point in Joachim's Expulsion from the Temple (Fig. 18). It is not only our knowledge of the scriptures that dictates this, but also the suggestion within the individual frescoes of a stately procession from left to right leading from one image to the next. But this is not the only order in which the cycle can be read.[43] Several of the chapters are centred compositionally and even perspectivally, implying that one can take them in while standing in the centre of the chapel. In a large chamber like the Scrovegni Chapel where the pictures on both main walls are arranged on a rectilinear grid (Fig. 19) and where the direction of the sunlight is constantly changing, drawing one's attention to a particular scene by throwing an intense if momentary spotlight upon it (Fig. 38), it can be difficult to keep one's attention strictly focused upon the chronological order. Sometimes, moreover, Giotto intended to draw one's attention away from the sequence, or at least to remind one of other scenes and images by means of visual rhymes, repetitions and similarities.[44] The kneeling figure in the Death Sentence (Fig. 33) is paying homage to the prisoner, a mocking echo of Jesus' true humility in washing the feet of the bemused Peter after the Last Supper, or of the oldest Magus kneeling before the infant Jesus. So too Scrovegni emulates the Magus as he kneels to offer his gift of the chapel to the Virgin in hope of salvation. The allegorical figure of Hope (Fig. 40) is represented nearby. Our attention is constantly being drawn to the Virtues and Vices who do not belong to the narrative sequence. Even if we try to adhere rigidly to the sequence our eyes have to cross the wall of the Last Judgement three times (Fig. 17), providing a grim reminder, in mid-story, of the fate of those responsible for the Massacre of the Innocents and for the mis-trial of Jesus (Figs 33–35). In addition, almost as if playing a game of snakes and ladders, Giotto will sometimes draw our attention vertically upwards from a picture on the lowest tier to one in the highest: from the Ascension to Jesus' Entry into Jerusalem to the Betrothal of the Virgin, for example (Fig. 19). The very layout of the frescoes, with the Virtues and Vices lined up in opposition, encourages one to infer contrasts and similarities between the images.

There were, however, two fixed points of entry upon which Giotto could depend. One was the door on the left-hand or north wall near the chancel, blocked up till recently but now re-opened as the main entrance for visitors, which may well have been used by the Scrovegni family to enter from their nearby palace.[45] From there, looking upwards, they would have seen the first fresco of the cycle, Joachim's Expulsion (Fig. 22), encouraging them to begin at the beginning. The other door, at the far end under the Last Judgement was the main entrance for visitors and pilgrims[46] (Fig. 17) and that provides one with an alternative starting point, entering in the midst of things, *in medias res*,[47] a term used by the Roman poet Horace who said that for familiar subjects it is pedestrian to begin at the beginning, the poet should plunge the hearer into the heart of the story.

From the bright sunlight outside, one's first impression is of gloom. The main chamber is in fact quite well lit by seven windows, but until one's eyes have fully adjusted, it is difficult to make out much more than the great archway over the high altar (Fig. 16), twenty yards away at the far end. Perhaps one can just discern the shadowy red figures of the Archangel Gabriel and the Virgin silently enacting the Annunciation across the top of the chancel arch. Instinctively I find myself turning to my right (Fig. 31) and catch sight of the scene of the Death Sentence closest to the door with the Massacre of the Innocents directly above. Both scenes depict Jesus' adversaries and are set beneath the Meeting at the Golden Gate with its ominous woman in her black cloak. Because of their position these two frescoes are momentarily put in the spotlight by the daylight pouring in from the door, before it closes behind one. Indeed Giotto incorporates this effect in the Death Sentence (Fig. 34) with a highlight on the pink robe of the High Priest closest to the viewer, as if the opened door were casting some momentary brightness in that gloomy courtyard at the break of day. One also notices two men busily writing at their desks painted in quatrefoils on the extreme right of the same wall (Fig. 32). The lower, identified as St Jerome, translator of the Latin Vulgate, looks upwards at the scenes of the Massacre and the Death Sentence. Upon his lectern rests a book in which we can read the opening words of the 'Ave Maria'. The other, probably St Luke the Evangelist, the patron saint of painters, glances downwards at the Death Sentence as he writes. The words 'Ave Maria' are also visible on his manuscript.[48] Of the four twinned pairs of evangelists and doctors in the four corners of the chapel, only the books of this pair display legible texts, providing support for the hypothesis that Giotto did indeed conceive of this as a point of entry into the cycle. The choice of the Ave Maria, derived as it is from the Angelic Salutation in the Annunciation with which the chapel is associated, is an appropriate text for this point of entry.

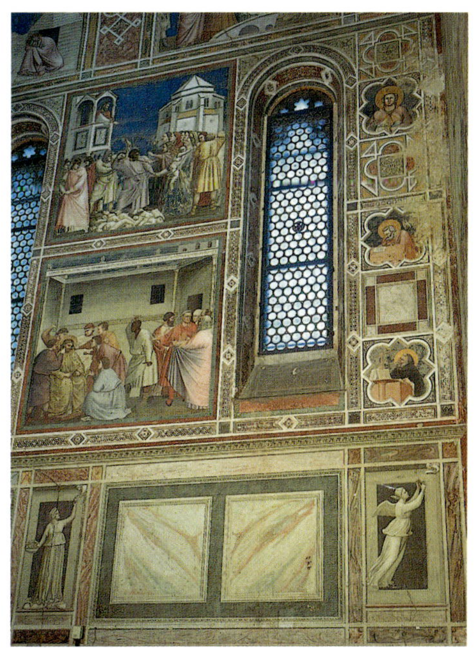

31. Giotto, view of the south wall of the Scrovegni Chapel from the main door showing The Massacre of the Innocents in the middle tier (corresponding to 20 in Fig. 18) and of The Death Sentence in the lower tier (32 in Fig. 18). In the lowest tier are the virtues of Charity and Hope.

The Massacre and the Death Sentence are among the most problematic and challenging images in the chapel. Such a view contrasts with the clichés about Giotto's naturalism and his down-to-earth approach to telling stories full of human interest. This simple-minded conception of Giotto's art actually makes him harder to appreciate, because we expect his work to be more approachable than it is. Better to be prepared for an artist who did not always make a direct appeal to the spectator.

Because it is closest to us when we first enter the chapel, the Death Sentence (Fig. 33) makes the stronger impact of the two. At first glance it seems like another of Ruskin's subdued pictures. The subject is less obvious than it appears. It is usually identified as the Mocking of Jesus after the trial by Pilate based upon Matthew 27, vv. 19 and 27–30. I suggest that Giotto has combined certain details of this account with others from John 19, 2–6 often referred to as the Ecce Homo. Perhaps the subject has been best described by Geza Vermes as The Death Sentence.[49]

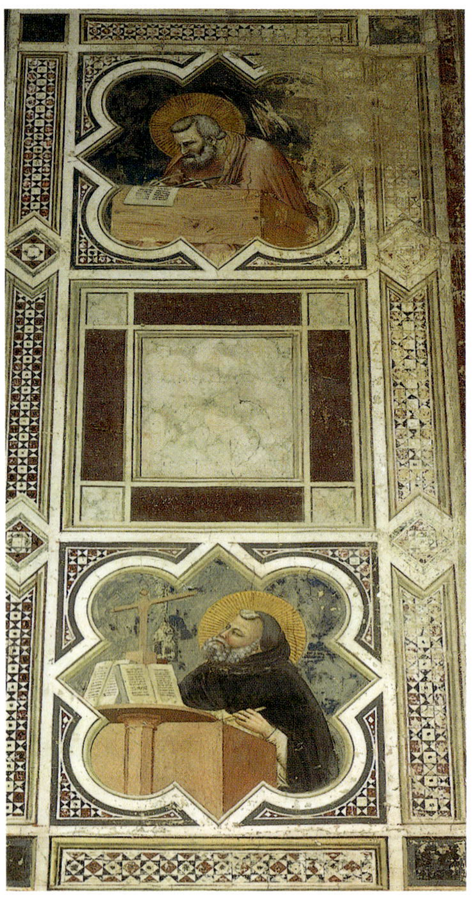

32. Giotto, St. Luke, above, and St. Jerome beneath, to the right of The Massacre of the Innocents and The Death Sentence, on the south wall of the Scrovegni Chapel.

When he was set down on the judgement seat, his wife sent unto him, saying, Have thou nothing to do with that just man: for I have suffered many things this day in a dream because of him [Matt. 27, v. 19]. Then the soldiers of the governor took Jesus into the common hall, and gathered unto him the whole band of soldiers. And they stripped him, and put on him a scarlet robe. And when they had plaited a crown of thorns, they put it upon his head, and a reed in his right hand: and they bowed the knee before him, and mocked him, saying, Hail, King of the Jews! And they spit upon him, and took the reed, and smote him on the head [Matt. 27, v. 27–30]. Pilate therefore went forth again, and saith unto them, Behold, I bring him forth to you, that ye may know that I find no fault in him. Then came Jesus forth, wearing the crown of thorns, and the purple robe. And Pilate saith unto them, Behold the man! [Ecce Homo] When the chief priests therefore and the officers saw him, they cried out, saying, Crucify him, crucify him [John 19, 4–6].

To the left the seated Jesus is being humiliated, on the right Pilate's outstretched arm appears to signify, 'I find no fault in him', to which the priest seems to reply in a gesture echoing that of Pilate, 'Crucify him, crucify him.' The actions of the men surrounding Jesus seem tame compared to Giovanni Pisano's later relief in Pisa Cathedral (Fig. 85), and Jesus' slumped body is rather ineloquent. The painting seems so straightforward as barely to merit a second glance. Unlike Duccio's Mocking (Fig. 14) there is no irony in the mocked Jesus transformed into the figure of the just judge. The incident seems to take place in a very matter-of-fact way.

Seen from the doorway (Fig. 34), however, the fresco looks less familiar but seems to make more sense visually, and exemplifies many features of pictorial storytelling.

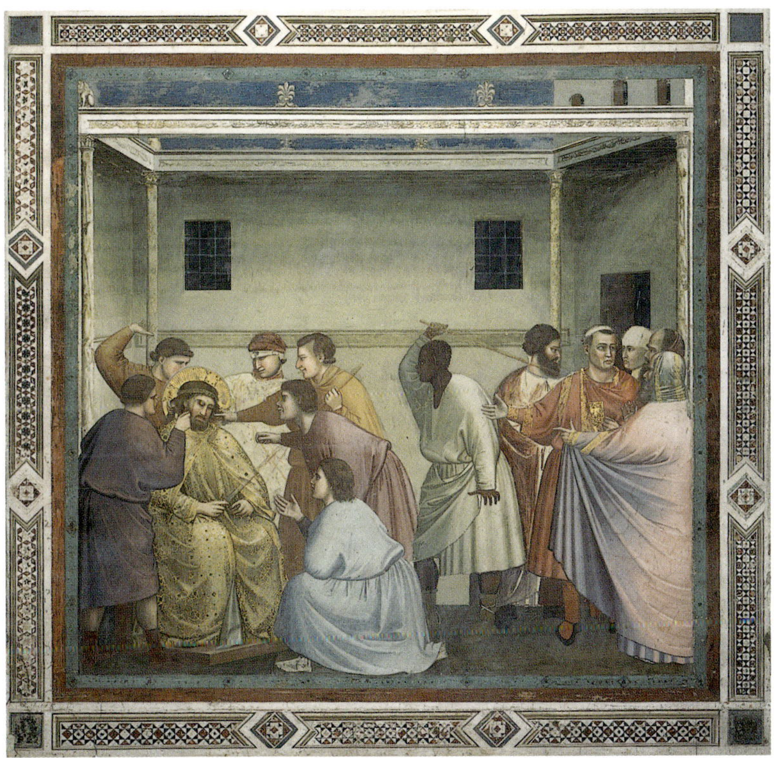

33. Giotto, The Death Sentence, lower tier of the south wall of the Scrovegni Chapel, (32 in Fig. 18). This photograph was taken on a scaffold directly in front of the fresco.

There are two specific visual adjustments which suggest that it was Giotto's intention that the picture could also be viewed from this unusual angle. The first, already mentioned, is the appearance of bright sunlight, as if from the open doorway, on the High Priest's pink robe. Second, a perspectival subtlety: the tops of the heads of the figures on the right-hand side of the picture are slightly higher than the horizontal dado rail which runs across the courtyard, and the heads of the men on the left are slightly lower. Almost unnoticeable from a frontal viewpoint, from here this reinforces our sense of Pilate and the priests as larger, brighter and closer to us, compared to Jesus and the figures around him who seem to be located in a more distant and gloomy corner of the courtyard.[50]

The very fact that one has just entered the chapel puts one in the position, in time as well as in place, of an eyewitness just entering the courtyard.

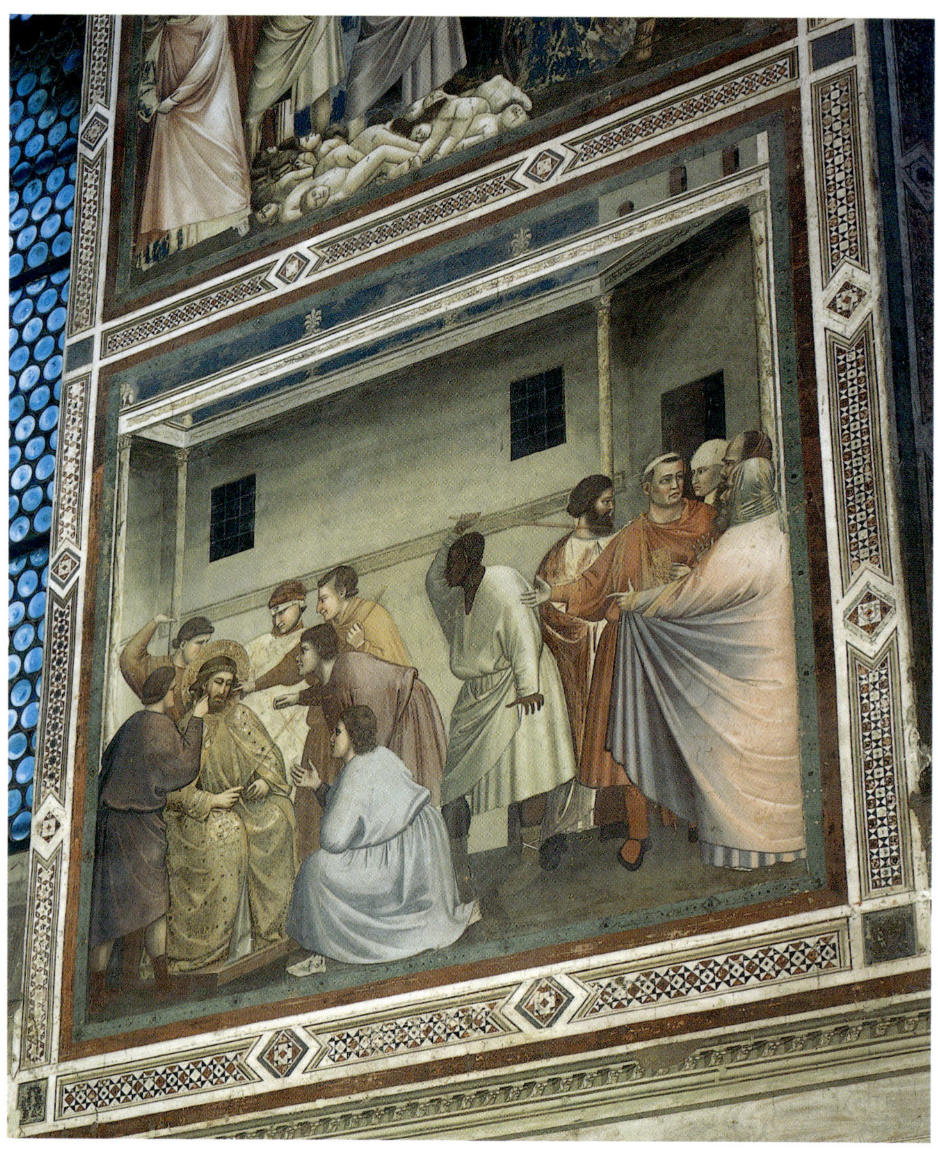

34. Giotto, The Death Sentence, lower tier of the south wall of the Scrovegni Chapel, (32 in Fig. 18). This photograph has been taken from the main door as in Fig. 31.

Although one seems to look at Jesus frontally from this position, he appears to be far away, for not only is he on the other side of the courtyard but one also observes him across a screen of partially overlapping figures – the High Priest, Pilate, the black man, the man spitting. In addition the colours of the clothes of the men surrounding Jesus are dingy and the corner of the courtyard is in half-shadow. Hence Jesus' remoteness, emphasised by his posture, slumped on his chair, head bowed, eyes almost closed, seemingly in a coma so that he has withdrawn psychologically into another world. More immediate are the grandees around Pilate in the foreground, wearing bright silk robes dyed with costly colours. While pointing at Jesus, they are neither looking at him nor at the scene of his torture but at one another, haggling over the prisoner's fate. But who is the one figure almost concealed amongst them who is staring at Jesus, immediately to the right of Pilate, head covered in a white shawl, framed in a dark doorway? This may be Pilate's wife who tells him, 'Have thou nothing to do with that just man: for I have suffered many things this day in a dream because of him.'[51]

From the viewer's position the horror of the incident lies in the detachment of the grandees and their blithe disregard for the way the prisoner is being treated – another example of negation. It is not so much a matter of extreme physical violence as of a continuous merry-go-round of blows and insults indicated by the bodies radiating around Jesus, who looks as if he has already been beaten senseless. But why is he in such a condition? We can only guess. And that, surely, is the point. We have to infer what Jesus has suffered since the previous scene (Fig. 35), the night before, where he was interrogated by the priests Annas and Caiaphas, separated by the space of a window from the present scene. What has brought about the transformation of the erect, even defiant man who refused to answer questions? Once again we have to supply the causal link to explain the change which has taken place between the two adjacent pictures, just as in the first two frescoes of Joachim. The full horror emerges slowly as our suspicion is confirmed that having just entered the courtyard in the early morning, at the tail-end of a sequence of events, we are witnessing the consequences for Jesus, as for many a more recent political prisoner, of a sleepless night of incessant physical and mental torture as well as the flogging which he has just endured.[52] Like a reporter arriving too late at the scene of a crime or a miscarriage of justice, one is forced to piece together retrospectively what had been going on in the 'cognitive space' between the two pictures. The worst atrocities are hidden from public view. Jesus' far-away expression and his posture are the clues. What makes this fresco so terrible is the contrast between this and the detached haggling between the Roman governor and the Jewish leaders in their fine clothes.

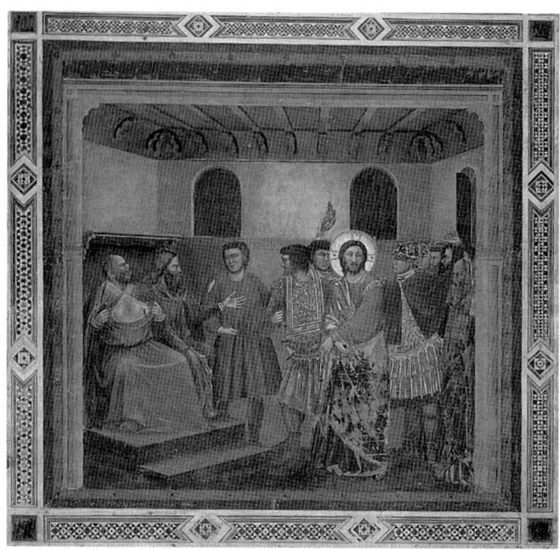

35. Giotto, Jesus interrogated by the Priests, lower tier of the south wall of the Scrovegni Chapel (corresponding to 31 in Fig. 18).

As depicted by Giotto, it is the story of a drawn-out miscarriage of justice and of the judge's disregard for the safety of the accused. It comes fully to life when, as spectators, our extended process of decoding supplies a temporal and logical dimension to the drama.

The oblique viewpoint from the main entrance is of course not the only one. Standing before the central scene of the Betrayal, the Death Sentence also provides a conclusion to the chapter which began with the Last Supper (Fig. 29). Likewise there is nothing to prevent one looking at the fresco from directly in front. But the viewpoint from which I have described it seems intended by Giotto to encourage the spectator to reflect upon the circumstances of the final stages of Jesus' trial in a new way, as well as providing a point of entry 'in medias res'.

The Massacre of the Innocents (Fig. 36) is still more perplexing in its understated opacity. So much so that John Ruskin rated it as the weakest of all Giotto's frescoes.[53] He sought to excuse it, however, on the grounds of decorum: such unspeakable deeds ought not to be represented realistically but merely as a shadow of the event for the imagination to dwell upon. A student of mine once provided a similar explanation: Giotto conceived of the mothers as numb with horror. Both explanations accord with what we have seen of Giotto's restrained approach. Herod's men are coldly efficient. They display no ferocity, the mothers little emotion.

The following interpretation turns on two points. First – the phase of the Massacre which Giotto has chosen. Giotto often represents the period just *before* the climax of an event as in the Last Supper or the Betrayal, so that our imagination is engaged and our attention sustained, as recommended by the eighteenth-century German writer Gotthold Lessing in what he called the pregnant or suggestive moment.[54] Here, however, Giotto chose a stage when the Massacre is all but *finished*, the pile of babies' bodies resembles the dead on a battlefield. This is the time of irreconcilable loss, the silence after the killing, when one is almost too numb to vent one's grief. Moreover this scene showing two of the mothers attempting to wrench the bodies of their children out of the clutches of their assassins concludes a sequence which

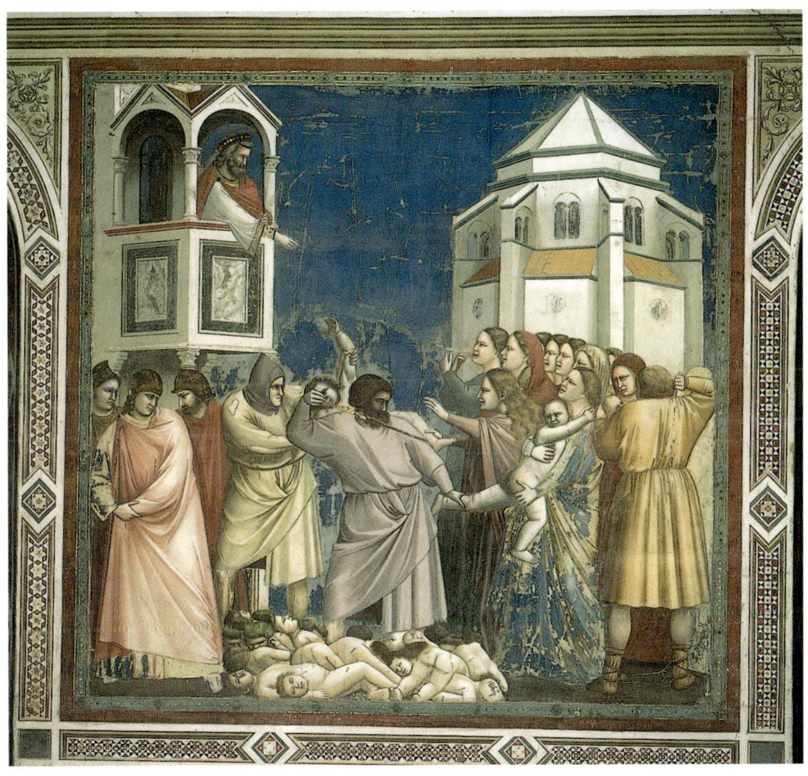

36. Giotto, the Massacre of the Innocents, middle tier of the south wall of the Scrovegni Chapel (20 in Fig. 18). This photograph has been taken on a scaffold directly in front of the fresco.

began with the infant Jesus being handed gently into the frame of the fresco of the Nativity.

The second point turns upon the same oblique viewpoint as in the Death Sentence. Once again the composition is subtly transformed (Fig. 37). The tug-of-war over the child partially hidden behind the bearded man in the centre, seems all the more vivid and immediate. We seem to catch a glimpse of the child's head just being dragged into our field of vision from behind the head of the bearded man, and we observe that the child's foot is just on the point of slipping from his mother's grasp and out of sight. There is neither hope nor charity – represented in the two Virtues below (Fig. 31). The child is about to die. This intensifies the horror at the tail-end of the atrocities. Again one is placed in the role of an eyewitness, and by virtue of having to

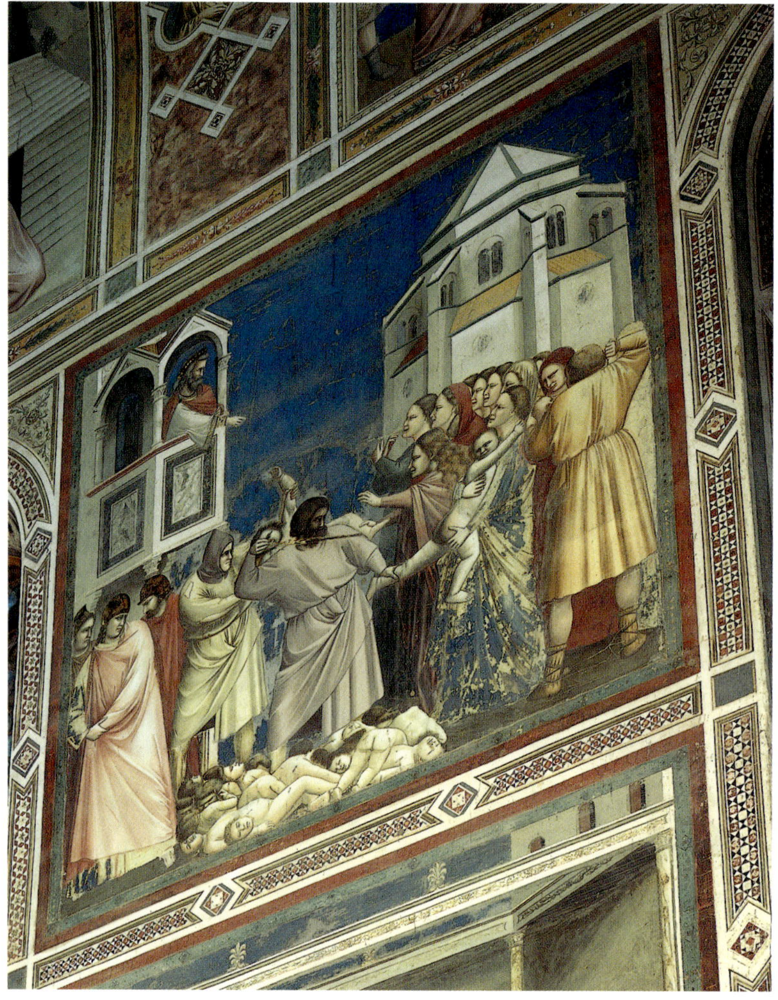

37. Giotto, The Massacre of the Innocents, middle tier of the south wall of the Scrovegni Chapel (20 in Fig. 18). This photograph has been taken from the main door as in Fig. 31.

puzzle out an action that is visually obscure we are made to linger over the scene and to identify with the feelings of this one *individual* mother. This observation requires one to modify the earlier statement about the phase Giotto has chosen. Although this is the end of the Massacre as a whole, it is, of course *just before* the last three victims are killed. It is the beginning of the end. In addition, by virtue of the enhanced perspectival effect, the actual distance across which the poor child's body is being dragged appears all the greater, as if he is being stretched on the rack, a foretaste of what is about to happen in the tug-of-war just begun in the foreground. From this viewpoint, moreover, the spatial depth in general is more ample, more crowded with figures, Herod's balcony seems much higher up and Herod himself more remote.

Perhaps the most powerful effect gained from our oblique point of view is that instead of feeling that our standpoint is midway between the crowd of mothers on the right and the men on the left, we seem to be standing in line with the women, though at some distance, like them craning upwards plaintively towards Herod who shows no mercy. As a result not only do we identify more closely with them but we also feel that the two babies are being dragged inch by inch out of our reach.

This analysis indicates how Giotto provided for the frescoes to be read in more than one order, how one can plunge into the story *in medias res*, reading backwards to the beginning of a chapter and of the cycle as a whole. We also find that oblique viewpoints can throw fresh light upon the subject. The two scenes also exemplify Giotto's employment of vertical juxtaposition: both show rulers committing acts of gross injustice towards innocent victims. Both represent Jesus' oppressors. The analysis also illustrates some general ideas about pictorial narrative, concerning the spectator's role both as eyewitness and as narrator, and the way that one's perceptions unfold as one dwells upon the image.[55] In the Massacre we experience a transition from numbed incomprehension at the sight of that pile of dead bodies to entering into the feelings of the mother whose baby is slipping out of her reach and of the helplessness of all the women in the face of the almost mechanical power of Herod's militia and its imperviousness to human sympathy. In the Death Sentence we shift from mere recognition of what is taking place, to a dawning realisation of what must have happened overnight in the space between Jesus' trial by the priests and his trial by Pontius Pilate.

The spectator's orientation to the pictures contributes to the temporality of this unravelling.[56] In both these scenes we feel that we have come in at the tail-end of a sequence of events and are compelled to work out what has been happening. Each picture concludes its chapter. By placing these two scenes in such a position by the main entrance, Giotto encourages us to search back over the preceding scenes for explanation.

* * *

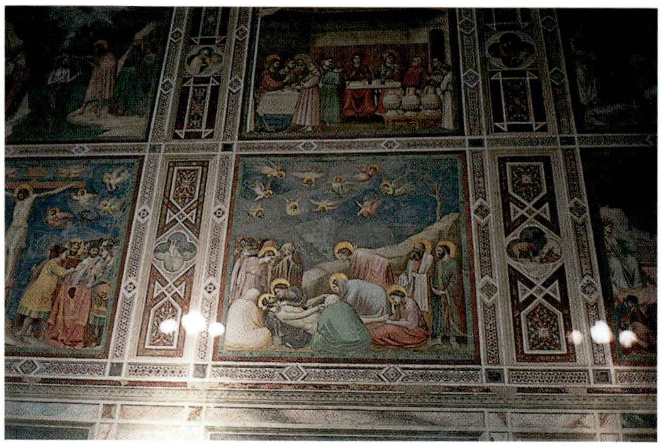

38. Giotto, The Lamentation, lower tier of the north wall of the Scrovegni Chapel (35 in Fig. 18). Unlike the other photographs of frescoes in the Scrovegni Chapel this has been taken by natural light to provide some indication of how the frescoes change as the sun moves around the chapel during the day, spotlighting particular frescoes.

The concluding sequence

The sixth and final chapter demonstrates Giotto's concern for bringing to a conclusion the intricate and carefully organised structure of the whole. In the opening fresco, Jesus is expelled from the gates of Jerusalem, carrying his cross to his own crucifixion.[57] The scene of the Lamentation over the body of Jesus (Fig. 38) takes place in a wilderness reminiscent of that into which Joachim made his retreat. Even the solitary tree is leafless. The mourners are relatively undemonstrative; Giotto has other means for communicating their feelings. His use of colour, for example, is remarkable for its discordance and gloom. The body of Jesus and particularly his head is the green of death and decay. It stands out stereoscopically. The woman behind the Virgin wears a dark green robe highlighted in an acid lemon yellow, the shadows a ruddy umber – colours which clash with one another and with the pale lilac of the woman next to her as well as with Mary's bright blue robe. The man on the extreme right wears a dark greeny-blue cloak with sienna red shadows over a dark blue gown. These chromatic disharmonies suggestive of a thunderstorm contrast with those of the next scene (Fig. 39), Jesus' Resurrection and his appearance to Mary Magdalene by the tomb, the Noli me Tangere, which is connected to it by the rock which appears to run up behind the frame and down the other side. The predominant colours of this fresco are white and

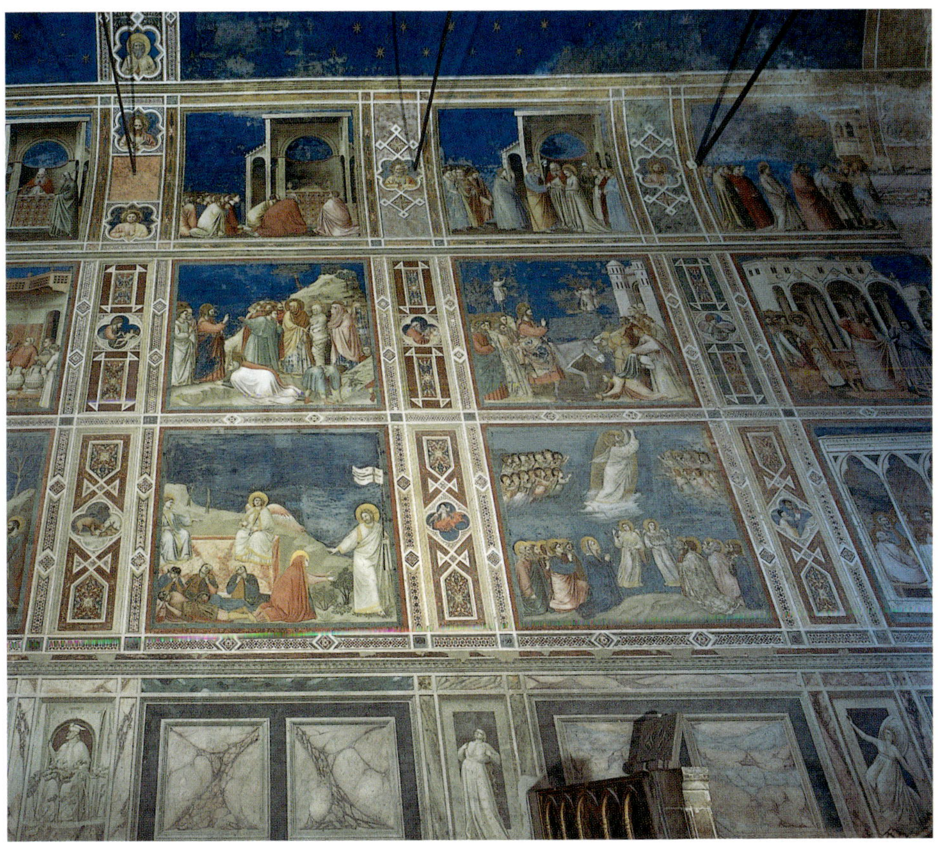

39. View of a section of the north wall of the Scrovegni Chapel from the same position as in Fig. 19. This photograph demonstrates how the boundary marked by the altar draws our attention to a shift in the frescoes above between the terrestrial and the sacred domains: - between The Suitors praying for their Rods to blossom and The Betrothal of the Virgin Mary; between The Raising of Lazarus and Jesus's Entry into Jerusalem; between the Noli Me Tangere and the Ascension.

rose, the colours of sunrise, also the symbols of Faith and Charity. Even the rock is devoid of shadow. Between the kneeling Magdalene and Jesus the shrubs and flowers burst into green leaf, the colour of Hope, as would the trees had not the pigment flaked off. All three theological virtues are suggested. Literally, 'the desert shall rejoice and blossom as the rose'.[58] Beneath, the Vices are tottering; the tyrant's castle in which Injustice is enthroned cracks, crumbles and is overgrown as Jesus returns from the grave, while in the space between the Resurrection and the Ascension, Anger tears her

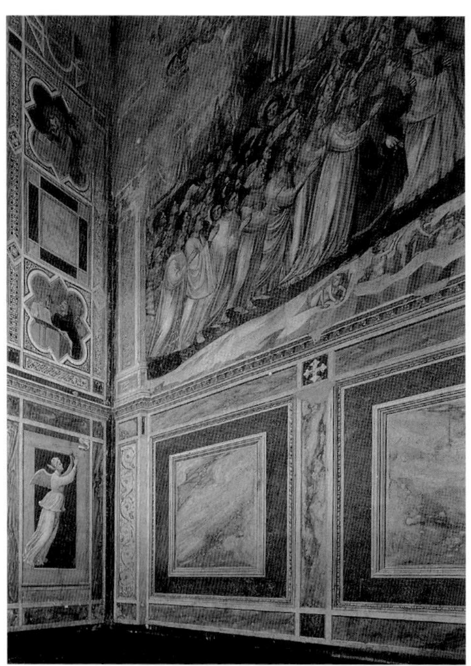

40. The south west corner of the Scrovegni Chapel showing the the figure of Hope, whose posture echoes that of Jesus in the Ascension (Fig. 39), seeming to join with the company of the blessed in The Last Judgement on the west wall.

clothes in rage, echoing the actions of Caiaphas (Fig. 35) when Jesus admitted to being the Son of God. Finally, in the next fresco, as Jesus rises into heaven so Inconstancy totters, overbalances and falls. A further connection is made between the scene of the Lamentation and the Raising of Lazarus, for if the line of the sloping rock in the former is continued upwards it joins up with the rock in the upper scene (Fig. 19). Moreover, the Lazarus incident, devised by Jesus to give proof of the resurrection, is placed directly above the scene of his own resurrection.

In the Resurrection and Noli me Tangere Jesus is placed at the very right-hand edge of the frame. 'Touch me not; for I am not yet ascended to my Father' (John 21, 17): he is just on the point of moving out of the frame into the next scene, that of his Ascension into heaven. In terms of the layout of the frescoes, he also moves out of the terrestrial domain in which he has conducted his ministry and suffered his Passion, back into the sacred domain. In the border between the two pictures a small quatrefoil of Elijah rising in his Chariot links the two images of Jesus and enhances his upward ascent, literally towards the gates of the Temple of Jerusalem in the picture immediately above, that of his Entry, the same gates from which he had been ejected at the start of this chapter. Symbolically he is ascending towards the heavenly Jerusalem. With both arms raised heavenwards he echoes the figure of Hope (Fig. 40) in the far corner of the chapel, diagonally opposite, which may be read as representing our hope of inclusion in the company of the blessed at the Last Judgement, depicted on the adjacent wall.[59] Chronological sequencing, our own progress through the story, the use of colour, juxtaposition, rhyme and the interrelationship between the narratives and the allegorical figures all work together in the grand conclusion. When we turn to leave the chapel we face the Last Judgement (Fig. 17), the conclusion to a momentous journey.

★ ★ ★

Giotto's temperance of style

Throughout this discussion the issue has arisen of Giotto's restraint, particularly in the way he depicted highly dramatic, emotional and violent events. Is this a limitation or was it deliberate, in reaction perhaps to the expressiveness of his older contemporary, Giovanni Pisano, who also contributed to the chapel? Moderation was one of the most important artistic virtues that Leon Battista Alberti in his *De pictura* enjoined artists to follow in their compositions. In his only reference to a work by a modern artist Alberti celebrated Giotto for his mosaic of the Navicella (Fig. 102) as a paradigm of good narrative composition.[60]

To answer this, let us return to Ruskin's point about the Massacre – that Giotto refused to represent such unspeakable deeds in all their gory realism, so that our imagination would better be able to dwell upon their significance. Is that the only reason?

In almost all Giotto's paintings physical actions are controlled, and the

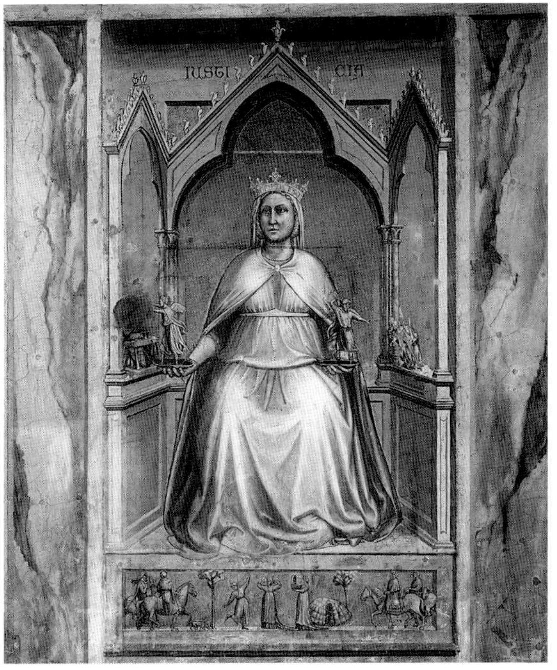

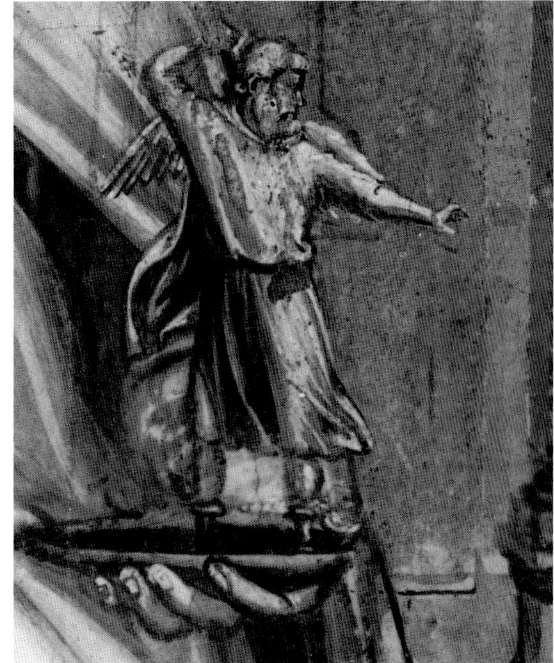

41. (*above left*) Giotto, Justice, centre of the lowest tier of the south wall of the Scrovegni Chapel (corresponding to d in Fig. 18).

42. (*above right*) Giotto, Commutative Justice (or criminal law), detail of Fig. 41.

expression of emotions is understated. The Virtues, like the behaviour of Jesus himself in the Betrayal, are all impassive, with the exception of Hope who flies delicately upwards. Giotto's brushstrokes correspond; the modelling of surfaces is smoothly graduated and inexpressive. The chief exceptions are the Vices who are very active – gesticulating, tottering and ripping their clothes apart, or inflicting injury upon themselves, as if already in Hell. They might well be described as intemperate. Nevertheless such actions are almost never permitted to intrude into the narrative in its stately progress round the walls; not even in the story of Jesus driving the money-changers from the Temple (Fig. 104). Only in some of the more ghastly scenes in Hell is physical violence let loose – one devil is castrating a man with a pair of blacksmith's pincers, a dragon-like creature is gnawing another man's penis, but these images are on so small a scale that only photography or scaffolding makes them accessible. One final instance is suggestive. The small figure of Commutative Justice (criminal law, in effect) held by Justice (Fig. 41) in her left hand, vigorously swings his sword to behead a criminal (Fig. 42). Giotto's brushstrokes swirl in sympathy. It is important to observe that not only are such figures engaged in violent actions but Giotto also painted them in a more vigorous and expressive manner. Elsewhere it is impossible to detect the gestural brushstrokes of the painter.

Giotto even seems to have controlled his skill in the depiction of nature, such a marvel to his contemporaries. For example, the artist who could paint the two vaulted chapels on the chancel arch (Fig. 16) in such convincing perspective and shading that as the sun moves round the chapel during the day they seem to be illuminated first from one side, then from the other – such an artist must have made a deliberate choice to employ toy-town buildings and interiors.[61] Likewise the painter who could depict the gesticulating hands of the High Priest in the Death Sentence (Figs 33–4) or the outstretched hand of the man in the Lazarus (Fig. 28) so as to look startlingly stereoscopic, must have chosen to organise most of his compositions in fairly shallow, flat friezes of figures close to the picture surface and parallel to it.

The following explanation of Giotto's pictorial style turns upon the moral virtues which the cycle is intended to instil. The central Virtue who is enthroned on the right-hand wall is Justice (Fig. 41), who looks across the chapel at Jesus' ascent into heaven. To either side stand six auxiliary Virtues, like magistrates on their bench or patron saints in an altarpiece.[62] Chief among these, on the right-hand side of Justice, is Temperance (Fig. 43), her mouth bridled, binding up the straps of her sword and thereby enacting the very words spoken by Jesus to St Peter during his Betrayal (Fig. 30), the fresco of which is placed just above and to the right.

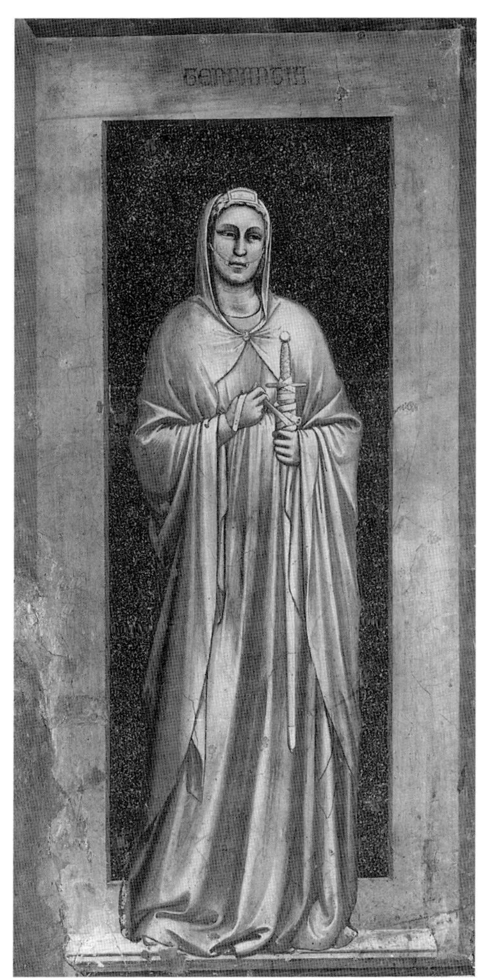

43. Giotto, Temperance, lowest tier of the south wall of the Scrovegni Chapel, (corresponding to c in Fig. 18) the Virtue placed on the immediate right-hand side of Justice and below the fresco of the *Betrayal* and to its left. Temperance is binding the belt of her sword around its hilt so that it cannot be drawn, thus enacting Jesus's command to St Peter in the Betrayal: 'Put up again thy sword into his place: for all they that take the sword shall perish with the sword.' Temperance is not only a key virtue in the Scrovegni Chapel but also reflects Giotto's restrained style of painting and his characterisation of the episodes of the life of the Virgin and of Jesus.

> Put up again thy sword into his place: for all they that take the sword shall perish with the sword.[63]

This episode, it will be recalled, was omitted from the fresco of the Betrayal itself, but the juxtaposition with Temperance alludes to it. Thus Temperance is characterised by Giotto as Christian self-restraint in desisting from immediate personal revenge against an aggressor.[64] Injustice, in contrast, has his hand on his sword. The moral seems to be that whenever the true Christian suffers injustice and violence, he or she should turn the other cheek, for the wicked will ultimately be punished by the just God at the Last Judgement. Then, and only then, will the wrath of God be let loose on that *Dies Irae* – Day of Anger.

Commutative Justice is a foretaste of that. This moral is left for the spectator to work out.

Opposite Temperance is its antithesis, Anger, on the left hand, the sinister side of Injustice (Figs 19 and 39), King of the Vices, whose tyrant's castle cracks as he looks towards the scene of the Last Judgement. Anger, or intemperance, is the key vice who rips her clothes in response to the scenes immediately above her where Hope of Salvation is fulfilled and Virtue appears to triumph: the Betrothal of Joseph and Mary, Jesus' Entry into Jerusalem, Jesus' ascent into heaven.

My contention is that Giotto's overall style of painting, including the gestures and actions of his figures as well as the compositions, was intended to be temperate. Not only should the good Christian, even when suffering terrible injustice, behave temperately, like Jesus, but the Christian artist should paint in such a style as to forestall emotions of anger and revenge.[65] Except in the depiction of the Vices and God's final and terrible punishment, the artist should aim to make the spectator stand back and think calmly and rationally about the higher significance of these events, not to react instantaneously, passionately, intemperately and blindly as Vices do.

Returning to the Massacre (Fig. 37) for a moment – can it be seen, perhaps, as a carefully 'argued' rejoinder to Giovanni Pisano's Massacre (Figs 66–9) in his Pistoia pulpit of 1298–1301, to be examined in the next chapter – both to Giovanni's emotional intensity and to his practice of involving the spectator closely in events? Giovanni almost seems to invite the Christian to take justice into his own hands, to pursue vendettas.[66] It seems that Giotto wanted his paintings to appeal more to the reason and intellect than to the emotions. His approach bears similarities to that advocated by Plato in *The Republic* and to St Augustine's reflections on tragedy in his *Confessions*.[67] Everything leads to this conclusion, the analytic approach to the depiction of individual episodes and the brilliant ingenuity with which he finds the means to represent the inner life, as well as the complex interrelationship between architecture and painting, the careful arrangement of the chapters upon the wall, and the tempo of his sequences.

Conclusion

Although Giotto's Scrovegni Chapel is physically on a far larger scale than Duccio's Maestà, there are many points of comparison in the two artists' approach to narrative. Both worked within the Gregorian doctrine of Christian Art, pursuing a detached 'platonic' approach in which the spectator's emotional involvement in the events is secondary to reflecting upon their significance. The intellectual demands upon the spectator are considerable. Events follow one another according to probability and necessity, and every detail relates directly to the action, even if it takes time for us to appreciate the connection. Their visual portrayal of the scriptural and apocryphal accounts is far more than mere illustration, it presents the stories in a new guise and invites us to interpret them afresh.

One major difference between the two artists, which arises from the nature of the commission, is that Giotto not only uses architecture to assist the narrative within individual scenes, but these are also related with great effect to the interior architecture of the chapel. The story begins with Joachim's despair at being ejected from the sanctuary of the Temple, located within the sanctuary zone of the chapel, and it concludes with the Pentecost opposite, also within the sanctuary, in which the Holy Spirit enters the disciples. The cycle begins with despair at rejection and ends with the hope of resurrection, justice and salvation at the Last Judgement.[68]

A second difference between Duccio and Giotto can be found in the different ways that they establish logical relationships both within individual scenes and between them. Giotto's handling of this is more complex. Take antithesis as an example. The whole chapel is structured on the antithesis between Vice and Virtue. The Vices are placed on the wall adjacent to Hell (Fig. 17), the Virtues opposite, juxtaposed with the Blessed. The Council in Heaven to decide the fate of mankind, faces the Last Judgement. Each of the six chapters is structured with a well-defined beginning, middle and end. Likewise individual frescoes. Several other types of logical relationship are suggested in the Chapel, cause and effect in particular, epitomised in the Betrayal (Fig. 30). In addition Giotto uses vertical juxtapositions to draw one's attention to similarities between different scenes. Above all he employs negation to good effect: Joachim does *not* respond to his dog, the disciples do *not* see Judas dipping with Jesus in the bowl. But we have to read this logic into the images and the juxtapositions between them, in the absence of any visual equivalent to conjunctions and other syntactical features of language. Nonetheless Giotto establishes his compositions and sequences in such a way that it is as if there were a syntax – or to use St Augustine's phrase about miracles – Giotto's images 'have a tongue of their own', they constitute a 'verba visibilia', a visual language.[69] In Gregorian terms, they can indeed be 'read' like a book. This is also true of Duccio, but Giotto seems perhaps to operate at a higher level of complexity.

Another distinctive feature of Giotto's approach to pictorial narrative is found in those individual frescoes which seem at first sight peculiarly refrac-

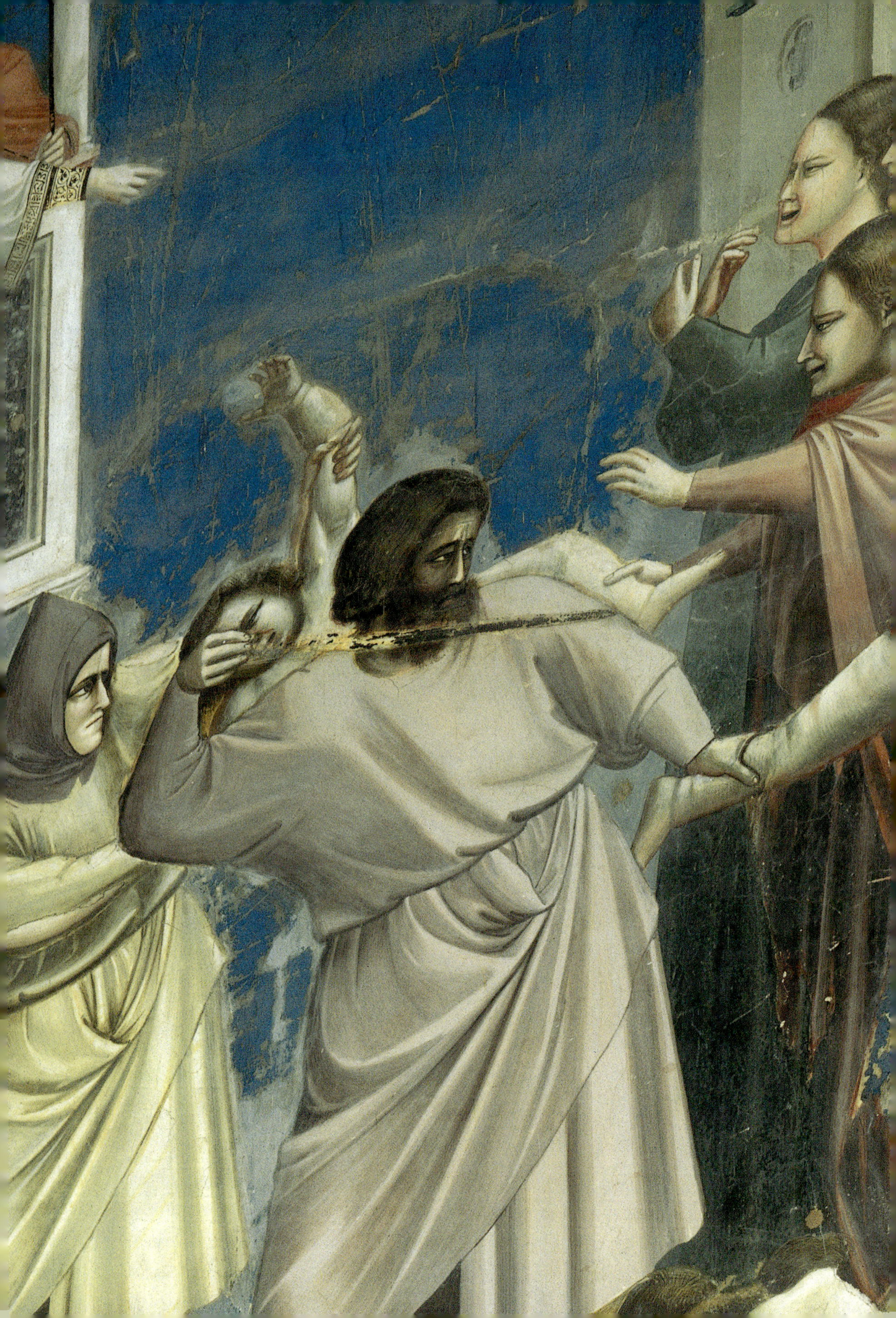

tory, such as the Massacre, the Last Supper and the Death Sentence, or another fresco which has not been discussed, the Marriage at Cana. Such images have struck observers as enigmatic, cryptic, inert or even boring. But extended contemplation is repaid by discovering how deeply Giotto had pondered the significance of such events, representing a familiar story in an unfamiliar way. In addition, the significance of the relationships between frescoes, such as that between Temperance and the Betrayal, may at first escape one. Even Giotto's more accessible images bear repeated and extended examination.

Giotto's employment of obscurity to set the spectator a puzzle is closely allied to his extraordinary acuity to the complexities of visual perception. I refer here not to the geometric perspective construction developed by Alberti in 1435, but to other aspects of perception.[70] Giotto's sleight of hand in the Last Supper (Fig. 29) depends upon the space between Judas and the figure to his right through which the spectator can glimpse the two hands in the bowl. Were the spectator's implied standpoint a little further to the right or to the left, his view of this would be obstructed. Likewise in the Massacre (Fig. 37) Giotto has once again employed movement parallax as well as masking and overlapping of figures so that we catch a glimpse of the child's body being pulled away from his mother. The Betrayal is full of partially masked details which, once we begin to notice them, encourage us to scrutinise the fresco with close attention.

Within a framework of seeming simplicity, then, Giotto operates with great guile. The dominant order of the cycle is the chronological movement spiralling around the chapel, but this is criss-crossed by rhymes, parallels, juxtapositions and many other devices of which we gradually become aware, and which immeasurably deepen our understanding of the story.

Finally, despite the restrained, detached and predominantly frontal presentation of his paintings, a feature shared with Duccio, Giotto sometimes ventured further in seeking to involve the spectator in the drama though the use of oblique viewpoints, though this is more the exception than the rule. Very different was the approach of Giovanni Pisano, to whom we turn next.

Detail of Figure 37

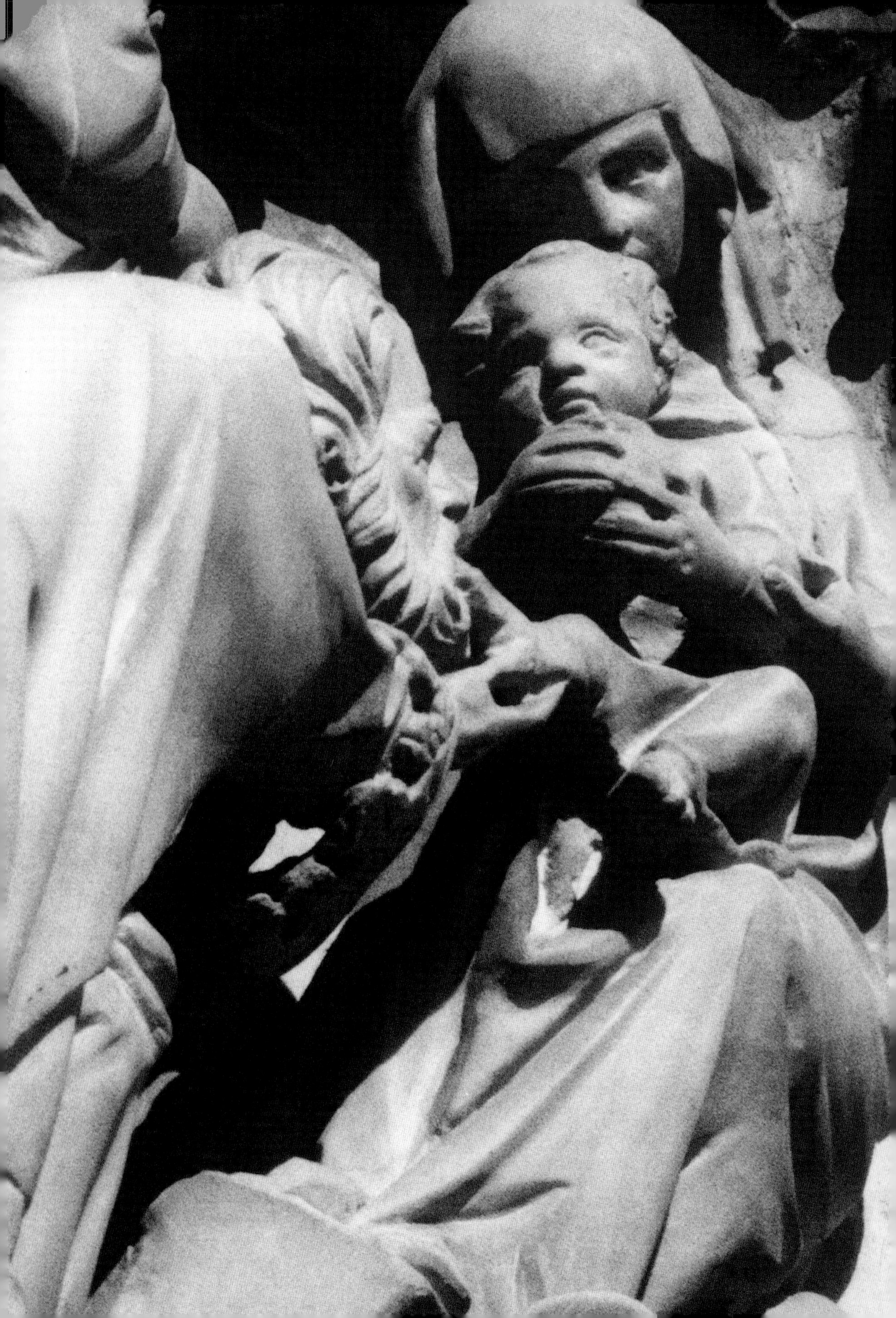

III

GIOVANNI PISANO'S PISTOIA PULPIT

With the work of Giovanni Pisano (c.1250–1319), who was almost a generation older than Giotto, we turn from painted panels and frescoes to relief sculpture. Tourists and scholars have somewhat neglected Giovanni's two pulpits. The first (Fig. 44), finished in 1301, is situated in the small Romanesque church of St Andrea in the city of Pistoia, the second (Fig. 72) (1302–11) stands in the grand cathedral of Giovanni's home city of Pisa a few paces from the leaning tower. Even in these days of mass tourism neither pulpit attracts the crowds to be found in the main tourist sites of Florence, Venice, Rome or in Giotto's Scrovegni Chapel in Padua. In Pisa visitors seem to have drifted into the cathedral after looking at the leaning tower, while one can spend hours all alone with the Pistoia pulpit.

Among art historians too, Giovanni Pisano does not enjoy the same reputation as Giotto and this may contribute to his omission from crowded tourist itineraries. Here it will be argued that he was as great an artist, and although his work was quite different in character, he made an equal contribution to the tradition of pictorial narrative.[1]

One reason for Giovanni's neglect may arise from the way his work has been photographed.[2] Almost exclusively, photographers have worked from scaffolds erected directly in front of the relief panels, so that we get the

Detail of Figure 64

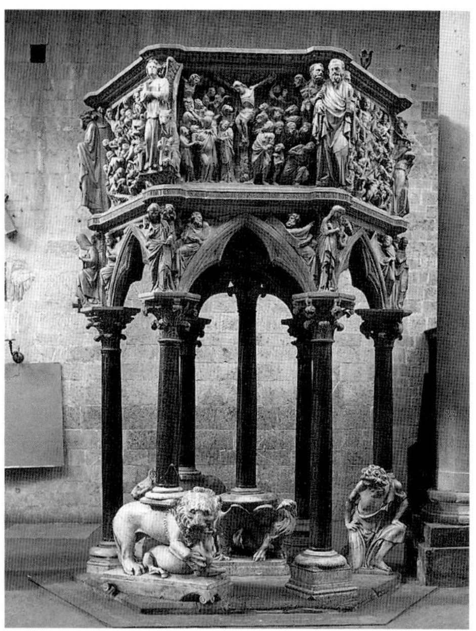

44. Giovanni Pisano, Pulpit in Sant' Andrea, Pistoia, 1298–1301, marble.

impression of looking at them as if they were hanging at eye-level upon the walls of an art gallery (Figs 60 and 73). This is also true of the way frescoed chapels are photographed, but it has, in my view, a more detrimental effect upon high relief sculpture, as I hope to demonstrate. In their actual locations the panels are about nine to twelve feet above the ground, so that if we stand close enough to see the figures clearly we have to look upwards. Because we are free to move around the pulpits, which we have to do in order to follow the story, we also look across the panels obliquely from various angles. With this in mind, Giovanni designed his reliefs specifically to be seen from a range of viewpoints, and only when they are so viewed do they fully make sense. Conventional photographs make the composition of the reliefs look messy, confusing and flat, off-putting to expert and tourist alike. Moreover, such photographs adversely affect the ways in which we perceive the sculptures even when we are in their presence. *In situ*, they are indeed somewhat confusing at first glance, and visitors might well feel frustrated by the effort of sorting out what they see, wishing they had a ladder so as to obtain views similar to those on postcards. On the one occasion I was able to do this, I found the composition of the reliefs fading before my very eyes, even as I climbed. Giovanni designed the reliefs to be seen from the ground. One has to make the effort to see these sculptures as they were intended.[3]

Before discussing how Giovanni tells the stories it is therefore necessary to examine his approach to relief sculpture.

Spatial representation in sculpture

This issue is of great importance not only for Giovanni Pisano but for all the sculptors discussed subsequently. Most art-historical writing on relief sculpture makes the assumption that until Donatello's reinvention of very low or squashed relief in the 1420s (Fig. 124) and the development of geometric perspective, to be discussed in Chapter 6, it was far harder, if not impossible, for sculptors to represent figures within a convincing physical and spatial setting than for painters, who, in fresco particularly, had a large surface to work upon. A sculptor with his small panel had to make his figures large if they were to be seen clearly, but the result was that the figures had to be crammed together with little space separating one from the other. This explanation is based on the assumption that without low relief and artificial perspective it is impossible to create much sense of the separation of figures beyond what can be achieved through overlapping one figure in the foreground against another behind; basically, the only depth possible is that provided by the volume of marble – by the actual depth of the panel. Sculptors, therefore, were limited to making friezes of figures which might be solid and substantial but could do little to suggest spaces between and behind them. The late John Pope-Hennessy, a leading expert on Italian Renaissance sculpture, in his account of Giovanni Pisano and of his father Nicola, refers in passing, and then only once, to Nicola's 'unceasing effort to produce a space illusion in the relief field', giving as an example the Adoration of the Magi in the Pisa Baptistry pulpit where 'the figures are disposed across three demarcated planes'.[4] Even John White, historian of the rebirth of pictorial space, did not seem to think that Giovanni's efforts in this area were worthy of mention.[5]

This account of relief sculpture is based upon the incorrect assumption that we look at these reliefs at eye-level. Seeing them obliquely from beneath has major implications for high relief sculpture which Giovanni exploited to great effect, not only technically and spatially as the following diagrams indicate, but also dramatically.[6]

When viewed from the front it is true that the depth within such a relief is limited to the thickness of the marble panel, from A to B – a few inches (Figs 45a and b). But from beneath (Fig. 46) a new potential is opened up because the relief is at an oblique angle to the onlooker.

The lower edge of the relief A is much closer to the eye than the upper edge C. It is as if the spectator were looking at the relief at eye-level but tilted away (Fig. 47).

Figures and objects at the lower edge are *actually* considerably closer (Fig. 67) to the eye and through the judicious overlapping of forms a far stronger impression of depth and the space between figures can be conveyed. It is as if the sculptor had used a deep block of marble (Fig. 48) from which to excavate his figures and by this means he could overcome the limitations of his medium.

The effect of looking up is further extended by virtue of the fact that it is also possible to view the reliefs from oblique angles (Fig. 49), providing the sculptor not just with the depth from A to D (Fig. 47), but also the depth across

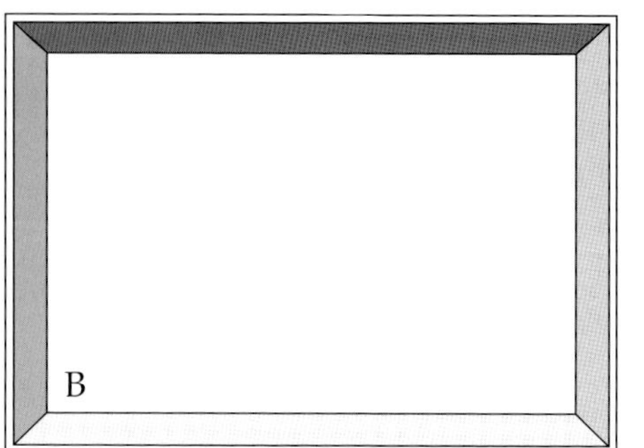

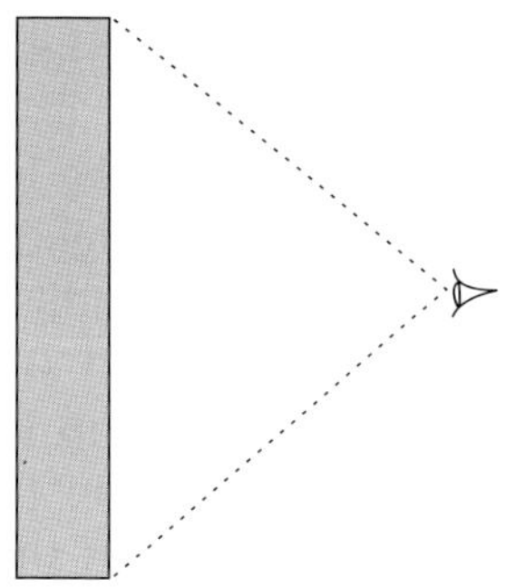

45a. (*far left*) Diagram showing the depth of an excavated block of marble from the front.

45b. (*left*) Diagram showing the depth of an excavated block of marble from the side.

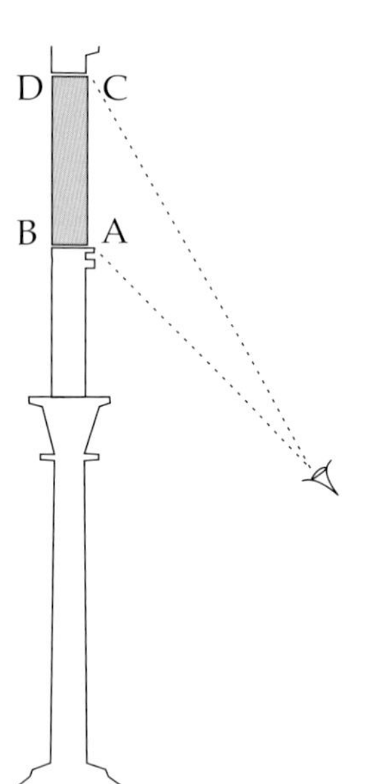

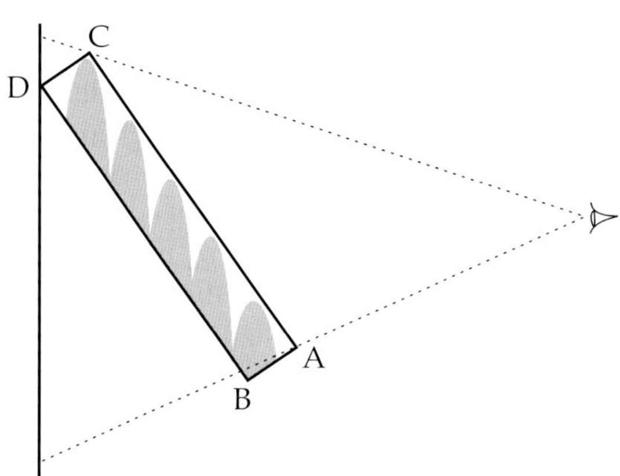

46. (*left*) Diagram showing a spectator looking up at a block of marble on a pulpit.

47. (*above*) Schematic diagram of a carved block of marble tilted away from the spectator.

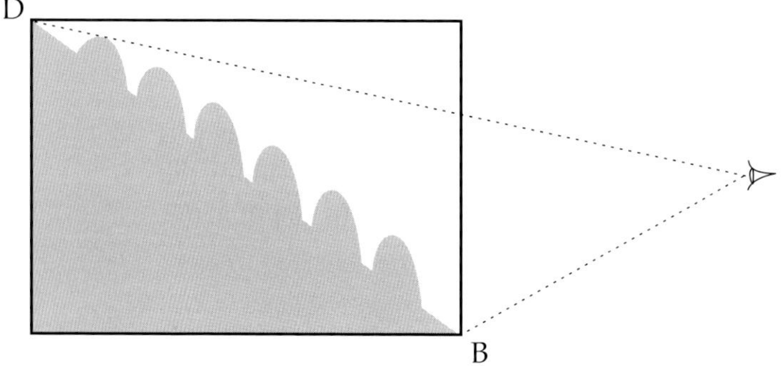

48. (*left*) Cross-sectional diagram of a deep block of marble with figures carved in it.

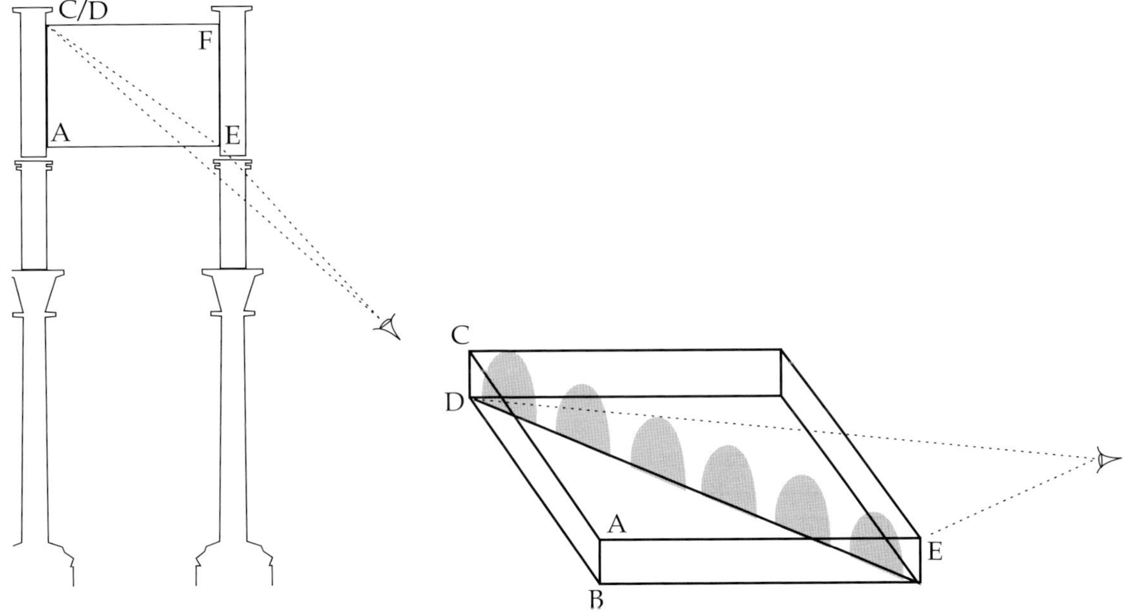

49. (*above left*) Diagram showing spectator looking up obliquely at a marble relief on a pulpit.

50. (*above right*) Oblique view of a block of marble.

the much longer length of the diagonal of the piece of marble from E to D (Figs 50 and 54).

By placing figures outside the relief at its corners, as well as upon different levels of the pulpit, the depth of field is extended still further. In addition Giovanni employed a number of illusionistic and perspectival devices to focus his compositions from particular viewpoints (Fig. 76). In short, Giovanni's reliefs can be viewed from a range of viewpoints at ground level. Those employed in standard photographs can therefore be ruled out, although, of course, the further away one stands, the closer one's angle of vision approximates to the eye-level view. One must surmise that in order to carve the pulpits so as to give rise to these different viewpoints, full-size preparatory models must have been made in clay or wax, with figures and limbs on swivels to enable Giovanni to work out the optimal arrangement before carving began.

By grasping these potentialities and exploiting them, Giovanni extended the resources of relief sculpture, though he must have learnt from the many

Roman sarcophagi carved in high relief still to be seen in the Camposanto in Pisa.

Another technical innovation should be mentioned, one which enabled Giovanni to use these oblique planes for dramatic ends to a degree that had eluded his father Nicola in the Siena Cathedral pulpit (1265–7) where the diagonal had already been employed. Careful examination of Nicola's sculpted figures shows that they can be viewed predominantly from a single viewpoint, usually from the front, though sometimes from the side as well. Giovanni's figures on the other hand can be viewed from different aspects, 'in the round' as it is called. How did Giovanni achieve this?[7]

A pillar showing three saints (Figs 51a and b) from Nicola's workshop, now in the Victoria and Albert Museum, helps us answer this question, particularly when we examine the heads, and try to work out how they were carved. It is clear that each head has been carved from a roughed-out cube of marble whose front plane has been used for the front of the face – brow, eyes, nose, cheeks, chin and mouth, while the sides were used for the sides of the face – ears, hair and jaw. Each surface has been carved in low relief and then the

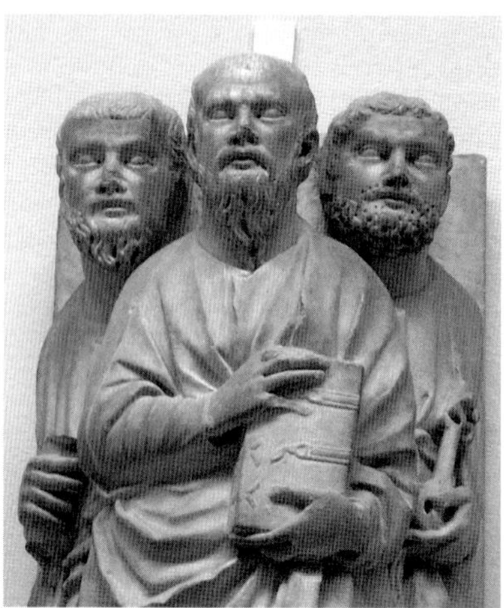

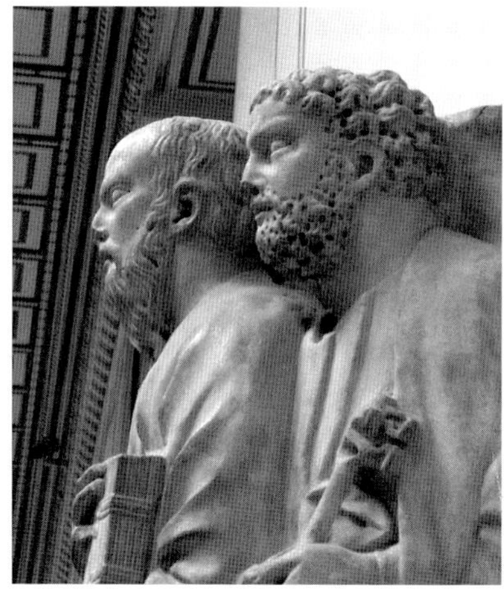

51a. (*above left*) Workshop of Nicola Pisano, Saints Peter, Paul and James, c. 1260–70, marble, Victoria and Albert Museum, view from front. One can observe that the heads have been carved from a rectangular block of marble with the front of the face of each saint aligned parallel to the front of the block.

51b. (*above right*) Workshop of Nicola Pisano, Saints Peter, Paul and James, Victoria and Albert Museum, view from the side. Because of the way in which the carving of each head has been conceived in relation to the block the side view is less satisfactory than the front view.

edges of the block chiselled away in order to create the rounded shape of the head. Viewed from the front this works quite well, but as soon as one adopts an oblique view the illusion falls to pieces since the edge is simply chamfered. The same technique was applied to Nicola's relief sculptures, as an unfinished example from his workshop demonstrates. Basically these were drawings upon the surface of the marble, which were then excavated to give them depth and solidity. Even at his best in the Siena Adoration this accounts for the somewhat stolid, boxy quality of Nicola's figures, but above all for the fact that he cannot fully exploit the possibilities of the oblique viewing position.

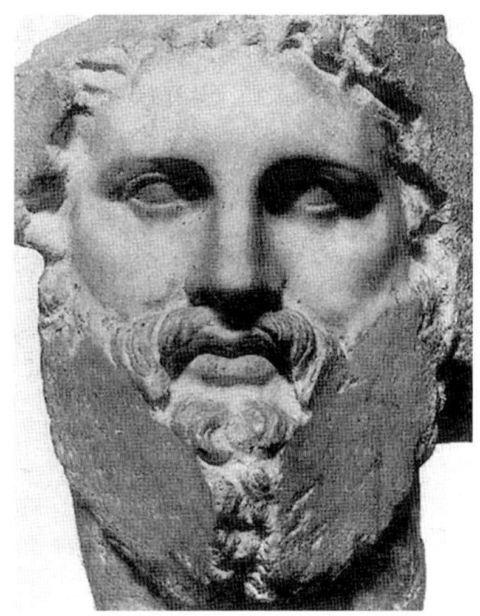

52. Unfinished bearded head, 3rd to 2nd century B.C., Alexandria. Unlike the heads in Fig. 51, this head has been carved from a rectangular block of marble positioned at 45° to the front of the face so that the nose and chin are aligned with the edge of the block. It is possible that Giovanni Pisano may have studied some such antique carving.

Giovanni's solution to the problem was as simple as could be. He orientated the block of marble at an angle of 45 degrees to the front of the face (Fig. 52) so that the bridge of the nose would lie along the foremost edge of the block.

The beauty of this depends upon the fact that it corresponds better to the anatomy of the face, where the cheeks and sides of the face are not at right angles to the brow but lie in two planes approximately at right angles, meeting along the bridge of the nose. When we look at such sculpture (Fig. 53) in the round from any angle, there are no discontinuities between one plane and the next such as those created by the chamfering of the edges of Nicola's cube, because the sharp edges and flat planes of the head correspond closely to the shape of the marble block – the nose to an edge, the cheek and jaw to a side. It goes without saying that what applies to the carving of a head also applies to whole figures as well as to sculpture in high and medium relief.

The Pistoia Pulpit

We shall begin our journey around Giovanni's first pulpit in Sant' Andrea Pistoia[8] at the beginning, with the Annunciation and the Birth of Jesus (Fig. 54). What we encounter, however, is not only a scene from the Gospels but to its immediate left, the figure of a priest. For the richness of Giovanni's narrative to be fully appreciated, this figure needs to be identified and explained.

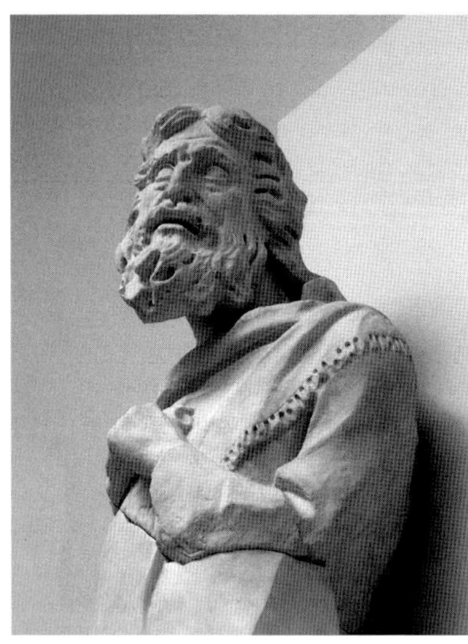

53. Giovanni Pisano, Head of the prophet Haggai, between 1285 and 1297, marble, originally from the façade of Siena Cathedral, now in the Victoria and Albert Museum. As in the antique head in Fig. 52 Giovanni has positioned Haggai's head so that his nose and the centre of his beard lie along the edge of a rectangular block. This makes it easier to carve the sides of the face so that the head makes sense from a variety of oblique viewpoints from ground level as the spectator walks around the figure placed high up on the façade. This approach to carving heads and figures gives rise to the rich variety of viewpoints in Giovanni's relief sculpture on his two pulpits.

Giovanni goes to great lengths to *begin* the story, to draw us into it by creating a visual equivalent to 'in the beginning' or 'once upon a time'.

The figure of a deacon carrying a bound volume in his left hand and swinging a censer in his right stands immediately to the right-hand side of the entrance to the pulpit (Figs 54–5), on the corner next to the panel of the Nativity. To grasp how any worshipper at the time would have understood this figure it is necessary to explain a little about the Mass and the use to which pulpits such as these were put.[9]

They were originally located adjacent to the wall between the sanctuary containing the high altar and seating for priests, monks and choir, and the main body of the church where the lay congregation assembled. The priest could climb into the pulpit and address the congregation.[10] These pulpits, however, were not used for sermons, which were delivered from movable, wooden pulpits which could be positioned inside or outside the church,[11] they were lecterns for reading the Epistles and the Gospels as part of the ritual of the Mass (Fig. 56). In the Pistoia pulpit the corner figures of the Evangelists and of the writers of the Epistles alludes to this function.[12] The pulpit was used at fixed points in the Mass before the Creed and Holy Communion. First the sub-deacon chants the epistle for the day, shortly followed by a deacon or a priest who sings the Gospel. A prescribed intonation was strictly enforced, the *tonus rectus*, which permitted no changes of pitch, so that the deacon was unable to give personal expression to his reading of the sacred text.

The lessons are preceded by an elaborate ceremony. The volume of the Gospels, often richly adorned with jewels and precious metals, lies upon the altar and the deacon calls upon God 'to cleanse my heart and lips . . . that I may be able fitly to proclaim thy holy gospel'. In the words of the Roman Missal, 'he then goes in procession, with lights and incense to the place where the gospel is to be sung', in this case the pulpit; 'he censes the book three times, and then sings the gospel'. Immediately after the lesson the sub-deacon takes the open volume to the cele-

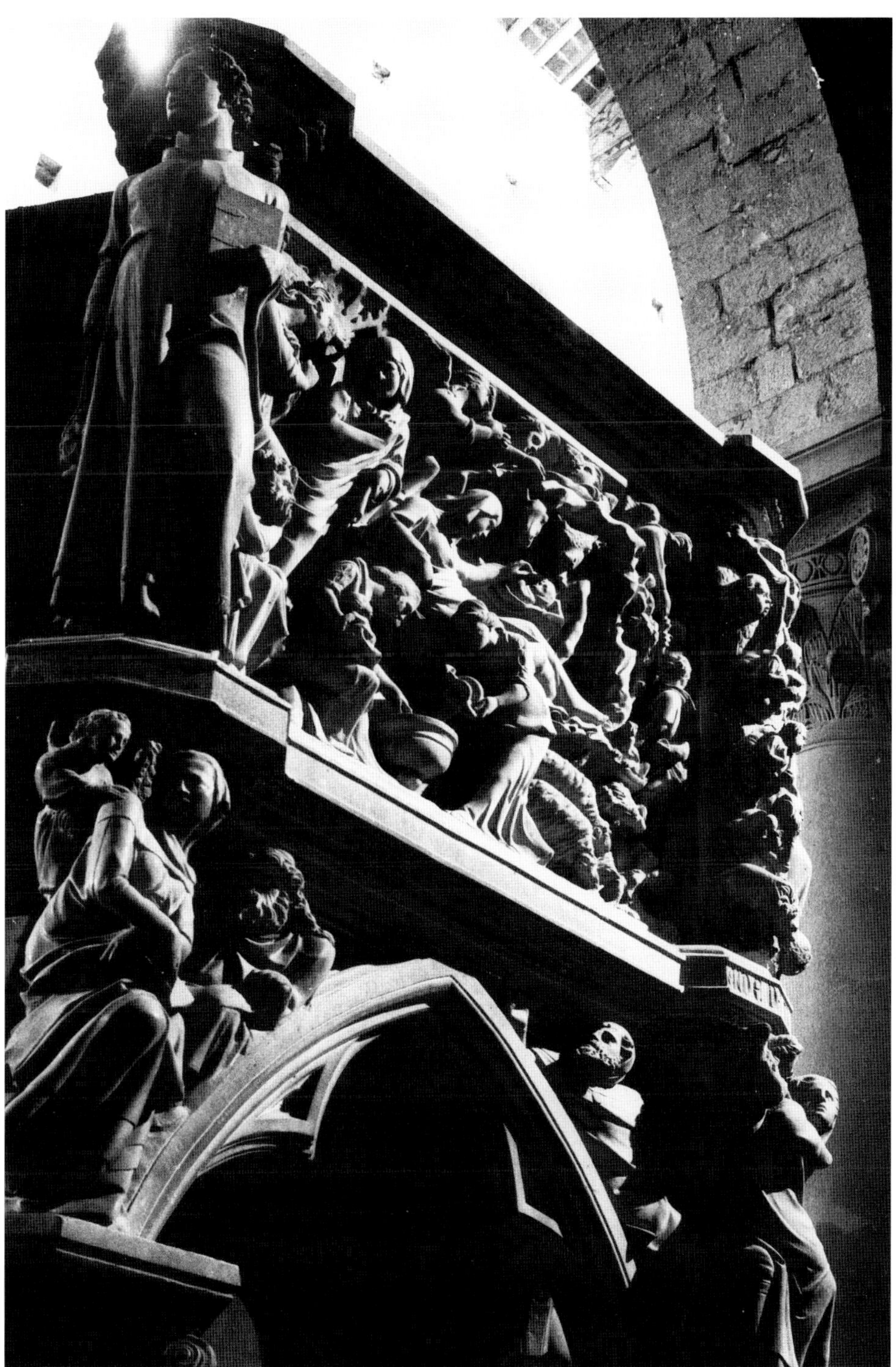

54. Giovanni Pisano, oblique view of the first panel of the Pistoia pulpit showing the Annunciation, St Joseph in the lower left hand corner, the Nativity, the midwives washing Jesus, the Annunciation to the Shepherds and the Adoration of the Shepherds. On the corner to the left of the relief is the figure of the Deacon carrying a book, probably a bible, and a censer. On the level beneath him the first Sybil is being roused by an angel.

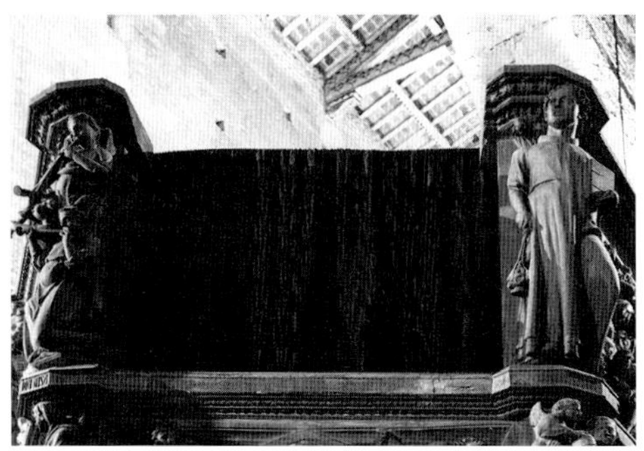

55. Giovanni Pisano, the entrance to the Sant' Andrea pulpit showing the deacon on the right and angels sounding their trumpets in the Last Judgement on the left.

brant of the Mass, who kisses it and says, 'Through the words of the gospel may our sins be wiped away.' The reading of the Gospel is a solemn and splendid ritual. A sermon may follow – a commentary in the vernacular upon that day's Gospel, applying its lessons to the issues of the day.

The figure of the deacon may be identified, then, as engaged in the act of carrying the Gospels and swinging the censer.

By placing the deacon at the start of his cycle, what was Giovanni trying to achieve? First, the figure links the liturgical reading of the Gospel with the visual depiction of the story of Christmas and Easter. Second, because the gospel was sung in Latin and was probably unintelligible to many in the congregation,[13] the carved images enabled the congregation to meditate upon the stories, if only at Christmas and Easter, while the sermon in Italian would have explained their significance. Perhaps Giovanni was also offering some personal reflections upon the relationship between the verbal and the visual accounts of Jesus' life. The presence of the deacon refers directly to the Gospels, but what relationship with the images is implied? Did Giovanni share the view of his fellow Pisan, Fra Giordano, that images can have equal authority to the scriptures? Or do the images show us the words springing into life? Or does Giovanni imply that the words of the scripture were partly based upon the canonic images, as suggested by Fra Giordano?

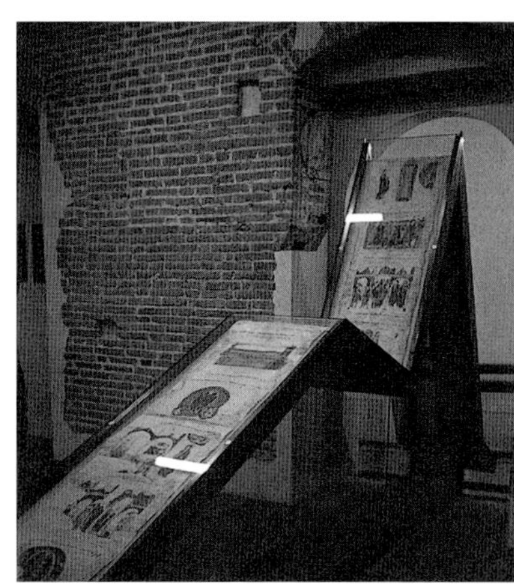

56. Illuminated pulpit scroll, 12th century, Museo dell' Opera del Duomo, Pisa. Such scrolls were visual aids. The images on this scroll are upside down in relation to the words. As the priest read the words the appropriate image hung over the pulpit facing the congregation, who could view it the right way up. Carved pulpits made by the Pisano family were monumental and very expensive versions of pulpit scrolls.

More can be extracted from Giovanni's device. One of the many difficulties faced by pictorial storytellers is that of representing the narrator in the act of telling a story. An important aspect of much traditional storytelling is to stress the fact that a story is being told.

One recalls the opening of the Gospel of St Luke.

> Forasmuch as many have taken in hand to set forth in order a declaration of those things which are most surely believed among us, Even as they delivered them unto us, which from the beginning were eyewitnesses, and ministers of the word; It seemed good to me also, having had perfect understanding of all things from the very first, to write unto thee in order, most excellent Theophilus, that thou mightest know the certainty of those things, wherein thou has been instructed.

Also apposite to this scene are the first words of St John's gospel echoing the first verse of Genesis:

> In the beginning was the Word, and the Word was with God, and the Word was God.

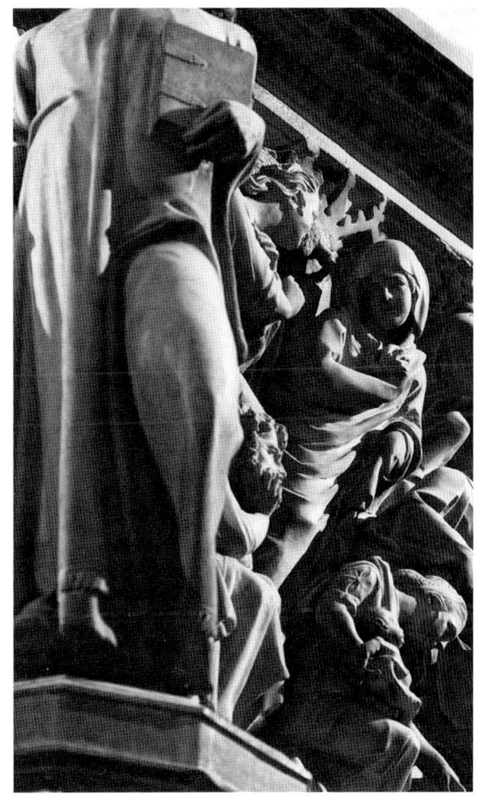

57. Giovanni Pisano, the Annunciation, close up of the first of the Pistoia pulpit. Gabriel appears to emerge from the fold of cloth over the hand of the deacon carrying the book.

It may seem a somewhat corny comparison but the device of showing the book being carried by the deacon has a parallel with the conventional title sequence of a 1930s movie of a novel, showing the book being opened, the pages turned, and the narrator's voice fading into the cinematic drama before our eyes. Here when we look up from behind the Angel Gabriel (Fig. 54), his wings outstretched, hair flying, face alight with joy and full of the urgency and excitement of his mission, as he springs into action from behind the hand of the deacon carrying the Gospels, it is as if those very words that he is about to chant are coming to life in front of us. This impression is enhanced by the way that Giovanni has carved the two figures, particularly the draperies of their arms, so that Gabriel seems to be emerging from a cavity in the deacon's side (Fig. 57). But this is not the only means by which Giovanni gives us the feeling of the story coming to life, as if we are eyewitnesses to the Annunciation.

On the corner of the pulpit, immediately beneath the Deacon, at the same level as the arches, sits the first of a series of six female figures (Fig. 58), those

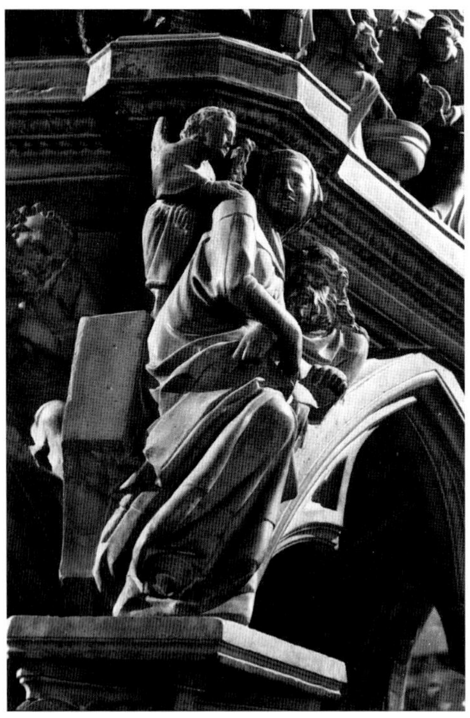

58. Giovanni Pisano, the first Sybil, close up of the Pistoia pulpit from approximately the same position as Fig. 54.

of the non-Jewish Sibyls who, like the Jewish prophets, foretold the coming of Christ. Giovanni uses them not only to proclaim their particular prophecies but as participants in his dramatisation.[14] A small angel behind her shoulder is nudging this first Sibyl, who is looking away from the scene taking place above her head, apparently oblivious. We can almost hear the angel saying, 'Turn around, look up, those momentous events you foretold are actually about to take place.' And the Sibyl on the next corner of the pulpit (Fig. 61) is indeed craning upwards, an active spectator and eyewitness. Like the deacon the first Sybil is calm and detached, in contrast to Gabriel's energetic arrival.

Second, within the panel itself, half-hidden, tucked behind the deacon's knee and just beneath the Archangel Gabriel, sits a fourth introductory figure, St Joseph (Figs 54 and 57), deep in thought, his chin resting in the palm of his hand, seeming to gaze across at the scene of the Virgin Mary lying after childbirth with Jesus in his crib.

Giovanni, then, opens the story using these four carved figures – deacon, Gabriel, Sybil and St Joseph. They are all in the foreground, closer to us than the Virgin Annunciate and the Nativity, so that to see the other events we have to look past them, over their shoulders, as if through their eyes, their words, their thoughts and their prophecies. Closest of all on the lowest level is the Sibyl, roused to witness the fulfilment of her prophecy. On the second level is the deacon reminding us of the Holy Writ and of the Mass. Then on the third level there is Gabriel making his announcement. Finally one of the characters who participates in the events themselves, St Joseph, acts as an intermediary, something of an observer himself, reflecting upon the meaning of what he sees. One can see the Sibyl as representing the prophecy of the future; the Annunciation as the initiation of the action in the present; Joseph the humble carpenter reflecting upon its significance and the deacon carrying the sacred history of the event.

The calm figures of the deacon, Sybil and Joseph create an air of expectancy and anticipation, fulfilled by Gabriel's dynamic entry (Fig. 59). I have dwelt upon them partly to show how self-conscious Giovanni was of his professional role as a storyteller, but also because the three figures, which overlap one another, also illustrate Giovanni's methods for extending the spatial resources of relief sculpture. Next we will see the full implications of those techniques for pictorial narrative.

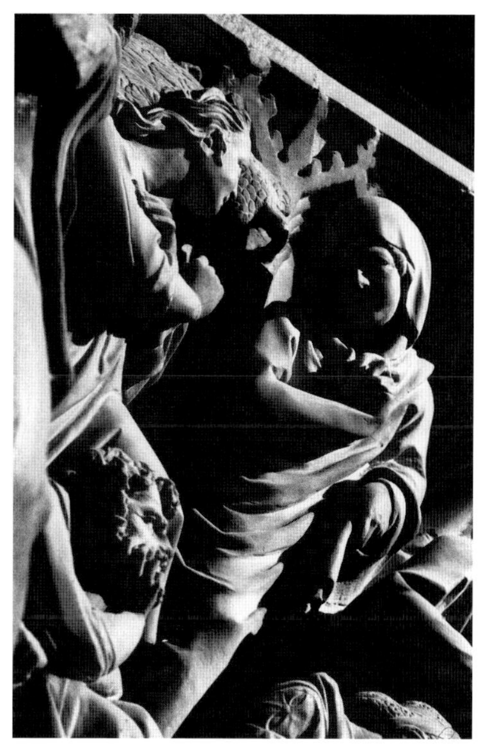

59. Giovanni Pisano, the Annunciation, close up of Gabriel and Mary, Pistoia pulpit.

The importance of new photographs is apparent. In the standard photo (Fig. 60) of the first panel everything seems to be taking place simultaneously: Annunciation, St Joseph, Mary on her bed adoring baby Jesus, the midwives washing him, the angels summoning the shepherds. This exemplifies one of the conventions for suggesting the sequence of events – continuous narration as it has been called. Here it looks a mess. The figures seem out of proportion with one another and the interactions between them are stilted. What a change takes place when we are in St Andrea and begin our own journey anti-clockwise around the pulpit (Fig. 54). We look up over Gabriel's shoulder and observe Mary's reaction through his eyes as he rushes in post-haste with his salutation, 'Ave, gratia plena' – 'Hail, thou that art highly favoured', in fulfilment of the prophecies of the Sibyl and of Isaiah. The Virgin recoils violently away from us – 'troubled at his saying', almost falling over.[15] The turbulence of the action, and the character of our involvement, is unlike anything in the work of Duccio or Giotto. From this position the juxtaposed scene of the Nativity seems remote. The figure of the Virgin is not only physically further away from us, but because she is reclining and much of her body is concealed by the head and shoulders of one of the midwives, she appears to be small and hence more distant. She is, moreover, looking away from us and in the opposite direction to the figure of the Virgin in the Annunciation. This contrast, in addition to the viewpoint that we share with Gabriel, concentrates the immediate, the here and now, where all is life and action, upon the Annunciation. Immediacy is powerfully suggested: things close to us, actions taking place along our line of sight, are in the here and

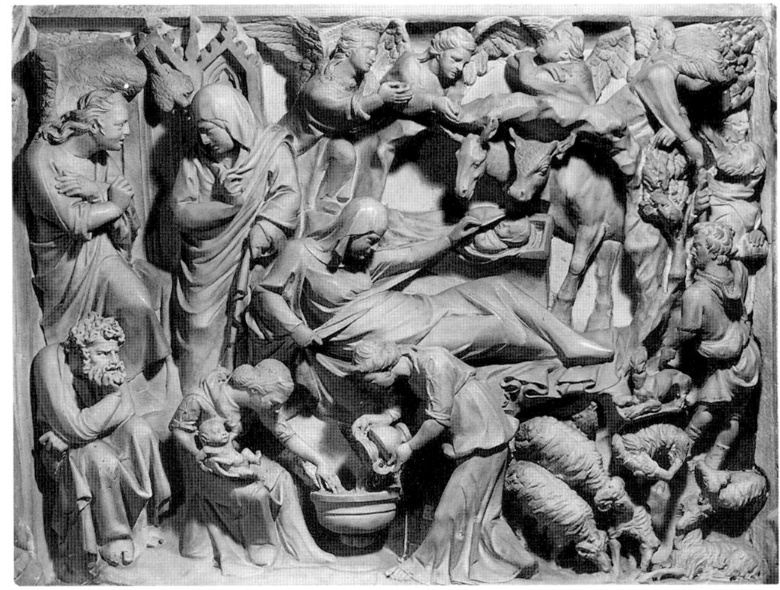

60. Giovanni Pisano, first panel of the Pistoia pulpit. This was photographed frontally from a scaffold at the height of the panel on the pulpit. It shows the same scenes as in Fig. 54.

now; things further away and more detached are in the future.* Distance is here used to suggest the order of events.

The interconnection between the scenes is more than a matter of sequence. Gabriel is telling Mary that she will give birth to the Son of God. It is hard to represent speech in pictures, it is harder to represent prophecy.[16] This is Giovanni's solution: the Nativity, more remote and 'in the future', *is* the manifestation of Gabriel's speech – 'Thou *shalt* conceive in thy womb, and bring forth a son, and *shalt* call his name Jesus . . . he *shall* be called the Son of God.' And the result of Gabriel's message issues from behind the hand of the Virgin Annunciate, just as Gabriel himself emerged from behind the deacon's hand. Three levels of narrative are suggested – the deacon's reading

*The equation of distance with the future certainly does not apply in all cases, as will become apparent.

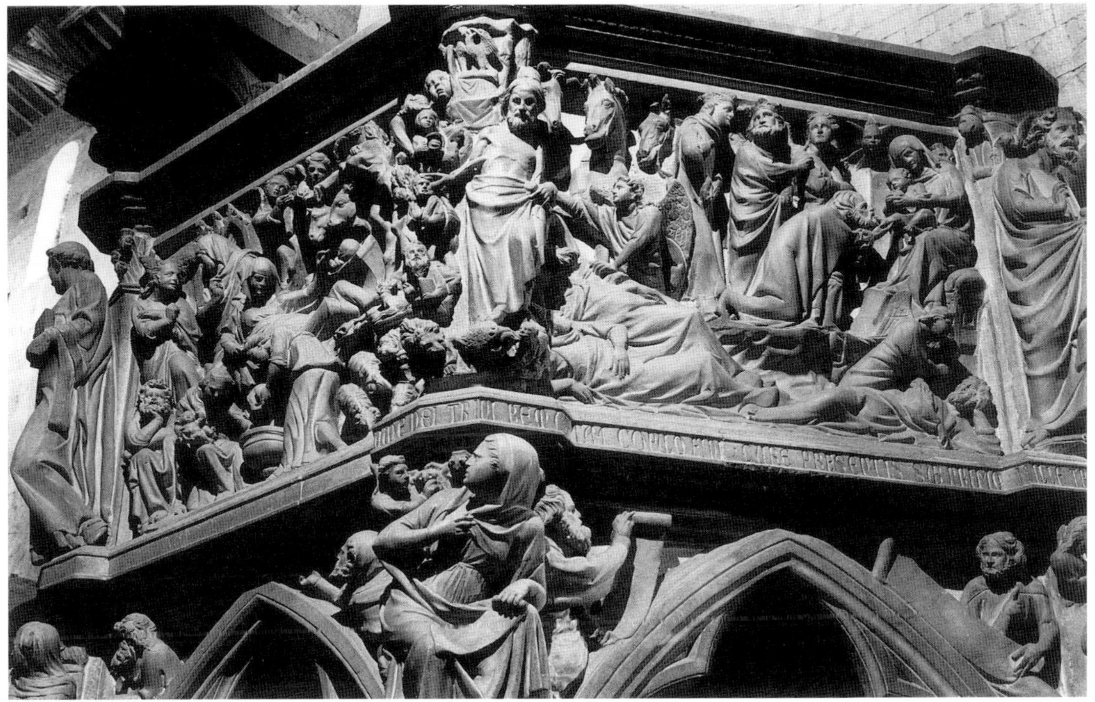

61. Giovanni Pisano, the first and second panels of the Pistoia pulpit. The second panel shows the Adoration of the Magi on the upper right, with the Magi's Dream on the lower left and Joseph's Dream on the lower right. On the corner beneath the two panels sits the second Sybil.

of the Gospel story, its prophetic message enacted by Gabriel and the fulfilment of that prophecy in the Nativity. All this, as well as the causal relationship between Annunciation, in the course of which the Incarnation occurs, and the Nativity, can be read into this overlapping sequence of scenes.

Finally, from this viewpoint, there are the midwives, not mentioned in the Gospels, filling the font-like basin and testing the temperature of the water before washing the baby. Above their heads, in the last scene of this sequence, Mary raises herself and cranes forward as she lifts – another hand in the sequence – the blankets to examine her swaddled baby. But now we have already entered the next episode in the story, best seen by moving to the front or slightly to right of centre. As we do so the figures and episodes change their position relative to us. The effect is striking. The Annunciation, no longer seen obliquely over Gabriel's shoulder, appears less turbulent and intense, Mary recoils less violently, possibly suggesting a later stage in their encounter as we now see Gabriel through *her* eyes: 'Behold the handmaid of the Lord.' As we move further to the right (Fig. 61) the Annunciation shifts from foreground to background in our field of view, and into the past. Our involvement with the Annunciation is defocused, and the next episode becomes focal, a perspectival and perceptual device which Giovanni was later to refine considerably, particularly in the Passion relief (Fig. 76) of the Pisa cathedral pulpit.

Now we observe Mary lifting the veil-like blanket to look at Jesus and to display him. Mary the mother has become the centre of our attention and Giovanni has so arranged her body that from this angle (Fig. 62) she leans forward out of the surface of the panel, her breasts heavy with milk, and we look straight up into her face, turned slightly away from our gaze in order

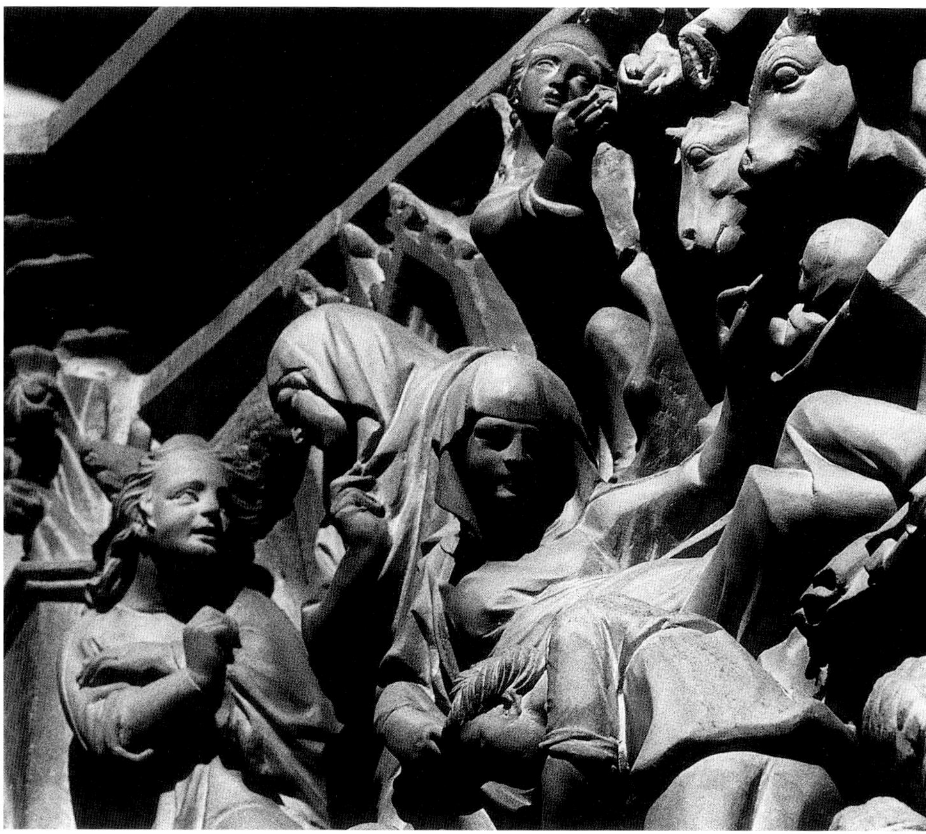

62. Giovanni Pisano, close up of the Nativity on the first panel of the Pistoia pulpit, viewed obliquely from the right. From this position the Annunciation recedes into the background.

to inspect her child. Her manifestation in the Annunciation is now almost hidden behind her head and shoulders, the head veiled. Even so St Joseph, now seeming to belong to the Nativity, continues to ponder upon the significance of these events.

Mary and the baby Jesus are the focus not only of our attention but also of the ox and ass, the angels and shepherds, as well as Joseph, Gabriel and the prophet on the right-hand side of the arch, a circle completed by the spectator.

Strikingly, the second Sibyl in the foreground below, now closest to us, also prompted to look up by an angel on her shoulder, has turned right round to watch the Nativity over her shoulder and join in the rejoicing at the birth of the Saviour. This Sybil, looking up at the panel obliquely from below is also perhaps a cue for spectators of the viewpoints we need to adopt.

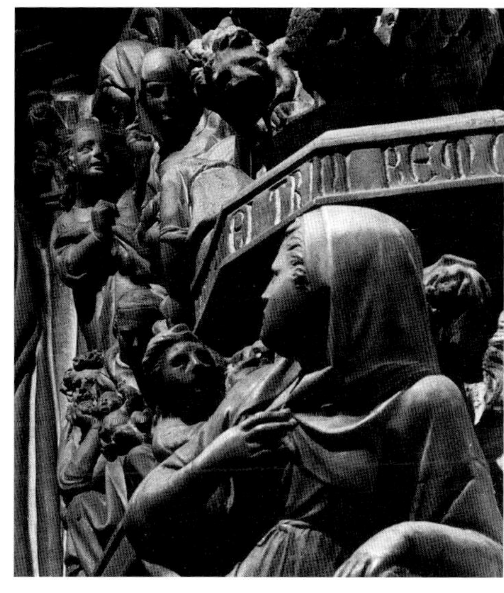

63. Giovanni Pisano, raking view of the first panel of the Pistoia pulpit from behind the second Sybil's head showing St Joseph, the Annunciation and Mary in the Nativity.

From a position behind the Sibyl's head (Fig. 63) Giovanni provides us with a series of raking views of overlapping heads and figures, seen as if in retrospect, forming a magnificent coda to the first act of the sacred drama, an echo of its elaborate opening, and, with the Sibyl's body turning in the opposite direction to her head (Fig. 61), a link to the next scene of the Adoration of the Magi.

Before moving on, it is worth observing that Giovanni's panel of the Annunciation and Nativity bears a suggestive relationship to Dante's description of an image of the Annunciation, carved in relief on the rockface of the mountainous road through Purgatory, written about 1314.

The Angel, who came down to earth with tidings
  Of peace, that had been wept for many a year,
  And opened Heaven from its long interdict,
In front of us appeared so truthfully
  There sculptured in a gracious attitude,
  He did not seem an image that is silent.
One would have sworn that he was saying, 'Ave';
  For she was there in effigy portrayed
  Who turned the key to open the exalted love,
And in her mien this language had impressed,

'Ecce ancilla Dei,' as distinctly
As any figure stamps itself in wax.
'Keep not thy mind upon one place alone,'
The gentle Master said . . .
Whereat I moved mine eyes, and I beheld
In rear of Mary, and upon that side
Where he was standing who conducted me,
Another story on the rock imposed;
Wherefore I passed Virgilius and drew near,
So that before mine eyes it might be set.[17]

Dante's glimpse of the next sculptured story beyond Mary corresponds so closely to Giovanni's procedure in the Nativity panel that one might reasonably imagine Dante had seen it. This would have been possible before Dante's exile from Florence in 1302. Even if Dante did not know the pulpit itself, the passage indicates his awareness of how a sequence of carved reliefs could lead one from one scene to the next, evidence that Giovanni could count upon spectators who were alert to such devices. In addition Dante bears witness to the notion that it was possible for visual images, silent as they were, 'imagine che tace', to enable one to infer what they were saying: 'One would have sworn he was saying, "Ave"'. Dante reflects upon the way in which Mary's words are imprinted in the movements of her body – 'in atto impressa' – in the same way that a shape is stamped into a piece of wax. The spectator has only to look in order to imagine that he is hearing the words. Later in the canto Dante calls this divine sculpture 'visible language' – 'visibile parlare' – a precise Italian translation of St Augustine's 'verba visibilia'.[18] Also significant is that Dante does not offer any explicit observations about the temporality of the image, in which two separate stages are compressed, although he is interested in the passage of time as the spectator moves from one relief to the next.[19]

The first panel exemplifies the dynamics of relief sculpture. To grasp the unfolding story we are called upon to make constant readjustments to our viewpoint. As we look back over the second Sibyl's shoulder there is a new sense of urgency suggested partly by her furrowed eyebrows, by the twist of her body, by her fingers delicately and swiftly gathering her shawl. There is fear: the Magi are arriving, and Herod is planning to follow them. Danger! Be swift. Giovanni shows the Adoration (Fig. 64) taking place almost furtively in a threatening atmosphere. This is an unusual approach, the subject was customarily portrayed as a symbol of the recognition of Christ's divinity by the gentiles. To understand Giovanni's treatment we have to examine the scriptural account in the second chapter of St Matthew's Gospel.

> [1] Now when Jesus was born in Bethlehem of Judæa in the days of Herod the king, behold there came the Magi from the east to Jerusalem, [2] saying, 'Where is he that is born King of the Jews? For we have seen his star in the east, and are come to worship him?'[3] *When Herod the king heard these things, he was troubled, and all Jerusalem with him.* [4] And when he had gathered all the chief priests and scribes of the people together, he demanded of them where Christ should be born. [5] And they said unto him, 'In Bethlehem of Judæa, for thus it is written of the prophet, [6] "And thou Bethlehem, in the land of Juda, art not the least among the princes of Juda: for out of thee shall come a Governor, that shall rule my people Israel."'[7] Then Herod, when he had privily called the wise men, inquired of them diligently what time the star appeared. [8] And he sent them to Bethlehem, and said, 'Go and search diligently for the young child; and when you have found him, bring me word again, that I may come and worship him also.' [9] And when they had heard the king, they departed; and lo, the star, which they saw in the east, went before them, till it came and stood over where the young child was. [10] When they saw the star, they rejoiced with exceeding great joy. [11] *And when they were come into the house, they saw the young child with Mary his mother, and fell down, and worshipped him: and when they had opened their treasures, they presented unto him gifts: gold, and frankincense, and myrrh.* [12] *And being warned of God in a dream that they should not return to Herod, they departed into their own country another way.* [13] *And when they were departed, behold, the angel of the Lord appeareth to Joseph in a dream, saying, Arise, and take the young child and his mother, and flee into Egypt, and be thou there until I bring thee word: for Herod will seek the young child to destroy him.'* [14] When he arose, he took the young child and his mother by night, and departed into Egypt. [15] And was there until the death of Herod: that it might be fulfilled which was spoken of the Lord by the prophet, saying, Out of Egypt have I called my son. [16] Then Herod, when he saw that he was mocked of the wise men, was exceeding wroth, and sent forth, and slew all the children that were in Bethlehem, and in all the coasts thereof, from two years old and under, according to the time which he had diligently enquired of the wise men.[20] [my italics]

Told concisely in fifteen sentences and 445 words, in Latin only 312, almost entirely in reported speech, Plato would surely have approved the style of narrative. But imagine yourself as an artist asked to illustrate this story, even in a sequence of images, and you run into problems. 'When Herod the king heard these things, he was troubled': at issue is the fact that an eyewitness report of the activities of the Magi worried the king, and his reaction is the

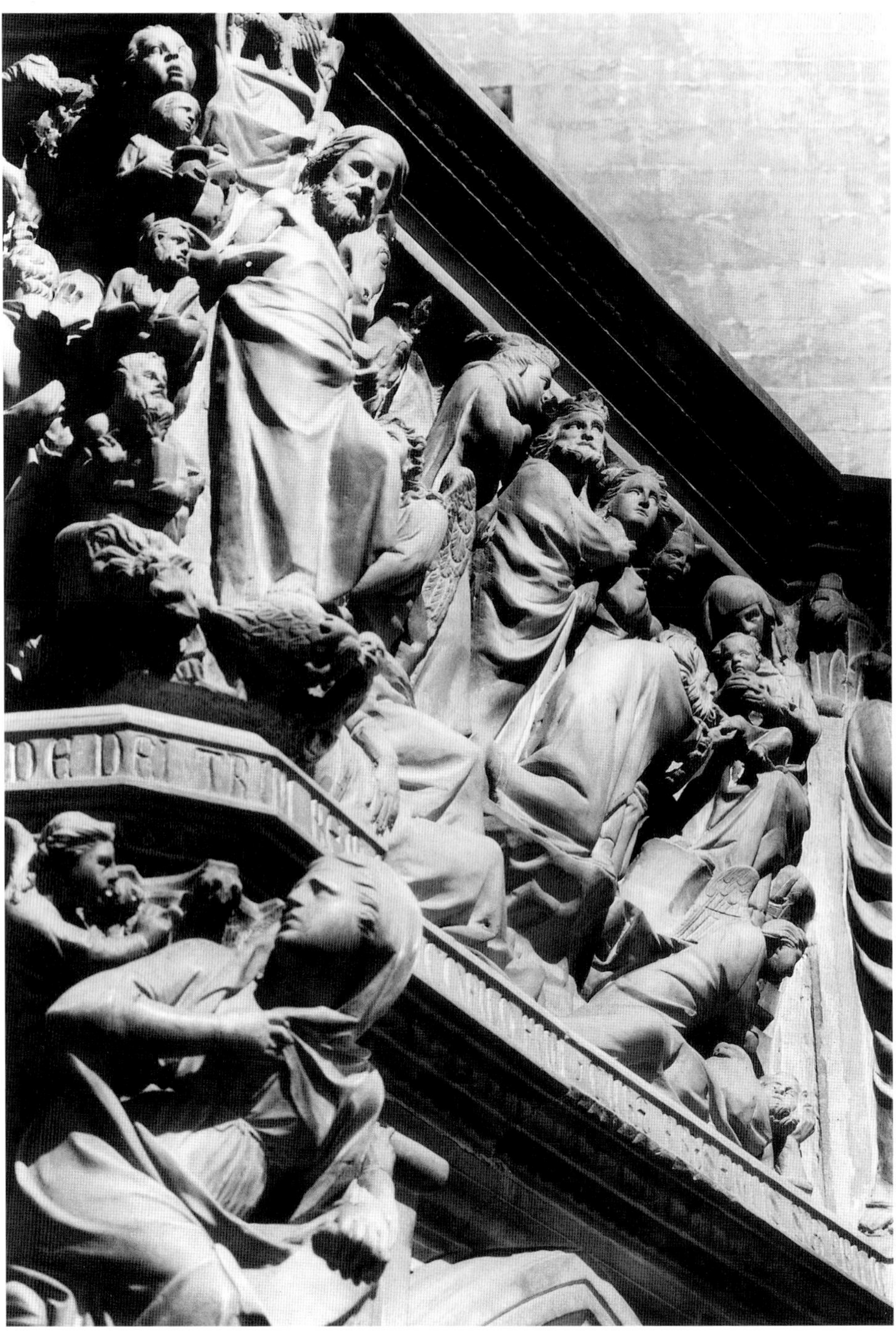

64. Giovanni Pisano, oblique view of the Adoration of the Magi with the second Sybil in the foreground, Pistoia pulpit.

basis for all that follows. The problems of representing this supposedly simple story in visual images are great. In fact the story itself is not so simple.[21]

The heart of the story is Herod's plot to murder Jesus. His plot is deeply duplicitous and covert. Apart from God, only Herod knows of it; he employs no accomplices. What is more, the story is told in such a way as to mirror that deception by deceiving the reader, initially at least, about what is going on. This is achieved by elision, by omitting various links in the chain of events, and by an absence of any explanation of what Herod is up to, leaving the reader to fill in the gaps. It is easy to skim the story casually without fully understanding it, to assume that Herod summons the Priests in order to provide the answer to the Magi's questions and then simply informs the Magi, intending to send his armed men after them. That is the gist, but the essence lies in the word 'privily' – the Latin word *clam*, related to *clandestinus* from which the English 'clandestine' derives, is even more suggestive. Herod summons the Magi without anyone knowing he has done so or why.

Herod summons the Priests openly to discover the expected whereabouts of the Messiah's birthplace. He dismisses them. Apparently, he takes no further action. Secretly, however, he calls a second meeting to which only the Magi are invited, making sure that no one at the first meeting knows. He gives the Magi the information they have been seeking, asking in return for them to inform him afterwards of Jesus' whereabouts so that he too can worship the Messiah. The reason for his secrecy is that he can use the Magi as his unwitting spies so that after their departure he can send assassins to murder Jesus without anyone knowing who was responsible – a mysterious attack on a single child in a small provincial town. Nobody would have the evidence to connect the death with Herod, the threat to his authority would be removed without any stain on his reputation. His conspiracy having been foiled, through God's intervention, Herod was compelled to massacre all the infants in the town.

St Matthew reveals not a word of these calculations passing through Herod's mind; they have to be reconstructed by the reader on the basis of that single word 'privily'. Herod aims to regain his mastery of events, threatened by the unexpected appearance of the Messiah, by making sure that only he knows the full story. The story turns upon deception, secrecy and conspiracy. Herod's plot would have worked had it not been for God, who *did* know the full story. God is the all-seeing and highly manipulative detective in this case, who thereby rescues the Holy Family and, incidentally, causes the massacre. It is apparent that the plot of this very short story is far from simple and it is difficult to represent pictorially.

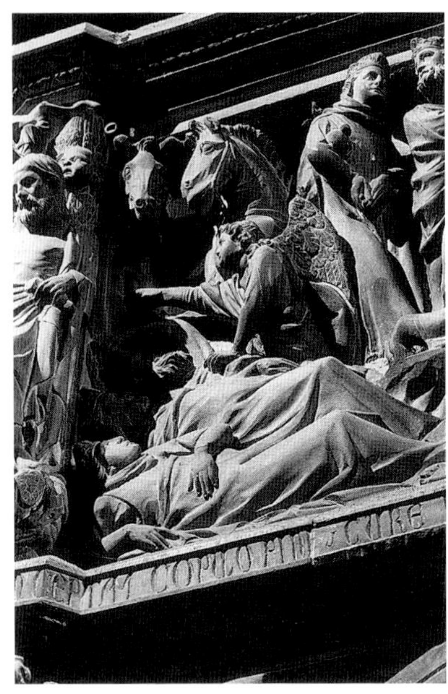

65. Giovanni Pisano, the Angel appearing to the sleeping Kings in their Dreams, warning them not to return to Herod, second panel of the Pistoia pulpit.

Giovanni's Adoration (Fig. 64) is unusual in that the act of homage is pushed into the upper right-hand background and the foreground is occupied by the two dreams which occurred subsequently warning the three Magi, sleeping on the left and Joseph on the right, to escape Herod's trap. The winged angels leaning over the slumbering figures point urgently in opposite directions (Fig. 61).

For the time being, however, we shall put aside our knowledge that the sleepers belong to a subsequent episode depicted in continuous narration, and approach the relief naïvely. Reading the scene as a whole, we receive a powerful impression that the ceremony is taking place while people are sleeping, in the dead of night. Even if we *do* know that the sleepers are the same individuals as those taking part in the Adoration, and hence that foreground and background are intended to suggest different stages of the story, this first impression of simultaneity is inescapable, whatever viewpoint we adopt.

We first see the scene over the head of the anxious Sibyl, being alerted by her guardian angel. From whichever angle we look at this scene, so often joyfully and magnificently depicted as a grand ceremony of homage paid to Jesus by the gentiles, it is viewed through a screen of figures, who point in different directions (Fig. 65), and it takes place hurriedly, furtively, in an atmosphere full of danger. The Magi are urgently ushered in by an angel and seem barely to have time to kneel in homage before everyone must be away to escape Herod's wrath. Even the Sibyl's expression has subtly changed as if to say, 'Hurry! Herod will be after you.' Turning the next corner we look up into Herod's face (Fig. 66).

Such a reading prompts a reflection on the nature of the various conventions for suggesting the sequence of events. As we have already seen in the case of Giotto, these should not be regarded as cut and dried. The Adoration illustrates the richness which can arise from this indeterminacy. Our first impression, in which we read everything as occurring simultaneously, conveys the danger which comes under the cover of night, the knock on the door before dawn. But it is also open to us to use our knowledge of the biblical story, in which case we regard the foreground events as taking place in the here and now and the background event, the Adoration, in the more tran-

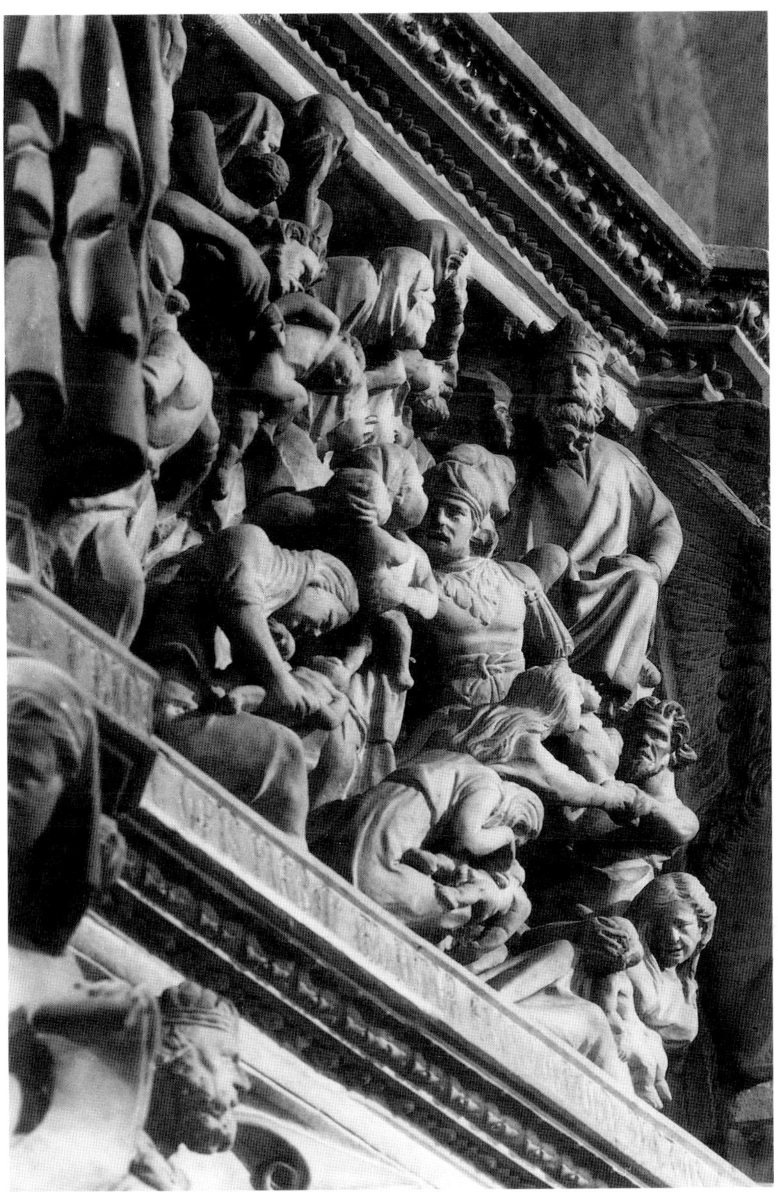

66. Giovanni Pisano, the Massacre of the Innocents, third panel of the Pistoia pulpit, seen obliquely from the left.

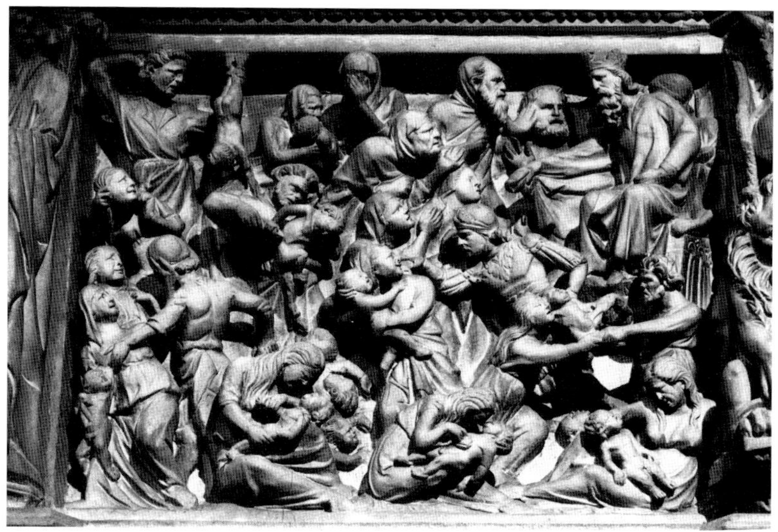

67. Giovanni Pisano, the Massacre of the Innocents, third panel of the Pistoia pulpit, seen centrally from beneath.

quil past. The absence of the focusing devices used in the Nativity panel to suggest sequence implies that Giovanni did not want these two readings to be fully separated; the whole is richer for the presence of both.

So while Giovanni does not represent Herod's conspiracy directly, he implies it by sandwiching the tense Adoration between the Nativity and the Massacre.

We gaze into the face of the personification of tyranny and evil, enthroned like Mary in the Adoration in the top right-hand corner of the panel, over the backs of the mothers pleading for mercy or trying to protect their babies. Sharing their viewpoint, we also look into the expressionless faces of the soldiers, only five of them. Here too, Giovanni has carefully designed oblique views across the diagonal both to create depth as well as to integrate our viewpoint with the direction of the action, fully exposing us to the horror of such violence. We are drawn to details: the furrowed expression in Herod's eyes, his arm outstretched in a gesture of command but wrapped in robes of state so as to seem limp as cloth (Fig. 67), perhaps haunted by his action, possibly even sharing the response of one councillor whose hand is juxtaposed in protest, a contrast to the murderous violence of the soldier beneath who executes the command without hesitation. We infer a chain of cause and

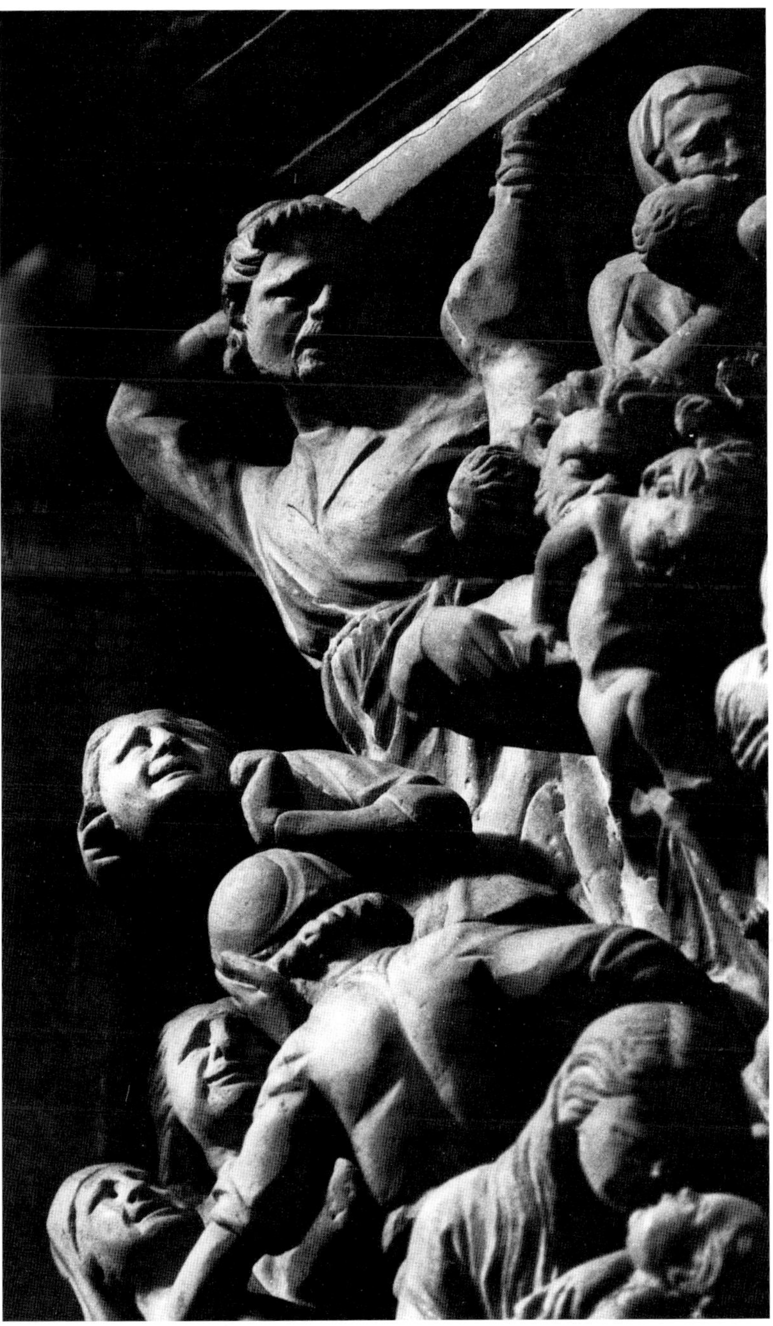

68. Giovanni Pisano, close up of the Massacre of the Innocents, third panel of the Pistoia pulpit, seen obliquely from the right.

effect: command, hunt and execute – Herod, the soldier in question and the soldier at the bottom left, about to grab and slaughter a child.

The rough chiselled carving of some of the mothers and their infants (Fig. 68), contrasting with the soft folds of Mary's robes, is expressive beyond the reach of words. Perhaps the chipped character of the marble* suggests the daggers hacking the victims. In the upper left corner there is a literal representation of the act of butchery; the child hangs upside down, his feet seemingly attached to the upper frame of the panel like those of a chicken hanging from a meat-hook, trussed together by the soldier's hand. The soldier's expression can be read either as ferocity or as horror at his own deed. The angelic child twists his head up to look at his assassin. Giovanni has endowed the head of one soldier with the features of a satyr (Fig. 69) from some Roman carving to suggest the savagery of his deeds in contrast to the features of the grieving mother beneath. Finally, the mothers along the bottom cradle their dead infants, whom shortly before they would have been nursing, their breasts heavy with milk, like Mary in the Nativity.

It is possible to entertain doubts about whether Dante saw the pulpit, but it is almost inconceivable that Giotto did not visit Pistoia to study such an important work. Instead of these terrible acts of carnage and butchery Giotto focuses our attention on the very personal act of a child slowly being dragged out of his mother's grasp (Fig. 37). Instead of showing the violence at its height, Giotto shows the very end; instead of Giovanni's milking mothers bewailing their infants, Giotto's are numb with grief. Giotto's depiction of the Massacre is the antithesis to Giovanni's riotous slaughter. I would argue that this was a carefully thought out response to certain issues in pictorial narrative, part of a developing debate.

The Massacre is the climax to this section of the story, the Christmas story to which Giovanni devoted three of the five available panels. Round the next corner he compressed the entire Easter story in the Crucifixion (Fig. 70a). The vivid temporal sequence is halted by the very device that Giovanni had so inventively

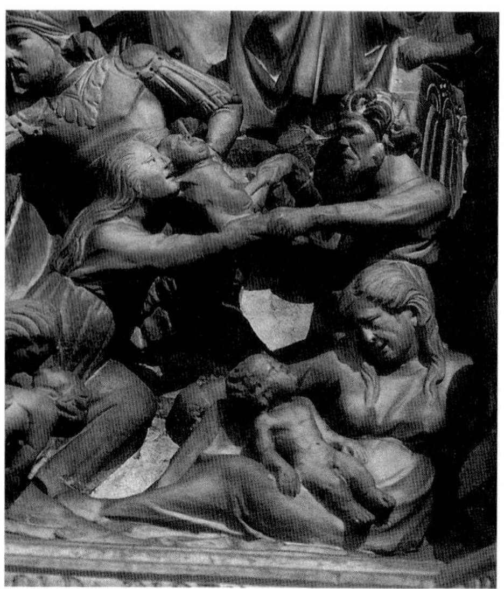

69. Giovanni Pisano, close up of the Massacre of the Innocents, third panel of the Pistoia pulpit.

*In fact, the excavation would largely have been done with drills.

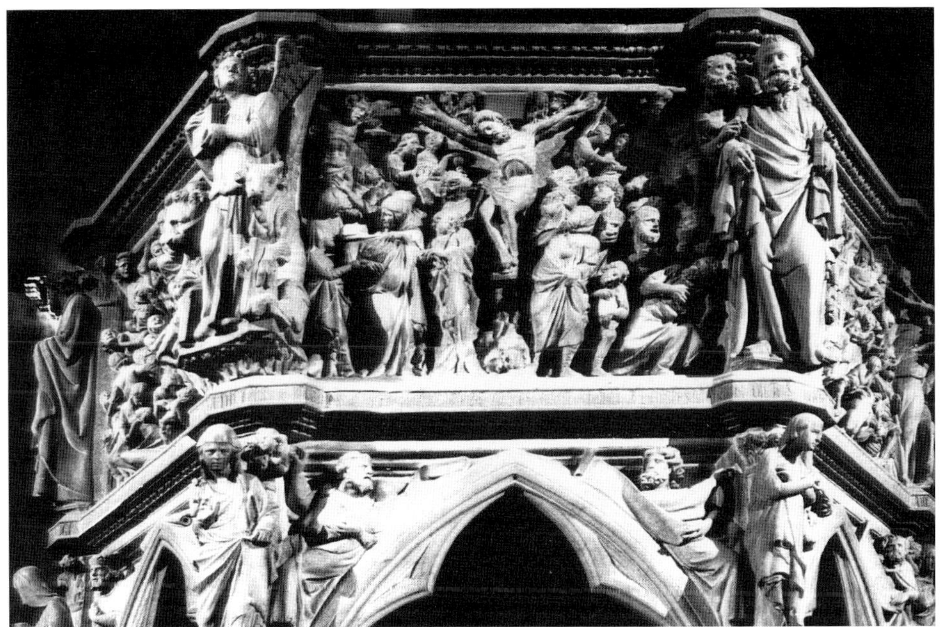

70a. Giovanni Pisano, the Crucifixion, fourth panel of the Pistoia pulpit. Because of the protruding corner figures, from this position one can only see the left-hand side of the Massacre on the left and the right-hand side of the Last Judgement on the right of the central panel of the Crucifixion. Thus the mothers seem to be pleading to Jesus on his cross, and the damned seem to be fleeing from him. The Crucifixion and the Last Judgement are, in a sense, merged as in Fig. 70b.

avoided in the three previous panels, the centralised frontal view. The crucified Jesus is central and all is arranged symmetrically around him. The Sibyls stand, one poised momentarily in a movement towards us, with her hand raised as if admonishing us to pause for worship and reflection.[22]

Although there is a further scene, the Last Judgement, the Crucifixion is the climax and resolution of the cycle. In the pulpit's original position the Crucifixion probably faced the congregation with the lectern above it or to one side. It may have been the first panel to be seen when one entered the church. In addition to its centralisation Giovanni employed the shape of the hexagon in another way. To left and right we see the panels of the Massacre and of its heavenly antithesis and retribution, the Last Judgement, splayed out like the wings of an open altarpiece, only backwards. Only the left-hand side of the Massacre and the right-hand side of the Last Judgement are visible. Herod is masked from view. Thus the mothers join the Virgin, St John and

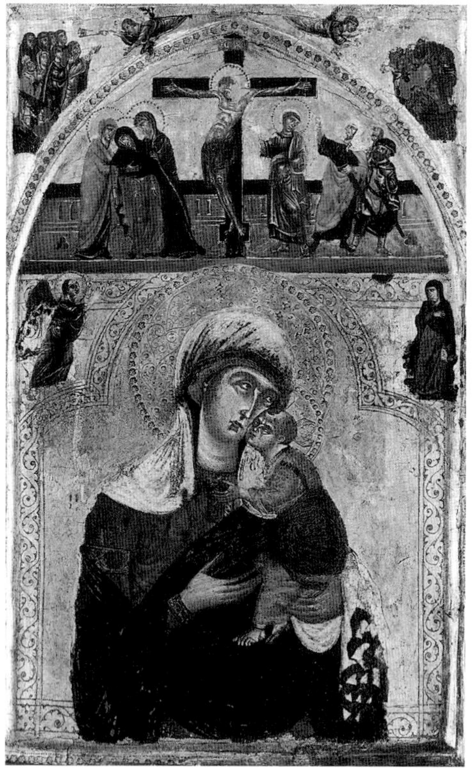

70b. Clarisse Madonna, the Virgin and Child, late 13th century, National Gallery, London. In this small devotional image, painted perhaps twenty years earlier than the Pistoia pulpit, the figures of the blessed and the damned are summoned by trumpeting angels in the spandrels to the left and right of the Cruxifixion. Thus the scenes of the Last Judgement and the Crucifixion are compressed.

the good thief on Jesus' right-hand side, and seem to appeal to the just king. All that is visible of the Last Judgement are the figures of the damned fleeing their punishments as 'the trumpets doth sound'. The Crucifixion and the Last Judgement are compressed (Fig. 70b). Out of the moral confusion of this world a moral order is established in which good triumphs and evil is punished.

The Crucifixion is a devotional set piece with a fixed viewing point, more like an altarpiece than part of a continuous narrative sequence. For us to begin the story involves breaking away from this compelling focus and walking round to the opposite side, at the back of the pulpit where the steps once stood for the priest to climb.

A fanfare concludes the cycle (Fig. 71). On the right-hand corner of the Last Judgement are three angels exuberantly blowing their trumpets, situated immediately to the left of the entrance of the pulpit (Fig. 55), opposite the deacon. Thus the beginning and the end of the story are brought together as Giovanni himself indicated in his inscription 'In praise of the divine Trinity

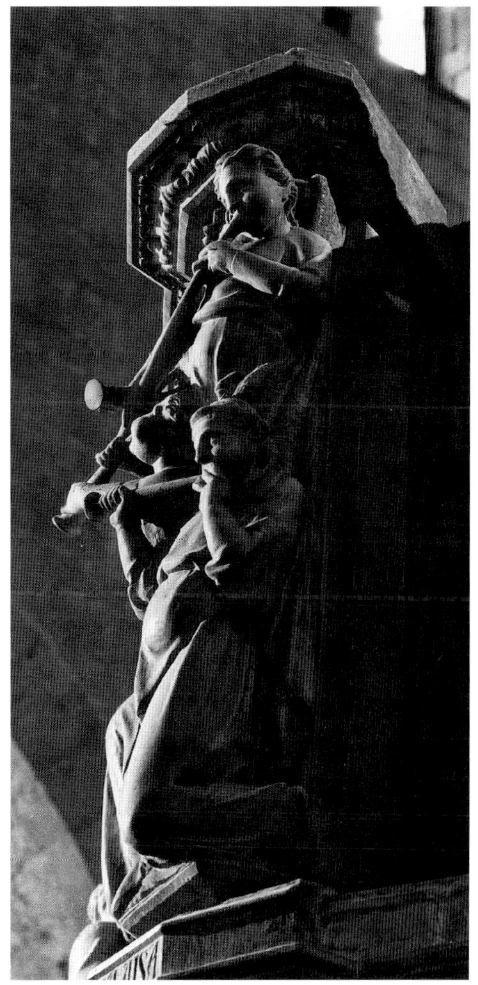

71. Giovanni Pisano, Angels sounding their Trumpets, figures on the corner between the Last Judgement and the entrance to the Pistoia pulpit.

I link the beginning with the end of this task in 1301.' But what exactly is this link? The trumpeters surely mark 'the new heaven and the new earth' and the passing away of the 'first heaven and the first earth' of the Apocalypse. Another antithesis.

In this pulpit, within the compass of five panels, Giovanni uses an extraordinary range of narrative devices from the layered subtlety of the introduction to the concluding triptych, which displays the divine moral order which Jesus came to establish.

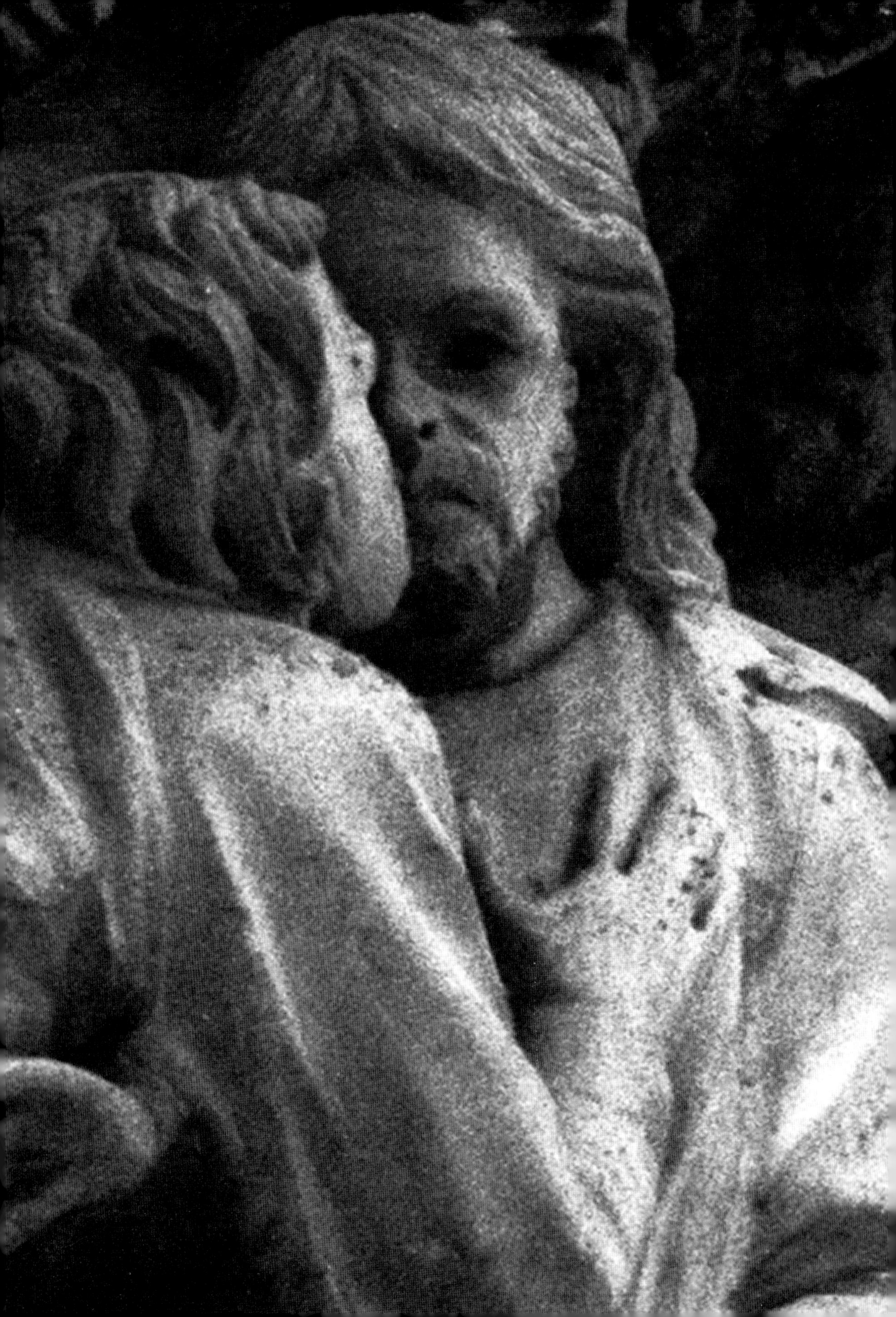

IV

THE CORRECT LAW: GIOVANNI PISANO'S PISA PULPIT

The Perspective

It might be felt that no sooner has the narrative got under way in the first three panels of the Pistoia pulpit, than it is brought to an abrupt conclusion in the Crucifixion. The five sides available for carved reliefs, enriched though they are by oblique views with the potential for subsidiary episodes, were too constricted a field for Giovanni's imagination. A greater opportunity soon appeared. Barely a year after completing the Pistoia pulpit he was commissioned in 1302 by the cathedral of his own city of Pisa to make a magnificent octagonal pulpit (Fig. 72).[1] This provided seven sides for the Christian story, but he added a further two panels on either side of the platform leading into the pulpit so that he had nine sides, almost double the number at Pistoia.

Recent writers have all but dismissed this work, except for the parts they happen to like. 'Where the narrative reliefs traverse the same ground as at Pistoia, their qualitative level is debased. Elsewhere, as in the Passion scenes shown in the sixth relief, we are confronted with ideas of great expressiveness inadequately executed.'[2] The meaning of this is not altogether clear. The more sympathetic author of another standard work, has observed that, 'It must have greatly taxed the artist's powers of invention to embark upon a second pulpit almost as soon as the first was finished.' He continues, 'The lack of a

Detail of Figure 76

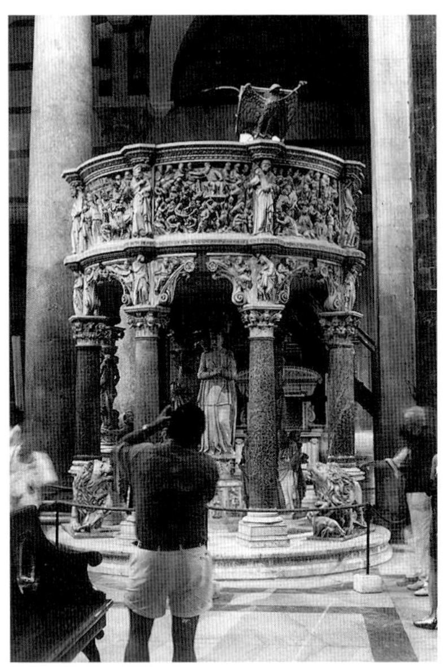

72. Giovanni Pisa, Pulpit in Pisa Cathedral, 1302–10, marble.

sufficient interval in which to refresh his mind and consolidate new ground must undoubtedly have been a major factor in keeping Giovanni from complete success in achieving a new synthesis.'[3] This is a strange explanation. J. S. Bach completed the St Matthew Passion in 1727 only three years after the first performance of his St John Passion in 1724. This is but one example of a great artist who was able to recast the same subject matter within a short period of time, without repeating himself.[4] More recently it has been argued that the fact that the Pisa pulpit took more than twice as long to complete as its predecessor suggests 'a lack of purpose and motivation which contrasts vividly with the fierce, determined vigour of Giovanni's carving on the Pistoia pulpit'.[5] These comments neglect the fact that twelve of the twenty two episodes on the Pisa pulpit had not previously been depicted at Pistoia, and the remaining ten were freshly recast.* Besides, Giovanni had almost double the number of panels to carve, in addition to the free-standing figures which support the pulpit. Whereas Giotto's reputation is such as to encourage scholars to struggle to make sense of every apparent weakness, Giovanni's relative lack of critical esteem, makes it easier for us to explain away his most taxing innovations as failures, rather than the result of our own interpretative shortcomings.

Giovanni himself seems to have had few doubts about his achievement at Pisa. There are two inscriptions on the pulpit. One, inscribed on the platform supporting the pulpit's columns, declares that, 'Giovanni has travelled to all the rivers and corners of the globe endeavouring to learn as much as possible, making his preparations with arduous labour yet without recompense. He now cries out, "I have not been on my guard. The more I have distinguished myself, the most hostile are the criticisms I have suffered . . . He who con-

***Pistoia**: 1st panel – Annunciation, Nativity, Midwives, Annunciation to the Shepherd, Adoration of the Shepherds; 2nd panel – Adoration of the Magi, Magi's Dream, Joseph's Dream; 3rd panel – Massacre of the Innocents; 4th panel – Crucifixion; 5th panel – Last Judgement.
Pisa: 1st panel – Annunciation, Visitation*, Birth of the Baptist*, Naming of the Baptist*; 2nd panel – Nativity, Midwives, Annunciation to the Shepherds; 3rd panel – Procession of the Magi*, Adoration, Magi's Dream; 4th panel – Presentation*, Herod's conspiracy*, Joseph's Dream, Flight into Egypt*; 5th panel – Massacre; 6th panel – Betrayal*, Peter's Denial*, Caiaphas*, Mocking*, Jesus whipped at the column*; 7th panel – Crucifixion; 8th and 9th panels – Last Judgement. The new episodes are marked with an asterisk.

demns the person who is worthy of the diadem, proves himself unworthy."' The second, higher inscription, beneath the narrative panels, declares Giovanni to be 'endowed above all others with command of the pure art of sculpture . . . He would not know how to carve ugly things even if he wished to do so . . . He has made famous sculptures and diverse figures. You who marvel, judge by the correct law!'

Clearly, Giovanni was not a modest man, but had his powers of invention been running dry it would have been surprising for him to have blown his own trumpet so loudly.[6] Oddly, few have hazarded a guess as to what Giovanni might have meant by the term 'by the correct law' – 'recto jure'.[7] Few of his contemporaries would have been able to read the inscription in Latin verse. In addition, it is gnomic, and I suggest that it was designed, in emulation of a literary convention, to tease the learned spectator to reflect upon the nature of the correct law, and hence upon the distinctive character of Giovanni's art.[8] There may be no single answer to the riddle. My interpretation is that the law in question is perspectival, that which governed the oblique views of the panels in Pistoia, but here developed by two major refinements: first, the curvature of each panel (Fig. 75);* second, a more sophisticated technique for focusing the viewer's attention upon individual episodes (Fig. 76). Other important features of the Pisa pulpit are Giovanni's approach to naturalism in his treatment both of the human figure and of space, as well as his extensive employment of rhyme and antithesis. These do not consort easily either with Giovanni's more literal approach in Pistoia or with the notion many people entertain of the unimpeded progress of naturalism in the Renaissance.

Let us put ourselves in Giovanni's position in 1302. He had just spent three or four creative years on the first pulpit to be made by the Pisano family since the completion of his father's for Siena cathedral in 1267. These pulpits were expensive and infrequent. Pistoia was also Giovanni's first essay in narrative. His mind overflowed with ideas which could not be fully accommodated in a single pulpit so small in compass. Pisa cathedral provided the scope for the realisation of those ideas.[9]

Giovanni's innovations were so bold that they do pose the spectator with considerable problems, particularly when one is looking at the work in a photograph taken upon a scaffold; the problems are exacerbated by Giovanni's originality. This is especially so to eyes accustomed to a particular kind of

*Each panel is curved to form a segment of a circle, but the radius of each segment is smaller than that of a circle passing through the eight corners of the octagon. As a result the surface of the drum is not circular but somewhat corrugated in appearance.

visual order. To define Giovanni's innovations and to examine their implications for narrative we shall look first at the most problematic relief, one that art historians disparage by attributing it to inferior assistants – the sixth panel containing five scenes of Jesus' Passion from his Betrayal to the Flagellation. When one first looks at the standard photograph (Fig. 73) one is tempted to accept the judgement that Giovanni's 'powers of invention' seem to have run dry, and that 'ideas of great expressiveness' have been 'inadequately executed'. The composition seems to collapse into episodic fragments stuck all over the place. How is this to be explained?

First one must draw attention to some implications of Giovanni's use of curved panels (Figs 74a and b). As one approaches each panel from the left

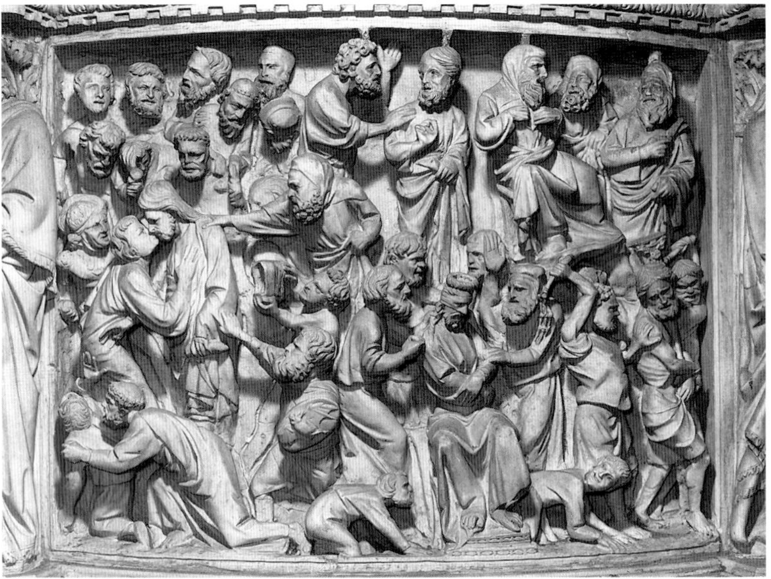

73. Giovanni Pisano, Passion panel of the Pisa pulpit. This photograph, like Fig. 60, was taken frontally from a scaffold at the height of the panel on the pulpit. It shows the Betrayal on the left; St Peter's Denial in the upper centre; the Mocking of Jesus in the lower centre; Caiaphas at the top right and Jesus being flogged tied to the column at the lower right. Compare this image with Fig. 82.

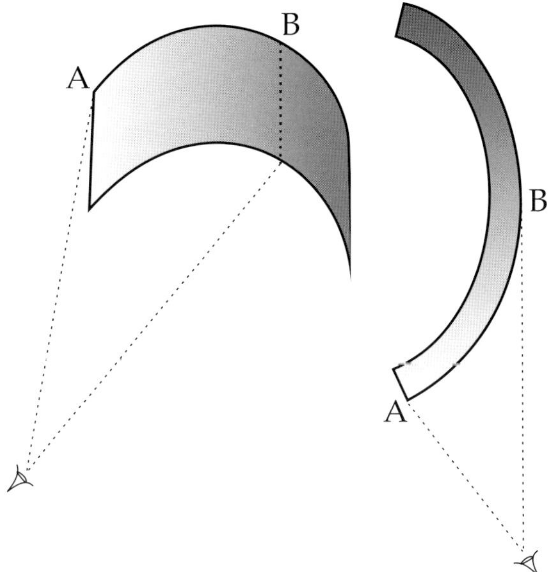

74a. and b. Diagrams showing the area of each curved panel on the Pisa Cathedral pulpit that is visible when the spectator looks up at it from the left.

walking round the pulpit, it is not possible to see more than half the relief. This is marked by point B:

Figures beyond that point are condensed or concealed by the curve and by other protruding figures closer to us (Fig. 88). An additional factor is that more distant figures are seen from so oblique an angle that they appear to collapse upon one another like a house of cards. Thus, walking round the pulpit in chronological order, the individual episodes of each of the seven curved reliefs reveal themselves sequentially and are subsequently concealed.[10]

This helps to focus the spectator's attention upon one episode at a time. But its effect is greatly enhanced by Giovanni's second innovation, a device for focusing the dramatic composition of each individual episode as it comes into view, adumbrated in the Pistoia Nativity (Fig. 54). Nowhere is this better exemplified than in the Passion panel, particularly in the left-hand scene of the Betrayal of Jesus, whose composition from the front, and particularly in eye- level photographs, looks so stilted and flat.[11] Seen obliquely from beneath, however, from a position directly in front of the preceding scene of the Massacre of the Innocents (Figs 72 and 75), what meets us is a dramatic and, in this case, a highly naturalistic composition in which Judas and Jesus

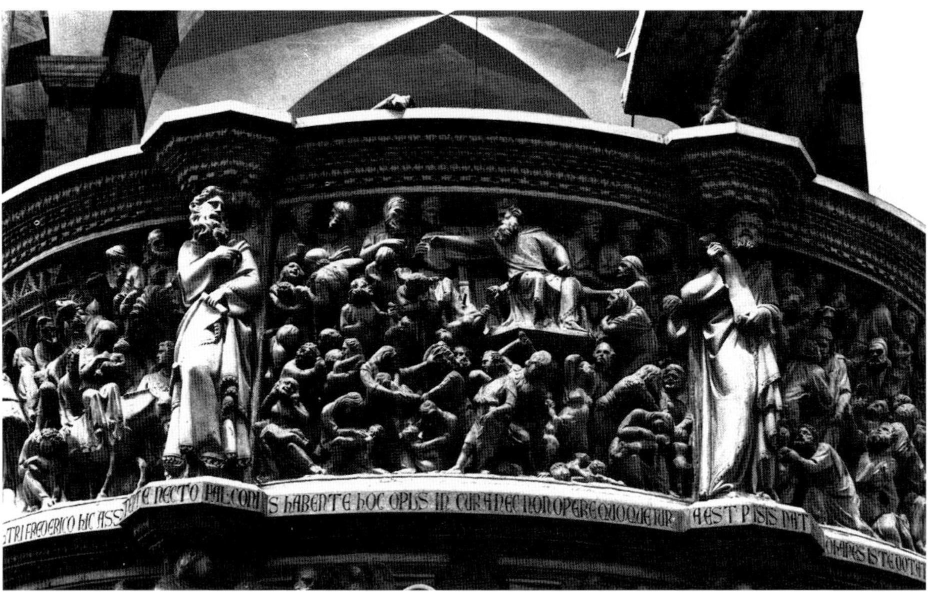

75. Giovanni Pisano, the Massacre of Innocents, Pisa pulpit. The photograph is taken centrally from beneath. On the left of the Massacre one can see the right side of the previous panel showing the Flight into Egypt, while on the right of the Massacre one sees the Betrayal in the succeeding panel of the Passion. The Betrayal comes into focus from this viewpoint.

are surrounded by a convincing circle of figures, who reach out to grab Jesus (Fig. 76).[12]

This convincing perspective depends upon more than the fact that one figure overlaps and masks the one behind it. It is enhanced by a favourite device of Giovanni's which we have already encountered (Fig. 57): our view into Jesus' face from behind Judas's back as he reaches forward to kiss Jesus. Thus the illusion of space between the figures, the composition and the dramatic climax come into focus simultaneously from this viewpoint. A few steps further to the right (Fig. 77) and the illusion of a circular composition flattens out, the dramatic intensity and our privileged viewpoint are lost and we are lured into the focus of subsequent episodes.

The Passion relief exemplifies this focusing device at its most successful and refined, but throughout the pulpit our involvement in the narrative is successively focused and defocused by this means – so long as one is aware of the 'correct law'.

How did Giovanni achieve both the illusion of the circular composition and the fade? First, the figures are carved deeply into the marble panel so that some are almost free-standing statuettes. Second, when viewed from the side and from below, the actual distance between the foreground and the background figures in the circle around Jesus is considerable. Third, as a ground plan indicates, they are arranged in a flattened ellipse around Jesus. Finally, in real space, the heads of these figures are arranged in an ellipse inclined at an angle of about 45° to the horizontal, and also at approximately the same angle to the front of the panel (Fig. 78).

Seen from below and from the left (P) along the longer axis of the ellipse (AB) this elliptical ring of heads foreshortens into a circle.

The illusion is further enhanced by Giovanni's angling the heads so that from this viewpoint each faces Jesus (Fig. 76). In addition the feeling of measurable depth is defined by the delicately calculated overlapping of figures from foreground to background. The crouching figure of St Peter at the very front overlaps the figures of Judas and Jesus; Judas overlaps and indeed almost covers Jesus, both of them partially concealing those behind them. St Peter overlaps a kneeling figure, who overlaps another, who overlaps another. Thus, in all directions there are four tightly integrated overlapping levels occupied by substantial bodies. The carving, in deep relief, is designed to accentuate the overlapping and to compensate for the diffused light of Pisa cathedral with some windows made of translucent sheets of alabaster. Deep undercutting defines the contours of the forms by creating as much contrast as possible, highlighted surfaces are juxtaposed with shadowy ones, eye-sockets and other features are also deeply carved. In addition, the polygonal cornice at the corner protrudes and extends towards us, providing a stage-like ground plane

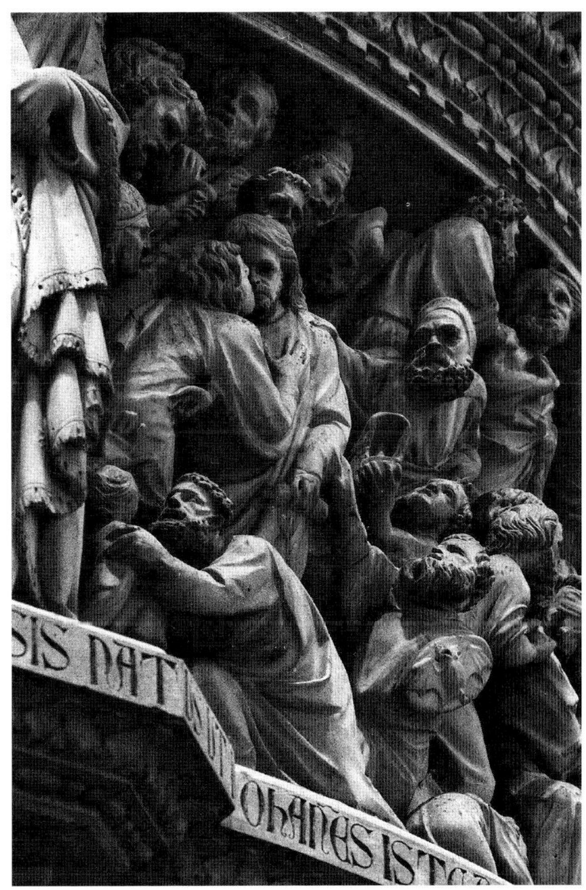

76. Giovanni Pisano, close up of the Betrayal on the Passion panel of the Pisa pulpit, viewed obliquely. See Fig. 78.

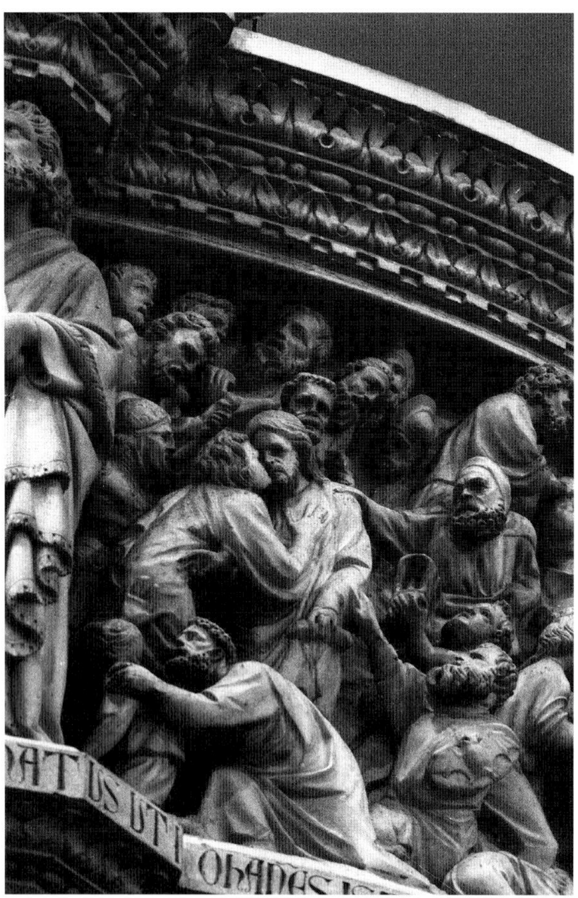

77. Giovanni Pisano, less oblique view of the Betrayal, Pisa pulpit. From this viewpoint the illusion of a three dimensional ring of figures around Jesus and Judas has flattened out for reasons indicated in Fig. 78.

for the figures to stand upon, as well as introducing a piece of 'real' architecture between ourselves and the figures, blocking parts of their bodies from view and defining the relationship between spectator and panel.

Now to explain the fade. As we move to position Q (Figs 77–8), the foreshortening of the ellipse across its shorter axis CD transforms it into a yet flatter ellipse, rather than a circle. Moreover the real depth from foreground to background is smaller. Fewer figures overlap, and we no longer look up into Jesus' face over Judas's back, nor are the faces of the captors angled around the circle towards Jesus' head. The protruding cornice does not figure so prominently from this viewpoint.

Giovanni achieved his effect by several self-reinforcing methods.* But most important was the illusionistic foreshortening of the ellipse into a circle. Giovanni speaks of encircling all the rivers and parts of the world to learn his rules, and it would be surprising had he not seen Trajan's Column in Rome where in one scene (Figs 79a and b) the frontal view of a forum enclosed by Corinthian columns seems to employ a crude form of geometric perspective in which the supposedly rectangular space looks like a parallelogram. Seen from the side, however, the perspective is more effective as is the composition of the figures.

*See appendix.

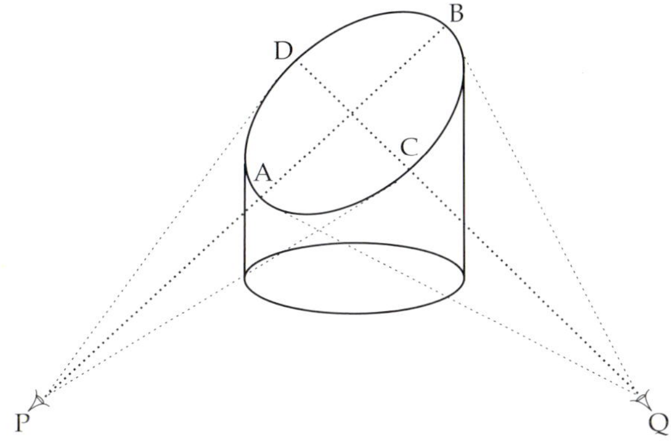

78. Schematic diagram of the arrangement of figures in a tilted ellipse ACDB around Jesus in the centre. Viewed from P to the left, as in Fig. 76, the ellipse, seen along its longer axis AB, foreshortens into a circle apparently in three dimensions. Viewed from Q, as in Fig. 77, the ellipse, seen along its shorter axis CD, foreshortens into an ellipse, and the illusion vanishes. The overlapping of forms and the orientation of the faces towards Jesus also contribute to the effect in Fig. 76.

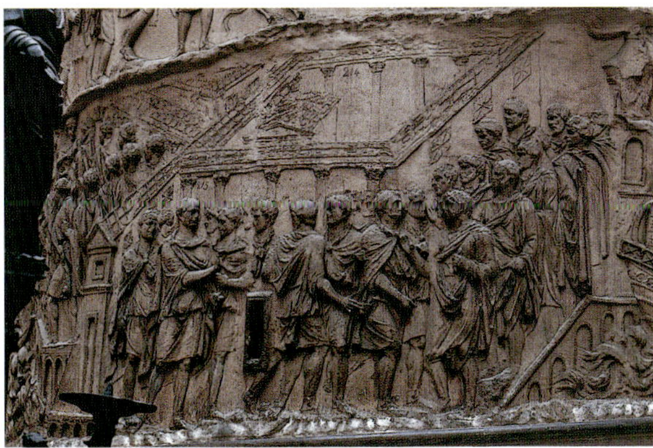

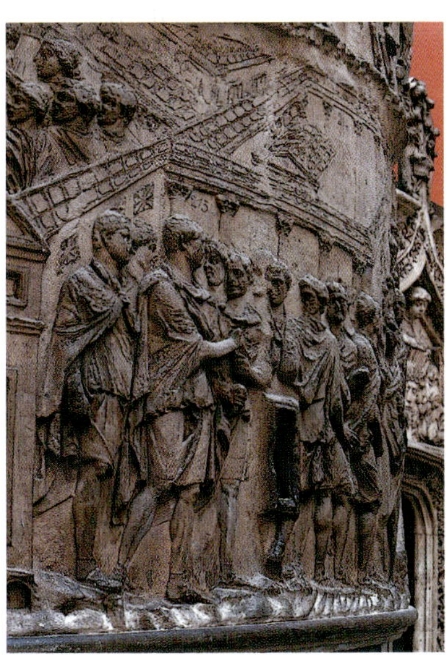

79a. (*above*) and b. (*left*) Scene from Trajan's Column, 113 A.D., the Imperial Forum, Rome. This scene is approximately half way up the column and was photographed from the plaster cast in the Victoria and Albert Museum. 79a shows the carving from the front and 79b from the left side, from where the perspective of the colonnaded courtyard comes into focus and the figures overlap to create a more convincing sense of depth than in 79a. Giovanni Pisano might have derived his anamorphotic system of focusing and defocusing individual episodes, the 'correct law', on the curved panels of the Pisa pulpit from an examination of Trajan's Column.

The narrative

This provides an explanation of how Giovanni's employment of the rounded panel and perspectival foreshortening helps the spectator to organize the apparently chaotic composition of the Passion panel. Far from being 'inadequately executed' the Passion relief is the culmination both of Giovanni's technical achievements and of his approach to pictorial narrative. So far, however, only one episode has been examined, but the panel is crowded with no fewer than five (Fig. 83) – the Betrayal and Capture, Peter's Denial, Caiaphas's wrath and Jesus' Mocking, Flagellation and being led away to crucifixion. Also at issue is the subtlety of Giovanni's carving. In an age dominated by photography it is comprehensible that Giovanni's perspectival devices should have been overlooked by art historians, but it is surprising that people have failed to appreciate the exquisite sensitivity of his carving in this panel – Jesus' blindfold in the Mocking (Fig. 85) is one example we shall examine.

So much, at this moment, for Giovanni's technical wizardry. We shall now analyse the narrative structure of the Passion relief, beginning at the beginning with the Capture (Fig. 76). This was not the first time that Giovanni had used the 'over-the-shoulder' device, here masterful in the way it establishes the contrast of Jesus' upright body, flowing locks and steadfast gaze with Judas's sinuous, snake-like, perhaps even hunchbacked body insinuating itself in a half-stooping bow into his master's presence and favour, his right hand on Jesus' breast seeming to stroke him, paw him, caress him or even to claw him in an embrace so ambiguous, so full of duplicity as to be the very essence of what we mean when we call someone a 'Judas' (Fig. 80). His hand and arm and the profile of his face are highlighted whereas the left-hand side of Jesus' face is in shadow. Jesus barely responds; he seems to look through Judas, his attention focused elsewhere as we notice his right hand, half hidden in the folds and shadows (his left hand grasps a scroll possibly symbolising his role as judge) emerging from under Judas's armpit in a sign of healing to restore the ear of Malchus, the High Priest's servant, just severed by St Peter. The primary focus of Jesus' attention is neither Judas nor the spectator but Malchus. Malchus's hand, palm outwards, is carved in a block-like manner upon Judas's behind. The intertwining of the bodies of Jesus and Judas around Jesus' act of healing and forgiveness at the very moment of betrayal is one of the great scenes of pictorial narrative. The ring of figures plucking at Jesus' robe heightens the power of the relationship between Jesus and Judas. One of these characters is very striking, with his beard of curly locks, overhanging brows and a stubby nose he stands immediately to the right of Jesus. In contrast to Judas's duplicitous caress he grabs Jesus' shoulder to arrest him.

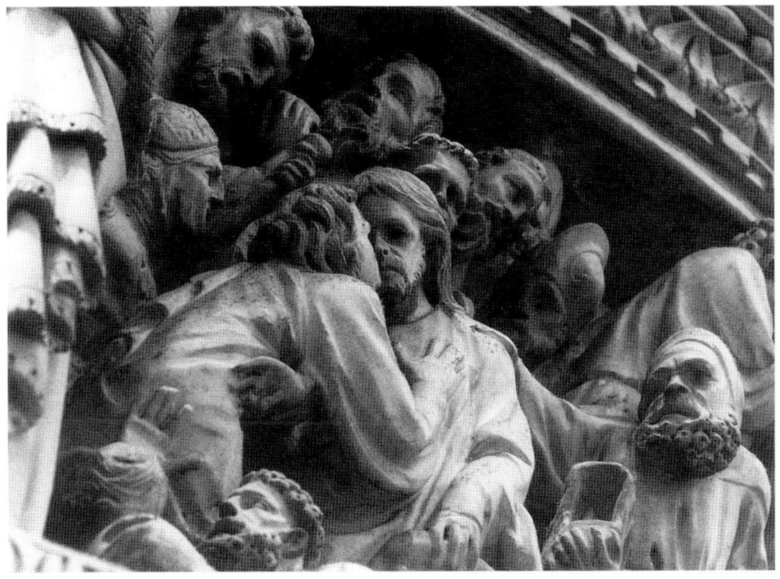

80. Giovanni Pisano, close up of Judas's Kiss, the Betrayal, Pisa pulpit, viewed obliquely from the left.

Giovanni has drawn his face from a classical source, that of an ugly, comic actor's mask, perhaps even without being aware of its significance. One is also struck by the crouching man beneath who holds a lantern up to Jesus, which could have housed a real oil lamp to illuminate him on special occasions.

One is, however, repeatedly drawn back to the contrast and antithesis between hunchbacked Judas, fawning and insinuating, and Jesus' authority, not responding to Judas but seeing through and past him as he heals the victim of his own disciple's violence.

From this standpoint, we may begin to discern the Mocking, the blindfolded Jesus in profile, Peter's Denial immediately above it, and in the far distance Jesus being whipped.

Moving now to the right, the scene of Judas's kiss fades, though even the side view is revealing (Fig. 81), particularly Judas's amorous embrace and his grotesque, seemingly faceless face – no nose, no eyes, no mouth – in contrast to Jesus' noble features, until one perceives the features of a satyr in his slanting protruding lips, curly locks and pointed nose. Perhaps our attention is then caught by the images at the top of the panel (Fig. 82), St Peter, so fervently loyal in the Capture, now playing the Judas himself in denying all association with Jesus, his face contorted and strained around the mouth and eyes,

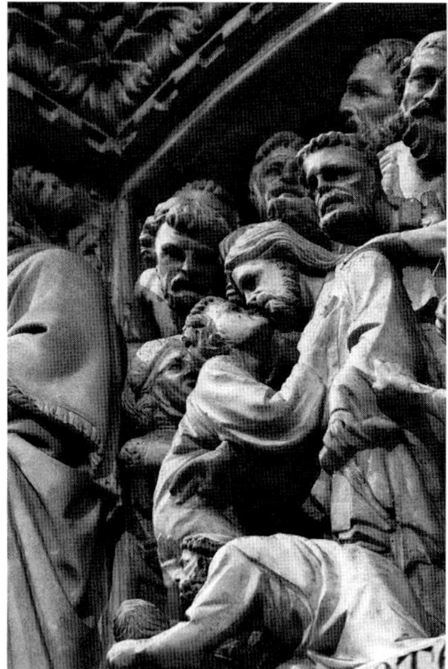

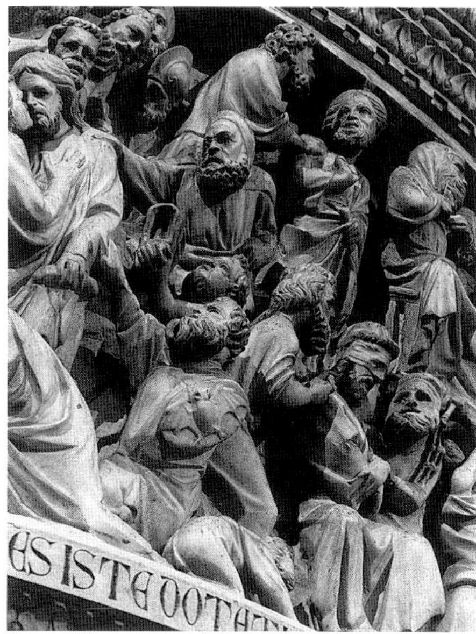

81. (*above left*) Giovanni Pisano, Judas's Kiss, Pisa pulpit. From this viewpoint, seen more to the right, the illusion of a circle of figures flattens out; even so Giovanni provides us with a fascinatingly grotesque depiction of Judas's face, seen in profile.

82. (*above right*) Giovanni Pisano, Peter's Denial in the upper centre of the Passion panel, Pisa pulpit. From this viewpoint the Denial comes into focus as the Betrayal fades, while the Mocking has not yet come into focus.

cringing in fear for his own life as his interrogator lays a hand on his shoulder, in a mirror image of the character who is grasping Jesus in the Betrayal (Fig. 76).

This juxtaposition exemplifies another of Giovanni's innovations – his seemingly deliberate non-naturalism in marked contrast to much of the Pistoia pulpit.* Giovanni's overriding concern in this instance is with the set of antitheses and contrasts between the behaviour of Peter and that of Jesus rather than with the form of the human body, or even narrative. Whereas Jesus accepts his destiny with nobility, Peter displays cowardice and treachery in the cause of self-preservation. The vertical juxtaposition between Peter's Denial and the Mocking of Jesus, also found in Duccio's Trial (Fig. 6), con-

*The first Sybil is exceptionally graceful and anatomically accurate.

trasts Peter's behaviour with Jesus' calm acceptance of his humiliation and torture.

Next we could proceed to explore the panel in the sequence of the biblical story and the arrangement of the episodes from left to right. This would be perfectly legitimate. But bearing in mind that there is no absolutely correct order, I propose to begin the analysis of the panel afresh, looking up at it from a standpoint right in the centre (Fig. 83). From here it appears least focused and most confused, similar to the eye-level photographs, which I have criticised, though significantly different. The reason for choosing this counter-example to my argument about the importance of oblique viewpoints is to demonstrate that Giovanni did not restrict himself or his spectator to a single system. Whereas the relief was never intended to be viewed from eye-level, it was clearly designed to be intelligible from here. Even this point needs some qualification, however. Seen from afar, one's angle of vision approximates to eye-level. We can imagine ourselves approaching the pulpit down the nave of the cathedral, finding as we come closer that the totally unfocused visual confusion gives way to something less disordered though still puzzling. Initially though we see a profusion of figures and groups spread over every inch of the panel. No figure addresses us directly apart from Jesus being whipped on the extreme right, and the composition of no single group is perspectivally focused. Nor does any scene appear to be central: even the Mocking of Jesus is off centre.

The subject of the scenes have already been identified purely for the convenience of description, but to the spectator approaching the relief for the first time, even that basic level of recognition is difficult, such is the turmoil. This was surely deliberate, and is a factor which may have contributed to contemporary criticisms of Giovanni's work, to which the quoted inscription refers. I suggest that Giovanni wanted us to be as confused as if we had walked onto a battlefield, just as we are confused by the sculptured battle scenes on the Roman sarcophagi in Pisa's Campo Santo, familiar both to Giovanni and to his original audience.[13]

Here is an excellent example of the use of intricacy employed to make us linger and dwell upon the image until we have puzzled it out. Beginning, then, as confused eyewitnesses, what do we see?

The Betrayal, occupying almost all the left-hand half, presents no problem using as it does the conventional formula. To right of centre the blindfolded and seated figure crowned with thorns and surrounded by his tormentors is also a conventional composition for the Mocking of Jesus (Fig. 82). But on which occasion? Jesus is mocked on four different occasions during his trial by the priests, Herod and Pilate. It is not immediately clear which episode is

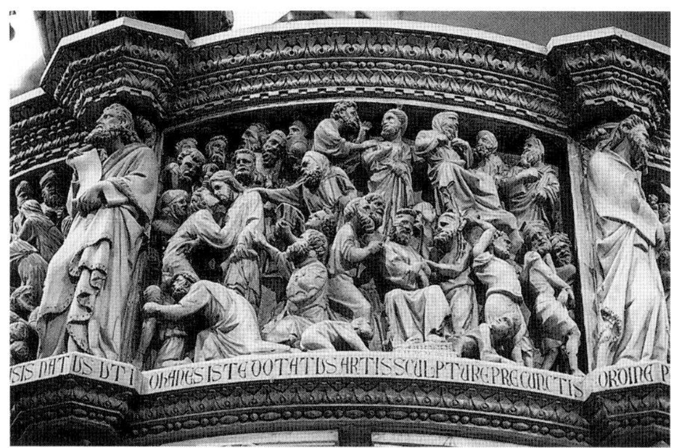

83. Giovanni Pisano, Passion panel, Pisa Pulpit. This photograph was taken from a central viewpoint looking up at the relief. Compare this with Fig. 73.

represented by the two figures in the top centre of the panel, one laying his hand on the other's shoulder. And the seated figure to their right, pulling or tearing apart the garments on his chest may well be Caiaphas the High Priest enraged by Jesus' blasphemous replies, but even this identification is obscure by virtue of being divorced from its customary association with Jesus' Trial. The removal of each episode from the context of the conventional composition makes identification problematic.

Finally, what exactly is the scene of Jesus' flogging on the extreme right? In the biblical account only Pilate has Jesus flogged, but here there is no trial before Pilate. Even if the spectator knew the *Meditations of the Life of Christ* which tells how Jesus, after his interrogation by the priests, is tied to a column in their dungeons and tortured throughout the night until dawn, even then the problem is not fully solved, because it looks as if Jesus is stumbling out of this panel into the next (Fig. 92), the Crucifixion, carrying the column as if it were his cross, whipped on his way while casting a backward glance towards us.[14]

One's attention, nonetheless, settles upon the seated figure of Jesus surrounded by his tormentors, particularly upon the two figures standing on the left who leer and snarl and the bearded figure on the right who holds Jesus' forearm in his left hand and whose right arm can just be discerned raised vertically, fingers outstretched, palm forward, crudely carved and straight as a paddle, anatomically disjoined from the man's body. With this 'weapon' he is about to hit Jesus – they 'smote him with the palms of their hands,' says the gospel.[15]

In contrast to their aggression and contorted faces sits their victim. The ornamented platform of his seat tips to the left, as if they are rocking it so as to unbalance him. But he is not thrown off balance. Everything about him is calm, inward, impassive – he neither resists nor responds. His crossed and bound hands and long delicate fingers hang limply down, his robes are unagitated and his eyes are blindfolded with a cloth so fine and subtle that it moulds itself to his features like a mask, reinforcing the impression that he is meditating. The logic of these similes and contrasts hardly needs to be spelt out – violence contrasted with passivity, agitation with calm. One's attention is so caught up with the ring of four figures radiating about Jesus' head that at first one barely notices two further figures crouching at his feet to either side of his throne. To the left is a very small figure snarling at Jesus' heels like a cur about to snap. To the right a man with a grotesque face, who appears to be reclining on one elbow, his fingers overlapping the frame, twists his head around to watch in a rather languid manner as if enjoying the show. Here perhaps we, the spectators, are drawn in as more than bystanders, since the viewpoint of this witness and his physical contortion somewhat resembles our own as spectators. This is particularly so if we look up into the eyes of the adjacent episode of Jesus being thrashed (Fig. 84), the only figure to look directly at us. Jesus' appeal is so direct that I find myself placed in a morally disturbing position. Would I have intervened to protect him against so many enemies as St Peter had done at the time of his capture, or would I, like St Peter juxtaposed immediately above Jesus' head, deny that I had anything to do with him? Would I join the torturers? Or would I, like the reclining grotesques, enjoy the show?

No longer are we confused eyewitnesses. Giovanni has so organised his figures that the more sense one makes of them the more one is involved as a participant, in such circumstances that one's moral dilemma is inescapable.

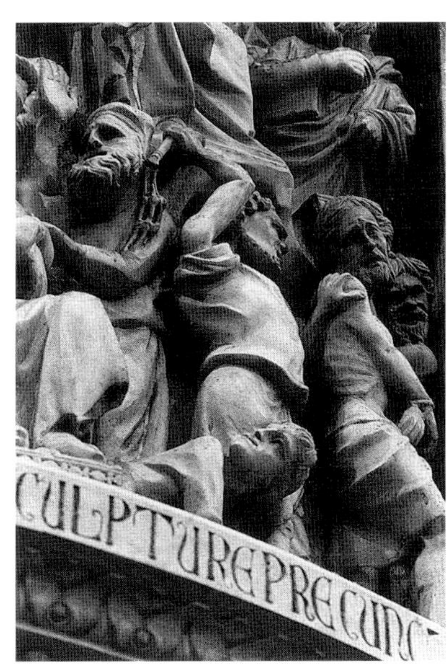

84. Giovanni Pisano, Jesus flogged, right hand lower episode on the Passion panel, Pisa pulpit.

Maybe one's attention now fans out to other figures, to the man with the whiplash which overlaps the shoulder of the man with the paddle-like arm, who is thereby framed between paddle and lash. They are like caryatid columns supporting their master the High Priest Caiaphas upon his throne, which seems to sway violently as a result of their violence and his anger. His disequilibrium seems even more pronounced by the way that his head is tilted away from us and by his contrast with Jesus. 'His throne is tottering,' one might reflect, like Herod's in the previous panel of the Massacre (Fig. 75) which can still be seen from here. One may reflect upon just and unjust rulers. One may look upwards at St Peter, the vertical folds of whose robes form a backcloth to Jesus' 'throne', and to his interrogator, whose head from this angle overlaps the edge of the frame of the panel. St Peter's gesture of negation occurs simultaneously to the tormenting of his master. Echoing arms reinforce the contrast between St Peter and Jesus being betrayed, as already noted. And now one becomes aware of a sequence of episodes arranged across the panel from upper left to lower right: Jesus betrayed, Jesus derided, Jesus scourged and driven to his execution, a sequence of cause and effect. Jesus, lofty and noble, staring into Judas's eyes, seeing through him; Jesus patient under duress; Jesus bent and broken.

This sequence also reinforces a transition for the spectator–narrator from a more detached observer of the Betrayal, to a participant in the Mocking to the object of Jesus' final appeal for compassion. And here, to speak personally, I may pause for reflection upon this unpromising viewpoint. I have also passed from a state of disorientation in which it was hard even to recognise what was going on, to an involved eyewitness and a morally engaged, if perplexed, participant in these events. So much has come to my attention, so many details, so many similes, so many juxtapositions, echoes and rhymes generating such a complexity of logical relationships that I begin to feel that the work is inexhaustible in its richness of meaning and its appeal to the emotions.

It is possible to proceed in either of two directions. A few paces to the left and one might explore the Betrayal; to the right, one's perception of the panel is once again transformed as the Mocking comes into focus (Figs 85–6) around the figure of Jesus and all other episodes fade.

The four faces are now turned directly towards him along the radii of the semicircle on which they are arranged; Jesus seems to be looking directly towards me through his blindfold, returning my gaze. This veil is extraordinary, so delicately moulded to the contours of Jesus' eyes and nose that if we could not see its border running across Jesus' cheeks and the tip of his nose, we might almost be tempted to interpret it not as a blindfold at all but as a passage of soft carving emphasising Jesus' unruffled emotions and patience, in contrast to the deep-set eyes of the thugs. It is like a veil; it is as if Jesus' feelings were veiled; as if his feelings were as soft and gentle as the material. It shrouds him. Yet it is a blindfold, so that though I can see him he cannot see me, but it clings so closely to his eyes and particularly to the ridge of his eyebrows, and the eye-sockets are so veiled in shadow, that one can easily be mistaken in believing that one can discern his eyes looking out at us. Thus Jesus seems to see me through his blindfold, and he also seems to see through me as he sees through Judas. Jesus seems all-seeing.

The other episodes (Fig. 86) are arranged in a semi-circle around the calm figure of Jesus: St Peter attacking Malchus, Judas betraying Jesus, Jesus' capture,

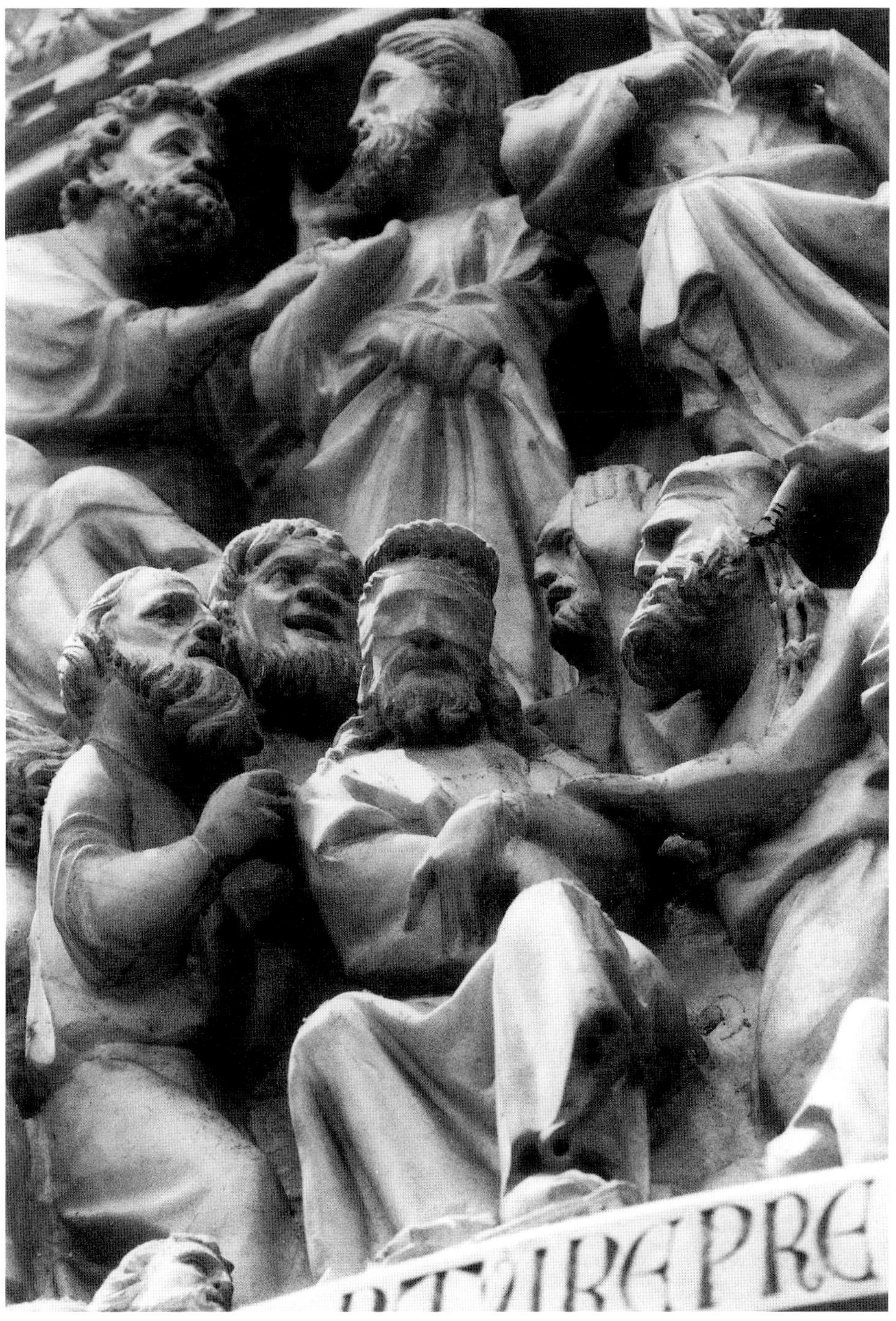

85. Giovanni Pisano, the Mocking of Jesus, Passion panel, Pisa pulpit. From this viewpoint, corresponding to that in Fig. 85, the Mocking becomes the focus of our attention.

St Peter's denial and escape from capture, Caiaphas's wrath and Jesus being whipped. Intemperance, treachery, violence, deception and cowardice, injustice, anger and cruelty – all the vices surround and assault Blind Justice.

The great panel of Jesus' Passion, then, only comes to life when we are armed with knowledge of the correct law – not limited simply to oblique viewpoints. It is difficult. It demands of the spectator a major creative effort to make sense of apparent chaos, even to identify the subject matter – so much of the story has been elided. We have to supply the logic, which is unusually complex. We are constantly having to shift our viewpoint both physically and psychologically. The reward for our labours is an extraordinary interpretation of the Passion.

It could be argued that the elision of so many key episodes such as the trial scenes, leaves us with a panel of images which is less a narrative with all the interconnections of logic and plot and more like a prompt for meditational exercises upon Jesus' sufferings, something similar to this 'Meditation on the Passion of the Lord, in General':

> What should we think that our Lord, blessed God above all things, from the hour of His capture at night until the sixth hour of His Crucifixion, was in a continuous battle, in great pain, injury, scorn, and torment, that He was not given a little rest! But in what battle is He tormented? You will hear (and see). One of them seizes Him, (this sweet, mild, and pious Jesus) another binds Him, another attacks Him, another scolds Him, another pushes Him, another blasphemes Him, another spits on Him, another beats Him, another walks around Him, another questions Him, another looks for false witnesses against Him, another accompanies the one that searches, another gives false testimony against Him, another accuses Him, another mocks Him, another blindfolds Him, another strikes His face, another goads Him, another leads Him to the column, another strips Him, another beats Him while he is being led, another screams, another begins furiously to torment Him, another binds Him to the column, another assaults Him, another scourges Him, another robes Him in purple to abuse Him, another places the crown of thorns, another gives Him the reed to hold, another madly takes it away to strike His thorn-covered head, another kneels mockingly, another salutes Him as king. These and many similar things were done to Him, not just by one but by many. He is led back and forth, scorned and reproved, turned and shaken here and there like a fool and an imbecile; like a thief and a most evil malefactor He is led now to Annas, now to Caiaphas, now to Pilate, now to Herod, and again to Pilate, now in, now out. O my God, what is this? Does this not seem a most hard and bitter battle?[16]

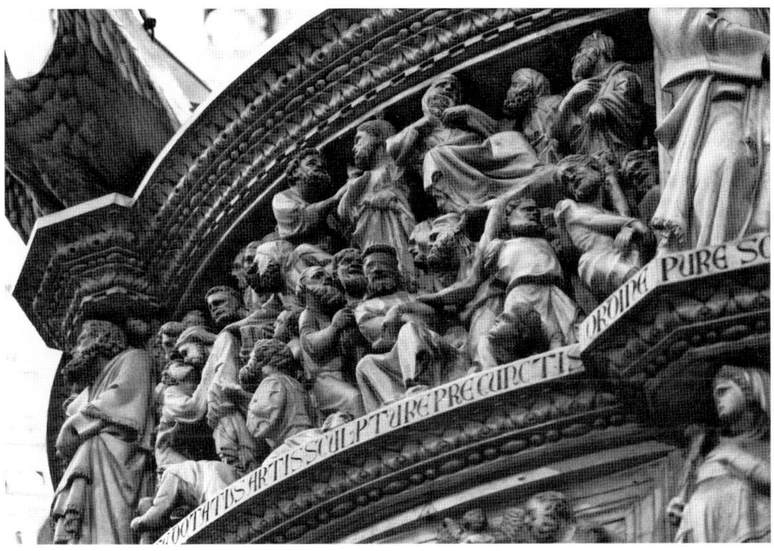

86. Giovanni Pisano, Passion panel, Pisa pulpit. This has been photographed from a viewpoint to the right.

Certainly Giovanni's Passion relief has affinities with this. It is different to the more sequential narratives of Pistoia. But it would be wrong when discussing the visual arts to draw too clear a distinction between the lyric or meditational mode and narrative. In the Passion panel there are strong narrative elements – the Capture, the Mocking, the Flogging – and one can discern a logical and temporal sequence between them. But its lyrical features are unusually important – the elisions, the startling contrasts and juxtapositions, the rhymes, the combination of naturalism in both figures and space with extreme anti-naturalism, the employment of simile and metaphor, the complex perspectival shifts and fades and the different narrative points of view.

Emotionally intense thematic interpretation, rather than smooth, multi-layered, unfolding narrative seems to be the key to the Pisa pulpit as a whole. Giovanni concentrates upon stimulating the spectator to engage in Devout Meditation, the term used in the *Meditations of the Life of Christ*, rather than retelling the stories in pictorial form.[17] This relates in turn to the Gregorian conception of pictorial narrative as a means of stimulating study and a deeper understanding of the scriptures. This is substantiated when we turn to the earlier scenes on the pulpit and try to summarise the cycle as a whole.

One cannot claim that every panel is a complete success nor do all display the intensity of the Passion. But this was neither the fault of uninspired assis-

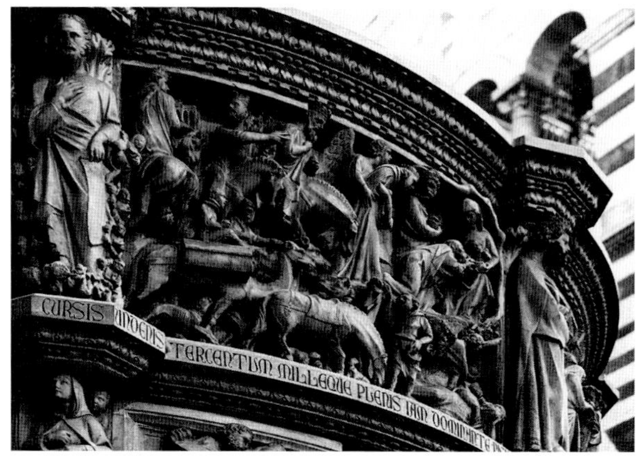

87. Giovanni Pisano, the Adoration of the Magi, Pisa pulpit, seen from the left.

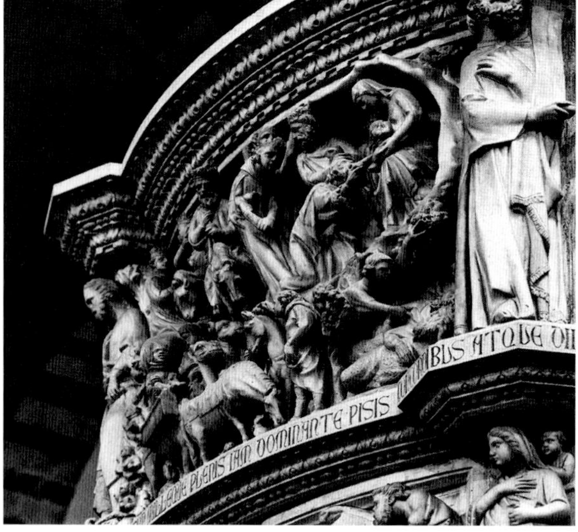

88. Giovanni Pisano, the Adoration of the Magi, Pisa pulpit, seen from the right.

tants nor of Giovanni's flagging inspiration but a result of his bold experimentation, of which he was so proud, on the one hand, and on the other of the fact that like any artist he had his failures.

At first sight the Adoration of the Magi seems to be one of his most successful sequential narratives. From the left, we watch the Magi on their horses wheel around as if picking up the trail of the guiding star. Moving round a step or two further (Fig. 87), we look up into the cave, characteristically over the backs of the Magi, participating in their worship – a sophisticated reworking of Nicola's Siena Adoration. The Magi's dream is tucked away in a lower cave in the right hand corner which we notice only when we cast a lingering backward glance on the panel (Fig. 88). From this position we become aware of the rationale for the composition of the whole panel in which the Adoration, contained within the soft edge of the cave, forms a crescent shape which runs backwards in a sweeping loop down through the heads of the Magi's attendants, their horses and camels. This almost pretty compositional flourish seems uncharacteristic of Giovanni. I would suggest that he wanted to convey a feeling of otherworldliness, of the miraculous birth of the divine in human form, by transforming the cave into something suggestive of a cloud formation in which the Holy Family and the Magi seem raised above the earth, and which draws the attendants into its vortex. That the angel emerges from the base of this 'cloud' to warn the Magi in their dream, supports this interpretation. Giovanni may even have intended to suggest that the cloud above the heads of the dreaming Magi, containing the Adoration, represents their dream of the wondrous events of the previous day, in the midst of which the angel appears to warn them of the danger.[18]

The next panel (Figs 89–90) resumes the narrative – a hurried Presentation, Joseph's dream, the escape of the Holy Family taking place immediately beneath the figures of Herod and his councillors, bringing to mind the gospel text. 'Then Herod, when he saw that he was mocked of the wise men, was

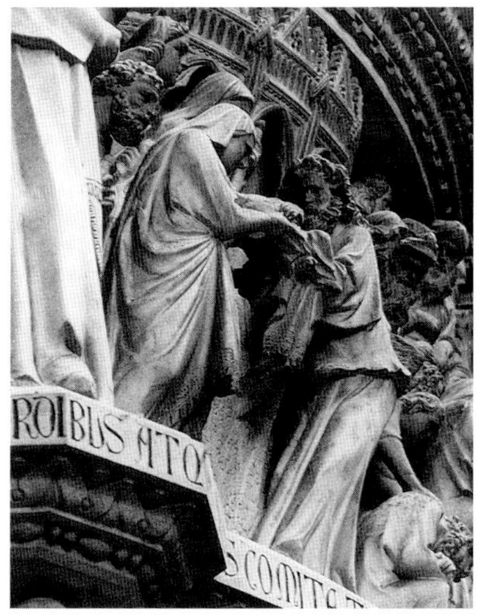

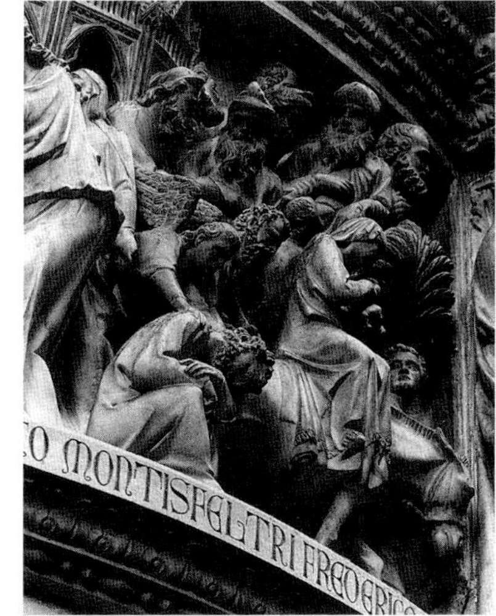

89. Giovanni Pisano, the Presentation in the Temple, Pisa pulpit.

90. Giovanni Pisano, the Flight into Egypt, Pisa pulpit. To the left we see the angel appearing to Joseph in his dream, warning him to take his family to Egypt to escape Herod's wrath, and on the upper right Herod conspires to trap the infant Jesus. See Fig. 75 for another viewpoint.

exceeding wroth, and sent forth, and slew all the children that were in Bethlehem.' In the next panel (Fig. 75) we reach the Massacre, where non-naturalism reigns in the huge figure of the enthroned Herod dominating a panel of confused and confusing little figures.

By superimposing a 'close-up' of Herod upon the panoramic battle-scene of the Massacre, Giovanni conveys the sense of Herod's exceeding wrath. It requires of us a disconcertingly shift of focus: when we look at Herod it is hard to read the details of the victims. Yet we have to do this. In addition, the panel is not composed along the easily identifiable diagonal axis of the Pistoia Massacre (Fig. 67), which emanates from Herod's command. Here Herod stretches across the field pointing at no one in particular, except perhaps the fleeing Holy Family in the previous panel. He is just 'in a rage', *not* connected with the havoc he is causing. We need to refocus to attend to what is happening in the town of Bethlehem beneath, where the stocky figure standing in the centre is the pivot of the composition (Fig. 91). Take just two scenes from a position slightly to the right of centre: the figure has his back to the soldier about to hack a baby boy in half; he also watches, impassive, not intervening, as a woman courageously fights back, momentarily blinding a soldier with the palm of her hand. We have to switch uncomfortably between the apoplectic rage of a tyrant furious at being thwarted; the cool eye of his lieutenant ensuring that the king's commands are implemented; and the individual scenes of butchery, torment, bravery, grief, all of them mediated by the figure of the lieutenant. The tiny figures, so out of scale with Herod, might have been intended to suggest their insignificance in his scheme of things.

A king's throne is a symbol of power, and Herod's throne is in peril. It rests upon the heads of his subjects, who secure his position, but his vengeance endangers his authority, supported though it appears to be by his seven councillors, pillars of state, to either side. Herod's evil command has shaken his power to its foundations, he has over-reached his authority. His outstretched arm unbalances him, and the turmoil beneath causes his throne to tilt and wobble, like that of Caiaphas in the next panel.[19]

The Passion panel brings to a climax the breakdown of order and good rule, gathering pace over the previous panels. We pick our own way through the battlefield till we emerge into the clarity and triumph of the Crucifixion (Fig. 92) where Giovanni reasserts the full field of the marble panel in a spatially unified panoramic composition. If one is looking for such things, this is the grandest illusion of space in Giovanni's career. He arranges the figures fully in the round in the foreground along the curved rim of the piece of marble, many with their backs towards us to give the impression of their

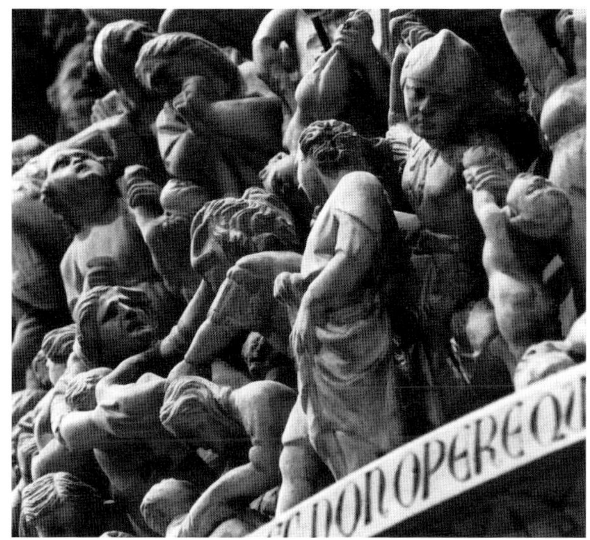

91. Giovanni Pisano, the Massacre of the Innocents, Pisa pulpit. This detail shows one of Herod's officials supervising the Massacre. This figure is in the centre of the panel just below Herod's throne (Fig. 75).

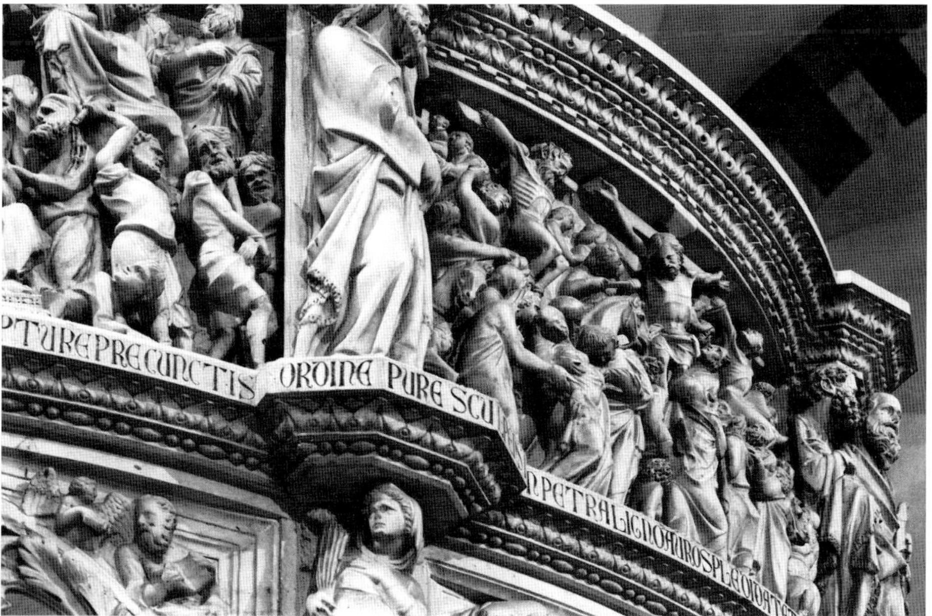

92. Giovanni Pisano, the Crucifixion, Pisa pulpit. To the left is the episode of Jesus being flogged from the adjacent Passion panel.

standing in a circle which appears to continue behind the cross, whose centrality and height over their heads is enhanced by our vantage point below. This impressive illusion was not introduced as a demonstration of technical skill, but for its contribution to the cycle, to emphasise the re-establishment of order in Jesus' triumph upon the cross.

This has been an abbreviated account of the pulpit, neglecting many panels and the supporting figures beneath and between the panels. The reader's patience has been taxed enough, and my descriptions are suggestive rather than exhaustive.

Giovanni's two pulpits conceived and executed in succession over a period of only thirteen years deal with broadly the same subject matter treated in very different ways. The Pistoia pulpit is a sophisticated attempt to rival the artifice of literature, and was, at this period, well in advance of Italian literary narrative. It focuses on the conflict between Herod, the anti-Christ and Jesus within the Christmas story.

The Pisa pulpit employs major new techniques to focus our attention. It is also more sermonic and less historical in character. The caryatid figure of Jesus holds a scroll on which is inscribed verse 11 of Psalm 85: 'Truth shall spring out of the earth; and righteousness shall look down from heaven.' It has been wisely suggested that the whole pulpit is a 'thought-edifice' focused upon this verse and upon Psalm 85, a key text for theological commentators from St Jerome to the author of the contemporary *Meditations*. A crude summary of their interpretations is that Jesus, the bringer of truth, justice, mercy and salvation, will forgive our sins and iniquities.[20]

Giovanni's subtle insights into the shifting treacheries of the Passion and the varieties of human cruelty and evil certainly conform to the significance of the psalm, as well as marking out the Pisa pulpit as the more mature, ambitious and the greater work of the two.

Conclusion

Giovanni Pisano's narratives are unlike those of Duccio and Giotto in several respects. While all three artists conform to the doctrines of Christian Art, creating cycles linked by probability and necessity without redundant details, making considerable interpretative demands upon the spectator, Giovanni's pulpits are not temperate, detached or platonic. From the Pistoia Annunciation to the Pisa Last Judgement, Giovanni sought to draw the spectator into the drama not as a dispassionate observer or some kind of reporter piecing together what was going on, but as an emotionally and morally involved participant. He accomplished this partly through oblique, over-the-shoulder viewpoints which help the spectator to see events through the eyes of the participants, and to identify with them, but also through the energy of his figures and the demonstrative way in which they display their emotions – stamped in their actions, to use Dante's phrase. Giotto occasionally employed similar viewpoints, but to different effect because his figures are reserved; they keep us guessing about what they might be thinking and feeling. There is little of the pregnant or suggestive moment in Giovanni's work. He overwhelms one with the sense of being there at critical moments in the Annunciation, the Massacre or the Passion. In the Pistoia pulpit his emphasis is more upon eyewitness, and the spectator's sense of identification is fairly straightforward. In the Pisa Passion, however, it is more complex. In the Betrayal, the Mocking and the Flagellation, Giovanni positions us so that we are compelled to face the moral dilemma of how we might have responded had we been present. Giovanni enables us to understand what it is like to betray someone, or how we might behave watching a prisoner being tortured.[21]

Not only are Giovanni's figures expressive, so too is his style of carving, unlike the painting of Duccio or Giotto where the handling of paint does not, by and large, vary in accordance with the subject matter. The folds of the vestments of Giovanni's Deacon (Fig. 54), one of his most temperate figures, are smooth and polished; Jesus' blindfold (Fig. 85) is fine, soft and almost transparent, reflecting his patience and contrasting with the crude carving of his tormentors. These similes embedded in the marble also activate the spectator's emotions. In addition Giovanni makes fuller use of metaphor and personification. The 'butchery' of the Massacre (Fig. 68) is personified in the actions of the soldier butchering the child; Judas is serpentine (Fig. 77); the figure crouching at Jesus' feet in the Mocking snarls like a cur; and the thrones of Herod and Caiaphas totter. Unlike Giotto's Vices, those of Giovanni are not separated from the narrative but actively participate in it.

In short, our engagement with Giovanni's narrative panels is far less intellectual and abstract. Whereas Duccio makes us think about the social forces that impinge upon the administration of justice, and Giotto leads us to reflect upon the nature of Temperance and Hope in the Resurrection, Giovanni arouses our passions about such concepts. Thus Malchus's ear is healed by Jesus at the very moment Judas is kissing him; the two actions are simultaneous and interwoven, and we feel the nobility of his charity and forgiveness. Likewise with vicious actions. So too with the overall pattern of the two pulpits, each displaying the breakdown of order and its subsequent reassertion. This, however, is not presented analytically, but emotionally – we experience this breakdown on our journey from Annunciation through Massacre and Passion as the sculptures become progressively more fragmented and difficult to read.

The difficulty presented by some of Giotto's frescoes is as much intellectual as visual, whereas that of Giovanni's reliefs is more visual, especially in the Passion panel. We have to learn to apply the correct law which he devised to bring scenes into perspectival, compositional and dramatic focus from a particular standpoint, to find order in apparent confusion. Giovanni's intelligence operated in a different way to that of the two painters.

His employment of the correct law is related to the fact that he does not use architecture as a controlling mechanism within the reliefs, whose compositions are almost exclusively constituted by the figures alone. There is nothing similar to Duccio's use of architecture as an extended metaphor for the breakdown of justice (Figs 6–15), or the subtle interaction of the frescoes and the interior architecture of Giotto's Scrovegni Chapel. Instead Giovanni has to employ the arrangement of the figures to create spatial illusions as the means of structuring the overall rhythm of his cycles. This is particularly apparent in the Pisa pulpit where the harmonious sense of ordered space in the Nativity and the Adoration breaks down in the succeeding panels until in the Massacre and the Passion the spectator only catches glimpses of small fragments of visual order in the individual episodes amongst the chaos of a battlefield. Then in the Crucifixion the spatial field of the whole panel is once again integrated.

Postscript

The painters' response to Giovanni Pisano

In an age dominated by the photograph, the complexity of the dynamics of viewing relief sculpture is one reason, perhaps, why Giovanni has not received his full due as Giotto's equal. It is not just a matter of having to rediscover the importance of oblique viewpoints but of Giovanni's complex visual field in general and the demands it makes upon the spectator. One has to search for those viewpoints from which the composition coheres and becomes intelligible. Even though it is sensible to read the reliefs sequentially we constantly find ourselves having to re-adjust, to backtrack, to look ahead, to come close and to move away. One has to learn a complex art of navigation.

Painting is more straightforward. Usually there is a single viewpoint and where it is above eye-level or has to be seen obliquely adjustments are made.

We are not required to tack back and forth across the picture plane.

A case can be made, however, that Giotto and his immediate successors did respond to certain of Giovanni's innovations while steering clear of Giovanni's emotional intensity, or intemperance. Jacob Burckhardt went so far as to claim that Giovanni Pisano 'was Giotto's true teacher'.[22] In the Scrovegni Massacre and Death Sentence (Fig. 31), Giotto may have been experimenting with such methods of engaging the spectator. In his later work in the family chapels of Sta Croce in Florence he did not have the walls of a large chamber into which spectators could enter; he and his pupils in Florence were confined to the humbler scale of chapels (Fig. 93) only one-fifth the size of the Scrovegni. This presented special problems in that these chapels were like small sanctuaries which could be entered only by priests and family. Entrance was barred by wrought iron screens. The chapels were, moreover, very tall and narrow. The paintings on the lateral walls would, therefore, be very difficult to see unless artists made careful adjustments for the oblique angles from which they would be viewed. Here Giovanni Pisano had something to teach them, and the solution they adopted also influenced their pictorial compositions and their approach to narrative.

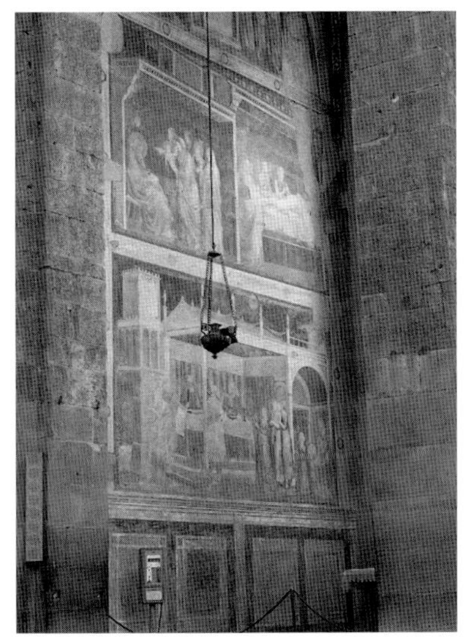

93. Giotto, View of the north wall of the Peruzzi Chapel, S. Croce, seen from outside, after 1310 and before 1337.

The simplest example is in Giotto's scene of the Apparition of St Francis to the brothers at Arles, in the middle tier of the Bardi family chapel in Sta Croce. At first sight this is a straightforward architectural setting and centralised composition. However, from outside the chapel the painting springs to life, and we seem to be present in the cloister looking into the Chapter House. Close observation reveals several carefully calculated but almost imperceptible optical corrections which make this possible.[23]

In the later Peruzzi Chapel next door (Fig. 93), Giotto's technique was more developed and integrated with the composition. The paradigmatic scene is Herod's Banquet.[24] Our starting point is the standard photographic reproduction (Fig. 94), which serves to give us some idea of the *actual* design of

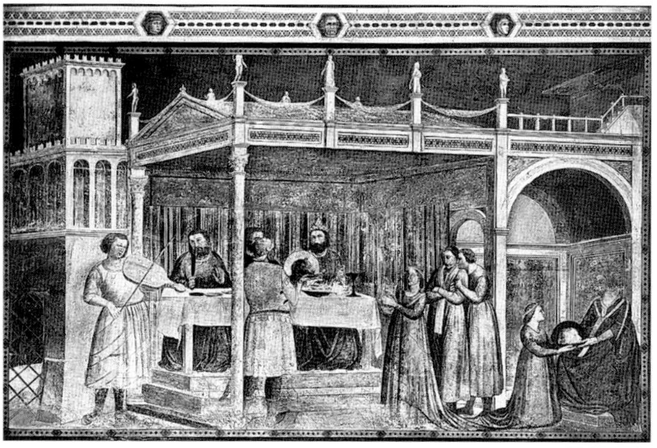

94. Giotto, the Feast of Herod, Peruzzi Chapel, S. Croce, dry fresco. This photograph was taken from scaffold directly in front of the fresco. Made before its restoration in the late 1950s, it shows the fresco heavily repainted and is reproduced to make the image of the restored fresco in Fig. 95 more legible.

the painted surface of the wall. Here the buildings, as in several of the scenes in the Scrovegni Chapel, are depicted as if they were set at a slight angle to the surface of the real work. But the perspective, particularly of the prison tower and the triangular pediment of Herod's banqueting loggia, seems, at first sight, typical of efforts preceding the developments of the mid-1420s: the receding lines seem to run in slightly different directions, without converging.

Seen from outside the chapel (Fig. 95) everything comes into focus, however, on account of the calculated adjustments Giotto made to compensate for the oblique viewpoint. The elongated loggia foreshortens into a square chamber, and we get a powerful impression of looking *into* spaces behind the painted surface of the wall, unlike much of Giotto's previous work where the action usually takes place across a rather shallow stage parallel to the real wall surface. This effect of a roomy interior is enhanced by three features: the coincidence of the shadows on the walls of the painted architecture with the light cast by the real window of the chapel giving a strong sense of shadowy interiors; the interconnecting withdrawing chamber in which the queen's daughter hands the Baptist's head to her mother; third, the depth of the roof of the loggia and the glimpse of the cornice of the main palace above and to the far right, as well as the prison tower to the left. This is a remarkable achievement scarcely surpassed by the seemingly more systematic perspectives of a century later.

But we must beware the language of pictorial technology for its own sake; the Feast of Herod is one of Giotto's greatest narrative paintings.

First the story. Against his better judgement and to placate his wife Herodias, Herod had John the Baptist imprisoned for condemning their marriage on the grounds that Jewish law forbad marriage to a sister-in-law even after her husband had died. Herodias urged Herod to have John executed, but Herod resisted.[25] At his birthday banquet, attended by all his high officials and nobility, Herodias's young daughter so delighted Herod with her dancing that he promises to reward her with anything she wants. Asked by the girl for suggestions, her mother replies, 'the head of John the Baptist'; the girl then asks Herod for the head 'on a charger'. Herod regretfully agrees, and orders the execution. Afterwards the head is given to the daughter who gives it in turn to her mother.

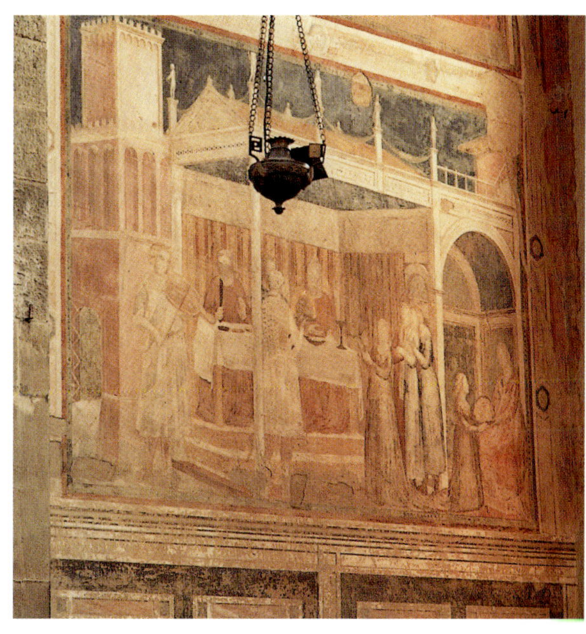

95. Giotto, the Feast of Herod, Peruzzi Chapel, S. Croce, after 1310 and before 1337, dry fresco, after restoration. This is viewed obliquely from outside the chapel.

Such is the power of images to supplant the words of these biblical stories that it is important to observe that there is no mention in the gospels of the head being brought to *Herod* at the banquet. It is brought to the daughter, who then gives it to her mother. Even on this issue there is disagreement between the gospels. In Mark it is clear that Herodias was *not* present at the banquet since the daughter leaves to ask her mother what to demand for her reward and returns to tell Herod. In Matthew, the whereabouts of Herodias are unspecified. Giotto, however, has clearly adopted the account in Mark, which is also that used in the *Diatesseron*, insofar as he shows Herodias in another room.[26]

Giotto includes three episodes, two of which are compressed into one – the daughter is apparently still dancing to the viol player's music as the head is brought in upon the charger; the third episode takes place in the withdrawing chamber where the kneeling girl delivers the head to her mother.

The key issue is the way Giotto designed the composition to 'come into focus' from the observer's position outside the chapel. From there the overlapping of objects in the picture makes sense. We seem to be standing slightly to the right of the diagonal axis of the loggia; from this position the freestanding column barely overlaps the executioner's left shoulder, and his head in turn overlaps that of the nobleman sitting on the other side of the table, so that we are looking over the executioner's right shoulder past the severed head of John the Baptist which conceals the upper part of Herod's body. This is exactly the kind of 'over-the-shoulder-into-the-eyes-of' composition favoured by Giovanni Pisano – we share the viewpoint of the executioner looking into the face of Herod confronted with the consequences of his rash promise. In addition, Giotto has employed his own device of implied movement parallax, as in the Scrovegni Last Supper (Fig. 29) and the Massacre of the Innocents (Fig. 37), but in a more developed form. The overlapping and occluding locates the spectator precisely – a little further to left or right and the relationship between the figures would change substantially. So there is only one correct viewpoint. We stand at a distance to the scene. At right angles to our line of sight the daughter, on the right, is continuing to dance to the tune of the viol player, the swing of whose bowing arm is suggested by the stripes on his gown. Is the head being handed to Herod or to his step-daughter? Are we to understand that she had simply resumed her dance while Herod's order was being carried out, or are we meant to read the juxtaposition as two discrete events compressed into one image?

The actions of the figures are inexpressive. The atmosphere of the picture, akin to that of the Last Supper or the Marriage at Cana, is frozen – with horror, in this case, as a result of the macabre appearance in the midst of the birthday party of the severed head. Here Giotto is in his element. Even though he drew upon Giovanni Pisano for elements of the perspective and composition, his characterisation of the drama is different. We can imagine how Giovanni might have represented this story. I shall subsequently examine Donatello's solution (Figs 124–6) a century later.

For as long as painters were obliged to work within the constraints of these confined family chapels so they continued to draw upon Giotto's ingenious solution, derived in part from Giovanni. This remained the case even in the following century, as in the Brancacci Chapel (Fig. 133). The key was not simply an optical adjustment for an awkward viewing position, more important was the narrative and compositional richness that could flow from this.

A final example is important not only in itself but also for its bearing upon the work of later artists. The Baroncelli Chapel painted by Giotto's senior assistant, Taddeo Gaddi, in the right transept of Santa Croce, is a lexicon of cunning devices not only in perspective but also in lighting.[27] The porch of the Temple in the Presentation of the Virgin is a virtuoso example of anamorphic perspective. But as normally reproduced, the scene next to it, that of the Betrothal of the Virgin, seems to demonstrate that all Giotto's economy and control has gone to riot in the work of his chosen successor – the surface is awash with figures to the extent that it is almost impossible to see the ceremony. In this respect it is very similar to Giovanni's Massacre and Passion panels at Pisa. But seen obliquely from outside the chapel (Fig. 96) (one needs to imagine the intricate wrought iron grille through which one would have had to peer at the lower tier of paintings) one finds oneself looking along a diagonal axis into the far corner of the courtyard, over the backs of two of the disappointed suitors, to the site where the High Priest performs the ceremony. It is as if we were immediately in line with these two suitors, craning past them to catch a glimpse of the joyful and momentous event. What at first appears confusing and lacking in clear composition is a deliberate attempt by the artist to convey the confusing experience of actually being present in a crowd, trying to catch sight of the source of the excitement. Our efforts to unravel the apparent visual confusion of the painting mimic and remind us of the real effort to see through the heads of a crowd, making the artistic experience more real. The demands made upon the spectator by such a fresco are similar to those encountered in Giovanni's reliefs.

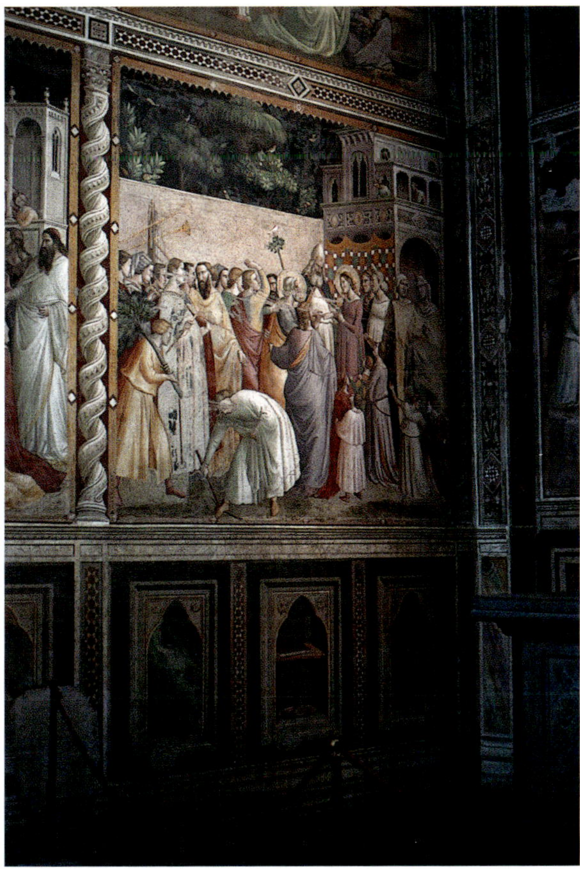

96. Taddeo Gaddi, the Betrothal of the Virgin, Baroncelli Chapel, S Croce, late 1430s, fresco. Photograph taken obliquely from the left from a position outside the chapel.

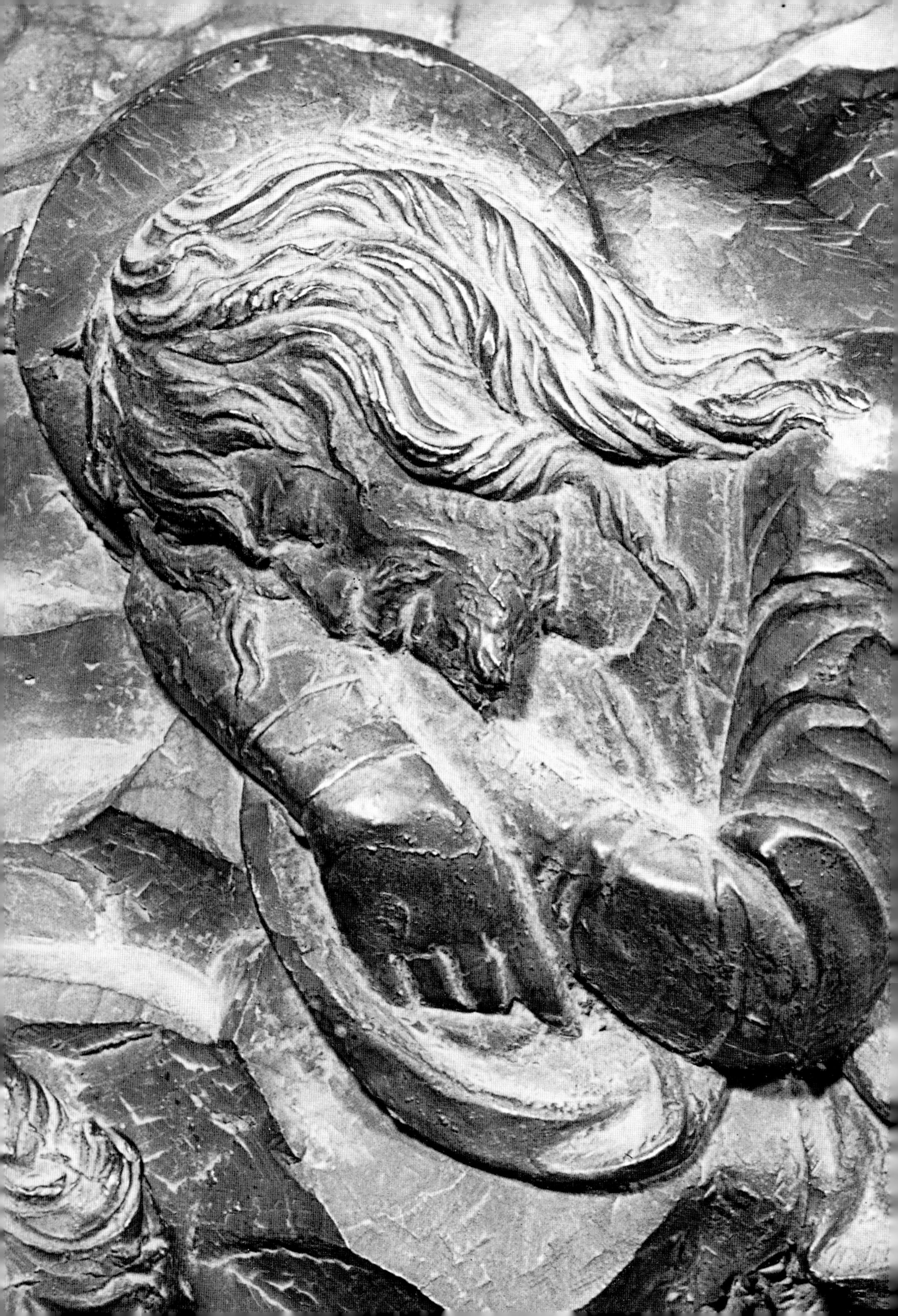

PART 2

1401–1465

Detail of Figure 148

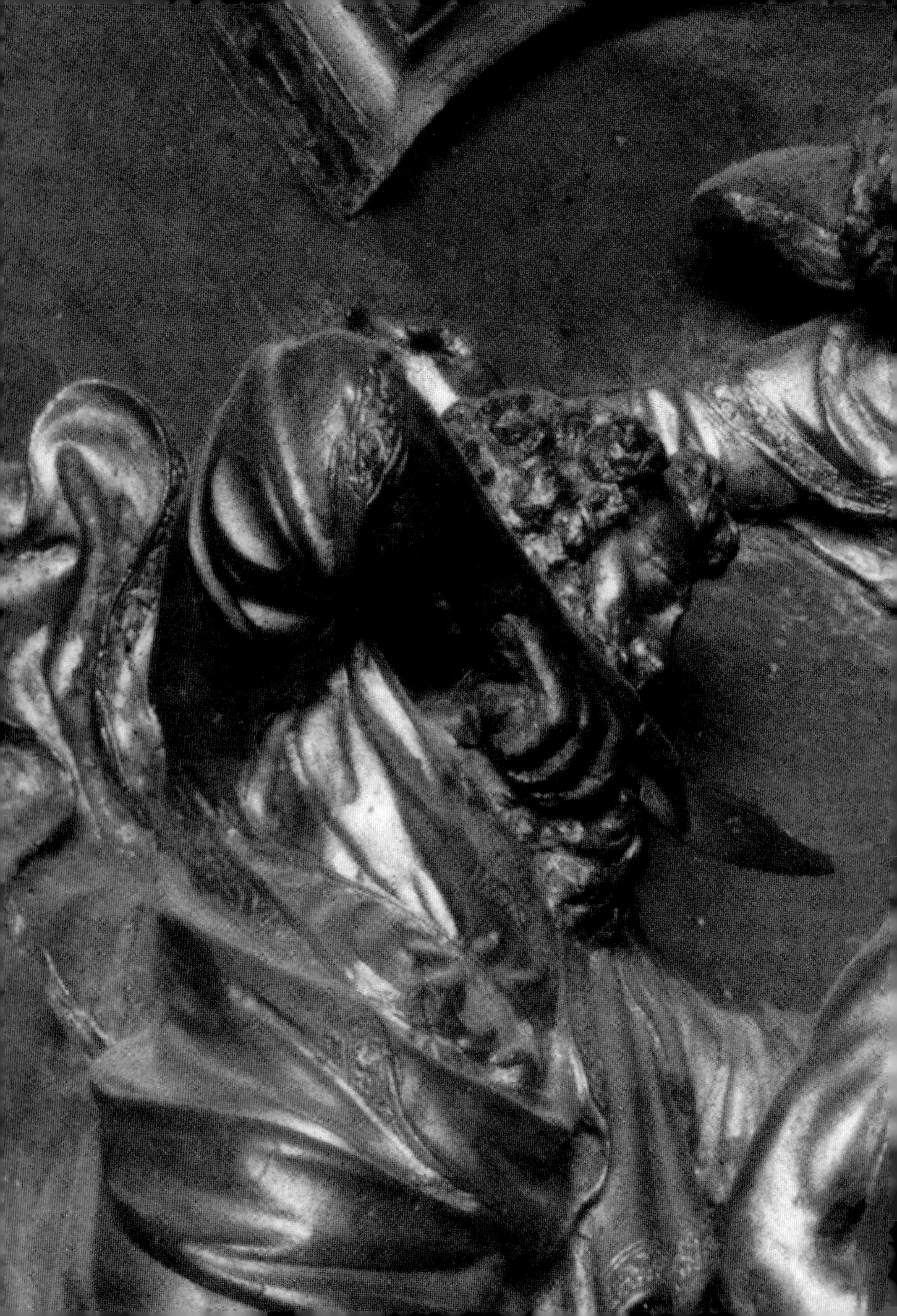

V

THE SECOND BAPTISTERY DOORS: GHIBERTI AND BRUNELLESCHI

The competition for the second Baptistery doors

In 1401 Lorenzo Ghiberti, Filippo Brunelleschi and five others took part in a competition to choose the sculptor to make the second pair of bronze doors for Florence's Baptistery (Fig. 97). These were for the east entrance opposite the new cathedral, nearing completion. One set of bronze doors had already been made by Andrea Pisano for the south entrance more than half a century earlier, between 1330 and 1336. The new doors were to follow the same design, twenty-eight panels in seven tiers, twenty panels devoted to stories, the eight lower panels representing single figures. Each panel was enclosed in a frame in the shape of a pierced quatrefoil and was slightly taller than it was wide.[1]

The subject for the competition was the Sacrifice of Isaac.[2] Only two competition reliefs survive – by the winner, Ghiberti (Fig. 100), and by Brunelleschi (Fig. 99). They were probably the two finalists. Two very different approaches to narrative and to the sculptural treatment of depth and distance are exhibited.

The story tells of God testing Abraham's faith by commanding him to sacrifice his only son, Isaac. They travel three days into the mountains with two young men and an ass. Leaving them behind, Isaac helps his father choose a

Detail of Figure 100

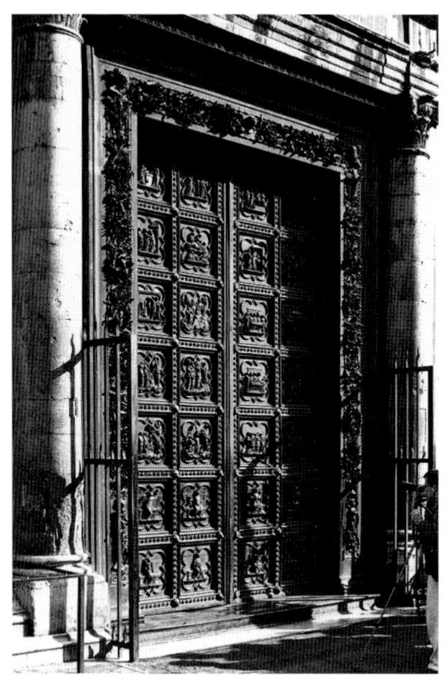

97. Lorenzo Ghiberti, North Doors of Florence Baptistery, gilded bronze, 1403-24.

site and only then discovers that he is to be the sacrificial victim. However, just as Abraham is stretching out his hand to take the knife with which to kill Isaac, the angel of the lord calls to him from heaven ordering him to stop 'for now I know thou fearest God'. Seeing a ram caught in a bush Abraham sacrifices that instead. Because Abraham was prepared to sacrifice his son God blesses him, promising that his seed will multiply 'as the stars of the heaven'.[3]

Both sculptors chose the episode when the angel speaks to Abraham, and both have shown the angel actually appearing to Abraham, though the text only mentions a voice; both show the ass and two young men, but there any similarity of treatment ends. Both are excellent in their different ways. It must have been hard for the judges to choose. Perhaps that is why both reliefs were preserved. Let us put ourselves in the position of one of the judges.

Brunelleschi has set his scene in a schematic landscape, similar to those by Andrea Pisano or Giotto. He has created little spatial depth to separate the servants from Abraham and Isaac – the two scenes are set one above the other with no explicit relationship between them. If Brunelleschi were the inventor of geometric perspective, and it will later become clear that I do not think his claim can be substantiated,[4] then it is surprising that he shows so little interest in the relationship between his figures and their setting, less than Giovanni Pisano, certainly less than the mid-fourteenth-century painter and sculptor Andrea Orcagna, whose octagonal relief of the Birth of the Virgin on the Or San Michele tabernacle (Fig. 98), dating from 1352–60, is an important antecedent of the kinds of perspective to be found in Donatello's relief of the Head of St John (Fig. 124). and Ghiberti's Gates of Paradise (Figs 138–9).[5] The

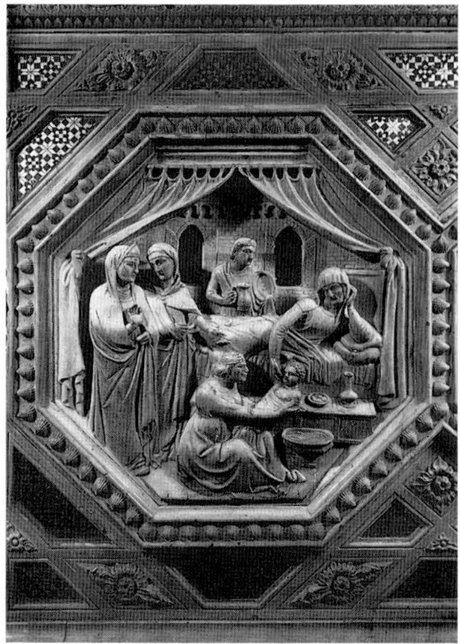

98. Andrea Orcagna, Birth of the Virgin, Or San Michele, Florence, marble, 1352-60.

octagonal frame of Orcagna's relief serves as a window behind which most of the figures and furniture recede. A curtain, hanging in loops from a rail on the uppermost edge of the octagon and hooked back to reveal the bedroom, enhances the sense of space in the chamber. In the foreground the midwife holding up the baby Mary for our inspection is located on a platform stage which extends somewhat into our space. Behind her the other figures and objects are arranged in carefully overlapping planes leading back to the servant holding a jug and bowl on the far side of the bed, the rear wall with its two lancet windows behind him. There are about twelve planes from the moulded frame to the rear wall of the chamber. This compares to approximately fifteen overlapping planes in Donatello's Head of St John. Sited so prominently in the centre of Florence there can be no doubt that Brunelleschi was aware of Orcagna's experiments in this kind of framed perspective as he would have been of Giovanni Pisano's, and he must have made a deliberate decision to keep his relief as flat as possible and to arrange the figures so carefully 'that they do not overlap'.[6] Perhaps the competition required uniformity with Andrea Pisano's earlier doors as the similarity of landscape suggests. Brunelleschi's relief does seem, however, to indicate an eye-level for the spectator halfway up the panel on a line running through the points of the left- and right-hand triangles of the quatrefoil. This is defined by the foreshortening of the cornice of the altar. The implication is that our eye-level is slightly above the altar, at about the level of Isaac's heels, and this is reinforced by the suggestion in the foreshortening of the figures that we are looking up at Isaac's head and down upon the bodies of the two servants and the ass. Our viewpoint is fixed – little advantage is gained by changing our position to obtain oblique views – and it is dramatic.

Among the factors contributing to the minimal sense of depth is the predominant placing of the bodies and objects parallel to the backplate. The figures are restricted to two shallow strips of space – that containing the ass and the young men and, just above and behind them, that containing Abraham, Isaac, the angel and the ram. The figures moreover are largely aligned with the frontal plane of the relief. The chief protagonists, furthermore, engage with one another from left and right in a frieze across the plane of the relief. Maybe, like Giotto, Brunelleschi wanted to concentrate the viewer's attention upon the action without any distracting display of naturalistic virtuosity. Unlike Giotto, however, he chooses the very climax of the event, or so it seems: Abraham is rushing forward, his momentum bearing upon the knife point placed at the pit of Isaac's throat, and Isaac's head is prised back by Abraham's thumb. The angel is exerting an equal and opposite force on Abraham's right forearm and has thus prevented the sacrifice

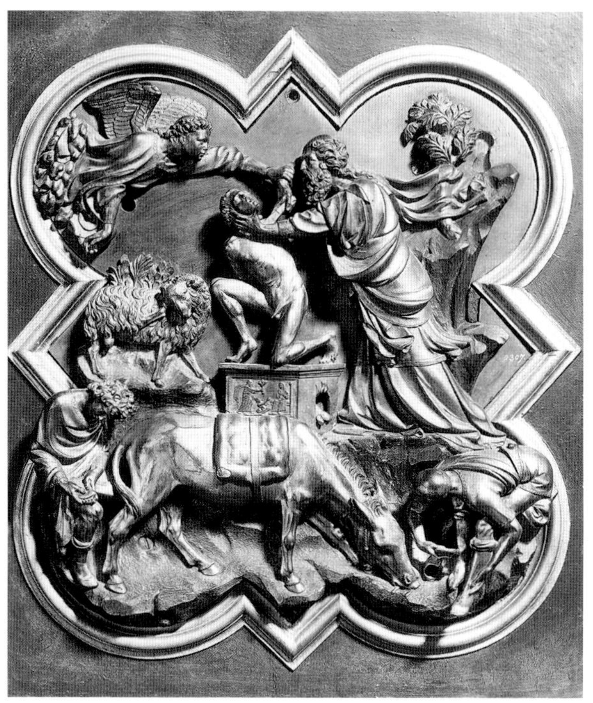

99. Filippo Brunelleschi, The Sacrifice of Isaac, competition panel for the North Doors of Florence Baptistery, gilded bronze, 1401, Museo Nazionale del Bargello, Florence.

occurring. Isaac screams, tortured both by the prospect of death as well as by the heat of the flames beneath forcing him into contortions to support himself. Each muscle, each fold of drapery is adjusted with mechanical precision to create the suspense. This is the very instant at which the event reaches its climax: an instant later the knife would have entered Isaac's throat. So it would seem, though on closer inspection it is clear that the angel has just pushed the knife away. Yet Brunelleschi has had to manipulate both the biblical text and the conventional depiction of the story to achieve this effect. The Bible clearly states that 'Abraham stretched forth his hand, and took the knife in order to slay his son.' Abraham had only just reached out to pick up the knife, he had not yet directed it at the boy, a point reinforced by the angel's command, 'Do not stretch forth your hand towards the boy, nor do anything to him.' The convention of earlier depictions on the other hand, also departing from the scriptural text, show Abraham with the knife or sword poised, about to do the deed, as in Ghiberti's relief.[7]

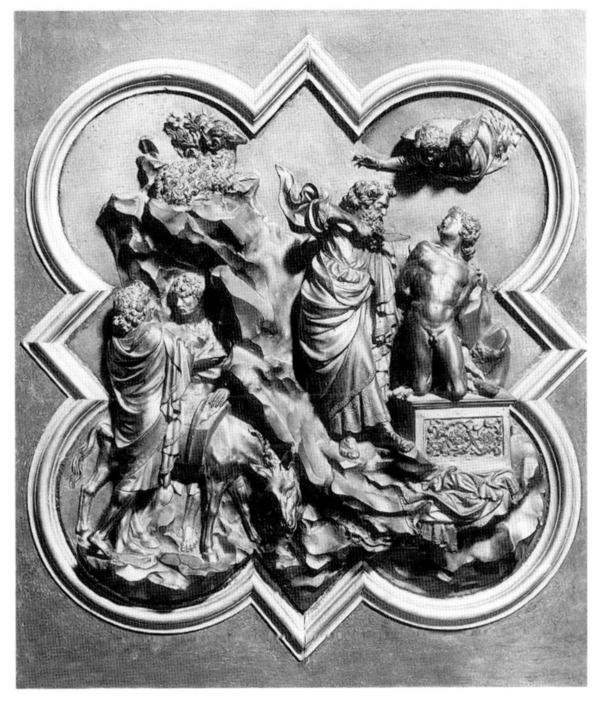

100. Lorenzo Ghiberti, The Sacrifice of Isaac, competition panel for the North Doors of Florence Baptistery, gilded bronze, 1401, Museo Nazionale del Bargello, Florence. This photograph was taken from below and to the left.

Brunelleschi's focus upon the 'knife-edge' between life and death was original; his conception of the terrible deed Abraham was required to do was the result of an exercise in Devout Meditation. In contrast, the ass and the two servants are totally absorbed in the process of relaxing and recuperating after their long journey while they wait for Abraham to return; their actions are leisurely. The viewer is also encouraged to linger over the minutely observed naturalism of the worn saddle or the strands of the rope round the ass's neck. But these apparent distractions and this sense of what is happening meanwhile only serve to emphasise the instantaneity and intensity of what is happening above, where Brunelleschi has conveyed speed of action and agonised expression through flying draperies and tense bodily movement.

Brunelleschi has subordinated everything to the precise representation of an instant in time viewed from a well-defined frontal position. This was a very unusual approach.

Ghiberti (Fig. 100) produced something more intricate and arguably more progressive. His landscape is also schematic, supporting the hypothesis that this feature was specified by the competition, but less so than Brunelleschi's, and Ghiberti makes an effort to suggest that the servants are some distance from the sacrifice, even though they seem aware of it, especially when we view the relief from the left and from below (Fig. 101), which it is rewarding to do. Ghiberti had studied Giovanni Pisano attentively.

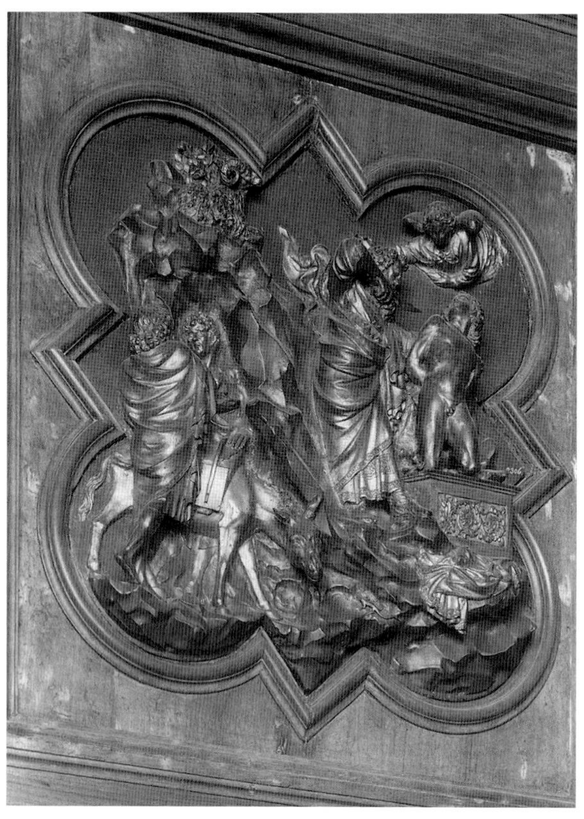

101. Lorenzo Ghiberti, The Sacrifice of Isaac, competition panel for the North Doors of Florence Baptistery, gilded bronze, 1401, Museo Nazionale del Bargello, Florence.

From the left we see the scene across many overlapping planes, seven in all – the back of the first servant, the ass, the second servant, the ridge of rock, Abraham, Isaac and, farthest away, the angel flying towards us out of the sky. We are encouraged to move around the little panel by the way that the figures are each turned at different angles to one another and to the surface plane. The bodies of Abraham, Isaac and the angel approach one another from different directions, likewise Isaac's limbs, suggesting that they can move freely in the space which surrounds them. This too contrasts with Brunelleschi's treatment. A major difference, however, is Ghiberti's treatment of the event itself. Unlike Brunelleschi, Ghiberti chose to represent not a moment but a *phase* in the action, as was customary. Ghiberti moreover follows pictorial precedent, if not the Bible, in representing the stage before Abraham attacks his son, before the angel speaks but as he is emerging from the sky. We are therefore able to witness Abraham steeling himself to carry out God's command, his awkward stance reflecting his indecision, his body both advancing and recoiling. The beauty of Isaac's young body indicates the gravity of Abraham's task. In the midst of Abraham's equivocation and emotional conflict, the angel arrives, already noticed by Isaac although Abraham remains oblivious.

Ghiberti's scene is very sensitive to Abraham's psychology, to his inner feelings, similar in that respect to Giotto's approach to pictorial storytelling, even though Ghiberti has employed the resources of relief sculpture so richly developed by Giovanni Pisano. Thus one participates in the scene through the oblique over-the-shoulder views, as a somewhat detached spectator, able nonetheless to imagine Abraham's dilemma. We are not thrown into the fury of the event, however, but encouraged to turn the story over in our minds, to meditate upon it, seeing it from different angles and viewpoints.

What a difficult choice for the jury. Knowing the result of the competition, it is all too easy for us to come down on Ghiberti's side on account of the sophistication of his figures and landscape, his dramatic subtlety and his psychological richness in conveying Abraham's inner turmoil. Brunelleschi, on the other hand, by imagining that the event continues until the point at which Abraham was about to kill Isaac, drives home the horror of what Abraham is prepared to do for the God in whom he has total faith. Ghiberti, following convention in representing an earlier phase, loses the clear impression that Abraham really *is* going to kill his son. His Abraham might almost be playing for time.

Brunelleschi's first biographer, Antonio Manetti, writing in about 1480, claimed that the judges wanted to share the commission between the two, and only Brunelleschi's refusal to accept this compromise prevented it.[8] Such compromise results of competitions had occurred in the previous century, indeed something of the sort was imposed upon Brunelleschi and Ghiberti twenty years later in the building of the cupola of Florence Cathedral.[9]Manetti gives us the impression that Brunelleschi was a 'control freak' in his conduct in building the cupola, seeking total autonomy over the execution of his design, which was unusual in building at that time, or indeed any other.[10]Manetti's account of the competition has a ring of truth about it, more so perhaps than Ghiberti's own song of self-praise:

> The palm of victory was conceded to me by all the judges and by all the other competitors. Universally the glory was conceded to me, without a single exception. To all it seemed that I had surpassed all others of that time by the consultation of a tribunal of learned men . . .[11]

Recent arguments that Ghiberti won, 'on points' as it were, for the technical reason that his work was cast in only three pieces as opposed to Brunelleschi's seven, which would have cost more to make because of the extra bronze, are conjectural; no evidence survives to suggest that the small extra cost relative to the whole disqualified Brunelleschi.[12] My own conjecture is that the two artists were neck and neck, but there is no documentary evidence for this, only Manetti's statement, the precedent of earlier compromise results and the implications of the foregoing analysis.

The key point is that the two competition panels represent different approaches to pictorial narrative, as different as those between Giotto and Giovanni Pisano a century earlier, though in different ways because the terms of the debate had altered. In Sta Croce Giotto and his successors had adapted

Giovanni's oblique perspective to their temperate style. Following their example, Ghiberti's approach is open and many-sided: like Giovanni, Ghiberti gives the spectator the freedom to view the work from many angles, although unlike Giovanni there are no privileged viewpoints where everything comes into focus, as in Giovanni's Pisa Betrayal. Yet the overall character is temperate and Ghiberti has also chosen the suggestive or pregnant phase of the action so that we can participate in the inner feelings of the protagonists. Brunelleschi's approach, on the other hand, is focused and instantaneous, inviting the spectator to react emotionally *to* the event rather than to muse upon it or to enter into the inner feelings of the characters, who are highly expressive and passionate. Correspondingly he chose a point in time and one very close to the climax of the story.[13] The relief is also intended to be seen from a fixed viewing position and it is planar and in certain respects more like a painting.

Thus we find each artist seeking a different resolution between certain key parameters set by Giotto and Giovanni in the earlier debate. Ghiberti follows Giovanni Pisano in adopting a multi-faceted and highly three-dimensional form of relief which encourages the spectator to share the viewpoints of the figures, to see what they see. In three other key issues, however, he does not follow Giovanni but Giotto: he chooses to depict the pregnant or suggestive phase of the action while adopting a generally temperate handling of the subject, so that we are able to enter into the inner feelings of the characters to some degree. Brunelleschi, while adopting Giotto's flat and frontal disposition of the figures, though purged of his overlapping, and rejecting Giovanni's obliquity, is nonetheless similar to Giovanni in the passionate actions of his figures and in the way we are led to react to them rather than to share their feelings. His use of the single climactic moment, however, is a refinement of Giovanni's energetic figures, and seems to be an innovation.

The 1401 competition between Ghiberti and Brunelleschi was important for pictorial narrative in the fifteenth century. But it is worth pointing out that Ghiberti's own conception of competition was, however, as much collaborative as combative. In his *Commentaries* he remarks that in the building of the cupola 'Filippo [Brunelleschi] and I were competitors [*concorrenti*] for eighteen years, with equal salaries, and in this way we carried on the work.'[14] Donatello (b.1386) and Masaccio (b.1401) adopted elements from both artists in addition to drawing upon Giotto, Giovanni Pisano and other artists of the fourteenth century, as well as contributing their own ideas. The issues within the debate were complex and multi-dimensional.

For example, a fixed viewpoint need not necessarily be tied to a momentary, climactic representation of the action – although such a connection is found in Brunelleschi's competition relief.[15] But this relationship is far more complex in Donatello's Head of St John (Fig. 124) and in Masaccio's frescoes (Figs 127, 130 and 132). A flat or planar image does not preclude our entering into the minds of the characters but neither is it inevitably related to a temperate approach. On the other hand, high relief like that of Giovanni Pisano that afforded the spectator a variety of oblique viewpoints was not necessarily tied to his kind of passionate and dynamic figures. The situation I wish to convey is of a vital tradition in which an artist of the fifteenth century was able to draw upon a large stock of procedures and approaches to pictorial narrative, which he could develop and to which he could add his own inventions. There were no definitive solutions to problems of narrative, of composition, or perspective. This freedom was possible in part because of the very different approaches to narrative of Giotto and Giovanni Pisano. This is one reason why it is important historically to place Giovanni alongside Giotto, to give sculpture its due place as well as painting and to correct the still dominant Vasarian picture that Giotto was the sole fount of everything that followed. The work of the early fourteenth-century artists, moreover, was not superseded by developments in the early fifteenth century, nor indeed at its end – Michelangelo made drawings in the Peruzzi Chapel and his figures of St Peter and St Paul for the Piccolomini Altar in Siena Cathedral made between 1501 and 1504 are evidence of his study of Giovanni Pisano. There was no single orthodoxy and no single path of development. Even within a small city like Florence and a small region like Tuscany artists were very different from one another, were highly individual and very experimental. This is what makes the art of the period so exhilarating. There was no single Quattrocento style.[16]

The second doors

Ghiberti was a competitive artist, even though the word carried collaborative connotations, and in the doors, for which he received the commission in 1403, he seemingly set out to compete subject by subject with his predecessors, both painters and sculptors, most of whom, however, on the evidence of his later *Commentaries*, he held in generous esteem, particularly Giotto and Ambrogio Lorenzetti. Ghiberti was a brilliant man in his early twenties, bent upon demonstrating, a little cheekily perhaps, where earlier artists had gone wrong and how the treatment of a subject could be improved. Giotto seems to have been a particular target. The twenty narratives of the bronze doors cover roughly the same episodes in the Life of Jesus as the twenty-three in the Scrovegni Chapel.

One detail of the programme in particular indicates that he also regarded Giotto, like Brunelleschi, as his *concorrento*. Ghiberti included the Navicella among his twenty panels. This is a surprisingly rare subject. The most prominent image was, of course, Giotto's huge mosaic made for the portico of Old St Peter's (Fig. 102) in the first decade of the fourteenth century and reassembled in 1675 on the inside face of the porch of the new St Peter's where it can still be seen, considerably altered to fit the arch.[17] In 1435 Alberti included a description of Giotto's Navicella in *De pictura,* the only modern work he mentioned, alongside his account of one of the most famous paintings of antiquity, the Sacrifice of Iphigenia by Timanthes. Even in its present condition Giotto's Navicella remains highly impressive. As Alberti observed, 'Giotto represented the eleven disciples struck with fear and wonder at the sight of their colleague walking on the water, each showing such clear signs of his agitation in his face and entire body that their individual emotions are discernible in every one of them.'[18] The mosaic is on a large scale. The waves swell up above the heads of the disciples on the right and seemingly above

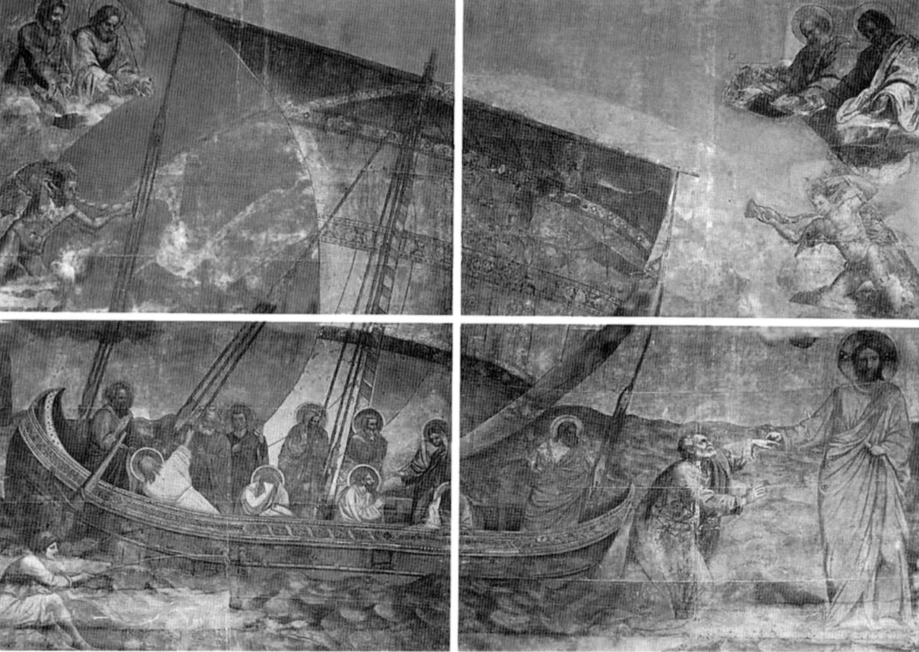

102. After Giotto, full size copy of Giotto's Navicella, tempera on paper, 1630, Fabbrica of St Peter's, Rome. Giotto's very large mosaic of the Navicella stood above the main portico of old St Peter's, Rome and was made after 1300. It is now installed, cut down and altered, but still magnificent, within the atrium of St Peter's facing the main door.

the spectator. The mast and billowing sail seem vast in proportion to the disciples and tilt dangerously, as if about to overturn. One disciple is pulling with all his might on the ropes to prevent this. Jesus, appearing on the waves, is the only person or object to remain vertical. The disciples indeed show a wide range of emotions, superbly expressed: one seems to have withdrawn into himself, another wrapped in his cloak with his head in his hands is completely panicking, another seems almost out of his mind and another clings to the side of the boat while looking at Jesus. Others show more faith. One prays and another holds up his hands in astonishment at the miracle. As in Giotto's Lazarus (Fig. 28) it seems to have been his intention to show a certain development from the figures in the stern of the boat who are either petrified or resorting to physical remedies for their plight to those in the prow, closer to Jesus and St Peter, some of whom begin look to Our Lord for their salvation.

Ghiberti (Fig. 103) lacked the scale on which Giotto had worked, so one cannot have the same sense of almost being in the capsizing boat. That the relief was, nonetheless, intended as a critique of one of the greatest works of the period is suggested by a small detail – unlike Giotto, Ghiberti shows the disciple hauling on the rope in order to *furl* the sail, an operation that he has just completed. This is what sailors do in a storm.[19] They do not leave their sails billowing as in Giotto's Navicella. It seems as if Ghiberti was suggesting that Giotto knew nothing about sailing. In addition, whereas Giotto's mosaic is more a doctrinal symbol of Jesus' protection of the storm-tossed church, Ghiberti sticks more literally to the text of St Matthew 14, 22–31 in which St Peter puts to the test Jesus' apparition, which some of the disciples believed to be a spirit.[20]

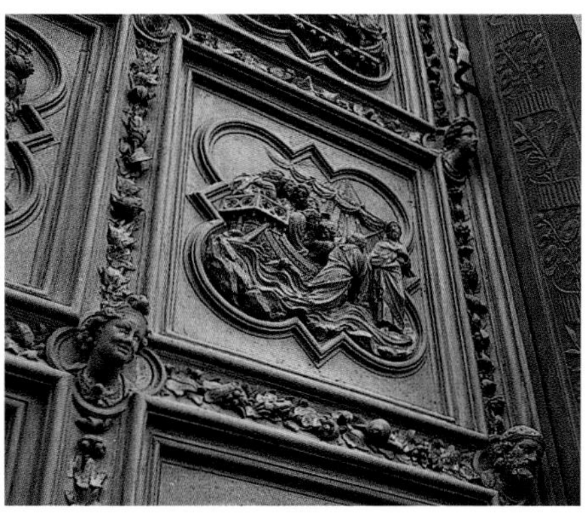

103. Lorenzo Ghiberti, the Navicella, gilded bronze relief from the North Doors of Florence Baptistery, 1403-24, in situ.

> 27. But straightway Jesus spake unto them, saying 'Be of good cheer; it is I; be not afraid.' 28. And Peter answered him and said, 'Lord, if it be thou, bid me come unto thee on the water.' 29. And he said, 'Come.' And when Peter was come down out of the ship, he walked on the water, to go to Jesus. 30. But when he saw the wind boisterous, he was afraid; and beginning to sink, he cried, saying, 'Lord, save me.' 31.

And immediately Jesus stretched forth his hand, and caught him, and said unto him, 'O thou of little faith, wherefore didst thou doubt?'

Whereas Giotto depicts Jesus as a strong and compassionate figure rescuing St Peter, Ghiberti shows Peter sinking into the waves, his hands raised in prayer, beseeching Jesus to save him, while Jesus stretches out his hand somewhat disdainfully, as if he is saying, 'O thou of little faith, wherefore didst thou doubt?' Ghiberti's more scriptural emphasis is upon the episode between St Peter and Jesus; the disciples sit in a ring in the stern of the ship, looking on. Giotto's image is more concerned with the disciples' individual reactions to the event. For so young a man to respond in this way to such an image took courage. While the nature of Ghiberti's argument is clear enough, nonetheless my personal view is that he didn't fully measure up to the formidable competition.

In Giotto's Expulsion of the Merchants from the Temple (Fig. 104), however, his habitual restraint results in a painting which is barely adequate in conveying the Bible's account of Jesus' rare expression of physical and verbal aggression.

And Jesus went into the temple of God, and cast out all them that sold and bought in the temple; and overthrew the tables of the moneychangers, and the seats of them that sold doves, And said unto them, 'It is written, My house shall be called the house of prayer; but ye have made it a den of thieves.'[21]

Giotto's Jesus lifts a clenched fist and with his other hand pushes one of the merchants; an upturned table lies tidily on its back, while a small child who has bought a dove shelters within St Peter's robes.

Ghiberti did not change the composition significantly (Fig. 105). Giotto's Jesus is the starting point for his own, but revised. Jesus' right arm is raised well above his head, his left hand is outstretched, energetically shoving the salesmen out of the Temple but, above all, Jesus charges at them, he might almost be whirling a battle-axe. This is the Church Militant. Driven by his violence the crowd falls over itself, a young man, derived from a Roman battle relief, has fallen and is in danger of being trampled and of toppling to his death over the ledge on which he is lying precariously, struggling to cling on. Ghiberti employs the 'real' ledge which is the base for his relief. A woman on the right is about to faint, next to her a man clutches his money bag all the tighter rather than helping the fallen man. It is an extraordinary artistic performance, perhaps Ghiberti also intended to show that he was the equal of his other *concorrento*, Brunelleschi (Fig. 99), in the depiction of momentary action and violence, but only when the subject demanded. Decorum, appro-

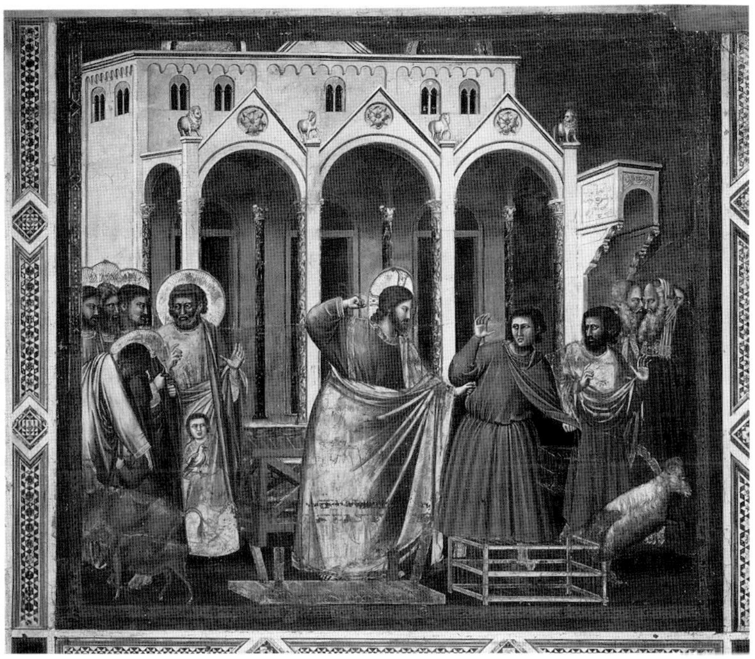

104. Giotto, Expulsion of the Merchants from the Temple, Scrovegni Chapel, Padua, fresco, middle tier of the north wall (26, Fig. 18) 1303-5.

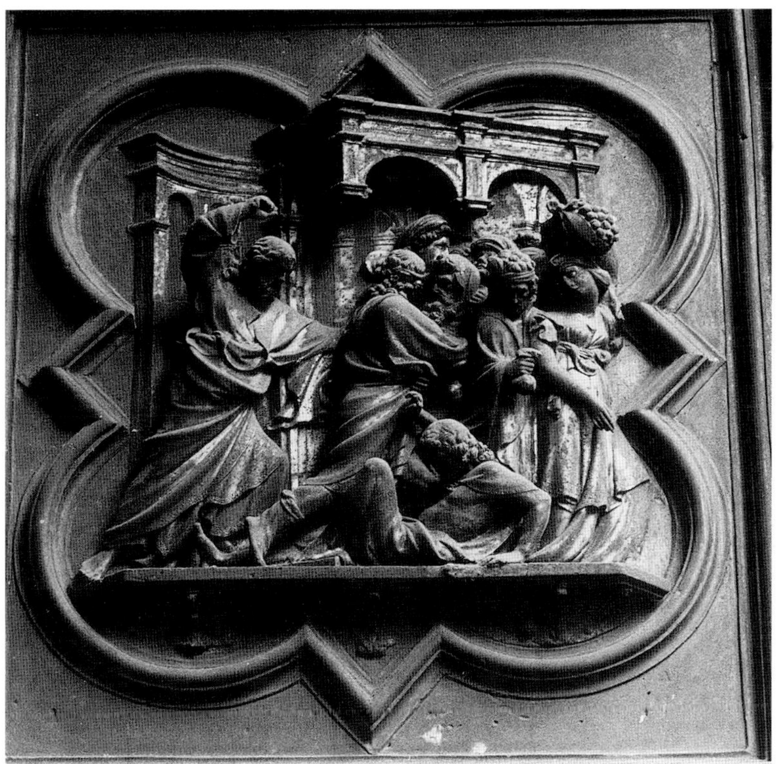

105. Lorenzo Ghiberti, Expulsion of the Merchants from the Temple, gilded bronze relief from the North Doors of Florence Baptistery, 1403-24, in situ.

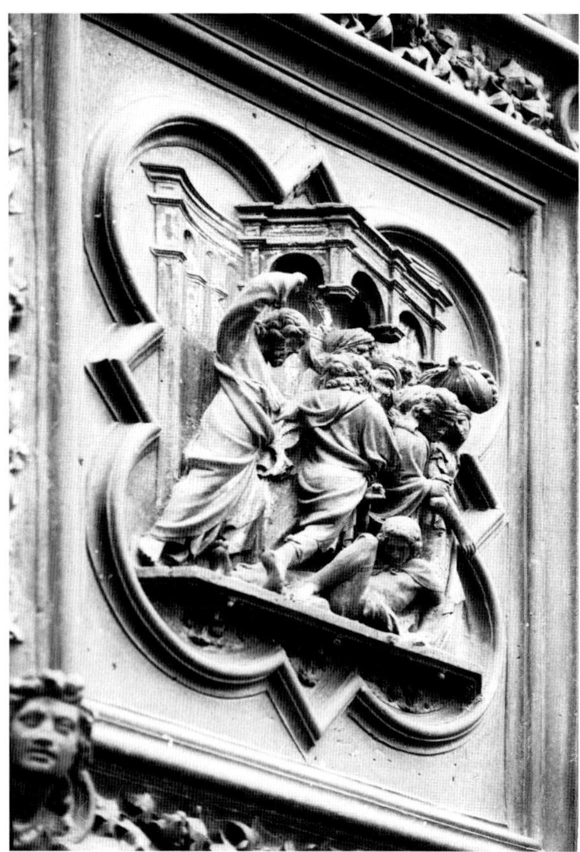

106. Lorenzo Ghiberti, Expulsion of the Merchants from the Temple, gilded bronze relief from the North Doors of Florence Baptistery, 1403-24, in situ. Photograph taken from the left.

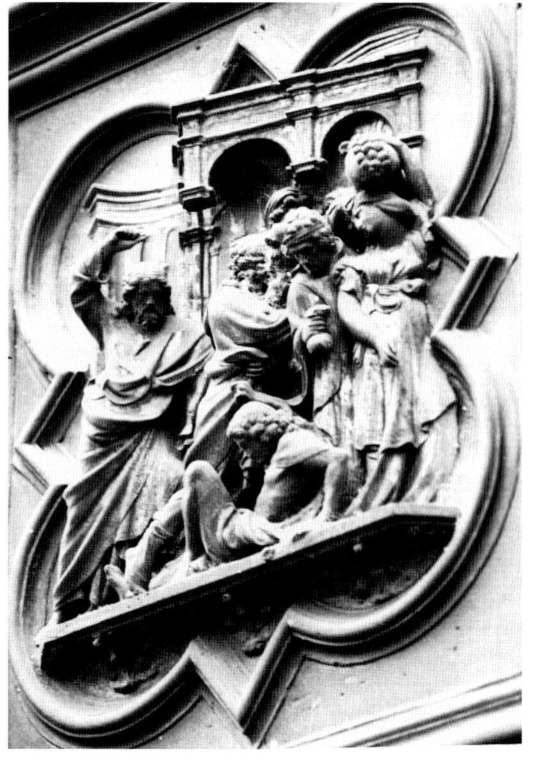

107. Lorenzo Ghiberti, Expulsion of the Merchants from the Temple, gilded bronze relief from the North Doors of Florence Baptistery, 1403-24, in situ. Photograph taken from the right.

priateness, is central to Ghiberti's art. How brilliantly the oblique views (Figs 106–7), Pisano-like, enhance the excitement of Jesus' action. Seen from the left the figures seem caught in the moment of falling over one another. From the right we are in their position, identified with the fallen youth and in fear for our lives for the sins we have committed. Giotto's fresco looks almost feeble in comparison. Here we see an artist who has made a careful study of Giovanni's pulpits and the 'correct law' of oblique narrative composition. But he has also incorporated something of Giotto's psychological inwardness.

Ghiberti even has implicit criticisms of one of Giotto's most successful scenes, the Raising of Lazarus (Fig. 28). Like Giotto he broadly follows the conventional formula, which he reverses (Fig. 108). Yet somehow Ghiberti is more successful in conveying the impression that Lazarus has just 'come forth' out of the cave-tomb in response to Jesus' words and is actually alive. How was this accomplished?

For one, he made full use of the three-dimensionality of relief sculpture. From our viewpoint, below and to the right-hand side, the scene of Martha on her knees pleading with Jesus to cure her brother, and Jesus responding

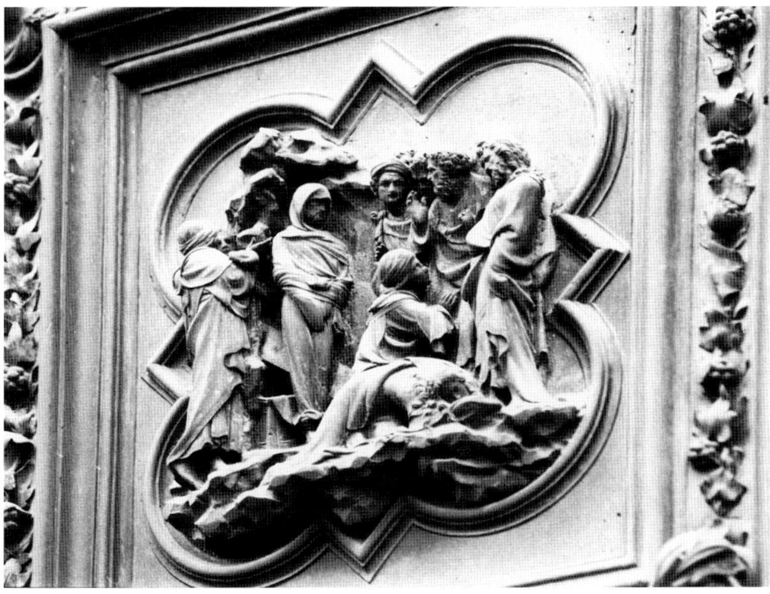

108. Lorenzo Ghiberti, the Raising of Lazarus, gilded bronze relief from the North Doors of Florence Baptistery, 1403-24, in situ. Photograph taken from the right.

by looking down, in profile, into her eyes, is composed on an axis at right angles to our line of sight, and as such it is the primary focus and the first thing to catch our eye. But through the paired figures of Jesus and Martha we see another pair, the bearded figure next to Jesus and the risen Lazarus, whom he has just seen. All the other characters are concentrating on Jesus to see what he will do next. Unlike Giotto, Ghiberti does not show Jesus issuing his injunction to Lazarus. Only the bearded man's raised hand and startled expression, as if he were seeing a ghost, directs our attention to Lazarus, who is indeed, from behind the heavy folds of his hood, gazing dolefully back at him. Even though Lazarus is still wrapped in his winding sheet the folds seem to be loosening, and depending upon the different angles from which one views him, his limbs seem to be stirring with life, emerging from the mummy-like wrapping. Finally, one small detail – there is a loop of drapery overlapping the edge of the coffin attached to Lazarus's feet to indicate that he has indeed, just a moment earlier, 'come forth' from the cavernous gloom of the cave.

All this provides one with an even more subtle sense of the transition of Lazarus from death to life, and of the recognition of the miracle by the spectators, than in Giotto's fresco. Ghiberti was attempting to improve upon an ingenious and excellent work of art, tightening up the pictorial composition, thinking the scene through again, perhaps using little clay puppet figures such as Giovanni Pisano must have used, so that he could turn heads and bodies until he hit upon exactly the right effect. Different aspects of the event come into focus when one looks at the relief from the centre or from the left – the standard photograph from a scaffold makes little sense.

In one relief in particular Ghiberti went beyond mere improvement. In the scene of Jesus among the Doctors (Fig. 109) Ghiberti tackled a story which had been a favourite over the preceding century, having been portrayed by Giotto, Duccio, twice by Taddeo Gaddi, as well as by Simone Martini and Barna da Siena. It was subsequently depicted by Giovanni di Paolo, Fra Angelico and Butinone in the fifteenth century. The fourteenth-century artists had used a similar formulaic composition, with the possible exception of Taddeo Gaddi's fresco in Sta Croce, which Ghiberti admired,[22] each successively making variations and improvements upon their predecessors, as we have seen Ghiberti doing himself. On this occasion Ghiberti radically revised the formula, going back to the text and thinking out the composition afresh, as in the Navicella.

> 41. Now his parents went to Jerusalem every year at the feast of the passover. 42. And when he was twelve years old, they went up to Jerusalem after the custom of the feast. (**1**) 43. And when they had fulfilled the days,

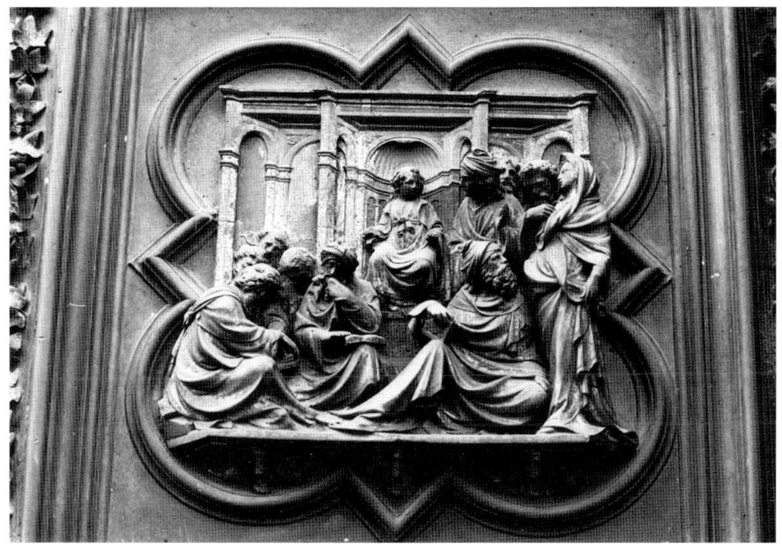

109. Lorenzo Ghiberti, Jesus amongst the Doctors, bronze relief from the North Doors of Florence Baptistery, 1403–24, in situ.

(**2**) as they returned, (**3**) the child Jesus tarried behind in Jerusalem; (**4**) and Joseph and his other knew not *of it*. 44. But they, supposing him to have been in the company, (**5**) went a day's journey; (**6**) and they sought him among their kinsfolk and acquaintance. (**7**) 45. And when they found him not, (**8**) they turned back again to Jerusalem, (**9**) seeking him. (**10**) 46. And it came to pass, that after three days they found him in the temple, (**11**) sitting in the midst of the doctors, hearing them, and asking them questions. 47. All that heard him were astonished at his understanding and answers. (**12**) 48. And when they saw him, they were amazed: and his mother said unto him, 'Son, why hast thou thus dealt with us? behold, thy father and I have sought thee sorrowing.' 49. And he said unto them, 'Why is it that ye sought me? wist ye not that I must be about my Father's business?' 50. And they understood not the saying which he spake unto them. (**13**) 51. And he went down with them, and came to Nazareth, (**14**) and was subject unto them: but his mother kept all these sayings in her heart. (**15**) 52. And Jesus increased in wisdom and stature, and in favour with God and man. (Luke, chap. 2)

As indicated this story can be broken down into at least fifteen subsidiary episodes. Almost all the fourteenth-century paintings represent episodes ten to twelve, the finding of Jesus. A fourteenth-century Italian manuscript (Fig.

110) of the Franciscan *Meditations on the Life of Christ* depicts the whole story in eleven separate images, several of them invented elaborations on the Bible story, following the advice given in the *Meditations* on the use of Devout Meditation. Ghiberti, however, kept to the tradition of depicting the three central episodes: the finding of Jesus in the Temple, Jesus disputing with the doctors, and Mary reproaching her son. The image, therefore, required a compression of three episodes, each complex in itself, and two key meanings or morals: Jesus' intellectual and spiritual precocity and his teaching on the need to sever family ties in the pursuit of one's relationship to God. To understand Ghiberti's treatment we need to examine the pictorial tradition.

Giotto's fresco in the Scrovegni Chapel (Fig. 111) is one of his most frozen. Jesus sits in the centre of the doctors. They are almost motionless, and the four doctors on the right are like clones. His hands are raised in argument. His authority is indicated by his position beneath the rounded arch of the apse of the basilican temple, which frames him as a niche does a statue. Mary and Joseph seem to have just entered and only one doctor on the left has noticed them, turning his head towards them. Jesus may be looking at them or at the doctor next to him – the direction of his glance is ambiguous. That is the point – we are left to work out for ourselves whether or not Jesus is ignoring his parents. Giotto, characteristically has chosen a transitional phase so that we have the sense both of Jesus holding the doctors spellbound by his learning and, at the same time, of his reluctance to respond to his mother's distress. In this way Giotto conveys Jesus' austere refusal to place family before God.

Barna da Siena's version (Fig. 112) in the Collegiata church in San Gimignano tries to liven up the event. An animated seminar is in progress – witness the intensity with which the man on the left leans forward to question Jesus, brows knitted and so absorbed as to be oblivious to the interruption behind him. Jesus' gesture, his finger pointing upwards conveys not only the sense of his answer, 'wist ye not . . . ?' but also suggests that he is raising a finger to his lips to quieten them down. By depicting such energetic intellectual debate Barna's painting conveys the conflict between religious duty and family values with greater immediacy.

Ghiberti seems to have been dissatisfied with all these performances. None fully conveyed the sense of Jesus' divinity and hence of his separation from his parents and from Mary in particular; none therefore really conveyed the richness of the dialogue between Jesus and Mary: her reproach, his answer, and above all the parents' incomprehension of that answer. In addition Ghiberti seems to have been critical of the depiction of the seminar; its intellectual and spiritual character was lacking – the doctors' amazement at the young

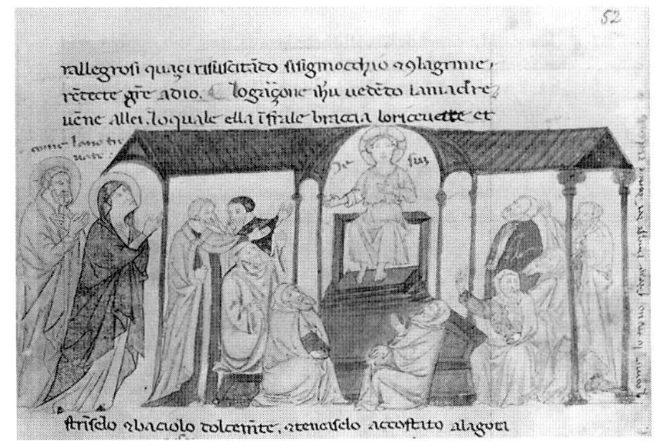

110. Jesus amongst the Doctors, 14th century Italian manuscript, Ms. Ital. 115, Bibliothèque Nationale, Paris.

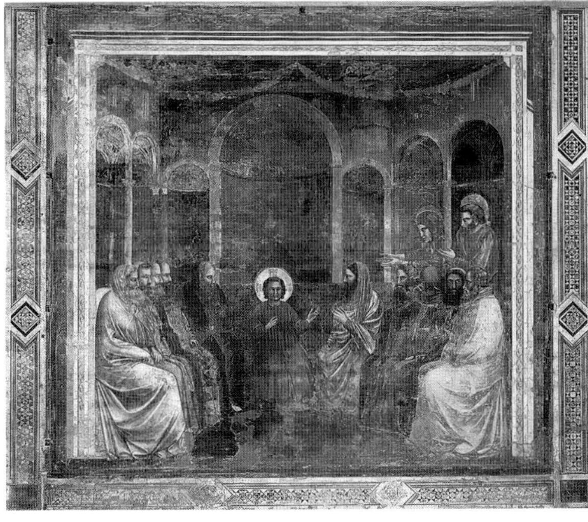

111. Giotto, Jesus amongst the Doctors, Scrovegni Chapel, Padua, middle tier of the north wall, (21, Fig. 18) 1303–5, fresco.

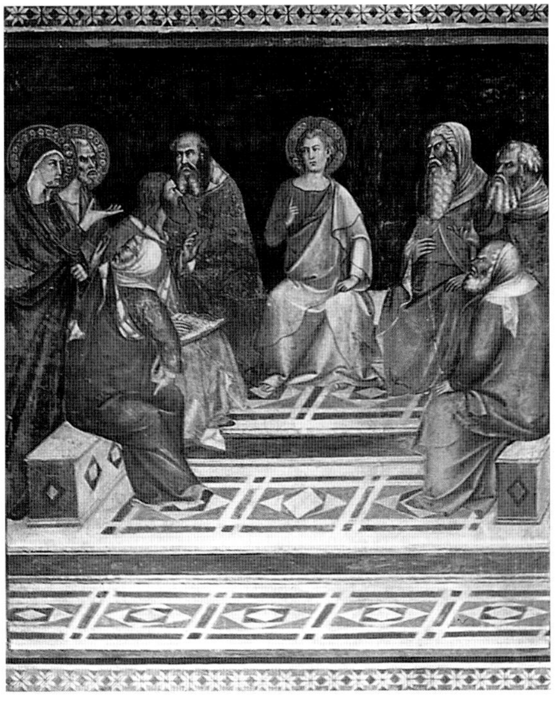

112. Barna da Siena (attrib.), Jesus amongst the Doctors, Chiesa della Collegiata, San Gimignano, fresco, mid. 14th century.

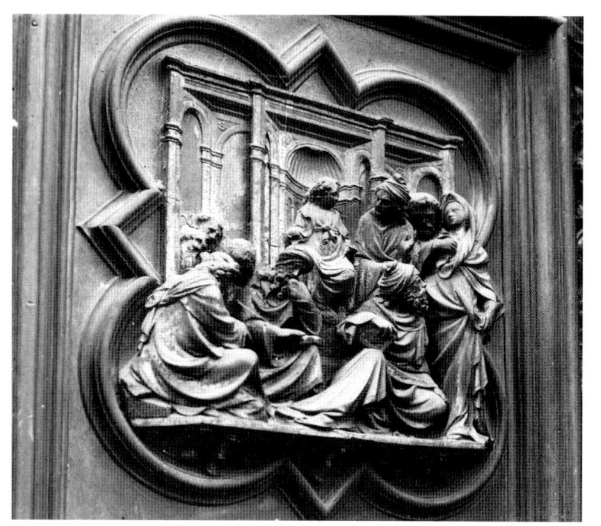

113. Lorenzo Ghiberti, Jesus amongst the Doctors, gilded bronze relief from the North Doors of Florence Baptistery, 1403-24, in situ, photographed from the left.

Jesus' 'prudentia', his knowledge of theology and his sound judgement, at which they are 'struck dumb'. It is perhaps significant that Ghiberti's St Luke (Fig. 2) shows the artist-evangelist carefully studying and collating different texts, a procedure Ghiberti must have followed himself.

Taking a cue perhaps from an illustration like that in a manuscript of the *Meditations* or from Taddeo Gaddi's fresco in Sta Croce, he first raised Jesus upon a throne, a sign of kingship and by analogy of divinity but also the traditional furniture for a teacher. The figure may derive from an early Christian statue whose scroll may symbolise the law. Everything serves to emphasise Jesus' role as teacher, ruler and Son of God. The doctors are not given benches but are seated humbly at Jesus' feet like pupils, again a suggestion which possibly derives from the manuscript illustration. They are in a huddle, deep in discussion between themselves, consulting their books over some profound point of interpretation which the prodigy had raised, and on account of our viewpoint slightly below the relief, we almost feel included among them. We are also led to infer that the bearded and turbaned doctor on the right, who is glaring angrily at the Virgin, has just swung round

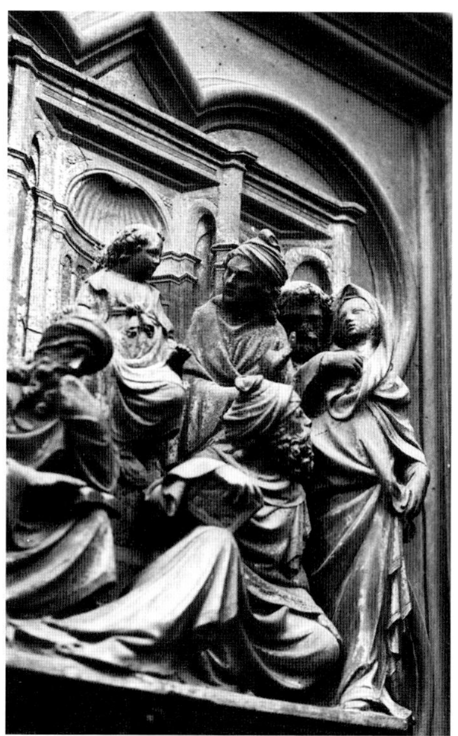

114. Lorenzo Ghiberti, Jesus amongst the Doctors, gilded bronze relief from the North Doors of Florence Baptistery, 1403-24, in situ, detail of old doctor and the Virgin.

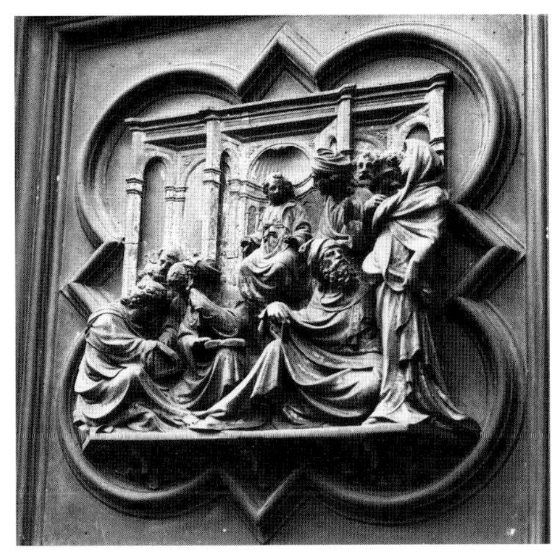

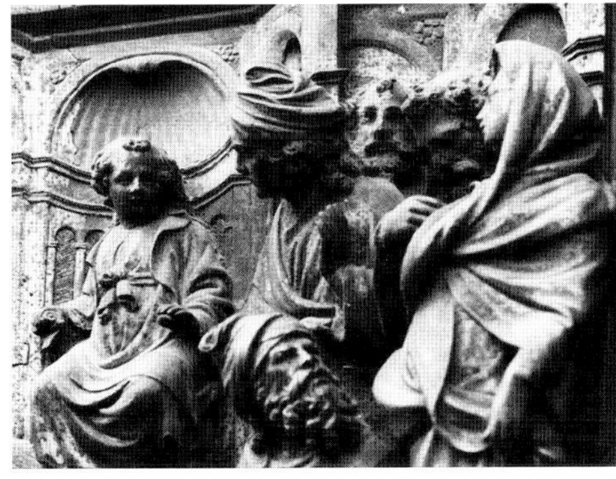

115 (*top*). Lorenzo Ghiberti, Jesus amongst the Doctors, gilded bronze relief from the North Doors of Florence Baptistery, 1403-24, in situ, photographed from the right.

116 (*bottom*). Lorenzo Ghiberti, Jesus amongst the Doctors, detail of Jesus, the steward and the Virgin Mary, gilded bronze relief from the North Doors of Florence Baptistery, 1403-24, in situ, photographed from the right.

on his haunches from his position within the scholarly circle, which earlier he completed: the loop of drapery running from his knee back to the gap in the circle provides a trace of his former position. The effect upon the scholarly proceedings of the Virgin's intrusion, for that is how it is portrayed, has been completely rethought. Where in earlier depictions there were one or two crosspatches looking grumpily at Mary, here we have both the sense of their intense concentration *before* her entry as well as the irritation of the old man whom she has disturbed (Fig. 113). The silent conflict between these two is well portrayed and is not without comedy; the seated, pug-faced, old patriarch, whose viewpoint we share (Fig. 114), having to look up at the upright young woman whose pos-ture and drapery convey not only a sense of intense sorrow but of wou-nded pride – for there lies Ghiberti's other major invention, he has introduced to the story an additional character neither mentioned in the Bible nor found in previous depictions where Mary bursts into the Temple and speaks directly to Jesus. Here she is kept at a distance and *ushered* into his presence by some kind of steward who speaks to Jesus (Fig. 115), his hand waving in the general direction of the Virgin, with all the arrogant deference of such officials (nowadays the PA on the telephone) as if to say, 'There's this woman outside, Sir, who claims to be your mother. Will you see her, Sir?' And Jesus, enthroned in a posture of great dignity and authority regally inclines his head and raises his left hand to indicate both a sense of his own train of thought being interrupted and as if he were saying, 'Just a moment, could you?' Thus the Virgin is trebly snubbed, first by finding Jesus enthroned as a teacher and ruler, second by the old scholar barking at her heels and finally by being made to dance attendance upon her own son enthroned in the hierarchy of his court. No wonder she looks aggrieved. Ghiberti, particularly when one looks at the scene from the right-hand side, from the Virgin's viewpoint (Fig. 116), uses the overlapping figures of Mary, the doctor, the steward and Jesus to suggest the courtly procedure keeping Mary away from her son. This is an exemplary case of the artistic exercise of Devout Meditation.

So powerful is the sense of her exclusion that one imagines that Ghiberti also had in mind Jesus' many commands to his followers to put faith before family, in particular the episode in Mark 3, vv. 31–5 immediately following the calling of the twelve disciples.

> There came then his brethren and his mother, and standing without, sent unto him, calling him. And the multitude set about him and they said unto him, 'Behold, thy mother and thy brethren without seek for thee.' And he answered them, saying, 'Who is my mother, or my brethren?' And he looked round about on them which sat about him, and said, 'Behold my mother and my brethren! For whosoever shall do the will of God, the same is my brother, and my sister, and mother.'

To sum up. The relief of Jesus among the Doctors is but one of many fine performances on these doors. Ghiberti studied the text to imagine exactly how each event occurred, matching its intricacies and significance against the works of his predecessors. These he corrected, or, in the case of the Doctors, he substantially recast the composition so as to suggest a broad time-span within which the event unfolds. In addition he finds means for subdividing the episodes, while compressing them into a single image, hence making the story more fully articulate. Finally he excels not only in scenes of action and the physical expression of emotion like Giovanni, but also, in the psychological expression of inner thoughts, like Giotto. He was fascinated by the psychology and the politics of experience: Abraham playing for time, Jesus holding his mother at bay. Ghiberti displays a somewhat cynical understanding of the world. On the other hand he seems to have been less concerned than Duccio, Giotto or even Giovanni with communicating religious doctrine or abstract ideas, far more interested in the details of how an event happened and what an eyewitness might have seen and experienced. This bent is also evident in Ghiberti's written descriptions of his own works and those of others in his *Commentaries*.[23] Perhaps for this reason we do not find him making much use

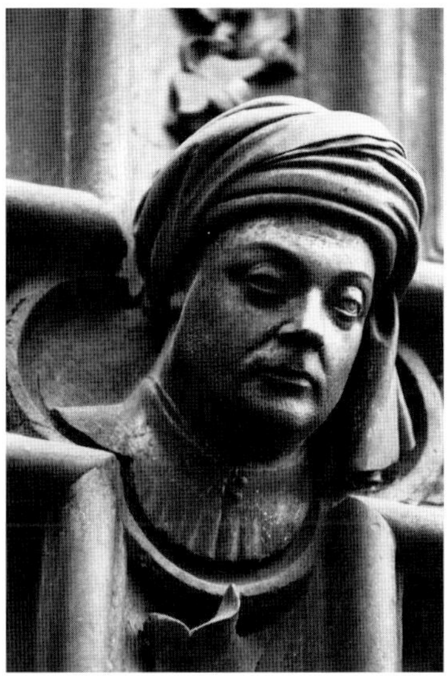

117. Lorenzo Ghiberti, Self Portrait, bronze bust from the North Doors of Florence Baptistery, 1403–24, in situ.

of antithesis. His interest in the logic of an event was restricted to the chain of cause and effect linking episodes together. As we have also noted he tended to employ the pregnant phase. Yet unlike Duccio and Giotto his reliefs on these doors are not intellectually taxing to any great degree, though they do sustain our attention through the intricacy of the story. Although the twenty reliefs form a cycle of the Life of Jesus, Ghiberti treats each panel more as a self-sufficient story than as part of an interlinked sequence of the kind produced by all three artists discussed in Part I.

His approach to many-sided high relief derived from Giovanni Pisano, but Ghiberti enriched it with very low surface relief so that figures and settings sometimes seem to be emerging out of the background. In contrast to Giovanni, moreover, his compositions are not unruly but are tempered by Giotto's disciplined and temperate pictorialism. Finally his figures, for all the voluminous loops and folds which have led some people to see Ghiberti as a somewhat old-fashioned, gothic artist, whatever that means, are correctly proportioned and anatomically articulated with the most subtle gestures to give voice, as it were, to the subject matter. These draperies are often miraculously eloquent as in the case of Lazarus, the Virgin and the Doctors, yet they are similar to Giotto's temperate handling of paint in their overall harmony.

Even so this was the work of Ghiberti's youth, the reliefs were probably completed, but uncast, by 1412, when he was less than thirty-five years old

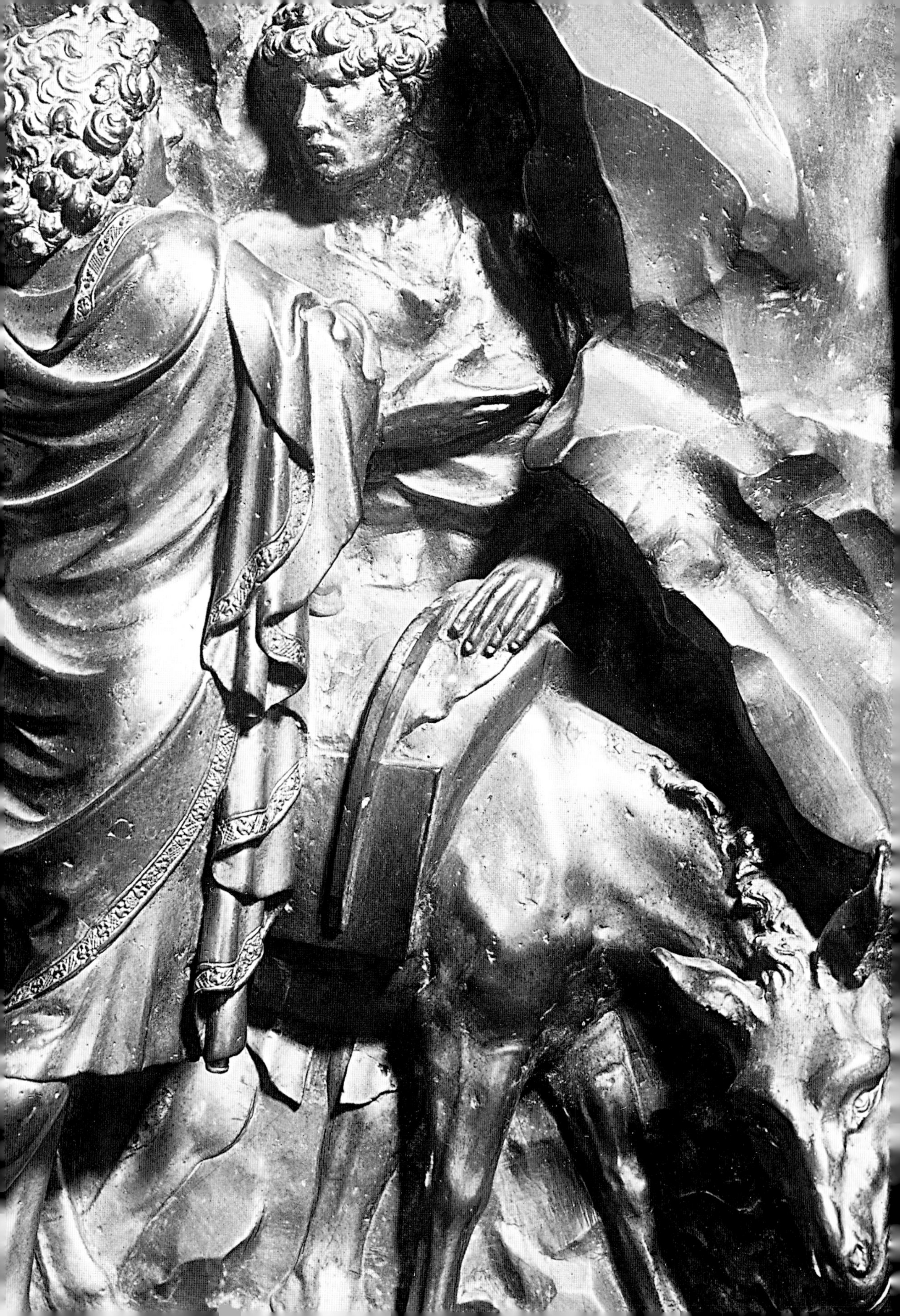

(Fig. 117), even though the doors were not finally erected till 1424.[24] Still to come were his reliefs for the third doors of the Baptistery, the Gates of Paradise, the designs for which were to occupy him for just over a decade in his late forties and fifties. But by that time his own achievements had inspired the competitive and collaborative energies of a younger generation, Donatello and Masaccio. Thus the Gates of Paradise have to be seen not only as a development of Ghiberti's own powers but as a response to Donatello and Masaccio, to whom we now turn.

Detail of Figure 101

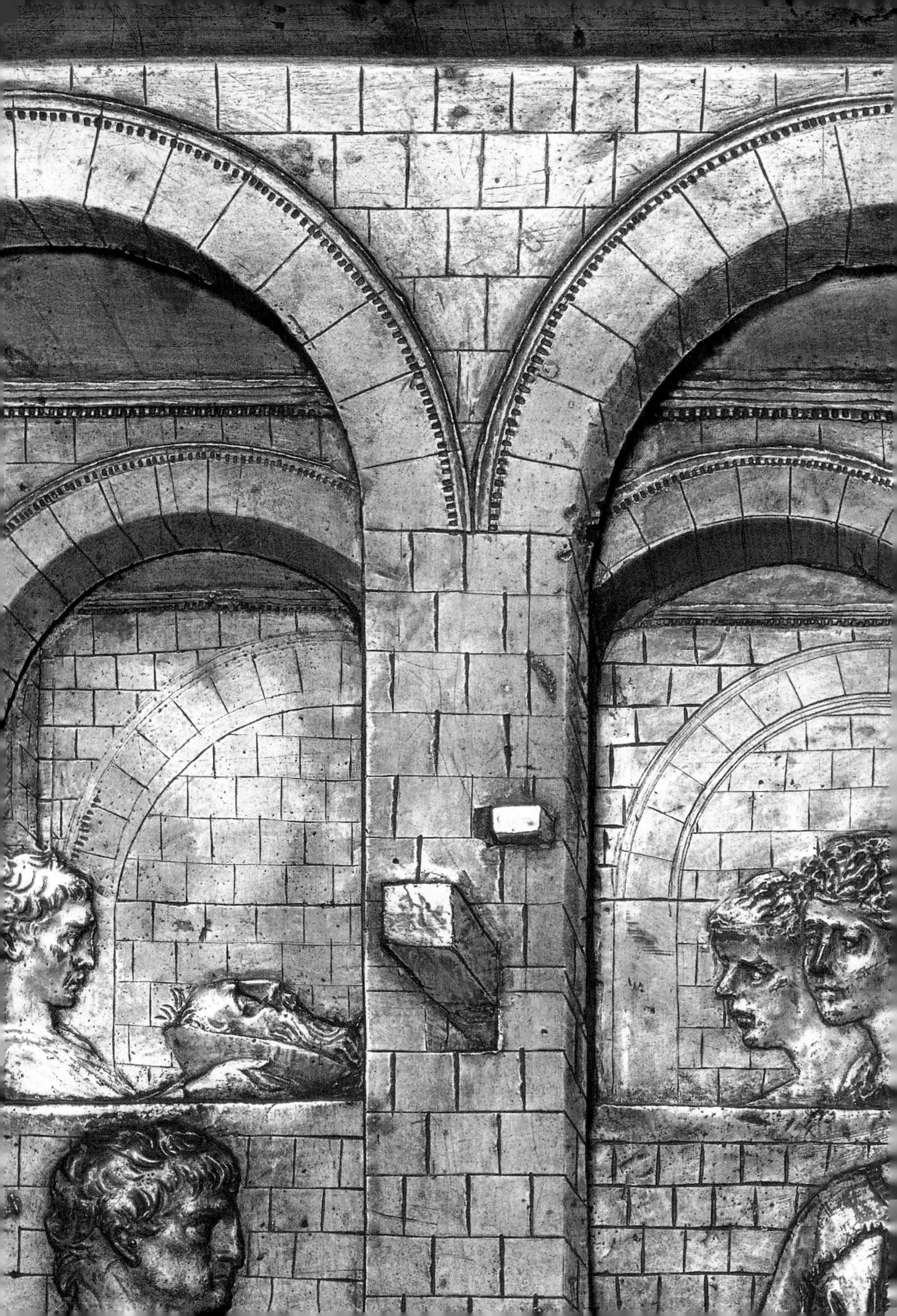

VI

DONATELLO'S HEAD OF ST JOHN AND THE INVENTION OF GEOMETRIC PERSPECTIVE

On 19 April 1424 Ghiberti's gates were ceremonially unveiled on the main door of Florence's Baptistery opposite the West Front of the cathedral. By the start of the following year, Ghiberti had secured the contract to make the Baptistery's third and final pair of bronze doors, apparently without any further competition.[1] Opportunities on this scale to depict the Life of Jesus or the Old Testament story were rare and hard to come by. With few exceptions – the Scrovegni Chapel is one – they were sited on or in the most important churches of a city – a cathedral or baptistery.[2] Donatello, for example, did not get such an opportunity until he was in his seventies. One reason was that such cycles, particularly in bronze, were extremely expensive. Moreover the occasion for such monumental works arose infrequently even during this period of civic expansion and monumental embellishment. Once the Baptistery of Florence was fully equipped with three pairs of bronze gates by the mid-fifteenth century it needed no more, to this day. The bronze doors of Hadrian's Pantheon remain *in situ* after 1800 years. Yet Ghiberti received two such commissions, the only two since the mid fourteenth century and the last until Donatello's aborted project for the doors of Siena Cathedral in the late 1450s and his subsequent pulpits for San Lorenzo, restricted to the Passion and Resurrection.

Detail of Figure 124

In the mid-1420s, however, in the interval between Ghiberti's two sets of doors, Donatello and Masaccio made works in bronze relief and fresco which, although they did not constitute monumental cycles of the Life of Jesus, made very important contributions to the 'debate' about pictorial narrative and particularly to the key issue in 1401 between Brunelleschi's highly focused approach, both visual and temporal, and that of Ghiberti. So they need to be discussed. The works in question are Donatello's bronze relief of the Head of St John being brought to the King's Table for the baptismal font in Siena's Baptistery (Fig. 124), probably made between 1423 and 1425, and Masaccio's contribution to the frescoes in the Brancacci family chapel painted between 1422 and 1428 (Figs 127, 130 and 132). These works are generally regarded as the first manifestations of a coherent geometric perspective construction, and of images where the central vanishing point plays a major role in their composition.[3] The question of who invented the geometrical perspective construction, if any single person were responsible, and when this happened, is inescapable in providing an account of these works. The consensus is that Brunelleschi was its inventor, probably some time in the early to mid-1420s, and that he worked in close collaboration with the two younger artists helping them to apply his system to their images, as well as assisting in their representation of architecture.[4] Supposedly his system was similar to that described in *De pictura* published subsequently in 1435 by Alberti, who should be regarded as Brunelleschi's mouthpiece. The collaboration between the three artists is moreover seen as constituting some kind of avant-garde to which Ghiberti did not belong. Indeed one is given the impression that there was vigorous competition, even hostility, between the conservative Ghiberti, attached to the International Gothic Style, and the innovators of the Renaissance.

That is not my sense of the situation. There is no evidence for a 'eureka' moment when Brunelleschi, or anyone else before 1435, discovered the geometrical perspective construction. Indeed, there is no primary documentary evidence other than that of the works themselves and Alberti's *De pictura*. What seems to be the case is that Ghiberti, Masaccio, Donatello and maybe Brunelleschi, were all experimenting with ways of making the relationship between figures and setting more plausible and naturalistic in relief sculpture and in painting; so too were the Salimbeni brothers, Sassetta, Gentile da Fabriano and Masolino.[5] But this did not necessarily involve the systematic application of geometric perspective, which, as we shall see, is not fully in evidence in the work of Donatello and Masaccio. People find it there because the conventional history of perspective encourages them to do so. Surprisingly, there is no primary evidence of Brunelleschi's involvement either in the invention of the technique or of his collaboration with Donatello and Masaccio in their designs. Because geometric perspective is considered to play so important a part in the composition of the narrative image and has held such a pivotal role in the scholarly commentary upon this important group of works, a digression is necessary to distinguish between what is certain, what is probable, what is possible, what is uncertain and what is conjectural.

Who invented geometric perspective and when?

First it is necessary to define what is meant by the 'correct geometric perspective construction', or the *construzione legittima* as Erwin Panofsky called it.[6] This is a method, using a geometric construction alone, for representing on a picture plane the appearance of a pavement of square tiles diminishing in size correctly according to their distance from the spectator (Fig. 118). While it involves the convergence to a single point (or the centric point, to use Alberti's term) of all lines at right angles to the picture surface, often called orthogonals or later vanishing lines, that is only a necessary but not a sufficient feature of the construction. The merit of the technique lies in the fact that it enables an artist to represent accurately the apparent diminution in size of all figures and objects in the picture so that wherever they are placed, laterally or in depth, they will be in scale with one another. There is no dispute that the method was first explained in writing in Book 1 of Alberti's 1435 *De Pictura* [On Painting]. What is at issue is whether the method was Alberti's own invention or whether, in the view indicated above, it had been invented earlier by Brunelleschi, then applied, with his assistance, by Donatello and Masaccio to their works of the 1420s, and that Alberti subsequently explained that technique in writing.

As already stated, there is no primary documentary or material evidence to support the claim that Brunelleschi was the inventor of geometric perspective, nor that he assisted Masaccio and Donatello in their use of perspective. That ought really to settle the matter even though the absence of hard evidence does not, of course, rule out either possibility. The burden of proof should be upon those who support Brunelleschi's claims. The myth of Brunelleschi's role, however, is so deeply embedded in the history of art, goes back so far and has been so greatly elaborated by distinguished scholars since the early twentieth century that in a field of such significance it is prudent to treat secondary sources with caution and stick to what primary contemporary evidence, material and documentary, is known to survive. In chronological order this is:

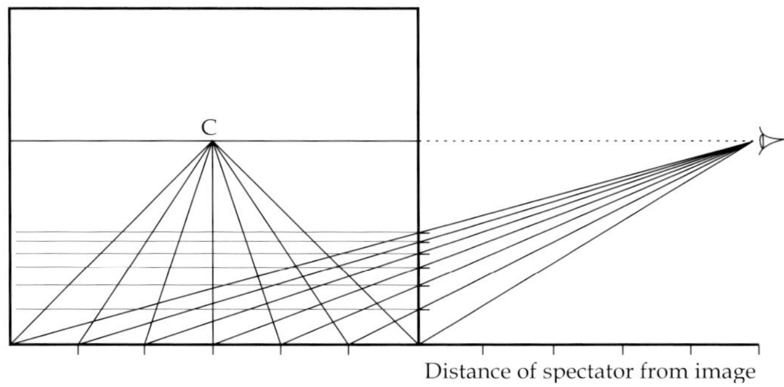

118. Diagram of the correct perspective construction, 'costruzione legittima' described by Alberti in *De Pictura* [On Painting], 1435. First one draws a rectangle – the picture surface – equivalent to a window through which the subject is seen. One divides the bottom line into divisions corresponding, in scale, to one third of the height of a man, about two feet - the Florentine braccia. One places the centric point C at the height of a man, three divisions, above the base line and draws straight lines from C to the divisions. These lines represent the receding or orthogonal lines of a pavement of squares tiles. In order to establish the correct diminution of these tiles according to the spectator's distance from the picture surface, Alberti claimed to have invented the following method. One places a point, representing the eye of the spectator at the same height as the centric point above the extended base line. If, for example, one intends the spectator to be standing five braccia, or ten feet, from the window, as in this diagram, then the point is placed five divisions distant from the side of the rectangle. One then draws straight lines from the spectator's eye to the divisions on the base line. Where these intersect with the right-hand side of the rectangle, one draws lines parallel to the bottom line of the rectangle. The intersections of these lines with the receding lines establish the apparent diminution in the size of the squares of the pavement. If the spectator were to stand further away then the squares would diminish more rapidly. Using this method any figure or object can be represented in scale with its surroundings according to its distance from the spectator.

1. A letter of 6 August 1413 from a poet Domenico di Prato, refers to his interest in some perspectives by Brunelleschi, who is described as a 'clever man . . . remarkable for his merit and fame'.[7] This is the *only* primary evidence, documentary or material, dating from Brunelleschi's lifetime to link him with perspective of any kind. But the nature of Brunelleschi's perspective is not described. Perspective was a term in common use, meaning optics in general, and did not necessarily imply what has come to be known as the 'correct geometrical construction'.
2. In the years 1423–5 Donatello was probably working on his bronze relief of the Head of St John (Fig. 124) for the Baptistery font in Siena which shows a tiled pavement with receding lines.[8]
3. In 1426 Masaccio painted an altarpiece for the Carmelite Church in Pisa, the Pisa Altarpiece, whose surviving central section shows the Virgin seated on a throne whose orthogonals converge to a central area.[9]
4. Sometime between 1422 and 1428 Masaccio and Masolino were painting frescoes (Fig. 133), which include perspectives with converging lines,* for the Brancacci family chapel in Sta Maria del Carmine in Florence. While there is no document confirming this, the Brancacci Chapel is universally accepted as their work and there is no reason to doubt that.[10]
5. At an unspecified date before his death in Rome probably in 1428, Masaccio painted a fresco of the Trinity in Sta Maria Novella. Here the convergence of the orthogonals approximates more closely to a point. This has been widely claimed as the first fully systematic application of Brunelleschi's new method.[11]
6. Between 1425 and 1436/7 Ghiberti was working on the designs and wax models of the ten bronze narrative panels for the third doors of the Florentine Baptistery. These had all been cast by the latter date.[12]
7. Leon Battista Alberti probably finished *De pictura* in August 1435. Book 1 contains the first written account of the 'correct geometrical construction' for perspective. Book 2 provides instructions for two other methods, the veil and the circumscribed-rectangle method.[13]
8. A year later in 1436 Alberti made an Italian translation, *Della pittura*, of *De Pictura*, which he dedicated to Brunelleschi in a letter. He says that he had 'recognized in many, but above all in you, Filippo, and in our greatest friend the sculptor Donatello, and in the others, Nencio (Ghiberti), Luca (della Robbia) and Masaccio, a skill for every laudable enterprise in no way infe-

*This term is used to refer to orthogonals which converge to a general central area though not to a single point.

rior to any of the ancients who gained fame in these arts.'[14] He claims to have *translated* his Latin text into Italian for Brunelleschi[15] and asks him to suggest any corrections.

In addition to this contemporary evidence there are, to my knowledge, seven subsequent written accounts of the invention of geometric perspective dating from between the mid-fifteenth and the mid-sixteenth centuries. Selective quotation from some of these has been the basis for the Brunelleschian foundation myth enshrined in more recent histories.

1. Between 1460 and 1464 the architect and sculptor Antonio de Piero Averlino, known as Filarete, published his *Treatise on Architecture*. He provides an accurate account of Alberti's perspective construction, correctly attributed, and one manuscript includes a delicate line drawing of Alberti's diagram, probably the earliest such drawing.[16] In answering a question raised by his fictional pupil as to why the squared paving stones do not appear as squares in the perspective projection, Filarete explains that 'it is because you see these things on a plane [the picture plane]. If you saw them frontally i.e. looking down on them from above] they would appear to be squares to you. To prove that this is so, look at the pavement where square pieces of wood have been spread out, or better look at a ceiling from below (Figs 119-20). All the beams are equidistant, the one from the other [i.e. parallel and equally spaced]. To the sight they seem to be more and less. Where they are close to you they appear to be more equal, and when they are further from you the more they seem to gather together, one on top of the other so that they all seem to be one. If you wish to consider this more closely, take a mirror and look at them in it. You will see clearly that this is so . . . I believe that [*credo che*] Pippo di Ser Brunellesco, the Florentine, discovered the method of making the plane in this way. It certainly was a subtle and beautiful thing to discover the rule for what the mirror shows you.'[17]
2. Around 1480, over thirty years after Brunelleschi's death in 1446, his biography was written, probably by Antonio Manetti. It claims that Brunelleschi developed in his youth, before the 1401 Baptistery competition, the 'science' of perspective which deals with 'setting down properly and rationally the diminution and increase in the apparent size both of near and distant objects as they appear to the eye . . . according to their distance from the spectator'. Manetti claims without qualification that Brunelleschi gave birth to the rule followed in these matters ever since. Manetti also describes in great detail two peepshows which he claims were made by Brunelleschi, the first of the Florence Baptistery and the second of the

Palazzo dei Signori. The same author was probably responsible for a subsequent brief life of Brunelleschi.[18]

3. In 1481 Cristoforo Landino, a Florentine humanist and friend of Alberti, wrote of him, 'What branch of mathematics did he not know? He was geometrician, arithmetrician, astronomer, musician, and more admirable in perspective than any man for many centuries.'[19] On Brunelleschi's role in the discovery of perspective, Landino cautiously observes that 'the architect Brunelleschi was also very good at painting and sculpture; in particular he understood perspective well, and some people maintain that he was either the inventor or the rediscoverer of it . . .'[20]
4. The *Libro di Antonio Billi*, probably written between 1516 and 1530, states that Brunelleschi rediscovered perspective and made perspectives of the Baptistery and the Palazzo dei Priori; that he collaborated with Donatello on the statues of St Mark and St Peter for Or San Michele, and that he was a close friend of Masaccio, whom he taught many things. Donatello is said to have understood perspective very well.[21]
5. Two decades or so later, the anonymous *Codice Magliabechiano*, probably dating from between 1537 to 1546, more or less repeats the statements in the *Libro di Antonio Billi*.[22]
6. Shortly after, Vasari, in the first, 1550, edition of his *Lives of the Artists*, credits Brunelleschi with the discovery of a method of perspective using ground plans, sections and the intersection. Vasari links this directly with the two peepshows mentioned by Manetti, which he describes.[23] Following the *Libro di Antonio Billi* and the *Codice Magliabechiano*, Vasari also claims that Brunelleschi was a close friend of the young Masaccio, but is more specific about what Brunelleschi taught Masaccio, namely perspective, 'as can be seen in the buildings in his works'.[24] In addition Vasari claims that Brunelleschi and Donatello were extremely close friends, but does not claim that Brunelleschi taught Donatello perspective. Alberti is criticised for being too bookish and insufficiently practical, and his role in the discovery of perspective is virtually dismissed.[25]
7. In the second, 1568, edition of the *Lives*, however, Vasari credits Uccello with 'having brought to perfection' the method of perspective using ground plans and sections, 'through the intersection of lines, making them foreshorten and diminish to a centre, having first fixed how high or low one wishes to have the viewpoint . . . so that he introduced the means, the method and the rule for placing figures on the plane, so that they stand on their feet, so that they are foreshortened and diminish in proportion, which previously had been done in an unsystematic fashion.[26] In other words, in the 1568 edition, Vasari seems to give Uccello the credit for finally

systematising central point construction, and Brunelleschi the credit only for the use of ground plans and sections.

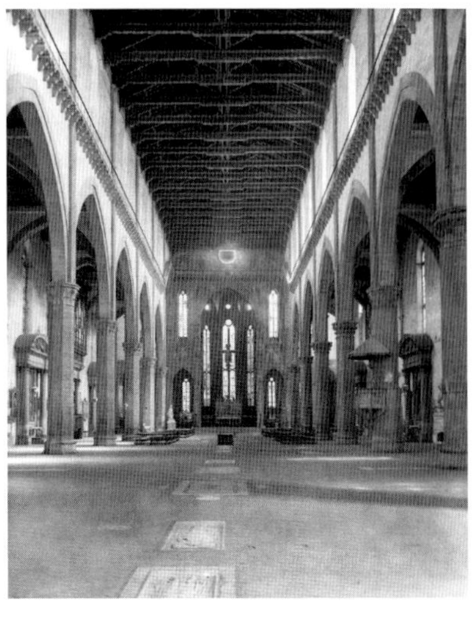

119. The nave of S. Croce, Florence, 1294–1385. The diminution of the apparent distance between the roof beams that run from side to side of the nave of S. Croce may have been the basis for Brunelleschi's observation reported by Filarete.

Apart from Filarete's description of Alberti's perspective construction and Landino's statement about Alberti's prowess in perspective, none of these statements in the early secondary literature can be corroborated by any surviving primary documents or material evidence. The peepshows do not survive and are not mentioned at all in the earliest, and arguably most accurate, account of the discovery, written by Filarete. Among the fifteenth-century sources only Manetti states unequivocally that Brunelleschi discovered perspective, but Manetti's description of the rule lacks specificity, while he provides no clear account of the method used to make the peepshows. Furthermore, Filarete's statement that he 'believes that' Brunelleschi discovered the method of 'making the plane' by looking at the diminution of the distance between ceiling beams parallel to the picture plane requires careful interpretation. He explains that when one looks 'at a ceiling from below: all the beams are equidistant, the one from the other [i.e. parallel and equally spaced]. To the sight they seem to be more and less. Where they are close to you they appear to be more equal, and when they are further from you the more they seem to draw together, one on top of the other so that they all seem to be one.' This must refer to roof beams running *across* the width of a room at right angles to one's line of sight and hence *parallel* to the picture plane (Figs 119–20). The distance between the beams seems to get closer and closer the further away they are from the spectator until 'they all seem to be one'.

This (Fig. 120) cannot refer to the convergence to a point of vanishing lines (Fig. 121), of parallel rafters running along the length of a room, parallel to one's line of sight, because Filarete is unequivocally talking about beams which appear to converge not in a point but in a line, which would be absurd, especially as an empirical observation. While it is true that the apparent diminution of the distance between the beams is indeed the crucial issue for which Alberti's construction provided the answer, Filarete only credits

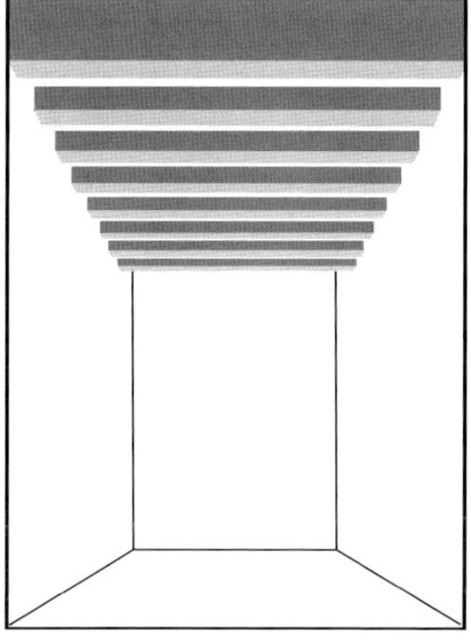

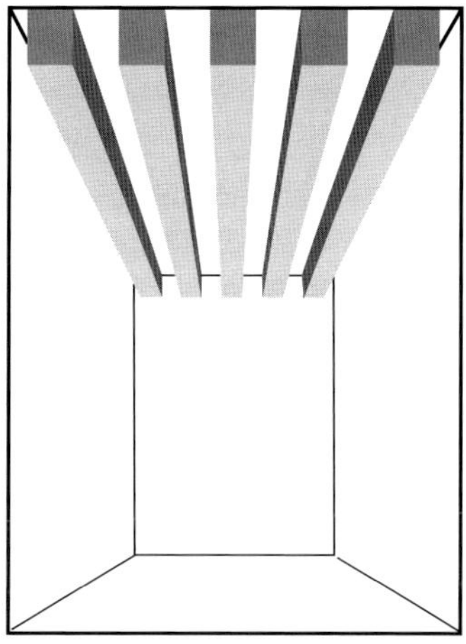

120 (*above left*). Diagram, corresponding to Fig.119, showing the diminution of the distance between traverse beams.

121 (*above right*). Diagram showing the convergence of beams at right angles to the picture surface.

Brunelleschi with the empirical observation using a mirror, not with the geometric construction.[27]

Given, moreover, that Filarete's treatise, the only other contemporary book on architecture apart from Alberti's *De re aedificatoria*, appeared during Alberti's lifetime, Filarete's caution is surely significant: he only 'believes' – 'credo che' – that Brunelleschi discovered the method. In any case, Filarete firmly attributes the geometric construction to Alberti.[28] Landino, scholar that he was, introduces Brunelleschi's claim with the still more cautious phrase 'some people maintain that'.[29] Vasari, however, accepts Brunelleschi's claim in 1550 but not to the geometric construction; in 1568 Uccello is given the credit for a method in which lines diminish to a point depending upon the position of the spectator, yet Vasari's account of that method is vague. Vasari also introduces the idea that Brunelleschi taught perspective to Masaccio who was, along with Donatello, a close friend. This, along with the statements in the *Libro di Antonio Billi*, is the source of the current idea that these three formed some kind of avant-garde. Vasari's account is second-hand and cannot be substantiated.

Only one document dating from Brunelleschi's lifetime, the 1413 letter, connects Brunelleschi directly with some, albeit unspecified, form of perspective in a period when many artists were experimenting with means of creating greater optical veracity in the depiction of the human figure and its relationship to landscapes and buildings.[30] There is no positive, primary contemporary evidence that Brunelleschi was the inventor of the geometric perspective construction. His claim depends upon vague statements, which often contradict one another, made several decades and over a century after his death in 1446.[31]

The case for Brunelleschi, however, is seriously undermined by one crucial piece of primary evidence and that happens to be the only other incontrovertibly dated document relating to this issue that we possess from Brunelleschi's lifetime: Alberti's dedicatory letter of 1436 to Brunelleschi in *Della pittura*. Several writers have had to explain away this negative evidence. In spite of lavish praise for Brunelleschi's achievements and the implicit assumption of close friendship with him, Alberti does not acknowledge Brunelleschi's contribution to the system set out in *De pictura*, nor to any other, neither does he make any statement to the effect that he, Alberti, is simply acting as the spokesman or mouthpiece of the real inventor, Brunelleschi.[32] According to Manetti, his admittedly unreliable biographer, whose testimony is in this instance confirmed, Brunelleschi was a notably prickly character who was highly secretive about and protective of his inventions, for which he was one of the first to try to obtain patent protection,[33] and of his architectural designs, which he kept as secret as possible to prevent others from stealing his ideas or claiming credit for them. If so, it is especially hard to believe that Alberti, in a public document addressed directly to Brunelleschi in the very year of the consecration of Florence's Duomo and of Brunelleschi's personal triumph in raising the cupola,[34] would have claimed personal credit for the perspective construction if that discovery were Brunelleschi's. At the very least, in giving his own exposition Alberti would surely have credited Brunelleschi if that were the real state of affairs.[35]

There is, therefore, not only an absence of any firm textual or documentary evidence to support Brunelleschi as the inventor of geometric perspective, but the only piece of primary evidence we do possess enabling us to attribute the discovery to a specific individual, counts strongly against Brunelleschi's claim and in favour of Alberti.[36]

In addition Alberti makes an unequivocal claim in Book 1 that he is the first person to deal with this difficult subject 'which as far as I can see has not before been treated in writing by anyone else'.[37] He also takes great care to be quite specific and limited in his claims for his construction. He does not claim to be the first person to employ a centric point, as he calls it, to which the orthogonals converge. As we have seen, Masaccio steadily developed towards this and possibly achieved it in his Trinity.[38] Alberti carefully but firmly restricts his claim to having invented a geometric construction for accurately representing the diminution in the apparent size of an imaginary pavement of square paving stones laid parallel to the baseline of the picture.[39] His method (Fig. 118 above) was to use a cross-section through the picture plane to relate the apparent distance between the tiles to the spectator's position. While Masaccio progressively developed the convergence of orthogonals towards a vanishing point, he did not employ a consistent method for establishing diminution, nor did Donatello or anyone else at this time. In Book 2 dealing with composition, Alberti also makes the implicit claim that his method will ensure that figures will be accurately proportionate to the buildings in which they are set.

> Another thing I often see deserves to be censured, and that is men painted in a building as if they were shut upon in a box in which they can hardly fit sitting down and rolled up in a ball.[40]

There are many inconsistencies of scale between figures and buildings in these works by Masaccio and Donatello (Figs 124, 127, 130 and 132), and although they handled the problem better than Ghiberti in the second doors (Figs 105 and 109) they do not appear to have used a geometric construction like Alberti's; certainly they did not apply such a construction consistently through the whole field of the image. This also indicates that Alberti was not putting in writing a method already in use.

We come next to the question of the two peepshows attributed to Brunelleschi by Manetti.[41] There is no evidence for Manetti's claim that either of these was the product of any rule or system. The first panel could well have been an empirically drawn picture of Florence's Baptistery, certainly made with great precision, possibly using one eye and maybe utilising some kind of trigonometrical system and apparatus.[42] Nonetheless, highly detailed and accurate representations of buildings and urban space were nothing new. Manetti is silent about the nature of any of the techniques which Brunelleschi employed. The image was apparently made from a fixed position, three *braccie* or about six feet inside the central door of the cathedral in Manetti's estimation. It was designed to be viewed, using a hand-held mirror, from a distance 'more or less' corresponding, in scale with the size of the drawing, to the distance from the draughtsman's original vantage point to the Baptistery. But the crucial point is that this was a *view* of an existing building for which geometric perspective is not necessarily required and to which perspective is indeed difficult to apply, as well as being not absolutely necessary.[43] There is simply no evidence that any perspective *construction* was employed. Geometric perspective may be required to represent an imaginary building. Nonetheless Manetti's description indicates that the painting involved a fixed viewpoint, and hence a fixed distance both between the draughtsman and the object, and a corresponding but only approximately fixed distance between the spectator and the panel. The crucial step in the invention of the perspective construction, however, was to provide a method involving a set of geometric rules and procedures for the establishment of a perspectival framework, enabling one to represent the apparent size of objects, buildings, people, animals or nature in an imaginary scheme, as they appear to the eye according to their distance from the spectator. This is what Alberti provided in *De pictura* (Fig. 118). There is no evidence that such a system was employed in the peepshows.

It is also important to emphasise that the peepshows presented views of a free-standing or nearly free-standing building, of irregular shape. The view of the Palazzo dei Signori, moreover, was an oblique one. Orthogonals and transversals would have been barely in evidence. There are a host of very good depictions of buildings and urban space from Ambrogio Lorenzetti's cityscape of 1338–40 onwards, including the Andrea da Firenze image of the painters' and goldsmiths' model for the Florence Duomo in the Spanish Chapel of Sta Maria Novella, Altichiero's frescoes in Padua of the 1370s, and Agnolo Gaddi's Legend of the True Cross in Sta Croce of around 1390. Fine, detailed and naturalistic, they nonetheless lack the framed focus of the system developed by Donatello and Masaccio in the 1420s. The view through a 'window' and the alignment of its base with the pavement or ground plane is also necessary to Alberti's construction. Manetti's descriptions indicate that neither of these features was present in the peepshows. What is more, the peepshows, as described, did not include people, and the key feature of the new construction was that it enabled figures to be represented in proportion to their surroundings. Related to that, there seems to have been almost no overlapping of one form by another, also absent in Brunelleschi's competition relief (Fig. 99), but which was central to all other painting and sculpture from Giovanni Pisano to Donatello. Manetti describes unimpeded views of the Baptistery and the Palazzo dei Signori, such as one might expect from an architect.

Returning finally to the status of Manetti's description as evidence concerning the peepshows: we only have his descriptions and his word that Brunelleschi made them. There is no corroborative evidence for Brunelleschi's authorship. Surprisingly, they are not mentioned by Filarete who is the earliest to sketch an account of the history of perspective,[44] nor in any other early source. The panels themselves do not survive. However, because Manetti describes them in such detail and claims to have held the view of the

Baptistery in his hands and 'seen it many times in my days and can testify to it', it seems certain that the panels did exist.[45] But with only Manetti's description to go on, it is hard to infer much about the originals, although many have tried. The peepshows may have little bearing if any upon the geometric construction, their authorship is uncertain and their date is unknown. It would be pure conjecture to link them with Domenici di Prato's letter of 1413. Perhaps they were made after 1436, which would be consistent with Alberti's silence in his letter of dedication. Finally, as we have seen, Brunelleschi's 1401 competition relief exhibits little interest in perspective beyond the suggestion of a fixed eye-level. Like Ghiberti he showed no interest in a view through a window or frame.

Turning to Brunelleschi's supposed collaboration with Donatello or Masaccio on their works of the mid-1420s: there is no documentary evidence for this, which derives from the unsubstantiated statements in the *Libro di Antonio Billi* and Vasari's *Lives* a century or more later, and from more recent conjecture. Yet there is documentary evidence of the key protagonists working together at various dates in the first three decades of the fifteenth century, though not on perspective. Donatello, Masolino and Uccello all worked for Ghiberti on the second set of Baptistery doors after 1407. In 1415 Donatello and Brunelleschi worked together on making a 'little figure in stone, clad in lead gilt' as a test piece for large statues for the buttresses of Florence Cathedral.[46] In 1418 Brunelleschi was assisted by Donatello and Nanni di Banco on his model for the cupola of Florence's Cathedral.[47] Brunelleschi and Ghiberti collaborated as well as competed on the design of the cupola. In 1426, while Masaccio was working on the Pisa Altarpiece, Donatello was in that city and drew money on Masaccio's behalf on two occasions, which implies some relationship between the two artists, though of what kind it is impossible to say.[48] There is also the strong suggestion in Alberti's dedicatory letter to *Della pittura* that Alberti, Brunelleschi and Donatello were close friends or associates and that they admired the achievements of Ghiberti, Luca della Robbia and the deceased Masaccio.[49]

When, moreover, we examine the architectural settings in these works of the mid-1420s, the internal visual evidence provides no support for the idea that Brunelleschi had any hand in their design, in fact it counts against it. The evocative and bizarre architecture of Donatello's Head of St John (Fig. 124) has nothing in common with Brunelleschi's architecture. In Masaccio's Pisa Altarpiece, the top-heavy, two-storey design of the Virgin's throne, flanked on either side with an attached Corinthian column supporting a cornice on which there stands a pair of half-size attached columns, is without parallel in any of Brunelleschi's works. The framework of Corinthian pilasters and the dentilated cornices surrounding all the frescoes in the Brancacci Chapel (Fig. 133) are simply classical in the most general way and cannot be described as specifically Brunelleschian.[50] The architectural settings within the frescoes are almost entirely generic depictions of the Florentine townscape, with the exception of the palace of Theophilus (Fig. 130) which is more classical, but again dissimilar to any building by Brunelleschi.

The strongest claim for Brunelleschi's collaboration rests upon the architecture of Masaccio's Trinity. Once again, however, neither the monumental Roman character nor such details as the Greek key decoration of the frieze, the coffered barrel vault, the strange Ionic capitals of the attached columns, and the design of the roundels set between the arch and the entablature belong either to Brunelleschi's system of design or to his lexicon of ornament.[51] The Corinthian pilasters, however, are close to those on Brunelleschi's Innocenti Loggia, and the Ionic capitals of the attached columns are similar, but far from identical to those in the Barbadori Chapel in Sta Felicità, probably by Brunelleschi and probably built between 1419 and 1427,[52] but also to those of the Guelph Party niche possibly by Donatello from 1423–5.[53] They are similar, certainly, but markedly different in design. In the absence, therefore, of any authoritative textual documents, this negative evidence, visual and stylistic, is compelling. All that can be said of the Trinity is that Masaccio, like the designer of the Guelph niche, used elements of the newly fashionable Brunelleschian *al antico* style and other classical elements to create a chamber classical in character.

The conclusion to be drawn from the evidence of architectural style is that there is nothing to support the hypothesis that Brunelleschi contributed to the architectural features of these works. It follows that he was unlikely to have had any hand in the perspectives.

By a process of elimination, therefore, it is probable that Donatello and Masaccio worked out their own methods for creating a more convincing sense of diminution and sense of scale as well as greater naturalism, and that they designed their own architecture. There is no evidence that they collaborated with one another, though they might have done so. Most significant, however, is that the perspective in these works does not constitute an overall geometric system, but applies elements of earlier perspective derived from Giotto, Giovanni Pisano, Ambrogio and Pietro Lorenzetti, Andrea Orcagna, Ghiberti himself as well as the contemporary work of Gentile da Fabriano and possibly Sassetta, together with an increasingly close approximation to a central vanishing point. This will become apparent when we examine the works in detail.

There is a weak argument for Brunelleschi's involvement and a strong one. The weak one is that Brunelleschi worked alongside Donatello and Masaccio at each stage. But what we find over a period of about ten years is a step-by-step development from the relative clumsiness of Donatello's relief of St George and the Dragon, through the increasing sophistication of the Head of St John and Masaccio's Pisa Altarpiece, to the Trinity.[54] If Brunelleschi were involved in this somewhat fumbling development towards convergence of orthogonals in a point, it would indicate that he was no further advanced than the other two. In the absence of evidence it is unnecessary to posit his involvement. The strong claim, on the other hand, is that Brunelleschi had a 'eureka moment' and that he instructed the younger artists in his new method. But the evidence of gradual development in their works, rules out that possibility.

In the absence of any evidence to the contrary, and there is always the possibility that new evidence may come to light, we can say with some assurance that in 1435 Alberti was not putting Brunelleschi's earlier discoveries into writing, let alone those of Masaccio or Donatello; Alberti was introducing his own geometric construction in order to remove a fundamental shortcoming from the vanishing area procedure which had been employed. A single system of geometrical perspective, invented by Brunelleschi or by anyone else simply did not exist before 1435. Moreover, it is probably misguided to think in terms of a single *construzione legittima* or of a single inventor at this time.[55] There were several competing and complementary methods. There had to be. For example – Alberti's geometric perspective is of little help in the foreshortening of figures or of complex architectural forms. Because of this Alberti, himself, provides instructions for three different methods in *De pictura*: the geometric construction, the veil and another system later adopted by Piero della Francesca for translating a geometric figure such as a circle onto a foreshortened surface. It must not be forgotten, either, that perspective geometry is only one of many cues which suggest the distance of an object from the spectator and its diminution in apparent size, as will be apparent in the analysis of the works themselves.*

There remains the question of what Brunelleschi's experiments in perspective, referred to in the 1413 letter, might have been. While that is not strictly relevant to the subject of this book it is reasonable to outline an approach to the problem. We know for certain that he produced something,

*See Appendix.

though not what, in 1413, and he probably made the peepshows, though we don't know when – as already mentioned, they might have been made after 1436. Filarete tells us that, using a mirror, Brunelleschi made an empirical observation of the diminution of the apparent distance between transverse rafters – perhaps those in S. Croce (Fig. 119). Beyond that we must admit that, in the absence of further evidence, we simply cannot say for certain what exactly he did or what influence he had upon his contemporaries. It is best to assemble the available evidence while resisting the all-too-human craving to force the pieces of the jigsaw into a picture, especially when so many pieces are missing.

Laborious though it has been to clear the ground in this way, it nonetheless makes it possible to examine the works by Masaccio, Donatello and Ghiberti between the mid-1420s and the mid-1430s empirically, without preconceptions about the type of perspective employed or its implications for composition.

The Head of St John being brought to the King's Table

Donatello's bronze relief of 1423–5 (Fig. 124) is one of six on the hexagonal font in Siena Baptistery (Fig. 122), to which Ghiberti himself contributed two panels: the Baptism and the Arrest of the Baptist (Fig. 123), possibly cast by 1420, which precede Donatello's in the sequence on the font. None of the Florentine reliefs appears to have been delivered until 1427, much to the fury of the Sienese.[56] This commission placed Donatello in competition with the older artist, for whom he had worked as a well-paid assistant on the second doors of the Florence Baptistery fifteen years earlier. One should not, however, exaggerate the conflict; Donatello seems to have designed reliefs to fit in with Ghiberti's. A comparison of the two works indicates that Donatello echoed the three arches of Ghiberti's depiction of Herod's court in the three main arches of Herod's banqueting chamber. When we stand in front of the Arrest of the Baptist with the Head of St John to our right, Donatello's use of low relief helps to distance the Head of St John from the earlier episode both in place and time. Finally, it is notable that Donatello so angled the head of Herodias's daughter that she is looking directly at a spectator positioned in front of the Trial. Thus, despite his innovative use of the window frame, of very low relief and greater perspectival coherence, Donatello also made the effort to harmonise his relief with its neighbour. Since the font itself was incomplete at the time, and both artists were working in Florence, this suggests some degree of collaboration as well as competition between them.

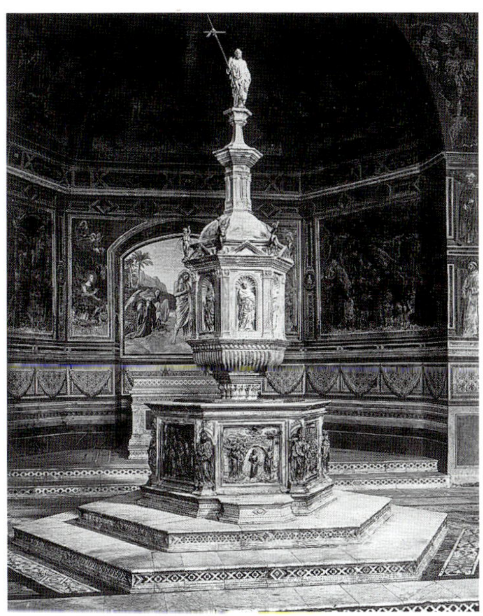

122. The Baptismal Font in the Baptistery of Siena, marble with bronze reliefs and figures, c. 1416-31. Many sculptors including Jacopo della Quercia, Lorenzo Ghiberti and Donatello contributed to the work. Ghiberti's relief of the Baptism, 1417-27, can be seen on the front.

Indeed an important theme in these chapters is the 'parallel development' of Donatello, Ghiberti and Masaccio.[57] It must also be noted that Donatello was also in competition with Giotto, who had depicted the story in the Peruzzi Chapel (Figs 94–5) a century earlier, as well as with other artists who had represented the subject.

It will be recalled that there were certain gaps and inconsistencies in the two accounts of the story in the Gospels of St Mark and St Matthew.[58] This provided artists with the latitude to develop their own accounts, as the author of the *Meditations* recommended. The late thirteenth-century mosaic in the Florence Baptistery shows Herodias seated at table next to her husband – she is presented with John the Baptist's head by her daughter, behind whom stands the executioner. Giotto, however, shows Herodias off-stage and behind the scenes. In Giotto's main scene the soldier presents the head perhaps to the daughter – still dancing – perhaps to the king. The ambiguity seems deliberate. In the adjoining room the daughter presents the head to her mother.

What does Donatello show (Fig. 124)? About this there has been much debate,[59] but the following is certain. In the fore-

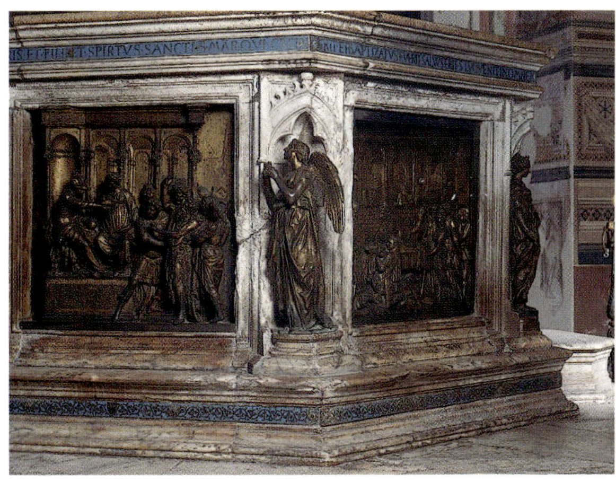

123. View of the Siena Baptistery Font showing Ghiberti's Arrest of the Baptist, 1417-27 on the left, and Donatello's Head of St John being brought to the King's Table, c.1423-5, seen obliquely on the right, both gilded bronze.

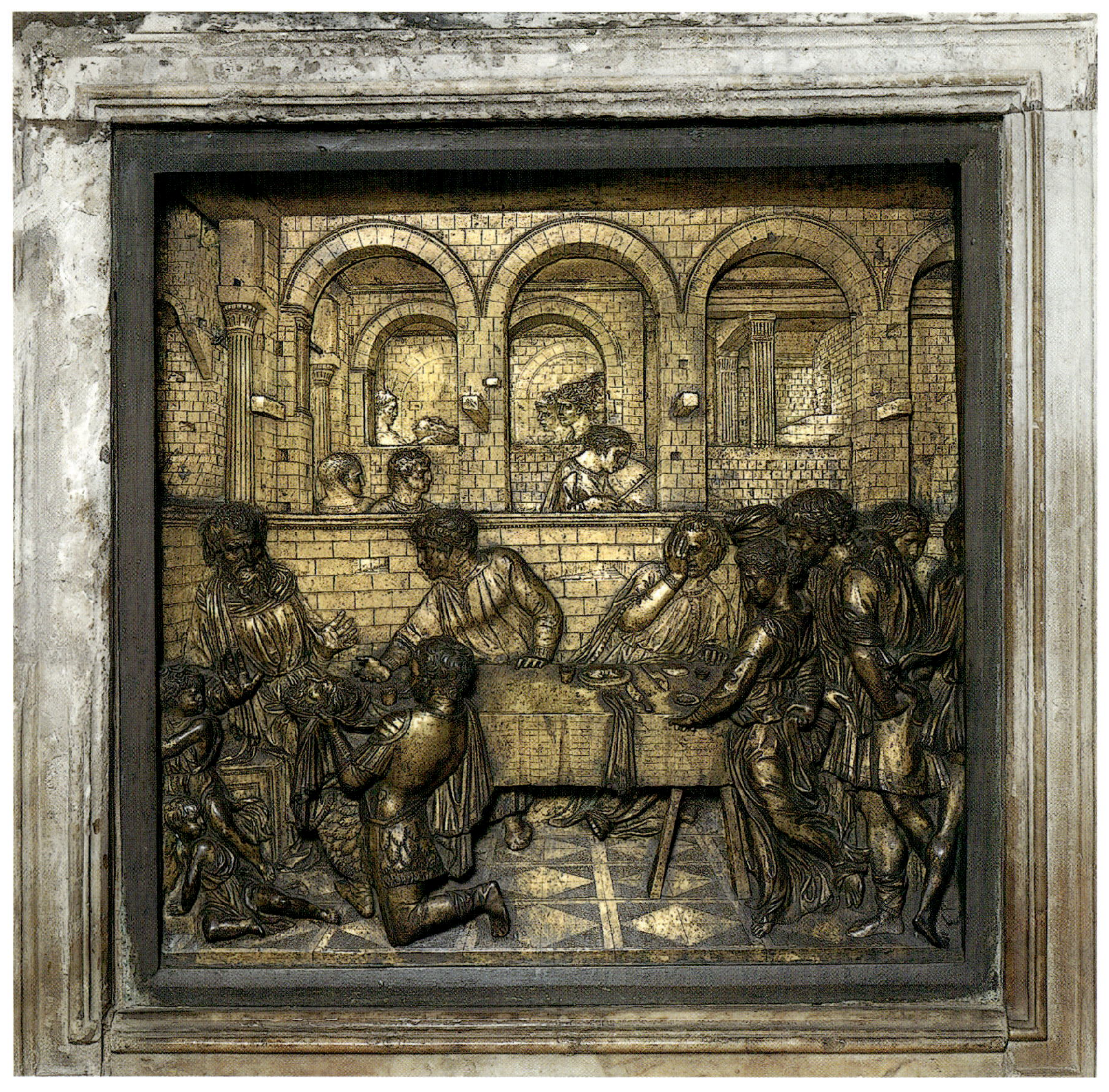

124. Donatello, the Head of St John being brought to the King's Table, gilded bronze, c. 1423–5, Siena Baptistery Font, frontal view.

ground a soldier presents the head directly to Herod, not to Herodias nor to her daughter. As in Giotto's fresco the daughter's dance continues, while the viol player plays in the gallery. None of this corresponds to either Gospel. They both tell us explicitly that after the execution the head is first brought to the daughter, in an unspecified location, then she (Mark 6, 28) *gives it* to her *mother* who was in another room or (Matthew 14, 11) *carries it* to Herodias elsewhere. What is uncertain about Donatello's relief is whether the figure seated next to Herod, gesticulating at the head, is a male guest or Herodias herself. The latter is more likely for no other reason than that there are small breast-like protuberances on its chest which Herod and the other male figures do not have. In addition Ghiberti's Arrest of the Baptist (Fig. 123) shows Herod and Herodias sitting together on their dais, a further indication of Donatello's efforts to harmonise his relief with the pre-existing work. Herodias's outstretched arm can be interpreted as her saying something like, 'Look! Here's his head! We're rid of him at last. I had the courage to do this.' Herod recoils in horror, for, according to Mark, he respected the Baptist. Herod's guests recoil with him and even the daughter seems to have frozen at the sight of the head, all except for the revengeful Herodias.

Also uncertain is the action seen through a pair of arches in the far background showing a figure who holds out the head on a platter to three others. Is this Herodias being given the head by her daughter possibly after the foreground episode? Or is this the executioner displaying the head to the daughter, surrounded by companions, having brought it to her immediately after its decapitation, marking the start of its stately progress, like some succulent and regal delicacy – such as a boar's head – from the kitchens to the banqueting hall? The latter seems more likely and better accords with the Gospels which are in agreement that the head is brought first to the daughter in an unspecified location.

In the main scene the soldier presents the Baptist's head directly to Herod, rather than to Herodias or to her daughter. As a result all the action is focused upon this gory climax with Herod at its centre. In this it differs from earlier depictions of the subject where the dramatic focus, and the guilt, is placed upon Herodias and her daughter. It may be significant that a 1427 document of the Sienese authorities describes the subject as 'the head of St John being brought to the king's table'.[60] To this end Donatello has rewritten the script in a manner somewhat similar to Brunelleschi's treatment of the Sacrifice of Isaac (Fig. 99), imagining a climax not described in the biblical narrative, indeed at odds with it, thereby going somewhat beyond the normal limits of Devout Meditation. In this, Donatello's emphasis differs from that adopted by Giotto (Fig. 95), who is more ambiguous, as we have seen. Nonetheless, although the main action is climactic and instantaneous Donatello has set it within a broad temporal context showing both the daughter continuing her dance in the foreground and the scene of the head in the background, thereby alluding to the rest of the story. Donatello's approach also differs from Brunelleschi's in that the dramatic focus has not been coupled with a fixed viewpoint, despite one's first impressions and claims that geometric perspective with a central viewpoint has been employed.[61] Insistent clues and our own preconceptions may lead us to think that it has, but closer examination throws new light on the relief.

Although the scene is presented to us through a frame into which we look, as Alberti was to recommend a decade later,[62] and although the architecture recedes in an apparently well-regulated perspectival fashion, there are so many anomalies that it is very unlikely that Donatello employed anything like Alberti's construction to control diminution and scale. It has often been pointed out that there are two central 'vanishing' points defined by the receding lines of the architecture: a higher one relating to the background, located at the point where the violist's elbow meets the ledge, and a slightly lower one relating to the tiled floor and tablecloth located two courses of masonry below. In fact none of the vanishing lines for either section meet in a single point but their intersections are scattered in a wide area around the centre of the relief. In addition, another viewpoint somewhat to the left of centre is suggested by the fact that the masonry pier above Herodias completely hides the corresponding pier behind it (p. 174). Even stronger evidence against the use of geometric perspective is found in the incorrect scale of the figures to one another and to the architecture. Were Herod or his seated companions to stand up they would be far taller than the figures already standing, and the sizes of the heads in the two galleries do not diminish with distance. The reader will notice other oddities.

Nonetheless we must not lose sight of the fact that, compared to any earlier relief sculpture or painting, one obtains a greater conviction that the figures are acting out the drama in a more naturalistic architectural setting than before, greater than in Ghiberti's adjacent Arrest of the Baptist (Fig. 123) which was possibly modelled though not cast by 1420, or in Donatello's earlier relief of St George and the Dragon of around 1417. There is a clear, even decisive, difference between this work and its predecessors. This arises, however, not as a result of the employment of a single device, geometric perspective, but through the accumulated effect of several.

First, and most important, the image is presented to us through the simple moulding of an ungilded bronze frame (Fig. 124). This is set directly behind the more elaborate moulded marble frame of the font, common to all six reliefs on the font. Ghiberti's adjacent relief has no such inner frame, the dais is skewed at a small angle to the marble frame and actually protrudes into the spectator's space. In Donatello's relief the tiled pavement comes right up to the lower edge of the bronze frame and the orthogonals of the pavement recede directly from it. Second, the frame, and particularly its lower edge, is the reference line for every single figure and object in the relief; nothing overlaps this edge except, significantly, the little toe of the figure retreating from view behind the frame on the extreme right. Every single form, every limb, is overlapped and partially masked by another closer to the spectator, with the exception of the foreground figures of the dancing daughter and the soldier presenting the head. Yet even their limbs, draperies and the soldier's sword overlap other parts of their bodies. Thus Donatello has provided us with a precise sense of where every form in the relief is located in relation to every other. The daughter, for example, is positioned between the front edge of the pavement and the table; her left hand almost touches the tablecloth; a small bowl rests immediately above it; a knife whose handle rests on the far edge of the table points towards the bowl; behind the far edge of the table sits the recoiling guest directly in front of the masonry wall, his head overlapping the cornice; the viol player is immediately behind this wall, and so on right up to the masonry wall with its blind arches in the depths of the chamber. From whichever point one begins it is possible to count as many as fifteen planes overlapping one another from the front frame to the back of the relief. The overlapping of forms was one of Giovanni Pisano's major innovations (Figs 64 and 76) to provide more space between figures in relief sculpture and became central to the tradition of painting and sculpture set out in this book. The three crucial devices, the framing, its conjunction with the pavement or ground and the overlapping were also adumbrated in Donatello's earlier relief of St George and the Dragon and probably derive from Orcagna's marble relief of the Birth of the Virgin (Fig. 98), derived in turn from Pietro Lorenzetti's 1342 altarpiece of the same subject, which Donatello would have seen in Siena Cathedral, above the Baptistery for which his relief was destined. These devices are largely responsible for the impression of spatial coherence and pictorial unity set in a new pictorial world somewhat distanced and separated from that of the spectator.

Nonetheless these are not the only means by which Donatello provides us with a sense of the space between figures and objects and with a sense of recession. Closely related is the way Donatello sets his figures so ingeniously into the furniture and the architecture that they seem to inhabit the place. Donatello also makes far more use of levels of relief carefully graduated from the nearly three-dimensional soldier, daughter and the trestle table in the foreground, to the very low cameo relief of heads and architecture in the deepest levels of the building. The foreground figures seem closer because they are more substantial. This technique had been pioneered by Ghiberti in the Second Doors (Figs 105 and 109). Donatello himself had developed this device further in the landscape background of his St George and the Dragon.

Yet another device is Donatello's use of the bronze frame to cut off from view the jumble of features glimpsed through the opening above Herod's head as well as the fourth arch on the right-hand side and any further arches beyond it. A man is walking out of view beyond the right-hand edge of the frame. Because we can see only part of the complex of chambers stretching to either side and into the distance, we are better able to imagine that what lies beyond is but a small part of the interior of an immense and forbidding fortress. Donatello dispensed with the practice of depicting entire buildings, which were inevitably out of proportion with the figures unless the buildings were very large or the figures very small. Hence it became possible to improve upon the scale of figures to buildings. Correspondingly, Donatello was able to employ quite large figures, while still maintaining a sense of scale, something that Ghiberti had not been able to achieve in his adjacent relief.

A seventh device is found in the way that the foreground figures in higher relief shift convincingly in relation to objects further back from us, particularly when we move around the panel – so-called movement parallax further developed by Ghiberti in his Gates of Paradise (Figs 135, 137, 138, 140 and 142). Finally, a feature that is not in itself cue for distance but which adds conviction to the scene – the architecture is massive. The masonry walls and arches look heavy, substantial and capable of bearing loads, more so than in most earlier painting or sculpture.

To summarise, the powerful effect of coherence is not the result of Donatello's employment of a single device such as the convergence of orthogonals to a point, nor even of some additional construction to control apparent diminution but of many interrelated ones. Above all it is the result of Donatello's handling of the encompassing bronze frame and the foremost edge of the tiled pavement so that the intricate overlapping and masking of all the forms relate to the frame and to the spectator. In addition there is the incompleteness of the architecture masked by the frame, the graduated levels of relief, the way that the figures inhabit the spaces at all levels, the convincingly massive quality of the architecture, and movement parallax in addition to the use of converging lines in the tiled pavement and tablecloth. Because of the way that these factors are interlinked we do not immediately become aware of the many anomalies of scale and 'correct' geometrical perspective, whose importance has been vastly over-emphasised (see Appendix).[63]

Donatello's employment of movement parallax relates to the fact that while our dominant viewpoint is from the front of the panel there are, in addition, a number of subsidiary viewpoints, just as we found earlier in the work of Giovanni Pisano and Ghiberti, and which Donatello did not jettison despite his employment of very low levels of relief in the background.[64] Set on a hexagonal structure, like Giovanni's Pistoia pulpit, the Head of St John being brought to the King's Table is one of a cycle of six panels which can be viewed sequentially as one walks round. I would single out two of these subsidiary viewpoints. The first is to the right of centre (Fig. 125), at a point where the napkin hanging over the table aligns with the line of the pavement and the protruding beam above the head of the horror struck guest is seen head on. These curious beams may have been designed to act as cues for these subsidiary angles. From this point we feel as if we belong to the right-hand group of spectators surrounding the daughter and the seated diner. Across a gulf, standing back and indeed recoiling with them from the group around Herod, we view the action over the back and shoulders of the soldier, looking directly into Herod's face. The second viewpoint is the corresponding one on the left (Fig. 126) where we complete the group of figures surrounding the presentation of the head to Herod. From here we share Herod's isolation from the horrified guests. There are other viewpoints when we stand up and look down upon the scene, as if we were located in a gallery opposite to the one in which the musician is standing. Some apparent anomalies in the modelling of the figures make sense from these lateral views. The head of the man with his hand covering his face (p. 200) looks odd from the front, but foreshortens convincingly from the side views; likewise the back of the kneeling soldier. It is fair to say, however, that unlike Giovanni Pisano or Ghiberti, Donatello makes the central, frontal viewpoint (Fig. 124) the dominant one, while the oblique viewpoints serve to enrich our understanding of the story.[65] Nonetheless, it was Donatello's great achievement to combine the advantages of the framed, somewhat flattened sculptural image, derived from Orcagna, with those of the dominant tradition stemming from Giovanni and used both by Ghiberti and Brunelleschi.

The effect of looking into the hall through the frame concentrates the drama. But the character of Donatello's architecture is also highly original. We *appear* to be looking into a cavernous underground place, some kind of vaulted dungeon supported by masonry piers and round arches forming an 'endless' vista as they recede one behind the other, creating a strange sense of claustrophobia enhanced by the fact that no windows are visible. There is no escape. The architecture is dramatic with a powerful emotional effect. Maybe Donatello was trying to create the impression of a tyrant's castle as

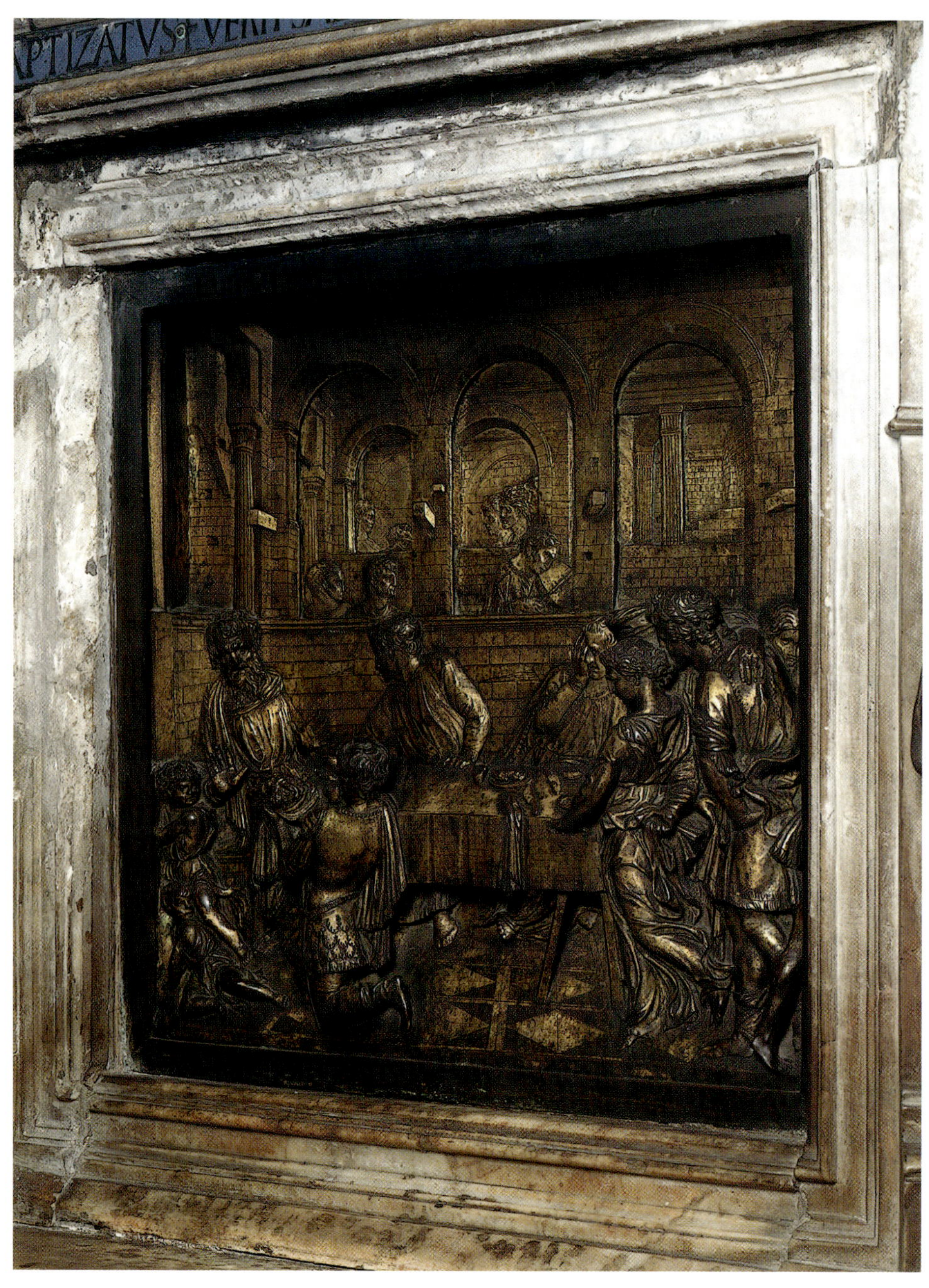

125. Donatello, the Head of St John being brought to the King's Table, gilded bronze, c. 1423–5, Siena Baptistery Font, photographed from the right.

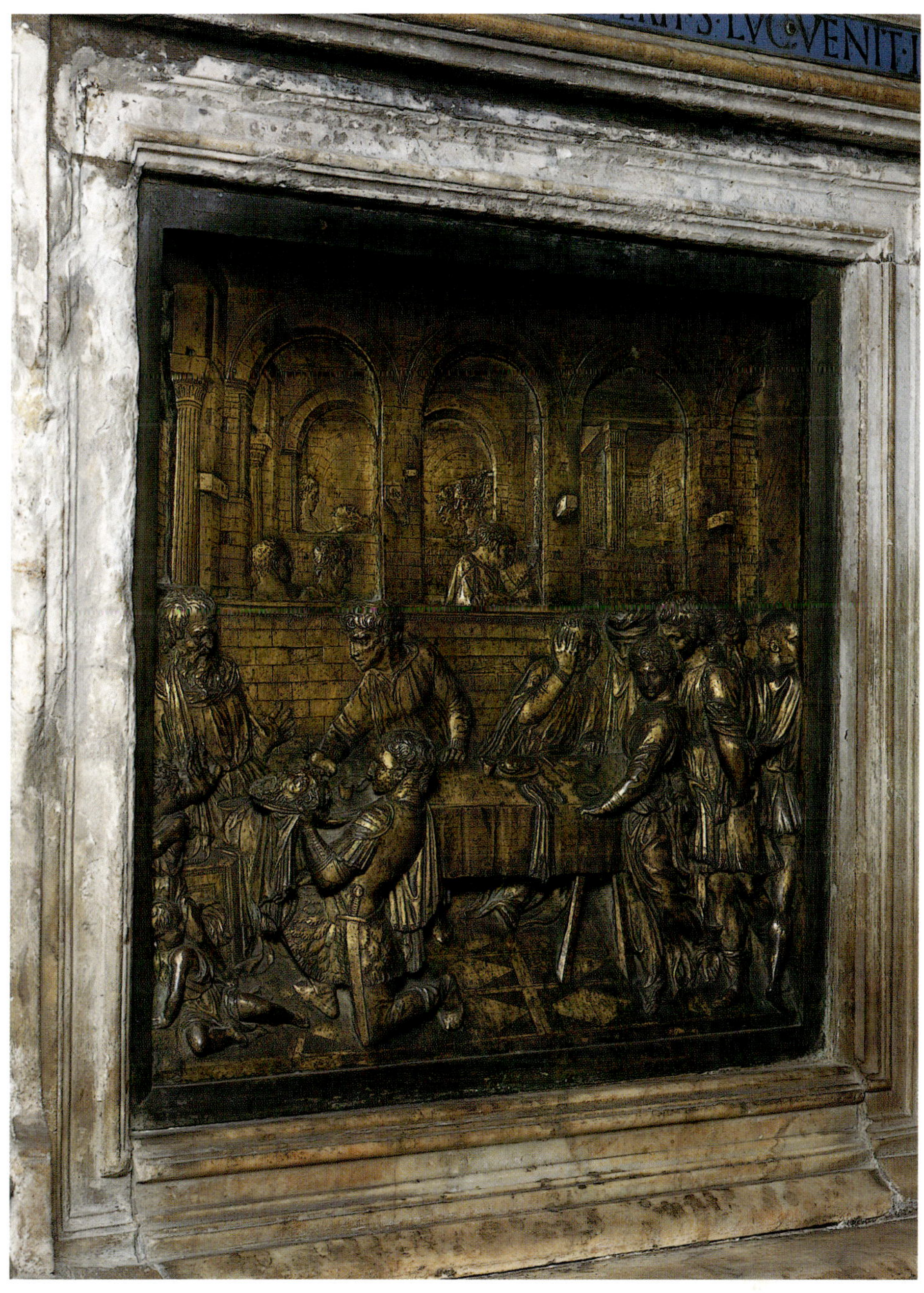

126. Donatello, the Head of St John being brought to the King's Table, gilded bronze, c. 1423–5, Siena Baptistery Font, photographed from the left.

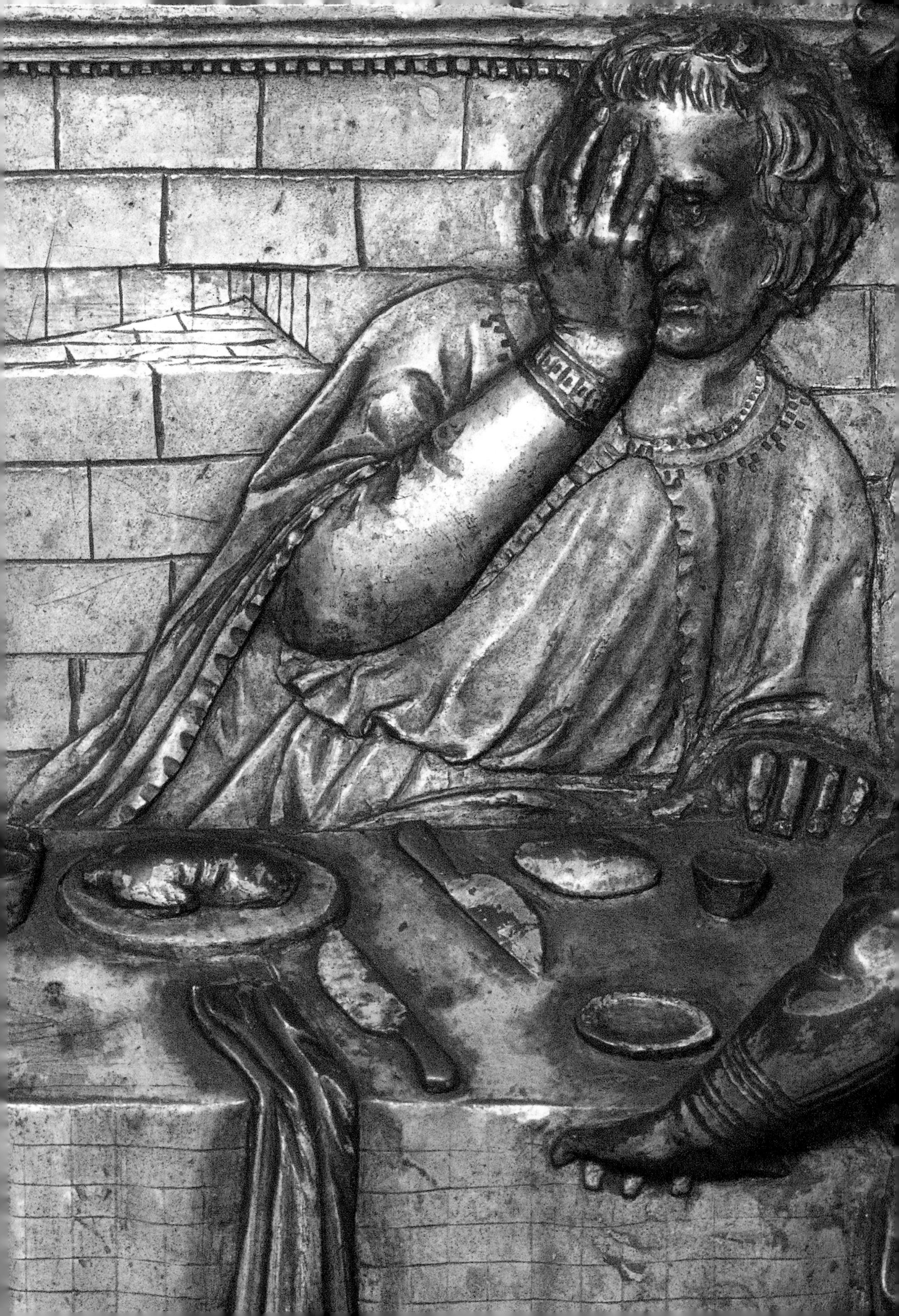

characterised a quarter of a century later by Alberti: 'We should not omit one contrivance very convenient for a tyrant, which is to have some private pipes concealed within the body of the wall, by which he may secretly hear everything that is said either by strangers or servants.'[66] The strange holes in the masonry may be such surveillance devices as well as serving to emphasise the thickness of the walls. The relief would originally have been seen by candle or oil light which, as it flickers on the surface of the gilded bronze gives the impression of the banquet lit by flares. But this description of the architectural setting is only one possibility. It may not be an underground vault but a courtyard with an arched loggia.

Turning next to the compositional implications of the converging lines of the tiled pavement – these somewhat divert the viewer's attention away from the climax on the left into the depths of the building, which is almost a character in its own right. The fact that the dramatic focus is to the far left whereas the focus for the orthogonals, imprecise as it is, lies in the centre may also have been intended to give emphasis to the fact that the central emptiness is the consequence of the climax,[67] for it is possible to imagine that the napkin and knife marks the place of a guest who has jumped up from his seat in horror. It can even be imagined that the viewer is that guest, mirroring the man opposite recoiling from the Baptist's head with his hand shielding his eyes from the sight.[68]

This figure draws attention to another feature of Donatello's handling of his medium which unlike either that of Ghiberti or Brunelleschi was not purely naturalistic, but exploited the metaphorical qualities of bronze rather as Giovanni Pisano had done with marble (Fig. 68). The face of this figure, examined closely, is an extraordinary fusion of a profile and full face, but it also seems to have melted – the mouth, the nose, the eye in particular seem like the half-molten wax from which the bronze was originally cast. It looks as if his features have collapsed under the horror of what he has seen. This is intensified by the curiously slimy object on his plate, like a piece of liver, which closer inspection reveals to be a decapitated chicken, and which itself echoes the Baptist's head and platter. Indeed this echo is reinforced by the rhyming of the table knife with the soldier's sword and the napkin with his cloak which he uses to hold the platter. This also makes sense of the scene in the far background: the Baptist's head is indeed being carried to the birthday feast in ceremony as dishes are still marched into state banquets from the kitchens with a musical accompaniment. Kitchen and execution cell have become indistinguishable in this travesty of a festive banquet. Herod, we've seen, admired the Baptist and was overcome with remorse when he was

Detail of Figure 125

forced by his oath to order the execution. Here remorse turns to horror and indeed doom; Herod's hands do not quite belong to his body as he gazes down upon the bearded head which mirrors his own. He is, literally, 'cornered' by his action and cannot escape the consequences. The two half-naked babies or cherubim, whatever they are, are like symbols of the Holy Innocents, or of innocence itself trying to escape the sight.

And thus while the viol player plays on, Herod's birthday celebration has been transformed into the Baptist's day of martyrdom; a birthday has become a death-day, a grand palace has become a dungeon, a king is transformed into a tyrant and his banqueting chamber into an inferno, where he will suffer the consequences of his evil actions. Finally this interpretation also explains the sexual indeterminacy of Herodias; we cannot tell for sure which sex she is, because like the wife of a later tyrant she had un-sexed herself in her power lust. And the two children evoke the following passage in Shakespeare's play about a tyrant who 'out-Herods Herod'.[69]

> And pity like a naked new-born babe,
> Striding the blast, or heaven's cherubim, hors'd
> Upon the sightless couriers of the air,
> Shall blow the horrid deed in every eye . . .[70]

This, then, is another drama focusing upon the themes of tyranny and earthly versus heavenly justice, like Duccio's Maestà (Fig. 14) on the high altar of Siena cathedral immediately above the Baptistery. Perhaps this also explains Donatello's recasting of the Gospel story and the difference between his image and earlier representations: Herod is a villainous tyrant and the scene is a foretaste of his future punishment.

Donatello aims to strike us with a sense of immediacy as powerful as Brunelleschi's Isaac or the reliefs of Giovanni Pisano. But despite the instantaneity of the dramatic climax, Donatello, unlike Brunelleschi, did not sacrifice the capacity of relief sculpture to provide oblique viewpoints, though these were probably meant to be subsidiary to the central ones. Nor is the action purely momentary as in Brunelleschi's Isaac – several episodes of the story are represented. Neither do we experience the event from a purely external standpoint, even though we are looking into the hall from the other side of the frame; Donatello enables us to enter into the experiences of Herod and of his guests, partly by means of the lateral views. At the same time the subtle metaphors discovered in the medium of the bronze, suspended there, half-concealed, hinted at, work upon our imagination to suggest deeper tragic realities, as in the work of Giovanni. Donatello has been eclectic in the stock of devices upon which he has drawn and the way he has positioned himself in the debate. The issues posed by this work called for a response from Ghiberti in the Gates of Paradise, which we will examine in chapter 8.

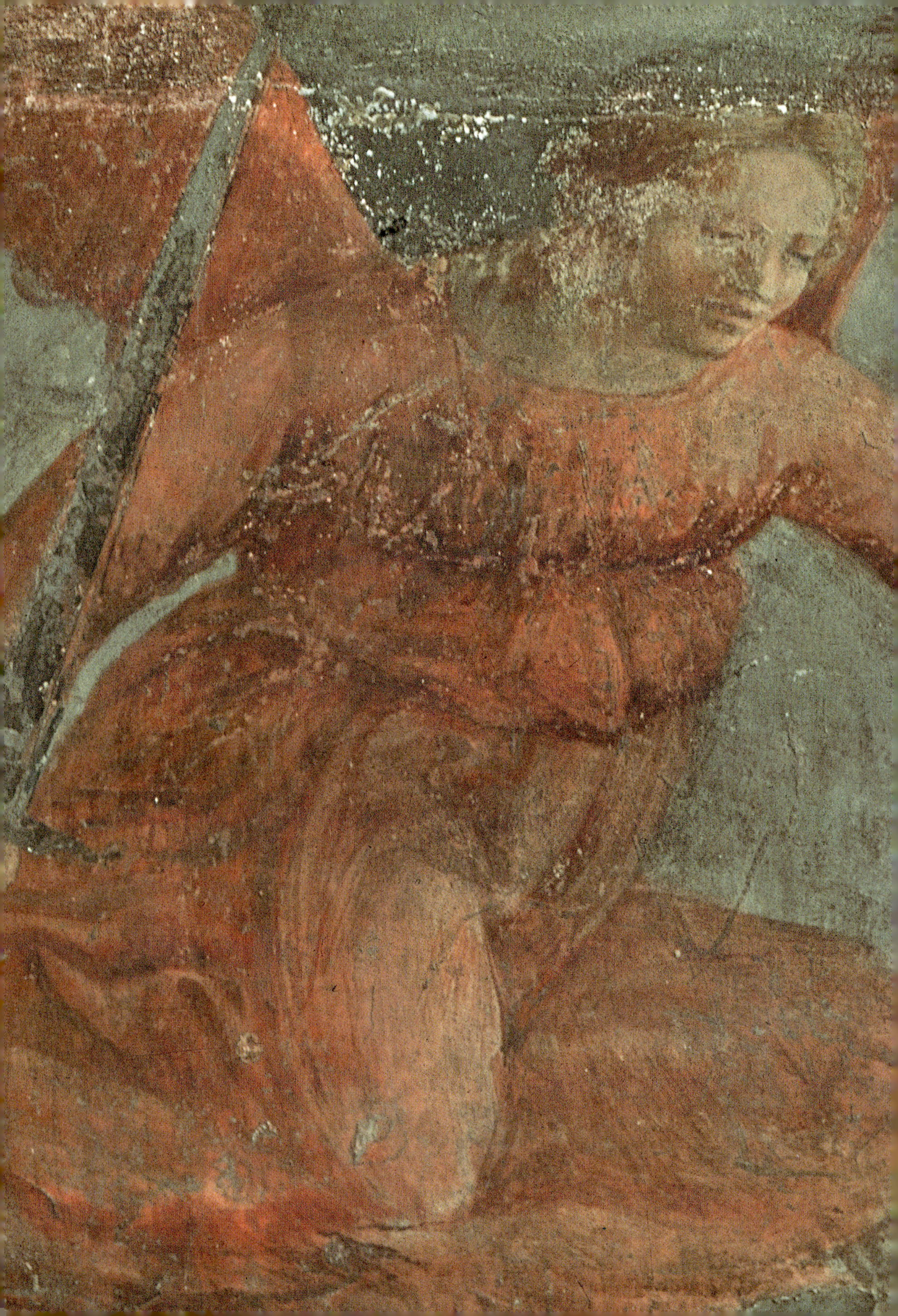

VII

MASACCIO'S BRANCACCI CHAPEL FRESCOES

It is not possible to determine the precise dates when the Brancacci Chapel was painted (Fig. 133). Masaccio and Masolino worked on it at some time between 1422 and 1428.[1] The subject of the chapel was the life of St Peter, regarded as the first pope, and the Acts of the Apostles. According to Vasari, Masolino painted the four evangelists in the vaults. He also painted Jesus calling Andrew and Peter; Peter weeping after his denial; Feed my Sheep and the Navicella in the lunettes.[2] These have been destroyed and were replaced by eighteenth-century frescoes.[3] Masolino also painted scenes of St Peter Preaching on the altar wall and SS Peter and Paul curing Tabitha and a cripple on the upper part of the right-hand wall opposite the Tribute Money. He painted the Temptation on the entrance pilaster on the same side. In the background of the Tabitha there is a very fine view, painted on a single 'giornata' or day's work, of one side of a typical Florentine piazza with two streets leading off into the distance. Several writers believe Masaccio painted this, perhaps in the role of a subcontractor initially employed as a specialist in perspective. But it is possible that Masaccio was Masolino's collaborator or partner from the start, although, if Vasari's attributions of the vaults and lunettes to Masolino is correct, it would suggest that Masolino began the work, since the process of fresco painting has to start from the top of a chamber. In Sep-

Detail of Figure 129

tember 1425 Masolino received a far more lucrative contract from a very important mercenary general, Pippo Spano, who worked for King Sigismond of Hungary, and went off to Hungary. He did not return to Florence until almost two years later in July 1427.[4] We do not know what happened next. Masaccio may have been asked to complete the chapel in Masolino's absence. If so it seems likely, on the visual evidence, that his work was in two phases: first, the completion of the altar wall in 1425; the second and larger part, the left-hand wall showing the Tribute Money and the Raising of Theophilus's Son, in 1427. There is documentary evidence that Masaccio spent much of 1426 painting an altarpiece for a chapel in the Carmelite Church in Pisa.[5] There are indications that this work was made in Pisa, though we cannot be certain. The Theophilus may have been finished by Masaccio, but it might have been damaged by the removal of Brancacci family portraits after their exile from Florence in 1435, later to be repaired in the early 1480s by Filippino Lippi, who also repainted St Peter's Martyrdom opposite, or painted it from scratch.[6] There are many uncertainties. I shall concentrate upon the left-hand wall, probably conceived by Masaccio and largely painted by him, both as a set of individual frescoes and as a pictorial unity.

The depiction of the stories of St Peter and the Acts of the Apostles was quite rare in monumental Italian art, so for some scenes Masolino and Masaccio were probably faced with the absence of ready-made pictorial formulae to adapt and improve upon. They may have had to work directly from the text. In other cases their problem was not difficult. Scenes of St Peter preaching or baptising, distributing alms to the poor or raising people from the dead could easily be derived from corresponding scenes in the lives of Jesus and the Saints. But the story of the Tribute Money (Fig. 127) is extremely complicated, earlier depictions in manuscripts were rudimentary, and a surviving fresco in the church of San Piero a Grado near Pisa of about 1300 concentrated upon the scene of the miracle of St Peter obtaining money to pay the tax from the mouth of a fish. As far as we know there was no compositional formula, so Masaccio in all likelihood had to invent the image from scratch.[7] It was a splendid opportunity for this brilliant but as yet unproven painter in his mid-twenties.

As told only by St Matthew (17, vv. 24–7) the story runs as follows:

> 24. And when they were come to Capernaum, they that received tribute *money* came to Peter, and said, 'Doth your master pay tribute?' 25. He saith, 'Yes.' And when he was come into the house, Jesus prevented him, saying, 'What thinkest thou, Simon? of whom do the kings of the earth take custom [dazio – municipal tolls[8]] or tribute? of their own children, or of strangers?' 26. Peter saith unto him, 'Of strangers.' Jesus saith to him. 'Then

are the children free. 27. Notwithstanding, lest we should offend them [*scandalizziamo* – not to create a scandal][9], go thou to the sea, and cast an hook, and take up the fish that first cometh up; and when thou hast opened his mouth, thou shalt find a piece of money: that take, and give it to them for me and thee.'

Let us try to imagine Masaccio's problems in visualising this story. Short though it is, there are in fact thirteen subsidiary episodes or speeches:[10]

1. The disciples and Jesus arrive at the city of Capernaum.
2. The tax collectors stop St Peter to ask him whether Jesus is liable to pay the municipal toll. (This suggests that Jesus and the disciples tried to march into the town without stopping to pay.)
3. St Peter replies, 'Yes.' (Even though he may not have been certain in his own mind whether this was the right answer.)
4. St Peter enters the house where Jesus is, presumably within the town, intending to ask Jesus whether he is liable to pay the toll.
5. Jesus anticipates St Peter's query with his own question, 'Do kings collect taxes or tolls from their own children or from foreigners?'
6. St Peter replies, 'From foreigners.'
7. Jesus sums up, 'Then the children must be exempt from the toll.'
8. Jesus then adds a qualification to his assessment of the legal position that he should not pay the toll: 'In order to avoid making this into an incident, we *will* pay it, but I will obtain the money by performing a miracle.'
9. Jesus then explains how the miracle is to be performed. He orders Peter to do two things.
10. Go to the sea (of Galilee), catch a fish (Peter had been a fisherman after all).
11. Open the fish's mouth and there find a coin.
12. Go to the tax collectors.
13. Give them the coin in payment of our taxes.

Of course the story could be depicted cartoon fashion in many scenes as in earlier manuscripts,[11] but even so, severe problems arise on account of the difficulties in representing speech in images. How does one represent the question, 'Is your master liable to taxation?' That is hard enough, but how can one depict the very complex dialogue between Jesus and St Peter in episodes five to eight? In any case what is Jesus talking about? It is all in riddles and analogies.

The easy parts, however, can be disposed of quickly. There is no problem in showing Jesus and his disciples arriving at Capernaum which was a small town of about two thousand people on the shores of the Sea of Galilee. Nor is there much difficulty in representing Jesus' practical solution to the problem, telling St Peter to catch the fish and pay the money. Gestures of command and instruction were commonplace and the content of the instruction could be represented by showing these actions taking place.

The real difficulty lies with Jesus' dialogue with St Peter, for what had to be depicted was a complex and abstract train of legal reasoning, in other words intellectual ideas of a specialised character. Let us look at the problem.

St Peter's first response was to admit, maybe reluctantly, that Jesus was liable to pay the tax. When they meet, Jesus voices St Peter's doubts on the point of law, but he uses a concrete example or analogy to establish the principle upon which he will base his decision. Kings collect tolls and taxes from foreigners, outsiders, not from members of their own family. What is referred to is some kind of customs toll on entry to a town which was commonplace both in biblical times and in the Renaissance. In effect Jesus is drawing a parallel to indicate that God is King and that because Jesus is his son he is not liable to pay this tax, likewise the disciples who are the children of God. Jesus, however, is anxious to prevent an outcry so he adds a qualification to this interpretation of his 'real' legal position: 'Let us pay the tax, however, for diplomatic and political reasons.'

This interpretation of the episode provides us with the germ of Masaccio's solution to this problem of pictorial representation. Jesus as judge is adjudicating between the law of God and the law of this world, in particular that of the small town of Capernaum. It is a conflict of laws. One must assume that Felice Brancacci and his, presumably, Carmelite advisers had special reasons for choosing this story, just as they had for choosing the St Peter cycle as a whole, and these must have been explained to Masaccio. Recent writers have convincingly argued that the Tribute Money was chosen for the chapel because of its relevance to the burning contemporary issue of the proper relationship between the Christian Church and the states which made up the Christian world – also involving a conflict of laws.[12]

It is not my wish to divert attention from the painting and the problems of pictorial narrative with a lengthy historical digression. Suffice it to say that in these very years the western Church ruled over by a monarchical pope was under severe threat, one that would culminate a century later in the Reformation and the breakaway of Protestant churches in England, Scotland, France, the Low Countries, Germany and elsewhere. Even at this period the followers of John Huss in Bohemia had set up their own 'protestant' state, and the Church was divided by schism resulting only recently in three rival popes whose claims had been resolved at the 1417 Council of Constance shortly before Felice Brancacci commissioned his chapel. Since the removal of the papacy to Avignon in 1307, even after its 'return' in the 1370s, it had been prevented from re-establishing its physical presence in Rome by the city's leading families, indeed in the 1420s Pope Martin V and his court, or curia, were resident in Florence inside the Dominican monastery of Santa Maria Novella in apartments that Ghiberti claimed to have designed. Both Felice Brancacci and the Carmelites were supporters of the papacy of Martin V. In these circumstances it is probable that the papacy itself was involved in the programme of the Brancacci Chapel. The issue of whether the Church should be subject to the laws of the State or have its own independent courts was a live one, concerning the issue of whether church bodies should pay state taxes. A related issue was whether the pope should enjoy monarchical powers or be subject to a council.[13]

In the western Church St Peter was considered to be the first pope and therefore symbolised the leadership of the Church on earth. In that light and in this context the significance of the Tribute Money for the contemporary situation is clear: Jesus is shown making a legal judgement between Church and State to the effect that in terms of God's law the Church should be tax-free but in practice it needs political friends and allies here on earth. The Church must pay the tax, though God would provide the money. Jesus is also designating St Peter, and hence his successors, as pope, his vicar on earth.[14]

Because these broad historical circumstances within which Masaccio was asked to depict the Tribute Money are now generally accepted, we have a rare opportunity to reconstruct the kind of relationship that must have existed between an artist and the client for this kind of commission. The Brancacci family, the Carmelites and maybe the papacy must have suggested the subject, possibly supplying a translation of the text and an explanation of the significance it held for them. It was for Masaccio to provide a visual solution to the problem, much as an architect nowadays provides a solution to a brief. Masaccio's response was highly inventive. For scenes of judgement there *was* a recognizable formula and a precedent – that of Jesus as judge in the Last Judgement seated in the midst of his disciples (Fig. 17). That is how Masaccio shows them, only here they are all standing. Next Masaccio had to show the conflict between Church and State. St Peter, on Jesus' right-hand side represents the Church on earth and the papacy. The tax collector standing on the town side of the picture represents the State. Masaccio thereby compresses the three scenes of the disciples' arrival at Capernaum (episode 1); the tax collector questioning St Peter (episodes 2 and 3); and Jesus' subsequent legal analysis and adjudication (episodes 5–7, 8–13) into a single judgement scene outside the town gate on the shores of the Sea of Galilee. Jesus stands in the centre arbitrating the opposing claims of Church and State and announcing his verdict.

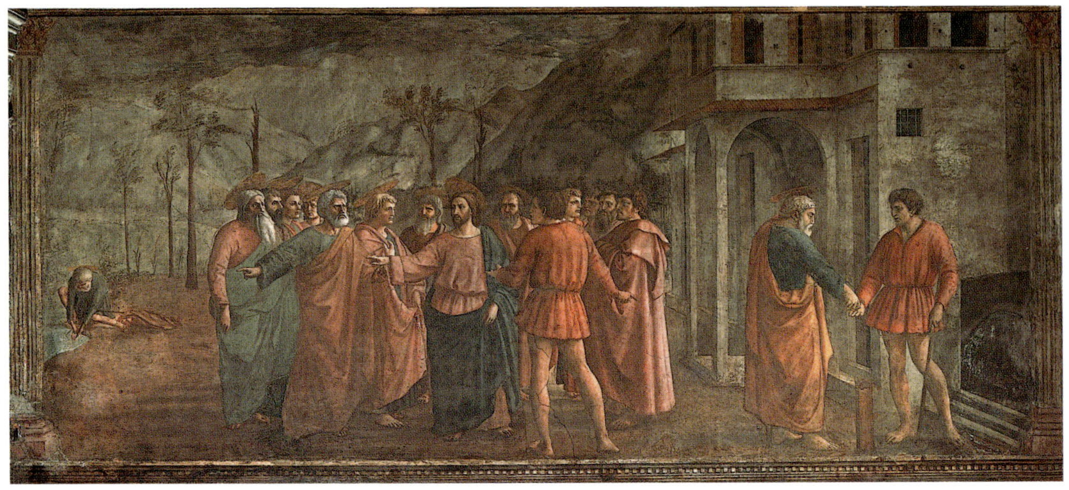

127. Masaccio, the Tribute Money, Brancacci Chapel, Sta Maria del Carmine, Florence, fresco, c.1424–28. Frontal view photographed on a scaffold before the cleaning of the late 1980s.

Masaccio makes a seemingly small but important change to the story. In the Gospel St Peter seems to have conceded the tax demand, even though he was in two minds about the justice of the claim. There is nothing to imply that he was angered by the demand. But in Masaccio's painting St Peter's facial expression appears to suggest outrage. It is Jesus, in the Gospel, who articulates an objection to the demand, which he does without rancour. The reason for Masaccio's change may have been to give expression to those voices within the Church at the time who strongly objected to paying State taxes.[15]

Thus everything falls into place. The scene is set up as an open-air court of law with Jesus adjudicating between the rival claims of the Church and the State, whose representatives, St Peter and the young tax collector, defendant and plaintiff, stand on opposite sides of the judge.[16] The tax collector looks at St Peter and points to Jesus with his left hand as if to ask whether 'Jesus', and with his right hand pointing towards Capernaum 'pays the tax to enter the city?' The taxman's mouth is open and his gestures are agitated. St Peter looks stormy (Fig. 128) and his left hand seems raised in query or protest. Here a relatively new factor has entered into the depiction of stories, not just atmospheric lighting but the use of colour and brushstroke to convey the emotional reactions of the characters. Between the two vehement adversaries stands Jesus, unemotional, looking at neither contestant, even though he is the object of their dispute as well as judge. Jesus dominates the scene.

He is not, however, placed in the centre of the fresco, neither do the orthogonal lines of the building meet in a point nor in Jesus' face. But it is fair to say that Jesus is the still centre of the drama and of the composition, and would remain so even if the building were removed.[17]

Masaccio emphasises the authoritative nature of Jesus' judgement by an intriguing use of overlapping and juxtaposed hands. The tax collector's agitated left hand is adjacent to Jesus' left arm whose hand hangs down in a very relaxed manner. Jesus' right arm, raised and pointing imperatively is directly juxtaposed to St Peter's protesting left hand. Jesus' judgement and order countermands St Peter's expostulation. Risking a small pun, one could even say that Jesus is dispensing even-handed justice, dismissing both claim and counterclaim and defusing the situation. It has been suggested that Jesus is striding forward to part the assailants before their quarrel explodes into physical violence.[18] Surrounding the protagonists stand the other disciples, their eyes focused upon the drama, particularly the two either side of Jesus, tensely awaiting his decision and the resolution of the conflict.

Masaccio's pictorial solution to the remaining details of the story is given by St Peter's right arm echoing Jesus' imperative gesture as if to say, 'Is that really what you command me to do? Of course I will obey you, but your decision astonishes me.'[19] Peter's gesture points in turn to the fishing scene which is balanced by the payment scene on the other side.

Jesus' adjudication is represented, therefore, as actually being carried out.[20] But the scene of the payment is itself interesting, for the way in which the two figures are placed on either side of a post in the ground ('to pay upon the post'). The pairing of St Peter framed by the town gate and the tax official standing on the town side of the post brings to mind the pictorial convention for a contractual agreement or a betrothal, which are of course the same thing. The two representatives in effect shake hands upon Jesus' judgement, even if their animosity has not fully subsided.[21]

This constitutes the bare bones of the composition devised by Masaccio to convey the essential features of a rarely depicted story of great narrative and doctrinal complexity, which he distilled with all its intricate subsidiary episodes into what looks like a single episode and a single decisive moment, the act of judgement.[22] But although Jesus' act of judgement is decisive, and although the orthogonals point in his direction, it would be wrong to claim that this is an example of the climactic approach to narrative seen from a fixed point of view, adumbrated by Brunelleschi in his Sacrifice of Isaac (Fig. 99). Jesus' gesture is interlinked with those depicting the preceding argument between the two contestants; the decisive moment is combined with other stages in the story, as in Giotto's Betrayal (Fig. 30), Ghiberti's Doctors (Fig.

109), Donatello's Head of St John (Fig. 124) and many other images. It is also claimed that the Tribute Money is an example of continuous narration, on account of the two flanking episodes of St Peter fishing for the money and paying the tax collector.* But this classification is also simplistic, so carefully has Masaccio integrated these episodes with the central composition. In the way the figures are arranged everything centres on Jesus and his decision: both the earlier quarrel and the resulting actions.[23] In short, Masaccio's solution to this complex problem of narrative representation is a highly sophisticated, thoughtful and intelligent response to the issues arising from the 1401 competition between Brunelleschi and Ghiberti. The fresco has the sense of immediacy, or *prontezza*, the feature that Manetti admired in Brunelleschi's relief, but it also succeeds in compressing several episodes into a single image.

The Tribute Money, however, is not all bare narrative bones, important though composition, physical gestures and facial expressions are. Masaccio was not the first artist to suggest different qualities of light. We find that in Duccio (Fig. 8), Giotto (Figs 24, 34 and 38), Taddeo Gaddi, Pietro and Ambrogio Lorenzetti, Gentile da Fabriano and Sassetta. But he was probably the first to show light so precisely sourced and focused, which he uses to model the figures, to differentiate them one from the other, particularly by overlapping bright and shadowy forms, and to direct the spectator's attention. However he went beyond this rational and naturalistic lighting not only to show different colours of light but also to use it for expressive effect in conjunction with different modes of handling fresco paint. Thus the light is sharply focused upon St Peter's face (Fig. 128) and upon his grey locks and beard, like sunlight on clouds before the storm breaks, in this case echoing the bleak rocky Apennine-like mountains in the distance rising above the figures and the spectator. Moreover, as can be seen in raking light, the actual *painting* of Peter's face seems to have something of an impasto to it which reinforces this feeling of elemental power.[24] This is in contrast to the tax collector, his face in shadow, short-haired, functionally attired, lacking personal dignity. In their midst, Jesus, not only calm in expression but painted so smoothly, with such even gradation in the modelling of his face, as to suggest the inner serenity or temperance conveyed by his posture and actions. Masaccio must have studied both Giovanni Pisano's variety of sculptural finish (Figs 68 and 85) and Ambrogio Lorenzetti's varied facture in the Good and Bad Government frescoes in Siena's town hall. Where Giotto had painted almost all his scenes

*When we consider the layout of the whole wall, the payment or contract scene will be seen to underline the broader doctrinal message as much as to conclude the story of The Tribute Money.

and figures in a uniformly smooth and inexpressive manner, Ambrogio painted the figure of Peace with serene, diaphanous robes, but the figure of Timor, Fear, who presides over the landscape ravaged by war, seems to be formed from the dark clouds of smoke coming from the fires burning the countryside beneath him. It can be argued, if only tentatively, that Masaccio gave the very surface of the plaster on which he painted an element of relief as well. The plaster surface of Masaccio's frescoes is more uneven than that of Masolino's, and it somewhat resembles the surface of Donatello's marble reliefs of the St George and the Dragon and the Ascension and Giving of the Keys.

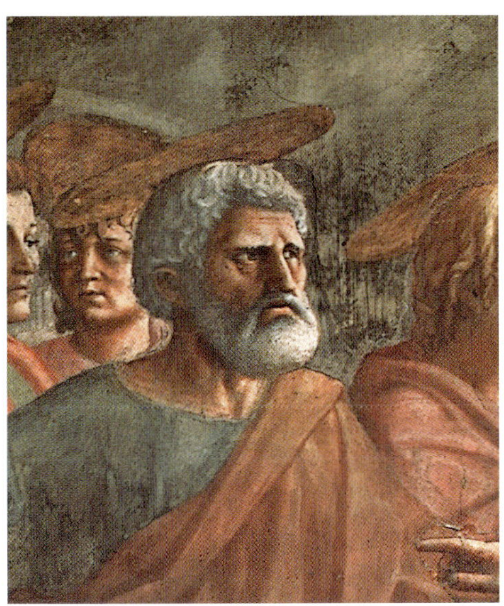

128. Masaccio, detail of St Peter's face in the central section of the Tribute Money, Brancacci Chapel, Sta Maria del Carmine, Florence, fresco, c. 1424–28.

The range of methods Masaccio used to naturalistic effect in the Tribute Money is similar to those in Donatello's Siena relief (Fig. 124). We view the judgement scene through a frame provided by the painted pilasters and cornices which cuts off our view of complete buildings and landscape features such as the lake. The ground comes up to the edge of the frame, just behind which the taxman's heels are placed, similar to the heel of the man disappearing off to the right in the Head of St John. The forms are carefully overlapped and this is enhanced by the way they are lit by focused directional light. The orthogonal lines on the building converge to something nearer to a point, though its construction is less credible than Herod's banqueting hall – the piers of the porch are barely able to support their own weight and the building as a whole is out of scale with the figures. These are also less integrated with the setting than in Donatello's Head of St John – the central composition could almost be extracted from the landscape and building, if not from the frame. Masaccio has employed a simple form of aerial perspective so that the more distant mountains are lighter and merge with the clouds.

Immediately to the left of the Tribute Money, on a raised pilaster marking the entrance to the chapel, is the scene of Adam and Eve's Expulsion from Garden of Eden (Fig. 129 and 133). Masaccio's treatment of this pilaster has an important bearing on the issue of relief to which we will return when

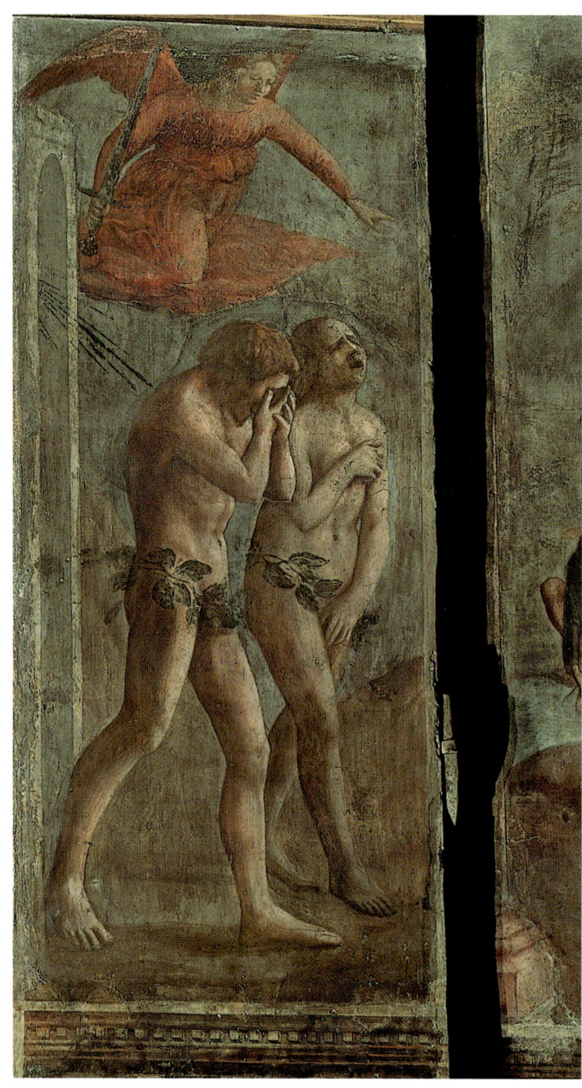

129. Masaccio, the Expulsion of Adam and Eve from Paradise, Brancacci Chapel, Sta Maria del Carmine, Florence, fresco, c.1424–28. Frontal view photographed on a scaffold before the cleaning of the late 1980s.

we consider the unity of the whole wall. Here we will simply observe a further example of Masaccio's inventiveness and flexibility in the handling of fresco painting and colour which differentiates him not only from his predecessors but also from many of his immediate successors. Giotto had used fresco in an almost totally uniform way, as already remarked in the discussion of his temperate style. But as we have observed, even within the single picture of the Tribute Money Masaccio varied his handling to suggest the characters and emotional states of different individuals. Here this is even more pronounced, particularly in the face of Eve whose eyes and mouth are like shadowy holes in the surface as she faces the cold light of the world outside paradise, as if embodying God's curse, 'In the sweat of thy face shalt thou eat bread.' The similarity of the shape of Eve's head to certain heads by Giovanni Pisano, particularly the bereaved mothers in the Massacre scene of the Pistoia pulpit (Fig. 68), has often been noted, but even more to the point is the way that Masaccio has sought in the roughness of his paint an equivalent to the rough-hewn, chipped and 'unfinished' character of Giovanni's carving, used so effectively to convey their inconsolable grief. In addition, within the same small fresco, Masaccio varies the quality of the light reflected off the bodies of the different figures. On Adam and Eve it is cold, stark, comfortless; but the angel above them, is warm, like fire, and perhaps in the arch formed by the angel's arms over Adam and Eve there is a hint of

God's subsequent redemption of Man. A similar handling of light and colour can also be observed in the scene of St Peter Baptising on the altar wall where the man on the right-hand side awaiting his turn for baptism shivering with his arms crossed, is painted in a cold light so that he seems almost like a spectre, whereas the body of the man who is receiving baptism is warm and seems to glow in the light coming from the golden bowl which St Peter is using to baptise him.

The subject of the painting (Figs 130, 132–3) occupying the whole lower wall immediately underneath the Tribute Money is also unusual, but for this there was a formula since it tells how St Peter performed the miracle of restoring to life the son of the governor of Antioch. For this the prototype of the Raising of Lazarus was available. Here, then, Masaccio was in competition, as it were, not only with two of Giotto's most successful frescoes, the Scrovegni Lazarus (Fig. 28) and the Peruzzi Drusiana (quite apart from Masolino's Tabitha on the opposite wall of the Brancacci Chapel itself), but also with Ghiberti's recent critique (Fig. 108) of Giotto's Lazarus. Even so, Masaccio never ceases to surprise us as he must have surprised his contemporaries.

Preliminary to a discussion of the painting, however, an assessment has to be made concerning its condition. As already noted, Felice Brancacci was exiled from Florence following Cosimo de Medici's triumphant return from exile in 1434. It has been argued that as a result of Felice's exile the portrait heads of members of the family in this fresco, which had been completed by Masaccio before his death, were hacked out of the plaster as an act of revenge and iconoclasm.[25] After the Brancacci were allowed to return from exile they employed Filippino Lippi in the 1480s to repair this fresco and either to complete the Martyrdom of St Peter opposite or to paint it from scratch. One reason for this complicated hypothesis is the shape of the area painted by Lippi in the Theophilus. It comprises a block of ten figures in the centre of the fresco, including Theophilus's son, and another group of five on the far left, all of whom are obviously portraits. Since fresco painters painted from the top of a wall downwards, spreading as much fresh plaster each day as they could paint during the day before the plaster dried, one would not expect this to be the pattern of Lippi's work had Masaccio left the fresco unfinished at his death. One would have expected a more or less uniform strip at whatever level Masaccio had abandoned the fresco. That, at any rate, is the argument, one which is not, however, universally accepted.[26] Whatever the truth, the son was not painted by Masaccio but by Filippino. I suggest that the figure of the son would have been depicted by Masaccio at a far earlier stage of resurrection, consistent with the treatment of this type of subject by his predecessors. Evidence for this is to be found in the direction in which those figures who were painted by Masaccio are looking and pointing. For example the seven men behind the kneeling figure of St Paul (Fig. 131), who is himself looking upwards to heaven praying for the miracle to occur, are clearly looking down at the ground below the head of Lippi's son and even their eyelids are correspondingly lowered. The man in the 'baseball cap' sitting on the left-hand side of Theophilus's throne is pointing towards the *ground*, not towards the kneeling figure by Filippino Lippi.

The story is a simple one:

> The governor of Antioch, Theophilus, had St Peter thrown into prison for preaching to his people. Hearing of his plight St Paul, disguised as a talented artist, went to Theophilus to plead for him. Eventually Theophilus reluctantly agreed to free St Peter if he were able to bring back to life his son who had died fifteen years beforehand. Somewhat daunted St Peter went to the tomb, prayed and the boy came to life immediately. Theophilus and the citizens of Antioch were converted, and built a magnificent church in which a high throne was erected on which St Peter was enthroned.[27]

The narrative has been abbreviated by Masaccio. On the pilaster, subsequently painted, or repainted, by Lippi, St Paul talks to St Peter through the bars of his prison cell (Fig. 133), presumably saying that he will do his best to obtain St Peter's release. St Paul's negotiations with Theophilus are not shown and the scene at the boy's tomb is transferred to the palace courtyard where the miracle takes place as another kind of trial, before an earthly magistrate on this occasion, of St Peter's delegated powers to bind and to loose. The consequences of the successful miracle are shown on the right-hand side in a partially separated scene where St Peter is represented as a ruler on a high throne in his new constructed basilica (Fig. 132), and the converted people of Antioch, depicted in contemporary Florentine dress with Theophilus himself kneeling in the centre, surrounded by Carmelite monks, pay homage at his feet.[28] The fact that Theophilus pays homage to St Peter reinforces Jesus' judgement in the Tribute Money above, that God's law is the highest authority even though an accommodation between Church and State is politically expedient.

The key feature of Masaccio's treatment of the miracle is the way that he shows the very beginnings of the boy's revival through the expressions on the faces of the citizens of Antioch and of the governor's men. The governor, with his orb and sceptre of office, neither surmounted by a cross, a wonderful portrait of confident worldly power in his fur hat, stares resolutely ahead across his palace courtyard, immovable in his scepticism. Clearly then, what-

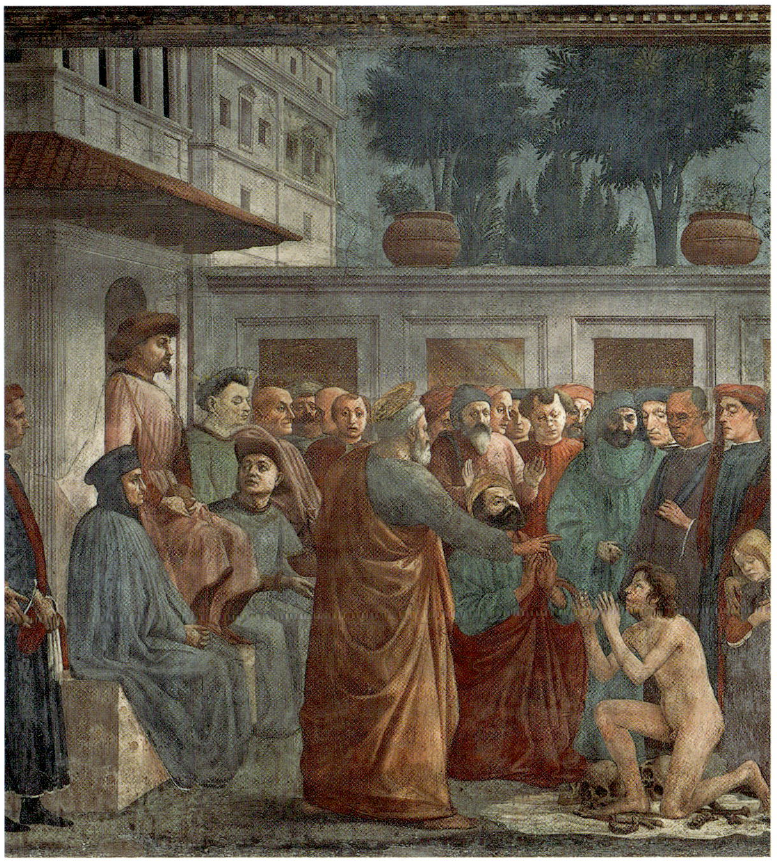

130. Masaccio, the Raising of Theophilus's Son, Brancacci Chapel, Sta Maria del Carmine, Florence, fresco, c.1424-28. Frontal view photographed on a scaffold before the cleaning of the late 1980s.

ever is taking place is barely visible to him or to most of the crowd. Even the figures behind St Paul, looking downwards at the body though they are, seem to have noticed little to surprise them. Only the red-capped man with the beard in the background has his eyebrows raised (Fig. 131). Only the figure immediately to the left of St Peter, whose eyes are popping out of his head and whose mouth has fallen open in a mask-like expression, has seen something to make him start, as well as the figure in the foreground to St Peter's right whose hands are raised in surprise. It is sad that we no longer have Masaccio's painting of the son to see for certain how the son's resuscitation was depicted so as to give rise to such varied reactions.

Their reactions, wonderfully picked out from the depths of the crowd by Masaccio's use of spotlighting and the skilful overlapping of the dark side of one face with the bright side of another, one of the lessons possibly acquired from Giovanni's Pisa pulpit (Fig. 76), are the real subject of the painting. As they see the miracle happen so they are converted – the stubborn Theophilus last of all, whose deferential private secretary, perhaps derived from Ghiberti's steward (Fig. 116) in Jesus among the Doctors, attempting to draw his attention to what is occurring.

But Theophilus's gaze can also be understood as his staring across the courtyard at the scene of another 'miracle', St Peter seated in the new basilica on a throne not only higher than his own but facing outwards (Fig. 132–3). The son's resurrection is framed between the two enthroned rulers. St Peter's enthronement is also an artistic miracle. It is not as simple as it seems. The seat of his throne is roughly at the level of the shoulders of the people standing around him, and the wall behind it is hung with a green cloth of honour. It is a hurriedly improvised and simple throne. But when we look at it carefully we begin to wonder where the throne actually is. St Peter certainly seems seated securely enough, but upon what is he seated? In truth he hovers unsupported above the heads of the kneeling men in front of him.

I would suggest that Masaccio's painting is a visual double-take. It represents St Peter enthroned in the new basilica in Antioch, receiving homage from the newly converted citizens, but it can also be read as a *painting of a painting*: St Peter painted upon a banner or cloth, a common contemporary practice, hung upon the wall of the courtyard of the Carmelite Church in Florence around which Carmelite monks and parishioners are standing and kneeling in prayer, perhaps on the feast day of St Peter's Chair at Antioch, 22 February to which the story of Theophilus's Son is related in the *Golden Legend*. Note that although we are presumed to have a viewpoint to the left, the right-hand knee of St Peter does not protrude as far as one might expect over the border of the green backcloth but just touches it. One tiny fold, hanging from the knee, overlaps that edge by a few millimetres (p. 268). By virtue of the fact that Masaccio has applied the same naturalism

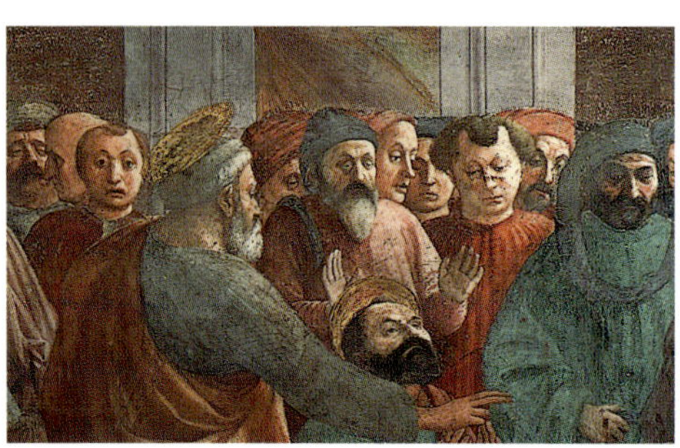

131. Masaccio, detail of the faces of seven men behind the kneeling St Paul in the Raising of Theophilus's Son, Brancacci Chapel, Sta Maria del Carmine, Florence, fresco, c.1424-28.

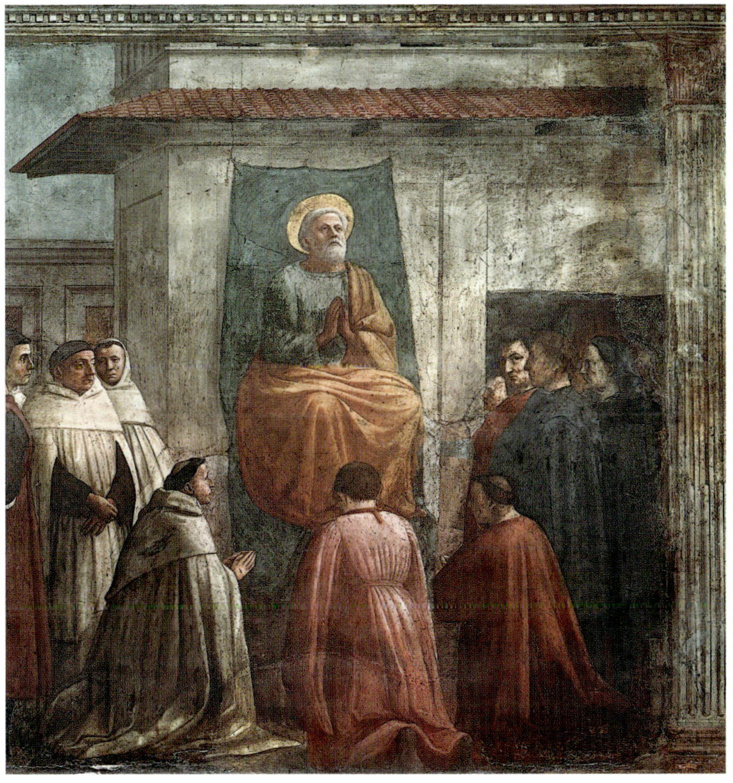

132. Masaccio, St Peter in Cathedra, Brancacci Chapel, Sta Maria del Carmine, Florence, fresco, c.1424–28. Frontal view photographed on a scaffold before the cleaning of the late 1980s.

both to the image of St Peter and to the figures around him it is impossible for the spectator to be certain whether to interpret it as a straightforward depiction of St Peter in Cathedra, or as contemporary Florentines around a painted banner of St Peter.

What is the point of this artistic trickery? Perhaps it was intended as a pictorial colophon, coming at the end of the story sequence on this wall and hence a manifesto of Masaccio's art. The banner is painted so as to make it hard for viewers to tell whether they are looking merely at a painting of St Peter enthroned or at a painting of a painting of St Peter. Masaccio's art came to be renowned for confounding the onlooker. Vasari describes a lost fresco of St Paul near the bell-ropes in the Carmine in which Masaccio 'exhibited extraordinary ability . . . the saint's head expressing a sense of awe [*terribilità*] so great that it seems only to lack the power of speech'.[29] Here, within the Brancacci Chapel, the figure of St Peter is painted not so much to deceive the eye but to invite the canny spectator to reflect upon the nature of such painting. At the same time one can also read the fresco as a depiction of the kneeling figures having a vision of St Peter appearing before them, his brow shining with light which seems to glow from within it rather than to be reflected. Another example of Masaccio's non-naturalistic use of lighting.[30]

If this interpretation is correct then the standing figure of a young man with the pointed nose and bushy hair almost immediately to the right of St Peter, in three-quarters profile looking somewhat slyly out of the picture directly at the spectator and with something of a twinkle in his eye, may, as some have suggested, be the self-portrait of Masaccio wittily taking credit for his formidable achievements.[31]

Finally we turn to Masaccio's planning of the whole wall (Fig. 133), the only wall in the chapel for which he had sole responsibility.[32] Till now, we have discussed these images as if we were looking at them in photographs taken from a scaffold. But as with all such chapels so also with this, gates and grilles excluded the public from entering, and the pictures had to be seen obliquely and of course from below, except for the lower paintings on the altar wall. Those who consider that Masaccio was employing a geometric perspective construction argue that this does not accord with one of its fundamental principles, namely that the spectator should stand at the presumed viewpoint from which the perspective was constructed. But as we have seen Masaccio did not employ that construction and we find that from outside the chapel the foreshortened compositions work in much the same way as Giotto's in the Bardi and Peruzzi chapels (Fig. 93).

From this position, moreover, all the paintings on the wall and pilaster coalesce into one grand scene. The landscape behind Adam and Eve seems to merge with the equally barren ground on the shore of the Sea of Galilee, the wall of Peter's prison with the massive buildings of Theophilus's palace. In this latter case, however, the wall of the prison painted upon the pilaster does not so much *merge* with the palace in the adjacent fresco as emphasise the illusion that we are looking at real scenes. This requires a more detailed explanation. The pilaster is raised a few inches above the surface of the main wall, enough to be noticeable. Upon it is painted a stuccoed wall lying parallel to its own surface. Windows are painted into this 'wall', behind one of which sits St Peter in his cell, and in front of which stands St Paul. Immediately adjacent, and also in the same plane as the wall, is the painted pilaster and the side wall of Theophilus's palace. Between the two, five men are

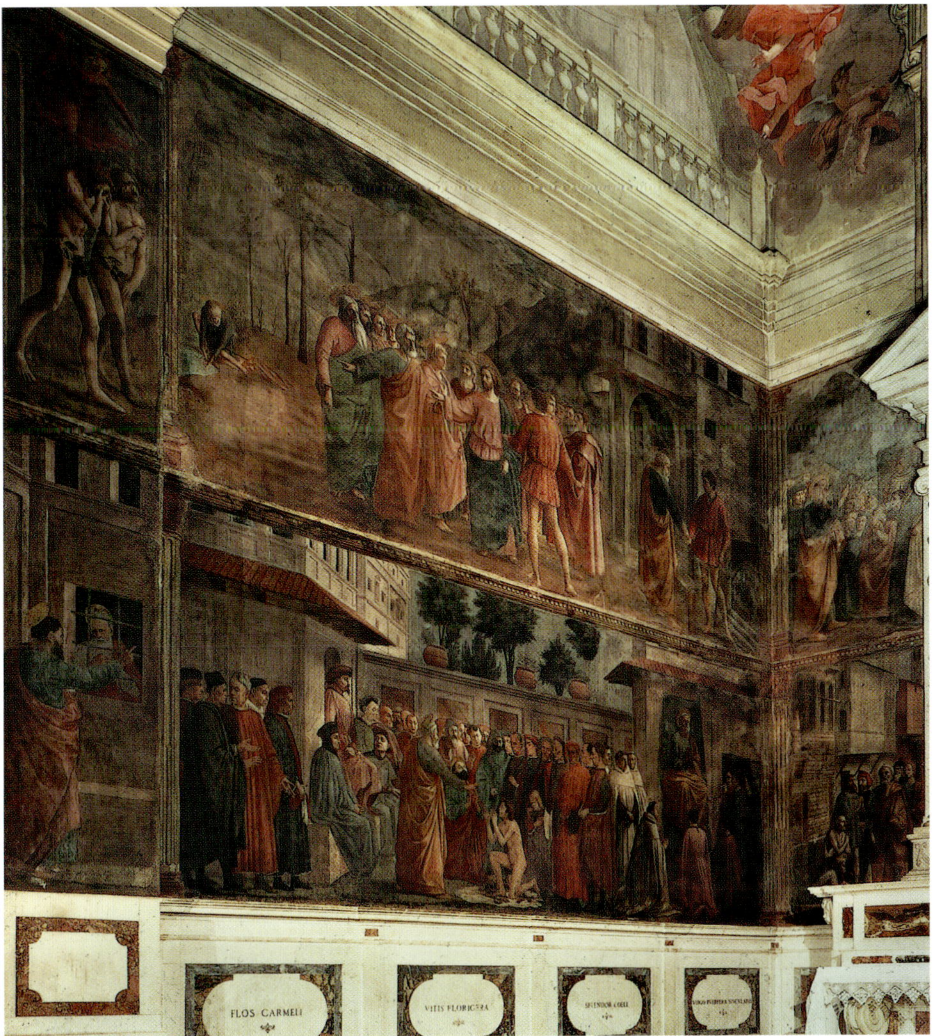

133. Masaccio, the south wall and part of the west wall of the Brancacci Chapel, Sta Maria del Carmine, Florence, fresco, c.1424–28, oblique view from outside the chapel photographed before the cleaning of the late 1980s. The frescoes on the south wall would have been designed to be seen from this position.

emerging into the courtyard. Because the painting of the prison wall on the pilaster has no frame, and because it really does stand out from the surface of the main wall, the impression of it being a solid building is enhanced, and we get the vivid sense that between it and the wall of the palace there is a passage through which the figures are entering the scene. Although all these figures as well as St Peter and St Paul are definitely by Filippino Lippi, this is another example of the way that features of low relief sculpture such as we find in Donatello's Head of St John (Fig. 124) have been integrated into fresco painting – incomplete views of the architecture, its habitability, and the freedom with which figures enter into the framed opening from the sides. All these factors contribute to the coherence and convincing nature of the image.

Thus the paintings upon the pilasters are not separated from those properly inside the chapel but integrated both visually and through their subject matter. In addition, the use of a very thin cornice to separate the upper from the lower tier of frescoes, facilitates the possibility of reading the whole wall as one, which the broader patterned bands used in earlier frescoed chapels would have prevented, though, as we have observed, Giotto related vertically aligned images to one another thematically.

The statement that The Expulsion from Eden is integrated with The Tribute Money by subject matter as well as landscape may seem surprising. But in looking at the wall as a whole (Fig. 133) this is the case. Adam and Eve are included, together with Masolino's scene of The Temptation on the opposite pilaster, to suggest the Fall of Mankind, whose remedy was the purpose of Jesus' mission.[33] In Masaccio's fresco Adam and Eve are walking away from the Gates of Paradise at an angle to the surface of the wall, as if they were about to walk diagonally across the chapel towards the altar – fallen man and woman like ourselves, the worshippers, seeking redemption through the celebration of the Mass and the Resurrection.

That is easy to grasp. But more important perhaps is the fact that from our distant vantage point the character of the Tribute Money as a whole changes. The scene of St Peter crouching by the sea shrinks into relative insignificance. The Tribute judgement dominates the whole register, its pendants to left and right become the figures of Adam and Eve and on the far side the contract between Peter and the tax collector, between Church and State. One can read the upper register then as Jesus giving his judicial decision that it is only through an even-handed and diplomatic agreement between Church and State that mankind can be redeemed from original sin and saved from eternal damnation at the Last Judgement. The Raising of Theophilus's Son is located directly beneath, so that the wall as a whole bears an affinity to the Last Judgement: aloft Jesus in majesty is surrounded by the apostles, while below is a scene of the dead being raised to life (Fig. 17). These images concern the power of the church in *this* world, suggested by the Gospel reading for the Feast of St Peter's Chair at Antioch:

> Thou art Peter, and upon this rock I will build my church; and the gates of hell shall not prevail against it. And I will give thee the keys of the kingdom of heaven: *and whatever thou shalt bind on earth shall be bound in heaven: and whatever thou shalt loose on earth shall be loosed in heaven* [my italics].[34]

The italicised passage is key to an understanding of the doctrine spelled out on this wall: what St Peter has raised on earth – Theophilus's son – shall be raised in heaven. What St Peter binds on earth – Ananias in the fresco of almsgiving on the altar wall – shall be damned. Moreover, where the Tribute Money shows St Peter in a state of confusion, the lower shows him fully in command, emulating Jesus in raising the dead just as Jesus had raised Lazarus. This is the apostle's inheritance.

The whole wall, the whole chapel indeed, is a major example of Carmelite propaganda for the primacy of the papacy against its many adversaries. It is interesting to note that in 1404 two English theology students at the University of Prague, who were suspected of Wycliffite tendencies, had some paintings made for their lodgings. On one wall were scenes of the life of Jesus shown in great simplicity, on the opposite wall, scenes of the life of the Pope in all his pomp and luxury. In his sermons, John Huss referred to these paintings with approval.[35] Perhaps the Brancacci Chapel frescoes are a response to such criticisms of the papacy. St Peter is depicted as a figure of gravity and moral dignity, he receives his charge directly from Jesus, whose mission he imitates in the execution of good works for the benefit of the poor and needy, and even his throne in the governor's former palace is devoid of costly ornament. In the words of Cristoforo Landino, Masaccio's art was 'pure without ornament', not only in its visual style but also in moral significance.[36]

This wall is a magnificent artistic accomplishment both in pictorial storytelling of the most complex kind and in the propagation of Church doctrine.

Conclusion

These works of the mid-1420s by Masaccio and Donatello indicate the wide range of possibilities open to artists making narrative images in the aftermath of the 1401 competition and Ghiberti's doors. As we can see, the situation was far from a simple case of a Brunelleschian avant-garde pursuing a perspectivally and compositionally centralised approach, focused upon a fixed moment in time, in opposition to the open-endedness and reflective nature of the reliefs of the more traditional Ghiberti. There is no evidence of Brunelleschi's involvement either in the works themselves or in the invention of the correct geometrical perspective construction. The types of perspective employed by Donatello and Masaccio were not fully systematic and although there was progress towards an approximation to central point perspective, the geometric construction described by Alberti to control apparent diminution is not in evidence, certainly not in the figures that are more often than not out of scale with their surroundings. The perspective appears systematic only with hindsight. This is not to say that these images are incoherent, but their coherence is not dependent solely or even largely upon the imperfect perspective construction but upon the precisely defined frame through which and in relation to which all the images are presented to the spectator. In addition to this, both artists employed a battery of mutually reinforcing devices: the use of the frame to mask some elements of the setting so that we see only incomplete parts of buildings and landscapes, the overlapping of forms, the way that figures inhabit the architecture, the massive nature of many of the buildings, Donatello's use of diminishing levels of relief and Masaccio's aerial perspective, oblique viewpoints and movement parallax in Donatello, directional lighting, strong modelling and cast shadows in Masaccio.

Both artists exploited the possibility of oblique and, in the case of Donatello, of multiple viewpoints (Fig. 124–6). Indeed Masaccio could not have avoided doing so because he had to deal with the constraints of the family chapel, the same as those faced by Giotto and his successors. The most momentary, climactic and physically expressive of these images, Donatello's Head of St John, can, nonetheless, be looked at from a range of viewpoints, as in Ghiberti's reliefs. Donatello's relief is not presented in an externalised manner; through different viewpoints he enables us to enter into the feelings of several different characters in the drama. Nor is the focus exclusively upon the presentation of the head and the immediacy of Herod's reaction. Masaccio, however, adopted an even more complex approach to suggesting the sequence of events in the Tribute Money (Fig. 127) where he compresses the moment of Jesus' verdict with the earlier episode of the argument between St Peter and the taxman, relating this central composition to the consequences of Jesus' act of judgement. While the converging lines of the building help to focus attention upon Jesus, they only serve to reinforce what is primarily determined by the arrangement of the figures, with Jesus at their centre. The actions of Masaccio's characters are far calmer than those in Donatello's relief, similar in this respect to Giotto or Ghiberti, yet although there are elements of a psychological drama in the Tribute Money, the narrative basically serves to spell out a doctrinal message. Many of these points also apply to the Raising of Theophilus's Son (Fig. 130), except that the converging lines, that are in any case less insistent, actually point *away* from the focus of the drama, while the architectural setting to which the perspective is applied constitutes a flat screen in front of which the action takes place, which had been standard practice for the preceding century.

So, apart from the employment of a collection of methods to establish a greater sense of naturalism, including an unsystematic form of perspective, these works by Donatello and Masaccio of the mid-1420s have little else in common with one another or with Brunelleschi's 1401 competition relief. Donatello in some respects continues the tradition of Giovanni Pisano and Ghiberti in the three-dimensionality of his relief, drawing the spectator into the action from a variety of viewpoints. In the passionate behaviour of his figures he resembles Giovanni, while he follows Ghiberti in the way that he draws the spectator into their inner feelings. Only in the climactic presentation of the head is there much similarity to Brunelleschi's Sacrifice of Isaac. Masaccio on the other hand is very similar to Giotto and even more so to Duccio in the way that he creates a sense of detachment and distance between the spectator and the image, in the temperate demeanour of his figures and his employment of the pregnant moment. Yet unlike Giotto or Ghiberti we are not led to enter into the minds of the characters: Masaccio's primary concern, in these works, is with the doctrinal message.

Finally, both artists have more affinity to Giotto than to Ghiberti in the kind of logic they employ. Ghiberti was above all interested in telling a story in its psychological subtleties, and hence he focuses upon the causal relationships between his figures, as we shall see again in the next chapter. But while the story is obviously important in Donatello's Head of St John, the moral consequences of Herod's actions predominate. So, in addition to cause and effect Donatello has suggested a set of antitheses or inversions: birthday, death-day; palace, dungeon etc. This is even more the case in the Brancacci Chapel where, much as in Giotto's Scrovegni Chapel, narrative is a vehicle for doctrine. Thus Masaccio sets up the antitheses between the Expulsion from Paradise and the contract between Church and State, between St Peter confused and St Peter enthroned and in command, between the spiritual leader St Peter, and the worldly ruler, Theophilus. At the same time Masaccio provides evidence of his outstanding intellectual agility and ingenuity in suggesting the conditional relationship between paying the tax, thereby reaching an accommodation with the State, and maintaining the mission of the Church to redeem mankind: a rare example of an 'if . . . then . . .' represented in a visual image. Finally, perhaps the most difficult problem of all, Masaccio found the means to convey the complex legal reasoning in the abstruse dialogue between St Peter and Jesus on tax liability in a single, powerful visual image.

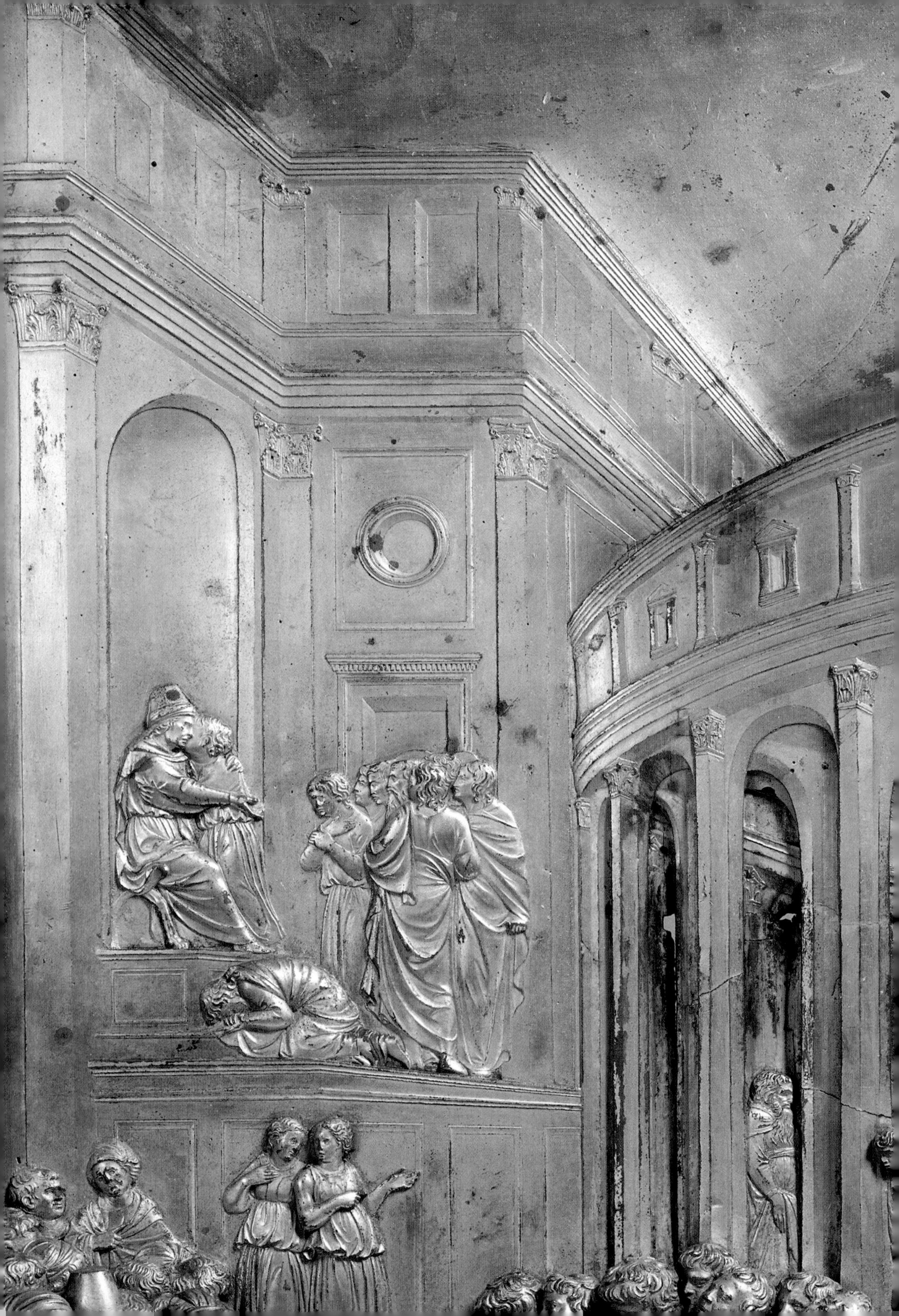

VIII

GHIBERTI'S GATES OF PARADISE

Ghiberti, meanwhile, had been working on the third gates for the Florence Baptistry (Fig. 134), for which he was awarded the commission in January 1425, though he probably began work in earnest upon the final format in 1428.[1] Donatello and Masaccio's recent work, which he must have known, was a challenge to him both in its more coherent naturalism and in the way the two artists tackled narrative. But before discussing Ghiberti's response it is necessary to establish a few dates. By April 1436 or 1437 all the ten panels had been cast in bronze. But the period during which Ghiberti actually composed and modelled the ten reliefs may have been shorter. This can be inferred from the fact that at least two changes were made to the format of the doors and to the number of panels, before it was agreed to have only ten. In June 1424, before Ghiberti got the job, the humanist scholar and Chancellor of Florence, Leonardo Bruni, was writing a narrative programme for the new doors on the same model as the earlier doors, with twenty-eight panels: twenty depicting the stories from the Old Testament and eight showing prophets.[2] The existing back frame of the doors, however, originally cast to serve as the front frame, allows for only twenty-four panels and obviously must have been made some time between 1425 and 1437. There is no evidence for an exact date but Richard Krautheimer, author of the main mono-

Lorenzo Ghiberti, Joseph and his Brothers, 1425–52, gilded bronze. Detail from the original of the right-hand relief in the central tier of the Gates of Paradise. Museo dell'Opera del Duomo, Florence.

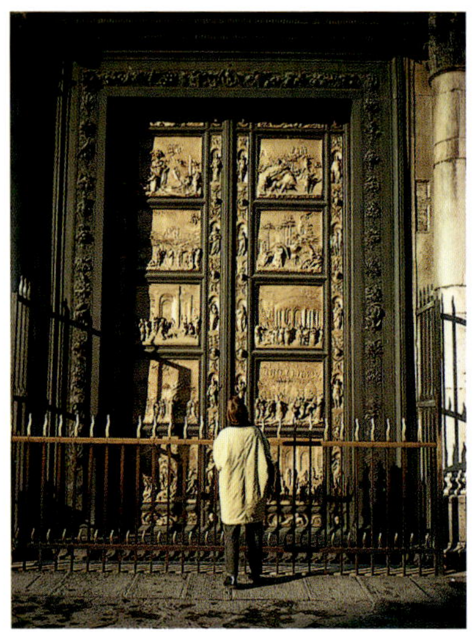

134. Lorenzo Ghiberti, the Gates of Paradise, the third gates of the Florence Baptistery facing the main entrance to the Cathedral, gilded bronze, 1425–52.

graph on Ghiberti, argues that this occurred in 1428 or 1429, as plausible a guess as any.

The implication is that Ghiberti did all the creative work on the final format of the Gates of Paradise within eight or nine years, much the same period as he spent on the second doors. It took a further fifteen years to finish the doors, which is also comparable to the twelve years it probably took to finish Ghiberti's earlier set.

What was Ghiberti doing in the three years from 1425 to 1428? In the summer of 1425 he was commissioned to make a full-size bronze statue of St Stephen for the niche belonging to the biggest guild in Florence, the Wool Guild or *Arte della Lana*, on the guild church of Or San Michele. This was ready for casting in August two years later in 1427. Over the same period he was being pressed by his Sienese clients to deliver his two reliefs for the Baptistery font, commissioned in 1417, though it is quite possible that he had started work and cast one of these, the Arrest of the Baptist, by 1420. Both reliefs were delivered in 1427. But heavy though the demands upon his time must have been, it would be strange had he not begun to plan and design the third gates of the Baptistery, the so-called Gates of Paradise. If his starting point were a twenty-eight panel format, as envisaged by Bruni in 1424, then he would have had to work through the implications of three different formats before agreement was reached upon the final ten relief scheme.

The old format with twenty quatrefoil panels, 45 × 38 cm, for the stories, would have provided too small an area for Ghiberti to respond to a work like Donatello's or to develop the innovations he had made in his own reliefs for the Siena font (Fig. 122–3). Even the revised format of sixteen panels envisaged when the rear frame was cast was inadequate – 50 cm square. The size of panel finally adopted for the new gates, 73 cm square, was similar to that of the Siena font reliefs which were 79 cm square – Ghiberti must have been a formidable negotiator to obtain these changes of format.[3]

We can infer the nature of Ghiberti's response to the younger artists primarily from the visual evidence of his reliefs on the Gates of Paradise and also from the writings of his old age, the *Commentari*. He embraced several of their innovations but did so in a critical spirit, and he also attempted to surpass them. In the central panels of Jacob and Esau (Fig. 139) and Joseph and his Brothers (Fig. 138), the fine loggia of Isaac's mansion and the circular granary, are more ambitious than any earlier representations of architecture, and the figures are better proportioned to the buildings. Like both Donatello and Masaccio, however, Ghiberti does not employ a precise vanishing point, and there is no evidence of his having either learned or discovered the correct geometrical method for constructing the framework to govern the diminution in the apparent size of objects with distance.[4] To take just one example: in the Joseph panel the figures within the granary are half the size of Joseph's brothers on the plinth to the left, even though they are all the same distance from the spectator.

In two fundamental aspects, however, Ghiberti diverged from his younger contemporaries. One of these relates to visual aspects of the image, the other to the narrative. First, he rejected the all-encompassing frame employed by Donatello, with all the figures lying behind it, most in very low or half relief. Even though oblique views are essential to the Head of St John, they are seen through the frame (Fig. 125–6). Ghiberti, however, seems to have wanted to retain the full range of different points of view which he employed in the second Baptistery Doors and which Giovanni Pisano has used on his pulpits. He may have thought that to pursue Donatello's path would negate the distinctive advantages of relief sculpture, pioneered by Giovanni, reducing it to a form of painting. Ghiberti adopted what seems to be a compromise. There is a frame but the lower part of the panel projects towards the spectator in the form of a apron stage upon which the free-standing figures are placed. The figures in lower relief are behind the frame, which does not, however, mask either figures or setting to any extent. In particular, the frame is not used to mask buildings and interiors so that only parts are visible; Ghiberti likes to show his buildings in their entirety. Consequently, for his figures to be in scale they have to be correspondingly smaller than those in Donatello's St John, about two-thirds the size. They are also better scaled to their surroundings than those of his predecessors.

In the depiction of the stories Ghiberti's practice diverged still more from that of Donatello and Masaccio, and from his own earlier work. Even though they had incorporated several episodes within the single frame, those scenes were so subordinated to the main subject and composition that one's first impression is of a single event, arising in part from the unifying effect of the frame. But in all but two of the ten panels on the Gates of Paradise Ghiberti adopted so-called continuous narration even more enthusiastically than Giovanni Pisano, showing as many as eight separate episodes in the panel of Jacob and Esau (Fig. 139).[5] He was quite explicit about this in his description of the work in the *Commentari* where he enumerated the number of scenes in each: thus in the Cain and Abel (Fig. 135), he says four stories are enacted. In most panels moreover it is not immediately possible to discern which of these episodes is the dominant one, indeed it is sometimes difficult to work out what is happening at all, as we shall discover. It is as if Ghiberti were arguing that in reality events must unfold in a sequence of episodes and these should be set out in a single panel, as Giovanni Pisano had done. His long description of every single episode in Ambrogio Lorenzetti's Franciscan Martyrdom shows how enthusiastic he was about such an approach.[6]

Ghiberti's Gates of Paradise are a carefully considered critique of Donatello and Masaccio's recent achievements and part of a continuing dialogue. Ghiberti could see the value in the innovations of his younger contemporaries. Very low cameo-style relief as in Donatello's Siena relief had been pioneered by Ghiberti himself. Now he extended its use to great open landscapes, buildings and indeed figures, but unlike Donatello he also used the full gamut of relief sculpture. The effect of this is to imitate nature more closely since it enables sculpture more fully to suggest the effects of movement parallax – the movement of nearby and distant objects relative to one another as the spectator changes position, as when one looks out of the window of a moving railway carriage. Hence, in Ghiberti's sculptures background objects in very low relief do not change their position relative to the spectator when one moves around them while those in the foreground and in high relief do. This is one of the most important elements in our perception of the distance between objects (see appendix).

These technical matters of perception and representation were not pursued for their own sake but for that of the narrative, as Alberti was to write, 'The greatest work of the painter is the historia.'[7] To this we will now turn.

All the reliefs have been designed to be seen according to their position on the doors, as Alessandro Parronchi demonstrated.[8] In the story of Cain and Abel (Fig. 135), positioned on the highest tier, this greatly enhances the effect of the landscape setting. The rocky outcrop in medium relief in front of which Cain is ploughing masks the bottoms of the trunks of the trees in the valley behind, in lower relief, so that they appear convincingly tall, and the platform of the hill upon which Cain and Abel make their burnt offerings is observed behind the tops of those trees in still lower relief, a long way off. The figures in low relief of Cain and Abel sacrificing are small and the two altars before which they are kneeling are represented in perspective foreshortened from below, which enhances the effect of their height above us and of our craning up to look at them. On the left still further away and in lowest relief, is the scene of Adam and Eve in front of their circular thatched hut, the first human shelter, with their infants, Cain and Abel. The surface of the area representing the sky is slightly uneven to suggest light cloud. Because we are able to move around the panel the overall effect of parallax is particularly striking.

The story itself is told backwards, that is to say, the foreground represents the present – Cain on the left is called from his plough and God asks him, 'Where is Abel thy brother?' The rest of the story, the murder, the sacrifice, the brothers' childhood is conceived as a progressive series of flashbacks temporally positioned in accordance with the distance of each episode from the spectator. Thus, very simply, distance in space represents distance in time. This is a sophisticated development of what Giovanni Pisano had done in the Nativity and Adoration panels of the Pistoia pulpit (Fig. 61), particularly in the Adoration where we look at the Adoration from the vantage point of the dreaming Magi and Joseph. But the faintness of Ghiberti's very low cameo relief enhances this effect and acts as a metaphorical suggestion of memory, fainter and less immediate than the three-dimensionality and solidity of the here and now. Let us take note in passing that Ghiberti does not invariably use the lowest relief to this end. The Creation of Adam (Fig. 136) in the first panel is in the highest relief while the scene of the serpent tempting Adam and Eve is in the lowest relief, taking place in a grove of trees. In that case low relief is used to give emphasis to the furtiveness of their act of disobedience. Ghiberti, therefore, subtly employs different levels of relief for a variety of narrative purposes, and to suggest different kinds of 'voice' – something not attempted in the works of either Masaccio or Donatello.

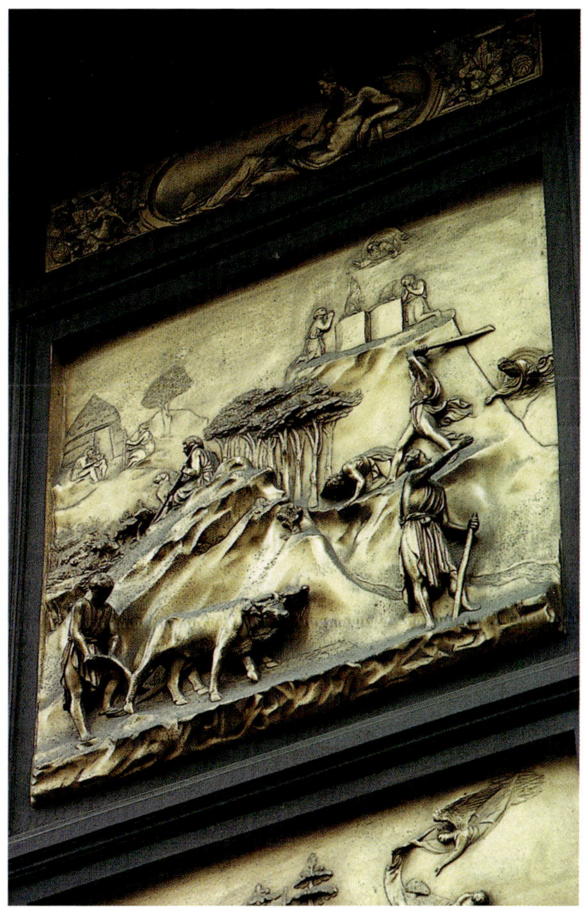

135. Lorenzo Ghiberti, the Story of Cain and Abel, top right-hand relief on the Gates of Paradise, 1425–52. This photograph was taken from the right-hand side and from beneath. The relief in situ is a facsimile of the original which is now in the Museo dell' Opera del Duomo, Florence.

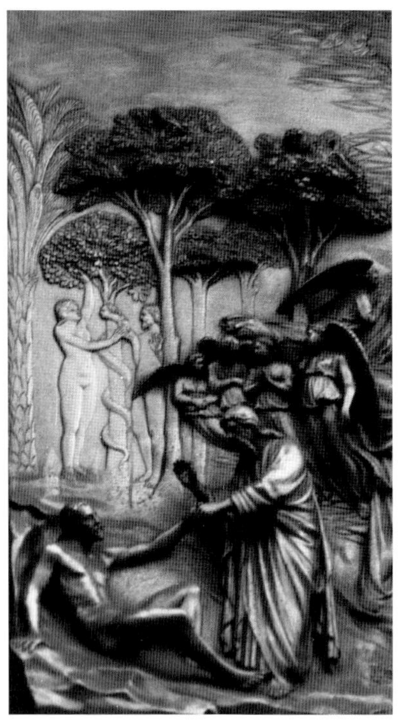

136. Lorenzo Ghiberti, the Fall and the Creation of Adam, detail of the Creation, top left -hand relief on the Gates of Paradise, 1425–52. This photograph was taken from the left-hand side and from beneath. The relief in situ is a facsimile of the original which is now in the Museo dell'Opera del Duomo, Florence.

But in the Cain and Abel relief levels are used to establish sequence. And here Ghiberti is ingenious. What has been said so far implies that one should read the panel as God questioning Cain in the 'present', the murder having taken place in the *immediate* past and the sacrifices in the more *remote* past. The very adjectives we use to describe time suggest the close metaphorical connection between time and distance. But to an artist so thoughtful about pictorial narration there was a problem, one already encountered. How could one *show* God asking Cain about the whereabouts of his brother who was now dead? Ghiberti's solution (Fig. 137) was to place the murder scene in the 'recent past' above Cain's head in close juxtaposition to God emerging out of the sky looking down on Cain while pointing with his right arm towards the murder. In this way Ghiberti suggests the content of the question as well as God's subsequent statement when Cain denies all knowledge: 'What hast thou done? The voice of thy brother's blood crieth unto me from the ground.' This is conveyed with great precision. It is an elegant solution to a difficult problem, possibly derived from Giovanni Pisano's method of visualising Gabriel's prophecy to Mary in the Annunciation of the Pistoia pulpit (Fig. 54).[9]

There is more to this relief. Normally, as we have seen, Ghiberti did not like to depict the climax of an event, but here, in this of all stories, his decision not to foreground the first murder seems almost perverse. When we look casually at the scene the first thing to catch our eye is the murder, superbly portrayed with Cain on the point of bringing his bludgeon down with all the force of his lithe body upon the head of Abel cowering upon the ground. Almost all the other figures are looking away from us, into the picture, self-absorbed in less dramatic workaday activities set in a beautiful and innocent pastoral landscape. So there is a paradox in the presentation of the murder scene. Its violence, even though the moment when the club hits Abel has not been chosen, makes it the most vivid scene in the panel; whereas its position, distancing and level of relief make it somewhat remote. It seems almost like a memory in Cain's mind, his guilt of the crime of fratricide, the result of fraternal rivalry. This, perhaps, explains why this relief is so moving. These suggestions would have been lost had Ghiberti foregrounded this episode. It would have been merely a murder, neither a guilty memory nor a guilty fantasy which God is uncovering. Ghiberti was a subtle psychologist.

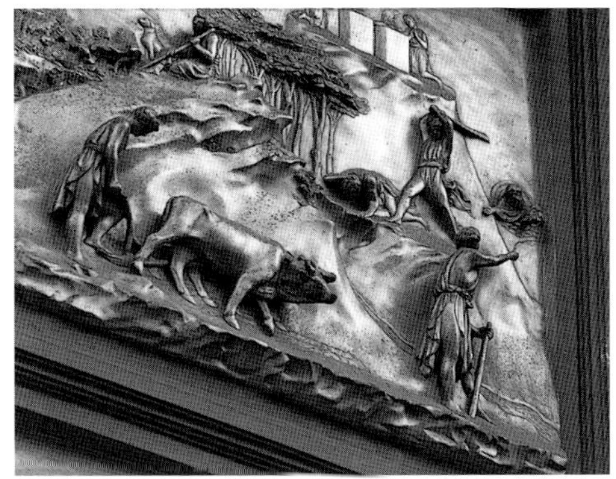

137. Lorenzo Ghiberti, God accusing Cain of murdering his brother, close up from the Story of Cain and Abel, top right-hand relief on the Gates of Paradise, 1425-52. This photograph was taken from the left-hand side and from beneath. The relief in situ is a facsimile of the original which is now in the Museo dell'Opera del Duomo, Florence.

Pursuing this train of thought, Ghiberti's critique of the decisive moment, and of active gesticulation or excessive violence, can be restated: if we wish to convey either in images, or indeed in words, the deeper and more intangible aspects of human experience we cannot use the direct approach. In order to allow the spectator the time and freedom to become inward with the work we have to adopt an indirect approach, and sometimes we have to lower our voice rather than rant at the audience. Perhaps this was a criticism of Donatello's Head of St John. The triumph of Ghiberti's indirect approach, the manifesto of his masterly pictorial narrative and perhaps one of the cleverest images in Western art – even a little too clever – is the panel of Joseph and his Brothers (Fig. 138), another story of fratricidal jealousy, attempted murder, conspiracy and revenge. This work has not enjoyed a good press in recent art-historical writing, but Vasari claimed that the scene 'on account of the expressions and the variety of incidents which it contains, is considered by all to be the most worthy, the most difficult, and the most beautiful in the whole work'[10] – a judgement I shall try to justify. First, however, we shall examine the recent criticisms.

The first by Richard Krautheimer and Trude Krautheimer-Hess emerges from a comparison of the Joseph with the Jacob and Esau panel (Fig. 139), which they much prefer.

> The composition [of the Joseph] is sustained by two large groups in the foreground, each of which is formed by a dozen or more figures. Though the two are far apart in content, they are designed as one throng of people, joined together by the complementary movements of the two 'leaders'(Fig. 141) a woman from the Distribution of Grain who turns inwards, and one

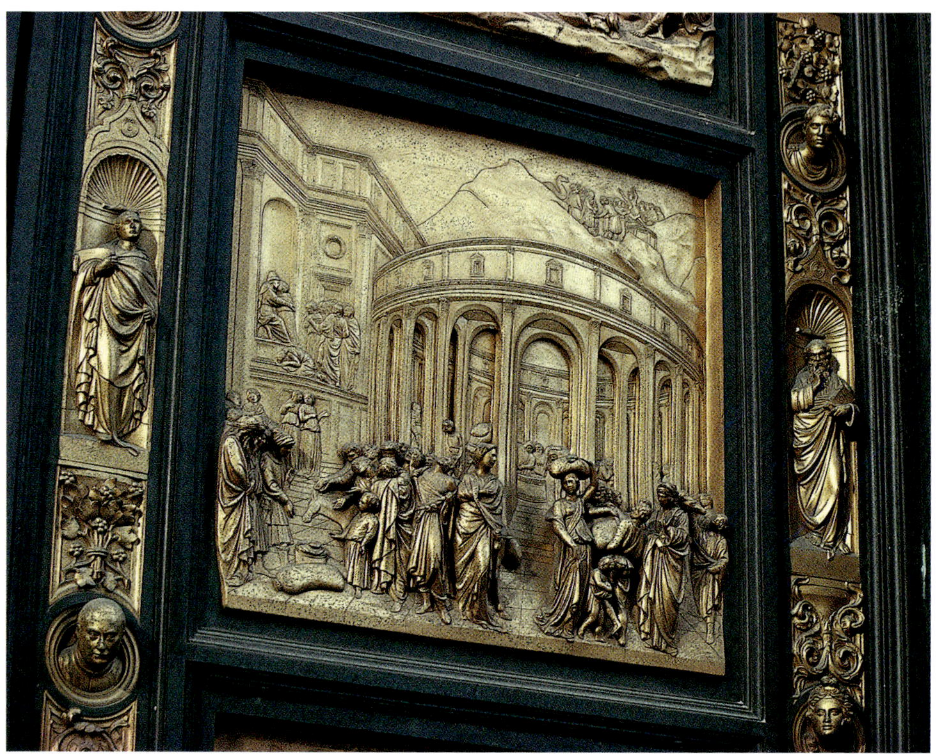

138. Lorenzo Ghiberti, Joseph and his Brothers, right-hand relief in the central tier of the Gates of Paradise, 1425–52. This photograph was taken from the left-hand side and from beneath. The relief in situ is a facsimile of the original which is now in the Museo dell'Opera del Duomo, Florence.

> of the brothers from the Discovery of the Cup who turns outwards. Ghiberti's attention was centered on these crowds to the extent that the individual has lost importance. Stances and movements have turned mechanical, the invenzione less rich, the draperies less articulate and free.[11]

They condemn the lack of narrative clarity. The crowds of figures in the centre foreground are so much the focus of Ghiberti's attention 'that the individual has lost importance'. E. H. Gombrich in a somewhat earlier article went even further in arguing that Ghiberti's overriding objective was to present his solution to a perspectival problem akin to the peepshows attributed to Brunelleschi by Manetti.

> . . . this introduces us most vividly into the mentality engendered by the idea of progress. The artist works like a scientist. His works exist not only

for their own sake but also to demonstrate certain problem-solutions. He creates them for the admiration of all, but principally with an eye on his fellow artists and the connoisseurs who can appreciate the ingenuity of the solution put forward. We are reminded of Brunelleschi's lost panels with views of Florentine buildings, which were made with no other purpose in mind than to prove the validity of his perspective construction.[12] Alberti, too, devised some kind of peepshows to display the powers of art in creating illusions. He and his biographer call these exercises '*dimostrationi*', demonstrations.

Something of this spirit of experimentation is also exemplified in the Second Door. The round building in the story of Joseph contributes nothing to the narrative. On the contrary, it rather muddles it. But it is displayed in the centre of the work as a *dimostratione*, a token of the master's skill in applied geometry which, we may assume, surpassed anything done before along these lines.[13]

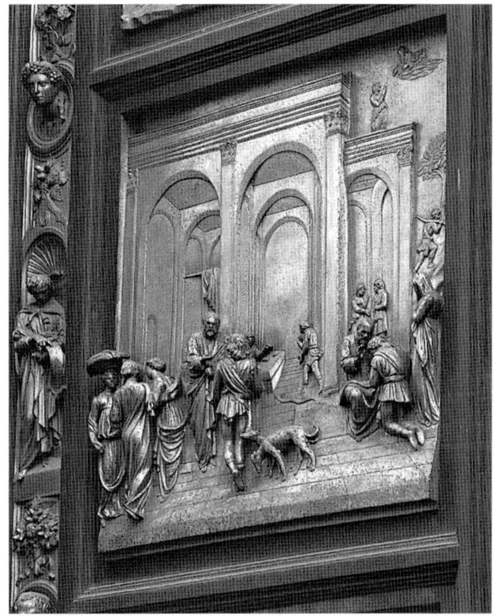

139. Lorenzo Ghiberti, Jacob and Esau, left-hand relief in the central tier of the Gates of Paradise, 1425–52. This photograph was taken from the right-hand side and from beneath. The relief in situ is a facsimile of the original which is now in the Museo dell'Opera del Duomo, Florence.

The nub of Gombrich's criticism is that Ghiberti's primary concern was not the narrative but the perspective of the magnificent circular granary which detracts from the narrative.

There are three issues which an answer needs to address. The first concerns the fine perspective of the granary; the second and most important, as well as the most difficult, relates to the pictorial narrative; last of all we need to consider what role Ghiberti intended the granary to have within the narrative.

The granary is magnificent architecture. It captures one's attention immediately. Likewise the perspective of the granary is also a demonstration of Ghiberti's skill, far and away the most complex representation of a building to have been made to date. But that does not necessarily imply that Ghiberti lacked interest in the narrative, nor that the granary contributes nothing to it or muddles it. In the Gates of Paradise (Fig. 134) Ghiberti not only depicted a variety of different landscapes, he also produced a kind of history of architecture, each building depicted in perspective, showing its development from Adam and Eve's simple circular thatched hut through the post-and-lintel hut and the pyramidical Ark in the Noah to the magnificent loggias of Isaac's house and the granaries of Pharaoh's Egypt, concluding with views of the cities of Jericho and Jerusalem and, in the final panel, of Solomon's Temple.

To understand the significance of this sequence of buildings, it has to be recalled that until the second half of the nineteenth century all but a few sceptics believed that the Bible gave a true account of the history of mankind since the Creation. It was only reasonable to see architecture as a yardstick of mankind's progress from the simplicities of Adam and Eve's life outside Eden. A careful reader of the Old Testament will find that buildings are relevant to the stories. Whereas Abraham dwelt in tents, as Ghiberti shows him, his son Isaac, an immensely wealthy and successful livestock farmer, lived in a city at one stage of his life.[14] The airy loggia of his mansion can be interpreted as Ghiberti's method of signifying his huge wealth, the inheritance of which is the central theme of the story. Even more significant in the panel of Joseph are the granaries which Joseph built to store the corn accumulated during the seven years of boom harvests. These are absolutely central to the story as well as an indication of the wealth and civilization of Egypt with all its cities. Joseph's grandfather, Isaac, was merely a rich cattle farmer with a fine ranch house; Joseph himself, according to the Bible, was the second most important man in the wealthiest, most powerful and best organised state in the world. In architectural terms, the granary Ghiberti imagined Joseph as building is a wonderfully elaborate structure. It is similar to Or San Michele, the palatial grain market and loggia that the Florentines had built in the fourteenth century, only circular, enclosing a piazza. It is a highly inventive architectural composition in its own right testifying to Ghiberti's fertility in the field of architectural design.

A circular building is more difficult to represent than a rectangular one, whatever perspectival approach is used, and with its arched colonnade running around the inside of the circular loggia, this would have been intricate and very time-consuming indeed. To understand the full significance of the building we must first consider Ghiberti's treatment of the story.

The story of Joseph is long, complex and rambles somewhat over fourteen chapters of Genesis.[15] Let us remind ourselves of its bare bones. Joseph was the youngest of the eleven sons of Jacob and his favourite, to whom Jacob gave a coat of many colours as a token of his affection. Joseph was also a prophet and interpreter of dreams who dreamt of his brothers and parents paying homage to him. For all these reasons his brothers envied him, and when the occasion arose they captured him, putting him in a dry well in the desert, leaving him to die. However some Ishmaelite merchants were passing and the brothers decided instead to sell Joseph as a slave, taking his coat of many colours back to Jacob covered with animal's blood, claiming that Joseph had been killed and devoured by wild animals.

Meanwhile Joseph is sold in Egypt and becomes a slave to Potiphar, captain of Pharaoh's bodyguard. Joseph's great abilities result in his promotion to chief officer in Potiphar's household. When Pharaoh has two dreams, Joseph alone is able to interpret them as forecasting a famine of seven years following seven years of good harvests and he advises Pharaoh accordingly to store grain during the seven good years for distribution during the famine – the first recorded instance of counter-cyclical economic policy!

Pharaoh appoints Joseph as his Chief Minister. The famine arrives and Jacob, who has since had another son, Benjamin,* sends his ten older sons to Egypt to buy corn, but he does not send Benjamin for fear of anything happening to him. Now Joseph has his opportunity for revenge. His brothers come to him to buy corn. He recognises them but does not reveal his own identity. He accuses them of being spies sent by Jacob to report on the depth of the famine in Egypt. He puts them in prison for three days and only agrees to sell them corn on condition that one brother stays behind, making any further sales conditional upon their bringing Benjamin the next time. Meanwhile he arranges for their money to be returned to them covertly in the sacks of corn.

When their corn runs out Jacob sends them to Egypt again and is forced this time to send Benjamin. On their arrival in Egypt Joseph has the brothers brought to his palace. They are terrified of being accused and punished for taking the money on the first occasion. But Joseph wines and dines them, asks whether their father is still alive, sees Benjamin and is so overcome with emotion that he has to leave the room. This time he tells his chief steward once again to put their money back in their sacks but in addition to put his own silver cup in Benjamin's sack. When the brothers depart, the steward, on Joseph's orders, overtakes them and accuses them of stealing Joseph's cup. So strongly do they deny the accusation that they make an offer: if the cup is found in any sack they will agree to its owner being executed, and all of them will voluntarily become Joseph's slaves. The cup is found in Benjamin's sack, the brothers are brought back in grief and anguish to Joseph, who torments them further by insisting upon keeping Benjamin. Finally, having exacted sufficient revenge, he reveals himself to them:

*The age of Benjamin is problematical.

Then Joseph could not refrain himself before all them that stood by him; and he cried, Cause every man to go out from me. And there stood no man with him, while Joseph made himself known unto his brethren. And he wept aloud: and the Egyptians and the house of Pharaoh heard. And Joseph said unto his brethren, I am Joseph; doth my father yet live? And his brethren could not answer him, for they were troubled at his presence. And Joseph said unto his brethren, Come near to me, I pray you. And they came near. And he said, I *am* Joseph your brother, whom ye sold into Egypt. Now therefore be not grieved, nor angry with yourselves, that you sold me hither: for God did send me before you to preserve life . . . And he fell upon his brother Benjamin's neck, and wept; and Benjamin wept upon his neck. Moreover he kissed all his brethren and wept upon them . . .[16]

It is an emotional story, a real tear-jerker, particularly the passage where Joseph asks after his father before revealing his identity, and afterwards when he has to tell his brothers *twice* that he is Joseph. It is a story not only of fraternal jealousy but also of conflict between father and son, for even Jacob was enraged when Joseph, his brilliant and arrogant son, recounted his dream of lording it over his father as well as over his brothers. And while Joseph exacts his revenge upon his brothers' guilty consciences, toying with them over Benjamin, he is also knowingly torturing his father, as well as taking pride in showing him all the success that his intelligence and prophetic gifts have brought him.

'And ye shall tell my father of all my glory in Egypt'

Finally, of course, Joseph forgives, having exacted his revenge and savoured it to the full.

What is special about Ghiberti's visualisation? Much is straightforward. In the far distance, in the mountains, the brothers take Joseph out of the well and sell him to the merchants. The brothers come and buy corn, they load their sacks, the cup is discovered, Joseph reveals himself to them. And Ghiberti tells this in six simple episodes, highly selective certainly, but providing a compressed account of the full story which is depicted in fifteen scenes on the inside of the dome of the Baptistery. The next episode is the granary itself, Ghiberti's magnificent architecture, the very image, in Joseph's words 'of all my glory in Egypt'. Far from 'contributing nothing to the narrative' it is central to it and appropriately located. Ghiberti created the most magnificent architecture of which he was capable, and presented it in the most intricate foreshortening in order to make manifest those words of Joseph. It is hard not to entertain the suspicion that the granary was also intended as a symbol of Ghiberti's glory here in Florence, close to Brunelleschi's cupola.

Within the structure, on the left, the well-head of the store is being filled with corn from the sacks, while to the right people are carrying away full sacks on their shoulders during the famine. The fourth scene in the foreground to the right shows the brothers loading their full sacks onto their camel, while on the left-hand side the cup is discovered in young Benjamin's sack, and the brothers react with expressions of grief. Finally in low relief on a dais in Joseph's palace he falls on Benjamin's neck and weeps (Fig. 143). It is all depicted with perfect clarity since all these episodes concern straightforward actions and emotions which are easily represented. Moreover the sequence of episodes follows a roughly clockwise order from the top right around the panel. The only oddity, to which no one has drawn attention, let alone explained, though perhaps Vasari hints at its significance in his reference to difficulty, is the scene that first catches one's eye, taking place in the centre foreground (Fig. 140) between the young man, the young woman with a bag of corn on her head and a child at her feet; the Krautheimers call them 'the two leaders', and the other tall man just to the right of her. These three figures are the largest, as well as the most prominent in the panel. Who are they and what are they doing?

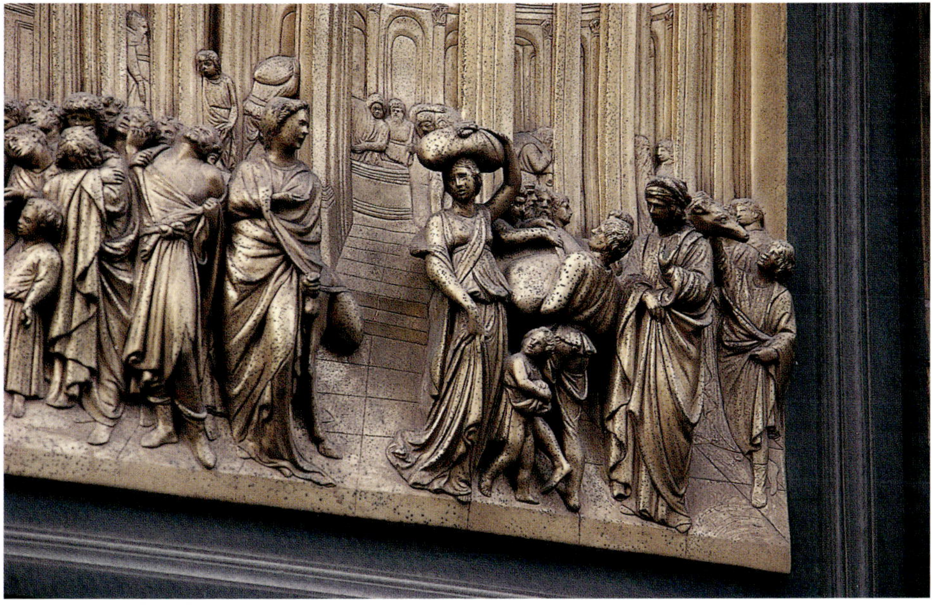

140. Lorenzo Ghiberti, the Three Leaders, close up from Joseph and his Brothers, right-hand relief in the central tier of the Gates of Paradise, 1425-52. This photograph was taken from the left-hand side and from beneath. The relief in situ is a facsimile of the original which is now in the Museo dell'Opera del Duomo, Florence.

We need to re-examine the story of Joseph's revenge and revelation. It all turns upon secrecy and upon Joseph's conspiracy to deceive his brothers. It is a complex story, and conspiracies are hard to represent visually. When his brothers first arrive Joseph recognises them but they do not recognise him and he keeps his identity secret. In addition he gets his steward to put their money and later his silver cup into their sack without their knowing. The pictorial representation of negatives, of absences, of deception are some of the most difficult for a visual artist to accomplish, since images must necessarily show the viewer things that are *present*, not things that are absent.[17] But here it is a matter not only of representing things absent but things deliberately *concealed* as part of Joseph's stratagem to have his revenge. In addition, to be effective, the artist like the good detective writer, must be able to pull the wool over the spectator's eyes in order to suggest the deception of the characters within the drama. And this feat, I suggest, Ghiberti has successfully accomplished. How?

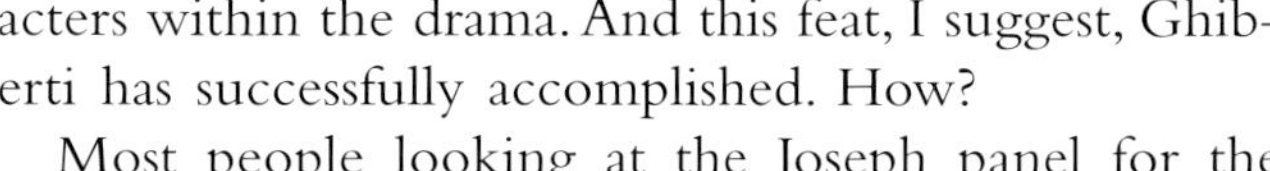

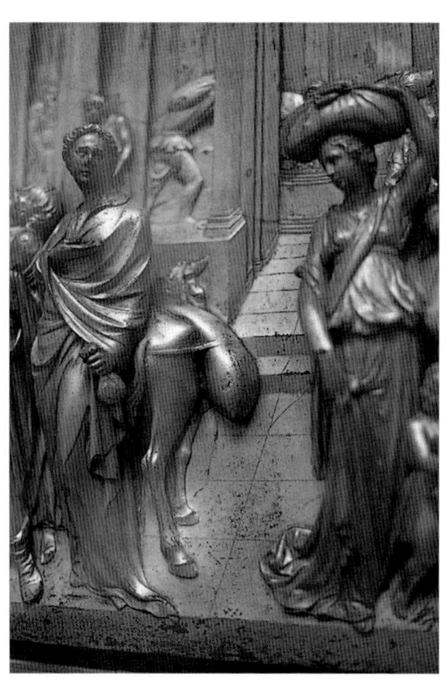

141. Lorenzo Ghiberti, the two central figures from Joseph and his Brothers, right-hand relief in the central tier of the Gates of Paradise, 1425-52. This photograph was taken from the right-hand side and from eye level. The relief is the original in the Museo dell'Opera del Duomo, Florence, gilded bronze.

Most people looking at the Joseph panel for the first time would agree that it is a bit of a muddle, and not just because of the dominance of the granary. But maybe it was a deliberate muddle. One's eye is first caught both by the splendour of the architecture and by the two central foreground figures of the young man and woman to either side of the entrance to the granary (Fig. 141). There seems to be something going on between them; maybe he is making a pass at her, maybe she is giving him the eye. Both are tall and handsome, and there seems to be some kind of body language between them. There is nothing of this in the Bible. And what of the third figure in the turban on the right-hand side (Fig. 142) gesturing in the direction of the central pair as if he were blessing them? The Krautheimers identify the young woman as an Egyptian who has just bought grain, and the young man as one of Joseph's brothers. Are they correct? The turbaned figure they do not even mention.

We notice that the handsome young man in the centre is carrying a small, unobtrusive leather bag in his left hand. It is a money bag like that in Ghiberti's Expulsion of the Merchants. Ignoring the woman for a moment; we can also see that there is also some relationship between the two men. I suggest that the man in the turban, who is surely Joseph, is gesturing to the young man, who must be the steward, telling him to put the bag he is holding back into the brothers' sacks. So what is the young woman doing? She is a decoy. She is simply a young woman leaving the granary having collected grain for her family, as the Krautheimers suggested. Ghiberti has, so to speak, 'frozen' the action at the moment that she crosses the path between Joseph and his steward. She turns round to look at him, perhaps because she fancies him, perhaps because she wonders what is going on. But the prominence of their pairing in the centre foreground suggests that there is a close connection between them. We are encouraged to try to make sense of their relationship. The two central and also the two largest figures are accidentally captured in a relationship of apparent complicity which diverts our eye from what is really going on: Joseph setting up the plot to trap his brothers and exact his revenge.

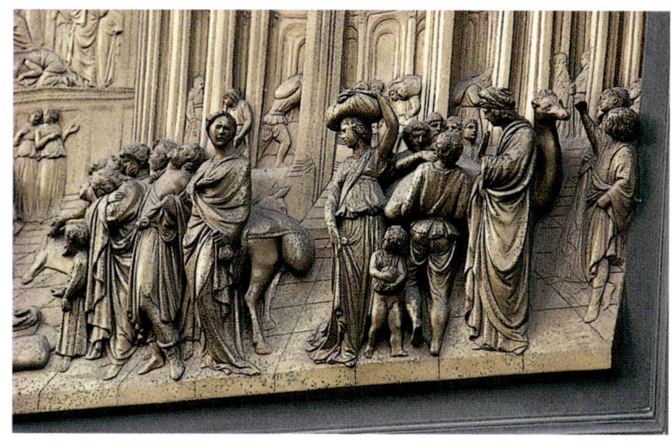

142. Lorenzo Ghiberti, the Three Leaders, close up from Joseph and his Brothers, right-and relief in the central tier of the Gates of Paradise, 1425–52. This photograph was taken from the right-hand side and from beneath. The relief in situ is a facsimile of the original which is now in the Museo dell'Opera del Duomo, Florence.

It is a very clever piece of pictorial storytelling, one moreover that employs to advantage one of the apparent weaknesses of images, their muteness, indeterminacy and our pleasure in overcoming the difficulty of puzzling out exactly what they represent. Ghiberti himself plays a trick upon his audience, just as Joseph plays a trick upon his brothers. Here, perhaps, is Ghiberti's response to Masaccio's achievement in representing the complex legal judgement handed down by Jesus in the Tribute Money (Fig. 127). Indeed here, on one level, Ghiberti outdoes all his contemporaries and predecessors and shows how artists can rival writers such as Boccaccio in the story of Gillette de Narbonne[18] or indeed the Bible itself. It is the kind of artistic sleight-of-hand which Florentines, who revelled in what we call Machiavellian politics and the art of conspiracy, would have much appreciated. Indeed we have reason to believe that Lorenzo Ghiberti was extremely wily in pressing his own advantage in negotiations. But there are several pictorial precedents upon which he may have drawn. In Giotto's Last Supper (Fig. 29), the spectator has a privileged view of Judas dipping with Jesus, which the disciples cannot see. In his Feast of Herod (Fig. 95) it is not altogether clear whether the executioner carrying the head is about to present it to the daughter, watched by

Herod who sits between them, or to Herod watched by the daughter of Herodias. The pairings are ambiguous. In Taddeo Gaddi's Baroncelli Chapel (Fig. 96) we have to search through the confusion of the crowd to find the three chief figures enacting the Betrothal of the Virgin. In addition we have met with many other examples where we have had to make sense of an apparently disorganised composition (Fig. 83). Ghiberti knew that he could depend upon an audience with highly developed visual skills in deciphering complex pictorial patterns so as to read the story. Here those skills are put to their greatest test. Hence, perhaps, Vasari's praise: 'The most worthy, the most difficult and the most beautiful of the whole work.'

To conclude our account of Ghiberti's consummate artistry we must turn finally to the scene, in lowest relief but prominently displayed in the middle ground, of Joseph revealing himself to his brothers (Fig. 143). In this case once again the level of relief is not used to suggest sequence or temporal distance, which is achieved by the clockwise arrangement of scenes. Here low relief suggests the complete privacy of their reconciliation, and like the lowered voice of an actor or orator it also conveys Joseph's intense emotion, perhaps even his own voice, roughened with tears, repeating the words, 'I *am* Joseph, your brother.' It is a beautiful visual analogue to the words of the Bible. At the same time the mutual embrace of Joseph and his youngest brother Benjamin is as moving as any earlier scene except perhaps for the embrace of Joachim and Anna in the Scrovegni Chapel (Fig. 25), upon which Ghiberti may well have drawn. It is almost as if Ghiberti went out of his way to design a composition in which the dramatic and visual focus is as far as possible from being the climax to the story. It is a bluff. Yet the deception points to the very heart of the story.

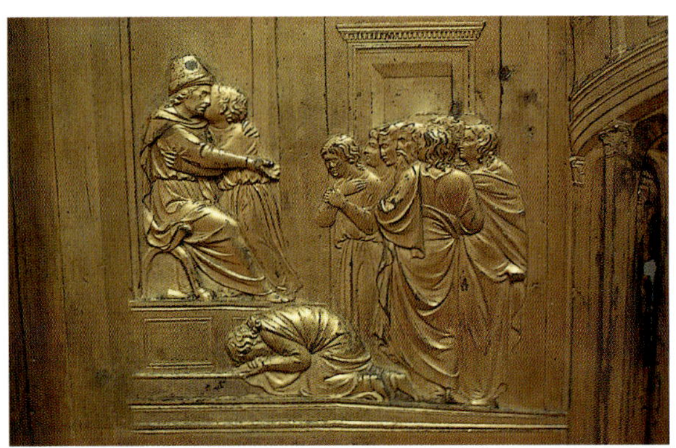

143. Lorenzo Ghiberti, Joseph weeps before his Brothers, from Joseph and his Brothers, right-hand relief in the central tier of the Gates of Paradise, 1425-52. This photograph was taken at eye level. The relief is the original in the Museo dell'Opera del Duomo, Florence, gilded bronze.

Finally, it is clear that the granary plays a most important and integral role in the panel; it is not just an isolated demonstration of Ghiberti's skill in perspective. First of all it draws our attention to the panel through the splendour of its design and the intricacy of the perspective; second, it encourages us to linger on the scene; finally, it makes manifest Joseph's power and glory while the conspiratorial Joseph himself remains concealed

(Fig. 138). It is also a manifestation of Ghiberti's pre-eminence.

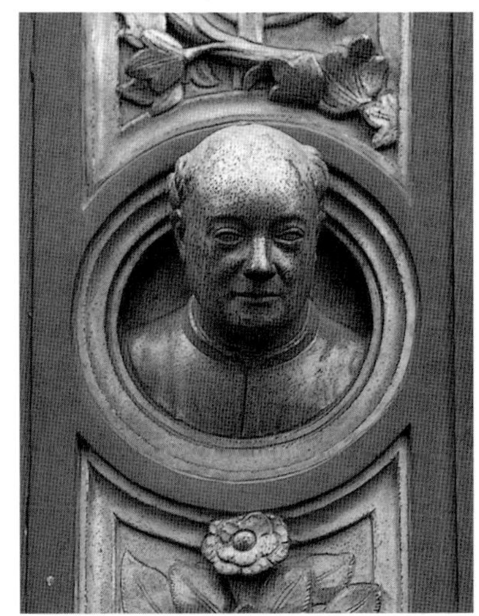

144. Lorenzo Ghiberti, Self Portrait, bronze bust from the Gates of Paradise, Florence Baptistery, 1425–52.

The Joseph is a powerful response to the work of Donatello and Masaccio. Ghiberti adopted their converging perspective, but made no advances in discovering the key to regular diminution, though he was somewhat more successful at relating the scale of his figures to the buildings. His architecture and landscapes are more elaborate and complex, and he employs free-standing figures in the foreground so as to create the effect of movement parallax in relation to the low relief backgrounds. In this respect his reliefs are more convincing than Donatello's. Yet Ghiberti jettisons their major innovation of the all-encompassing frame, which distances the spectator from the image as well as operating as a point of reference for the position of every object in the picture. He preferred to retain the three-dimensionality of his own earlier work, derived in part from Giovanni Pisano.

Ghiberti also avoids any focus upon the momentary, except in the Solomon and Sheba, whose clasping hands bring the series to an appropriate end.[19] He prided himself upon crowding each panel with several episodes so as to relate all the stages in a story within the same relief, using different levels of relief, among other methods, to suggest the sequence as well as give emphasis to particular aspects of the story: Adam and Eve's furtive act of disobedience (Fig. 136) or Joseph's emotional outburst in the privacy of his palace.

Perhaps most significant in the Gates of Paradise, however, is the way that this highly literate, self-taught humanist–artist (Fig. 144) attempts to meet the challenge of literature by representing complex concepts and states of mind in a silent medium, aiming to outdo all his predecessors and contemporaries in the highest branch of art, narrative or history, overcoming the most difficult pictorial problems, especially that of representing deception and also reversal, Aristotle's *peripateia*, upon which all plots turn, doing so in a story which touches upon some of our deepest emotions: jealousy, rivalry, revenge, forgiveness. In doing so he was also setting the spectator considerable problems in interpretation.

It was a remarkable achievement and a hard act for his only surviving *concorrento*, Donatello, to follow. His response is the subject of the final chapter.

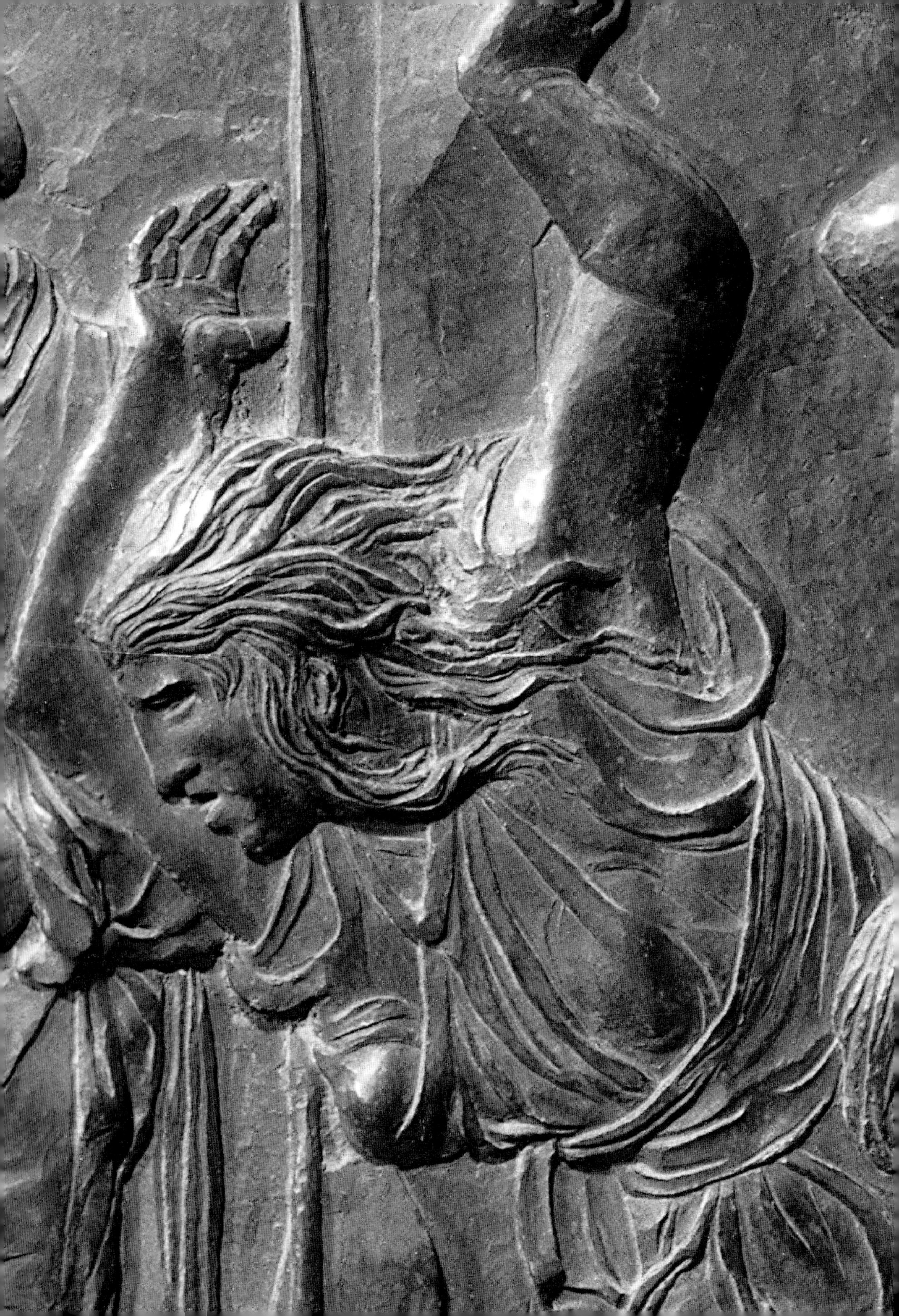

IX

DONATELLO'S PULPITS IN SAN LORENZO

There were, as we have seen, few opportunities for artists to tackle major cycles of the biblical stories, Old Testament or New. Once Ghiberti had secured the commission for the third doors of the Baptistery in 1425 it was unlikely that further opportunities in Florence would arise in the near future, if at all.

Donatello, having made a brilliant debut in narrative relief in his Head of St John (Fig. 124) of the mid-1420s, had subsequently produced several individual works: an Ascension of Christ, an Ascent of the Virgin, and a relief of the Feast of Herod all in marble, an Annunciation in *pietra serena* as well as four stucco reliefs of the life of St John the Evangelist in Brunelleschi's Sacristy for the Medici family in San Lorenzo, all probably in the late 1420s and 1430s. But work seems to have dried up, even in the field of monumental stone and bronze statues for the cathedral and Or San Michele, and this may have lain behind his decision to work in Padua in the decade between 1443 and 1453. Even there he did not obtain a major narrative cycle – the four predella scenes of the life of the Franciscan St Anthony of Padua on the bronze altarpiece he made for the Santo in Padua, splendid as they are, did not present an artist of Donatello's stature with the highest challenge in narrative: a major biblical cycle where, paradoxical though it may appear, the

Detail of Figure 155

wealth of precedent could assist an artist in developing his own interpretation.

Returning to Florence in 1453 to see Ghiberti's Gates of Paradise (Fig. 134) installed in the main entrance to the Baptistery may have fuelled his ambition. The doors seem to have had that effect upon the Sienese government, for in October 1457 Donatello moved to Siena saying that he wished 'to live and die' in that city.[1] In April 1458 he is referred to as the 'master of the doors' of the cathedral of Siena, its final embellishment.[2] A list dated 1467 mentions two panels in wax by Donatello, and some writers have associated a bronze relief of the Lamentation of Christ in the Victoria and Albert Museum with the doors. But something went wrong. By 1459 Donatello was back in Florence, his rent paid by the Cathedral Office of Works.[3] It is not known when he started upon his last work – a pair of so-called bronze pulpits (Figs 145–6) for the church of San Lorenzo then in the process of rebuilding at Medici expense.[4] There has been much scholarly debate, still unresolved, about the nature of these objects, their function and their genesis.

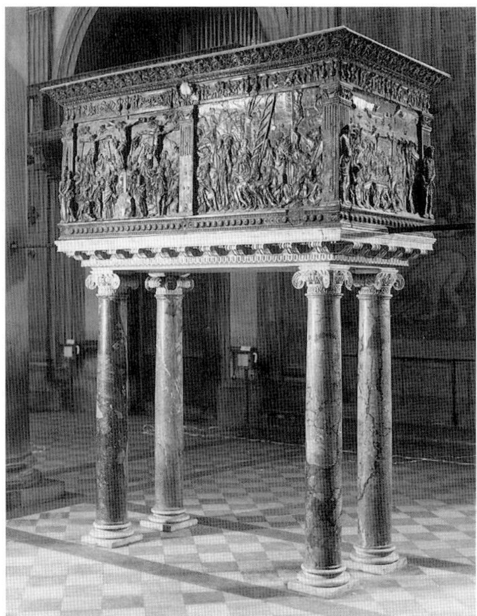

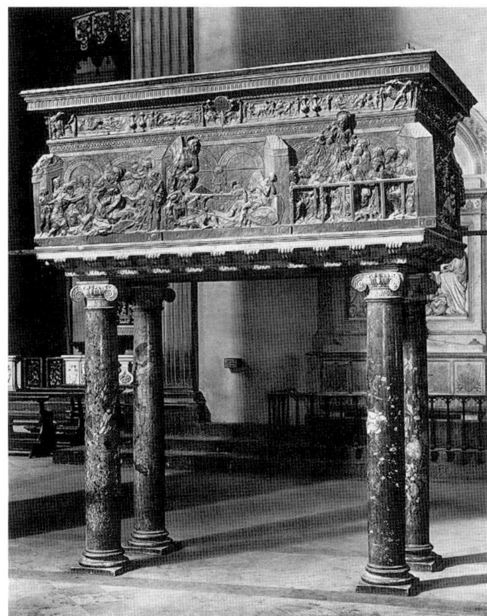

145 (*above left*). Donatello, South Pulpit, San Lorenzo, Florence, bronze, 1459-65, the Crucifixion, the Lamentation and the Entombment.

146 (*above right*). Donatello, North Pulpit, San Lorenzo, Florence, gilded bronze, 1459-65, scenes of the Resurrection and Ascension.

There are grounds for believing that they were associated with some kind of memorial to the ailing Cosimo de Medici, who died in 1464.[5] The date of 1465 is inscribed upon one of the bronze reliefs. Donatello himself died in 1466 and was buried in the same crypt close to the tomb of Cosimo directly beneath the crossing of the church, a burial place of great honour. They are the last great sculptural cycle of the type treated in this book, effectively bringing that tradition to a close. For two-dimensional images the tradition of great biblical cycles was magnificently revived in the decoration of the Sistine Chapel between the 1480s and 1541, but thereafter it effectively disappears.

We cannot say what brought the project for the Siena cathedral doors to an end. Vasari tells us that a Florentine goldsmith visited Donatello and reproached him for letting the Sienese enjoy such a grand source of pride. Donatello then spoilt his work and escaped to Florence during a public holiday. If there is a germ of truth in this tale, one imagines that he would have been promised some equally grand project in Florence since he needed to earn a living, quite apart from entertaining his remaining artistic ambitions. Cosimo de Medici must have offered him the opportunity to compose a 'last testament' for their joint burial place and memorial in the half-completed church. Vespasiano da Bisticci, Cosimo's bookdealer, claimed that Cosimo commissioned the pulpits to provide Donatello with work.[6] We know that throughout the latter half of 1458 the Lord of Mantua, Lodovico Gonzaga, was trying to employ Donatello.[7] Were the two magnates bidding for his services? Some people might think that the bronze doors of one of the grandest cathedrals in central Italy would have been a greater enticement to working either for the Gonzagas or the Medici. Maybe some insurmountable problem had arisen with the project for the Siena doors – lack of money, for instance. But in addition to the patriotic appeal of being honoured in his own country, the incentive of being given a relatively free hand by a friendly patron could have influenced him. The Siena doors would probably have involved covering the full story of Jesus' life, as had Ghiberti's; the pulpits, on the other hand, concentrate exclusively upon Jesus' death and resurrection.

This emphasis is itself surprising, and the pulpits are unusual in many other ways: in the choice of subjects, in the treatment of narrative and composition, in the way that the possibilities of relief sculpture are explored, in the unique use of varied light and colour in bronze relief and, most important, in their intense focus upon death and resurrection.

To start with the subject matter. No other cycle dealing with the Passion, the Easter story, places so great an emphasis upon Jesus' death, mourning, funeral and resurrection. Of the ten scenes relating to Jesus (the eleventh shows the martyrdom by fire of St Lawrence to whom the church is dedicated) seven concern his death and resurrection, only two treat the events leading up to his death. While there was no invariable rule about the scenes included and the balance between the episodes, by and large earlier artists had depicted more of the events after the Entry into Jerusalem and before Jesus' crucifixion. Giovanni Pisano at Pisa has four episodes before death as well as the Crucifixion. Giotto showed nine scenes leading up to Jesus' death and only four after; Duccio nineteen before, twelve after; Pietro Lorenzetti an equal number, five before and five after; Ghiberti, nine before and three after; Fra Angelico thirteen before and five after. These dry statistics simply reinforce the obvious point that the sculptor and his probable client were very old men. This work is a profound meditation upon death in the light of the Christian doctrine of the resurrection of the body.

The choice of particular scenes is also unusual. Surprisingly, the Trial of Jesus had previously been depicted only by Duccio, Giotto and Fra Angelico; only Giotto and Fra Angelico had represented the Lamentation; only Duccio and Pietro Lorenzetti depicted the Entombment, a subject that Donatello himself had handled twice before in other contexts. Only Duccio and Fra Angelico had shown the Maries visiting Jesus' tomb on Easter morning, only Giotto and Fra Angelico had depicted the Ascension, again a subject Donatello had previously treated in isolation. Moreover Donatello's representation of all these episodes was a complete recasting of the approaches taken by his illustrious predecessors. Donatello's treatment of the more common subjects such as Jesus' Descent into Limbo (if that *is* its subject), his Resurrection and the Ascension are rethought. In fact, only the Agony in the Garden, the Crucifixion and the Pentecost adhere to pre-existing compositional formulae. Donatello, therefore, was putting a major effort into making the most of his only opportunity to compete, and to conclude his dialogue with his predecessors and contemporaries.

And yet, oddly in spite of Donatello's originality in the depiction of each episode, the reliefs have great directness and simplicity – with perhaps one exception, the Trial. Donatello turned away, it seems, from the ever-increasing sophistication in pictorial storytelling which we have traced from Giovanni Pisano to its climax in Ghiberti's Joseph. It is easy to describe the subject of each scene in a few words, a short sentence.

Jesus faces his forthcoming death.
Jesus is unjustly sentenced to death.
Jesus is crucified.
Removed from the cross, Jesus' disciples grieve over his corpse.

Jesus is buried and mourned.
The Maries visit his grave and find it empty.
The bodies of the saints awake after Jesus' resurrection.
Jesus rises from the dead.
He ascends to Heaven.
The Holy Spirit descends upon his disciples.
St Lawrence suffers martyrdom for Jesus.

Everything takes place in the here and now. There are few complicated ideas, thoughts or doctrines to express. There are no super-subtle conspiracies. The subject of the first pulpit (Fig. 145) is death: fear of death, the injustice of a wrongful sentence of death, death by torture and the grief of the mourners, the process of mourning, the funeral. This is the triumph of death as experienced by the convicted man and by the survivors. In the second pulpit (Fig. 146) Donatello presents the specifically Christian consolation of the hard-won triumph *over* death in Jesus' resurrection. Christian martyrs like St Lawrence endured agonies because of Jesus' example on the Cross and their own faith in resurrection. In Donatello's simplicity and strength of feeling he was turning aside from the intellectualism of Duccio, Giotto, Ghiberti and Masaccio towards the emotional power of Giovanni Pisano, to whom he also looked in the great variety of his artistic and sculptural treatment of relief.

We have traced the debate concerning the framed view and the employment of different levels of relief in sculpture. In his own reliefs following the Head of St John and particularly in the most recent Miracles of St Anthony in Padua, Donatello closely adhered to the framed image to which the ground plane is conjoined; he used very low relief and grand perspectival architectural settings. Ghiberti in his Gates of Paradise had rejected such an approach in favour of an eclectic employment of different levels of relief with statuettes protruding beyond the surface towards the spectator in addition to very low relief (Figs 135–43); Donatello often emphasised the grand climax of a story, Ghiberti by and large did not use such an approach, preferring a more episodic form of narrative.

Regarded as a response to and commentary upon Ghiberti's masterpiece, Donatello's pulpits seem to be conceding much ground to his former master. Some of the panels are in very low relief (Figs 155–60), but almost as if Ghiberti's example had liberated him from a rigid adherence to the encompassing frame and centralised perspective; Donatello develops every possible variation on the theme. There is usually more than a single viewpoint for each panel arising from a variety of partially contradictory cues. He places high relief statuettes in front of the framing pilasters of low relief panels, as in the Trial (Fig. 149), Lamentation (Fig. 155) and Entombment (Fig. 158), somewhat akin to Giovanni Pisano's framing caryatids (Figs 61 and 70a); he has figures spilling out of the frame in the foreground of the Agony (Fig. 147); in the Maries at the Tomb (Fig. 161) he builds up a house tomb in front of the surface of the relief, placing the figures within. Whereas in the Gates of Paradise Ghiberti follows a similar pattern for each panel, Donatello plays fast and loose with the spectator's relation to the image, as the subject and feeling move him.

This, together with our uncertainty about Donatello's intentions regarding the overall physical character of the project, makes it difficult to determine the physical viewpoints from which it was intended that the reliefs were to be seen. The internal evidence of the reliefs themselves suggests shifts in viewpoint as we move from one scene to the next, from a low eye-level to a normal one to a very high one to a very low one, and so on. The Agony in the Garden could be understood as having a viewpoint from below looking up, but it could equally well be seen straight on. The receding lines of Pilate's praetorium (Fig. 149) converge just below the eye-level of the figures, but we also have a sense of looking up from a low viewpoint into the barrel vaults. In the Crucifixion (Fig. 154) we might imagine ourselves either standing on the ground looking up or even on a level with Jesus on his cross, whereas in the Lamentation (Fig. 155) we seem to have moved down to a point just below the level of Jesus' body, looking up at the crosses and ladder above us, though equally we could be standing. The recessional lines of the tomb and the cave in the Entombment (Fig. 158) as well as the foreshortening of some of the figures around Jesus suggest an eye-level at the very bottom edge of the frame, whereas the figures at the edges and in front of the pilasters suggest that we are standing on their level. In the Resurrection pulpit (Fig. 146) all the scenes are framed to either side by pedimented and tiled portals. With the exception of the St Lawrence we seem to be looking down upon the roofs of these structures from above. In the panel of the Maries (Fig. 161) this viewpoint relates to the fact that they are descending the steps into the tomb, even though their figures are not foreshortened. Likewise the figures in the first two scenes of the resurrection are also seen at eye-level, whereas in the Ascension (Fig. 165) we seem to be looking down upon the disciples from the level of Jesus' head, even though this scene is just one section of a single panel and shares the same architecture as the previous two. There are so many implied viewpoints in the panels and they are so contradictory that it seems impossible on this basis to reconstruct any alternative framework, whether a funereal monument or a pair of pulpits, that would enable these viewpoints to be reconciled with the physical position of each relief. In neither of the pulpits did Donatello use a single consistent rational system of perspective and foreshortening.[8]

We have already observed something similar in the Head of St John but there was also a precedent a decade or so later in his career, probably in the 1430s, in a location where there is no doubt about the intended position of the reliefs and of the spectator, namely the stucco roundels he made for the vault of the Old Sacristy of the same church, San Lorenzo. Michael Podro has observed that whereas the perspective of St John's Ascension coincides with our viewpoint craning upwards as we stand on the floor of the Sacristy, in other roundels 'the perspective is dissociated from our bodily position'.[9] Similarly the effect of looking at Donatello's images, whether we are looking up at them in the church in their present framework or whether we are examining photographs taken upon a scaffold, the perspectives and the foreshortenings within the reliefs seem to position us imaginatively in relation to each scene, regardless of our actual standpoint. This is not to say that there is no advantage to be gained from looking at the reliefs from different points of view, either from below or from the sides or even from above, as has been suggested.[10] But, as we have seen the new perspective did not necessitate the spectator to be placed at the implied viewpoint.[11] However, the images on these pulpits are the first we have examined which date from after the publication of Alberti's correct geometrical construction in 1435. It is fascinating that not only does Donatello not use it, but he seems to reject it in an almost ostentatious manner.

Donatello also breaks free from the constraints of a coherent naturalism which had been increasingly adopted by most artists over the course of the previous century, reaching its culmination in Ghiberti's consistently graceful and naturalistic figures. Donatello possessed all the skills to do likewise, as we know from his earlier statues of St George and the bronze David, so here he must have *chosen* not to, as and when it suited him. Some figures are elegant and well proportioned; others are short and stumpy like some of Giovanni Pisano's; others are extraordinarily lithe and elongated; some faces are carefully and naturalistically modelled; others within the very same relief are crude but very effective cuts in the wax. This is clearly not the result of any lack of skill or knowledge, nor, I believe, the intervention of assistants, but Donatello's deliberate rejection of naturalistic coherence as an invariable rule and his openness to the use of every contrivance within the tradition of the previous two hundred centuries. In particular there are parallels to Giovanni Pisano's last pulpit in Pisa Cathedral.[12] Maybe Donatello's primitivism was also a reaction against Ghiberti's uniform elegance and beauty.

Turning to the cycle of reliefs itself, it is necessary to discuss practically every relief, such is their quality,[13] variety and the integration of the series as a whole, but also because Donatello has reverted to the practice of Duccio,

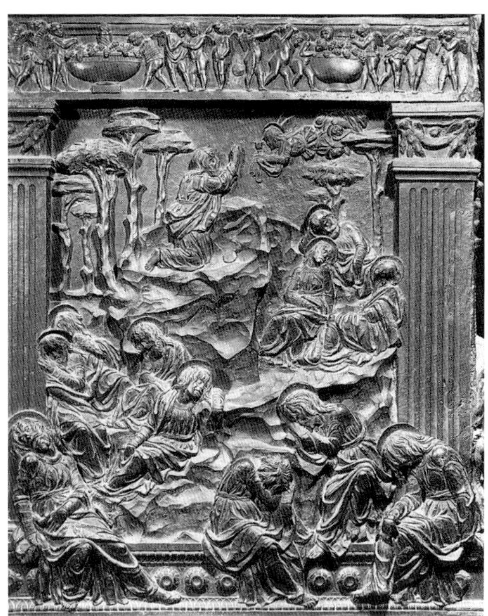

147. Donatello, the Agony in the Garden, South Pulpit, San Lorenzo, Florence, bronze, 1459–65.

Giotto and Giovanni in relating all the panels in an interdependent sequence, unlike Ghiberti where the individual scenes can stand alone.[14]

No other Passion sequence begins with the Agony in the Garden (Fig. 147). All begin with the Entry into Jerusalem except for Giovanni's Pisa pulpit which starts with the Betrayal. Donatello's decision to reject that convention must have been made to focus attention upon Jesus as a man facing up to his forthcoming death: in the words of the Franciscan *Meditations on the Life of Christ*, which Donatello may have read, Jesus 'appears to have forgotten that he is God and prays like a man. Like any other little man of the people he prays to God.'[15] Giovanni had begun his Passion sequence with the Betrayal (Fig. 76) probably because he wanted to emphasise personal treachery and injustice and to place the spectator in the position of one of Jesus' betrayers or assailants. But here, and throughout the scenes of Jesus' death and burial, there seems to be a strong element of Imitatio Christi – the imitation of Christ – the title of a fifteenth-century northern European volume of religious meditations written by an almost exact contemporary, Thomas à Kempis. This was an idea fundamental to St Francis's mission, but also a long-standing element in Christian doctrine.[16] In effect this is Jesus as a *man* receiving the last rites before his death. Donatello has omitted the conventional scenes of Jesus admonishing his disciples for sleeping. They just sleep (Fig. 148), each in a state of total exhaustion and abandon, perhaps the sleepiest sleepers ever portrayed, so sleepy that they are able to sleep despite their rocky beds and horribly uncomfortable postures. The mouth of one hangs open, the hair of another hangs over his face in greasy locks, another leans against the pilaster clutching it in a childish gesture in his sleep. The colour of the bronze itself is black as night, intensified by the fact that this side of the pulpit receives no direct and little ambient light.[17] All of them seem to be slipping off the rock so that the fact that the four foreground sleepers overhang the bottom frame of the pulpits suggests that the whole group could start slithering towards us out of the picture.

This is also perhaps the least naturalistic and most primitive panel. The figures are stunted, the draperies clumsy, the landscape out of proportion, the

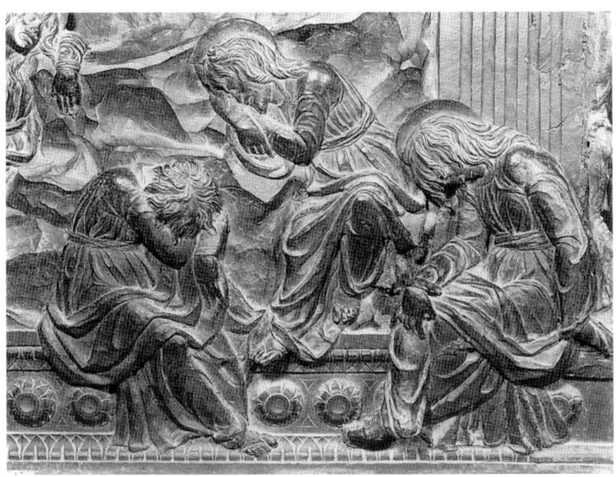

148. Donatello, close up of sleeping disciples in the Agony in the Garden, South Pulpit, San Lorenzo, Florence, bronze, 1459-65.

trees as stumpy as Giotto's even though the figures do diminish in apparent size according to their distance from us, and although some of the faces are very carefully modelled. This selective rejection of naturalism is highly sophisticated.

What is the point of this chorus of exhaustion and unconsciousness? I suggest Donatello wanted one to focus upon Jesus' isolation in the face of death – and of our own. Only the individual is awake to his own agony and fear; nobody can tell one what it will be like to die. Jesus' isolation is dramatised by the sleeping disciples. One with his head thrown back in the left foreground echoes the sleeping soldier who can be seen from here in the left foreground of the Resurrection (Fig. 164) on the north pulpit. Thus Donatello draws a parallel between the disciples sleeping during Jesus' agonised prayer and the soldiers sleeping through his resurrection from the dead. He also suggests a parallel between Jesus praying to his Father and his Ascension (Fig. 165).

In sharp contrast the Trial (Fig. 149) shows Jesus sunk from his position on high praying to God to an abject figure below Pilate's throne, overwhelmed by the imperial grandeur of his palace. The bronze itself appears multicoloured, more brown than black. The figures seem to shrink in scale to the architecture, though not in actual size. Our implied viewpoint, suggested by the converging lines of the courtroom, rises to a level just beneath the eye-level of the figures standing in the scene, and we see a Roman building with its coffered barrel vaults of such majesty as truly to suggest Pilate's Praetorium. Yet the relief also works well when viewed from below. In its claustrophobic character and absence of windows onto the outside world it resembles Herod's Banqueting Hall (Fig. 124). This is the first scene shift, each of which is highly dramatic. What is striking is the conjunction of the grandeur and the visual stability of the perspective with the authoritative monumentalism of the Roman architecture, in contrast to the tormented confusion of Jesus' Agony. From craning upwards at the dark cliff face of Gethsemane, the haunt of the abandoned sleepers clinging to the surface like sea birds, occluding our

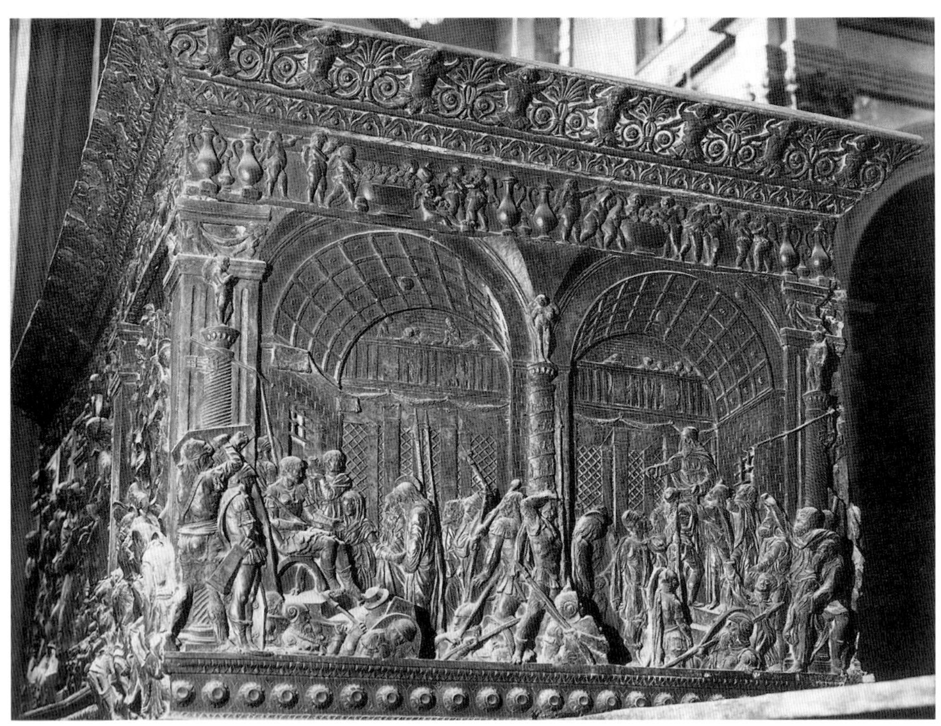

149. Donatello, the Trial of Jesus, South Pulpit, San Lorenzo, Florence, bronze, 1459–65.

view of sky and space, we move to a richly ornamented scene of spacious vaults high up over our heads, of depth, distance, recession, ordered by our perspectival viewpoint. Pilate is seated upon his X-shaped throne, a symbol of imperial power. This is how Donatello characterised the august setting of Roman justice in all its order and magnificence.

Once we enter into the Praetorium, so to speak, and begin to examine more closely what is taking place, this sense of order begins to collapse. There is a parallel here with Duccio's treatment of the same subject (Fig. 14–5) which Donatello could have studied in Siena. The figures are confusing, some of the soldiers rise up out of the floor, and it is not at all clear what they are doing or what is going on. Jesus is clearly identifiable in the left-hand scene before Pilate (Fig. 150) but he practically merges into the bronze (Figs 151–2) in the right-hand scene, the subject of which is uncertain. One's expectation is that this side shows the Trial of Jesus by Caiaphas and the High Priests. But this identification is unclear for a number of reasons – the scene is apparently located in Pilate's palace; 'Caiaphas' moreover is pointing across

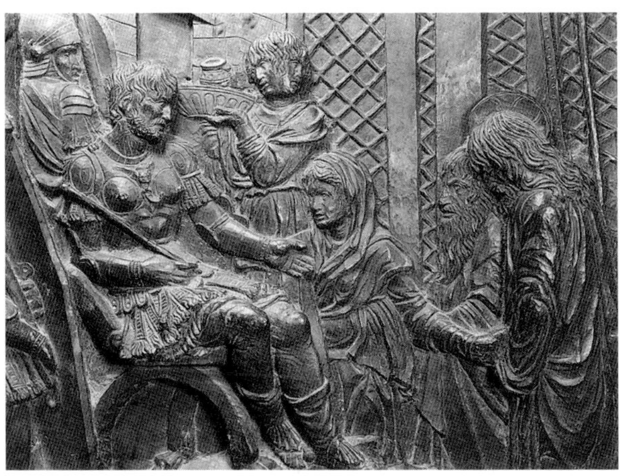

150. Donatello, Pilate, Pilate's wife and Jesus, detail of the Trial of Jesus, South Pulpit, San Lorenzo, Florence, bronze, 1459–65.

towards Pilate's chamber; in addition 'Caiaphas' is standing upon a dais, whereas the convention had been to show him seated and often tearing his clothes (Figs 7, 35 and 85). The sequence of events in the biblical text, in which the trial by Caiaphas precedes the trial by Pilate, leads one to expect the Caiaphas scene to be on the left and the Pilate on the right. Nonetheless it almost certainly does represent the trial by Caiaphas, surrounded by 'false witnesses'.[18] One of the two figures to the right of Jesus, one wearing a turban, pointing at him with one hand and looking up towards Caiaphas, could well represent the witness who finally says, 'This *fellow* said, I am able to destroy the temple of God, and to build it in three days.' (Matthew 26, v. 61) At first Jesus refuses to answer, but when pressed, his words are taken to imply that he is the Son of Man, at which they all cry out that Jesus is guilty and must be condemned to death (Fig. 152). Caiaphas's gesture, then, would be his verdict and a command for Jesus to be taken to Pilate, towards whose court Caiaphas is pointing. The bearded figure crouching behind another man on the extreme right by the column might even be St Peter who followed Jesus 'afar off unto the high priest's palace, and went in, and sat with the servants, to see the end' (Matthew 26, v. 58). If so, this emphasises Jesus' complete desertion by his disciples in his hour of need.

The left-hand scene (Fig. 153) also condenses several episodes into one: Pilate asking Jesus 'Are you King of the Jews?'; Jesus refusing to answer; the Jewish priests repeatedly calling for crucifixion; and Pilate's wife physically interceding between them and her husband, advising him to have 'nothing to do with that just man: for I have suffered many things this day in a dream because of him' (Matthew 27, v. 19).[19]

Pilate's strange, uncomfortable posture (Fig. 150), shifting in his throne, strongly conveys his judicial discomfort. His left arm, rather lamely outstretched towards Jesus in half-echo of his wife's heart-felt pleading, gives expression to his reiterated but ultimately ineffective judgement that he can

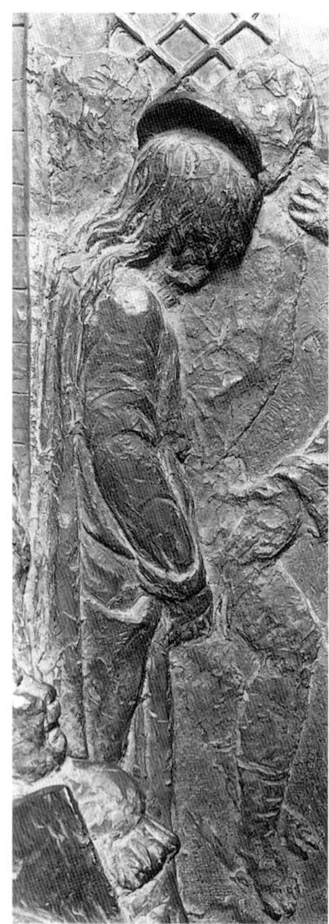

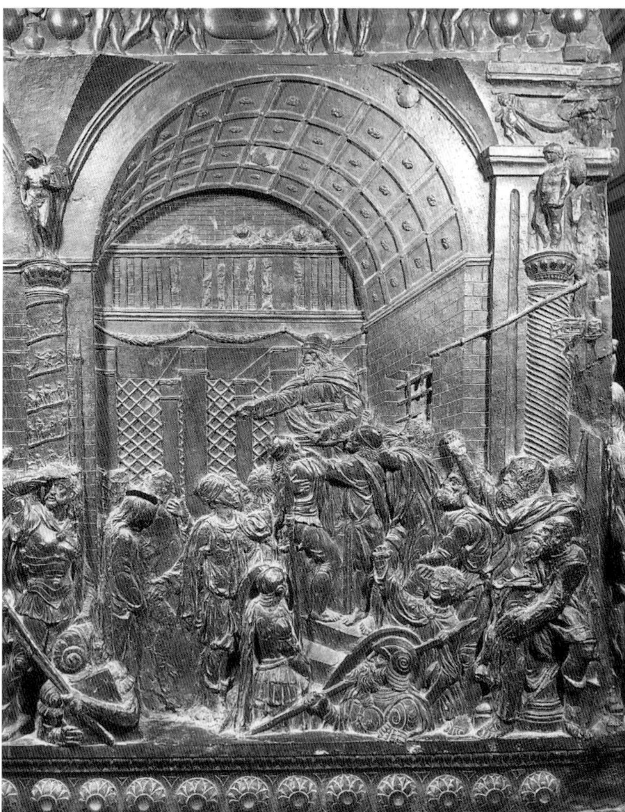

151 (*above left*). Donatello, close up of Jesus in the scene of Caiaphus condemnings Jesus, detail of the Trial of Jesus, South Pulpit, San Lorenzo, Florence, bronze, 1459–65.

152 (*above right*). Donatello, Caiaphus condemning Jesus, right side of the Trial of Jesus, South Pulpit, San Lorenzo, Florence, bronze, 1459–65.

find no fault in the prisoner. At the same time the two-faced youth behind him, hovering with the water in which Pilate will shortly wash his hands, has been convincingly interpreted as a symbol of Pilate's vacillation and hypocrisy.[20] Much of the shifting courtroom drama portrayed by Duccio in his sequence on the back of the Maestà has been condensed in two paired images. Pilate's grasp of justice is on the point of slipping into the hands of the High Priest and his mob. As in the Duccio (Fig. 12), Donatello's Pilate is losing control of his courtroom.

This perhaps explains the reason for the dual composition of the two trials, which might be derived from Masaccio's Theophilus (Fig. 133), and why the

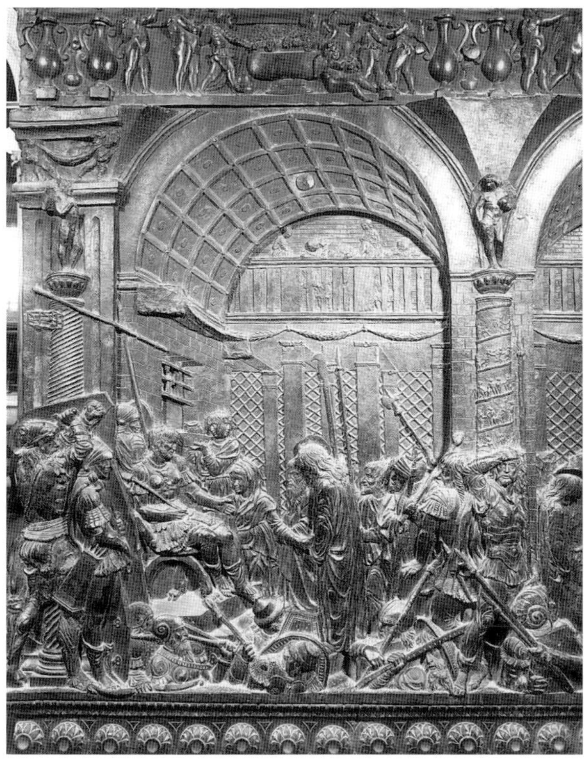

153. Donatello, Pilate interrogates Jesus, left side of the Trial of Jesus, South Pulpit, San Lorenzo, Florence, bronze, 1459-65.

figure of Caiaphas is shown standing high up, pointing accusingly across and down toward Jesus before Pilate (Fig. 149). The whole relief is thus dominated by Caiaphas surrounded by his henchmen who seem to do more than merely bring pressure to bear on Pilate from the ante-room to his audience chamber. It is Donatello's Caiaphas who seems to be the one who, with his outstretched arm, passes judgement upon Jesus, whereas Pilate is indecisive, almost pleading with the prisoner. The most extraordinary figure in all this hubbub is that of Jesus, bowed but visible before Pilate even though his head is downcast and in shadow. But in the right-hand scene Donatello has modelled Jesus' figure so indistinctly and incompletely (Fig. 151–2), and juxtaposed him with the striking figure of a bearded Roman soldier in the very centre staring out of the panel, that Jesus' spirit seems almost to have left his body, leaving behind only a few rags and a skull-like face (Fig. 151). The dual composition symmetrically mirrored around the central wall supporting the two barrel vaults also conveys the sense of the text in *Meditations* – Jesus 'is led hither and thither with downcast gaze and shamefaced walk'.[21]

The Trial of Jesus is the most intricate and subtle narrative on the pulpits, very far from the climactic nature of Donatello's Head of St John or his Paduan reliefs. Several episodes are condensed; the interaction between Pilate and Jesus is surprisingly low-key; figures and subjects are hard to decipher; we do not look through a frame, and the figures themselves are graded from very low relief to almost free-standing statuettes. While the relief could never be mistaken for the work of Ghiberti (Fig. 139), it does suggest that Donatello had absorbed certain lessons from the Gates of Paradise and responded in his own magnificently creative style.

The next scene, the Crucifixion (Fig. 154), is also symmetrical in composition; Jesus is now raised high on his cross, in contrast to the rags-and-bones figure of the trial, and is modelled almost in three dimensions so that Jesus on his cross replaces the monumental architecture of Roman authority. This is a moment of triumph as well as of death at which the three figures at the foot of the cross begin their lamentations, in the words of the *Meditations*, 'Everyone wept inconsolably.'[22]

The next scene, the Lamentation (Fig. 155), perhaps Donatello's most adventurous, presents a contrast with the Crucifixion. Our initial sense is of a panorama. But while in the Crucifixion we are able to imagine ourselves

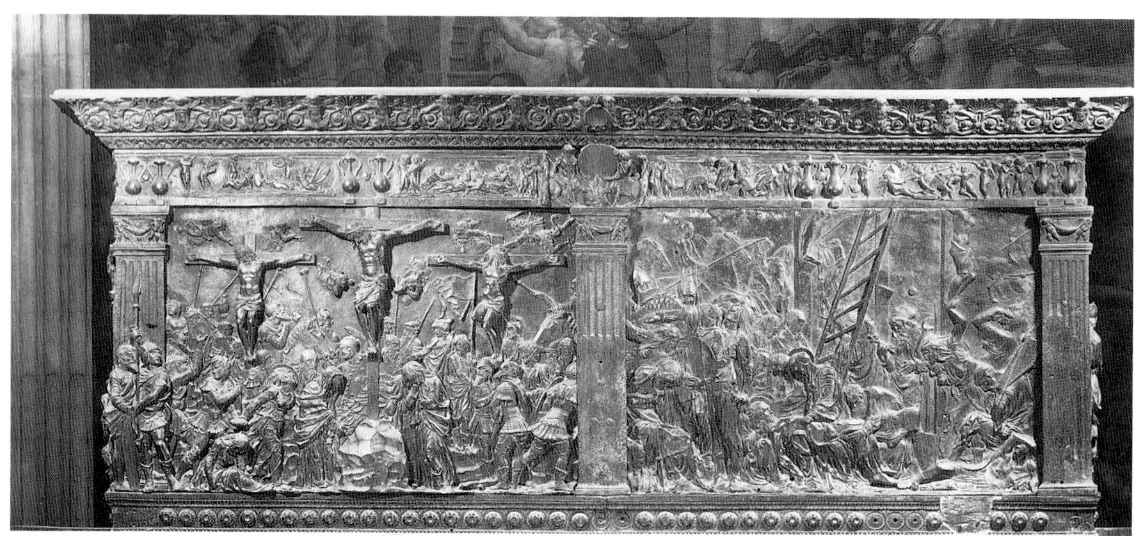

154. Donatello, Crucifixion and Lamentation, South Pulpit, San Lorenzo, Florence, bronze, 1459–65.

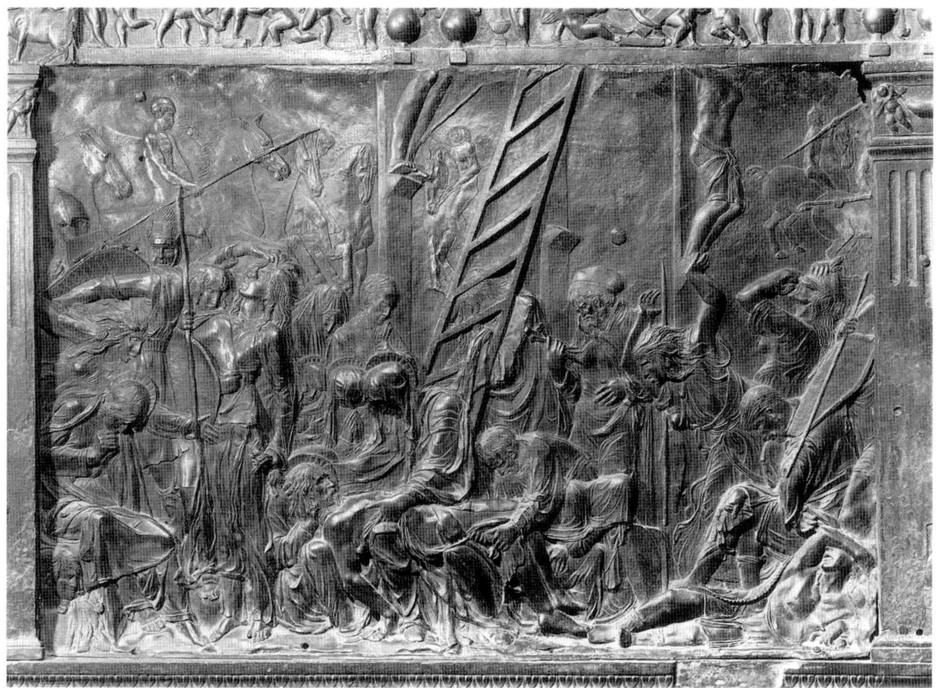

155. Donatello, Lamentation, South Pulpit, San Lorenzo, Florence, bronze, 1459-65.

hovering at the same level as Jesus on the cross, in the next panel, in the Lamentation, we come down to the level of Jesus' outstretched body, with the three crosses and the ladder towering over us. We close in upon his recumbent body, in far lower relief than in the Crucifixion, and the people immediately adjacent to him. At the same time we seem to have just entered the scene from the left-hand side so that the three crosses and the ladder recede from us obliquely into the distance on the right. The most imaginative feature is the way that the upper parts of the three crosses, the bodies of the two thieves and the oddly placed ladder are cut off by the upper border of the frame. The whole panel is depicted in low relief.

The subject is the lamentation over the dead body of Jesus, coupled with a suggestion in the ladder, the empty cross and the man gazing at the three nails in his hand of Jesus' previous descent. Neither of these episodes was recorded in the Bible, both derive from pictorial tradition and devotional texts such as the *Meditations*. There is little story as such. The process of mourning begun at the foot of the cross reaches its climax – the disciples in every

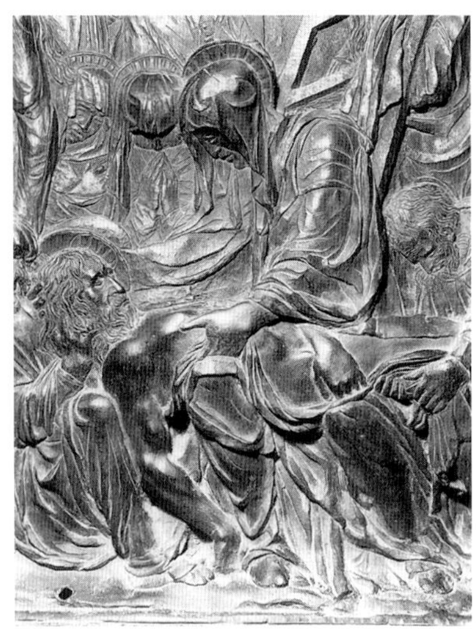

156. Donatello, Mary and Jesus, detail from the Lamentation, South Pulpit, San Lorenzo, Florence, bronze, 1459-65.

posture of grief and prayer, from the women with wildly flowing tresses tearing at their hair and shrieking with grief to the peace, gentleness and silent loss of the Virgin and her companions supporting the body of Jesus, his tortured features now at rest (Fig. 156). The range of their expressions of grief contrasts with Giotto's more restrained Lamentation (Fig. 38).

Donatello's handling of the shift between this scene and that of Jesus' funeral or entombment is one of the most inventive in the cycle (Fig. 157). The two reliefs are at right angles, and when we stand looking towards the corner pillar, each panel recedes from our line of sight at approximately 45 degrees, so that the two scenes seem to be fused into one panorama stretching behind the seemingly solid square pillar at the corner. We become acutely conscious of the two thieves to either side of the empty cross who seem to face us from this viewpoint, while the foreshortening of Jesus' body in the Lamentation is so acute that it is hard to decipher. Thus our attention is directed towards the next scene, the Entombment. This is Donatello's equivalent, using low relief, of Giovanni Pisano's method of fading the perspectival and compositional focus on each scene as we move around the Pisa pulpit.

The Entombment (Fig. 158) is once again a very simple subject which is recorded in all four Gospels. Our eye-level sinks even lower, to the very base of the relief, to the floor of the tomb 'hewn out in the rock'. The level of relief, in the centre of the panel, becomes still shallower while we now seem to have moved farther away from the action as if Jesus' body, being lowered into his

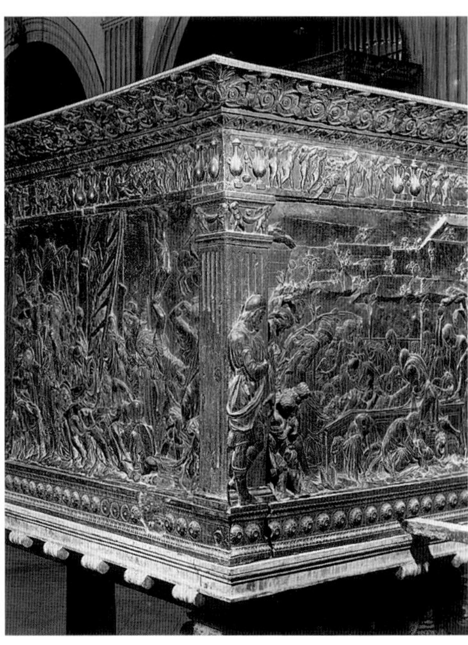

157. Donatello, corner of the South Pulpit, San Lorenzo, Florence, bronze, 1459-65. showing the Lamentation seen obliquely from the right and the Entombment from the left.

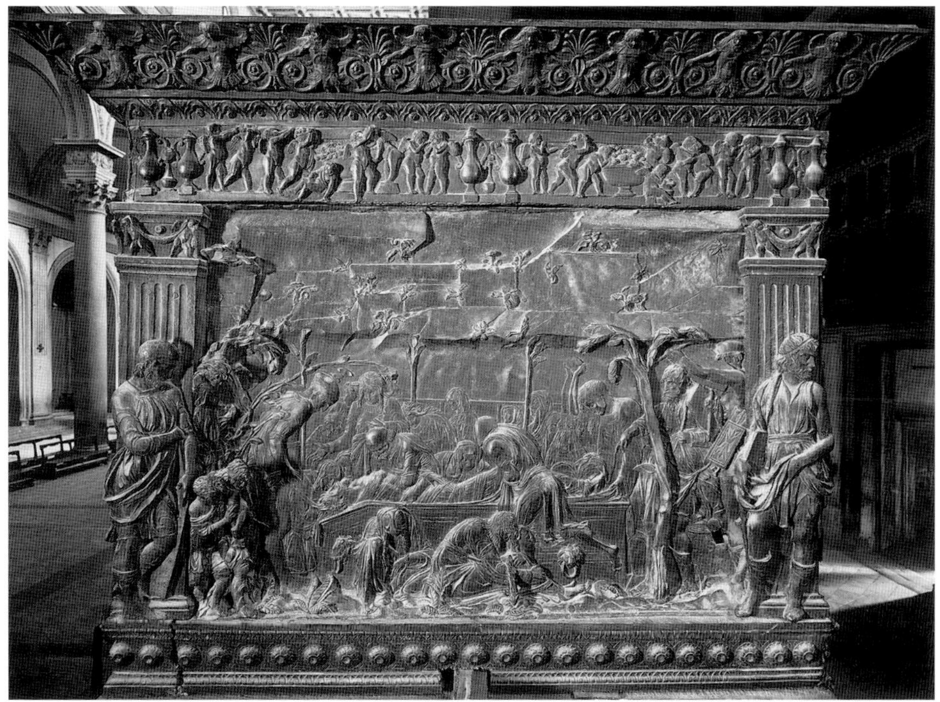

158. Donatello, the Entombment, South Pulpit, San Lorenzo, Florence, bronze, 1459-65.

sarcophagus, is growing fainter as it is taken away from us. This effect is enhanced by the fact that in this panel the figures at the edges, standing in front of the pilasters, situated in the spectator's space, are in far higher relief than those at the centre. Thus there is a progressive gradation of relief from these figures in the round to the very lowest relief in its centre. This emphasises another effect – that of Jesus being lowered into the sarcophagus. The sequence of diminishing relief on the left-hand side (Fig. 157) parallels the sequence of the postures of these figures, progressively bending down till we reach the tall man lowering the winding cloth. Thus we seem to be standing outside the frame and behind these figures and looking at the scene from that side, particularly when we stand to the left. From this position the scene is moderately well illuminated by light coming from the south windows of the church reflected off the surface of the relief. Even so, it is difficult to make out Jesus' head or that of the Virgin kissing him. Here again Donatello has found his own way, distinct from Ghiberti's, of combining Giovanni's approach to relief sculpture with very low cameo-relief.

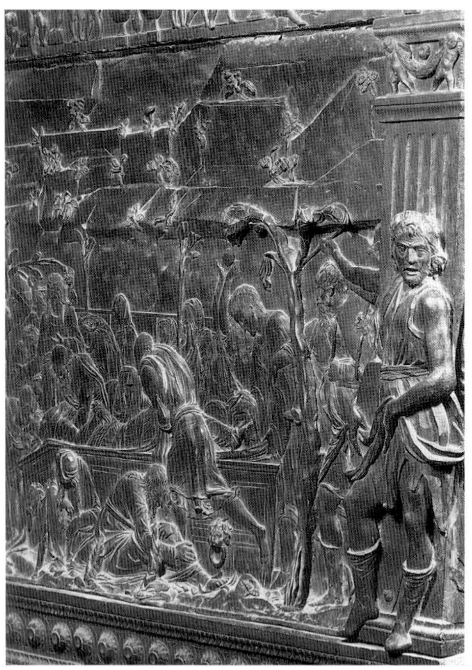

159. Donatello, the Entombment seen from the right, South Pulpit, San Lorenzo, Florence, bronze, 1459-65.

Looking from the sides (Fig. 159) we seem to be standing outside the rocky tomb looking in at the body of Jesus disappearing from view. From the centre (Fig. 158), however, our viewpoint appears to be almost on the ground looking up at the roof of the tomb at the figures leaning over, lowering Jesus into his sarcophagus, looking up into the anguished gaze of the Virgin's face kissing her son for the last time (Fig. 160). Here Donatello achieves an odd effect. Because Jesus' head has fallen backwards so that it is almost upside down we identify all the more closely with him. It is as if *we* are being lowered into the tomb beneath the overhanging rock, as if we are experiencing our own burial with all the heads of our friends and family looking down on us. And yet in the same panel we can look in upon the scene from outside seeing Jesus disappear – we are both mourners and mourned. Finally, when we look at the panel from the right-hand side it is so dark as to be almost invisible. This is because the light source does not reflect at all from this angle – an effect which is well-nigh impossible to represent in a photograph. The physical presence of Jesus has diminished almost to nothingness and even the light has been extinguished.

The Passion or Crucifixion pulpit (Fig. 145) tells the story of the disappearing body of Jesus in a repeated sequence, from the Agony to the Trial and from the Crucifixion to the Entombment. Because of its location relative to the source of light in the church, the pulpit never receives direct light and is always in shadow, but Donatello has contrived it so that the scenes grow progressively more invisible as the levels of relief diminish and darkness descends – also unphotographable.

When we walk across to the Resurrection pulpit (Fig. 146), the first thing we see is the front panel telling the story of Easter morning, of the Resurrection, and of the Ascension. Its rich gilding shines in the light from the south-facing windows. But to pick up the thread of the narrative we have to begin with the panel at the end of the pulpit (Fig. 161), corresponding to the Entombment opposite. We move from the extreme subtleties of the most del-

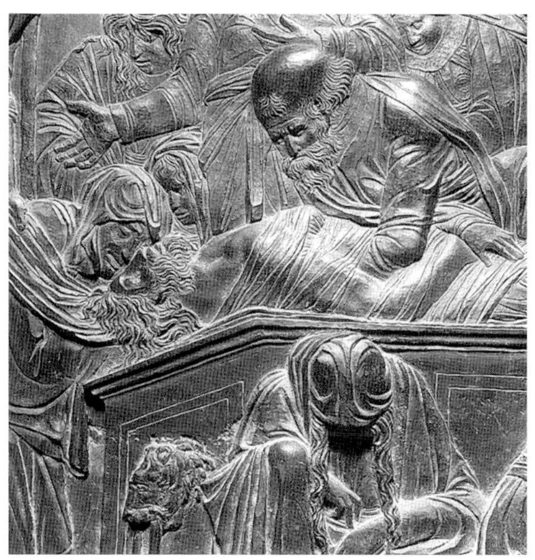

160. Donatello, the Entombment, detail of Mary and Jesus, South Pulpit, San Lorenzo, Florence, bronze, 1459-65.

icately diminishing cameo-relief receding into the surface of the bronze to a building, almost a three-dimensional model, built up *in front* of the surface, with figures inside behind an arcade of pillars through which we peer. Again the story is simple. The Maries visit the tomb after the Sabbath to anoint the body with spices, but on entering the sepulchre they are met by an angel who terrifies them, and tries to calm their fear. Jesus is not in his grave, he is risen, they should tell the other disciples and go to Galilee where they will see the risen Lord.

What is extraordinary about Donatello's treatment of this simple but crucial episode is that his model tabernacle suggests the very *emptiness* of Jesus' tomb. The soldiers sleep by the tomb and even the shrouded Maries are like sleepwalkers. This final descent is the most chilling point in the story – the Maries have not only lost their Lord, now they discover that they have also lost his physical remains (Fig. 162). The very tangibility of the setting in contrast to the diminishing levels of relief in the Lamentation and the Entombment conveys their sense of loss, of empty space and dark shadow into which the Maries have descended to seek their Lord's body.[23] Again, by virtue of its orientation, the end relief is one of the darkest of those on this pulpit. But when we turn the corner (Fig. 163) there is Jesus fully illuminated and silhouetted against the glittering gold background: He is risen, indeed he is rising.

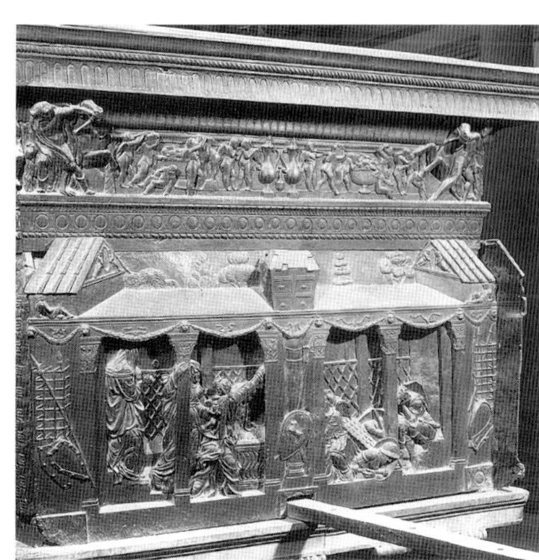

161. Donatello, the Maries at the Tomb, North Pulpit, San Lorenzo, Florence, bronze, 1459-65.

The same pedimented portals divide the single panel on the front (Fig. 146) into three scenes, but there is no foreground arcade, the figures are built up in front of the masonry wall of blind arches, projecting into our space, except in the Ascension where a railing par-

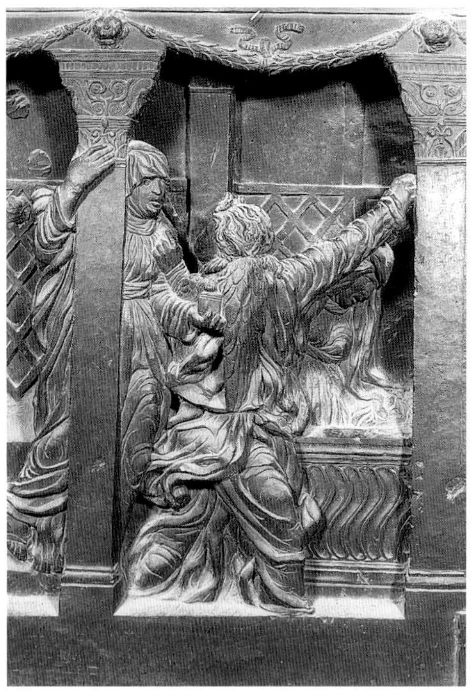

162. Donatello, detail of the Maries at the Tomb, North Pulpit, San Lorenzo, Florence, bronze, 1459-65.

tially distances us from the disciples. Again the subject matter is simplicity itself. The first episode shows Jesus clambering through a crowd of haloed figures, before climbing onto his own tomb in the second scene. Often indentified as Christ in Limbo, perhaps it is better described as a literal representation of the event recorded in Matthew 27, 52–3: 'And the graves were opened; and many bodies of the saints which slept arose, and came out of the graves after his resurrection'.[24] Maybe Donatello was attracted by the notion of the sleepers awakening and extended this to Jesus, who also seems heavy with sleep, being urged forward with the Baptist extending a helping hand. In the next scene (Fig. 164), still weary, Jesus climbs up onto his own tomb echoing the weary Jesus of the Agony (Fig. 147). Finally, after appearing to his disciples, he rises into heaven (Fig. 165). The progress of Jesus from the first to the third compartment of the pulpit, rising as he does from a bowed, struggling figure to the upright figure ascending above the cornice into heaven, suggests the triumph of the resurrection of both body and soul over death as he grows progressively more palpable in increasingly higher relief. The railing in front of the Ascension distances us from Jesus as he stands on a rock blessing the disciples while the angels are waiting to carry him up to heaven. Yet because the heads of some of the disciples are foreshortened from above, and we are able to see the upper surface of the rail, we also gain the impression of sharing Jesus' standpoint looking down on them as he bids them farewell.

The surface gilding of this triumphant progress is in sharp contrast to the dark shadows of the tomb. But the most striking and starkest feature of this sequence is the shrouded, bedraggled, battle-weary figure climbing onto his own tomb, like an arctic explorer or mountaineer, his eyes almost closed in weariness after his war against the forces of evil and death.

Standing in the middle of the nave beneath the crossing looking towards the entrance of the church, as we might do returning to our seat after receiv-

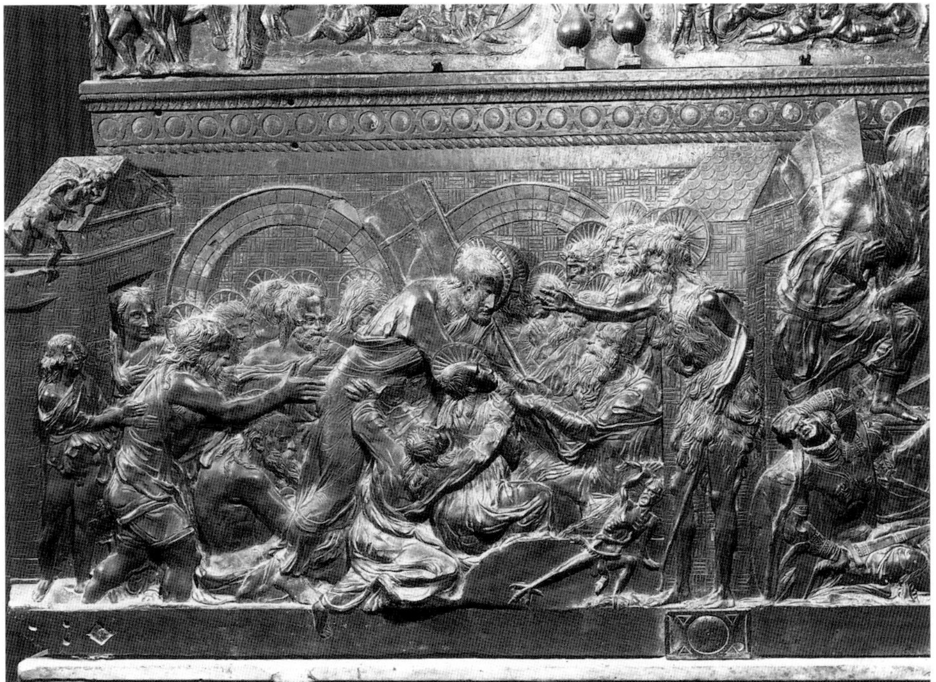

163. Donatello, 'And the graves opened', North Pulpit, San Lorenzo, Florence, gilded bronze, 1459-65.

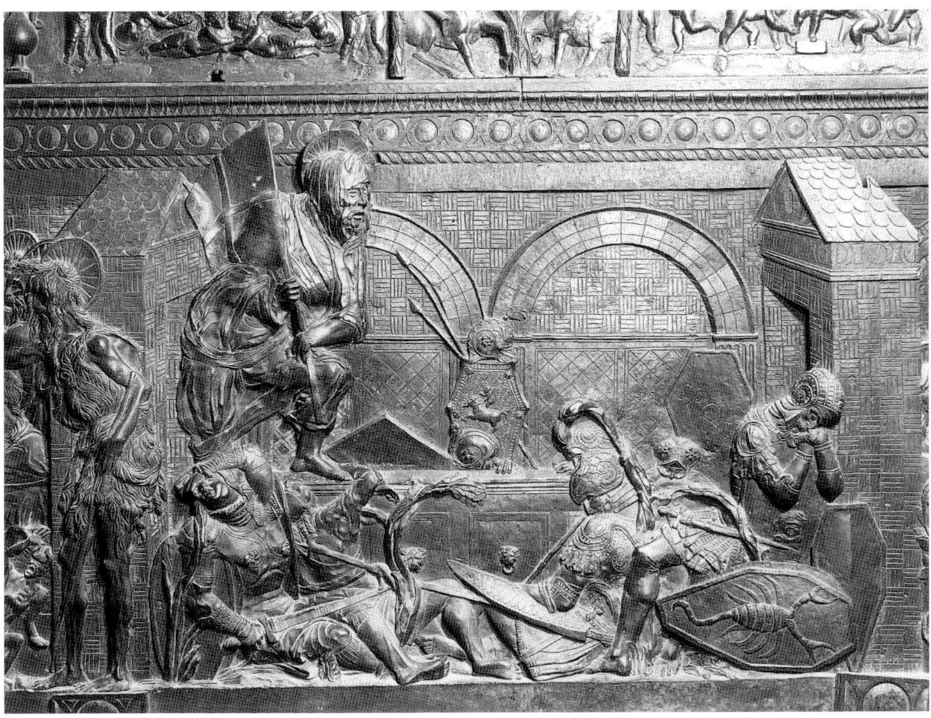

164. Donatello, the Resurrection, North Pulpit, San Lorenzo, Florence, gilded bronze, 1459-65.

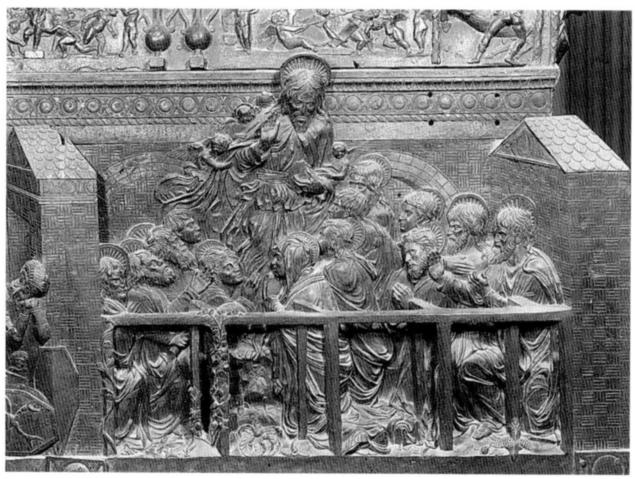

165. Donatello, the Ascension, North Pulpit, San Lorenzo, Florence, gilded bronze, 1459-65.

ing communion, we can observe a kind of synopsis of the two pulpits. To our right, shrouded in shadow, we see Jesus' descent from his cross into his grave, each scene growing more shadowy and indistinct. To our left, from the Maries' descent into the dark emptiness of the tomb, the lowest point, we see Jesus ascending in glory, growing brighter and more palpable, rising with one's own progress towards the Ascension.

I have concluded this book with Donatello's San Lorenzo pulpits because they bring to a close a long phase in the early Renaissance tradition of pictorial narrative, while referring back to and incorporating many features in the work of earlier artists such as Giovanni Pisano, Duccio and Giotto. They are also the final act in the more recent debate initiated by the 1401 competition concerning the relationship between the spectator's point of view and the temporality of the image. In the pulpits Donatello developed a more subtle and flexible control of the relationship between spectator and image than in his own earlier work or in that of Ghiberti, Masaccio or anyone else. The panels avoid the assimilation of relief sculpture to painting at the same time as rejecting the miniature stage-set with figures fully in the round that Ghiberti employed in his Gates or Paradise. In many respects Donatello finally resolved the problems of making narrative images in relief that had confronted everyone from Giovanni Pisano onwards. These reliefs are fully sculptural, using all levels of relief both to establish the image and to articulate the story; one's experience of them is enriched from many different viewpoints, yet they also give rise to a variety of imaginary standpoints regardless of one's physical orientation. Donatello avoids the contortions of Giovanni's efforts to create perspectivally focused compositions in high relief, as well as the distancing effect of the encompassing frame which he himself had employed from the mid-1420s onwards. To be seen correctly the reliefs of the pulpits do not depend upon any particular standpoint, even though different standpoints can enrich our experience.

The Agony, the Trial, the Crucifixion and the Lamentation are interrelated through contrasts of many kinds; while the Crucifixion, Lamentation and Entombment enact Jesus' changing position as he moves downwards from cross to sarcophagus, reinforced by the gradual fading of his body as it sinks into lower and lower relief into the surface of the bronze, while the spectator's viewpoint follows Jesus in his descent. This diminuendo contrasts with the reliefs of the Resurrection pulpit where Jesus becomes progressively more corporeal, starting with his total absence from the tomb and concluding with his Ascension – these scenes being projected towards us in front of the apparent surface of the panel.

The exception is the Trial. The two scenes of Jesus before Caiaphas and Pilate bear a complex relation to one another, at the same time as forming a single scene; several episodes are compressed, the two figures of Jesus are obscure, there is the contrast between the magnificence of the building and the confusion of the courtroom, so that the spectatator is involved in a process of puzzling out what is happening almost as demanding as in Ghiberti's Joseph or Giovanni Pisano's Passion. But in the remainder of the panels Donatello does not to confront us with intellectual problems, not even perceptual ones, but draws us into a sustained meditation upon the central Christian doctrine of the resurrection.

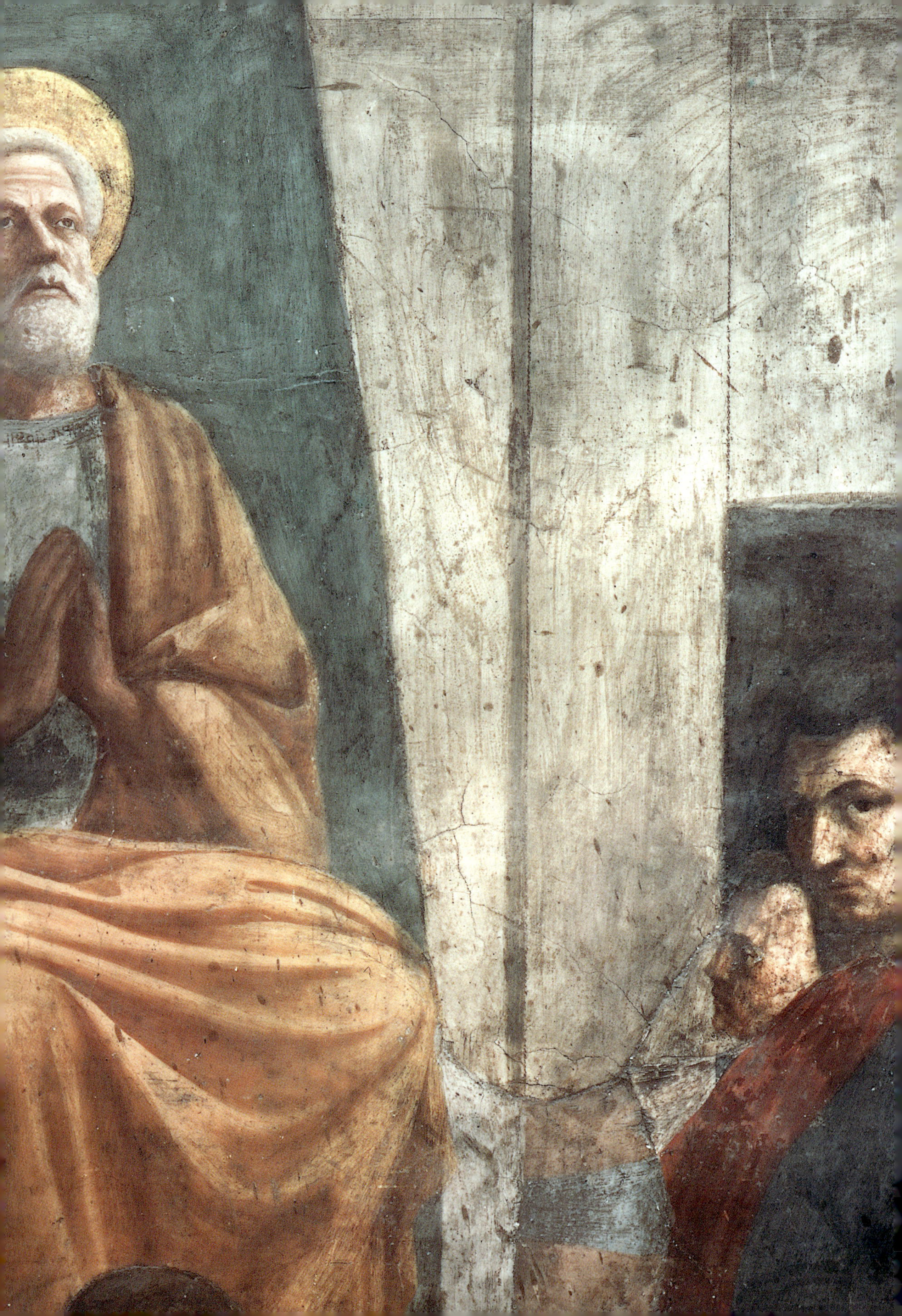

CONCLUSION

VISIBLE SPEECH

These images make considerable demands upon the spectator. But are there grounds for believing that people at the time looked at them in this way? The evidence is scanty – that cannot be denied. Art criticism did not exist, printing had not yet been invented and there were no newspapers; few artists issued manifestos, made statements about their work or wrote letters or journals,[1] and the comments of the public are not recorded. But the little written material which does exist suggests that this kind of spectatorship was indeed practised in the early Renaissance. I shall use this evidence to indicate that artists could count upon spectators to linger over and puzzle out their images; that in their approach to depicting the biblical narratives artists enjoyed a measure of freedom; and that this was a society with a fairly high degree of literacy in which leading artists shared. I will also touch upon issues of pictorial temporality, logic and the role of the spectator which have been implicit in the preceding chapters.

Capturing and holding the spectator's attention

Alberti was as much concerned with how a spectator reads a picture, as with how an artist makes one. Most commentators upon Alberti's *De pictura*, however, concentrate upon the rules and procedures he lays down for artists:

Detail of Figure 132

orderly composition, geometric perspective and the lifelike depiction of nature.[2] But Alberti justifies almost all his recommendations in terms of their effect upon the spectator. First of all a picture must capture our attention; then it must hold it long enough for us to make sense of it.

To capture the eyes of spectators Alberti insists that a painting must be strikingly beautiful and bear a close resemblance to nature.[3] He also stresses the importance of copiousness (*copia*), variety (*varietas*), novelty (*nova*) and an abundance (*exuberantia*) of things in the image and of the colours in which they are depicted.[4]

For a picture to continue to hold the attention of spectators so that they dwell (*morentur*) on the image, Alberti lays special emphasis upon copiousness and variety.

> A historia you can justifiably praise and admire will be one that reveals itself to be so charming and attractive as to *hold the eye of the learned and unlearned spectator for a long while* with a certain sense of pleasure and emotion. The first thing that gives pleasure in a historia is copiousness and variety [*copia et varietas rerum*]. Just as with food and music novel and extraordinary things delight us for various reasons but especially because they are different from the old ones we are used to, so with everything the mind takes great pleasure in variety and copiousness [*varietate et copia*]. So in painting variety of bodies and colours is pleasing. I would say a picture was most copious [*copiosissimam*] if it contained a mixture of old men, youths, boys, matrons, maidens, children, domestic animals, dogs, birds, horses, sheep, buildings and provinces; and I would praise all copiousness provided that it relates to the action that is taking place [*ad rem de qua illic conveniat*]. *When the spectators dwell on examining all the details* [my italics], then the painter's copiousness [*pictoris copia*] will acquire favour.[5]

This frequently quoted passage has usually been interpreted as a set of stipulations for the artist to observe; less attention has been paid to Alberti's view that the reason for an artist to follow them was in order to capture and then to retain the spectator's interest.[6]

While Alberti provides the most explicit statement that an artist had to fashion his images so as to encourage spectators to dwell upon them for an extended period, this notion is also implicit in the writings of Dante and of Ghiberti. Indeed the idea that it is necessary to attract the spectator's attention through the sensuousness of an unusual, splendid, rich or very beautiful image in order to set the mind to work interpreting its meaning derives from St Augustine.[7] Alberti, however, is the first writer we know to have applied these concepts directly to visual images in general.

Part of the reason for Alberti's emphasis was his firm belief that painting, like literature, should depict complex stories and allegories of a philosophical nature for which there were no ready-made formulae.[8] Both the painter and the spectator had to be problem-solvers. The artist had to encrypt his ideas in the expectation that the learned spectator, at least, would decipher them.

To illustrate this point Alberti drew upon the example of The Sacrifice of Iphigenia, a famous lost painting of antiquity by Timanthes of Cyprus. Timanthes won a competition for this picture because he solved the problem of how to express the overwhelming grief of the girl's father, Agamemnon. His solution was to cover Agamemnon's head in a veil while contriving a composition so organised as to guide the spectator to determine for himself the depths of Agamemnon's sorrow.[9]

> When he had made Calchas sad [*tristem*] and Ulysses even sadder [*tristiorem*] at the sacrifice of Iphigenia, and displayed all his art and skill on the grief-stricken [*maerore affecto*] Menelaus, consumed by emotion [*consumptis affectibus*], being unable to devise a suitable means [*quo digno modo*] by which to register the face of the extremely sad [*tristissimi*] father, Timanthes covered the father's head in drapery, *in such a fashion as to leave traces of his grieving soul which could be better inferred* [*meditaretur*] *by the mind than discerned by the eye* [my italics].[10]

Alberti's specificity about the mental activity required of the spectator to puzzle out the emotions represented by the signs of the father's emotional state in the folds of his veil indicates the importance he attached to the spectator's role. Timanthes is commended for setting up the scale of progression in the intensity of grief experienced by the other characters as well as the signs in Agamemnon's veil so as to encourage the spectator's active participation.

Alberti's artist was a problem-solver. Painters, like writers, should invent complex stories and allegories rather than follow conventions. It was hard to represent a smiling face; it was even harder to work out an effective means to depict Agamemnon's grief; hardest of all was to fit all the figures together in a composition that explained the story to the spectator. That, precisely, was the painter's job – to solve difficult problems of pictorial expression and communication in compositions which employed purely visual language with the utmost economy and which were not allowed to run riot.

The corollary is that this made far greater demands upon the spectator, who could no longer rely exclusively upon established compositional formulae to signify the subject of a composition, nor upon gestures whose meanings were almost as well established as words. The spectator also had to become a problem-solver, using the free play of mind to interpret the visual images representing the complex mental states that Alberti wanted artists to depict, such as Ulysses portrayed as 'not really mad but only pretending'.[11] And in order for him to do this the painter had to ensure that, once having gained the spectator's involvement in the contemplation of a picture, that interest was sustained.

Such time-consuming attention was thought to be necessary because the visual arts were considered as intellectual pursuits through which complex thoughts, feelings, speech and ideas could be represented by means of visual signs. This was essential to meet the didactic requirements of Christian Art. It took time for the spectator to interpret such images. The earliest expression of this idea during our period is also the earliest description of a fresco from Giotto's Scrovegni Chapel, written between 1308 and 1312 by the poet Francesco da Barberino.

> Animosity: it suffers this, indeed with endurance, as where Envy is consumed inside and out with enviousness – this Giotto painted excellently in the Arena at Padua.[12]

Brief though this is, Barberino clearly believed such images were as capable as writing of expressing complex ideas.

At about the same time, Dante, in his famous description of the marble reliefs that he sees in Purgatory, quoted in the chapter on Giovanni Pisano's Pistoia pulpit, is quite explicit about the capacity of these sculpted narratives both to tell stories – the Annunciation, David dancing before the Ark and Trajan and the Widow – as well as to exemplify ideas and doctrines, such as the virtue of humility.[13] The phrase that Dante uses to characterise visual images that are open to being read this way, is visible speech, 'visibile parlare'.[14] In effect this is a translation of St Augustine's term, 'verba visibilia' – visible words or language.[15] Almost a century later Cennino Cennini talks of the capacity of painting 'to discover unseen things, hiding themselves under the shadow of natural objects and to give shape to them with the hand'.[16] Alberti's slightly later formulation in *De Pictura* is along similar lines: 'We will now go on to instruct the painter how he can represent with his hand what he has conceived with his mind.' He continues, 'a historia will move spectators when the men painted in the picture outwardly demonstrate their own feelings as clearly as possible . . . these feelings are known from the movements of the body.'[17]

* * *

The literacy of artists and audiences

If artists were to understand the intellectual and spiritual content of the biblical texts and other doctrinal material they were required to depict, they needed to be literate and generally well educated, as well as skilled in their own art. Equally they had to be able to count upon an audience that was moderately well educated and literate.

The requirement that artists must be literate is found in the preamble to the 1355 regulations of the Siena Guild of Painters, quoted in the introduction: painters are professional visualisers of biblical events for the benefit of those who do not know how to read.[18] Implicit is the claim that Sienese painters, like their patron saint St Luke *did* know how to read and write – but so too did many members of their audience, as we shall see. There is explicit evidence of several artists who could both read and write. Although Cennino Cennini, author of the early fifteenth-century *Libro del arte,* describes himself as a 'humble painter' but was nonetheless able to write a book.[19] Alberti and Ghiberti take the literacy of artists for granted, and both expect artists to be learned in the Liberal Arts as well – to be both well read and well educated.[20] Ghiberti is even more insistent about this than Alberti, perhaps because he lacked Alberti's advantages of birth, and he criticises unlettered painters and sculptors, thanking his parents for taking care 'to have me instructed in the arts in which one cannot prove oneself without the discipline of letters and a grasp of all the theories. Thus, through the care of my parents and the teachings of my instructors, I have grown in knowledge of literature and in the disciplines of philology and technics and I delight in commentaries on these things.'[21]

What evidence is there that other artists fulfilled these requirements? First, contrary to what is commonly believed, Italians of the time were far from illiterate. Literacy was exceptionally high and a substantial minority, perhaps a quarter of the population, was able to read and write Italian. For males, the figure is higher, perhaps as high as a third.[22] This means that a substantial majority of the population had access to writing through being read to. Giovanni Villani's claim that 75 per cent of all men in Florence in 1338 were literate was vastly exaggerated, but it indicates his overall impression that this was essentially a literate society.[23] Villani, moreover, was proud of the high educational attainments of his fellow citizens, pride that was further justified by the fact that parents had to pay for this education themselves – there was no state subsidy.[24]

So the audience for art was highly literate by the European standards of the time. But were painters and sculptors among the 33 per cent of literate males? Paul Grendler has claimed that all male nobles, professionals, middling merchants and the women of those classes could read and write as a matter of course, but so too could the sons of skilled artisans such as butchers, bakers and candlestick makers. Further down the scale there is evidence from the 1480 Florence tax returns that even woolworkers and mattress makers paid for their children's education.[25] If these more menial artisans were literate, then artists certainly were. Ghiberti's own parents were not well-to-do.

Specific evidence for literacy amongst the leading artists themselves is strong. Giovanni Pisano's Latin inscriptions on his two pulpits do not prove that he could write Latin himself, but he must surely have been the author of such personal and complex statements even if he had to have them translated. It would also be surprising if Giovanni was unable to make sense of the Latin inscriptions. The same applies to Giotto, whose Latin inscriptions to the Virtues and Vices in the Scrovegni Chapel may have been composed in a similar way. His depiction of St Jerome, whose book is open on his lectern showing the text of the Ave Maria (p. 38 and fig. 32), strongly suggests that Giotto could make sufficient sense of major liturgical Latin texts, and had expectations that many of his spectators could do so too, certainly the members of the Scrovegni family.[26] Ambrogio Lorenzetti must have been able to read the Italian inscriptions on his frescoes of Good and Bad Government, even if he did not compose them himself – though he probably did. Ghiberti, a century later, like Cennino Cennini, could write Italian; it is also significant that in describing his relief of David and Goliath, he quotes directly from the Latin Vulgate – 'Saul percussit mille et David decem milia' [Saul hath slain his thousands, and David his ten thousands. 1 Samuel, 18, v. 7],* suggesting that he could also read some Latin.[27] Ghiberti's near contemporaries, Fra Lorenzo Monaco, Fra Angelico and Fra Filippo Lippi, were all monks and must have been literate in both Latin and Italian. The 1436 will of a painter from Crete provides direct evidence of his educational ambitions for his unborn child: 'I wish him first to learn to read and write and thereafter the art of painting . . . And my books I bequeath to my child, if it is male, so he may learn to read'.[28]

That is the direct evidence about individual artists. Masaccio and Brunelleschi were both the sons of legal notaries so it is inconceivable that they were not educated in Italian and had some Latin. Brunelleschi himself served as a Prior of the Florentine Republic. Alberti's letter dedicating *Della pittura,* the Italian version of *De pictura,* to Brunelleschi, mentioning Ghiberti, Luca della Robbia, Donatello and Masaccio, is persuasive evidence that all

*The Vulgate has 'Percussit Saul mille . . .'. The inversion suggests that he was quoting from memory.

those artists were able to read the book in Italian, but that their Latin was perhaps not up to the task of reading the Latin version.[29] There is, however, evidence that the architect Filarete read *De pictura* rather than *Della pittura*.[30] Only Duccio's literacy is unsupported by direct or circumstantial evidence, but it is hard to believe that the painter of the Trial of Jesus was unable to read.

The balance of probability is that all the artists discussed in this book could read and write Italian and maybe some Latin. Their audience was also fairly literate and well educated. Later in the fifteenth century the evidence is unequivocal. Botticelli was a keen student of Dante; Leonardo and Michelangelo were both talented writers as well as artists.

Subject matter: The challenge of a silent medium

To communicate complex events and ideas through the medium of 'visible language' is difficult because a visual image cannot speak – Dante called it 'an image which is silent'[*imagine che tace*][31] – nor can it show the human body in movement. Artists are therefore denied the three major signs for effective human communication – words, bodily movements and changing facial expressions. Furthermore, without accompanying text, captions, cartoon bubbles, cinematic movement, mime or speech visual imagery seems a somewhat clumsy medium for telling stories, let alone for conveying Christian doctrine. It is open to misinterpretation. Anyone who has had the experience of encountering a painting of an unfamiliar subject in an art gallery or has tried looking at newspaper photos without reading the captions, will appreciate this. Most people look for the label. Indeed, exactly this shortcoming was held against painting by a leading humanist in the mid-fifteenth century.[32]

The absence of words, moreover, makes it difficult to convey thoughts and feelings, dreams and prophecies – the very stuff of religious stories.[33] It also poses apparently insuperable problems in communicating negative statements, deceptions and conspiracy – problems for which our artists nonetheless found successful solutions (Figs 6 and 138).[34] Finally, without words it seems to be 'impossible to draw the little connections of speech or to give the picture of a conjunction or an adverb' upon which written and spoken narrative depends.[35]

Yet artists have succeeded in operating a viable 'visual language'. How was this possible? We shall examine their use of compositional formulae, biblical texts and the exercise of what one writer termed Devout Meditation.

* * *

Compositional formulae

For many biblical stories there were standardised compositional formulae, some established in the first centuries of Christian Art. Like a caption or title, each of these patterns acts as a sign for the subject matter.[36] When in the sixteenth and seventeenth centuries painting became a display of the artist's virtuosity more for the benefit of private collectors than for Christian instruction in public places, these formulae disappear, sometimes making the subject matter almost impossible to identify, hence necessitating the use of titles. Titles were used only rarely in our period.[37]

Once one has recognized the overall subject, the identity of individual figures slots into place, though here too standard formulae or attributes were used to identify Jesus, Mary and the saints. Conversely, of course, knowledge of the identity of particular characters can sometimes help to identify the subject of the image as a whole. The basis for this is similar to that of spoken or written language, as explained by St Augustine: the meaning of these signs depends upon agreed social and institutional conventions.[38] In the early Renaissance virtually everyone would have learnt this visual language from infancy in the same way as one learns one's mother tongue, by being steeped in it, not by being taught the rules: 'Infants acquire speech purely by assimilating the words and phrases of those who speak to them.'[39]

We get a rare glimpse of how children did learn to recognize pictures from Giovanni Dominici's *Regola del Governo di Cura Familiare* of 1403, where he advises parents who do not want to have their homes so stuffed with religious paintings as to look like churches, that the nurse should take the children to church as often as possible, showing them the pictures and telling them the stories. Dominici, moreover, clearly expected that some parents of a lower social class, from whom the nurses would have been recruited, were able to perform this role themselves.[40]

This is how, at the simplest level, people must have begun the acquisition of visual literacy. In fact Dominici indicates that even for those who subsequently did learn to read, Christian education should begin with visual images.

Most of the images discussed in this book would have been easily recognisable. For example, in Duccio's Trial of Jesus, the placing of the scene of Jesus' interrogation by Annas above Peter's first denial was well established in Romanesque manuscript illustrations (Fig. 6). His images of the Flagellation and the Mocking of Jesus (Figs 13–14) are formulaic, so too Giotto's frescoes of Jesus driving the Moneychangers from the Temple (Fig. 104), the Raising of Lazarus (Fig. 28) and the Lamentation (Fig. 38). Recognising these would have been no problem for a contemporary spectator.[41] The story of Joachim and Anna (Figs 20–1) may have been less familiar. Most of Ghiberti's reliefs on his first Baptistery doors and his competition relief of the Sacrifice of Isaac would have been easy to identify (Figs 101, 103, 105, and 108–09). Almost all Giovanni Pisano's reliefs conform to pre-existing patterns adapted to his requirements. Perhaps the only exception is his Passion panel (Fig. 83), but its component parts such as the Betrayal and the Mocking adhere to formulae. The problem in making sense of this relief arises more from the demands made upon the spectator to view it from specific angles than from the obscurity of the subject matter. Exceptions to the rule would have been Masaccio's Tribute Money (Fig. 127), Ghiberti's Joseph (Fig. 138) and Donatello's Trial of Jesus (Fig. 149).

Biblical texts in translation

Artists did not always follow these formulaic compositions slavishly as we have seen. They often turned to written sources, in the scriptures and in the *Golden Legend*, the *Meditations on the Life of Christ* and other texts, to enrich the inherited conventions without any loss of intelligibility. But while we can be confident that the major artists were literate, is there any evidence that they had access to such texts in Italian? It is commonly believed that before the Reformation, translations of the scriptures were banned by the Catholic Church, but this is untrue, a slur seemingly perpetrated by English reformers.[42] A famous example of a pre-Reformation translation of the Latin Vulgate is found in the ninth-century Lindisfarne Gospels, which has an interlinear Anglo-Saxon translation made in the tenth century. The surviving evidence from the early Renaissance, meagre though it is, indicates that some artists owned translations and others had access to them. The Cretan painter, mentioned earlier, not only wanted his son to learn to read before learning to paint, but also owned a small library, which would have included such texts, presumably in Greek; no doubt western artists would have been similarly equipped. The 1497 inventory of the Florentine sculptor Benedetto da Maiano (c.1442–97) has survived. It includes no fewer than six bibles or bible anthologies in Italian as well as a book of the saints, the miracles of Our Lady, the virtues and vices, the *Life of St Bernard*, a Dante, the *Flowers of Virtue*, and *The Little Flowers of St Francis* among other Christian books. This list corresponds to the evidence of Florentine wills in general at the beginning of the fifteenth century.[43] These included copies of the *Golden Legend* and the *Meditations on the Life of Christ*. Major artists of the previous two centuries almost certainly had access to similar collections.

There is a great deal of corroborative evidence that the scriptures were increasingly available in Italian from the mid-thirteenth century onwards, particularly in Tuscany and especially in Florence. Gospel harmonies or synopses such at the *Diatesseron* compiled by Tatian (AD 120–73) in the second century, which weaves together a coherent narrative directly from the four Gospels, were especially popular and available in Italian translations. Most of the translations were made by Dominicans or Franciscans 'for the use of those who do not know Latin' ('non sae gramatiche') – the function of translation was similar to that of pictures of the biblical stories.[44] Although these Italian translations were not used in the liturgy of the Mass, they would have been employed for religious instruction, in sermons for example. Finally, it is noteworthy that there are fifty-two quotes from the Italian Bible in Dante's *Convivio* (1304–08), and the first six stanzas of *Purgatorio* XI consist of Dante's versified translation of the Lord's Prayer.

Individual scenes of Duccio's Trial sequence (Figs 6–15) followed conventional formulae, but the extended, step-by-step unfolding of the story had no pictorial precedent, and drew upon a close reading of the Bible or the *Diatesseron*, supplemented by the *Golden Legend*. The same is true of some of Giotto's frescoes, such as the Last Supper (Fig. 29) and the Betrayal (Fig. 30).

The artists of the early fifteenth century made more use of textual sources. Antoninus (1389–1459), the Dominican Archbishop of Florence, strongly objected to painters who embellished biblical subjects with non-biblical episodes and inappropriate figures:

> Nor are they to be praised who paint apochryphal tales, such as midwives in the Nativity, or the Virgin's girdle thrown down by Thomas the Apostle during her Assumption because of his doubt, and the like. To paint curiosities in stories of the saints or in churches, which have no value in stimulating devotion, but laughter and vanity, such as monkeys, or dogs chasing hares, or the like, or vain adornments of clothing, appears superfluous or vain.[45]

This call for strict scripturalism was by no means universally obeyed. Antoninus's fellow Dominican, Fra Angelico, perhaps went furthest in this direction in his cycle of the Life of Jesus for the silver cupboard of SS Annunziata dating from the early 1450s, where each scene is labelled with the appropriate text from the Vulgate. But three decades earlier Masaccio's Tribute Money (Fig. 127) was closely based upon the scriptures. Of course in this case it is probable that there was no specific compositional formula for the story, so Masaccio had to invent one. He based it upon a careful reading of the biblical text probably interpreted for him by members of the Carmelite Order and maybe the Papal Curia to draw attention to its contemporary political and ecclesiastical significance. Nonetheless Masaccio's solution to the problem was to adapt a pre-existing formula for a different event, the Last Judgement, while for the subsidiary scene of St Peter handing over the tax, Masaccio employed the composition used for depicting contracts and betrothals. The Raising of Theophilus's Son (Fig. 130) immediately below also lacked a precedent and Masaccio once again had to devise the scene directly from the text of the *Golden Legend*, basing the composition on the Raising of Lazarus.

Ghiberti in his Gates of Paradise, in the Cain and Abel (Figs 135 and 137), but above all in the panel of Joseph and his Brothers (Fig. 138) provides us with the most elaborate case of an artist translating a complex story into visual form, striving to find a visual equivalent not only for the sequence of events but also for Joseph's conspiracy to deceive his brothers, which is at the centre of the plot. Donatello's pulpits, on the other hand, are not based upon close textual readings since many of the scenes he chose to depict are only mentioned in passing in the scriptures. The single exception is the Trial of Jesus (Fig. 149), where one's difficulty in identifying the precise nature of the subject arises from the way in which Donatello combined the trial by Pilate with that by Caiaphas alongside elements taken from the *Meditations.*

Devout meditation

Did artists have any freedom to deviate both from formulaic canonical images and from scriptural texts? We have encountered many examples of their doing so, but was there any formal justification?

It is clear from scattered references from the early thirteenth century onwards that there was a spirited debate on this subject, some churchmen arguing that artists should adhere strictly both to the authority of pictorial tradition and to the Bible; Antoninus appears to put the Bible first; while others were in favour of some freedom so long as it did not conflict with the scriptures nor with Christian doctrine.[46] Evidence of how such freedom might be exercised is provided by the highly influential *Meditations on the Life of Christ* probably written by a Franciscan in about 1300. This guide to pious meditation on the Gospel story both elaborates upon the biblical text itself and encourages devout Christians to do likewise.

> Moreover you must not believe that all things which were said and done by him [Jesus], upon which we are able to meditate, were all put into writing: indeed, in order to make a greater impression, I will narrate these things in such a way *as they might have occurred* [my italics] or as I believe

> they could have happened, in accordance with certain imaginary representations which the soul perceives in a diversity of ways. For we can meditate upon the holy scriptures, expound them and understand them *in many ways, just as we believe it to be useful provided that it is not contrary to the truth of life, of justice and of doctrine as well as faith and good morality.* When, therefore, you find in my narrative 'The Lord Jesus said or did this in this way', and similarly in other cases, should it be impossible to prove it from the scriptures, you should not accept it otherwise than as what is determined by means of Devout Meditation [*devota meditatio*] . . .*[47]

The biblical texts of many of the stories such as the Adoration were indeed terse in the extreme, while others like the Tribute Money or even the Last Supper are enigmatic and demand interpretation. Other subjects such as the Lamentation or the Massacre of the Innocents are mentioned only in passing. This argument in favour of encouraging readers to elaborate upon the biblical account has a parallel in Fra Giordano's contemporary justification for using authoritative images to provide additional eyewitness accounts to flesh out the sacred story. This kind of activity also relates to St Augustine's requirement for the close reading and careful study of the scriptures.

An example from the *Meditations* shows how Devout Meditation could be practised. The writer describes how Jesus was nailed to the cross. First the cross itself was erected and then Jesus was made to climb a ladder, next his two hands were nailed before the ladder was removed. A nail was driven through his hanging feet. None of this is described in the Gospels. So the author continues:

> There are, however, those who believe that He was not crucified in this manner, but that the cross was laid on the ground and that they raised it up and fixed it on the ground. If this suits you better, think how they take Him contemptuously, like the vilest wretch, and furiously cast Him onto the cross on the ground, taking His arms, violently extending them, and most cruelly fixing them to the cross.[48]

The *Meditations* is primarily addressed to readers not to spectators, and it indicates that they were familiar with the practice of elaborating imaginatively upon the biblical narratives. By extension there is good reason to believe that they would have carried this into their reading of visual images. Correspondingly the procedures of the *Meditations* were transferable to the making

*Meditation, meditatio, should not be understood as a kind of hippy 'oooom', but as a disciplined process of intellectual inquiry and reflection.

of images; Benedetto da Maiano owned a copy of the book, and we have seen indications that artists as early as Giotto and Giovanni Pisano drew upon the text. The author's descriptions are highly visual and one is frequently recommended to place oneself in the position of an eyewitness to the event – a point to which we will return.

Inevitably problems could arise if artists exercised Devout Meditation without restraint. For example, a fresco of the Annunciation attributed to Ambrogio Lorenzetti showed the Virgin Mary so terrified by the appearance of the Archangel Gabriel that she has fallen to her knees clutching onto a column.[49] That the painter's exercise of Devout Meditation was considered to have gone too far, may be inferred from the fact that Mary's cowering figure was hacked out from the plaster and repainted in a more decorous posture. Although Lorenzetti's exercise of Devout Meditation appears to have been censored, this case supports the view that, so long as they did not contradict faith, doctrine or decorum, early Renaissance artists enjoyed considerable freedom in their visualisations and in adapting both pictorial formulae and the biblical record. That was their job, after all, set out in the Statutes of the Painters' Guild of Siena, Lorenzetti's home town. The corollary was that they were vulnerable to censorship if their meditations went too far and offended church or client. It appears that Lorenzetti was trying to get away with his new interpretation without having obtained prior approval.

Giovanni's Passion panel (Fig. 83) combines all three approaches to the identification of the subject matter. He used conventional compositions for the Betrayal and the Mocking of Jesus; he drew upon the *Meditations* for the scene of Jesus being whipped at the column on the night before his Crucifixion; and finally he included abbreviated events from the story. He combined and arranged these scenes so that the spectator feels he is an eyewitness, a case study of the meditational approach.

In his competition relief of Abraham and Isaac (Fig. 99), Brunelleschi appears at first glance to have employed the conventional and extremely ancient formula for this subject, dating back to frescoes in the Roman catacombs. But his interpretation of the subject accords neither with pictorial precedent nor with the scriptural text. His decision to depict the moment when Abraham is on the very point of plunging the knife into his son's throat was clearly the product of much thought. There is no warrant for this in the Bible, but it exemplifies the method recommended by the author of the *Meditations* of imagining what may have happened, and of filling in the scant scriptural story.

Similarly, Ghiberti's scene of Jesus among the Doctors (Fig. 109) on his first doors for the Baptistery, elaborates upon the biblical story and adapts the time-honoured composition (Fig. 111) both by introducing the figure of the steward to mediate between Jesus and his family, and by placing the doctors in a huddle on the floor. In this case Ghiberti, like Giovanni in the Passion panel, is employing all three approaches to the subject. So too Donatello in his Head of St John being brought to the King's Table (Fig. 124): the subject is recognisable through the presence of conventional elements such as the banqueting table, the head upon a platter, the dancing daughter and the king. But Donatello has imagined an episode which is not described in either of the two scriptural versions of the story and which is unusual in pictorial convention – that of the head being presented directly to Herod. Finally, almost all Donatello's reliefs for the San Lorenzo pulpits (Figs 147–65) involved him in elaborate and deeply Devout Meditation upon how each episode might have taken place, resulting in panels which while being broadly recognisable, are rich with new insight into Jesus' death and resurrection.

We have seen that there is indeed evidence to suggest that artists worked in the expectation that spectators could be counted upon to devote a sufficient amount of time to deciphering their images; that a considerable section of the population, including many artists, was literate enough to be able to read the Bible, which was available in Italian translations; and finally, that artists could depend upon their audience having the knowledge, visual and literary, to recognise the subjects of their images and to reflect upon them in an imaginative way. It only remains to examine three related issues: the treatment of time, of logic and the role of the spectator.

Time and the image

Much ink has been spilled on the representation of time in pictures. It has been argued that because visual images are static they are at a great disadvantage to the written or spoken word in the depiction of the flow of events, which is the very essence of storytelling. This was much discussed in the seventeenth and eighteenth centuries by writers such as the Earl of Shaftesbury in his *Characteristics* and by Gotthold Lessing in his *Laokoon*, but it is something of a red herring for the early Renaissance because, as Ruskin pointed out so deftly in a passage already quoted, 'a modern picture, isolated and portable, must rest all its claims to attention on its own subject: but the pictures of the early masters were almost always parts of a consecutive and stable series'. The issue does not figure at all in contemporary writing about art, even in the works of Alberti and Ghiberti. I suspect that the reason for this is that it was not regarded as a problem either for artists or for spectators. We have to guard against projecting the concerns of a later period onto an earlier one.

In addition, in discussions of time in pictorial narrative, three discrete issues tend to be confused: first, the time taken by the spectator to look at an image; second, the representation of the sequence of events; and finally the point, stage or moment in the story that the artist has chosen to depict. As we have seen, the first of these, the temporality of looking, certainly was a matter of contemporary interest to Alberti, to Ghiberti and it is also implicit in Dante's descriptions in of the bas-reliefs in purgatory. The second, the sequence of events, was not mentioned explicitly, though it is implicit in Ghiberti's longer descriptions. The reason once again is that given by Ruskin – it was a commonplace convention.

Partly as a corollary, the third issue is not referred to at all; but another reason for this neglect is that, as far as I can see, the aim of most narrative images of the period was not to represent some precise moment in the story from which one needed to infer what had preceded and what succeeded it, but to provide a visual digest or summary of the whole story or episode for didactic purposes. This is clear in all three of Dante's descriptions of the purgatorial bas-reliefs. In the Annunciation he observes that one can see both the angel Gabriel's opening salutation, 'Ave Maria', and Mary's final words of humble acceptance, 'Ecce ancilla dei' – 'Behold the handmaiden of the Lord'. The same is the case of a much later description of a real bas-relief of the Annunciation by Donatello, which Vasari praised highly for showing the Virgin's fear at the unexpected appearance of the angel, her timid and sweet gesture of reverence, the way she responds to his salutation and her humble gratitude – practically all the stages of the event compressed in a single image.[50]

These are a few examples of individual images which stand alone, but almost all the images discussed in this book belong to a sequence, and this made it possible for the artist to get in as much of the story as possible. He could break it down into a series of subsidiary events in framed cartoon-like images, as in Duccio's Trial (Figs 9, 10, 12–15); in the stories of Joachim and Anna (Figs 20–1), the Betrothal of the Virgin (Fig. 26), the Nativity of Jesus and his Passion in Giotto's Scrovegni Chapel; in the Baptist series on the Siena Baptistery font (Figs 122–3); or in the Passion and Resurrection on Donatello's two San Lorenzo pulpits (Figs 145–6). Alternatively several episodes might be included in a single relief panel or painting, the device often referred to as continuous narration, as in Giovanni Pisano's two pulpits (Figs 60, 83 and 89–90), Masaccio's Tribute Money and the Raising of Theophilus's Son (Fig. 133), Ghiberti's Gates of Paradise on which he prided himself for packing as many as eight episodes into a single relief (Figs 138–9), and Donatello's Trial of Jesus (Fig. 149). Sometimes, as in the case of the Annunciations already mentioned, different episodes might be compressed into a single framed image; this is also found in Giotto's Betrayal (Fig. 30) and the Death Sentence (Fig. 34), Ghiberti's Jesus among the Doctors (Fig. 109), Donatello's Head of St John being brought to the King's Table (Fig. 124) or the central scene of the Tribute Money (Fig. 127). Finally, we find some individual scenes showing a particular stage and, on occasion, even a moment in the story. But these are always part of a series or of a continuous narrative. Indeed, more often than not, all of these approaches are found in a variety of combinations in any particular cycle.

Even where more momentary images are employed we find no orthodoxy about which moment to employ. One reason for this has already been explained. Another is that the issue was more a matter of the emphasis that an artist wanted to give to an episode, than of any attempt to create a sense of time. At one extreme we do find that Giotto seems to correspond closely to Lessing's pregnant or suggestive moment, but this is part of his temperate approach to pictorial narrative, designed to allow the spectator to reflect at length upon the meaning of the story. At the other extreme, and almost unique, is the 'prontezza', or immediacy, of Brunelleschi's Sacrifice of Isaac (Fig. 99), designed perhaps to show Abraham's extreme zeal and obedience to God.[51] In between there were all manner of variations as well as combinations of different methods.

Logic

It is logic that primarily connects the episodes of a story not the passage of time. Indeed a long period of time can separate one event from another in the chain of cause and effect, but it clearly doesn't assist the story to recount all or any of the intervening events simply in the interests of temporal continuity. In his *Poetics*, Aristotle distinguished between bad stories, which he called episodic, in which the events merely succeed one another, and good stories in which they form a 'probable and necessary sequence'. Alberti uses a phrase, 'ad rem de qua agitur' – 'in accordance with the action being performed' – to stipulate that none of the figures in a composition should be superfluous to the logic of the narrative.

Nonetheless, the logical connections which we take so much for granted in verbal storytelling present problems to the pictorial storyteller because of the absence of those 'little connections of speech' mentioned by Addison, and it is the set of pictorial problems arising from this absence that must now be examined.

Lessing in his *Laokoon* of 1766 had observed that only poetry could represent negatives but it was Sigmund Freud (1860–1939), the founder of psychoanalysis, in his *Interpretation of Dreams* of 1899, who compiled a comprehensive list of the problems of visualisation in the chapter on the 'Means of Representation in Dreams' – perhaps the most painstaking account of the problem. He listed six types of logical relationship: simultaneity, causation, either–or, antithesis or contradiction, similarity, agreement and contiguity, and negative statements, to which one might add conditional as well as both – and statements.[52]

Freud showed that in dreams, and his point applies equally to painting and sculpture, juxtaposition and sequence are used to represent these connections.[53] But the juxtaposition of two images, for example, does not invariably signify a causal relationship between them, unlike the use of the conjunction 'because' linking two clauses. In the absence of verbal syntax the interpreter of images has to infer the sense of the overall logic and meaning. We, the spectators, have to supply the logic. This is a crucially important point.

There have been many examples of how this works in practice. In the first scene of the story of Joachim and Anna (Fig. 22), Giotto's juxtaposition of Joachim being pushed out of the sanctuary with the other man being blessed within it, encourages us to infer a set of antitheses between barrenness and fertility, between inclusion within the religious community and exclusion from it. Indeed the whole structure of the Scrovegni Chapel (Figs 16–17) is antithetical: the personifications of the Virtues on the west wall face those of the Vices on the east wall; alongside the Virtues, the blessed are on the right-hand side of the Last Judgement, the damned on the left. The juxtaposition between Joachim being expelled from the Temple and the next fresco, showing him among the shepherds (Fig. 23), can also be interpreted as an antithesis, but a more obvious reading is causal: as a result of Joachim's humiliation in the Temple, he withdraws into the wilderness.

In the first scene of Duccio's Trial of Jesus (Fig. 6), the juxtaposition of Jesus' interrogation with Peter's first denial in the hallway beneath invites us to draw a comparison between Peter's cowardice and Jesus' courage, once again an antithesis. In Donatello's Head of St John (Fig. 124) the presence of the viol player and the dancing daughter contrast with the horrific presentation of the severed head. This establishes a set of contrasts and inversions: Herod's birthday is the Baptist's death-day; Herod's palace is transformed into a dungeon and the King into a prisoner. We also infer a chain of cause and effect: Herodias has set the whole tragedy in progress by instructing her daughter to ask for the head as her reward. As a result, the soldier presents the head, Herod is horror-struck, and the guests recoil. Addison's 'little connections of speech' may indeed be absent from the visual arts, but the artist can so arrange his images that the spectator infers the appropriate logic in the picture. The words themselves may be lacking, but it is as if there were a syntax.

At its most complex, in Ghiberti's Joseph and his Brothers (Fig. 140), the spectator has to puzzle out, as in the investigation of a crime, exactly what relationships obtain between the figures, which of those relationships are significant and what they mean. Once this detective work has been accomplished, all is apparent – Joseph is surreptitiously ordering his steward to plant the brothers' money in Benjamin's sack in order to trap them, take his revenge and finally to forgive them. The very indeterminacy of visual images and the absence of logic-bearing syntax enable Ghiberti to place the spectator in the position of the brothers, as the victims of Joseph's conspiracy, utterly bewildered by what is happening to them.

The Joseph is perhaps the paradigm of an image designed to appeal to Alberti's problem-solving spectator and of the doctrines of St Gregory and St Augustine discussed in the introduction. Ghiberti's relief attracts the eye through the splendour, novelty and beauty of the architecture, and the copiousness, variety and elegance of the figures. This both holds the viewer's attention and stimulates the mind to try to make sense of the story. And once again we have to supply the logic. It is a crucially important point. The spectator is placed in the position of an eyewitness who has just arrived on the scene, trying to piece together what is happening, what has happened and what it all means. This leads us to the pictorial equivalent of the narrator and of the point of view.

The spectator as narrator

> Forasmuch as many have taken in hand to set forth in order a narrative of those things which are most surely believed among us, even as they delivered them unto us, which from the beginning they saw for themselves, as eyewitnesses and ministers of the word; it seemed good to me also, having had perfect understanding of all things from the very first, to write unto thee in order, most excellent Theophilus, that thou mightest know the certainty of those things, wherein thou hast been instructed.[54]

> Moreover, if you want to profit from this, you need to put yourself in the position of an eyewitness in relationship to those things which are

narrated as having been said and done. In addition, you must see it with your own eyes and hear it with your own ears.[55]

The second quotation is from the *Meditations*, the first comes from the opening of the Gospel according to St Luke. The author introduces himself to the reader before proceeding with his story. But although he declares that his narrative is based upon the eyewitness accounts of those who originally witnessed the events of Jesus' life, he, as compiler, does not attempt to give his narrative the immediacy of an eyewitness account. He recounts such events as Jesus praying in the Garden of Gethsemane while his disciples were asleep, or Jesus' forty days in the wilderness being tempted by the Devil, which no eyewitness other than Jesus himself, God or the Devil could have observed. St Luke's narrative, therefore, is really that of an external narrator, of whose presence one is barely conscious but who, like God, seems to know everything and to have been everywhere, often called the omniscient narrator. Basically one can distinguish between two main types of narrative, between those told in the first person and in the third – between those told by subjective narrators who enter into the mind of their chief character and those who adopt an external point of view.[56]

What of pictorial narrative in the early Renaissance? Are there equivalents to the types of literary narrator? At first sight there does not appear to be any place for a narrator at all. Pictures seem more akin to the dramatic, or what Plato termed the mimetic form of story. Because pictures are mute it is impossible to include a narrator who actually *tells* the story.[57]

The very inscrutability of images, however, puts the spectator in the position of attempting to tell the story to himself from the evidence supplied by the artist. First we have to identify the broad nature of the subject on the basis of the compositional formula. But then, as we look more closely, trying to puzzle out exactly what is going on, so we begin to tell the story to ourselves. Just as we have to supply the logic so also, in pictorial narrative it is *the spectator who is the narrator.*

We can see this process in the handful of extant contemporary descriptions of works of art. It is presented as something of a pleasurable game, in which a measure of guesswork is involved. Dante says of the angel Gabriel, 'one would have sworn that he was saying *Ave*'. Likewise in Ghiberti's lengthy description of Ambrogio Lorenzetti's Franciscan Martyrs, practically every scene is introduced with the Italian word 'come'; how: 'it is clear that the people standing watching are listening to the hanged friar who continues to preach; how the executioner is ordered to behead them; how the execution takes place in the presence of a great crowd . . .' and so on.[58]

But do we as spectator–narrators find ourselves assuming a role that is equivalent in any way to that of the literary narrator? Since these pictorial narratives are akin to the enactment of a drama in which the spectator cannot directly participate, it seems hard to identify any equivalent to the subjective narrator. By necessity, it would seem that the spectator must be a narrator who is external to the events, reporting and interpreting what is observed. This corresponds to Plato's ideal kind of distanced, terse and grave style of storytelling, and it is to be found, I believe, in many, but not all of Giotto's frescoes in the Scrovegni Chapel, in all Duccio's Trial scenes on the Maestà, in Giovanni Pisano's Crucifixion (Fig. 70a) at Pistoia, in Brunelleschi's Sacrifice of Isaac (Fig. 99) but not in Ghiberti's (Fig. 101), in most of Ghiberti's scenes on the Gates of Paradise, in almost all of Masaccio's Brancacci Chapel frescoes (Fig. 133). The action seems to take place behind a barrier separating us from the figures, and the figures themselves interact with each other across the front plane of the picture surface or parallel to it, oblivious of our presence. Gestures and expressions are restrained, notably in Giotto and Duccio, making it hard for us to identify with their inner feelings.

This type of reserved narration is the dominant mode, accounting for about three-quarters of my examples. It is also what one would expect in view of the orthodox Christian doctrine concerning images deriving from the Platonism of St Augustine and St Gregory. These images were didactic, designed to teach one what to worship and what to imitate.

Occasionally, however, we may be drawn into a more intimate relationship with the characters in a picture, by a figure who looks out at us directly, as in Giotto's scene of Joachim in the Wilderness (Fig. 23), where one shepherd appears to catch our eye in a complicitous glance – or perhaps he is looking at his painted companion. The double-take is deliberate and once noticed it makes us feel that we are a third shepherd sharing the puzzlement of the other two in their master's state of mind. But although it helps to usher us into the feelings of the painted characters, it hardly counts as subjective since its aim is to emphasise Joachim's deep withdrawal from the people and creatures around him. Significantly, it is only on rare occasions that we enjoy such eye-contact with a *major* character as with Jesus in Duccio's scene of his Mocking (Fig. 14).

Something more involved or subjective is found in images that set up the spectator's relationship so that he or she actually shares the viewpoint of one or more figures within the picture, most commonly where we feel that we are standing behind them, looking over their shoulders, seeing what they see, sharing their point of view and experience of the event. Giovanni Pisano was the main practitioner. Depending upon where we stand, usually at an oblique angle to the relief, we get drawn into the high emotional drama of the events and are not able to stand back to contemplate them dispassionately. Giotto, on the other hand, used this infrequently, in just a few of the Scrovegni Chapel frescoes, such as the Massacre of the Innocents (Fig. 37); more frequently in his later frescoes in Florence (Figs 95), though even so he kept the emotional temperature fairly cool. Ghiberti often emulated Giovanni Pisano but his figures are far less demonstrative.

Let us begin with the simplest case, Giovanni's Nativity panel in Pistoia. Seen obliquely from the left (Fig. 54), at the beginning of the story, we see Mary from behind Gabriel's shoulder; we see her recoil through his eyes. Nonetheless, for obvious reasons, we are not invited to merge our identity with that of Gabriel.[59] When we move around the relief we next see Gabriel through Mary's eyes (Fig. 61) in the background of a very intimate view of Mary displaying the baby Jesus to the shepherds, with whom we have become identified in turn. Thus Giovanni permits us to enter into the point of view of different figures in the carved relief depending upon our standpoint. At his most dramatic and subtle, in the Betrayal and the Mocking in the Passion panel at Pisa, Giovanni enables us to experience a close and disturbing identification with the insinuating figure of Judas (Fig. 76), so different from Giotto's detached presentation (Fig. 30), and with the witnesses to Jesus' humiliation (Fig. 85).

There is no need to multiply examples. Ghiberti in both sets of his doors for the Florence Baptistery as well as in his early competition relief (Fig. 101), uses this same device and so too does Donatello, particularly in the St John relief (Figs 125–6) and the pulpits. Even Giotto, though never Duccio, occasionally permits the spectator to become a participant as in the scene of the Suitors watching for the Rod to Blossom (Fig. 26), where we can imagine ourselves as being among the kneeling suitors, and in a more elaborate form in Giotto's later fresco of Herod's Feast, keeping us at a distance, even so.

But as with other aspects of pictorial narrative, sequence and logic, one must beware of being too categorical, of allowing generalisations to pre-empt observation and common sense. For, although in Giovanni's Pistoia pulpit we see a particular event more or less through the eyes of Gabriel, the shepherds or the mothers of the Holy Innocents, this first person viewpoint shifts from scene to scene and within each panel. It is not, indeed it cannot be, equivalent to a sustained, focused subjective viewpoint such as we find in a modern novel. Nor would that be appropriate. Insofar as these images are designed to arouse our feelings at all, their purpose is to encourage us to have feelings *about* Jesus or Mary and other saints and patriarchs, not to enter into their minds.

The corollary is that within a single panel the spectator's narrative standpoint may shift and change. In the case of relief sculpture, this is possible because the spectator is physically mobile, able to walk around the image, seeing it from different angles. Moreover, the fact that it takes time for us to unravel the image contributes to the possibility of what might be called a 'polyphonic' narrative. Giovanni's Passion panel is an excellent example of this. We start from the distanced viewpoint of a bewildering confusion of figures (Fig. 83), very much a detached and external observer; only gradually do we come to grasp that there are other more intimate ways of becoming involved in the story. Another complex example is Donatello's Head of St John where our initial perception is that of a detached spectator looking in upon a violent event from the other side of the frame (Fig. 124). Subsequently it may occur to us that we are actually in the position of a guest who has jumped backwards away from the table. Finally, we appreciate that there are lateral views (Figs 125–6) which we share with Herod, giving us insight into his isolation, or into the horror of the guests at the far end of the table.

Because of its inherent indeterminacy, a story told in images is open to being narrated in a range of rich and varied ways, from different distances and points of view. It is even possible for us to imagine our way into sharing the experience of different characters even though the artist does not have the capacity to represent their inner feelings directly through words. What can seem a weakness in the communicative power of images becomes a strength.

To conclude: Alberti emphasised the effect of a successful *historia* upon the emotions of the spectator. 'When the men painted in the picture outwardly demonstrate the movements of the souls as clearly as possible, the historia will move the souls of the spectators in turn.'[60] He went on to say that we feel the same emotions as the painted figures: 'we mourn with the mourners, laugh with those who laugh, and grieve with the grief-stricken'. So Alberti seems to have expected someone looking at Timanthes's Sacrifice of Iphigenia to feel in turn the mounting level of sadness and grief expressed by Calchas, Ulysses, Menelaus and Agamemnon; and the observer of Giotto's Navicella (Fig. 102) would have shared in the confused and turbulent feelings of each of the apostles. Yet, as we have seen, the majority of the images we have examined tend to discourage direct emotional identification with the figures in them, appealing more to the understanding than to the emotions. Partial exceptions to the rule are the pulpits of Giovanni Pisano and Donatello. Insofar as feelings are important it is our feelings *about* the characters – how patiently Jesus endures the injustice of his Trial in Duccio's Maestà (Figs 6–15), the humility of Joseph in Giotto's sequence of the Betrothal (Fig. 26), our horror at the actions of Herod and his soldiers in the Pistoia Massacre (Figs 66–9). That relates to one major function of these cycles, to teach us how to behave through the imitation of Jesus, Mary and the other saints and what behaviour we ought to avoid.

Most of the images we have examined are the product of a somewhat cerebral art. Michelangelo observed that Flemish painting will 'please the devout more than any painting of Italy, which will never cause him shed a tear'. He believed that 'at its best nothing is more noble or devout' than Italian painting, 'for good painting is nothing but a copy of the perfections of God and a recollection of his painting; it is a music and a melody which only intellect can understand, and that with great difficulty'.[61] This kind of art corresponds closely to St Augustine's idea of a fourfold response to miracles: the splendour and beauty of the image seizes our attention and arouses our senses, the senses arouse our minds; the mind interrogates the image in order to understand the doctrinal message manifest in the story.[62]

APPENDIX

Some factors affecting the perception of space between forms

In creating a convincing sense of recession, diminution and the sense of distance between forms a *combination* of factors is required.* Convergence of orthogonals to a central point and the Albertian diagram (Fig. 118) to control diminution are but two of these. Obviously, not all of these are necessary to a particular image. The presence of human figures is a precondition.

The following is a list of these factors.

1 View through a 'window' or frame.
2 Base of 'window' (as minimum) aligned with floor.
3 Masking and overlapping.
4 Figures inhabiting buildings/landscape.
5 Partial views of buildings.
6 Convincing massiveness of buildings/landscape.
7 Geometric perspective:
  i orthogonal convergence to a point.
  ii figures in scale with buildings/surroundings.
  iii geometrically controlled diminution.

*See Kenneth R. Adams, 'Perspective and the Viewpoint,' *Leonardo,* Vol., 5, 1972, pp. 209–17, partic. pp. 209–10. My list is an expansion of Adams's.

8 Foreshortening of figures and parts of figures; simple anamorphosis.
9 Light and shade.
10 Atmospheric perspective.
11 Graduated levels of relief (sculpture only).
12 Binocular parallax (sculpture only).
13 Movement parallax – actual (relief sculpture) or implied (painting).

NOTES

PREFACE

1 'Narrative is not a topic which has unduly engaged the attention of historians of Italian medieval painting, despite its self-evident analyticity, and despite the fact that it has been widely discussed by literary critics of the same period.' Julian Gardner, 'The Louvre Stigmatization and the Problem of the Narrative Altarpiece', *Zeitschrift für Kunstgeschichte*, 45, 1982, p. 237.

2 *Christianity and the Renaissance: Image and Religious Imagination in the Quattrocento*, ed. Timothy Verdon and John Henderson, Syracuse, 1990.

3 Christopher Green, in an unpublished inaugural lecture at the Courtauld Institute, 25 Feb. 1997 entitled 'Fictional Artists, Real Spectators: "Amico di Sandro, Roger Fry's Cézanne and the *Demoiselles d'Avignon*"', observed that active spectatorship and its record in prose is characteristic of English art history in a tradition going back to Ruskin and Pater, continued in the twentieth century by Roger Fry, Lawrence Gowing, John Golding and David Sylvester.

4 The positioning of paintings and sculpture in relation to buildings and the spectator is more studied now than previously, thanks to the pioneering work of Eve Borsook, Michael Podro, Thomas Puttfarken and Julian Gardner. See: Eve Borsook, *The Mural Painters of Tuscany from Cimabue to Andrea del Sarto*, London, 1960; revised second edition Oxford, 1980; Julian Gardner, 'The Decoration of the Baroncelli Chapel in Sta Croce', *Zeitschrift für Kunstgeschichte*, 1971, 34, H2, pp. 89–114; Thomas Puttfarken, *Masstabfragen: über die Unterschiede zwischen grossen und kleinen Bildern*, Hamburg, 1971; Michael Podro, *Piero della Francesco's Legend of the True Cross*, 1973 Charlton Lecture in Art, University of Newcastle upon Tyne, Newcastle upon Tyne, 1974, pp. 3 and 14–16; Thomas Puttfarken, *The Discovery of Pictorial Composition: Theories of Visual Order*

in Painting, 1400–1800, New Haven and London, 2000, pp. 137–47 on Titian's Madonna di Ca' Pesaro, partic. pp. 144–5.

5 Lorenzo Ghiberti, ed. Ottavio Morisani, *I commentari*, Naples, 1947.

INTRODUCTION

1 'Man is a storytelling animal,' observed the novelist Salman Rushdie on a BBC TV programme in July 2004.

2 For reflections upon some of the social and technological implications of state censorship in eighteenth-century France see Robert Darnton, 'Paris, the Early Internet', *New York Review of Books*, 29 June 2000, pp. 42–7.

3 Robin Dunbar, *Grooming, Gossip and the Evolution of Language*, London, 1997 (Ist pub. 1996), pp. 60, 79, 123, 171–2. See Carlo Ginzberg, 'Morelli, Freud and Sherlock Holmes: Clues and Scientific Method', *History Workshop Journal*, 9, Spring 1986, pp. 5–36, for the alternative 'bison down by the river' theory of the origins of language.

4 For an early Renaissance example of secrecy as a strategy for obtaining power over somebody see Boccaccio's story 'Gillette de Narbonne', the 9th story on the third day of the *Decameron*.

5 Plato, *The Republic*, Harmondsworth, 1987, 376–98 (Stephanus page numbers). The literature on Plato's treatment of the arts in *The Republic* is vast. A very good introduction is *Plato on Poetry*, ed. Penelope Murray, Cambridge, 1996, pp. 1-33. For an excellent recent account with good references for further reading see Ramona Naddaff, *Exiling the Poets: The Production of Censorship in Plato's Republic*, Chicago, 2002, pp. 39–40 and n. 8 on memorising Homer and its role in ancient Greek education. For her account of Plato's censorship of poetry see pp. 18–57. R. L. Nettleship, *Lectures on the Republic of Plato*, London, 1897 remains an excellent introduction.

6 Dante, *Inferno*, Canto v, 127–38. My colleague, Dr Jonathan White, kindly assisted me with the interpretation of this passage. The translation is Longfellow's. Not everyone shared Dante's Platonic theories of literary infectiousness. Boccaccio, in the afterword to the *Decameron* claims that whether love stories 'prove wholesome or noxious depends entirely upon the hearer'. In addition, Boccaccio may have alluded, ironically perhaps, to Dante's Canto v in subtitling *The Decameron* 'The book of Prince Galehaut'. See G. Boccaccio, *Decameron*, tr. Guido Waldman, Oxford, 1993, pp. xxi and 683.

7 Plato, *The Republic*, 398a–b. See Naddaff, op. cit., for the view that Plato was not actually exiling all poets from his republic, so much as setting himself up in competition with them, aiming to establish a new, more philosophical poetry. For Alberti's approach to this issue see Conclusion, p. 271 and n. 8.

8 For the passage in question, Plato, *Republic*, 393e–394a in the context of 392e–394b; G. Genette, *Narrative Discourse*, Oxford, 1980, pp. 161–73; ibid., 'The Boundaries of Narrative', *New Literary History*, 8, 1976–7, pp. 1–13 and 1–3 in particular; Naddaff, op. cit., pp. 58–66.

9 See Brecht's theory of alienation: B. Brecht, 'Alienation Effects in Chinese Acting' (first published in English in 1936) in *Brecht on Theatre*, ed. and tr. John Willett, New York, 1964, pp. 91–2.

10 Aristotle, *Poetics*, tr. Malcolm Heath, Penguin, London, 1996, pp. 6–7, Bekker page number 1448b.

11 Aristotle, op. cit., p. 16, 1451b, 'For this reason poetry is more philosophical and more serious than history. Poetry tends to express universals, and history particulars. The *universal* is the kind of

speech or action which is consonant with a person of a given kind in accordance with probability or necessity . . .'

12 'Tragedy is an imitation of an action which is admirable, complete and possesses magnitude . . .', Aristotle, op. cit., p. 10, 1449b. Other translations have 'serious' for admirable.

13 'Of all plots and actions the episodic are the worst. I call a plot episodic in which the episodes follow one another without either probability or necessity (ούτ εἶκοσ οὺτ ανάγκη).' (My translation), Aristotle, op. cit., p. 17, 1451b. In *The Poetics* Aristotle uses the term 'according to probability or necessity', or some variant on those words, several times – e.g. n. 6 above; p. 16, 1451a; p. 25, 1454a, where he uses the term three times in quick succession in extending the concept from plot to character. It is a key term. Several translations of the sentence after the next one, 1452a, talk about events following one another 'as cause and effect' (Aristotle, *Poetica*, ed. and trans. S. H. Butcher, London, 1896), 'as a consequence of one another', Aristotle, *The Poetics*, trans. W. Hamilton Fyfe, London & New York, 1927), 'logically' (Aristotle, *Poetics*, Gerald F. Else, Leiden, 1957). But Aristotle does not use such terms. The text is unusually elliptical at this point and translators have interpolated the words suggesting a strong *causal* relationship between events; this is not quite the same thing as Aristotle's term, 'probability and necessity'. Heath, loc. cit. interpolates the word 'because', which while suggesting cause and effect does so with a lighter touch, avoiding the implication of events following one another according to a rigid law. 'The imitation is not just of a complete action, but also of events that evoke fear and pity. These effects occur above all when things come about contrary to expectation but because of one another.' For Aristotle's conception of cause and necessity see the *Physics*, tr. Philip H. Whicksteed and F. M. Cornford, 2 vols, London, 1929, vol. I, II, V, 200a 32ff. and II, ix, 196b 10ff. Aristotle distinguishes necessary progression from luck or chance. He conceived of cause as an attribute of a thing or person and believed that 'the principle of causation is derived from the definition and rationale of the end . . .'

14 Neither Jews nor early Christians, however, were absolutely orthodox in their observance of this commandment. The most famous example is the extensive painted narrative decoration of the synagogue at Dura-Europos in modern Syria, probably dating to AD 244–56. See Carl H. Kraeling, *The Synagogue*, 2nd edn, Ktav Publishing House, 1979; Katrin Kogman-Appel, 'Bible Illustration and the Jewish Tradition', in *Imaging the Early Medieval Bible*, ed. John Williams, Pennsylvania, 1999, pp. 61–96, partic. 61 and 65–6.

15 For an introduction see Emile Mâle, *The Early Churches of Rome*, tr. David Buxton, London, 1960, pp. 42–8; John Beckwith, *Early Christian and Byzantine Art*, New Haven, 1993, pp. 19–24; John Lowden, *Early Christian and Byzantine Art*, London, 1997, pp. 18–41 and J. Elsner, *Imperial Rome and Christian Triumph*, Oxford, 1998, ch. 8 and pp. 251–9. For accessible illustrations of the catacombs, Fabrizio Mancinelli, *The Catacombs of Rome and the Origins of Christianity*, Florence, 1981.

16 See John Lowden in Williams, op. cit., p. 5 and n. 13. See my conclusion, p. 276 for a more extended discussion of this issue.

17 Lowden, *Early Christian and Byzantine Art*, p. 18 suggests that some reasonably sized churches existed before AD 312, instancing the church and baptistery at Dura-Europos, before AD 256.

18 For Constantine's toleration and his church building see Richard Krautheimer, *Rome: Profile of a City 312–1308*, New Jersey, 1980, pp. 3 and 18–31.

19 Ibid., p. 25; Beckwith, op. cit., pp. 27–30. Lowden, op. cit., points out that Sta Costanza was not a church but a mausoleum even though it was attached to the Basilica of St Agnese.

20 For St Gregory see R. A. Markus, *Gregory the Great and his World*, Cambridge, 1997 and F. H. Dudden, *Gregory the Great: his Place in History and Thought*, 2 vols, London, 1905. For Gregory's letters to Serenus I have drawn heavily upon Celia M. Chazelle, 'Pictures, Books and the Illiterate: Pope Gregory I's Letters to Serenus of Marseilles', *Word and Image*, vol. 6, no. 2, April–June 1990, pp. 138–53. For changing interpretations of the Serenus letters see Chazelle, 'Memory, Instruction, Worship: "Gregory's" Influence on Early Medieval Doctrines of the Artistic Image', in *Gregory the Great: A Symposium* ed. John C. Caradini, Notre Dame and London, 1995, pp. 181–215. Peter Brown explains the sixth-century context of the change from an emotional, quasi-pagan response to the presence of an image to its being read and puzzled out as recommended by St Gregory, in Peter Brown, 'Images as a Substitute for Writing', *East and West: Modes of Communication*, ed. E. Chrysos and Ian Wood, Leiden, 1999, pp. 15–34. Ian Wood's response, 'Image as a Substitute for Writing – A Reply', in the same volume, pp. 35ff., provides a more detailed historical account of the transition. Perhaps the change has never been complete, in practice. For a wide-ranging account of the use of devotional images see Sixten Ringbom, *Icon to Narrative: The Rise of the Dramatic Close-Up in Fifteenth-century Devotional Painting*, Doornspijk, 1984 (1st edn, 1965).

21 'Aliud est enim picturam adorare, aliud per picturae historiam quid sit adorandum addiscere. Nam quod legentibus scriptura, hoc idiotis praestat pictura cernentibus, quia in ipsa ignorantes uident quod qui debeant, in ipsa legunt qui litteras nesciunt; unde praecipue gentibus pro lectione pictura est.' See Chazelle, 'Pictures, Books and the Illiterate', 1990, pp. 138–53. At the Second Council of Nicaea in AD 787, which reinstated the cult of images in response to the Iconoclastic Controversy, it was resolved that images could be objects of veneration (*proskynesis*) but not of adoration (*latreia*), and any homage paid to the image was to the prototype, i.e. to Jesus, the Virgin or a particular saint, not to the image itself. See Jaroslav Pelikan, *Imago Dei: The Byzantine Apology for Images*, New Haven, 1990, particularly pp. 175–82 for the post iconoclastic doctrine.

22 'Idcirco enim pictura in ecclesiis adhibetur, ut hi qui litteras nesciunt saltem in parietibus uidendo legant, quae legere in codicibus no ualent.' Chazelle, op. cit., p. 139.

23 Herbert Kessler in *Spiritual Seeing: Picturing God's Invisibility in Medieval Art*, Pennsylvania, 2000, pp. 1 and 3, states that medieval writers distinguished between two categories of image, icons or portraits of people and narratives or *historiae*. He argues that both Jews and Christians could accept *historiae* more easily than icons because they avoided the problem of worship, and it could thus be claimed that they did not breach the second commandment.

24 Joyce Coleman in her *Public Reading and the Reading Public in Late Medieval England and France*, Cambridge, 1996 provides a critical account of the orthodox theory of the development of the history of literacy: there is a quasi-Darwinian evolution from 'primary orality' through to modern times, that as

writing becomes available orality simply survives as a relic to serve the under-privileged. In her view both the situation and the process were far more complicated, and perhaps remain so. She points out that Xenophon quotes Socrates describing himself working in his library on the texts of the pre-Socratic philosophers. Thus Socrates and his predecessors were literate as well as oral. She argues that literacy, the experience of texts stored as writing, encompasses aurality, hearing texts being read, as well as the private reading of texts both silently and aloud. She argues that even for those who could read for themselves, reading aloud in company was perhaps the primary form of literacy, instancing Chaucer, Henry VI, Elizabeth I, Cosimo de Medici and Federigo da Montefeltro. Her re-examination of the nature of literacy has implications for our interpretation of the Gregorian doctrine of art as the book for the illiterate. For an exhaustive account of the history of the Gregorian doctrine and of its interpretation by modern scholars see Lawrence G. Duggan, 'Was Art really the "Book of the Illiterate"?' *Word and Image*, vol. 5, no. 3, July–Sept, 1989, pp. 227–53. For an overview of the controversy about whether images were simply visual aids or the source of knowledge which could be read actively see Herbert L. Kessler, 'Reading Ancient and Medieval Art', *Word and Image*, vol. 5, no. 1, Jan, 1988, p. 1.

25 'Atque indica quod non tibi ipsa uisio historiae, quae pictura teste pandebatur, displicuerit sed illa adoratio, quae picturis fuerat incompetenter exhibita.' Chazelle, 'Pictures, Books and the Illiterate', p. 140.

26 Duggan's own view is at odds with Chazelle's interpretation of Gregory and that of others: 'my sympathies lie with the views of Coulton, Henry, Gombrich, and Schier . . . that pictures as instruments of precise communication fall far short of words, that a mark of that disparity is that pictures inevitably must be made intelligible in words to the intellect (though not necessarily to other parts of the psyche), and that pictures cannot be "read" in the same way as, or as fully as, books . . . Imagine a Tuscan peasant coming upon Masaccio's *Tribute Money* in the Brancacci Chapel . . . None of these people could learn from the painting . . . what it was about.' See conclusion, n. 36. Duggan, op. cit., pp. 243–4. Nicholas Gendle argues that the early texts are not primarily pedagogic but help to remind Christians of verbally imparted teaching, Nicholas Gendle, 'Art as Education in the Early Church', *The Oxford Art Journal*, 3, Oct, 1979, pp. 3–8. Duggan, Gombrich and others may or may not be correct, my concern, however, is not with some *universal* truth about the way in which we read narrative images but with the beliefs and opinions which obtained in the early Renaissance, e.g. the views of Fra Giordano below, and notes 27–31. Giordano and others took the view that the visual testimony of the canonical paintings of the events of the life of Jesus and that of the Gospels were equally authoritative and complementary.

27 Lina Bolzoni, *The Web of Images: Vernacular Preaching from its Origins to St Bernardino da Siena*, Aldershot, 2004, pp. 16–21.

28 *Prediche inedite del B. Giordano da Rivalto recitate in Firenze dal 1302 al 1305*, ed. Enrico Narducci, Bologna, 1867, Sermon XXXII, 6 Jan 1305, pp. 168–77; XXXIII, pp. 177–83.

29 'Di questi Magi fanno i santi molte quistioni; chè fanno quistione e domandano, che fu quello che gli mosse a venire; fanno quistione chi fuoro questi Magi, e

onde fuoro, e che condizione fu la loro, e quanti furono, e in quanto tempo vennono. Tutte queste quistioni fanno i santi, perocchè 'l Vangelo nol dice . . .', *Prediche inedite del B. Giordano*, p. 169.

30 'Fanno ancora i santi quistione, che condizione fu la loro. Questo si può comprendere pur per lo nome, che sonno detti Magi. Magi é a dire in quella lingua uomini savissimi e filosofi, e in altra lingua è a dire grandi signori di gente, o re, o grandi baroni . . . Avvene ancora un'altra grande testimonia, cioè le prime dipinture che vennero di Grecia di loro: onde le dipinture sono libro de' laici, ed eziandio d'ogno gente; perocchè le dipinture vennono tutte da' santi primamente: acciocchè se ne potesse avere più compiuta conoscenza, si faceano le figure de'santi prima come erano, e nella figura, e nella condizione e nel modo. Onde si truova che Nicodemo dipinse Cristo in croce in una bella tavola, primamente a quella figura e modo che Cristo fu, che chi vedea la tavola, si vedea quasi tutto 'l fatto pienamente, tanto era ben ritratta, secondo il modo e la figura; chè Nicodemo fu alla Croce di Cristo, quando vi fu posto e quando ne fu levato: e quella è la tavola onde usci poi quel bello miracolo, onde si fa la festa del santo Salvatore. Cosi altresi troviamo che santo Luca dipinse la Donna nostra in su una tavola ritratta, tutto appunto com'era, la quale tavola è oggi in Roma, e serbasi con grande divozione. Faceano i santi quelle dipinture per dare più chiara notizia alle genti del fatto; sicchè queste dipinture, e spezialmente l'antiche, che vennono di Grecia anticamente, sono di troppo autoritade; perocchè là entro conversaro molti santi che ritrassero le dette cose, e dierdene copia al mondo, delle quali si trae autorità grande, siccome si trae di libri. Onde di quelle dipinture che vennero di Grecia sapemo certamente che fuoro grandi signori; perocchè sono dipinti con corone di re in capo; e quindi altresi si può sapere quanti fuoro, che fuoro tre, e cosi sono dipinti tre insieme. Se dicesse: che mosse questi Magi? Fu grande fede e grande divozione. Fede gli mosse che Cristo fosse nata, e pero vennono; divozione gli mosse, chè credettono che non fosse re terreno, ma celestiale.' Op. cit., pp. 170–1.

31 See Hans Belting, *Likeness and Presence: A History of the Image before the Era of Art*, tr. E. Jephcott, Chicago, 1994 (German edition, 1990), p. 4. Unfortunately Belting does not provide a reference for the source of this legend.

32 Lowden quotes from the pre-iconoclastic *Life of St Pankratios*, possibly seventh century, in which St Peter is said to have given instructions that the entire picture-story of the life of Our Lord Jesus Christ should be painted in all the churches from Antioch to Jerusalem, *Early Christian and Byzantine Art*, op. cit., p. 151 and also pp. 17, 152.

33 Luke, 1, 2.

34 The Annunciation. Quoted in Cyril Mango, *The Art of the Byzantine Empire, 312–1453*, Toronto, 1986, pp. 176–7.

35 Pelikan, op. cit., pp. 86–9; Belting, op. cit., pp. 49 and 57; Dorothee Klein, *St Lukas also Maler der Maria*, Berlin, 1933; H. U. Asemissen and G. Schweikhart, *Malerei als Thema der Malerei*, Berlin, 1994, ch. 3, 'Lukas malt die Madonna'; Museum of Fine Arts, Boston, *Rogier van der Weyden, St Luke Drawing the Virgin*, Brepols, 1997, p. 6 argues that Mary Theotokos, the God bearer, 'approved and conferred her grace and power to these prototypes and their immediate variants'. See also Jacobus de Voragine, *The Golden Legend*, tr. W. G. Ryan, 2 vols, Princeton, 1993, vol. 1, pp. 247–54.

36 'Imperciochè noi siamo per la gratia di Dio manifestatori agli uomini grossi che no sanno lectera, de la cose miracolose

operate per virtù de la santa fede . . . venerabile et glorioso missere santo Luca, el quale fu non solamente figuratore della statura et de la portatura de la gloriosa vergine Maria, ma fu scriptore de la sua santissima vita et de suo santissimi costumi, unde' è onorata l'arte nostra.' G. Milanesi, *Documenti per la Storia dell'Arte Senese*, 3 vols, Siena, 1854, vol. 1, p. 1. For a translation of the statutes by Gabriele Erasmi see Hayden Maginnis, *The World of the Early Sienese Painter*, Pennsylvania, 2001, pp. 199ff. See also Evelyn Welch, *Art and Society in Italy 1350–1500*, Oxford, 1997, p. 137.

37 Chazelle, 'Pictures, Books and the Illiterate, pp. 145–8. See also Meredith J. Gill, *Augustine in the Italian Renaissance: Art and Philosophy from Petrarch to Michelangelo*, Cambridge 2005. Jacobus de Voragine, Boccaccio and Salutati as well as Petrarch were all well versed in Augustine's works and referred to *De doctrina cristiana*. See pp. 9, 13, 197 and 148.

38 See n. 44 below.

39 S. Augustini, *In Joannis Evangelium, Tractatus xxiv, 2*, London, 1895, p. 2 and tr. Revd H. Browne, London, 1895, pp. 2–3.

40 Saint Augustine, *On Christian Teaching*, tr. and intro. R. P. H. Green, Oxford, pp. 31–2. I am indebted to my colleague Dr Kay Stevenson for directing me to *De doctrina cristiana* as well as to a comparable reference in Basil's third homily 'On the Hexaemeron'.

41 Augustini, *Tractatus*.

42 'Nec tamen sufficit haec intueri in miraculis Christi. Interrogemus ipsa miracula, quid nobis loquantur de Christo: habent enim si intelligantur, linquam suam.' S. Augustini, op. cit.

43 Chazelle, 'Pictures, Books and the Illiterate', pp. 146–9.

44 *On Christian Teaching*, pp. 53–4. He even compares pictures unfavourably to dress and bodily ornament which are 'useful and necessary institutions' which enable us to distinguish sex and rank and without whose 'coded meanings', he argues, society could hardly function. In *De consensu evangelistarum* Augustine writes: 'They thoroughly deserve to err who have sought Christ and his apostles not in sacred books but in pictures on walls', see Chazelle, 'Pictures, Books and the Illiterate', p. 146.

45 Saint Augustine, *On Christian Teaching*, p. 31; see Augustine, *De Doctrina Christiana*, ed. and tr. R. P. H. Green, Oxford, 1995, vol. 2, 5, p. 58.

46 Saint Augustine, *On Christian Teaching*, pp. 33–4; see also pp. 106 and 111. However, St Augustine warns the expositor that he should not himself adopt the 'helpful and healthy obscurity' of the scriptures in his commentary or sermons but should adopt 'the greatest possible clarity'. Indeed he implies that obscure exposition amounts to setting oneself up as an equal to the writers of the holy scriptures. See pp. 114–16.

47 Giovanni Boccaccio, *Life of Dante*, tr. J. G. Nichols, Hesperus Press, London, 2002, p. 52, also p. 51; Gill, op. cit., p. 13.

CHAPTER 1

1 John White, *Duccio: Tuscan Art and the Medieval Workshop*, London, 1979, ch. 6, pp. 80–134. See also Dillian Gordon, 'Duccio', *Grove's Dictionary of Art*, London and New York, 1996, vol. 9, pp. 341–50. Jane I. Satkowski, *Duccio di Buoninsegna: The Documents and Early Sources*, ed. and intro. Hayden B. J. Maginnis, Georgia Museum of Art, 2000.

2 White, op. cit., pp. 96 and 196–7 for documents relating to the procession.

3 For double-sided altarpieces see Julian Gardner, 'Fronts and Backs: Setting and Structure', in *La Pittura nel XIV e XV Secolo: Il Contribuito dell'Analisi tecnica all storia dell'Arte*, ed. H. van Os and J. R. J.

Asperen de Boer, Bologna, 1983, pp. 297–322, partic. pp. 297–300. Gardner suggests that mass might have been celebrated on both sides of the Maestà. See also Donal Cooper, 'Franciscan Choir Enclosures and the Function of Double-Sided Altarpieces in Pre-Tridentine Umbria', *Journal of the Warburg and Courtauld Institutes*, 64, 2001, pp. 1–54.

4 The stained-glass oculus, long attributed to Duccio, is now attributed to Cimabue on stylistic grounds, and was begun in 1287–8, see White, op. cit., pp. 137–8.

5 Fifty-eight is strictly speaking an estimate, however. Fifty-two narrative scenes survive, thirteen from the front and thirty-nine from the back. It is possible that in addition to the nine predella panels on the back there was a tenth. John White argues reasonably that there were two additional narrative panels on the front and back above the Madonna and the Crucifixion respectively, but these do not survive. I have broadly followed White's reconstruction on pp. 80–102 and figs 51 and 52. However, the image of the Maestà *in situ* on a Biccherna cover of 1482, now in the Siena Archivio di Stato, and reproduced by White in fig. 57, shows the right-hand side of the altarpiece. We see an independent superstructure supported on a beam above the upper pinnacles of the main panel. This is an exceptional feature, not to be found on any surviving altarpiece of the fourteenth or fifteenth centuries that I can find. On the right there is a pinnacled panel which must have been balanced by a pendant on the left; presumably there was another in the centre. It is likely that these panels were double-sided. None of these six images is known to survive. But the height of the beam is such as to make it questionable that there was room for two images back and front in the centre of the main altarpiece. We do not know the content of the images on the beam, whether they were narratives, representations of saints, angels or something else. Whatever the case there might have been as many as sixty stories. See Satkowski, op. cit., p. 75.

6 It appears from an undated document some time after the contract of 9 Oct 1308 that at that point there were thirty-four narrative panels, or maybe thirty-eight, on the rear part of the altarpiece. It is not clear whether this number includes the predella. If it did, then Duccio must have added a minimum of three or a maximum of eleven scenes. Although his calculations are different from mine, White has inferred from this that a 'process of development' in the design of the altarpiece took place after the signing of the contract, possibly involving the addition of a predella, see White, op. cit., p. 82. This also opens the intriguing possibility that the unprecedented number of trial scenes was included at this development stage (see note 7 below). The truth of the matter, however, is that we simply do not know.

7 This is noted by John White, *Art and Architecture in Italy, 1250–1400*, Harmondsworth, 1966, p. 151. James Stubblebine, *Duccio di Buoninsegna and his School*, 2 vols, Princeton, 1979, vol. 1, pp. 48–50 also makes this observation, and suggests that this indicates Duccio's dependence upon manuscript illuminations – see also n. 15 below. Anne Derbes, *Picturing the Passion in Late Medieval Italy: Narrative Painting, Franciscan Ideologies and the Levant*, Cambridge, 1996, p. 85 argues that there are eight scenes of the trial. I have counted the Flagellation, Mocking and Pilate washing his Hands as part of the Trial, making eleven. White suggests that this expansion of the Trial reflected contemporary mystery plays, Derbes considers a Byzantine source and draws attention to

a fresco cycle at Staro Nagoričino of 1316–18 with five episodes. For a thorough discussion of the Trial see Derbes's chapters 3 and 4.

8 See William M. Bowsky, *A Medieval Commune: Siena under the Nine, 1287–1355,* Berkeley, 1981, pp. 55–6 for the oath each member of the ruling Council of the Nine had to swear on taking office in 1339: 'That law and justice be done and administered to the citizens subject to you . . . without discrimination by your rectors and officials. And that the statutes of your commune and its ordinances be observed for each person who demands it.'

9 I owe the observation concerning the embedding of the parchment to Val Fraser. The inscription, which also appears in Lorenzetti's frescoes in Sala del Nove, is the opening of the Wisdom of Solomon, *Apochrypha*, Ch. 1, v. 1. See also Bowsky, op. cit., p. 103; Andrew Martindale, *Simone Martini*, Oxford, 1988, pp. 14–17, 204–9.

10 These frescoes have spawned an enormous and fascinating literature since Nicolai Rubinstein's seminal article 'Political Ideas in Sienese Art: The Frescoes by Ambrogio Lorenzetti and Taddeo di Bartolo in the Palazzo Pubblico', *Journal of the Warburg and Courtauld Institutes*, vol. 21, 1958, pp. 179–207. For a more recent account see Jonathan White, *Italy, the Enduring Culture*, London, 2000, pp. 53–60. Hans Belting, 'The New Role of Narrative in Public Painting of the Trecento: Historia and Allegory', in *Pictorial Narrative in Antiquity and the Middle Ages*, ed. Herbert L. Kessler and Marianna S. Simpson, Washington, 1985, pp. 151–68, suggests that Giotto's fresco in Florence's Podesta's Palace of 'commune rubato da molti', as well as his figure of Justice in the Scrovegni Chapel, were sources for Lorenzetti's frescoes, see p. 158. Giotto's fresco in Florence no longer survives but is described in Vasari's *Lives*, ed. G. Milanesi, Florence, 1906, 1973 reprint, vol. 1, p. 400

11 For discussion of this issue see the Introduction to Creighton E. Gilbert, *Italian Art, 1400–1500: Sources and Documents*, Evanston, 1992, pp. xviii-xxvi, which argues that there was a wide variety of practice in which sometimes the artist and sometimes the client or church had most influence over the programme and its visual manifestation. Charles Hope, 'Visual Narrative in Renaissance Art', *Journal of the Royal Society of Arts*, Nov 1986, pp. 804ff. and particularly pp. 807–9 contend that it was the artist's job to visualise the story and that he often enjoyed considerable freedom in doing so. Perhaps, like writing the script of a film, the programme could be a collaborative effort. Florens Deuchler, 'Duccio Doctus: New Readings for the Maestà', *Art Bulletin*, 61, 1979, pp. 541–9 refers to 'Duccio's careful reading of the Gospels' on p. 545.

12 *Il Diatesseron in Volgare Italiano, Testi inediti dei secoli XIII–XIV,* ed. V. Todesco, P. A. Vaccari, M. Vattasso, Città del Vaticano, 1938. For further information on Italian translations see the conclusion pp. 277-8.

13 For information on literacy in general and artists' literacy in particular see conclusion pp. 273-5. See also introduction, pp. 6-11 and notes 24 and 26. Creighton Gilbert makes the interesting observation that the fifteenth century in Italy was unique in the number of books about art written by artists, listing Piero della Francesca, Leonardo da Vinci, Alberti, Ghiberti, to which one might add Cennino Cennini. Even though there is no parallel in the fourteenth century, it is nonetheless contributory evidence of a tradition of the literate

artist beginning earlier and flowering in the quattrocento: Gilbert, op. cit., p. xv.

14 Alberti observes that all the praise of the composition consists in its invention. Indeed, he believed that the invention had such force 'that even by itself and without the picture it gives pleasure'. L. B. Alberti, *De Pictura*, ed. and tr. C. Grayson, London, 1972, sect. 53, pp. 94–5.

15 This detail is recorded in Luke 22, v. 55. 'And when they had kindled a fire in the midst of the hall, and were set down together, Peter sat down among them'. John 18, v. 18 has them standing round the fire. Duccio's fidelity to the text of Luke down to the detail of showing Peter 'in their midst' strongly suggests that he did not rely upon the *Diatesseron* alone. It also indicates Duccio's scrupulously close reading. The image is also found in the twelfth-century *Eadwine Psalter* in the Victoria and Albert Museum, see Alexander Sturgis, *Telling Time*, London, 2000, p. 17 for illustration.

16 See introduction above pp. 4–5 and notes 12 and 13; also Aristotle, *Poetics*, 1996, pp. 15, 1451a, where Aristotle argues that when Homer 'composed the *Odyssey* he did not include everything which happened to Odysseus (e.g. the wounding on Parnassus and the pretence of madness during the mobilization: the occurrence of either of these events did not make the occurrence of the other necessary or probable)'. See also L. B. Alberti, *De Pictura*, ed. and tr. C. Grayson, London, 1972, II, 40, pp. 78/9: 'I would praise any great variety so long as it is appropriate to what is going on in the picture' – '. . . ad rem de qua illic agitur conveniat'.

17 The precise historical truth behind the Gospel account need not concern us, since to Duccio and his contemporaries it was understood to be a divinely inspired and true historical record, and even today it provides the main evidence for historians trying to reconstruct what actually occurred. For a historian's reconstruction of the Trial of Jesus see Paul Winter, *On the Trial of Jesus*, Berlin, 1961; and Geza Vermes, *The Passion*, London, 2005. For some current accounts of the historical Jesus see Geza Vermes, *Jesus the Jew: A Historian's Reading of the Gospels*, 2nd edn, London, 1983; E. P. Sanders, *The Historical Figure of Jesus*, Harmondsworth, 1993; *idem*, *Jesus and Judaism*, London, 1985.

18 Jacobus de Voragine, *The Golden Legend*, tr. W. G. Ryan, 2 vols, Princeton, 1993, vol. 1, p. 207.

19 The vertical juxtaposition of the two scenes is found in *The Eadwine Psalter*, though they are not linked by a staircase or any other architectural feature. See Sturgis, op. cit.

20 This verse is included in the Italian version of the *Diatesseron* cited in n. 12: 'Dissero i Giudei: a noi non è licito d'uccidere alcuno.' *Diatesseron*, p. 350. For a full discussion of whether the Jews did retain the right to capital punishment under the Roman imperium see Vermes, *The Passion*, pp. 103–8 and 16–27 and Winter, op. cit.

21 Voragine, op. cit., p. 205.

22 For a similar analysis of Duccio's use of architectural subdivisions in narrative see John Drury, *Painting the Word: Christian Pictures and their Meanings*, New Haven and London, 1999, p. 44 on Duccio's Annunciation from the Maestà in the National Gallery, London. See also pp. 43–7.

23 Dietmar Popp, *Duccio und die Antike*, Scaneg, München, 1996, pp. 171–6 and pls 90 and 92.

24 Ibid., p. 206.

25 See Conclusion, pp. 282–4.

26 The use of visual disorder to suggest the breakdown of justice is employed on a larger scale by Ambrogio Lorenzetti in his frescoes of Good and Bad Government, in Giovanni Pisano's Pisa Pulpit and also by Donatello in his own depiction of the Trial of Jesus in his San Lorenzo pulpits, for which, see Chapter 9, pp. 253ff.

CHAPTER II

1 The 'interior space of the church' has been admirably described as 'the carrier of an idea':- Pelikan, *Imago Dei: The Byzantine Apology for Images*, New Haven and London, 1990, p. 3 quoting J. Strzygowski in *Aesthetikos: Essays in Art, Architecture and Aesthetics,* ed. P. A. Michaelis, Wayne State, 1977, p. 133. By the end of the fourteenth century the walls of churches in Tuscany were so smothered with frescoes and other images that the form of the building could barely be discerned, see Samuel K. Cohn Jr, *The Cult of Remembrance and the Black Death,* Baltimore, 1992, pp. 244–80, partic. pp. 277–8.

2 For fastidious analyses of the evidence surrounding the chapel and its original appearance see Laura Jacobus, 'Giotto's Design of the Arena Chapel', *Apollo*, vol. 142, no. 406, Dec 1995, pp. 37–42; *idem*, 'Giotto's *Annunciation* in the Arena Chapel, Padua', *Art Bulletin,* 81, no. 1, March 1995, pp. 93–107. Robin Simon provides an account of Enrico Scrovegni's fortunes as well as a history of the physical condition of the chapel in 'Giotto and after: Altars and Altarpieces at the Arena Chapel, Padua', *Apollo,* v. 142, no. 406, Dec 1995, pp. 24–36. Scrovegni was in league with Cangrande della Scala of Verona who besieged Padua in 1319. When the siege failed Scrovegni fled to Venice where he remained in exile effectively until his death in 1336. The chapel was designed as his mausoleum, and at present it contains three images of him – the donor portrait below the Last Judgement, the effigy attributed to Giovanni Pisano, and a full-length statue now in the sacristy. Although Simon does not mention it, one might reasonably speculate about Scrovegni's ambitions to become the ruler of Padua. This could account for the grandeur of the Scrovegni Chapel, unprecedented for a private citizen, to my knowledge, and a cause for complaint by the neighbouring monks of the Eremitani Church, who protested in 1305 that the chapel had been built 'more for pomp, vainglory and wealth than for praise, glory and honour of God'. For documents see Claudio Bellinati, *La Capella di Giotto all' Arena, 1300–1306: Studio Storico-Cronologico Su Nuovi Documenti,* Padua, 1967; see too the same author's *Giotto: Padua felix – atlante iconografico nell' capella di Giotto, 1300–05,* Treviso, 1997 and *idem*, 'La Capella degli Scrovegni', in *Padova: Basiliche e Chiese,* ed. Claudio Bellinati and Lionello Puppi, 2 vols, Vincenza, 1975, pp. 247ff. See Eve Borsook's excellent account in *Mural Painters of Tuscany,* 2nd edn, Oxford, 1980, pp. 7–14; James Stubblebine's collection of seminal essays and documents in *Giotto: The Arena Chapel Frescoes,* London, 1969; and Creighton Gilbert in *Grove's Dictionary of Art,* London, 1996, vol. 12, pp. 681–96. Laura Jacobus's eagerly awaited monograph may well transform our understanding of the chapel.

3 See Jacobus, 'Giotto's Annunciation', for a fine analysis of the Annunciation and its possible relation to the annual performance of the Annunciation.

4 According to Jacobus, 'Giotto's Design', 1995, p. 40, the existing panel of God the Father was not part of the original

scheme, which probably had a stained-glass oculus of God the Father.

5 *Meditations on the Life of Christ,* ed. Isa Ragusa and Rosalie B. Green, Princeton, 1961 and 1977, pp. 5–9. The account of the council is derived from Bernard of Clairvaux, Sermon I in J.-P. Migne, *Patrologia Latina,* CLXXXIII, cols 387ff. Neil McKenna drew my attention to this reading of the subject matter, which makes sense in terms of the four white-robed figures to left and right of the throne. The figure closest to the throne on God's left, looking angry with arms folded, fits the characterisation of Truth who strongly opposes Mercy's pleas. For the issue of artists drawing upon such texts as the *Meditations,* see the conclusion, pp. 277–9.

6 The original location of the main altar is uncertain – see Jacobus, op. cit. and Simon, op. cit.

7 Jacobus, 'Giotto's Annunciation', 1995.

8 Ibid., p. 107.

9 Robin Simon, *op. cit.*, p. 27, argues that the chapel was originally empty of all the existing liturgical subdivisions and altars and that the high altar stood in the apse but somewhat forward of the existing one. Laura Jacobus in her forthcoming monograph on the Scrovegni Chapel will present an alternative and rigorous reconstruction of the original interior which helps to support my inferences.

10 For precedents for this arrangement see John Osborne, 'The Dado Programme in Giotto's Arena Chapel and its Italian Romanesque Antecedents', *Burlington Magazine,* CXLV, May, 2003, pp. 361–5. On p. 362 Osborne describes 'the dado as a form of visual commentary to direct the thoughts of the viewers pondering the meaning of the sacred narratives above'. For the Virtues and Vices see S. Pfeiffenberger, 'The Iconology of Giotto's Virtues and Vices', Ph.D. diss., Bryn Mawr College, 1966; Bruce Cole, 'Virtues and Vices in Giotto's Arena Chapel', in *Studies in the History of Italian Art, 1250–1550,* London, 1996, pp. 337–63.

11 Dr Lisa Wade, 'Representations of the Last Judgement and their Interpretation', Ph.D. diss., University of Essex, 2001.

12 *The Apocryphal New Testament,* tr. M. R. James, Oxford, 1966: The *Book of James,* or *Protevangelium,* pp. 39–40 and the *Gospel of Pseudo-Matthew,* p. 73.

13 See E. H. Gombrich, 'Action and Expression in Western Art', in *Non Verbal Communication,* ed. Robert A. Hinde, Cambridge, 1972, pp. 373–93, particularly pp. 381–2: 'One might in fact translate the pictograph into a sentence in which the protagonist is the subject, the action the verb and the tomb or rock the object [Gombrich's examples are the Resurrection of Lazarus and Moses Striking the Rock]. The pictograph . . . represents the "what" but not the "how", the verb but not the adverb or any adjectival clause.' Gombrich then proceeds to explain ways in which the subject can be enriched 'adverbally' or 'adjectivally', so to speak.

14 'Lord Lindsay speaks of the priest within this enclosure as "confessing a young man who kneels at his feet". It seems to me, rather, that he is meant to be accepting the offering of another worshipper, so as to mark the rejection of Joachim more distinctly.' John Ruskin, *Giotto and his Works in Padua,* London, 1900, p. 64. Ruskin's account of the Scrovegni Chapel frescoes, first published between 1853 and 1860 is rich with remarkable insights.

15 For a more extended discussion of logical relationships and temporality see conclusion pp. 282–6.

16 See introduction p. 6 For the spectator's role as narrator see conclusion pp. 286–90.

17 Lina Bolzoni, *The Web of Images: Vernac-*

ular Preaching from its Origins to St Bernardino of Siena, Aldershot, 2004, pp. 20–2. Fra Giordano uses a sermon on the Temptation of Jesus in the desert to recommend that fleeing the city and living in the desert should be a model for everyone, at least spiritually: 'Christ . . . fled the world to be an example to you: that you too must flee from men and go into the desert. This desert could be your cell, your house, your room.' For an analysis of the ambivalent significance of wilderness in the Old and New Testaments in the context of the archaeological study of John the Baptist see Shimon Gibson, *The Cave of John the Baptist,* New York, 2004, pp. 84–90.

18 Cf. Alberti's observation in *De Pictura:* 'Reflected rays assume the colour they find on the surface from which they are reflected. We see this happen when the faces of people walking about in the meadows appear to have a greenish tinge.' L. B. Alberti, *On Painting and Sculpture,* ed. and tr. Cecil Grayson, London, 1972, pp. 46–7. For an extended discussion of colour and light in Giotto, see Paul Hills, *The Light of Early Italian Painting,* New Haven and London, 1987, pp. 41–63.

19 M. R. James, op. cit.

20 'The Virgin was conceived not *ex coito* but *ex osculo*', according to Virginia L. Bush, 'The Sources of Giotto's Meeting at the Golden Gate and the Meaning of the Dark-Veiled Woman', in *Giotto and the World of Early Italian Art: An Anthology of Literature,* ed. Andrew Ladis, New York, 1998, pp. 164–6.

21 See L. M. Bongiorno, 'The Theme of the Old and the New Law in the Arena Chapel', *Art Bulletin,* 1968, vol. 50, no. 1, pp. 11–20. Bush, op. cit., pp. 176–9 confirms Bongiorno's identification of the woman as Synagoga. Stubblebine, op. cit., p. 77, however, describes the woman in black simply as a contrast to the 'gawking' young girls: 'the more prudent older woman at the center, who veils her face as though it were not quite proper to watch the couple'.

22 Simon Goldhill, *The Temple of Jerusalem,* London, 2004, p. 122 Eloise M. Angiola, 'Gates of Paradise and the Florentine Baptistery', *Art Bulletin,* 60, 1978, pp. 242–8.

23 I Kings 6, v. 2; likewise II Chronicles 3, v. 3. The two accounts agree on the length and breadth though not on height – Kings says 30 cubits while Chronicles says that the porch was 120 cubits high or around 60 metres. If the chamber were the same height as the porch this would have made the Temple so very tall and thin that modern scholars believe the height in Chronicles to be a textual error. Nonetheless the façade of the inner chamber of the Temple of Herod the Great, which followed the proportions of Solomon's, was 50 metres tall, Goldhill, op. cit., p. 68. According to the most recent measurements the interior of the Scrovegni Chapel is 8.41 m wide, and 12.65 m high to the top of the barrel vault. The length of the main chamber from the entrance to the chancel arch is 20.88 m and the total length to the original end of the chancel is 26.01 m: Adriano Verdi, 'L'architettura della Capella degli Scrovegni', *Giotto e il suo Tempo,* exhibition catalogue, Milan, 2000, pp. 118–39. These measurements provide almost the same proportions as the Temple described in I Kings 1 : 1.5 : 3. The length is 0.78 m, or 3.1 per cent, too long. But this is probably good enough. According to Richard Krautheimer, for a medieval church to be described as an imitation or copy of a prototype it was not necessary for all the precise features or measurements of the original to be observed; only a 'selective transfer' of architectural elements or measurements was required. By

medieval criteria of imitation, which were more concerned with meaning than with form, the Scrovegni Chapel as a copy of Solomon's Temple is vastly over-determined: see Richard Krautheimer's seminal article 'Introduction to an "Iconography of Medieval Architecture"', *Journal of the Warburg and Courtauld Institutes,* 5, 1942, pp. 1–31, partic. pp. 13–15.

24 Goldhill, op. cit., p. 26 estimates that a cubit was approximately half a metre, which makes the chapel 52 cubits long, 16.82 wide and 25 cubits high, almost the same dimensions as Solomon's Temple.

25 1 Kings 6, v. 4.

26 1 Kings 7; II Chronicles 9, v. 11.

27 This may reinforce the suggestion that Scrovegni had dynastic ambitions in Padua, see note 2 above. I am indebted to Eric Fernie for the point that Solomon's Temple was a palace chapel. See too Goldhill, op. cit., p. 30 on the significance of this. I am also grateful to Fernie for sharing with me his understanding of the significance of Temple imitations in the Middle Ages.

28 John Wilkinson, *From Synagogue to Church: The Traditional Design; its Beginning, its Definition, its End,* London, 2002, argues on the basis of careful measurement and analysis that most, if not all, synagogues and churches follow the proportions of the Temple very closely.

29 Ruskin, op. cit., pp. 48–9.

30 Pseudo-Matthew, 8, vv. 1–2; Bellinati, *Giotto: Padua felix*, text for appropriate frescoes.

31 Ibid., pp. 89–91 for Ruskin's sensitive description of this fresco.

32 According to the *Protevangelium*, pp. 42–3 and Pseudo-Matthew, p. 74, Mary returns to Joseph's house following her betrothal; the Annunciation takes place there. According to Jacobus de Voragine, *The Golden Legend*, tr. W. G. Ryan, 2 vols, Princeton, 1993, vol. 1, p. 197 she returns to her parents' house in Nazareth. Erwin Panofsky, *Early Netherlandish Painting,* 2 vols, Cambridge, 1966, vol. 1, pp. 131–2, seems to suggest that Melchior Broederlam's Annunciation takes place in or adjacent to the Temple, but he cites no source. I would suggest that the association of the location of the Annunciation with the Temple sanctuary is symbolic rather than historical.

33 John 11, vv. 1–45.

34 Emile Mâle, 'La Résurrection de Lazare dans l'Art', *La Revue des Arts,* 1, 1951, pp. 44–52; E. H. Gombrich, 'Moment and Movement in Art', *Journal of the Warburg and Courtauld Institutes,* vol. 27, 1964, p. 303 and pl. 29 a; and Gombrich, 'Action and Expression'; n. 13 above.

35 See conclusion p. 284.

36 In different Gospels Jesus mentions both signs. The author of the *Meditations on the Life of Christ* engages with this problem in his efforts to visualise the table arrangements of the Last Supper. He argues that the table must have been about four foot square, with Jesus in one corner and the rest tightly seated three to a side 'in such a manner that all could eat from one dish. Therefore the disciples did not understand when He said, "The one who has put his hand in the dish with me shall betray me", because all placed their hands there.' The writer provides a different solution. Op. cit., p. 277. See also Ruskin, op. cit., pp. 135–8.

37 *Diatesseron,* pp. 335–6. The translation is the Authorised Version.

38 See chapter. 8, pp. 233-42.

39 Luke 22, v. 48.

40 Matthew 26, v. 52.

41 Mark 14, vv. 50–2.

42 For an exhaustive account of the ordering of narrative cycles see Marilyn Lavin, *The Place of Narrative: Mural Decoration in Italian Churches, 431–1600,* Chicago, 1990, pp. 43–50 for the Scrovegni Chapel.

43 For order in literary texts see Gérard Genette, *Narrative Discourse,* tr. Jane E. Lewin, Oxford, 1980, (1st French edn 1972), pp. 33–85.

44 The *locus classicus* is Michel Alpatoff, 'The Parallelism of Giotto's Paduan Frescoes', *Art Bulletin,* 29, 1947, pp. 149–54, reprinted in Stubblebine, op. cit., pp. 156–69.

45 Jacobus, 'Giotto's Annunciation', p. 38.

46 Following the recent restoration it is no longer possible to enter through this door.

47 Horace, 'De Arte Poetica', in *Satires, Epistles and Ars Poetica,* ed. and tr. H. Rushton Fairclough, London and Cambridge, 1947, ll. 128–52, pp. 460–63. 'Nor does he begin Diomede's return from the death of Meleager, or the war of Troy from the twin eggs. Ever he hastens to the issue, and hurries his hearer into the story's midst, as if already known . . .' ll. 146–9.

48 C. Bellinati, 'La Cappella degli Scrovegni', in *Padova Basiliche e Chiese, a cura di Claudia Bellinati e Lionello Pappi,* 2 vols, Vincenza, 1975, vol. 1, pp. 252–3.

49 Geza Vermes, *The Passion,* London, 2005, pp. 62ff.

50 See chapter 4, note 23 below.

51 On the other hand this figure may be another soldier. A beardless figure wearing a similar white cap shoves the Virgin back towards the gate of Jerusalem in the next scene of the Carrying of the Cross.

52 It would not have been difficult for Giotto's contemporaries to have imagined this. Public life was a theatre of cruelty. Contemporary chronicles record many occasions of summary arrest and overnight torture. *Meditations,* 75, p. 326 provides an account of the prison where Jesus was held overnight standing bound to a stone column being mocked and tortured.

53 Ruskin, op. cit., pp. 113–15.

54 Gotthold Ephraim Lessing, *Laokoon,* ed. Dorothy Reich, Oxford, 1965, Section 16, p. 158: 'Die Malerei kann in ihren koexistierenden Kompositionem nur einem einzigen Augenblick der Handlung nutzen, und muß daher den prägnantesten wählen, ans welchem da Vorhergehende und Folgende am begreiflichsten wird.' (Painting in its coexisting compositions can only make use of a single instant of the action, and must therefore choose the most pregnant, from which that which precedes and that which follows can be comprehended.) Again, 19, p. 182: 'Diesen einzigen Augenblick macht er so prägnant wie möglich.' (This single moment he makes as pregnant as possible.) Many problems arise from the employment of this eighteenth-century terminology, which relates primarily, as Ruskin indicates, to single framed paintings not to cycles as in our period. No fourteenth- or fifteenth-century text refers to this aspect of temporality in painting or relief sculpture. For a discussion of this issue see the conclusion pp. 282–3. Lessing, moreover, does not actually use the term 'pregnant moment', but the phrase has entered the language. 'Prägnant' is probably best translated either as 'suggestive' or 'most laden with significance' – for the latter see Wolfgang Kemp, 'Narrative', in *Critical Terms for Art History*, 2nd edn, tr. David Britt and ed. Robert S. Nelson and Richard Shiff, Chicago, 2003, p. 68.

55 Conclusion pp. 269–72, 283, 286–90.

56 For Alberti's observations on this issue see conclusion pp. 270–1.

57 This follows St John's Gospel; the three Synoptic Gospels say that a passer-by, Simon of Cyrene, was compelled to carry the cross for Jesus.

58 Isaiah 35, 1. In the Vulgate it is not a rose but a lily. The Greek septuagint uses κρινον – flower or lily while the origi-

nal Hebrew 'Chabatseleth' can mean meadow-crocus, saffron or rose.

59 See Bruce Cole, *Studies in the History of Italian Art, 1250–1550,* London, 1996, pp. 371 and 393.

60 Alberti, op. cit., pp. 78/9, 82–7, 90–5 and 105. The Navicella is described on pp. 82/3.

61 Ruskin, op. cit., pp. 47–8.

62 See Jonathan B. Riess, 'Justice and the Common Good in Giotto's Arena Chapel Frescoes', in Ladis, op. cit., 1998, pp. 233–44. Is it too fanciful to see the organisation of this wall as a kind of inverted altarpiece? Whereas in an altarpiece the seated Madonna and Child flanked by standing saints occupy the main pictorial field with small narrative panels in the predella beneath, or in some cases above, as in Duccio's Maestà, here Justice and her companion Virtues are surmounted by three tiers of narrative frescoes on a monumental scale. Is Giotto also perhaps drawing a parallel between Justice and the Virgin of Charity, to whom the Scrovegni Chapel is dedicated?

63 Matthew 26, v. 52.

64 Selma Pfeiffenberger argues for a Ciceronian basis to Temperantia: 'All passions must be restrained', *De officiis,* I, 27 and 29, and Temperance is a 'firm and well considered control exercised by the reason', *De inventione,* II, liv, *164;* see Pfeiffenberger, op. cit., II. 2. 14–20 and V. 15. On Justice as the central virtue see II, 3, 13–14.

65 'As the underlying tone in Giotto is moderation, so the predominant virtue is temperance.' Richard Offner, 'Giotto, Non-Giotto', in Stubblebine op. cit., p. 140. Offner's two articles first appeared in the *Burlington Magazine,* 74, 1939, pp. 259–68 and 75, 1939, pp. 96–113. Both are reprinted in Stubblebine, op. cit., pp. 135–55. See Hayden Maginnis, *Painting in the Age of Giotto,* Pennsylvania, 1997, pp. 85–7 and 101–2 for a fulsome tribute to Offner's account of Giotto as an artist who eschewed mere naturalism. Maginnis's own view is that Giotto was a realist rather than a nominalist whose concern was with 'ideas, emotions, psychological states. For that purpose, he did not need or use the panoply of illusionism; in tempered illusionism he employed an economy of means that spoke more eloquently to ideas for being less encumbered by appearances.' *Idem,* op. cit., p. 101. This view of Giotto as a painter who controlled the naturalism of his images is at odds with the long tradition dating back to Boccaccio: 'his depiction looked not like a copy but like the very thing, so that more often than not the viewer's eye was deceived, convinced that it was looking at the real object and not at his depiction of it.' *Decameron,* Day 6, 5, tr. Guido Waldman, Oxford, 1993, p. 394.

66 For a recent treatment of the vendetta in the Renaissance see Lauro Martines, *April Blood: Florence and the Plot against the Medici,* London, 2003, pp. 7–12.

67 This is not to suggest that Giotto had read Plato or even St Augustine. However Pfeiffenberger, op. cit., II. 3. 14 does raise the intriguing possibility that Plato's *Republic* may have influenced the order of the Virtues with Justice at their centre. A contemporary Paduan scholar, Pietro d'Abano, knew Greek and had been to Constantinople, though she admits that does not mean he had read the *Republic.* John of Salisbury (1115–80) was apparently acquainted with the work. It was first translated into Latin by Manuel Chrysaloras and Uberto Decembrio in 1400–03, Gerard Boter, *The Textual Tradition of Plato's Republic,* Leiden, 1989, p. 261. For Plato's doctrine of aesthetic detachment see Introduction pp. 3–4. For St Augustine's critique of Aristotle's conception of pity and iden-

tification with the tragic hero, see *The Confessions,* Bk III, 2–3 and Wade op. cit. to whom I am indebted for these references and for her insight into St Augustine's discussion of this issue.

68 The figure of Despair faces Hope to either side of the main entrance.

69 See introduction, pp. 11-13.

70 Kenneth R. Adams in 'Perspective and the Viewpoint', *Leonardo,* vol. 5, pp. 209–17, usefully lists eight major depth or distance cues: 'binocular convergence (kinaesthetic), binocular parallax (visual), accommodation of the lense, movement parallax, geometrical perspective, partial masking, light and shade, and atmospheric perspective'. See Chapter 6 and Appendix.

CHAPTER III

1 'So many people think that Giotto was the forerunner of the Renaissance . . . but Giovanni was doing this earlier.' Michael Ayrton with Henry Moore, *Giovanni Pisano: Sculptor*, London, 1969, p. 9. See also n. 22, Chapter Four.

2 The overriding reason, though, was the scant notice given to Giovanni Pisano in Vasari's Florence-centred *Lives of the Artists* published in 1550, which established Giotto as the single most important artist spearheading the first phase of the Renaissance. Vasari's *Lives* established the historiography of Italian Renaissance art, and remains a powerful influence upon the canon. See Jane I. Satkowski, *Duccio di Buoninsegna*, Georgia Museum of Art, 2003, p. 34.

3 For a careful assessment of the issue which differs from my own see Francis Ames-Lewis, *Tuscan Marble Carving 1250–1350: Sculpture and Civic Pride*, Aldershot, 1997, pp. 61–4. See also Enzo Carli, *Il Pergamo del Duomo di Pisa*, Pisa, 1975 and M. Bergstein, 'Lonely Aphrodites: On the Documentary Photography of Sculpture', *Art Bulletin*, vol. 74, 1992, pp. 475–98. Robert Munman argues that Giovanni made optical adjustments to his figures for the façade of Siena Cathedral which can be paralleled in his two pulpits, but is uncertain whether these were made 'consciously or instinctively'. See his *Optical Corrections in the Sculptures of Donatello. Transactions of the American Philosophical Society*, vol. 75, pt 2, pp. 6–7, Philadelphia, 1985 My argument is that Giovanni was both conscious and calculating. See also Geraldine Johnson's forthcoming article, 'Representing Renaissance Sculpture in Two Dimensions'; and Geraldine Johnson (ed.), *Sculpture and Photography: Envisioning the Third Dimension*, Cambridge, 1998, pp. 8–9.

4 John Pope-Hennessy, *Italian Gothic Sculpture*, London, 1955, p. 5; Ames-Lewis, op. cit., p. 85.

5 John White, *The Birth and Rebirth of Pictorial Space*, 3rd edn, London, 1987 does not refer to Nicola or Giovanni Pisano. In his *Art and Architecture in Italy, 1250–1400*, Harmondsworth, 1966, White has little to say about the creation of space in the work of the Pisani, father and son. He grants that in Nicola's Adoration of the Magi on his Siena cathedral pulpit 'the actual carved depth of the relief and the space that is supposedly represented by it . . . are practically unrelated', in contrast to his Adoration in the Pisa Baptistery where there is little distinction between the two things, White, op. cit., p. 47. In his account of Giovanni Pisano's two pulpits the creation of an effect of space is simply not mentioned, White, op. cit. pp. 75–80 and 83–7. Ames-Lewis goes still further in arguing that Giovanni rejected his father's pictorialism in the Siena pulpit 'and evolved instead an individual variant on the traditional manner of

stressing the relief surface. In this he showed his concern to preserve the integrity of the actual depth of his blocks rather than to allow his figures to recede into pictorial depth.' Ames-Lewis, op. cit., p. 97.

6 White, ibid., p. 76 vividly describes how the angle figures of the Pistoia pulpit have been emancipated 'from the tyranny of the single viewpoint' so that the observer is required to explore the 'rich and studied lateral views that open out obliquely to either side'. He contrasts this with the angle figures of Nicola's Siena pulpit which 'still confirm the basic frontality of the square-headed capitals on which they sit'. White does not, however, extend this insight to the organization and spatial separation of the figures within Giovanni's relief panels at Pistoia.

7 See previous note.

8 For a summary of the known facts about the commission and of the church of St Andrea see Peter Kovaáč, 'Notes to Giovanni Pisano's Pistoia Pulpit,' *Umění*, 51, 2003, pp. 458–73, partic. pp. 458–9. The parish priest, Arnoldus, who is mentioned in the pulpit's inscription, was instrumental in having the church designated as second in importance to the cathedral. Nonetheless it remains a puzzle why a pulpit of such grandeur and costliness previously, and subsequently reserved for cathedrals or baptisteries should have been commissioned for a small parish church. Unfortunately Anita Moskowitz's *Nicola and Giovanni Pisano Pulpits*, Harvey Miller, Turnhout, 2006, appeared when it was too late for me to consult.

9 *The Missal*, London, 1957, pp. 665–7; J. A. Jungmann, *The Mass of the Roman Rite*, London, 1959.

10 See Fig. 22 in Chapter 2 for Giotto's depiction of this arrangement. See too the fresco, not by Giotto, of The Miracle at Greccio in the St Francis cycle in the Upper Church at Assisi.

11 There is one to be seen in Sto Spirito in Florence.

12 In 1619 the pulpit was moved from its original position on the choir screen as a result of the introduction of the Tridentine Mass. L. Mellini, *Giovanni Pisano*, Milan, n.d. (c.1969), p. 16 and Ames-Lewis, op. cit., p. 77. See Peter Kováč, op. cit., pp. 462ff. for a recent discussion of contending reconstructions by Géza Jászai, *Die Pisaner Domkanzel*, Munich, 1964, pp. 23–7; G. L. Mellini, *Giovanni Pisano*, Milan, 1970, p. 67; for Mellini's diagram of the original location see undated edition, c.1969, p. 16; Carli, op. cit., pp. 14–15; Piero Morselli and Anita Fiderer-Moskowitz, 'The Pistoia Pulpit's Uneven Supports: The Bases for a Hypothesis', *Source*, 22, 2003, no. 2, pp. 1–9.

13 Sometimes the lesson in Latin was followed by a reading in the local vernacular language. But this was not part of the rite of the Mass, only an introduction to the sermon. J. A. Jungmann, *The Mass of the Roman Rite*, London, 1959, p. 266.

14 My colleague, Valerie Fraser, has suggested that these six figures can also possibly be read in sequence as enacting the stages of the Annunciation as discussed by Michael Baxandall, *Painting and Experience in Fifteenth-Century Italy*, Oxford, 1972, pp. 49–56.

15 Luke 1, vv. 26–35.

16 Sixten Ringbom, 'Some Pictorial Conventions for the Recounting of Thoughts and Experiences in Late Medieval Art', in *Medieval Iconography and Narrative: A Symposium*, ed. F. G. Anderson, Odense University Press, 1980, pp. 38–69, partic. pp. 41–3, 52–5, 60–1.

17 L'angel che venne in terra col decreto
della molt' anni lagrimata pace,
che aperse il ciel dal suo lungo divieto,

dinanzi a noi pareva sì verace
quivi intagliato in un atto soave,
che non sembiava imagine che tace.
Giurato si saria ce' ei dicessse; *Ave*,
però che ivi era imaginata quella,
che ad aprir l'alto amor volse la chiave.
Ed avea in atto impressa esta favella,
Ecce ancilla Dei, propriamenta.
come figura in cera si suggella.
'Non tener pure ad un loco la mente,'
disse il dolce maestro . . .
per ch'io mi mossi col viso, e vedea
di retro di Maria, da quella costa
onde me'era colui che mi movea,
un' altra storia nella roccia imposta:
per ch'io varcai Virgilio, e femmi presso,
acciochè fosse agli occhi miei disposta.

Purgatorio, X, ll. 34–54. The translation is by Longfellow.

18 See Introduction pp. 12–13. The sculpture is divine because God made it. Dante says that it was 'new to us, for here it is not found' ('novello a noi, perchè qui non si trova', l. 96.) See J. A. Burrow, *Gestures and Looks in Medieval Narrative*, Cambridge, 2002, pp. 177–8.

19 See Conclusion p. 283.

20 Matthew 2, 1–16.

21 See Richard Trexler, *The Adoration of the Magi*, Princeton, 1997, pp. 5–6. See subsequent chapters for the history of the cult and iconography of the Adoration.

22 We are afforded oblique views of Jesus, which emphasise the contrast of the anatomical accuracy of his tortured ribcage with an outstretched arm more like a primitive woodcarving. But these views are strictly subsidiary.

CHAPTER IV

1 P. Bacci, *La ricostruzione del pergamo di Giovanni Pisano nel Duomo di Pisa*, Milan, n.d. (1926); Gert Kreytenberg, 'Vox Dei,' *FMR*, no. 76, vol. XX, Oct. 1995, pp. 69–85.

2 Pope-Hennessy, *Italian Gothic Sculpture*, London, 1955, p. 12.

3 White, *Art and Architecture in Italy, 1250–1400*, Harmondsworth, 1966, p. 85, supported by Michael Ayrton, *Giovanni Pisano: Sculptor*, London, 1969, p. 161 who claims that Giovanni lacked 'a sufficient interval to refresh his mind'. Ayrton does, however, acknowledge that the shortcomings of the pulpit arise from Giovanni's ambitions: 'the comparative failure of the work as a whole lies in a conceptual complexity so dense that it was self-defeating even in its own day'. *Idem*, op. cit., p. 162. Kreytenberg, op. cit., p. 78 argues, on the other hand, that for Giovanni the Pisa pulpit 'was never merely a slightly larger version' of Pistoia, 'rather his inexhaustible creative energy was revealed in all its abundance in the new and revolutionary conception of the Pisa pulpit'.

4 Christoph Wolff, *Johann Sebastian Bach: The Learned Musician*, Oxford, 2002, pp. 291–303. Bach also wrote a St Mark Passion for which only the libretto survives while his obituary mentions five Passions in all, *idem*, op. cit., p. 296.

5 Ames-Lewis, *Tuscan Marble Carving 1250–1350: Sculpture and Civic Pride*, Aldershot, 1997, pp. 118–9.

6 Ames-Lewis, op. cit., seems to suggest that the inscriptions were in the nature of defiant bombast: 'Furthermore, however they are interpreted, the Pisa Duomo pulpit inscriptions seem to imply some breakdown in Giovanni's relations with the Duomo authorities that may have lessened his commitment to the project. Despite what he was to write in the inscriptions about his high abilities, Giovanni did not here have the opportunity fully to satisfy the expressive drives innate in his artistic temperament.'

Kreytenberg, on the other hand, points out that it was usual for artists to sing their own praise in twelfth- and thirteenth-century Italy but quotes Harold Keller's observation that this was the first time that an artist 'addressed himself to the spectator in order to lay bare his soul'. *Idem,* op. cit., p. 78.

7 Ames-Lewis, op. cit., p. 83 suggests that the 'proper rules' may relate to a synthesis of medieval and classical styles. Ayrton, op. cit., p. 158 considers that the 'proper rules' are those governing the complex iconography.

8 There is another reference to law in the upper inscription in the passage relating to Nello di Falcone who 'not only exercised control of the work but also of the law (on which it is based)'. ('Nello Falconis habente/Hoc opus in cura nec non opera quoque jura'.) Nello di Falcone was the Operaio, or Master of Works of the cathedral. The translation is Pope-Hennessy's, who interpolated 'on which it is based': only a guess, even if an inspired one. If his translation is correct, could this mean that the Operaio collaborated with Giovanni in developing the artistic law? It is an intriguing possibility, and indeed a fulsome tribute from such a proud and prickly artist. The full Latin texts and translations are in John Pope-Hennessy, *Italian Gothic Sculpture*, London, 1955, p. 181. I have modified Pope-Hennessy's translations in some instances. The Latin text for the parts quoted above are as follows:

Circuit his amnes mundi
  partesque Iohannes
Plurima temptando gratis discenda
  parando
Queque labore gravi Nunc
  clamat : non bene cavi
Dum plus monstravi plus hostica
  damna probavi . . .
Se probat indignum reprobans
  diade mate dignum.

And

Ut Johannes iste dotatus
Artis sculpture pre cunctis ordine
  pure
. . .
Clara sculpturas fecit variasque
  figuras.
Quisquis miraris tunc recto jure
  pro baris.

For statistics on literacy in Italy during the Renaissance see the Conclusion pp. 273–4. While male literacy in Italian could be as high as 33 per cent, the number of those able to read Latin was far smaller and would have been restricted to clerics, lawyers, scholars and writers. The gnomic nature of the inscriptions has analogies with the Prologue to Gottfried von Strassburg's *Tristan*, tr. A. T. Hatto, Harmondsworth, 1960 which offers similarly enigmatic reflections upon the relationship between art and criticism.

9 It was easier for a painter like Duccio or Giotto to present a large number of separate episodes demarcated by distinct borders. In the Pistoia pulpit eleven episodes are presented on the five panels; in Pisa there are twenty-two episodes on the nine panels.

10 Sculpted scenes of the story of Joseph were depicted on a rotating circular drum which was part of the choir screen in Notre Dame, Paris dating from the mid- to late fourteenth century according to Alain Erlande-Brandenburg, *The Cathedral: The Social and Architectural Dynamic of Construction*, Cambridge, 1994, p. 280 (original publication, Paris, 1989). The revolving section disappeared at the beginning of the eighteenth century. Unfortunately the author provides no references.

11 Kreytenberg op. cit., p. 88 does not agree with the consensus that the Passion is especially weak.

12 Enzo Carli in his discussion of the Nativity panel refers to the effect of distance between the figures as 'quasi "prospettiva"'. He also discusses the issue of viewpoint. See Carli, *Il pergamo del Duomo di Pisa*, Pisa, 1975, p. 28.

13 P. E. Arias et al., *Camposanto monumentale di Pisa. Le Antichità*, Pisa, 1977; B. Andreae and S. Settis (eds), *Colloquio sul reimpiego dei sarcofagi romani nel mediovo, Pisa 5–12. September 1982*, Marburg-Lahn, 1984; B. Andreae (ed.), *Symposium uber die antiken Sarkophage, Pisa 5–12. September 1982*, Marburg-Lahn, 1984.

14 *Meditations on the Life of Christ*, ed. Isa Ragusa and Rosalie B. Green, Princeton, 1961 and 1977, p. 326.

15 St Matthew 26, v. 66.

16 *Meditations*, pp. 318–9; see also S. Ringbom, *The Rise of the Dramatic Close-Up in Fifteenth-Century Devotional Painting*, Doorspijk, 1984, pp. 11–58 (1st edn 1965); E. Panofsky, 'Imago Pietatis', *Festschrift für Max J. Friedländer zum 60*, Leipzig, 1927, pp. 261ff.; Michael Baxandall, *Painting and Experience in Fifteenth-Century Italy*, Oxford, 1972, pp. 46–8.

17 See *Meditations*, p. 5 and Sancti Bonaventurae, *Opera*, Venetiis, 1756, vol. 12, p. 381: '. . . si illud per scripturam probari non posit, non aliter accipias, quam devota meditatio exigit' (. . . if it may be impossible to prove it through the scriptures, you should not accept it otherwise than what Devout Meditation determines). The word *meditatio* has connotations of active examination or intellectural inquiry. For further discussion of the role of Devout Meditation for artists in enriching the sometimes scant narrative of the Gospels see the Conclusion pp. 279-82. The Passion relief has affinities to images of the Man of Sorrows surrounded with symbols reminding one of the conventional compositions for the various scenes of the Passion.

18 See Sixten Ringbom, 'Some Pictorial Conventions for the Recounting of Thoughts and Experiences in Late Medieval Art', in *Medieval Iconography and Narrative: A Symposium*, ed. F. G. Anderson, Odense University Press, 1980, pp. 38–69.

19 Frances Mattheson, 'Giovanni Pisano's Pisa Pulpit', unpublished BA. diss., University of Essex, 1996.

20 'Veritas de terra orta e Iustitia de coelo perspexit' – Herbert von Einem, *Das Stützengeschoss der Pisaner Domkanzel: Gedanken zum Alterswerk des Giovanni Pisano*, Köln, 1962, pp. 9–13. Perhaps this scroll relates to that held by Jesus in the Betrayal, see Niels Hannestad, 'How Did Rising Christianity Cope with Pagan Sculpture?' in *East and West: Modes of Communication*, ed. E. Chrysos and Ian Wood, Leiden, 1999, pp. 173-203, particularly pp. 147–7.

21 Ayrton, op. cit., pp. 127–8 relates Giovanni to the Franciscan Spirituals, Joachim da Fiore and the 'Dies irae' attributed to Tomaso di Celano. M. Alpatov also alludes to Giovanni's impassioned style: 'la chaire de Nicola a été faite pour qu'on y lise des écritures sacrées, celle de Giovanni plutôt pour qu'on y fasse des sermons passionés, pour entrainer les fidèles'. See 'Sur la chaire de Giovanni Pisano à Pisa', *Arte Lombarda*, special number, 1965, pp. 37–50, partic. p. 42.

22 Unfortunately he did not elaborate: Jacob Burckhardt, *Italian Renaissance Painting according to Genres*, tr. D. Britt and C. Beamish, Los Angeles, 2005, p. 95.

23 See Martin Kemp, *The Science of Art: Optical Themes in Western Art from Brunelleschi to Seurat*, New Haven and London, 1990, p. 10. Kemp argues that

the failure of all lines in Giotto's Confirmation of the Rule in the Bardi Chapel to converge may be the result of an accommodation to our seeing the fresco sideways: 'He has used his special sensitivity to the way in which appearances change from different viewpoints to suggest that we are witnessing the event not from the centre but from a relatively low position nearer the side wall of the room. This also has the effect of placing us, psychologically, with the kneeling friars in a position subordinate to the main actors of the drama. This sense of the eyewitness character of Giotto's scene reflects one of the main motives behind the new naturalism.' I would only qualify this account by claiming that the viewpoint would have been outside the chapel. See too references in the preface, n. 4 above.

24 The dating, and even the attribution, of the frescoes in these two chapels is much disputed. Rona Goffen adduces evidence to show that the two chapels must have been constructed simultaneously and suggests a date of 1310–16 for the Bardi, Goffen *Spirituality in Conflict: St Francis and Giotto's Bardi Chapel*, Penn State, 1988, pp. 54–9. Julia Clodell, 'Giotto's Peruzzi Chapel Frescoes: Wealth, Patronage and the Earthly City', in *Giotto, Master Painter and Architect in Florence*, A. Ladis, New York, 1998, pp. 150–1, summarises the dating of various scholars. There is no documentary evidence for date or authorship. My grounds for believing that the Peruzzi was later than the Bardi Chapel depend upon my sense that the adjustment to the viewer's position is more sophisticated in the frescoes of the Peruzzi Chapel. Julian Gardner in 'The Early Decoration of Santa Croce in Florence', Burlington Magazine, CXIII, 1971, pp. 391-2, n. 13

25 Jacobus de Voragine, however, argues that Herod and Herodias secretly plotted to execute St John through the stratagem of getting the daughter to ask for his head. See Jacobus de Voragine, *The Golden Legend*, tr. W. G. Ryan, 2 vols, Princeton, 1993, vol. 2, p. 133.

26 St Mark 6, vv. 16–28; St Matthew 14, vv. 1–11; *Il Diatesseron in Volgare Italiano*, Città del Vaticano, 1938, pp. 254–5.

27 A. Ladis, *Taddeo Gaddi*, University of Missouri Press, 1982, pp. 83ff.; Julian Gardner, 'The Decoration of the Baroncelli Chapel in Sta Croce', *Zeitschrift für Kunstgeschichte*, 34, 1971, pp. 89–113.

CHAPTER V

1 Richard Krautheimer and Trude Krautheimer-Hess, *Lorenzo Ghiberti*, 2 vols, Princeton, 2nd edn, 1970, (1st edn, 1956) pp. 31–43; Hanno Rauterberg, *Die Konkurrenz Reliefs: Brunelleschi und Ghiberti in Wettbewerb um di Baptisteriumstür in Florenz*, Münster, 1996; Lorenzo Ghiberti, *I commentari*, ed. Ottavio Morisani, Naples, 1947, pp. 42–3; *The Commentaries of Lorenzo Ghiberti*, tr. Peter Murray, Courtauld Institute of Art, London, n.d., p. 21; Antonio de Tuccio Manetti, *The Life of Brunelleschi*, tr. Catherine Engass, ed. Howard Saalman, Pennsylvania, 1970, pp. 46–50. The seven competitors included Jacopo della Quercia and Niccolo Lamberti, see Ghiberti, second commentary, section 19. The dimensions of the competition reliefs, without frames, is 45 × 38 cm. *Lorenzo Ghiberti, 'materia e ragionamenti'*, Florence, 1978, pp. 60 and 64.

2 Krautheimer, op. cit., p. 35.

3 Genesis 22 v. 1–19.

4 See Chapter 6 below.

5 Ulrich Middeldorf, review of H. Kauffmann, *Donatello*, in *Art Bulletin*, vol. 18, 1936, pp. 570–85, partic. p. 583, points out 'how conservative Brunelleschi is in his

composition compared with Ghiberti' and draws attention to 'a certain progressive tendency' in Or-cagna's reliefs. Gert Kreytenberg, *Orcagna's Tabernacle in Orsanmichele, Florence*, New York, 1994, is the most detailed account of a work that deserves more attention, see p. 24 and pls 12–15; Kreytenberg, 'La prima opera del Ghiberti e la scultura fiorentina del Trecento', *Lorenzo Ghiberti nel suo tempo, Atti del convegno internazionale di studi*, 1978, 2 vols, Florence, 1980, p. 62; Nancy Rash Fabbri and Nina Rutenberg, 'The Tabernacle of Or San Michele in Context', *Art Bulletin*, 63, 1981, pp. 385–405, partic. pp. 393–3. See also John White, *Art and Architecture in Italy, 1250–1400*, Harmondsworth, 1966, op. cit., p. 390; J. Pope-Hennessy, *Italian Gothic Sculpture*, London, pp. 196–8.

6 The phrase is Middeldorf's, op. cit., p. 583.

7 See, for example, the thirteenth-century mosaic in the cathedral of Monreale or the bronze doors of San Zeno, Verona. The earliest known depiction, the fresco above the niche for the scrolls in the synagogue of Dura-Europos, 244–56 AD, is quite faithful to the text, showing Abraham with the knife in his hand, held by his side and the voice of the angel represented by the hand of God, Carl H. Kraeling, *The Synagogue*, Ktav Publishing House, 2nd edn, 1979, pp. 56–7 and pl. LI.

8 Manetti, op. cit., pp. 48–51.

9 Antje Middeldorf Kosegarten, 'The Origins of Artistic Competitions in Italy', *Lorenzo Ghiberti nel suo tempo, loc. cit.*, pp. 167–86. She points to the example of the designs for the façade of Orvieto cathedral where the authorities arrived at a compromise between the two solutions, entrusting the project to Lorenzo Maitani but involving the author of the other drawing in the execution, pp. 176–8. Another example is the design of the columns and capitals for the Duomo in Florence in July and August 1357. In that case two designs were commissioned from Andrea Orcagna and from Francesco Talenti. A *consiglio* chose Orcagna's, but that was not the end of the story. A new *consiglio* was convened to consider three designs – Orcagna's old one, a new one by Talenti and a third by Giovanni di Lapo Ghini, who had been a member of the earlier *consiglio*. This time Talenti's design was finally chosen. It seems that Talenti's new design represented a compromise of some sort. The document is fascinating for including a record of the judgements of the individual members of the *consiglio*, providing us with unique insight into the criteria they applied, which included consideration of the visual effect of the capitals when seen from the ground. See C. Guasti, *Sta Maria del Fiore, la costruzione della chiesa e del campanile secondo i documenti*, Florence, 1887, pp. 97–109, pp. 100–01 for the *consiglio* of July 17th; Howard Saalman, *Filippo Brunelleschi: The Cupola of Santa Maria del Fiore*, London, 1980, pp. 41–2.

10 Manetti, op. cit., pp. 82–95. Saalman, however, pp. 24–8, considers that Manetti presented an overdramatised account of Brunelleschi's relationship with Ghiberti. Krautheimer, op. cit., p. 42 considers that there are grounds for believing that the competition ended in a tie.

11 Ghiberti, *The Commentaries*, op. cit. p. 21.

12 Krautheimer, op. cit., vol. 1, p. 46 gives weight to this argument, while admitting that 'within the final overall cost of the door 60 florins made little difference'. I calculate that the total difference in cost for bronze for the twenty-eight reliefs alone would have been 54 florins – the cost of bronze for Ghiberti's reliefs would have been 144 florins and for Brunelleschi's 197 florins. The final total cost of the doors was 16,000 florins. The extra cost of bronze for Brunelleschi's

reliefs would have been a mere 0.3 per cent of the total. Krautheimer, however, argues that no one on the jury in 1401–02 could have foreseen such an enormous cost. Yet if they were 'prudentes viri', as Krautheimer suggests, they must have had some idea of what they were letting themselves in for, especially since they would have had an estimate of the total weight of bronze, 34,000 lbs (Krautheimer, op. cit., p 110), which alone would have cost more than 3,000 florins. Even in terms of the cost of materials, the quantity of bronze for the reliefs, about 1556 lbs, would have been small in proportion to the bronze required for the armature and frame of the doors, about 4.5 per cent of the total. The extra weight of Brunelleschi's reliefs would have been 588 lbs, 1.7 per cent of the total cost of bronze alone. I have used Krautheimer's figures in my calculations and used the rate of exchange from Florentine soldi to florins as approximately 76 in 1401–02, see Peter Spufford, *Handbook of Medieval Exchange*, London, 1986, p. 12.

13 I cannot think of an earlier image depicting an instantaneous moment in an action. Some of Giovanni's reliefs come closest, but it would be more accurate to describe the actions depicted as dynamic than as instantaneous. Despite Augustine's discussion (or thought experiment) of an instant or a point of time in his *Confessions*, Book 11, 16, the notion of instantaneity in the visual arts does not appear to have been current. Perhaps Leonardo with his idea of a continuum composed of an infinity of instantaneous movements was the first to conceive, in concrete visual terms, of an infinitesimal moment in time. Brunelleschi's panel, therefore, seems to have been highly original. See Leonardo da Vinci, *Treatise on Painting*, tr. A. Philip McMahon, 2 vols, Princeton, 1956, vol. 1, pp. 137–8. See E. H. Gombrich, 'Moment and Movement in Art', *Journal of the Warburg and Courtauld Institutes*, vol. 27, pp. 293–306.

14 Ghiberti, *op. cit.*, II, 23. Obviously a very different impression is conveyed by Manetti's account both of the Baptistery competition and their collaboration on the Dome, but Saalman's fastidious analysis supplies no documentary evidence to support Manetti. See notes 9 and 10 above. In general, while competition was undoubtedly important, many of the major sculptors and architects of the period were employees of the Opera of Sta Maria del Fiore and of the Baptistery working together on what were, in effect, major state-funded projects financed through two of the most important guilds, the Arte della Lana and the Calimala.

15 It is often suggested that the development of central point perspective with a fixed viewpoint by Brunelleschi necessitated the representation of a single instantaneous moment in an event. This position, characterised as 'The Standard View' is summarised in Lew Andrews, *Story and Space in Renaissance Art: The Rebirth of Continuous Narrative*, Cambridge, 1995, pp. 4–8. Andrews demonstrates that, in practice, not only is there no correlation between single point perspective and the representation of a single momentary event, but that the development of perspective seems to have stimulated the development of continuous narrative rather than discouraged it. Andrews's expert decoupling of perspective and point in time is thoroughly welcome, but I would question his subsequent attempt to couple perspective and continuous narrative. There were many different positions an artist might take on this issue.

16 I do not intend this generalisation, or anti-generalisation, to extend beyond the

period. For a more extended discussion of the historiographical concepts underlying this complexity see my article, 'Walter Pater's *Marius the Epicurean* – the Imaginary Portrait as Cultural History', *Journal of the Warburg and Courtauld Institutes*, vol. 46, 1983, pp. 166–90, partic. pp. 170–5.

17 Helmtrud Köhren-Jansen, *Giottos Navicella: Bildtradition, Deutung, Rezeptiongeschichte*, Worms am Rhein, 1993.

18 L. B. Alberti, *De Pictura*, ed. and trans. C. Grayson, London, 1972, pp. 82–3.

19 I am indebted to Libby Armstrong, an experienced sailor, for this nautical information.

20 In St Luke's account of the Resurrection the disbelieving disciples think that the risen Jesus is a spirit or a ghost (Luke, 24, v. 38).

21 Matthew, 21, v. 12–13.

22 Ghiberti, *op. cit.*, II, 6: in Sta Croce 'above the sacristy door, was the twelve-year-old Christ disputing with the Doctors in the Temple, but it was three parts destroyed when a new wall was built: verily, the art of painting is of short duration'. From what survives we can see that Taddeo Gaddi seated Jesus on an elevated throne above the doctors' heads; this may well have influenced Ghiberti. See Amy Schwartz, 'Ghiberti's First Achievement', MA diss., University of Essex, 1977, pp. 3–11.

23 One example is Ghiberti's extended description of Ambrogio Lorenzetti's lost fresco of a Franciscan mission to convert Muslims: it shows 'how [come] a youth decides to become a friar. How he enters the Order, is vested by the Prior and how then with other friars fervently seeks permission to preach the Christian faith to the Saracens in Asia. How these friars set out and begin preaching, but are taken prisoner and brought to the Sultan who immediately orders them to be tied to a column and beaten with rods'. Lorenzo Ghiberti, *I Commentari* 2, 11. This may well seem novelettish, but Ghiberti clearly enjoyed art of this kind.

24 Based almost entirely upon internal stylistic evidence, Krautheimer produces an elaborate chronology for the production of the reliefs between 1403 to 1419. According to this Ghiberti develops from the International Gothic Style to the incipient Renaissance: op. cit., vol. 1, pp. 113–34; Richard Krautheimer, 'Ghibertiana', *Burlington Magazine*, August 1937, vol. 71, pp. 68–80. It would take too much space to discuss here in detail my view that it is equally possible, and more probable, that Ghiberti completed the design and modelling of all the reliefs as early as 1412 and that the remaining years were taken up with casting, chasing and all the other aspects of the doors. Given that the Calimala Guild, in the new contract drawn up in 1407, insisted upon Ghiberti working 'every working day, all day long, with his own hands like any journeyman' in order to speed up progress, it would seem odd for them to have commissioned from him the bronze statue of St John the Baptist in 1412 for their niche on Or San Michele if his main design work on the doors remained incomplete. The St John took three years to complete and was the first large bronze statue to be cast since antiquity. After 1412, moreover, Ghiberti was involved in other work which would have taken up considerable amounts of his time. This included two stained glass *occuli* for the façade of the Duomo in Florence in 1412, his work on two reliefs for the Siena Baptismal font, commissioned in 1416, his work on models for the cupola after 1418 and his commission to produce a bronze statue of St Matthew for the bankers' guild niche on Or San Michele in 1419. All this seems to point to the creative work on the reliefs being

finished by 1412. Those nine years correspond to what we know to be the case on the Gates of Paradise. Ghiberti received that commission in 1425, and twelve years later in April 1437 all the third reliefs were cast. It nonetheless took a further fifteen years or so before the third doors were installed. Krautheimer, vol. 1, p. 165.

CHAPTER VI

1 Richard Krautheimer and Trude Krautheimer-Hess, *Lorenzo Ghiberti*, vol. 1, p. 159.
2 The fact that the Scrovegni Chapel included such a cycle is perhaps additional testimony to Scrovegni's ambitions. See n. 2, Chapter 2.
3 Thomas Puttfarken in his *The Discovery of Pictorial Composition: Theories of Visual Order in Painting, 1400–1800*, New Haven and London, 2000, pp. 71ff. distinguishes between three aspects of perspective: the construction of a perspectival picture from a fixed position; second, the spectator viewing such an image from a corresponding position; and third, the compositional role of perspective, where, for example, Jesus' head in Leonardo's Last Supper is directly in front of the vanishing point. Puttfarken points out that this compositional effect of perspective was not discussed until the late seventeenth century in France. It is not referred to by Alberti or in subsequent Renaissance treatises. While Puttfarken is clear that we should not read Alberti in terms of later academic theory, he nonetheless argues that the compositional effect of perspective was central to the construction. Masaccio's Tribute Money 'very nearly realized a formula that we can describe as optimal, even as classic . . . that of using the compositional impact of the combined centric rays to display, frontally and centrally, the main protagonist, the figure of central significance' (pp. 87–8). While I agree with much of Puttfarken's argument I part company on the *necessary* compositional implications of perspective, particularly in the 1420s and early 1430s before Alberti produced his construction.
4 See Erwin Panofsky, *Perspective as Symbolic Form*, tr. Christopher Wood, New York, 1997 (originally pub. 1927); John White, *The Birth and Rebirth of Pictorial Space*, London, 1957; Hubert Damisch, *The Origin of Perspective*, tr. John Goodman, Cambridge, Mass., 1994 (French edn, Paris, 1987); Martin Kemp, *The Science of Art: Optical Themes in Western Art from Brunelleschi to Seurat*, New Haven and London, 1990. For more critical interpretations see James Elkins, *The Poetics of Perspective*, Ithaca, 1994 and Puttfarken, op. cit., pp. 69–97.
5 For example the frescoes in Oratorio di San Giovanni Battista, Urbino by the Salimbeni brothers; 1416, Donatello's relief of St George and the Dragon c.1417; the San Giovenale Triptych of 1422 sometimes attributed to Masaccio; the predella panels of Gentile da Fabriano's Strozzi altarpiece of 1423; Sassetta's Art della Lana Altarpiece, 1423–25 probably for San Pellegrino, Siena, now dispersed; the predella panels of Gentile's 1425 Quaratesi altarpiece, Masolino's Annunciation in the National Gallery, Washington.
6 Panofsky, op. cit., p. 62. Panofsky provides no source for the term which was introduced by Pietro Accolti in his *Lo inganno de gl'occhi prospettiva practica*, Florence, 1625, see J. V. Field, 'Masaccio and Perspective in Italy in the Fifteenth Century', in *The Cambridge Companion to Masaccio*, Diane Cole Ahl, Cambridge, 2002, pp. 195–6, n. 44.
7 'Se in questo luogo isterile d'ogni bene et fertile d'aspidi et di basilischi mi

turbo, anzi mi ramarichi, non è da meravigliarsi, né se tu, accompagnato da magnanima volontà nel vostro Fiore ti ralegri, trovandoti alcuna voltacol prespettivo, igegnoso uomo Filippo di ser Brunelesco, raguardevole di vertudi e di fama . . .' Giuliano Tanturli, 'Rapporti del Brunelleschi con gli ambienti letterari fiorentini', *Filippo Brunelleschi: La sua opera e il suo tempo*, Florence, 1980, p. 125.

8 H. W. Janson, *The Sculpture of Donatello*, Princeton, 2nd edn, 1963, p. 68 argues that the relief was probably modelled between 1423 and 1425, though Donatello might have received the commission as early as 1419 and certainly delivered the relief to Siena as late as 1427.

9 James Beck, *Masaccio, The Documents*, New York, 1978, pp. 17–23. The altarpiece seems to have been commissioned on 19 Feb and completed on 26 Dec 1426. On the possible doubts that can be raised concerning the identity of the painting referred to in the documents and the fragments which survive see Martin Davies's exemplary analysis of the evidence in *National Gallery Catalogues: The Earlier Italian Schools*, 2nd revised edn, London, 1961, pp. 347–51.

10 The attribution depends upon Vasari, based in turn upon the earlier *Il codice Magliabechiano* and *Il libro di Antonio Billi*. The rebuilt or rehabilitated Carmine was consecrated on 9 April 1422, and, according to Vasari, Masaccio painted a fresco of the ceremony. Masolino completed his frescoes of the Legend of the True Cross in Sto Stefano, Empoli in November 1424. He was paid for scenery probably for a miracle play in the Carmine on 8 July 1425. Masolino was working in Hungary for Pippo Spano from 1 Sept 1425 until the summer of 1427. See Beck, op. cit., pp. 12–13, 50–2 and Perri Lee Roberts, *Masolino da Panicale*, Oxford, 1993 and her essay 'Collaboration in Early Renaissance Art: The Case of Masaccio and Masolino', in Ahl, op. cit., pp. 98–101.

11 Beck, op. cit., pp. 29–30. Once more there is no documentary evidence of Masaccio's authorship but the attribution is accepted. For the perspective of the Trinity and the supposed collaboration between Brunelleschi and Masaccio see G. J. Kern, 'Das Dreifaltigkeitfresko von Sta Maria Novello. Ein perspektivisch-architectgeschichtliche Studie', *Jahrbuch der königlich preussischen Kunstsammlungen*, 22, 1913, pp. 36–58; White, op. cit., pp. 139–40; U. Schlegel, 'Observations on Masaccio's Trinity Fresco in S. Maria Novella', *Art Bulletin*, 45, 1963, pp. 19–33; H. Janson, 'Ground Plan and Elevation in Masaccio's Trinity Fresco', *Essays in the History of Art Presented to Rudolph Wittkower*, London, 1967, pp. 83–8; J. Polzer, 'The Anatomy of Masaccio's Holy Trinity', *Jahrbuch der Berliner Museen*, 13, 1971, pp. 18–58; Martin Kemp, 'Science, Non-science and Nonsense: The Interpretation of Brunelleschi's Perspective', *Art History*, 1, 2, June 1971, pp. 134–61; R. Lieberman, 'Brunelleschi and Masaccio in S. Maria Novella', *Memorie domenicane*, n.s., 12, 1981, pp. 127ff.; F. Garrieri, 'La Capella Cardini di Pescia di diritto nel catalogo brunelleschiano', *Bollettino d'Arte*, 30–1, 1985, pp. 102ff.; Jane Aiken, 'Renaissance Perspective', Ph.D. diss., Harvard University, 1986; J. V. Field, R. Lunardi and T. B. Settle, 'The Perspective Scheme of Masaccio's Trinity Fresco', *Nuncius: Annali di Storia della Scienza*, 4, 1989, pp. 31–118 and J. V. Field's summary 'Masaccio and Perspective in Italy in the Fifteenth Century', in Ahl, op. cit., pp. 177–201; Kemp, *The Science of Art*, pp. 16–21; John Shearman, *Only Connect . . . Art and the Spectator in the Italian Renaissance*, Princeton, 1992, pp. 62–6; V.

Hoffmann, 'Masaccios Trinitätsfresko', *Mitteilungen des Kunsthistorischen Institutes in Florenz*, 40, 1996, pp. 42–77.

12 Krautheimer, op. cit., vol. 1, pp. 162–4.

13 Michael Baxandall, *Giotto and the Orators*, Oxford, 1971, n. 11, p. 126.

14 L. B. Alberti, *De Pictura*, ed. and trans. C. Grayson, London, 1972, pp. 32–3.

15 '. . . this little work of mine, *De pictura*, which I did into Tuscan for you (quale al tuo nome feci in lingua toscana)'. Grayson in Alberti, op. cit., pp. 32–3. Grayson translates 'al tuo nome' as 'for you'; Spencer translates it as 'for your renown', J. R. Spencer, *Leon Battista Alberti on Painting*, New Haven and London, 1966, p. 40. Hubert Damisch, op. cit., p. 60, points out, correctly, 'that the phrase is ambiguous'. For the incorrect deductions that Damisch draws from this see n. 32 below.

16 *Filarete's Treatise on Architecture*, tr. and intro. John R. Spencer, New Haven and London, 2 vols, 1965, vol. 1, pp. 303–4 for the English translation; vol. 2, XXIII, fols 177v–178r for the Italian manuscript facsimile and the drawing of Alberti's construction. This statement about the way that Brunelleschi discovered perspective is repeated in almost the same words in ibid., vol. 1, p. 305 and vol. 2, fols 178v–179r.

17 Ibid., the Italian original for the section 'or better look at a ceiling' runs as follows: 'o vuoi guardare uno solare disotto su: tutte le travature sono equidistanti l'una dall'altra, & sguardando ti parrà che sieno e più & meno: secondo ch'elle ti saranno appresso ti paranno più equali, & quanto più ti si dilunghano, tanto più ti paranno accostate insieme l'una adosso all'altra in modo che ti paranno tutt'una . . .' The translation of this passage is mine, adapted from Spencer's.

18 Antonio de Tuccio Manetti, *The Life of Brunelleschi*, tr. Catherine Engass, ed. Howard Saalman, Pennsylvania, 1970, pp. 42–7. *Huomini Singularii in Firenze dal mccc innanzi* in G. Milanesi (ed.) *Operette istoriche edite di Antonio Manetti*, Florence, 1887, pp. 159–68, partic. p. 163.

19 Michael Baxandall, *Painting and Experience in Fifteenth-Century Italy*, Oxford, 1972, p. 116, tr. of *Comento di Christoforo Landino fiorentino sopra la comedia di Dante Alighieri*, Florence, 1481, p. iv r.

20 My adaptation of Baxandall's translation, Baxandall, *Painting and Experience*, p. 125. 'Maxime intese bene (*la*) prospettiua, e alcunj affermano, luj esserne suto o ritrouatore o inuentore', *Comento di Cristoforo Landino*, in *Il Codice Magliabechiano*, ed. Carl Frey, Berlin, 1892, reprinted, Farnborough, 1969, p. 120.

21 *Il Libro di Antonio Billi*, ed. Carl Frey, Berlin, 1892, pp. 16, 31–2, and 38.

22 *Il Codice Magliabechiano*, pp. 62, 66, 75, 82.

23 Giorgio Vasari, *Le vite de' più eccellenti architetti, pittori, et scultori italiani . . .*, edition based on the 1550, Florence edition, ed. L. Bellosi & Aldo Rossi, 2 vols, Turin, 1991, vol. 1, p. 279: '. . . egli trovà da sé un modo che ella potesse venire giusta e perfetta, che fu il levarla con pianta e proffilo e per via della intersegazione'.

24 Ibid., p. 280.

25 Ibid., pp. 355–6.

26 Giorgio Vasari, ed. G. Milanesi, *Le Vite de' più eccellenti pittori, scultori ed architettori*, 1973 reprint of Florence, 1906, vol. 2, pp. 204–5.

27 The confusion arises in the account given by Damisch, op. cit., p. 62: 'the problem was that of determining how to delineate *on a plane* the lines of a building (or any other object) in its designated spot, *con ragione*, in conformity with the rule stipulating that the lines of lateral facades converge toward a single point, or, as Vitruvius put it, toward a single "centre"'. Damisch then quotes Filarete's passage but omits the first two

sentences referring to transverse roof beams, providing his own paraphrase instead: 'a simple ceiling whose rafters seem to shrink as they recede into space'. Filarete is patently not describing the shrinking in the apparent width of the rafters but the shrinking of the apparent distance between them. Krautheimer, op. cit., vol. 1, p. 236 makes the same misreading.

28 Elkins, op. cit., p. 62, argues that while Filarete credits Brunelleschi with 'the way of making this plane', he does not credit him with the discovery of perspective in a more general sense. According to Anthony Grafton, *Leon Battista Alberti*, London, 2000, pp. 266–86, *De re aedificatoria* was largely composed in the 1440s and was completed, in some sense, by 1452. However, Grafton believes that Alberti continued to work on it well into the 1450s and beyond.

29 See note 20 above. The significance of Landino's phrasing lies in the fact that all his statements of fact and judgements in his brief account of the history of art are in the first person, except when he wishes to indicate that opinion is divided, for example in the various theories of the origins of painting. There statements are put in the third person, of the kind 'some say'. The only other instance is the statement about Brunelleschi's role in the discovery of perspective.

30 The scholarly focus upon developments believed to lead up to the classical perspective diagram, and upon major artists, misrepresents the historical situation. In the eighty years between Lorenzetti's Good and Bad Government in Siena Town Hall and the 1420s there were many Italian artists who were experimenting in this field including Orcagna, Giovanni da Milano, Andrea da Firenze, Bartolo di Fredi, Giusto de Menabuoi, Altichiero, Avanzo, Spinello Aretino, Agnolo Gaddi, Taddeo di Bartolo, Lorenzo and Jacopo Salimbeni, and Rosello di Jacopo Franchi. White, however, does include a chapter on Giusto de Menabuoi, Altichiero and Avanzo. The predella panels of Sassetta's Arte della Lana Altarpiece of 1423–5 tend to be passed over, but see Machtelt Israëls in the *Burlington Magazine*, 163, no. 1182, Sept 2001, pp. 532–43; so too the predellas of Gentile da Fabriano's Strozzi Altarpiece of 1423 and his Quaratesi Altarpiece of 1425, see Keith Christiansen, *Gentile da Fabriano*, London, 1982.

31 Cecil Grayson succinctly summarises this position: 'It is commonplace . . . to ascribe the initiative towards fixed-point perspective in painting to Brunelleschi, though there is no real evidence to support this view beyond the experiments described in his *Life* by Manetti. These are difficult to reconstruct exactly, and in any case do not offer or imply instruction on how to represent three-dimensional space on a two dimensional surface.' Alberti, op. cit., p. 11. The key issue, of course, was the construction to determine diminution not the fixed point.

32 Damisch, op. cit., tries to make this claim, but he bases it upon his own mistranslation and misreading of the text. Following the passage quoted in n. 15, he writes, '– *al tuo nome*: the turn of phrase is not, however, without ambiguity, but should it be understood that the author of *Della pittura* had some title to present himself as the spokesman of the dedicatee?' (– *al tuo nome*: mais la formule ne va pas sans ambiguïté: doit-on comprendre que, du dédicataire, l'auteur du *Della Pittura* ait-on quelque titre à se presenter comme le porte-parole? 1987 French edition, p. 68.) The impli-

cation of Damisch's rhetorical question, that Alberti was writing as Brunelleschi's mouthpiece, is false. Damisch, moreover, has mistranslated, or mis-paraphrased, the clause quoted in my earlier footnote 15; he refers to 'the little "work on painting" which Alberti had written in his name – *al tuo nome* . . .' But Alberti states without any ambiguity that what he has made 'al tuo nome' is his *translation* into Italian of his Latin work *De pictura*, not that he had *written* the text of either *De pictura* or *Della pittura* 'al tuo nome'.

33 Frank D. Prager and Giustina Scaglia, *Brunelleschi: Studies of his Technology and Inventions*, Cambridge, Mass., 1970, pp. 111ff. and 129; Isabelle Hyman (ed.), *Brunelleschi in Perspective*, New Jersey, 1974, pp. 30-2.

34 The Duomo was consecrated on 25 March 1436, Dale Kent, *Cosimo de' Medici and the Florentine Renaissance*, New Haven and London, 2000, p. 125. According to Baxandall, the best, though not necessarily the original manuscript of the Italian version was completed on 17 July 1436, Baxandall, *Giotto and the Orators*, n. 11, p. 126.

35 It has been argued that Manetti's statement that Brunelleschi developed in his youth, even before the Baptistery competition in 1401, the 'science' of perspective which deals with 'setting down properly and rationally the diminution and increase in the apparent size both of near and distant objects as they appear to the eye . . . according to their distance from the spectator' and that he gave birth to the rule (*la regola*) followed in these matters ever since, constitutes a riposte on behalf of Brunelleschi's camp to Alberti's claims. If so it is mild and much belated. Saalman, in his Introduction to Manetti, op. cit., pp. 29–32, argues that Manetti's whole account of Brunelleschi's architecture should be interpreted as an anti-Albertian polemic. Anthony Grafton argues that although Alberti's request that his 'learned friend' Brunelleschi should correct anything that required amendment was simply common humanist practice, it nonetheless backfired. Grafton states, without providing evidence, that 'Brunelleschi . . . presumably reacted with characteristic irritation when he saw that Alberti's work contained a long discussion of perspective but did not mention him or his model panels.' See Grafton, op. cit., pp. 144–5, 53–7.

36 John White recognizes the problem while nonetheless claiming that Brunelleschi 'developed a complete, focused, system of perspective with mathematically regular diminution towards a fixed vanishing point . . . All this is revolutionary in its novelty.' John White, op. cit., p. 120. However, in his section on Alberti he draws attention to the fact that despite the dedication of *Della pittura* to Brunelleschi 'there is no reference to him in the text itself. There is therefore nothing to connect his name with the creation of the new perspective which Alberti strongly implies is his own invention.' White argues that since the origins of the method must have been well known within the circles in which both men moved, 'there must clearly be a sense in which his claim is true. He could not otherwise have written in such terms in Florence, and in Brunelleschi's lifetime.' But White is unable to accept the forceful logic of his own argument because he wrongly accords equal weight to Manetti's secondary testimony: 'There are equally no grounds for a rejection of Manetti's factual account which was also written

during the lifetime of many who had known both Brunelleschi and Alberti.' There is nothing to prove that Manetti's account is 'factual', and the claims made both by Filarete and Landino are more circumspect. White op. cit., p. 124. White's solution to this conflicting evidence is that Brunelleschi made his peepshows by laboriously combining ground plans and elevations, which Alberti then abbreviated and improved through his geometric construction.

37 '. . . in hac plane difficili et a nemine quod viderim alio tradita litteris materia . . .', in Alberti, op. cit., pp. 36–7. It is possible to argue that by including the reference to 'litteris' Alberti was splitting hairs by restricting his claim only to being the first person to treat the subject in *writing*, thereby avoiding the charge of plagiarism that could have be made on behalf of Brunelleschi's earlier practical demonstrations of the system. But, for the reasons already stated, this is improbable. He is unlikely to have put himself in a position where his claim could have been so readily and authoritatively dismissed. It has been argued by Kim Veltman, *The Sources of Perspective*, n.d. p. 17, www.sumscorp.com/books that in the Italian translation, which Brunelleschi could have read, Alberti omitted this; but in fact he makes the same claim in both versions.

38 See n. 54 below.

39 He condemns the practice of some – *nonnulli* – who after connecting the receding lines, or orthogonals, to the centric point would then construct the diminution of the paving stones by first drawing a line at an arbitrary distance parallel to the base line, the next at two-thirds that distance, and each succeeding distance being diminished by two-thirds. Alberti, op. cit., pp. 54–5. On pp. 56–7 Alberti explicitly lays claim to having invented or discovered by himself the procedure shown in Fig. 118: 'optimum hunc adinveni modum [I invented the following excellent method]. This carefully chosen wording was clearly intended to leave one in no doubt about the originality of Alberti's precise contribution to the perspective construction. It makes it almost inconceivable that he was plagiarizing Brunelleshci.

40 Alberti, op. cit., pp. 76–7.

41 Manetti, op. cit., pp. 42–6.

42 Kemp, 'Science, non-science', and *The Science of Art*, pp. 14 and 345.

43 The seventeenth-century Dutch painter of church interiors, Pieter Saenredam, first made a freehand drawing which he then corrected by making a proper perspective construction based on measurements and sometimes ground plans. However, he may have been the first to combine drawing with perspective construction, according to Gary Schwartz and Marten Jan Bok, *Pieter Saenredam*, London, 1990, pp. 79–80.

44 Vasari's description of the peepshows was almost certainly based upon Manetti.

45 Milanesi published a description in the inventory of Lorenzo Magnifico of two objects, a perspective of the Palazzo de'Signori and its piazza, and another panel of San Giovanni. Milanesi suggested that these were the peepshows described by Manetti and Saalman in his edition of Manetti accepted this, op. cit., n. 22, p. 131; G. Milanesi (ed.) *Operette istoriche edite di Antonio Manetti*, Florence, 1887, p. 86, n. 1; E. Müntz, *Les Collections des Médicis au Xv[e] Siècle*, Paris and London, 1888, p. 62.

46 Charles Seymour Jr, *Michelangelo's David: A Search for Identity*, Pittsburgh, 1967, pp. 116–19. Brunelleschi is described as a goldsmith.

47 Howard Saalman, *Filippo Brunelleschi: The Cupola of Sta Maria del Fiore*, London, 1980, pp. 61–2.

48 James Beck, op. cit., p. 35.

49 Alberti's mention of Ghiberti in this list lends support to the view that the relationship between Brunelleschi and Ghiberti was nothing like so hostile as Manetti's portrayal of it.

50 Paul Joannides, *Masaccio and Masolino, A Complete Catalogue*, London, 1993, pp. 106 and 316. Keith Christiansen, 'Some Observations on the Brancacci Chapel Frescoes after the Cleaning', *Burlington Magazine*, 133, 1991, pp. 4–20 argues that, whether or not Vasari was correct in his first 1550 edition (op. cit., vol. 1, p. 270) that Masaccio received the Brancacci commission through the intervention of his 'closest friend' Brunelleschi, there is no doubting Brunelleschi's keen interest in the young painter. The mouldings and pilasters which frame the frescoes 'are entirely Brunelleschian', and it is Brunelleschian architecture that forms the backdrop to Masaccio's frescoes (pp. 16–17).

51 Gary M. Rodke points out that 'Nowhere in contemporary Florence would [Masaccio] have found a coffered barrel vault or a chapel with the precise form seen in his fresco. His painting, then, did more than replicate Brunelleschi's architecture: it gave vision to what no Renaissance architect had yet built.' See 'Masaccio's City: Urbanism, Architecture and Sculpture in Early Fifteenth-Century Florence', in Ahl, op. cit., p. 51.

52 Saalman, op. cit., pp. 82–96.

53 Janson, op. cit., pp. 51–6.

54 In his Healing by Shadow in the Brancacci Chapel, both the recession of the street and the scale between figures and buildings is rudimentary. In the Pisa Altarpiece Madonna of 1426 the orthogonals of the throne, as far as one can tell, and it is not an easy thing to work out from a small photograph, do not meet in a single point but are scattered in a central area. The foreshortened sides of the throne seem too shallow to provide the Madonna with a decent seat. While the throne and Jesus' halo are foreshortened as if seen from below, the bodies of Madonna, Child and the two lower angels are not foreshortened at all, nor are their haloes. What we find is a clever combination of methods, particularly the systematic overlapping and partial masking of forms. We also find quite a precise representation of the fall of light and shadow on the forms of the throne derived from Gentile's 1423 Nativity. In the Tribute Money the overall effect is better. The range of methods Masaccio used to achieve a naturalistic effect in the Tribute Money is similar to those used by Donatello in the Siena relief. While an improvement upon the Healing by Shadow, the figures however are less integrated with their setting than in Donatello's relief. In the Trinity, according to the most recent on-site examination and measurements, those of Field et al., there is a centric point within the step just below the donors, but the orthogonal ribs of the barrel vault deviate from it by as much as 10 cm to either side (Field, op. cit., pp. 37–8). The Trinity, therefore, exhibits a closer approximation to a centric point than its predecessors. The evidence of the Trinity, therefore, corresponds with Alberti's acknowledgement that he was not the first person to employ a centric point. But Field et al. do not believe that Masaccio employed Alberti's technique for controlling diminution (Field, op. cit., pp. 76–8). Another indication that such a construction was not used is the fact that the figures are out of scale with one another and do not diminish according to distance. The largest figures, were they to stand up, are the donors; Mary and St John are about 80 per cent of the size of the donors; God the Father and Christ are about 90 per cent. One

would expect apparent size to diminish with distance. In any case the distance between the donors and Mary and St John is small, roughly the diameter of the attached columns, which would not account for such a considerable diminution. Once again, the success of the effect of the Trinity substantially depends upon artful masking and overlapping of up to a dozen planes, the employment of foreshortened haloes, the diminution of the barrel vault and architecture which like that of Donatello's St John's Head is massive and convincing.

55 Elkins, op. cit., pp. 8, 41, 64, 67, 87. Michael Ann Holly drew my attention to the obsession of art historians with identifying a single inventor.

56 Janson, op. cit., pp. 67–8; Krautheimer, vol. 1, op. cit., pp. 139–41. In March 1425 the Sienese expressed their anger that 'i maestri da Firenze' had missed every deadline for the work for the Baptistery. This may suggest that the Sienese authorities saw the commissions for the three Florentine reliefs as connected.

57 Ulrich Middeldorf, review of H. Kauffmann, *Donatello*, in *Art Bulletin*, vol. 18, 1936, p. 584.

58 Chapter 4, p. 143.

59 Janson, op. cit., pp. 70–1.

60 Ibid., p. 66

61 Ibid., p. 69: 'That Donatello's perspective here is no longer empirical but based on theory, can no longer be doubted; if as White . . . has observed, the orthogonals do not all meet in a single vanishing point, the deviations are so slight they can be verified with a ruler and crept in during the process of chasing, rather than in the original design'. Janson's reference is to John White, 'Developments in Renaissance Perspective – II', *Journal of the Warburg and Courtauld Institutes*, 14, 1951, p. 45. Krautheimer, vol. 1, *op. cit.*, pp. 151–2, 244 while believing that Donatello incorporated certain elements from Brunelleschi's peepshows, considers that the relief is incommensurable. Kemp, *The Science of Art*, p. 16 considers that Donatello has only half understood Brunelleschi's 'more consistent perspective'.

62 Alberti, op. cit., pp. 54–5.

63 See White, 'Developments in Renaissance Perspective', p. 46, where he argues that the proportion of figures to architecture, the extension of the hall beyond the frame and figures disappearing out of the frame are more important facts about Donatello's use of perspective than the convergence of his orthogonals to a point.

64 Bruce Cole, *Masaccio and the Art of Early Renaissance Florence*, Bloomington, 1980, pp. 139 and 183.

65 Robert Munman, *Optical Corrections in the Sculptures of Donatello, Transactions of the American Philosophical Society*, vol. 75, pt. 2, pp. 35–9. It has been observed that 'pictorial perspective constructions are more tolerant of the spectator's movement away from the calculated point of sight' than the strictest theorists, such as Leonardo da Vinci, have argued, which is the reason 'why the fiction of Donatello's Feast of Herod works even when you stand and look down on it'. This assumes that there is a 'single vanishing point', and the recession is calculated with 'a fixed and precisely determined spatial relationship between the spectator and the fiction of the seen object'. As we have seen, it is not possible to make these assumptions, and the range of possible positions from which the spectator can view the relief are not that different from what we have found in earlier works. John Shearman, op. cit., pp. 60–6.

66 L. B. Alberti, *Ten Books on Architecture*, tr. James Leoni, reprint, London, 1965, bk 5, ch. 3, p. 86.

67 We must, however, bear in mind the

possibility that at this period converging lines were just that and that their effect as directional signs was an unintended by-product of the technique. See n. 3 for Puttfarken's view on this issue.

68 Sometimes tables are set on both sides as in the Scrovegni Last Supper, sometimes on one side only as in frescoes of the Last Supper painted in monastic refectories.

69 *Hamlet*, III, 2, 16.

70 *Macbeth*, I, 7, 16.

CHAPTER VII

1 Ch. 6, n. 10 above and Diane Cole Ahl, 'Masaccio in the Brancacci Chapel', in Diane Cole Ahl, *The Cambridge Companion to Masaccio*, Cambridge, 2000, pp. 138–57.

2 Giorgio Vasari, *Le Vite*, ed. Milanesi, 1973 reprint of Florence, 1906, II, p. 265. Until the cleaning of the 1980s when the underpaintings, the sinopie, revealed Feed my Sheep, its existence was not known.

3 The vaults and lunettes were repainted by Vincenzo Meucci, 1746–8; there was a fire in 1771.

4 James Beck, *Masaccio, The Documents*, New York, 1978, p. 52.

5 Ibid., pp. 17–23.

6 Felice Brancacci's second will of 1432 refers to unfinished frescoes in the chapel, Perri Lee Roberts, *Masolino da Panicale*, Oxford, 1993, p. 184.

7 See Herbert von Einem, *Masaccio's 'Zinsgroschen'*, Cologne, 1967, pp. 17–19 for precedents. Von Einem states that the frescoes in old St Peter's almost certainly included the Tribute Money, but there are no surviving drawings of it. Jacques Mesnil, however, in his *Masaccio et les Débuts de la Renaissance*, La Haye, 1927, p. 76 argues that the inclusion of so minor an episode as the Tribute Money and the omission of major ones is hard to explain. He also argues that Masaccio had to work out completely for himself the most appropriate methods of visualising the subject to make the theme as intelligible as possible. The fresco in the nave of San Piero a Grado shows not the central episode as in the Brancacci, but St Peter fishing for the coin. Von Einem, op. cit., p. 19, claims that the San Piero a Grado cycle derives from the cycle in old St Peter's. If so, that might have been the episode represented there too. Joseph Polzer suggests that a lost fresco in old St Paul's in Rome of St Paul preaching to the Hebrews, showing the saint in the centre of a group of standing figures, is a source for Masaacio's Tribute. The fresco is recorded in the Vatican manuscript Barb. Lat. 4406. fol. 119r. J. Polzer, 'Masaccio and the Late Antique', *Art Bulletin*, 53, 1971, pp. 36ff.

8 Dazio, municipal toll, is the word used in the fourteenth-century Italian translation of the text in the *Diatesseron*, which may provide some indication of the wording in whatever Italian text Masaccio may have worked from. *Il Diatesseron in Volgare Italiàno*, ed. V. Todesco et al., Città del Vaticano, 1938, p. 273.

9 Also *Diatesseron*.

10 For von Einem's breakdown of the episodes and his interpretation of the fresco as a statement of the obedience of Christians towards the Church; see von Einem, op. cit., pp. 23–4.

11 See von Einem, op. cit., plates 18–20 for examples.

12 Anthony Molho, 'The Brancacci Chapel: Studies in its Iconography and History, *Journal of the Warburg and Courtauld Institutes*, 40, 1977, pp. 50–98. Von Einem argues that it is a statement about the obedience of Christians to the Church as opposed to the State in a period of powerful challenges to the supremacy of

the Papacy from the followers of Wycliff and Huss. Astrid Debold-von Kritter shows, in great detail, the support given by the Carmelites to the doctrine of the primacy of the Papacy and argues that the theme of the Tribute Money is that St Peter is 'Universalis Magister post Christum'. Astrid Debold-von Kritter, *Studien zum Petruszyklus in der Brancaccikapelle*, Berlin, 1975.

13 Since the Florentine War of the Eight Saints of 1375 against the Papacy, the Florentine state had imposed heavy taxes, duties and confiscations upon the Florentine clergy; so too did the Papacy itself. In 1424 matters came to a head over the clergy's debts and a meeting of the Great Council of the clergy was held on 15 November 1424 to resolve the crisis, without much success. See David Peterson, 'Electoral Politics and the Florentine Clergy: A Meeting of the Maius Concilium in 1424', *Renaissance Studies*, vol. 5, no. 4, December 1991, pp. 359–97. For a broad survey of the fiscal situation of the clergy see Nirit Ben-Aryeh Debby, 'Political Views in the Preaching of Giovanni Dominici', *Renaissance Quarterly*, vol. LV, no. 1, Spring 2002, pp. 29ff. For the conciliar movement in the Roman church see Francis Oakley, *The Conciliarist Tradition: Constitutionalism in the Catholic Church, 1300–1870*, Oxford, 2003, pp. 20–110.

14 While acknowledging the wonderful scholarship of von Einem, Debold-von Kritter and Molho I would question whether they have given as much weight to the image as to contemporary documents in their view that the message of the Tribute Money is obedience to papal primacy. It seems a little too cut and dried. Jesus, surely, is the dominant figure and he is arbitrating an agreement between Church and State.

15 See Warman Welliver, 'Narrative Method and Narrative Form in Masaccio's Tribute Money', *Art Quarterly*, n.s., Autumn 1977, 1:1, pp. 40–58. On p. 44 n. 20. Welliver argues that the Latin of the Vulgate 'praevenit eum' can mean either 'he anticipated him' or 'he prevented him,' but he seems to prefer the latter as implying that Jesus prevented St Peter lunging forward to punch the official! Welliver uses this as the textual basis for arguing that St Peter 'raises his left hand to strike the collector; but Christ lifts His robe with His left hand so that He can move to His right and interposes His right arm just in the nick of time, for Peter's hand is already beyond the restraining arm' (p. 51). To me this seems to push the interpretation of the visual evidence a little too far. Was St Peter left-handed? His palm is open and appears hesitant, protesting or questioning, as if in reply to Jesus's commanding right arm – 'Surely you don't want me to pay the scoundrel?' The *Diatesseron* translates 'praevenit eum' simply as 'gli venne incontra' – 'he came towards him', which avoids all these problems.

16 The relationship between the almost identical postures of the two figures is one of rotational symmetry (rotation through 180 degrees). They do not mirror one another as Welliver seems to suggest.

17 The buildings are out of scale with the figures, and the doors and windows do not diminish correctly. The alignment of the heads of the figures at the eye-level of an assumed spectator is a feature found in Giotto, and the complex arrangement of figures derives from Giotto, Giovanni Pisano and many earlier artists.

18 My disagreement with Welliver, op. cit., on this point centres upon whether Peter really is about to punch the tax collector as Welliver believes, or whether Masaccio is trying to convey the passions simmer-

ing just below the surface, which is my impression. Were the physical violence to be made too literal the delicately balanced and suggestive compositional framework would be destroyed.

19 'Pierre le regarde, les sourcils froncés, le front plissé, se demandent s'il a bien saisi le sense des paroles: la main gauche levée et en arrêt marque la surprise, la main droite suit instinctivement le geste de Jésus; toute l'attitude est interrogative: "Est-ce bien là je dois aller? C'est vraiment dans la bouche du poisson que je trouverai cette pièce de monnaie?"' Mesnil, op. cit., p. 77.

20 Richard Woodfield argues convincingly that while continuous narrative is apparent in the double presence of the tax collector and St Peter and the subsidiary episodes, that they are to be interpreted not 'naturalistically as a continuation of the action in the middle but originate as the medieval indirect narrative device of separating off thoughts and dreams as amplificatory images.' 'Words and Pictures', *British Journal of Aesthetics*, vol. 26, no. 4, Autumn 1986, pp. 357–70, partic. p. 364. See ch. 3, n. 16 above for Sixten Ringbom's article on this subject.

21 For the significance of the handshake as faith, within or outside marriage, see Eloise M. Angiola, '"Gates of Paradise" and the Florentine Baptistery', *Art Bulletin*, 60, 1978, p. 246. For the transient significance of such signs and conventions see H. Roodenberg, 'The "Hand of Friendship": Shaking Hands and Other Gestures in the Dutch Republic', in Jan Bremmer and Herman Roodenberg (eds), *A Cultural History of Gesture*, Oxford, 1991, pp. 152–81.

22 Vasari describes this with precision: 'aspettando la resoluzione con gesti sì pronti'. Vasari, op. cit., vol. 2, p. 297.

23 See note 20.

24 'Masaccio preferred his pigments pasty, in order to build up the paint and attain a better sense of relief . . .', James Elkins, *Our Beautiful, Dry, and Distant Texts*, Philadelphia, 1997, p. 221 quoting Carl Friedrich von Rumohr, *Italienishen Forschungen*, ed. J. Schlosser, Frankfurt, 1920, vol. 2, p. 378. Joannides, op. cit., p. 336 also observes that the paint on Peter's face is 'fuller and thicker than elsewhere'. J. V. Field et al., 'The Perspective Scheme of Masaccio's Trinity', *Nuncius*, IV, 1989, op. cit., p. 36 n. 12 make similar observations about the Brancacci and the Trinity. The most recent restoration of the Scrovegni Chapel has revealed that Giotto previously used a similar impasto technique on the bushes in the figure of Injustice.

25 Heinrich Brockhaus, 'Die Brancacci-Kapelle in Florenz', *Mitteilungen des Kunsthistorischen Institutes in Florenz*, Dritte Band, Heft IV, III, 4, March 1930, pp. 160–82. In 1436 Felice Brancacci and his immediate family were, like the family of his father-in-law, Palla Strozzi, declared rebels. The family was not permitted to return until 1474. Brockhaus argues, op. cit., p. 173, on the basis of other cases where public portraits of exiles were destroyed that any portraits in the chapel of Felice Brancacci, his family, followers and friends 'must have been destroyed'.

26 Keith Christiansen, 'Some Observations on the Brancacci Chapel Frescoes after their Cleaning', *Burlington Magazine*, 133, 1991, pp. 4–20, thinks Brockhaus's argument remains 'open to debate'. Joannides, op. cit., p. 315 rejects the defacement theory. John Shearman, in a Courtauld seminar in the late 1960s, indicated that he accepted Brockhaus.

27 Jacobus de Voragine, *The Golden Legend*, trans. W. G. Ryan, 2 vols, Princeton, 1993, I, pp. 162–6.

28 Creighton Gilbert's identification of

Theophilus as the central kneeling figure is plausible because that figure is wearing a gown of similar colour and with similar pleats to the enthroned Theophilus, see 'Special Images for Carmelites', in Timothy Verdon and John Henderson (eds), *Christianity and the Renaissance*, New York, 1990, pp. 161–207, partic. p. 195. Gilbert also argues that the presence of the Carmelites is justified by the order's belief that it alone existed at the time of the apostles.

29 Vasari, op. cit., II, p. 295.

30 Paul Hills, *The Light in Early Italian Painting*, New Haven and London, 1987, p. 142 and more generally the chapters on Masaccio, pp. 115–45.

31 M. Salmi in *Masaccio*, Milan, 2nd edn, 1947, p. 73 identifies this figure with Masaccio and dismisses Vasari's identification of the figure to the right of Jesus in the Tribute Money as a fairy tale. Joannides, op. cit., p. 336 finds this 'most convincing'. The figure originally reached out to touch St Peter.

32 Though the upper lunette was probably painted by Masolino, and the scene of St Peter in Prison and other figures by Lippi.

33 Debold-von Kritter, op. cit., n. 21 p. 60 argues that St Peter's payment of the tribute makes mankind's access to salvation and hence paradise possible again. More generally, through the institution of the Church, St Peter is given the means to return mankind to the heavenly gates through which, figuratively speaking, Adam and Eve had been expelled.

34 St Matthew 16, vv. 18–19. Jacobus de Voragine refers to St Peter's power to bind and loose as part of the second reason for celebrating the Feast of the Chair of St Peter, Voragine, op. cit., vol. 1, p. 164.

35 E. H. Gombrich, 'Art and Propaganda', *The Listener*, 7 Dec. 1939, pp. 1118–20.

36 Michael Baxandall, *Painting and Experience*, Oxford, 1972, 122–3, 131–3. E. H. Gombrich, 'Visual Metaphors of Value in Art', *Meditations on a Hobby Horse*, London, 1963, pp. 12–29.

CHAPTER VIII

1 Richard Krautheimer and Trude Krautheimer-Hess, *Lorenzo Ghiberti*, 2 vols, Princeton, 2nd edn, 1970, vol. 1, pp. 159–66 and vol. 2, pp. 368 and 414, for his dating of progress on the doors.

2 Ibid., vol. 1, pp. 169–72; vol. 2, pp. 372–3; for a translation and commentary, Creighton E. Gilbert, *Italian Art, 1400–1500: Sources and Documents*, 2nd edn, Evanston, Ill., 1992, pp. 163–5.

3 For the dimensions of the Siena panels see *Lorenzo Ghiberti: 'materia e ragionamento'*, Florence, 1978, p. 227; on p. 60 the dimensions for the Competition Relief are given as 45 by 38 cm. For the dimensions of the Gates of Paradise panels see Krautheimer op. cit., vol. 1, p. 164 where the panels on the back frame are given as 50 cm square, Krautheimer, op. cit., vol. 1.

4 Krautheimer, vol. 1, pp. 248–51 claims that in the designing of these two panels, Ghiberti was instructed by Alberti on the basis of *De Pictura*, published in 1435. But by that date it is almost certain that all the reliefs would have been substantially complete, and in any case the visual evidence contradicts this. It is also apparent that Ghiberti had not learnt Alberti's method for foreshortening circles and semicircular arches lying in orthogonal places. See the whole of Krautheimer's Chapter XVI.

5 Lew Andrews, *Story and Space in Renaissance Art: The Rebirth of Continuous Narrative*, Cambridge, 1995, pp. 1–18; Lorenzo Ghiberti, *I commentari*, ed. Ottavio Morisani, Naples, 1947, pp. 45–6;

The Commentaries of Lorenzo Ghiberti, tr. Peter Murray, Courtauld Institute of Art, London, n.d., p. 23.

6 Ibid., Morisani, pp. 37–8; see also n. 23, Chapter 5; Murray, p. 18. See also n. 23 to chapter 5.

7 L. B. Alberti, *De pictura*, ed. and trans. C. Grayson, London, 1972, pp. 70–1.

8 Alessandro Parronchi, 'Le "Misure dell' Occhio" secondo il Ghiberti', in *Studi su la dolce Prospettiva*, Milan, 1964, pp. 313–48. This pioneering paper argues that Ghiberti's response to Brunelleschian and Albertian perspective was essentially antagonistic. Obviously I would challenge the notion of a systematic Brunelleschian perspective, and I believe that the reliefs were completed before the publication of Alberti's *De Pictura*.

9 See Ringbom cited in Ch. 3, n. 16 above.

10 Vasari's *Lives*, ed. G. Milanesi, vol. 2, p. 241, Florence, 1906, 1973 reprint.

11 Krautheimer, op. cit., vol. 1, p. 297.

12 As we have seen, these panels probably did not rely upon a geometric perspective construction, insofar as one can infer anything from Manetti's description alone.

13 E. H. Gombrich, 'The Renaissance Conception of Artistic Progress and its Consequences', *Norm and Form: Studies in the Art of the Renaissance*, London, 1966, pp. 7–8.

14 Genesis 26, 12–14.

15 Genesis chapters 37–50.

16 Genesis 45, 1–15.

17 See Conclusion, n. 52, p. 337.

18 Giovanni Boccaccio, *Decameron*, trans. Guido Waldman, Oxford, 1993, ninth story of the third day.

19 Eloise M. Angiola, '"Gates of Paradise" and the Florentine Baptistery', *Art Bulletin*, 60, 1978, p. 246.

CHAPTER IX

1 Volker Herzner, 'Regesti Donatelliani', *Rivista dell' Istituto Nazionale d'Archeologia e Storia dell' Arte*, Ser. 3, Ann. 2, Rome, 1979, p. 216.

2 Ibid., p. 218.

3 Ibid., p. 222.

4 H. W. Janson, *The Sculpture of Donatello*, Princeton, 2nd edn, 1963, p. 209.

5 The debate is summarised in Janson, op. cit., pp. 211–15. I incline to Irving Lavin's hypothesis that they are pulpits and formed part of a coherent plan for the crossing, modelled upon S. Lorenzo fuori le Mura which possesses twinned marble pulpits facing one another across the nave. See Irving Lavin, 'The Sources of Donatello's Pulpits in San Lorenzo, Revival and Freedom of Choice in the Early Renaissance', *Art Bulletin*, 41, 1959, pp. 19–38; 'Donatello's Bronze Pulpits in San Lorenzo and the Early Christian Revival', in Lavin, *Past-Present: Essays on Historicism in Art from Donatello to Picasso*, Berkeley, 1993, pp. 1–27. Volker Herzner, however, examines the evidence and the condition of the pulpits in great detail and suggests that the front panel of the north pulpit may originally have been intended for a project for Cosimo's tomb on which Donatello may have worked between his return from Padua and his departure for Siena. Cosimo rejected so ostentatious a memorial and the panel was re-employed as part of a new pulpit project: Herzner, 'Die Kanzeln Donatellos in San Lorenzo', *Münchner Jahrbuch der Bildenden Kunst*, Ser. 3, vol. 22, 1972, pp. 101–64. For a critique of Herzner, see Janis Clearfield, 'The Tomb of Cosimo de' Medici in San Lorenzo', *Rutgers Art Review*, 2, Jan 1981, pp. 13–30. Even so, whatever its origins, the Resurrection panel was incorporated into the project which we see today. Despite the obvious physical disparities and anomalies the sculptural programme of the two pulpits

makes sense, and, as is indicated by my argument, the reliefs seem to have been designed for the illumination which they receive in their present location, which also makes use of other features. See also Odette Livingstone-Smith, 'Donatello's Bronze Pulpits in San Lorenzo', MA diss., University of Essex, 1982, which provides accurate and detailed measurements of the pulpits on pp. 32–6

6 Janson, op. cit., p. 209; Vespasiano da Bisticci, *The Vespasiano Memoirs*, tr. W. G. and E. Waters, London, 1926, p. 224.

7 Herzner, 'Regesti Donatelliana', op. cit., pp. 218–21.

8 For a different hypothesis about viewpoint see Robert Munman, *Optical Corrections in the Sculptures of Donatello. Transactions of the American Philosophical Society*, vol. 75, pt. 2, pp. 50ff.

9 Michael Podro, *Depiction*, New Haven and London, 1998, pp. 49–50. If only the stucco reliefs survived and not the building, and we had no idea of their original location, a reconstruction based upon their internal perspectives would come up with some curious results. Because of the complexity of the implied viewpoints in the pulpit reliefs, because we do not know whether the existing pulpits follow the scheme Donatello had in mind and because there is insufficient evidence to make an alternative reconstruction, I have not felt the need to have new photographs taken in this case but have employed the very fine ones taken for Jenö Lányi by Alinari in the 1930s. In addition, because so much depends upon the very low levels of illumination and visual obscurity of many of the reliefs, as will be made clear later in this chapter, it is almost impossible to photograph the effect of viewing the pulpits *in situ*.

10 See also James Elkins, *The Poetics of Perspective*, Ithaca, 1994, pp. 139–44: Patrick Maynard, 'Perspective's Places', *Journal of Aesthetics and Art Criticism*, vol. 54, 1996, pp. 23–40.

11 Another example is the Ovetari Chapel by Mantegna and others in the Eretimani Church in Padua painted between 1448 and 1457, where the implied viewpoints of the upper frescoes are higher than those of the lowest tier. The young Mantegna was influenced by Donatello's work done during his residence in Padua.

12 See John White's fine observations on the pulpits, John White, *The Birth and Rebirth of Pictorial Space*, London, 1987, pp. 165–7: 'to him perspective was no spatial game with a value of its own. It was, for him, only the means to more important, and essentially artistic ends.' White writes of Donatello turning 'with new urgency' to Giotto's solutions; my view is that Giovanni's were equally important to him.

13 There is much discussion of the quality of some panels and the intervention of assistants, for a summary of which see Janson, op. cit., pp. 216–17. It is easy, however, to confuse quality with Donatello's bold experiments in primitivism. Maybe the Crucifixion and the Pentecost are defective in some ways. But it is noteworthy that Francesco Bocchi in his detailed and enthusiastic description of 1591 does not differentiate between the different scenes on artistic grounds and observes of the Pentecost (often rejected by connoisseurs) that 'it shows truly stupendous artistic power'. Quoted in Janson, op. cit., pp. 210–11 and Francesco Bocchi, *Le belleze della città di Fiorenza, Florence*, 1591, pp. 250ff.

14 Another artist who returned to Duccio's type of painted panel cycle was Fra Angelico in his doors for the silver cupboard in SS Annunziata probably dating

from the late 1440s. See L. Kanter and P. Palladino, *Fra Angelico*, New Haven and London, 2005, p. 145.

15 *Meditations on the Life of Christ*, ed. Isa Ragusa and Rosalie B. Green, Princeton, 1961 and 1977, p. 321.

16 Thomas à Kempis 1379/80–1471, was born in the diocese of Cologne. The *Imitatio* was first issued in 1418. For St Francis see John Moorman, *A History of the Franciscan Order*, Oxford, 1968, reprinted 1998, pp. 11, 58, 75–8; *The Life of St Francis*, chs 9 and 13.

17 Bronze is an alloy of copper and tin, but other metals and minerals can be added to change its characteristics. These include zinc, lead, aluminium, gold, silver, gold, antimony, phosphorus and manganese. Quite apart from the use of surface gilding on the south face of the north pulpit it seems as if Donatello varied the proportions of the alloy to change the colour.

18 Bocchi, op. cit., has no doubts about the subject.

19 Lavin, op. cit., 1959, p. 25.

20 Ibid., pp. 34–6.

21 *Meditations on the Life of Christ*, p. 328.

22 Ibid., p. 337.

23 John White, op. cit., p. 166, talks of 'the deep cutting, obeying the emotional demands of the scene'.

24 Many of the features associated with Limbo such as Jesus breaking open the gates of Hell are absent. Christ in Limbo is not a biblical episode. The passage from Matthew is the closest biblical account.

CONCLUSION

1 Even so Creighton Gilbert has pointed out that the fifteenth century was very unusual in the history of art in the number of books written by leading practitioners, see his *Italian Art, 1400–1500: Sources and Documents*, 2nd edn, Evanston Ill., 1992, p. xv.

2 Although Michael Baxandall argues that *De pictura* was 'a handbook in the active appreciation of painting for an unusual kind of informed humanist amateur', he nonetheless believes that the book is based upon 'the assumption that an art is by definition systematic and teachable through rules', Baxandall, *Giotto and the Orators: Humanist Observers of Painting in Italy and the Discovery of Pictorial Composition 1350–1450*, Oxford, 1971, pp. 129 and 135. Thomas Puttfarken, *The Discovery of Pictorial Composition*, New Haven and London, 2000, pp. 64–8, while disputing Baxandall's emphasis upon Alberti's conception of pictorial composition as fundamentally rule worthy, emphasises Alberti's interest in the artist rather than the spectator. Oskar Bätschman in his 'Looking at Pictures – the Views of Leon Battista Alberti' does deal with the importance of the viewer's pleasure, emotional involvement and imagination; see Antoinette Roesler-Friedenthal and Johannes Nathan (eds), *The Enduring Instant: Time and the Spectator in the Visual Arts*, Berlin, 2003, pp. 251–69.

3 *De pictura*, Alberti, ed. and trans. C. Grayson, London, 1972, pp. 98–101.

4 Alberti op. cit., pp. 86–9.

5 'Historia vero, quam merito possis et laudere et admirari, eiusmodo erit quae illecebris quibusdam sese ita amenam et ornatum exhibeat, ut oculos docti atque indocti spectatoris diutius quadam cum voluptate et animi motu detineat . . . Fit enim ut cum spectantes lustrandis rebus morentur, tum pictoris copia gratiam assequatur', *De Pictura*, Alberti, op. cit., II, 40, pp. 78–9. He returns to this point in Book 3: 'The aim of the painter is to obtain praise, favour and goodwill for his

work much more than riches. The painter will achieve this when his picture holds the eyes and mind of spectators and inspires them'. ('dum eius pictura oculos et animos spectantium tenebit atque movebit'). Alberti, op. cit., III, 52, pp. 94–5.

6 Immediately following this passage Alberti provides some elaborately hedged guidelines on how to achieve this through good composition so that the picture does not descend into confusion.

7 See introduction above 'Reading Pictures', pp. 11–12.

8 See L. B. Alberti, *De re aedificatoria* translated as *Ten Books on Architecture*, tr. James Leoni, London, 1755, reprinted London, 1965, bk. 7, ch. 16, p. 150: 'I look upon a Picture with no less pleasure . . . than I read a good History. They both indeed are Pictures, only the Historian paints with Words, and the Painter with his Pencil. All other Qualifications are common to them both, and they both require the greatest Genius and Application. But I would have nothing either on the Wall or Pavement of the Temple but what savours entirely of Philosophy.' In his *Dinner Pieces (Intercenales)* Alberti argued in favour of expressing important philosophical doctrines in a cryptic form: 'the greatest philosophers chose to utter [these] in veiled fashion . . . In this way, people would be struck with awe and listen more attentively', quoted in Anthony Grafton, *Leon Battista Alberti, Master Builder of the Renaissance*, London, 2000, pp. 102–3. See also Edgar Wind, *Pagan Mysteries of the Renaissance*, Harmondsworth, 1967, pp. 231–4. Among his many accomplishments Alberti made a major advance in cryptography. L. B. Alberti, *De componendis cyfris*, text in Latin and Italian, pref. David Kahn, Turin, 1994. There's an English edition, *A Treatise on Ciphers*, trans. Alessandro Zaccagnini, Turin, 1997.

9 This painting did not survive antiquity but there are several surviving descriptions of it. Alberti's was derived from *The Institutio Oratoria of Quintilian*, tr. H. E. Butler, 3 vols, 1921, 2, xiii, 13: '. . . pinxisset tristem Calchantem, tristiorem Ulixen, addidisset Menelao, quem summum poterat ars efficere maerorem, consumptis adfectibus, non reperiens, quo digne modo patris vultum posset exprimere, velavit eius caput et suo cui que animo dedit aestimandum.' '. . . having depicted Calchas sad [tristem], Ulysses sadder [tristiorem], and having given Menelaus, consumed with emotion [consumptis adfectibus], what grief he was able to convey using all his art, he was unable to work out how he could portray the father's face as it deserved [quo digno modo], so he veiled the father's head and left his feelings to be inferred.'

10 Alberti, *De Pictura*, pp. 82/3: '. . . tristem Calchantem, tristiorem fecisset Ulixem, inque Menelao maerore affecto omnem artem et ingenium expossuisset, consumptis affectibus, non reperiens quo digno modo tristissimi patris vultus referret, pannis involuit eius caput, ut cuique plus relinqueret quod de illius dolore animo meditaretur, quam quod posset visu discernere.'

11 Alberti, op. cit., 37, pp. 74–5. See Jules Lubbock in *London Review of Books*, 31.10.02, pp. 40–1.

12 'Inimica: inimicatur enim patientibus eam unde Invidiosus invidia conburitur intus et extra hanc padue in arena optime pinsit Giottus.' From *The Documents of Love*, c.1308–12, quoted in Stubblebine, *Giotto: The Arena Chapel Frescoes*, London, 1969, p. 109.

13 Caution is obviously required in the interpretation of this famous text. Dante

is not describing sculptures he had seen but is presenting verbal descriptions of events as if he were reading the story from sculpted reliefs. Of course he may have got the idea of viewing such reliefs in sequence from Pisano pulpits and particularly Giovanni's in Pistoia, as has already been suggested. Dante was clearly an experienced and admiring spectator of the visual arts. Nonetheless it is essential to note that these purgatorial sculptures are the works of God, which put to shame to work of the great sculptors of antiquities such as Polycletus; Dante describes them as being 'Novel to us, for here it is not found'.

14 *Purgatorio*, X, l. 95; J. A. Burrow, *Gesture and Looks in Medieval Narrative*, Cambridge, 2002, pp. 177–8.

15 St Augustine, ed. and tr. R. P. H. Green, *De Doctrina Christiana*, Oxford, 1995, vol. 2, 5, p. 58; also Oxford Classics pb. edition of the English translation also by Green, Oxford, 1999, p. 31.

16 Cennino Cennini, ed. D.V. Thompson Jr, *Il Libro dell'Arte*, New Haven, 2 vols, 1932, vol. 1, p. 2: 'di trovare cose non vedute, chacciandosi sotto umbra di naturali e fermarle con la mano'; Alberti, op. cit., I, 24, pp. 58–9: 'Sequitur ut pictorem institutuamus quem ad modum quae mente conceperit ea manu imitari queat.' See also Mary Pardo, 'Giotto and Things Not Seen, Hidden in the Shadow of Natural Ones', *Artibus et Historiae: an Art Anthology*, Vienna, No. 36, XVIII, 1997, pp. 41–53.

17 Alberti, op. cit., II, 41, pp. 80–1.

18 G. Milanesi, *Documenti per la Storia dell'Arte Senese*, 3 vols, Siena, 1854, vol. 1, p. 1.

19 Cennino, op. cit., 'si chome picholo menbro essercitante nell'arte di dipintoria'.

20 Alberti, op. cit., III, 52 and 53, pp. 94–5.

21 Lorenzo Ghiberti, *I commentari*, ed. Ottavio Morisani, Naples, 1947, I, 1, p. 2; II, 2, p. 18. See note 28 below.

22 Paul Grendler, *Schooling in Renaissance Italy, Literacy and Learning 1300–1600*, Baltimore, 1989, pp. 1–109.

23 While obviously exaggerated the statistic partly depends upon his definition of literacy which is not clear-cut. A household where one member can both read and write is clearly literate, unlike a household where no one has such skills. For the relationship between literacy, orality and aurality (i.e. reading aloud) see Joyce Coleman, *Public Reading and the Reading Public in Late Medieval England and France*, Cambridge, 1996, pp. 1–38.

24 Grendler, op. cit., pp. 71–3.

25 Grendler, op. cit., p. 103. See also R. A. Goldthwaite, *The Building of Renaissance Florence*, Baltimore, 1980, p. 419. Ghiberti, however, makes it clear that some artists were pretty dumb.

26 C. Bellinati, 'La Capella degli Scrovegni', in *Padova Basiliche e Chiese*, ed. Claudio Bellinati and Lionello Pappi, Parte Prima, Vincenza, 1975, pp. 252–62; Eve Borsook, *The Mural Painters of Tuscany*, Oxford, 2nd edn, 1980, p. 13, n. 50; C. Bellinati, *Giotto: Padua felix – atlante iconografico nell' capella di Giotto, 1300–05*, Treviso, 1997, pp. 132–7.

27 Ghiberti, op. cit., II, 22, pp. 46ff. See also E. H. Gombrich, 'The Renaissance Conception of Artistic Progress', *Norm and Form: Studies in the Art of the Renaissance*, London, 1966, pp. 5–6. A letter by the bibliophile scholar Aurispa implies that Ghiberti was a 'member of that codex-swapping crowd that included Aurispa, Traversari, Niccolò Niccolì and Poggio Bracciolino'. This implies that Ghiberti must have been a fairly fluent reader of Latin.

28 C. Mango, *The Art of the Byzantine Empire, 312–1453*, Toronto, 1986, pp.

258–9. Crete was a possession of Venice from 1204–1669.

29 Masaccio of course was dead by 1436, having died in Rome probably in 1428. Antonio Manetti, *The Life of Brunelleschi*, Pennsylvania, 1970, pp. 38–9, states that Brunelleschi had learned to read and write and learned some Latin, which Manetti says was unusual, but he did so possibly because his father was a notary. The *Codice Magliabechiana*, ed. Carl Frey, Berlin, 1892, reprinted, Farnborough, 1969, p. 62 states that Brunelleschi was a very learned student of the scriptures, particularly of St Paul, and of Dante.

30 *Filarete's Treatise on Architecture*, vol. 1, p. 301, n. 7. J. R. Spencer observes that certain passages on optics referred to by Filarete are only found in the Latin text, not in the Italian translation.

31 *Purgatorio*, x, l. 39.

32 Michael Baxandall, op. cit., p. 91. Guarino complained that paintings and sculptures were poor vehicles for transmitting personal fame 'because they are *sine litteris*, unlabelled'. James Hall kindly drew my attention to this reference.

33 Sixten Ringbom, 'Some Pictorial Conventions for the Recounting of Thoughts and Experiences in Late Medieval Art', in *Medieval Iconography and Narrative: A Symposium*, ed. F. G. Anderson, Odense University Press, 1980, pp. 38–69 for systematic discussion of some problems.

34 E. H. Gombrich, *Art Bulletin*, 31, 1949, p. 72.

35 Joseph Addison, 'Essays on Fancy and the Imagination', *The Spectator*, 27 June 1712, no. 416.

36 For the use of pictographic conventions in the didactic art of Imperial Rome and early Christian Art see E. H. Gombrich, 'Action and Expression in Western Art', in *Non Verbal Communication*, ed. Robert A. Hinde, Cambridge, 1972, pp. 373–93, particularly pp. 381–2. When the subject matter is unfamiliar and the conventions not well established it can be difficult even for the faithful to identify the stories. Many years ago, visiting the Brancacci Chapel early one morning an old woman told me what she thought the frescoes represented – the Distribution of Alms was the Circumcision and the Baptism of the Neophytes was the Baptism of Jesus.

37 One example is an extensive Old Testament fresco cycle in the Collegiata in San Gimignano, whereas the New Testament cycle is free of titles. Presumably it was considered that the compositional formulae for most Old Testament stories were less familiar. These titles were in Italian, in the form 'Come Dio creo el mondo' – How God created the first man, etc. This is further evidence of widespread literacy, for there must have been sufficient people to read the titles to women and children and other members of the family who could not read.

38 'All things which are meaningful to humans, just because humans have decided that they should be so, are human institutions.' St Augustine, op. cit., vol. 2, 96, p. 53.

39 Ibid., vol. 2, 134–5, p. 62; vol. 4, 6–13, pp. 102–3.

40 Giovanni Dominici, *Regola del Governo di Cura Familiare*, Florence, 1860, pp. 131–3. Also C. Gilbert, op. cit., pp. 145–6. For Dominici's life see Chapter 7, n. 13 above.

41 The problems which arise for the spectator when unfamiliar stories are represented or where familiar stories are represented in unfamiliar compositions can be seen in the case of the remains of the narrative scenes on the Westminster Retable of c.1270 and the mid-fourteenth-century carvings in the Lady Chapel of Ely Cathedral.

42 Kenelm Foster O. P., 'Vernacular Scrip-

tures in Italy', chs 9, 6, of G. W. H. Lampe (ed.), *The Cambridge History of the Bible, Vol. 2. The West from the Fathers to the Reformation*, Cambridge, 1969, p. 465: 'the vernacular Bible was a fairly important factor in the religious life of pre-Reformation Italy, at least in Tuscany and in parts of the North . . . It is, finally, noteworthy that, so far as our evidence goes, the Church in Italy in those centuries showed no hostility in principle to the translation of the Bible, and placed no serious obstacle in the way of rendering it accessible to people in their own language.'

43 C. Gilbert, op. cit., pp. 42–4; Grendler, op. cit., pp. 275–86.

44 V. Todesco, A. Vaccari and M. Vattasso (eds.), *Il Diatesseron in Volgare Italiano: Testi inediti dei Secoli xiii–xiv*, Vatican, 1938.

45 St Antoninus, *Summa Theologica*, c.1458, first printed, Venice, 1477, Pt. 3, Title 8, ch. 4, section. 11, quoted in Creighton Gilbert, op. cit., p. 148.

46 Rudolf Belmer, 'The Freedom of Mediaeval Art', *Gazette des Beaux-Arts*, 6e. ser., 28, 1945, pp. 264–88; for St Antoninus see C. Gilbert, op. cit., p. 147 and *Art Bulletin*, 41, 1959, pp. 76–7.

47 Translation adapted from Isa Ragusa and Rosalie B. Green, *Meditations on the Life of Christ*, Princeton, 1977 (1st edn 1961), pp. 4–5; *Sancti Bonaventurae Opera*, 13 vols, Venice, 1756, vol. 12, p. 381. See M. Thomas, 'Zur Rolle der "Meditationes Vitae Christi": Innerhalb der europäischen Bild-Entwicklung der Giotto-Zeit', in *Miscellanea Codicologica F. Masai Dicata*, ed. P. Cockshaw, M-C Garand and P. Jodogne, Ghent, 1979, pp. 319–30.

48 Ragusa and Green, op. cit., pp. 333–4; Sancti Bonaventurae *Opera*, op. cit., p. 495. See also Michael Baxandall, *Painting and Experience in Fifteenth Century Italy*, Oxford, 1972, pp. 45ff.

49 Millard Meiss, *Frescoes from Florence*, Hayward Gallery, London, 1969, pp. 60–5; V. Schmidt, 'Artistic Imagination versus Religious Function: Ambrogio Lorenzetti's Annunciation at Montesiepi', in *The Power of Imagery. Essays on Rome, Italy and Imagination*, ed. Peter van Kessel, Rome, 1993, pp. 133–48, 290–6. Schmidt claims that 'nowhere in the fourteenth century . . . does one find such wild panic'. The sinopia drawing was not uncovered till 1966.

50 G. Vasari, *Le Vite*, ed. Milanesi, 1973, reprint of Florence, 1906, op. cit., vol. 2, p. 397. Baxandall, *Painting and Experience*, pp. 49–56 adduces the evidence of a sermon by a popular mid-fifteenth-preacher, Fra Roberto Caracciolo da Lecce, who divides the Annunciation into five Laudable Conditions of the Blessed Virgin: Disquiet, Reflection, Inquiry, Submission and Merit, and Baxandall uses these to argue that these 'very exactly fit the painted representations' of the fifteenth century. But it can equally be argued that a spectator, tutored by Fra Roberto's sermon, might use a particular depiction to meditate on all or some of the five.

51 *Prontezza* is Manetti's term, op. cit., p. 49.

52 S. Freud, *The Interpretation of Dreams*, trans. A. A. Brill, London and New York, 1937, pp. 296-323. E. H. Gombrich observes in his review of Charles Morris, *Signs, Language and Behaviour*, in *Art Bulletin*, 31, 1949, p. 72, that 'Lessing observed almost two hundred years ago that negation cannot be expressed through the image.' Gombrich asks, 'Are there any "formators" corresponding to "logical words" in the language of the image?' See n. 15, chapter 8. The Lessing passage is the last paragraph of ch. 8 of the *Laokoon*. 'But it may be said the poet alone possesses the power of painting with negative traits, and, by mixing the negative and the positive together, of uniting two appearances in one. No longer is she the graceful Venus; no

longer are her locks bound with golden clasps; no azure robe is floating round her; her girdle is laid aside . . .' tr. E. C. Beasley, London, 1888, p. 63. In this passage Lessing is paraphrasing Statius, *Thebaid*, bk. 5, v. 61ff.

53 Ringbom, op. cit., pp. 41–7.

54 Luke 1, 1–14.

55 *Meditations on the Life of Christ,* op. cit., pp. 4–5; *Sancti Bonaventurae Opera,* 13 vols, Venice, 1756, vol. 12, p. 381.

56 Literary narratives have been categorised into two broad types: first person and third person narrators. These have been subdivided again into first person narrators who tell their own story autobiographically and those who are minor characters; likewise with third person narrators there is the omniscient narrator and one who is external to the events. This, however, seems excessively categorical and recent literary scholars have called it into question. For example, Jane Austen's *Pride and Prejudice* is, strictly speaking, a third person omniscient narrative, but so much of the story is seen through the eyes of Elizabeth Bennett that it is almost indistinguishable from a first person autobiographical account.

57 Alberti, op. cit., pp. 80-3 recommended the inclusion of 'someone in the historia who brings to the attention of the spectators what is going on, and either beckons them with his hand to look, or with ferocious expression and forbidding glance challenges them not to come near, as if he wished their business to be secret, or points to some danger or remarkable thing in the picture, or by his gestures invites you to laugh or weep with them'. But such a figure does not, indeed cannot, actually tell the story, instead he helps to engage the spectator and to prompt his reactions, to compensate for one's uncertainty in interpreting gestures and facial expressions.

58 Ghiberti, op. cit., II, 11, p. 37.

59 For this reason Giovanni's handling of the device is less personal than Antonello da Messina's in the fifteenth century where we are shown only the Virgin, so that to all intents and purposes we become Gabriel. Even so, the Virgin is not looking directly at us, but at someone to our left, presumably Gabriel, so that our role as witness to the Annunciation is maintained.

60 Alberti, op. cit., II. 41, pp. 80–1.

61 Francisco de Hollanda, *Diálogos em Roma (1538). Conversations on Art with Michelangelo Buonarroti*, ed. Grazia Dolores Folliero-Metz, Heidelberg, 1998, pp. 76–7. There are issues concerning the authenticity of these dialogues, see p. 9. Does God's painting refer to Dante, Purgatorio, x, ll. 94–9?

62 See above, introduction, p. 12.

INDEX

PHOTOGRAPH CREDITS

Musée du Louvre/Photo courtesy RMN, 1; John White, *Art and Architecture in Italy, 1250-1400*, Yale University Press, 4–5; Antonio Quattrone; the author 6–17, 19–38, 101–4, 111, 123–6; 38, 44, 51a and b, 53–9, 61–70a, 71–2, 75–7, 79a–92, 96–7, 103, 105–9, 113–17, 134–44; National Gallery, London, 70a, 70b; Nicolò Battaglini, 93, 95; Alinari, 94, 98, 100, 119, 122, 147–8, 150–65; Scala, 127–33. For permission to take photographs my thanks to the Commune di Padova, Settore Musei e Biblioteche; Opera della Metropolitana di Siena; Opera della Primaziale Pisana and the Soprintendenza per i beni artistici e storico per le province di Firenze, Pistoia e Prato.